Financial Management
for Nonprofit Organizations

NONPROFIT LAW, FINANCE, AND MANAGEMENT SERIES

The Art of Planned Giving: Understanding Donors and the Culture of Giving by Douglas E. White
Beyond Fund Raising: New Strategies for Nonprofit Investment and Innovation by Kay Grace
Charity, Advocacy, and the Law by Bruce R. Hopkins
The Complete Guide to Nonprofit Management by Smith, Bucklin & Associates
Critical Issues in Fund Raising edited by Dwight Burlingame
Developing Affordable Housing: A Practical Guide for Nonprofit Organizations by Bennett L. Hecht
Financial and Accounting Guide for Not-for-Profit Organizations, Fifth Edition by Malvern J. Gross,
    Jr., Richard F. Larkin, Roger S. Bruttomesso, John J. McNally, Price Waterhouse LLP
Financial Planning for Nonprofit Organizations by Jody Blazek
Fund-Raising: Evaluating and Managing the Fund Development Process by James M. Greenfield
Fund-Raising Fundamentals: A Guide to Annual Giving for Professionals and Volunteers by James
    M. Greenfield
*Fund-Raising Regulation: A State-by-State Handbook of Registration Forms, Requirements, and
    Procedures* by Seth Perlman and Betsy Hills Bush
Intermediate Sanctions: Curbing Nonprofit Abuse by Bruce R. Hopkins and D. Benson Tesdahl
The Law of Fund-Raising, Second Edition by Bruce R. Hopkins
The Law of Tax-Exempt Healthcare Organizations by Thomas K. Hyatt and Bruce R. Hopkins
The Law of Tax-Exempt Organizations, Sixth Edition by Bruce R. Hopkins
The Legal Answer Book for Nonprofit Organizations by Bruce R. Hopkins
A Legal Guide to Starting and Managing a Nonprofit Organization, Second Edition by Bruce R.
    Hopkins
Managing Affordable Housing: A Practical Guide to Creating Stable Communities by Bennett L.
    Hecht, Local Initiatives Support Corporation, and James Stockard
Nonprofit Boards: Roles, Responsibilities, and Performance by Diane J. Duca
The Nonprofit Counsel by Bruce R. Hopkins
The Nonprofit Guide to the Internet by Robbin Zeff
The Nonprofit Law Dictionary by Bruce R. Hopkins
Nonprofit Litigation: A Practical Guide with Forms and Checklists by Steve Bachmann
The Nonprofit Handbook, Second Edition: Volume I—Management by Tracy Daniel Connors
The Nonprofit Handbook, Second Edition: Volume II—Fund Raising by Jim Greenfield
The Nonprofit Manager's Resource Dictionary by Ronald A. Landskroner
Nonprofit Organizations' Business Forms: Disk Edition by John Wiley & Sons, Inc.
Partnerships and Joint Ventures Involving Tax-Exempt Organizations by Michael I. Sanders
Planned Giving: Management, Marketing, and Law by Ronald R. Jordan and Katelyn L. Quynn
Program Related Investments: A Technical Manual for Foundations by Christie I Baxter
Reengineering Your Nonprofit Organization: A Guide to Strategic Transformation by Alceste T.
    Pappas
Reinventing the University: Managing and Financing Institutions of Higher Education by Sandra L.
    Johnson and Sean C. Rush, Coopers & Lybrand, L.L.P.
Strategic Planning for Nonprofit Organizations: A Practical Guide and Workbook by Michael Allison
    and Jude Kaye, Support Center for Nonprofit Management
Streetsmart Financial Basics for Nonprofit Managers by Thomas A. McLaughlin
Successful Marketing Strategies for Nonprofit Organizations by Barry J. McLeish
The Tax Law of Charitable Giving by Bruce R. Hopkins
The Tax Law of Colleges and Universities by Bertrand M. Harding
*Tax Planning and Compliance for Tax-Exempt Organizations: Forms, Checklists, Procedures, Second
    Edition* by Jody Blazek
The Volunteer Management Handbook by Tracy Daniel Connors
International Guide to Nonprofit Law by Lester A. Salamon and Stefan Toepler & Associates
Private Foundations: Tax Law and Compliance by Bruce R. Hopkins and Jody Blazek
Financial Management for Nonprofit Organizations by Jo Ann Hankin, Alan Seidner and John
    Zietlow
*The Universal Benefits of Volunteering: A Practical Workbook for Nonprofit Organizations, Volunteers
    and Corporations* by Walter P. Pidgeon, Jr.
A Streetsmart Guide to Nonprofit Mergers and Networks by Thomas A. McLaughlin

FINANCIAL MANAGEMENT FOR NONPROFIT ORGANIZATIONS

Jo Ann Hankin
Alan G. Seidner
John T. Zietlow

JOHN WILEY & SONS, INC.
New York • Chichester • Weinheim • Brisbane • Singapore • Toronto

To family and friends who have been helpful along the way
Jo Ann Hankin

To my daughters, Melanie and Deborah Seidner
Alan Seidner

I dedicate my portion of the book to my parents, Harold and Miriam Zietlow, for their encouragement, support, and prayers.
John Zietlow

This book is printed on acid-free paper.

Copyright © 1998 by John Wiley & Sons. All rights reserved.

Published simultaneously in Canada.

No part of this publication may be reproduced, stored in a retrieval system or transmitted in any form or by any means, electronic, mechanical, photocopying, recording, scanning or otherwise, except as permitted under Sections 107 or 108 of the 1976 United States Copyright Act, without either the prior written permission of the Publisher, or authorization through payment of the appropriate per-copy fee to the Copyright Clearance Center, 222 Rosewood Drive, Danvers, MA 01923, (508) 750-8400, fax (508) 750-4744. Requests to the Publisher for permission should be addressed to the Permissions Department, John Wiley & Sons, Inc., 605 Third Avenue, New York, NY 10158-0012, (212) 850-6011, fax (212) 850-6008, E-Mail: PERMREQ@WILEY.COM.

This publication is designed to provide accurate and authoritative information in regard to the subject matter covered. It is sold with the understanding that the publisher is not engaged in rendering legal, accounting, or other professional services. If legal advice or other expert assistance is required, the services of a competent professional person should be sought.

Library of Congress Cataloging-in-Publication Data:

Hankin, Jo Ann.
  Financial management for nonprofit organizations / Jo Ann Hankin, Alan Seidner,
   John Zietlow.
    p. cm.—(Nonprofit law, finance, and management series)
    Includes bibliographical references and index.
    ISBN 0-471-16842-4 (alk. paper)
    1. Nonprofit organizations—Finance. I. Seidner, Alan G. II. Zietlow, John T.
  III. Title. IV. Series.
  HG4027.7.H356   1997
  659.15—dc21   97-8604
                                                                           CIP

Printed in the United States of America.
10 9 8 7 6 5 4 3 2 1

Subscription Notice

This Wiley product is updated on a periodic basis with supplements to reflect important changes in the subject matter. If you purchased this product directly from John Wiley & Sons, Inc., we have already recorded your subscription for this update service.

If, however, you purchased this product from a bookstore and wish to receive (1) the current update at no additional charge, and (2) future updates and revised or related volumes billed separately with a 30-day examination review, please send your name, company name (if applicable), address, and the title of the product to:

Supplement Department
John Wiley & Sons, Inc.
One Wiley Drive
Somerset, NJ 08875
1-800-225-5945

For customers outside the United States, please contact the Wiley office nearest you:

Professional & Reference Division
John Wiley & Sons Canada, Ltd.
22 Worcester Road
Rexdale, Ontario M9W 1L1
CANADA
(416) 675-3580
1-800-567-4797
FAX (416) 675-6599

John Wiley & Sons, Ltd.
Baffins Lane
Chichester
West Sussex, PO19 1UD
UNITED KINGDOM
(44) (243) 779777

Jacaranda Wiley Ltd.
PRT Division
P.O. Box 174
North Ryde, NSW 2113
AUSTRALIA
(02) 805-1100
FAX (02) 805-1597

John Wiley & Sons (SEA) Pte. Ltd.
37 Jalan Pemimpin
Block B # 05-04
Union Industrial Building
SINGAPORE 2057
(65) 258-1157

About the Authors

Jo Ann Hankin is chief finance and administrative officer at Whittier College in California. Her responsibilities include finance, accounting, telecommunications, and business enterprises. Prior to joining the college in September 1996, she served as Vice President of Finance of The UCLA Foundation and Associate Vice Chancellor of Finance and Information Management at UCLA.

Jo Ann has been active in the Financial Executives Institute, Los Angeles chapter, and has chaired various committees of that organization. She is involved with Consultant to Project Business, a program to teach the principles of business to junior and senior high school students, as well as the Committee of 200, an organization of women entrepreneurs and executives. She is founder and past officer of the Cash Management Society of Los Angeles, and has served as the UCLA/United Way Campaign Director in the capacities of Volunteer for the Center for Non-Profit Management and as President of The UCLA Child Care Services Advisory Board.

Alan G. Seidner is the founder of Seidner & Company of Pasadena, CA, an investment management and consulting firm whose roster includes high net worth private investors, healthcare organizations, major corporations, nonprofit institutions, and municipalities.

Alan is author of many financial reference works, and is a frequent speaker on investment techniques and strategies. He has also provided testimony before federal government agencies on the performance of pension fund investments.

John T. Zietlow is a professor of finance at Indiana State University, where he teaches introductory corporate finance, capital budgeting and structure, short-term financial management, and graduate finance survey. At the departmental level, he has served on various search and curriculum committees; he is currently Chair of the Personnel Committee.

John has been developing, overseeing delivery of, and executing multi-level executive education programs for just over ten years. He is a frequent speaker, as well as an author of several articles and academic presentations on the subject of financial management, and has co-authored a best selling financial management text. He is a member of the Association for Research on Nonprofit Organizations & Voluntary Action (ARNOVA), Financial Management Association, various regional financial associations, and the Treasury Management Association of Indiana.

Contents

Preface   ix

Acknowledgment   xi

Chapter 1   Understanding Nonprofit Organizations   1

Chapter 2   Using Financial Management to Accomplish
Your Mission   42

Chapter 3   Financial Roles and Responsibilities   67

Chapter 4   Long-Range Financial Planning and Strategy   104

Chapter 5   Developing and Managing a Financial Plan   146

Chapter 6   Financial Reports   182

Chapter 7   Technology Tools—Managing Information   236

Chapter 8   Types and Sources of Funding for Your Program   258

Chapter 9   Cash Management and Banking Relations   303

Chapter 10   Managing Your Organization's Liabilities   336

Chapter 11   Investment Policy and Guidelines   367

Chapter 12   Investing Principles, Procedures, and Operations
for Short-Term and Long-Term Endowment   407

Chapter 13   Fixed-Income Securities Portfolio Management
and Investment Operations   483

Chapter 14   Safeguarding the Organization's Assets, People,
and Property: Risk Management and Audit   537

Chapter 15   Financial Policy—Internal and External   558

Chapter 16   Evaluating Your Progress   568

Index   591

Preface

Financial Management for Nonprofits is a book written for use by those responsible for financial management in the nonprofit organization. There are many titles used to identify persons assigned these responsibilities including, but not limited to, the director of finance, chief financial officer, treasurer, controller, chief accountant, and financial secretary. Actually, the title of the position is not important; the responsibility is extremely important.

Our book is written from a managerial decision-making perspective for those in leadership and day-to-day management positions who have oversight responsibility for financial functions or are members of the Board. These leaders and managers may, or may not, be experienced financial managers. Most of the subjects and issues that confront those responsible for financial management and related functions in the small- to medium-sized nonprofit organization are not determined by size, but rather by the mix of assets and strategies employed to accomplish the organization's mission.

Another important focus of this book is to demonstrate that financial management functions are expanding—and when done well, these strategies will make a real difference in the organization's ability to achieve its mission. Effective and responsible financial management contributes toward accomplishing the mission in a number of significant ways, including:

- Strategic planning
- Evaluation of existing and new programs
- Marketing
- Fund raising
- Operational expertise
- Empowerment through the sharing of information
- Catalyst for cultural change in the organization
- Increase in investment income
- Preservation of investment assets

Depending on your nonprofit organization's size and scope of activities, the nature and complexity of its financial functions will range from simple to highly sophisticated and complex. In any case, the financial systems used must be designed to provide the information necessary to meet management, fiduciary, and legal requirements. The organization of the book into these four major sections is intended to emphasize the positive contributions of the financial and business functions to the organization and its mission:

• Managing Your Organization's Financial Resources
• Maximizing Your Organization's Cash
• Investing for the Short and Long Term
• Controlling and Managing Risk

Working for a nonprofit organization is an exciting and meaningful opportunity. There are many similarities and differences between nonprofit and for-profit organizations, and it is important to recognize and understand how they are similar as well as dissimilar. By virtue of their mission, nonprofit organizations benefit society by improving the public good.

Hundreds of thousands of nonprofit organizations of all sizes exist today, employing many people. Each nonprofit organization has a responsibility to its mission, its constituents, its employees, and its volunteers. The effective financial management of the organization's resources will enable it to succeed in fulfilling its mission and goals.

As you can see from the material covered in this book, those involved in managing the finances of the organization have a great deal of responsibility. In the process of carrying out these responsibilities, some members of the organization may feel disliked or undervalued by those they serve on a regular basis. Under these circumstances, it is critical for the responsible financial manager to be fair, to understand the interplay between facts and people, and to understand that accountability is not always popular with those being held accountable.

This book is intended to provide financial personnel with a clear sense of the technical expertise and skills needed to manage this function well for their organization. It will also reinforce the fact that you are part of a larger group in the nonprofit community who fulfill the same set of major responsibilities and uphold the same ethics and values. The authors hope that the information contained in this book will enable readers to better manage the financial resources of the nonprofit organizations they serve and enhance their overall financial health and viability.

Acknowledgment

Jo Ann Hankin thanks Clariza Mullins, currently Associate Treasurer, Pepperdine University, for her important contribution to Chapter 9 on Cash Management and Banking Relations. Clariza's technical expertise, hands-on experience, and communication style make this chapter an extremely useful one.

Alan Seidner, as co-author, wishes to thank the professional staff of Seidner & Company, Investment Management, for their help in researching and completing the material in this publication. Specifically, special thanks go to Joan West, Leah Romero, Sandee Glickman, Joe Flores, and Lina Macias.

John Zietlow greatly acknowledges the contributions of the following individuals who lent their expertise to specific areas of the book: John Webb, Darryl Smith, Darryl Deardorff, Jerry Trecek, Bob Reynhout, Dave McFee, Bob Bontrager, Phillip Purcell, Rob Licht, David Holt, Eric Lane, Gregg Capin, Dan Busby, Raj Aggarwal, and Kathleen Eisenhardt. Particularly, we are grateful to Marla Bobowick, who signed the book for Wiley, and to Martha Cooley, Anne Brunell, and Robert Carmenini, who were instrumental in directing the project from inception to publication.

A special thanks goes to Lilly Endowment, Inc., for initiating the study of the financial management of faith-based organizations by providing grant money to Indiana State University. The individuals responsible for evaluating and guiding the grant process are Fred Hofheinz and Jim Hudnut-Beumler. The advisory panel assembled as part of that grant project were invaluable in shaping the research project that underlies some of the significant findings presented in this book. They believed, as we do, that proficient financial management can greatly aid in the accomplishment of charitable missions. A heartfelt thanks goes to the 288 financial managers who took part in the exhaustive survey covering financial management practices employed by their organizations.

Lastly, we thank our families for bearing with us in the arduous process of putting this guide together. My contribution is dedicated to my parents, Harold and Miriam Zietlow, for their encouragement, support, and prayers.

CHAPTER ONE

Understanding Nonprofit Organizations

1.1 Definition of Nonprofit Organizations   2
   (a)   501(c)(3) Corporations   3
   (b)   Bylaws and Articles of Incorporation   4
1.2 Characteristics of Nonprofit Organizations   4
   (a)   Organizational Mission   5
   (b)   Organizational Structure   6
1.3 Understanding the Workforce   6
   (a)   Choosing Trustees/Directors   7
   (b)   Officers of the Nonprofit Organization   8
       (i)   President/Chair of the Board   8
       (ii)   Treasurer/Chief Financial Officer   8
       (iii)   Secretary   8
       (iv)   Board Committees   9
       (v)   Executive Director   10
       (vi)   Staff   11
       (vii)   Volunteers   11
       (viii) Independent Contractors   11
   (c)   Job Descriptions   11
1.4 Understanding the Language
   of the Nonprofit Organization   12

Appendix 1A: Sample Job Descriptions/Summary
                    of Responsibilities and Qualifications   14
Appendix 1B: Bylaws of the ABC Educational Foundation—
                    A California Nonprofit Public Benefit
                    Corporation   21

More than one million nonprofits are registered in the United States today, not including churches and small nonprofit organizations that are not required to register with the Internal Revenue

Service (IRS). The number of registered charitable organizations has exploded from roughly 300,000 in 1970 to 600,000 today. One-half of the nonprofit sector's revenue goes to the largest 15 percent of these organizations, some of which are large hospitals and universities. Faced with growing missions and shrinking resources, many organizations have turned to for-profit activities such as issuing credit cards with their logos and selling their mailing lists to advertising firms in order to augment their revenues. Most of these same organizations have overlooked the potential of better financial management to enhance revenues (from better investment management and faster cash collections) or reduce costs (from better negotiations with banks and process re-engineering).

Our framework is intended to be of immediate value to non-profit financial professionals. This handbook caters to the treasurer with little or no formal training, business-only training, or too little time (perhaps due to a multitude of responsibilities) or support staff to do the job the way he or she knows it can be done. This handbook specifically includes material for small, resource-constrained and large organizations presented in an easy-to-use format, including forms where helpful. The discussion goes beyond the "buzzwords" in order to provide reasonable steps toward more proficient treasury management. These techniques include:

- Learning organization, re-engineering, Total Quality Management (TQM), and benchmarking
- Executive bonuses
- Strategic alliances
- Advanced cash management
- Financial forecasting
- Fund-raising management and evaluation
- Fraud prevention and detection
- Program selection and cost-benefit evaluation
- Investment and other financial policies

1.1 DEFINITION OF NONPROFIT ORGANIZATIONS

In the broadest terms, *nonprofit* is a designation given by the IRS to describe a group of organizations that are allowed to make a profit but that are prohibited from distributing their profits or earnings to those in control of the organizations. If these organizations apply for and receive tax-exempt status from the IRS, they are not required to pay federal income taxes except in specific cases, which are discussed later in this book. This classification makes them distinctly different from for-profit corporations, which distribute profits to their owners or shareholders and must pay corporate income taxes on their earnings. In addition, contributions to some nonprofit organizations are tax deductible for donors. Further details regarding nonprofit organizations can be found in Sections 501 through 521 of the IRS code.

As reported in *The Charitable Nonprofit*,

> If one defines the nonprofit sector as all organizations recognized as tax exempt by the IRS, then in 1991 there were more than one million organizations in the nonprofit universe. These organizations accounted for about 6 percent of the GNP and 10 percent of total employment.
>
> The full universe of nonprofit entities is even larger in some respects. Very small nonprofit organizations with less than $5,000 in annual revenues, churches of any size, and charities that are incorporated by governmental bodies (such as state universities) do not have to apply for tax exemption, although they may make application. It is difficult to estimate the number of entities falling into these categories. The consensus seems to be that there are about 350,000 churches all told.
>
> Thus the total universe of nonprofit organizations defined most broadly appears to be on the order of one and one half-million entities, or conceivably even larger.
>
> This total can be compared with the total number of incorporated business establishments, which is estimated to exceed six million.[1]

(a) 501(c)(3) Corporations

Most organizations are qualified for tax-exempt status under Section 501(c)(3) of the IRS code. However, there are other ways to qualify.

> The 501(c)(3) corporations are those organizations which have qualified for tax exempt status under Section 501(c)(3) of the Internal Revenue Service code. These 501(c)(3) organizations are generally referred to as the 'charitable' nonprofit. The 501(c)(3) group generally consists of private foundations and educational, religious, scientific, literary, social welfare, and other charitable organizations. These organizations have been granted tax-exempt status and are entitled to receive tax-deductible contributions from donors.
>
> The rationale for allowing these organizations to enjoy the benefits of tax deductibility is that they are thought to serve broad public purposes which transcend the personal interests of their members and benefactors.
>
> When most people speak of nonprofit organizations, the 501(c)(3) are the organizations which they have in mind. 501(c)(3) is equivalent to the common meaning of the term

[1]William G. Bowen et al., *The Charitable Nonprofit* (San Francisco: Jossey Bass, 1994), 4–6.

nonprofit—but it most certainly does not capture the full range of nonprofit entities granted tax exempt status by the IRS.[2]

The 501(c)(3) includes less than half of all tax exempt organizations in the United States.

Of the more than one million tax exempt organizations, 516,554 were 501(c)(3) in 1991.

Of these, about one-quarter or 125,000 are independent entities working actively in substantive fields and reporting annual revenues of as much as $25,000.

(b) Bylaws and Articles of Incorporation

The Articles of Incorporation (or Charter) and Bylaws are the initial documents that spell out the rules, regulations, and procedures for nonprofit corporations and form the basis for subsequent policy setting. The Trustees are responsible for preparing, periodically reviewing, and amending these documents to keep pace with the mission and support structure of the organization.

The Articles of Incorporation are prepared and submitted when the organization first applies for state corporate status, and they are maintained in the state office responsible for corporate records (i.e., Secretary of State's Office).

The Board of Trustees (or Board of Directors) is also responsible for drafting the bylaws, which serve as the organization's operating rules. Bylaws are more detailed than the Charter and include information such as the number and tenure of Trustees, how and when meetings are to be called, when reports are to be presented, how Board vacancies are to be filled, and other details needed to ensure the consistent and efficient operation of the organization.

The Trustees are legally responsible for reviewing the nonprofit organization's bylaws and Articles of Incorporation to ensure that they accurately reflect what is happening in the organization. It is also the Trustees' responsibility to ensure that those provisions of the governing documents are followed.

Once these two documents are in place, the Trustees should develop policy manuals covering their own service, personnel, finances, equipment, and other areas. These policies should address issues related to the organizational mission such as conflict of interest, risk management, property, and facility use.

1.2 CHARACTERISTICS OF NONPROFIT ORGANIZATIONS

A nonprofit organization must have the following characteristics:

- Public service mission

[2]*Id.,* 4–6.

- Organizational structure of a not-for-profit or charitable corporation
- Governance structures that preclude self-interest and personal financial gain
- Exemption from paying federal taxes
- Special legal status stipulating that gifts made to the organization are tax deductible

(a) Organizational Mission

One essential difference between a nonprofit and for-profit corporation centers on its mission. The ultimate mission of for-profit organizations is to make money for the owners/shareholders, ranging from an individual, to sole proprietors, to corporate ownership through the purchase of shares.

A nonprofit organization does not include the concept of ownership and, therefore, has a completely different thrust. Its mission is to serve a broad public purpose which is clearly incompatible with ownership and personal gain. This does not prevent nonprofit organizations from paying salaries to their employees, including the Chief Executive Officer or Chief Financial Officer. The Board members typically donate their time as a public service and receive no compensation.

These requirements do not prevent nonprofit organizations from making money, however. Nonprofit organizations can and do make money in the same way as for-profit organizations. The difference is that the moneys earned must be directed to the public purpose for which the nonprofit organization was established, held in reserve, or turned over to another organization with a public purpose. Thus, a key element of all nonprofit organizations is the use of earnings from the endeavor to promote the organizational goals, not to enrich the owners or stockholders.

The customers of nonprofit organizations are as diverse as their missions. Its customers may not only include people, but also whales, forests, birds, and buildings, individually or collectively. In addition, the people who have given their time, money, and other types of assets to further the cause are as much customers of the nonprofit as the actual recipients of the service being provided. They ask the most difficult questions of the nonprofit, have the greatest knowledge of the asset base, and are able to measure it against the activity performed on behalf of the organization.

A for-profit organization has a clear mission (to make a profit) and a clear decision-making path for achieving it. However, the public service nature of a nonprofit poses a major challenge in terms of identifying and articulating its mission and developing criteria for measuring its success. The mission statement must not only define what the organization is and does, but it must also state these concepts in a way that enables its achievements to be measured and evaluated.

After developing its mission statement, a nonprofit organization faces two additional major challenges: identify its public, and identify its constituency and level of involvement. After clearly identifying the group it intends to serve, a nonprofit must design an organizational structure that reinforces its commitment to the target group. It must then establish an image in the community, provide direction to potential fund sources, and either attract or repel the people to be served by the nonprofit organization.

(b) Organizational Structure

The structure of an organization defines the roles and responsibilities of those charged with pursuing its mission—the Board of Directors/Trustees, committees, staff, officers, outside contractors, and volunteers. A nonprofit organization must be structured to meet its goals. Water reclamation projects will require a structure involving engineers and construction experts, while feeding the homeless requires a completely different set of skills and hard assets to meet its goal. Although both operate as nonprofits, one may need to retain a huge amount of capital-intense equipment, while the other may require only a portable cooking facility.

The type of nonprofit determines the organizational structure and complexity of its membership. Medical research, conducted in conjunction with commercial medical development, requires a strict accounting for the input of each member or contributor and an equally strict accounting for any profit or gain realized from the joint venture.

The organizational structure for financial management will be addressed in greater detail in Chapter 3.

1.3 UNDERSTANDING THE WORKFORCE

The success of a nonprofit organization is dependent on the workforce it assembles to accomplish its mission. Nonprofit organizations provide unique challenges in this area.

The Board of Trustees. The Board of Trustees/Directors of a nonprofit organization determine the mission and set the parameters under which the organization operates. Their major areas of responsibility are:

• Determine the organization's mission and establish policies for its operation, ensuring that its Charter and bylaws are written and being followed

- Develop the organization's overall program on an annual basis and engage in long-range and strategic planning to establish its future course
- Establish fiscal policies and procedures, and set budgets and financial controls
- Provide adequate resources for the activities of the organization through direct financial contributions and a commitment to fund raising
- Select, evaluate, and if necessary, terminate the Chief Executive Officer
- Develop and maintain a communication link to the community, promoting the work of the organization

The Board of Trustees/Directors must keep the nonprofit organization focused on its mission. While Board members do not ordinarily participate in day-to-day operational decisions, they may approve operating budgets and assess the productivity of the operational managers. Ordinarily, they receive no compensation, whereas operational managers are usually on the payroll of the organization.

Since the Board of Trustees/Directors can be held responsible for the operations of the nonprofit, it is imperative for each member to fully understand the oversight role and for the organization to protect them through the purchase of Board liability insurance. This is discussed in detail in Chapter 15.

(a) Choosing Trustees/Directors

It is critical for nonprofit organizations to choose Trustees who have the experience, skills, and knowledge base needed for the Board to carry out its fiduciary and programmatic responsibilities. The Board, as a whole, must work well together and demonstrate strengths in the following areas:

- Vision
- Strategic planning
- Organizational development
- Fund raising
- Financial management
- Human resources management
- Legal issues related to nonprofits, contracts, human resources
- Public relations
- Community representation
- Programs related to the organizational mission

- Monitoring of day-to-day operations
- Conflict-of-interest avoidance

(b) Officers of the Nonprofit Organization

State laws vary, but they generally require a nonprofit organization's Board of Trustees to have at least three officers: a Chair (or President), a Treasurer (or Chief Financial Officer), and a Secretary. Some organizations include additional officers. The number of officers, their titles, powers, and duties are spelled out in the bylaws, along with the timetable and process by which officers are elected.

The selection of the right individuals to serve on the Board of a nonprofit organization is a critical task. Only the most qualified persons should be considered for officer positions, with no one appointed on an honorary basis.

(i) President/Chair of the Board. The President/Chair of a nonprofit Board should be a person of authority who is respected by the other Board members, the organization, the staff, and the community and who has the time and other resources needed to complete the required work. Ordinarily, the President has previously served in several other Board positions and is familiar with and informed about the operation of the organization.

(ii) Treasurer/Chief Financial Officer. The Treasurer must be a person with financial experience related to the operation of nonprofit organizations. Accountants and business professionals are generally preferred for these jobs; however, many lack experience with nonprofits and may not be sensitive to the special needs and characteristics of financial management in this sector. It is most advantageous for these organizations to find a Treasurer with nonprofit experience.

(iii) Secretary. The Secretary must be well organized and able to record information accurately since this position is usually responsible for maintaining all records of the nonprofit, including the preparation of Board meeting agendas and minutes. Since minutes serve as the official record of Board deliberations and decisions, they must reflect the actual motions, who made and seconded them, and how they were voted.

The Secretary should draft the Board meeting minutes and distribute them to Board members in advance of the next meeting for review and correction, as necessary. After all corrections are noted, the Board votes to accept the minutes and make them part of the corporate record. Their importance cannot be overstated because, when the minutes are approved, the Board's action is official and binding.

(iv) Board Committees. When a nonprofit organization reaches a certain size, its operation becomes more complex and its Board may experience difficulty in meeting all of its responsibilities. When this occurs, the Board may decide to pursue its work in smaller groups or committees, permitting a more detailed analysis of specific functions or areas such as executive, finance, staff, fund raising, investment management, property management, and planning. The role of these committees is to delve into the issues in their respective areas in a detailed way and to bring the results of these activities to the full Board for discussion. The Board may require a recommendation for action from the committee, based on its in-depth review.

Advantages of a committee structure are the division of workload and the promotion of a more informal discussion of the pros and cons of matters before the Board. It also allows an organization to bring experts into the deliberation process without appointing them to the Board.

In general, such committees should be chaired by a Trustee or Board member and have a majority of Board members serving in combination with outside resource people and staff members, who are assets to the process.

The committees listed below are common in nonprofit organizations. The actual number of committees depends on the size of the organization.

- *Executive Committee.* Mandated to strengthen the efficiency and effectiveness of the governing board.
- *Trustee Committee.* Reviews recommendations from the nominating committee and makes final recommendations to the Board for new trustees.
- *Student Affairs Committee.* Deals with issues related to the welfare of students.
- *Academic Affairs Committee.* Ensures that an institution's actions and policies reflect its priorities, mission, and character.
- *Finance Committee.* Determines how the Board should oversee the fiscal operations of the institution most effectively.
- *Audit Committee.* Describes the roles and responsibilities of a well-managed audit committee, which include overseeing regular audits of financial activities, adhering to laws and regulations, and monitoring the organization's conflict of interest policies.
- *Investment Committee.* Develops strategies and guidelines to support the Board's larger investment programs.
- *Development Committee.* Develops sound policies and tasks that support successful fund-raising and related programs.

- *Nominating Committee.* Identifies potential trustees for the Board of Directors and may also focus on getting people involved in the nonprofit organization. (See also Trustees Committee.)
- *Planning Committee.* Develops long-range strategic plans for the organization.
- *Building and Grounds Committee.* Makes policy for the physical plant and addresses issues, such as deferred maintenance.
- *Marketing/Public Relations.* Determines policy for how the organization will be marketed and presented to the public.
- *Program Committees.* Assumes general responsibility for one or more major events that may involve mobilizing volunteers to plan and work the event.
- *Personnel Committee.* Sets personnel policies.

An important and useful printed resource on the roles and responsibilities of Board Committees is "Board Basics," available from:

Association of Governing Boards
    of Universities and Colleges (AGB)
One Dupont Circle
Suite 400
Washington, D.C. 20036
Phone 1-800-356-6317

(v) **Executive Director.** The character of every nonprofit organization is largely determined by its Executive Director, who speaks for the organization publicly and hires the staff who deal with the organization's constituents on a daily basis. Because this position is key to the nonprofit, the selection process should follow these guidelines:

- Trustees should agree on the kind of person they are seeking, the special qualifications desired, and their expectations of the Executive Director prior to the actual selection.
- The Board must outline everything that needs to be accomplished by the Executive Director in managing the day-to-day operations of the nonprofit organization by responding to the following questions:

    1. What tasks are being performed now, and are they necessary?

    2. What tasks are not being performed now that should be?

    3. What new activities are being added that will require additional work?

    4. What specific tasks are required to accomplish the new work?

5. Do existing tasks need to be redefined or reorganized in order to address staff concerns over job assignments?

6. What steps should be taken to locate/hire an Executive Director?

(vi) Staff. The Executive Director is responsible for hiring the staff. Before doing so, he or she must determine the tasks to be performed and distribute them among the salaried employees, volunteers, independent contractors, and outside service providers. The best workforce mix is one that achieves the organization's mission in the most effective and efficient way. Usually a number of configurations will achieve the goal, and each has its own set of advantages and disadvantages.

(vii) Volunteers. Volunteers are a source of free labor that can be extremely useful to the nonprofit organization. Since volunteers are unpaid, it is important to find other rewards that will keep them motivated and involved. The process of recruiting, training, and retaining volunteers is complex, and their interaction with paid staff must be handled with care. Many nonprofits would be unable to function without volunteers, who want meaningful responsibility. Providing ways to reward and recognize volunteers is one of the significant challenges of the nonprofit organization.

(viii) Independent Contractors. Independent contractors are often retained to perform work for the nonprofit organization because they have special expertise that is not available in existing staff, provide that expertise at a cost lower than hiring additional long-term staff to fill a short- to medium-term need, enable organizations to focus on core activities, and increase organizational flexibility.

Outsourcing to independent contractors initially began as a strategy used solely by large corporations, but the practice has become widespread among organizations of all types and sizes. Services commonly outsourced include payroll, taxes, employee benefits, claims administration, investment services, graphic services, organizational restructuring, and organizational development.

(c) Job Descriptions

All types of organizations, including nonprofits, need written job descriptions for every member of their workforce including salaried staff, volunteers, independent contractors, and outside service providers. Written documentation of what each member does for the organization in a specific job or position is essential.

A typical job description includes the following components:

- General description of the job
- Statement concerning to whom the person reports and whom she or he will supervise
- List of specific responsibilities and functions

1.4 UNDERSTANDING THE LANGUAGE OF THE NONPROFIT ORGANIZATION

These are some of the most commonly used terms, with working definitions, used in the nonprofit sector:

Board of Trustees	Governing board of the nonprofit corporation (trust or charity), see Board of Directors
Articles of Incorporation	Legal document used to create a nonprofit organization
Bylaws	Set of rules that govern a nonprofit organization's internal affairs
Board of Directors	Two or more individuals who serve as the governing body of an organization
Tax exempt	Not subject to income taxes
501(c)(3)	Section of IRS code which defines this type of tax exempt, nonprofit corporation
Nonprofit	Corporation that is not allowed to distribute profits or surpluses to its Board or those in control of the organization
Treasurer	Chief Financial Officer of nonprofit organization
Secretary	Officer of nonprofit Board responsible for preparing Board agendas, minutes, and other documentation of business of nonprofit Board
Officer of Corporation	Legal representative of the Board of nonprofit corporation; President, Vice President, Secretary

Chair of Board	Person selected by Board to be its leader
Volunteer	One who does meaningful, but unpaid, work for the nonprofit organization
Fiduciary	One who is legally bound to oversee the affairs of another using the same standards as one would employ to look after his or her own assets
Stewardship	Holding something in trust for another
Philanthropy	Good will, active effort to promote human welfare
Endowment	An accumulation of contributions that is held for investment; earnings, if any, can be distributed to programs
Deferred giving	A charitable gift made before one's death
Restricted fund	A fund which has been contributed to a nonprofit organization for a specific, designated, purpose and cannot be used for general operations
Unrestricted fund	A fund contributed to a nonprofit organization whose use is determined by the Board of Directors
Fund accounting	Technical accounting term that refers to a system of accounting for funds by project
Permanent fund	A fund in which the principal is never spent
Conflict of interest	State of affairs that looks suspicious and raises questions of appearances

SAMPLE JOB DESCRIPTIONS/SUMMARY
OF RESPONSIBILITIES AND QUALIFICATIONS

BOARD OF TRUSTEES

Summary of Responsibilities

Members of the Board of Trustees of a nonprofit organization must assume their role with a full understanding of the accountability and liability, both personal and organizational, resulting from their service in their particular state. Specific responsibilities include but are not necessarily limited to the following:

- Determine the organization's mission and ensure that it is being carried out, as documented by federal and state law
- Set policies for ensuring that the organization operates according to its bylaws, the law, and ethical standards
- Ensure compliance with the rules and regulations set by federal, state, and local governments which have jurisdiction over it (e.g., filing tax returns with the IRS)
- Make certain that donated funds are used for the purposes of the organization, as prescribed by the donor
- Fulfill the legal requirements of the organization as an employer, including the payment of payroll taxes for the organization's employees
- Develop the organization's overall program, and engage in long-range strategic planning to establish its general course for the future
- Oversee the financial health of the organization, and establish fiscal policy and boundaries, with budgets and financial controls
- Provide adequate resources to operate the organization through direct financial contributions and a commitment to fund raising
- Select and evaluate the performance of the Chief Executive Officer
- Develop and maintain a communication/link between the organization and the community in promoting its work
- Monitor the performance of the organization to maximize the welfare of the public

Qualifications

Trustees must possess the following qualifications:

- Strong commitment to the mission, goals, and objectives of the organization

- Time, energy, and expertise required to make a significant contribution
- Skills and experience in organizational, financial, and human resources management, and strategic planning
- Ability to address issues and problems analytically, creatively, and decisively
- Strong leadership, interpersonal, and networking skills
- Familiarity with federal, state, and local laws and regulations governing nonprofit organizations
- Honesty, integrity, dedication, and positive attitude

BOARD CHAIR

Summary of Responsibilities

The Chair's overarching responsibility is to lead and motivate the Board of Trustees in concert with the CEO. Specific responsibilities include:

- Focus the Board on fulfilling its short- and long-term responsibilities and developing a clear vision for the future
- Provide strong leadership and direction to the Board, and develop ways to enhance its effectiveness
- Represent and speak on behalf of the Board concerning its decisions, actions, and related activities in interactions with the media, donors, and other constituencies of the nonprofit organization
- Serve as the Board's conscience and disciplinarian in order to control inexperienced or misguided Trustees, prevent factionalism and other practices harmful to the Board's reputation, promote teamwork and collegiality, and uphold ethical standards

Qualifications

The Chair must demonstrate the following qualities:

- Exemplary record of service and contributions to the Board which has earned the respect and trust of the membership
- Clear understanding of the respective responsibilities of the Chair and the CEO, and the ability to work cooperatively with the CEO toward common goals
- Excellent command of all aspects of the nonprofit organization, including strengths and weaknesses, and the ability to focus the Board's attention on both short-term needs and a long-term vision
- Close ties with business leaders, potential donors, government agencies, and others who can be of assistance to the nonprofit organization

- Strong organizational, communication, listening, motivating, decision-making, and public-speaking skills
- Sensitivity, objectivity, foresight, loyalty, and discretion

CHIEF EXECUTIVE OFFICER

Summary of Responsibilities

The CEO of a nonprofit organization is appointed by and reports to the Board of Trustees and has primary responsibility for the day-to-day operations. Specific responsibilities are to:

- Manage the financial operations of the organization to include internal control, review of financial statements, and monitoring of all financial details to ensure their accuracy and integrity
- Ensure that all programs, services, and activities contribute to and are in synch with the organizational mission, goals, and objectives
- Implement and monitor compliance with policies related to the organizational bylaws, the law, and ethical standards
- Select, supervise, and evaluate the performance of key positions including the Chief Financial Officer
- Develop and maintain close working relations with Trustees, staff, donors, and the community at large

Qualifications

The CEO must possess the following qualifications:

- Master's degree in business or the equivalent in a related field
- Extensive skills and experience in providing leadership and direction for all aspects of a large, complex nonprofit organization
- Proven ability to effectively manage financial, human, capital, and other organizational resources
- Excellent organizational, motivational, and interpersonal skills
- Familiarity with federal, state, and local laws and regulations governing nonprofit organizations
- Honesty, integrity, dedication, and positive attitude

TREASURER/CHIEF FINANCIAL OFFICER

Summary of Responsibilities

The role of Treasurer/Chief Financial Officer of a nonprofit organization entails the following responsibilities:

- Develop a financial structure for the review and approval of the Board of Trustees

- Safeguard the financial assets and maintain the financial records
- Define appropriate standards of behavior for fulfilling the finance function within the organization
- Prepare timely and meaningful financial statements
- Plan and implement fund-raising program, and explore planned-giving opportunities
- Comply with external reporting requirements
- Develop and implement appropriate budgeting practices and procedures
- Respond to operational changes affecting financial needs
- Report financial results to the CEO and Board of Trustees
- Supervise and empower employees engaged in the organization's financial activities
- Serve as a key participant in teams engaged in addressing multifaceted organizational problems
- Play an integral role in organizational decision making and creative problem solving
- Develop and implement systems for internal and external information sharing related to the organization's finances
- Work with program heads to represent their interests, explain the story behind the numbers, and clarify the business impacts during every step of the planning and budgeting process
- Present to the CEO and Board of Trustees a balanced picture of what is happening, where the problems lie, and what actions need to be taken

Qualifications

The Treasurer/Chief Financial Officer must possess the following qualifications:

- Training and experience in financial management, generally accepted accounting principles, and internal control systems
- Knowledge about the organization's mission and programs, and their relationship to the financial requirements and components
- Technical expertise in developing budgets and preparing financial statements
- Operational expertise
- Interpersonal communication and decision-making skills
- Honesty, integrity, and commitment to the organization's mission, values, and goals

SECRETARY

Summary of Responsibilities

The responsibilities of the Secretary are reflected in the nonprofit organization's bylaws and standing orders and include the following major functions:

- Plan Board meeting calendar and individual meetings, develop and distribute agendas, and provide for the staffing needs of the Board and its committees
- Prepare and disseminate minutes, resolutions, policy statements, and Board correspondence
- Review and maintain bylaws and standing orders
- Serve as custodian of official corporate documents and records
- Coordinate and facilitate all Board meeting arrangements including travel, hotel, meals, and other logistical details
- Foster effective communication and good personal relations between the Board of Trustees and CEO

Qualifications

The Secretary must possess the following skills/strengths:

- Understanding of the Secretary's unique role and commitment to developing and enhancing it
- Experience in managing and organizing all aspects of the work environment
- Knowledge of the history and mission of the nonprofit organization
- Familiarity with the legal and ethical issues of concern to Trustees
- Superior writing, coordinative, and interpersonal skills
- Efficiency, flexibility, and detail orientation

NOMINATING COMMITTEE

Summary of Responsibilities

Members of the Nominating Committee must devote their efforts to insuring that the Board of Trustees possesses the optimal mix of skills, experience, and influence needed to meet the Board's wide-ranging challenges. Particular responsibilities include:

- Assist the Board in determining the desired composition with respect to skills, abilities, experience, diversity, and influence and in making periodic adjustments to meet the changing needs of the organization
- Develop and cultivate a list of top-notch candidates who possess the desired qualities and are willing and able to serve
- Design, implement, and oversee a program for orienting, educating, and motivating new Trustees
- Oversee the successful integration of new Trustees onto Board committees and other activities
- Assess the effectiveness of individual Board members at the end of their terms, and determine their re-election status
- Identify and acknowledge meritorious contributions to the Board on the part of individual Trustees
- Coordinate periodic reviews of the overall performance of the Board
- Nominate the officers of the Board, and evaluate their performance on an annual basis

Qualifications

Members of the Nominating Committee must possess the following qualifications:

- Track record of strong, effective, and dedicated service on the Board
- Access to prominent individuals in the business, financial, and other communities who are prospective recruits
- Clear understanding of the Board's role and the importance of its composition to the organization's future
- Excellent planning, networking, and persuasive skills
- Patience, perseverance, and commitment to the task at hand

FINANCE COMMITTEE

Summary of Responsibilities

The Finance Committee is charged with the following tasks:

- Undertake a detailed review of all financial statements and audit reports, and convey the results to the Board
- Make recommendations to the Board on policy matters and issues related to the financial management function of the non-profit organization

- Provide assistance and support to the Chief Financial Officer in the development of long-range plans for raising, managing, and safeguarding organizational funds in an optimal manner

Qualifications

Members of the Finance Committee must have the following qualifications:

- Clear understanding of the mission, goals, and respective roles of the Finance Committee and Chief Financial Officer for the nonprofit organization
- Skills and experience in the areas of financial management, communication, and planning
- Integrity, good judgment, and adherence to sound financial principles

VOLUNTEERS

Volunteers are invaluable resources who contribute to the mission of nonprofit organizations in a variety of important ways. They can assist in an optimal manner under the following conditions:

- All volunteers are required to participate in an orientation program in order to gain a thorough understanding of the mission, goals, and activities of the nonprofit organization as well as learn about available involvement opportunities.
- Volunteers are assigned to activities which match their particular experience, talents, and areas of interest.
- Staff members are assigned to oversee specific tasks performed by volunteers as well as to provide guidance and answer any questions that may arise.
- Job descriptions are used to clarify the specific duties, responsibilities, expectations, chain of command, and other details of the various volunteer positions.
- Periodic meetings with volunteers are held to solicit feedback on the progress made, problems encountered, and changes needed.
- Close working relations between volunteers and professional staff are fostered to ensure maximum effectiveness and productivity.
- Volunteers are treated with the utmost respect and appreciation, and complete their assigned tasks with thoughtfulness, flexibility, enthusiasm, and dedication.

BY-LAWS OF THE ABC EDUCATIONAL FOUNDATION— A CALIFORNIA NONPROFIT PUBLIC BENEFIT CORPORATION

ARTICLE I. NAME

The name of this corporation is THE ABC EDUCATIONAL FOUNDATION ("the Foundation").

ARTICLE II. OFFICES

Section 1. Executive Office

The executive office of the Foundation is hereby fixed and located at 1400 Main Street, Los Angeles, California 90000. The Board of Trustees is hereby granted full power and authority to change from time to time said executive office from one location to another. The location of the executive office of the Foundation need not be in the state of California. Any such change shall be noted in the By-Laws by the Secretary, opposite this section, or this section may be amended to state the new location.

Section 2. Other Offices

Other business offices may at any time be established by the Board of Trustees at any place or places where the Foundation is qualified to do business.

ARTICLE III. PURPOSES AND POWERS

Section 1. Purposes

The Foundation is a nonprofit public benefit corporation and is not organized for the private gain of any person. It is organized under the California Nonprofit Public Benefit Corporation Law for public and charitable purposes to do the following:

(a) Broaden participation in and access to higher education within the State of California

(b) Promote a better understanding of the community's role in improving access to higher education

(c) Provide financial assistance to schools and colleges, support groups, faculty, and students in support of activities to improve access to higher education

(d) Engage in a variety of activities related to the above purposes

Section 2. Powers

In furtherance of the purposes hereinabove set forth, the Foundation shall have and shall exercise, subject to any limitations contained in its Articles of Incorporation, these By-Laws, applicable law or applicable policy statements, all powers of a natural person and all other rights, powers and privileges now or hereafter belonging to, or conferred upon, corporations organized under the provisions of the California Nonprofit Public Benefit Corporation Law, including without limitation, the power to do the following:

(a) Adopt, make, use, and at will alter, a corporate seal, but failure to affix such seal shall not affect the validity of any instrument

(b) Adopt, amend, and repeal By-Laws

(c) Qualify to conduct its activities in any other state, territory, dependency, or foreign country

(d) Issue, purchase, redeem, receive, take, or otherwise acquire, own, sell, lend, exchange, transfer or otherwise dispose of, pledge, use, and otherwise deal in and with real and personal property, capital stock, bonds, debentures, notes and debt securities, and money market instruments of its own or others

(e) Pay pensions, and establish and carry out pensions, deferred compensation, saving, thrift and other retirement, incentive and benefit plans, trusts and provisions for any or all of its Trustees, officers, employees, and persons providing services to it or any other subsidiary or related or associated corporation, and to indemnify and purchase and maintain insurance on behalf of any fiduciary of such plans, trusts, or provisions

(f) Make donations for the public welfare or for community funds, hospital, charitable, educational, scientific, civic, religious, or similar purposes

(g) Assume obligations, enter into contracts, including contracts of guaranty or suretyship, incur liabilities, borrow or lend money or otherwise use its credit, and secure any of its obligations, contracts or liabilities by mortgage, pledge or otherwise encumber all or any part of its property and income

(h) Participate with others in any partnership, joint venture or other association, transaction or arrangement of any kind whether or not such participation involves sharing or delegation of control with or to others

(i) Act as a trustee under any trust incidental to the principal objects of the Foundation, and receive, hold, administer, exchange, and expend funds and property subject to such trust

(j) Receive endowments, devises, bequests, gifts, and donations of all kinds of property for its own use, or in trust, in order to carry out or to assist in carrying out, the objects and purposes of the Foundation and to do all things and acts necessary or proper to carry out each and all of the purposes and provisions of such endowments, devises, bequests, gifts and donations with full power to mortgage, sell, lease, or otherwise deal with or dispose of the same in accordance with the terms thereof

Section 3. Dedication of Assets

This corporation is organized and shall be operated exclusively for educational purposes (meeting the requirements for exemption provided for by California Revenue and Taxation Code Sec. 214), within the meaning of Section 501(c)(3) of the Internal Revenue Code of 1986, as amended, and Section 23701d of the California Revenue and Taxation Code, as amended. The property, assets, profits and net income of this corporation are irrevocably dedicated to said educational purposes (meeting the requirements for exemption provided for by California Revenue and Taxation Code Sec. 214), and no part of the profits or net income of this corporation shall ever inure to the benefit of any Trustee, officer, or to any individual. Upon the dissolution of this corporation, the assets remaining after payment of, or provisions for payment of, all its debts and liabilities, to the extent not inconsistent with the terms of any endowment, devise, bequest, gift or donation, shall be distributed to an organization which is organized and operated exclusively for educational purposes (meeting the requirements for exemption provided for by California

Revenue and Taxation Code Sec. 214), and which is exempt from taxation under Section 23701d of the California Revenue and Taxation Code, as amended (or the corresponding provision of any future California Revenue Law) and Section 501(c)(3) of the Internal Revenue Code of 1986, as amended (or the corresponding provision of any future United States Internal Revenue Law) or to the federal government or to a state or local government.

Notwithstanding any other provision of these By-Laws, the Foundation shall not carry on any activities not permitted to be carried on:

(a) By a corporation exempt from Federal Income Tax under Section 501(c)(3) of the Internal Revenue Code of 1986, as amended (or the corresponding provision of any future United States Internal Revenue Law)

OR

(b) By a corporation, contributions to which are deductible under Section 170(c)(2) of the Internal Revenue Code of 1986, as amended (or the corresponding provision of any future United States Internal Revenue Law)

No substantial part of the activities of the Foundation shall consist of the carrying on of propaganda or otherwise attempting to influence legislation, nor shall the Foundation participate in, or intervene in (including the publishing or distributing of statements) any political campaign on behalf of any candidate for political office.

ARTICLE IV. MEMBERSHIP CORPORATION

Section 1. Membership

The Foundation shall be a membership corporation as provided in Chapter 3 of the Nonprofit Public Benefit Corporation Law (California Corporations Code Sections 5310 et seq.). One class of voting membership is hereby created and all persons who are eligible and active members of the Board of Trustees or as Advisory Trustees on the date this By-Law becomes effective will constitute the membership of the Foundation for the remainder of the terms to which they were originally elected or appointed.

There shall be no multiple or fractional memberships, nor members who are not natural persons.

Section 2. Members Called Trustees

The members of the corporation shall be called "Trustees" and the membership as a whole the "Board of Trustees" (and are so referred to hereinafter) in recognition of the long association of these terms with the Foundation. The use of these terms implies no other or different relationship or responsibility than that provided for members in the Nonprofit Public Benefit Corporation Law and these By-Laws.

Section 3. Persons Associated with the Foundation

By resolution, the Board of Trustees may create any advisory boards, councils, honorary memberships or other bodies as it deems appropriate. The Board of Trustees may also, by resolution, confer on any persons not already Trustees in such classes all of the rights of a member of the corporation under the Nonprofit Public Benefit Corporation Law other than the right to vote.

Section 4. Liability of Trustees

Trustees of the Foundation are not personally liable for the debts, liabilities, or obligations of the Foundation.

ARTICLE V. TRUSTEES

Section 1. Powers

The Trustees shall have all of the powers conferred by law, the Articles of Incorporation, or these By-Laws on members of nonprofit public benefit corporations. Notwithstanding any other provision in these By-Laws, the Board of Trustees legally has the exclusive and nondelegable power to do the following:

(a) Elect the Board of Trustees of the Foundation

(b) Elect the President

(c) Dispose of all or substantially all of the assets of the Foundation

(d) Approve a merger or dissolution

(e) Amend or repeal the Articles of Incorporation or the By-Laws of the Foundation

Section 2. Number and Qualification of Trustees

The authorized number of Trustees shall be not less than twenty (20), with no upper limit on the number of Trustees.

Section 3. Manner of Selection of Trustees

The composition of the Board of Trustees shall be as follows:

3.1 Elected Trustees. Trustees (except for ex officio Trustees as provided in Section 3.2) shall be elected by majority vote of the Trustees in attendance in person or by proxy at the meeting held to conduct such election, provided that there is a quorum (as provided in Section 11 of this Article), or a majority vote of mail written ballots, provided the requisite number of votes are cast (as provided in Section 12 of this Article), and may be re-elected. No more than twenty (20) new Trustees may be elected each year. The election of Trustees shall take place at the last meeting of the Board of Trustees each fiscal year. The Board of Trustees shall vote upon the nominations submitted by the Nominations Committee and such other nominations as may have been submitted by any member of the Board of Trustees eligible to vote not later than a date set by the Board sufficiently in advance of the vote to enable the inclusion of such nominations on proxy forms or mail written ballots.

3.2 Ex Officio Trustees. The following persons shall be ex officio Trustees:
Former presidents of the ABC Educational Foundation.

Section 4. Term of Office

All elected Trustees shall serve on the Board of Trustees for a term of three (3) years and may be re-elected. Terms of office shall commence on the first day of the Foundation's fiscal year.

Section 5. Honorary Trustees

Subject to the provisions of Section 3 of Article IV (relating to Persons Associated with the Foundation), the Board of

Trustees may from time to time invite individuals to serve as Honorary Trustees. Such Honorary Trustees shall serve at the pleasure of the Board of Trustees and shall have all rights and privileges of Trustees other than the right to vote.

Section 6. Resignation and Removal of Trustees

6.1 Resignation.   A Trustee may resign at any time. Such resignation shall not affect the Trustee's obligation for any liabilities already or thereafter incurred to the Foundation.

6.2 Expulsion, Suspension or Termination.   A Trustee may be expelled or suspended, or membership on the Board of Trustees or any of the rights associated therewith may be terminated or suspended, for just cause and upon the delivery of notice to such Trustee no later than fifteen (15) days prior to the date of intent to take such action, by first-class or registered mail, postage paid, addressed to such Trustee's last known address. Such notice shall indicate the reasons for the proposed action to be taken, the proposed effective date thereof, and shall inform the Trustee of his or her right to a hearing, orally or in writing, no sooner than five (5) days before the proposed effective date of this action.

The intent to take such action against a Trustee shall be submitted on the motion of any Trustee to the Nominations Committee at a meeting specifically called to consider such action, and must be approved by the majority of the quorum in attendance at such meeting.

If the intent to take such action is approved by the Nominations Committee and notice is duly mailed to the affected Trustee, the President (or, if the President is the affected Trustee, the Vice President—Finance) shall appoint an *ad hoc* hearing committee of not fewer than ten (10) Trustees who are not members of the Nominations Committee to provide for the hearing, if one is requested, pursuant to Corporations Code §5341. The decision of the Nominations Committee, or, if a hearing is held, of the *ad hoc* hearing committee, shall be final.

Section 7. Vacancies

7.1 Elected Trustees.   There is no limit to the number of elected Trustees, and therefore, the resignation, removal or death of a Trustee shall not cause a vacancy unless the number of Trustees thereby falls below twenty (20), in which case a majority of the remaining Trustees shall fill the vacancy, or all of the vacancies shall be filled by a sole remaining Trustee.

7.2 Ex Officio Trustees. Vacancies created by the removal, resignation, or death of ex officio Trustees shall be filled by the persons who succeed them in the offices that qualified them as Trustees.

Section 8. Regular Meetings

The Board of Trustees shall meet at least two times during each fiscal year. Notice of such regular meetings shall be given pursuant to the provisions of these By-Laws.

Section 9. Special Meetings

Special meetings of the Board of Trustees may be called for any purpose at any time by the Chairman of the Board, the President, the Vice President—Development, the Vice President—Finance, or any five Trustees by delivering written notice to the President or Vice President—Finance. Notice of such special meetings shall be given pursuant to the provisions of these By-Laws for notice of regular meetings.

Section 10. Notice and Place of Meetings

Meetings of the Board of Trustees shall be held at the place which has been designated in the notice of the meeting, if any; or if not stated in such notice or if there is no notice, at the place designated by resolution of the Board; or, absent any other designation, at the executive office of the Foundation located at 1400 Main Street, Los Angeles, California 90000.

Whenever a notice of a meeting of the Board of Trustees is required to be given, the Vice President—Finance shall cause notice of such meeting to be delivered by personal service, first-class mail or telegraph to each Trustee. In case notice is given by mail or telegram, it shall be sent, charges prepaid, addressed to the Trustee at his address appearing on the Foundation's records, or if it is not on these records or is not readily ascertainable, at the place where the regular meetings of the Board of Trustees are held. Such notice shall be given not fewer than ten (10) nor more than ninety (90) days before the date of the meeting to each Trustee who is entitled to vote; provided, however, that if notice is mailed, it shall be deposited in the United States mail at least twenty (20) days before the meeting.

Such notice shall state the date, place and hour of the meeting and, whenever practical, the general nature of the business to be transacted. Any other business which properly comes before a meeting may be transacted, notwithstanding the preceding sentence.

Section 11. Action at a Meeting:
Quorum and Required Vote

One-third of all the Trustees eligible to vote shall constitute a quorum. Only Trustees eligible to vote may hold and vote proxies. A majority of those present in person or by proxy at a duly held meeting with a quorum may perform any act or make any decision vested in the Board of Trustees, unless a greater number, or the same number after disqualifying one or more Trustees from voting, is required by law or the Foundation's Articles of Incorporation or By-Laws, and may continue to transact business notwithstanding the withdrawal of enough members to leave less than a quorum.

Section 12. Action without a Meeting:
Mail Written Ballots

Any action which may be taken at any regular or special meeting of Trustees may be taken without a meeting if the Foundation distributes a mail written ballot to every Trustee entitled to vote on the matter. Such ballot shall set forth the proposed action, provide an opportunity to specify approval or disapproval of any proposal and provide a reasonable time within which to mail or otherwise return the ballot to the Foundation.

Approval by mail written ballot shall be valid only when the number of votes cast by ballot within the time period specified equals or exceeds the quorum required to be present at a meeting authorizing the action, and the number of approvals equals or exceeds the number of votes that would be required to approve the action at a meeting at which the total number of votes cast was the same as the number cast by ballot.

Ballots shall be solicited in a manner consistent with the notice requirements of these By-Laws. All such solicitations shall indicate the number of responses needed to meet the quorum requirement and, with respect to ballots other than for the election of Trustees or Directors, shall state the percentage of approvals necessary to pass the measure submitted. The solicitation must specify the time by which the ballot must be received in order to be counted.

Mail written ballots may not be revoked.

Trustees may be elected by mail written ballot if the Board so determines, in which case, the Board shall also fix a date for the close of nominations a reasonable time before the printing and distribution of the mail written ballots.

The use of a written ballot at a meeting of the Board of Trustees, which is intended to be voted upon at the meeting where it is distributed, does not invoke the provisions of this section as to mail written ballots.

Section 13. Validation of Defectively Called or Noticed Meetings

The transactions of any meeting of the Board of Trustees, however called or noticed or wherever held, shall be as valid as though transacted at a meeting duly held after regular call and notice, if a quorum is present and if, either before or after the meeting, each of the Trustees not present or who, though present, has prior to the meeting or at its commencement, protested the lack of proper notice to him, signs a written waiver of notice or a consent to holding such meeting or an approval of the minutes thereof. A waiver of notice need not specify the purpose of any regular or special meeting of the Board of Trustees. All such waivers, consents, or approvals shall be filed with the Foundation's records or made a part of the minutes of the meeting.

Section 14. Adjournment

A majority of the Trustees present in person or by proxy, whether or not a quorum is present, may adjourn any meeting to another time and place. If the meeting is adjourned for more than thirty (30) days, notice of the adjournment to another time or place shall be given prior to the time of the adjourned meeting to the Trustees who were not present at the time of the adjournment.

Section 15. Form of Proxy or Mail Written Ballot

Any form of proxy or mail written ballot shall afford an opportunity on the proxy form or mail written ballot to specify a choice between approval and disapproval of each matter or group of related matters intended, at the time the proxy or mail written ballot is distributed, to be acted upon at the meeting for which the proxy is solicited or by such mail written ballot, and shall provide that where the person solicited specifies a choice with respect to any such matter the vote shall be cast in accordance therewith.

In any election, any form of proxy or mail written ballot in which the Trustees to be voted upon are named therein as candidates and which is marked by a Trustee "withhold" or otherwise marked in a manner indicating that the authority to vote for the election of Trustees is withheld shall not be voted either for or against the election of a Trustee.

Section 16. Fees and Compensation

Trustees shall not receive compensation for their services as such. Trustees may, however, be reimbursed for reasonable out-of-pocket expenses incurred by them in the performance of their duties as Trustees.

Section 17. Council of Presidents

The president and all the former presidents of the Foundation shall constitute a Council of Presidents whose primary function shall be to recommend to the Nominations Committee a person to be President-elect at the appropriate time. The Council of Presidents shall meet on the call of the President and may serve to advise the President on other matters of importance to the Foundation as the President may from time to time request.

ARTICLE VI. STANDING BOARDS OF THE FOUNDATION

The Board of Trustees shall have certain Standing Boards as set forth herein.

Section 1. Executive Committee

The Executive Committee is a Standing Board of the Foundation.

1.1 Composition. The Executive Committee shall have not fewer than twenty-four (24) nor more than thirty (30) members, the exact number to be fixed from time to time by resolution of the Board of Trustees. All members of the Executive Committee shall be members of the Board of Trustees. Except for ex officio members, and except as otherwise provided in these By-Laws, the Executive Committee shall be elected annually by the Board of Trustees in accordance with the nomination and election procedures for Trustees in these By-Laws. Vacancies of elected members on the Executive Committee arising during the term of office may be filled by the Board of Trustees at a special election to be held at the discretion of the President, unless such vacancies reduce the number of Executive Committee members below twenty-four (24) in which case the President shall call for a special election to be held at the next regularly scheduled meeting of the Board of Trustees. The remaining members of the Executive Committee may temporarily fill vacancies until an election is held.

Any other provision of these By-Laws notwithstanding, at no time shall more than forty-nine (49) percent of the persons serving on the Executive Committee be any of the following: (i) persons compensated by the Foundation for services rendered within the previous twelve (12) months (whether as an employee, contractor or otherwise) other than reasonable compensation paid to a member for his service as an Executive Committee member or, (ii) the spouse, an ancestor, sibling or descendent to the first degree of consanguinity, or any person married to such relative of any person so compensated.

1.2 Ex Officio Executive Committee Members. The following Trustees are designated ex officio as members of the Executive Committee, to serve until their successors are named:

(a) The Chair of the Board of Trustees

(b) The President of the Foundation (who shall serve as the Chief Executive Officer and Chair of the Executive Committee)

(c) The President-elect of the Foundation (when one exists)

(d) The Vice President-Finance of the Foundation (who shall serve as Chief Staff and Financial Officer of the Executive Committee)

(e) The Vice President-Development of the Foundation

(f) The General Counsel of the Foundation

Any other provision of these By-Laws notwithstanding, at no time shall more than one-third of the persons serving on the Executive Committee be ex officio members as designated herein.

1.3 Term of Office. Elected members of the Executive Committee shall serve for a one-year term and may be re-elected for not more than six consecutive one-year terms. Ex officio members of the Executive Committee shall serve so long as they hold the positions that qualify them as members.

1.4 Duties and Powers. The Executive Committee shall manage the activities and affairs of the Foundation and have the full authority to act thereon except as limited by law, the Articles of Incorporation, and except as certain functions may be reserved to the Board of Trustees or may be delegated by the Board of Trustees to Standing Boards or special committees of the Foundation pursuant to these By-Laws.

Notwithstanding any other provision of these By-Laws, the Executive Committee is vested with the full fiduciary responsibility for the following:

(a) The prudent investment of and accountability for the assets of the Foundation

(b) The adoption of the Foundation's annual budget

(c) The power to approve self-dealing transactions, the power to issue checks, drafts and other orders for the payment of money, notes or other evidence of indebtedness and to receive the same on behalf of the Foundation, with such signature or endorsement authority as the Executive Committee determines

(d) The power to authorize any officer or officers, agent or agents, to enter into any contract or execute any instrument in the name of, and on behalf of, the Foundation. Such authority may be general or confined to specific instances and, unless so authorized by the Board of Trustees, no officer, agent or employee shall have any power or authority to bind the Foundation by any contract or engagement or to pledge its credit or to render it liable for any purpose or any amount, except for contracts or commitments in the regular course of business of the Foundation executed by an officer within the scope of his authority

Subject to any limitations of law, or the Articles of Incorporation, the Executive Committee shall manage and carry out the fiduciary responsibility vested in it by these By-Laws and in so doing shall have all the rights, powers and authority of the Board of Trustees.

1.5 Regular Meetings. Meetings of the Executive Committee shall be held at such times and at such places as the President may determine, but in no event fewer than three (3) times during each fiscal year of the Foundation. Notice of such meetings shall be given in the manner set forth in Section 8 of Article V of these By-Laws (relating to Notice and Place of Meeting), except that notice may be given by telephone not less than twenty-four (24) hours prior to the meeting and that notice sent by mail shall be given not less than forty-eight (48) hours prior to the meeting.

Actions may be taken without a meeting of the Executive Committee if all members individually or collectively consent thereto in writing. Such consents shall be filed with the minutes of the proceedings of the Executive Committee, and shall have the same force and effect as an action taken at regularly noticed meetings of the Executive Committee.

1.6 Quorum. Twelve (12) members present in person shall constitute a quorum for the transaction of business, except as expressly provided otherwise in the Articles of Incorporation, these By-Laws or by resolution of the Board of Trustees. The Executive Committee shall not conduct business by proxy or mail written ballot.

1.7 Meetings by Conference Telephone. Members of the Executive Committee may participate in a meeting through use of conference telephone or similar communications equipment, so long as all members participating in such meeting can hear one another. Participation in a meeting in this manner shall constitute presence in person at such meeting.

1.8 Special Committees and Organization. In discharging its responsibilities, the Executive Committee will establish appropriate policies for the investment and management of funds, for the conduct of audits, for the acceptance and management of planned gifts, for the grants and allocations of Foundation funds, and for the nomination of persons for election to the various posts established in these By-Laws for election by the Board of Trustees. The Executive Committee shall create special committees on investment, audit, grants and allocations, and nominations for the exercise of these respective responsibilities and may delegate to these committees such responsibility to act on behalf of the Executive Committee, to the extent permitted by law, as it deems appropriate, and each such committee shall report all actions taken to the next regular meeting of the Executive Committee. The Executive Committee from time to time may create such other committees and delegate to each such authority as the Executive Committee deems appropriate.

The Executive Committee shall, by resolution, establish the number of members, responsibility, title, and rules governing any special committees established hereunder. The members, and Chair, of all such special committees shall be appointed annually by the President, subject to approval by the Board of Trustees. The President, the Vice President—Development, and the Vice President—Finance shall be ex officio members of all special committees (except the Audit Committee); all other members of the special committees shall be appointed from the membership of the Board of Trustees, provided that the majority of each committee be comprised of Trustees who are not ex officio members.

The President shall appoint the Chairs and members of such committees established by the Executive Committee and shall assure that each committee shall have representatives of the Executive Committee and other groups represented on the Board of Trustees as a whole.

The Executive Committee shall establish rules and procedures for the conduct of its business and, except as already provided for in these By-Laws, appoint such officers as it deems appropriate for the conduct of its business.

1.9 Removal with Cause. The Board of Trustees may remove from office by majority vote an Executive Committee member who has been declared of unsound mind by final order of a court, or convicted of a felony or found by final order of a court to have violated a duty under Article 3 of the Nonprofit Public Benefit Corporation Law.

1.10 Removal without Cause. Any Executive Committee member may be removed from office without cause by the vote of a majority of the Trustees then in office.

Section 2. Board of Development

A Standing Board to be known as the Board of Development shall be vested with the Foundation's authority to raise private funds and other gifts to support its mission.

The composition of the Board of Development is intended to reflect the breadth of the development effort, with representatives from diverse areas of the community as well as central development activities. Its purpose is to serve as the senior advisory and volunteer management body for development. The President shall be Chair of the Board of Development.

2.1 Ex Officio Members of Board of Development: Term of Office. The following persons are designated ex officio as members of the Board of Development, to serve so long as they hold the position designated below, or as otherwise provided herein:

1. The Chairman of the Board of Trustees
2. The President of the Foundation (who shall serve as Chair)
3. The President-elect of the Foundation (when one exists)
4. The Vice President—Development of the Foundation
5. The Vice President—Finance of the Foundation
6. The General Counsel of the Foundation

2.2 Other Members of the Board of Development: Term of Office. The President may appoint other members of the Board of Development who may or may not be Trustees, to serve at the pleasure of the President. Consideration in making such appointments should be given to the person's strong history of financial support for the Foundation or whose experience, ability and leadership would be of great value to the Board of Development.

ARTICLE VII. OFFICERS

The Foundation shall have certain officers as set forth herein. The Foundation may also have such other officers as the Executive Committee may from time to time establish in order to conduct the business of the Foundation. Each officer of the Foundation shall have such authority and perform such duties as provided in the By-Laws or as the Executive Committee may from time to time prescribe.

Section 1. Chair of the Board

The Chair of the Board shall be the immediate past President of the Foundation. He or she shall preside at meetings of the Board of Trustees, the Executive Committee, and the Board of Development in the absence of the President.

Section 2. President

The President shall be an elected Trustee of the Foundation and is elected by the Board of Trustees as provided in these By-Laws for a term of two years, and may not be re-elected to a second consecutive term. The President shall be the Chief Executive Officer and shall preside at all meetings of the Board of Trustees, the Board of Development and the Executive Committee. A vacancy in the presidency will be filled by the President-elect or, if there is none, by special election of the Board of Trustees. An ex officio Trustee shall not serve as President.

Section 3. President-Elect

The President-elect shall be an elected Trustee of the Foundation and is elected by the Board of Trustees at the last meeting of the fiscal year before the anniversary of the President's assumption of office, and shall take office as President at the expiration of the President's term of office, or upon a vacancy in the office of President. The President-elect shall preside at meetings of the Board of Trustees in the absence of both the President and Chairman of the Board and shall perform the other duties of the President in the President's absence.

Section 4. Vice President—Development

The Vice President—Development shall serve as Chief Staff Officer of the Board of Development.

Section 5. Vice President—Finance

The Vice President—Finance shall serve as chief staff officer of the Executive Committee and Chief Financial Officer of the Foundation, and act as the Foundation's Secretary and Treasurer.

Section 6. General Counsel

The General Counsel shall be the legal advisor to the Foundation and all of its boards and committees, and shall exercise such other powers and perform such other duties as the Board of Trustees may from time to time determine. The President shall appoint the General Counsel, who shall serve at the pleasure of the President.

Section 7. Removal and Resignation

Any officer elected by the Board of Trustees or appointed by the President may be removed at any time with or without cause either by the Board of Trustees, by the President, or by any officer upon whom the power of removal has been conferred by the Board of Trustees, subject to the rights, if any, of the officer under a contract of employment with the Foundation. Without prejudice to the rights, if any, of the Foundation under any contract to which the officer is a party, any officer may resign at any time by giving written notice to the Foundation. Unless otherwise specified therein, any such resignation shall take effect at the date of the receipt of such notice.

Section 8. Vacancies

A vacancy occurring in any office shall be filled in accordance with the procedure for the regular selection or appointment of that officer under these By-Laws, although the President may appoint a person to act as that officer in the interval of time reasonably required before a regular appointment can be made.

Section 9. Compensation

Officers may receive such compensation for their services or such reimbursement for their expenses as may be determined by the Executive Committee to be just and reasonable. The Board of Trustees may, at the Foundation's expense, bond any officer and employee for the faithful performance of his duties in such amount and with such surety or sureties as it may determine.

ARTICLE VIII. PROCEDURES

The Board of Trustees, the Executive Committee, and the Board of Development may each prescribe appropriate rules, not inconsistent with the By-Laws, by which its respective proceedings shall be conducted. Unless provided otherwise in these By-Laws, the procedures regarding the notice and calling of meetings and the transaction of business of meetings of the Board of Trustees shall apply to the proceedings of all Standing Boards, special, and other committees of both the Board of Trustees and the Executive Committee, except for procedures regarding proxies and mail written ballots, which shall apply only to meetings of the Board of Trustees. Each Standing Board, special, or other committee shall prescribe its own appropriate rules, except as pertain to the notice and calling of meetings. Unless otherwise provided, Robert's Rules of Order shall apply to all meetings and proceedings of the Foundation.

ARTICLE IX. MISCELLANEOUS

Section 1. Inspection of Corporate Records

Every Trustee shall have the absolute right at any reasonable time to inspect and copy all books, records and documents of every kind and to inspect the physical properties of the Foundation. Such inspection may be made in person or by agent or attorney and the right of inspection includes the right to copy and make extracts.

Section 2. Representation of Shares of Other Corporations

The Chair of the Board, the President, the Vice President—Finance or another Trustee designated by the Executive Committee is authorized to vote, represent, and exercise on behalf of the Foundation all rights incident to any and all shares of any other corporation or corporations standing in the name of the Foundation, unless the Board of Trustees designates another person to exercise such rights, or unless the By-Laws of the other corporation otherwise provide. The authority herein granted may be exercised either in person or by proxy or power of attorney duly executed.

Section 3. Fiscal Year: Audit

The fiscal year of the Foundation shall be from July 1 to June 30. The financial books and records of the Foundation shall be audited at least once during each fiscal year by reputable and independent certified accountants.

Section 4. Standing Orders

Standing orders and rules of practice consistent with the Articles of Incorporation and the By-Laws, may be prescribed from time to time by the Board of Trustees in order to facilitate and expedite the carrying on of the business of the Foundation. The Vice President—Finance shall keep such orders and rules, if any, in permanent written form, properly indexed and same shall be part of the permanent records of the Foundation and shall govern and control the administration of the activities and affairs of the Foundation as far as applicable.

Section 5. Indemnification of Agents of the Corporation: Liability Insurance

5.1. Subject to any limitations contained in the Articles of Incorporation and to the extent permitted by the California Nonprofit Public Benefit Corporation Law, the Foundation may indemnify any person who was or is a party or is threatened to be made a party to any proceeding by reason of the fact that such person is or was a Trustee, officer, employee, member of a committee, or other agent of the Foundation, against expenses, judgments, fines, settlements, and other amounts actually and reasonably incurred in connection with such proceeding and the Foundation may advance expenses in connection therewith.

5.2. The Foundation may purchase and maintain insurance on behalf of any Trustee, officer, employee or other agent of the Foundation against any liability asserted against or incurred by such person in his or her capacity or arising out of his or her status as such, whether or not the Foundation could indemnify such person against such liabilities under the provisions of Section 5.1 of Article IX. Notwithstanding the above, the Foundation shall not purchase and maintain such insurance for a violation of Section 5233 of the California Nonprofit Public Benefit Corporation Law (with respect to self-dealing transactions).

5.3. Section 5 of Article IX (relating to Indemnification of Agents of the Corporation: Liability Insurance) does not apply to any proceeding against any Trustee, investment manager, or other fiduciary of any employee benefit plan in such person's capacity as such, even through said person may also be a Trustee, officer, employee, or other agent of the Foundation for purposes of Sections 5.1 and 5.2 of Article IX. The Foundation may indemnify such Trustee, investment manager or other fiduciary to the extent permitted by Subdivision (f) of Section 207 of the California General Corporation Law.

Section 6. Support Group Policy

Notwithstanding any provision of these By-Laws to the contrary, the Foundation shall comply policies relating to support groups as set forth in policy statements in effect from time to time.

ARTICLE X. AMENDMENTS TO BY-LAWS

The Board of Trustees may adopt, amend or repeal these By-Laws. Any proposed amendment, repeal or revision of these By-Laws shall be submitted in writing to the Vice President—Finance not fewer than fifteen (15) nor more than ninety (90) days prior to the meeting at which the same is to be considered. At least ten (10) days prior to such meeting, the Vice President—Finance shall mail or cause to be delivered copies of any such proposal to each Trustee in the manner provided in Section 10 of Article V (relating to Notice and Place of Meetings) of these By-Laws.

CHAPTER TWO

Using Financial Management to Accomplish Your Mission

2.1 Introduction 42
2.2 Financial Management and Its Importance 43
    (a) Financial Management Structure 43
    (b) Cash Flow System 44
    (c) Why Is Treasury Management So Important for Nonprofits? 45
2.3 Do Nonprofit Treasury Management Objectives Differ? 50
2.4 Preview/Principles 52
    (a) The Lilly Study 52
    (b) Keep the Mission First! 54
    (c) Management and Financial Objectives 54
        (i) Management Objectives 54
        (ii) Financial Objectives 54
        (iii) Achievement of Financial Objective—How Well Are You Doing, Regardless of Objectives Pursued? 54
        (iv) Is the Indicated Financial Objective Really Operational? 55
        (v) Hindrance to Achievement of Financial Objective 56
2.5 How Can Nonprofit Treasury Management Be Improved? 56
    (a) Scoring in the Short-Term Financial Management Categories 58
        (i) Performance Improvement Measures 64
    (b) A Useful Framework for Treasury Diagnosis 65
        (i) Cash Conversion Cycle 65
        (ii) Cash Budget 65

2.1 INTRODUCTION

Nonprofit financial management was rocked in 1995 by the New Era Philanthropy scandal. It appears, at the time of this writing, that some organizations turned over substantial sums to New Era, some of which they may never recoup: Young Life, $2.5 million; Messiah College, $2 million; Wheaton College and Houghton College, each $1.5 million; and Spring Arbor College, $1.1 million. Because of these debacles, we are hearing about the results of *not* attending to financial management matters. As suggested in the first chapter, the main goal of this guide is to enable the nonprofit financial manager, usually carrying the title of treasurer, to gain proficiency in each major area of financial management. A secondary goal is to equip board members and executive directors to grasp key financial concepts. We will try to achieve both goals by using examples and illustrating complex calculations wherever possible.

The best-in-class organizations we profile at various points in this guide show the upside to proficient financial management. Campus Crusade for Christ, Intl. (CCC), headquartered in Orlando, is one such organization. CCC is one of the largest nondenominational religious organizations in the United States, yet almost all its employees (including the Chief Financial Officer) are volunteers who must raise their own financial support from donors. CCC managers learned the importance of the financial function from a major financial catastrophe in the early 1980s, and they regularly implement new and innovative financial management methods like those presented in this guide. In this chapter, we will demonstrate how nonprofits can further mission accomplishment by improving financial management, especially in the treasury area.

We will demonstrate that proficient financial management can sustain and enhance mission achievement, using real-life examples from charitable, religious, art, education, and human services organizations. "Proficient" means "having or marked by an advanced degree of competence, as in an art, vocation, profession, or branch of learning." The proficient financial manager is one who is expert or adept at what he or she does. By using examples from the best of governmental, business, and nonprofit arenas, we engage the reader in better knowing how to administer his organizational type.

2.2   FINANCIAL MANAGEMENT AND ITS IMPORTANCE

(a) Financial Management Structure

Nonprofit administrators have difficulty maintaining strong financial control due to the following characteristics of nonprofit organizations that may hinder an effective internal control structure:[1]

- A volunteer governing Board, many of whose members serve for limited terms.

[1]American Institute of Certified Public Accountants (AICPA), New York, NY (1994).

- A limited number of staff personnel, sometimes too few to provide the appropriate segregation of duties.

- A mixture of volunteers and employees participating in operations. Depending on the size and other features of the organization, day-to-day operations sometimes are conducted by volunteers instead of employees. The ways in which responsibility and authority are delegated vary among organizations. This may affect control over financial transactions, particularly with respect to authorization.

- A budget approved by the governing Board. The budget may serve as authorization for the activities to be carried out by management in attaining the organizations' program objectives. Many nonprofit organizations prepare budgets for both operating and capital expenditures.

(b) Cash Flow System

Nonprofit organizations' financial processes can be accurately characterized as a cash flow system. Many charities and churches receive cash from gifts and grants, husband the cash for a while, then disburse the cash to other organizations, members, clients, or beneficiaries. Even food and medical charities, which transform cash into services or products (possibly receiving added revenue by doing so), benefit greatly from the cash flow system model (see Exhibit 2.1).

Organizations that primarily transfer funds from donor or grantor to clients or beneficiaries are labeled as *conduits*. Examples include foundations, denominations, association headquarters operations, and agencies sending personnel abroad to deliver a service. Proficient cash management is absolutely essential to the suc-

Exhibit 2.1. Cash Flow Model of Nonprofit Organizations' Finances

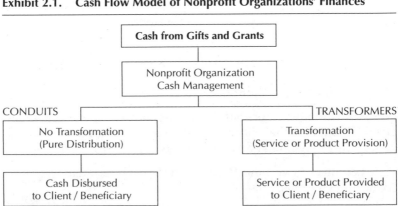

cess of conduits in that they are primarily cash gathering and distributing machines. *Transformers*, in turn, convert cash into one or more products or services, and distribute those outputs to clients and other beneficiaries. Transformers include churches, arts organizations, charities, educational institutions, and health and human service organizations. Cash management proficiency is still important prior to the conversion process, but the quality and quantity of service delivery assume greater importance. Overall working capital proficiency, which may include both receivables and inventories, is the appropriate focus in transformers.

(c) Why Is Treasury Management So Important for Nonprofits?

Financial management is rapidly gaining prominence in nonprofit organizations. Treasury management, enveloping all decisions affecting the cash position, is singled out for special attention in the well-managed nonprofit organization. Treasury management is critical for today's nonprofit organization for several reasons.

1. *Many nonprofits are in financial distress:* As businesses in Chapter 11 bankruptcy proceedings have discovered, daily monitoring and control of the organization's cash position is vitally important to preserve and prolong financial health.

   Cash is the lifeblood of an organization's operation. The entity that continues to generate cash and maintains its access to cash will survive and thrive. An organization that ignores or poorly manages its cash position has difficulty carrying out its mission and may fail. More businesses fail for a lack of ready cash than for any other reason, even firms with sound profitability. Resource-constrained nonprofit organizations are increasingly aware that proficient financial management sustains program initiatives, and may mark the difference between surviving and failing concerns. A fundraising letter from the general director of one religious nonprofit portrays this new awareness:

   > . . . Our fiscal year will end in just a few weeks. By faith, we are asking God to help us finish this year in the black. . . . [Our organization] must be financially strong as we enter the new fiscal year. That is the only way we can pursue the harvest God has given us with our full energy—and I can't bear the thought of doing anything less.

2. *Greater control of resources often means more resources:* Not only do managers know and protect financial resources, but their reputation for being accountable stewards enhances the probability of being granted more resources in the future. Next to their ability to gather the cash in the first place, their effectiveness and

efficiency as organizations are primarily related to how well they collect, manage, invest, and disburse their cash. Some local Red Cross organizations are hanging banners in front of their buildings trumpeting the fact that Red Cross was rated the #1 charity by *Money Magazine*. That rating is based on an analysis of their financial data.

3. Stewardship demands proficiency in treasury management: A steward is "one who manages another's property, finances, or other affairs." Longevity and bureaucracy in many nonprofits have spawned organizational cultures that disregard the facts that (1) management is essential, and (2) the property and finances *belong to* an organization only in a legal sense, and are better viewed as being managed *by* the organization. A big part of treasury management is investment and debt management. Nonprofit organizations often have very large sums of investable funds compared with firms of similar size in other industries. Nonprofit organizations are also more likely to have greater investment management needs than businesses for several reasons:

- Most nonprofit organizations must set aside funds for replacement of plants and equipment. Investor-owned firms, on the other hand, can rely on the issuance of new stockholders' equity to finance some of their replacement needs.

- Nonprofit organizations are increasingly beginning to self-insure all or a portion of their professional liability risk. This requires that rather sizable investment pools be available to meet possible actuarial needs.

- Many nonprofit organizations receive gifts and endowments. While these sums may not be large for individual nonprofit organizations, they can provide additional sources of investment. In the United Kingdom, a study of over 4,000 of the larger charitable organizations found that one-sixth of their revenues came from investments.[2]

- Many nonprofit organizations also have rather sizable funding requirements for defined benefit pension plans and debt service requirements associated with the issuance of bonds. These funds are usually held by a trustee.

- Nonprofits that rely on grants and gifts must raise those funds when they are most available, as opposed to when they are most needed. Funds are then invested or used to pay down borrowings until monies are distributed or trans-

[2]Stephen P. Osborne and Les Hems, "The Economic Structure of Charitable Sector in the United Kingdom," *Nonprofit and Voluntary Sector Quarterly* 24 (1995): 321–325.

formed into products or services. Businesses selling products or services experience a closer time match between revenues and expenditures. The cash flow timeline in Exhibit 2.2 illustrates the unsynchronized nature of donative nonprofits' revenue and expense cycles.

4. *Nonprofits' financial management is increasingly scrutinized by funding agencies, present and potential donors (and their advisors), and external philanthropic watchdog agencies:* Watchdog agencies such as the American Institute of Philanthropy (AIP), the Council of Better Business Bureaus (BBB), and the National Charitable Information Bureau (NCIB) (also trade associations ECFA and EFICOM) are often quoted in mainstream newspapers and magazines. Let's illustrate the type of reports being publicized. Exhibit 2.3 provides a tabulation of nonprofit organizations which was freely available to anyone with a computer and access to one of the on-line services. The website is run by the Internet Nonprofit Center.[3] One can download the financial statistics for all charities registered to do business in various states. Exhibit 2.3 shows the top five, overall average, and bottom five charities according to percent of total expenditures devoted to programmatic expenditures, using 1993 data as reported to the attorney general's office in Oregon (see middle column labeled Program percent). The selected organizations were all registered in Oregon, but represent only 128 of the more than 9,000 organizations registered in that state.

The "average" numbers in the middle row of Exhibit 2.3 serves as a point of reference for the reader. The numbers included here are being used to scrutinize organizational efficiency by the IRS, state regulatory agencies, foundations and other grant agencies, and even sophisticated individual donors. Yet, for a limited number of organizations, the figures in Exhibit 2.3 paint a partly unfair

Exhibit 2.2.   Cash Flow Time Line Shows Time to Convert Cash Back to Cash

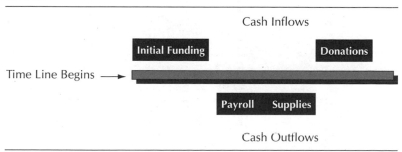

[3]The current web address is http://www.nonprofits.org/library/gov.html.

Exibit 2.3. Publicly Available Financial Information Accessed by the Internet

Name	Total Revenue	Program ($)	Program % of Total Expenditures	FundBalc	NetFxdAssts	TotalAssets
Valley Family Health Care	2,347,638	2,300,631	100.00	1,314,490	0	1,314,490
Assembly of God Expression of Marriage Encounter	482,498	451,595	100.00	57,785	4,519	59,167
300 Main	124,402	129,445	100.00	54,383	570,770	621,055
American-Foundation	121,546,994	120,102,344	98.53	2,258,615	287,553	5,137,199
Ronald McDonald Children's Charity	19,429,642	12,531,792	92.99	28,310,698	0	33,415,584
Average:	18,724,323	13,723,968	73.29	15,394,679	7,361,176	21,044,034
American Indian Relief Council	4,690,350	1,277,756	30.07	1,556,190	738,017	1,746,391
Find the Children	783,612	167,808	21.43	89,596	962	93,568
Athletes for Youth Foundation	556,562	95,335	19.18	71,606	0	73,306
Interstate Firehouse Cultural Center	251,737	47,034	17.97	0	0	9,653
Mission To Children	96,863	15,504	15.19	31,001	512	512

picture. Some organizations may use the accumulated fund balance to finance part of the program services spending, meaning that the percent of expenditures for this particular year was higher than normal. On the opposite end, for relatively young organizations the start-up costs require a relatively large investment in fundraising and administration. Smaller and younger organizations such as Mission to Children, therefore, often have lower program ratios due to their inability to take advantage of "economies of scale," in which salaries and other overhead expenses are spread across a larger service quantity or caseload. For the other organizations, however, the moral of the story is hard to miss; spend as much as possible on programs so as to be "above average" in their use of donated funds. This means you must manage your finance function efficiently and limit expenditures on it and other staffing functions in order to maximize the amount available for program spending that furthers the mission.

5. *Treasury management encompasses many of the managerial processes that are being re-engineered for greater efficiency and effectiveness today by businesses, and that are ripe for re-engineering by nonprofits:* In their guide *The Reengineering Revolution: A Handbook,* Michael Hammer and Steven Stanton devote an entire chapter to re-engineering in mission-driven organizations. Hammer and Stanton said:

> There are tens of thousands of them: government agencies, charities, hospitals, universities, schools, think tanks, benevolent societies, veterans' associations, communities of bird watchers. While improving their financial situation may be important, what really motivates them is performing their mission more effectively. Such institutions often consider finance a necessary evil, and not to be confused with their fundamental mission, which usually seeks to improve or even transform lives. Still, reengineering has much to offer these organizations, and some— the United States Army, the Church of Latter-Day Saints, and the Social Security Administration, to name just a few—have embarked on the adventure and are reaping its benefits. Reengineering is not just a capitalist tool. It enables any organization— those in the service of ideals as well as stockholders—to rethink its processes and find breakthrough ways of improving them.[4]

The resources available are primarily oriented to accounting and financial control—the controller's function. Although a

---

[4]Michael Hammer and Stephen Stanton, *The Reengineering Revolution: A Handbook* (New York: HarperBusiness, 1995), 275.

major portion of financial managers' time is devoted to cash management and other treasury management issues, relatively little space is devoted to them in most financial management resources available to nonprofit managers. Specific help has been available only for health care organizations and colleges and universities. The donative nonprofit organization, meaning one dependent to a large degree on donations for its revenue stream, is especially overlooked. The topics presented in this handbook—cash management, financial analysis and forecasting, bank relationship management, new opportunity analysis, and investing and borrowing—are important issues for your organization and the financial professionals working in it.

2.3 DO NONPROFIT TREASURY MANAGEMENT OBJECTIVES DIFFER?

Board members and financial executives who come to nonprofit organizations from the business sector are often frustrated and confused by the different environment. Consider the two polar extremes in Exhibit 2.4. At one polar extreme are organizations that are able to gain all of their revenue from product or service sales. These "commercial" organizations look much like businesses, and are sometimes labeled "businesses in disguise." But most nonprofits are religious organizations or charities, which find themselves at or near the opposite pole, with their revenues coming from grants and gifts. These are termed "donative" or donation-dependent nonprofits. They provide "public goods" free of charge to their clients. Why is this important?

1. Businesses have a numerical, specific objective: maximize stock price. This typically translates into maximizing long-run prof-

Exhibit 2.4. Spectrum of Nonprofit Organizations

| Hospitals | Arts Organizations | Charities |
| Educational Organizations | | Religious Organizations |

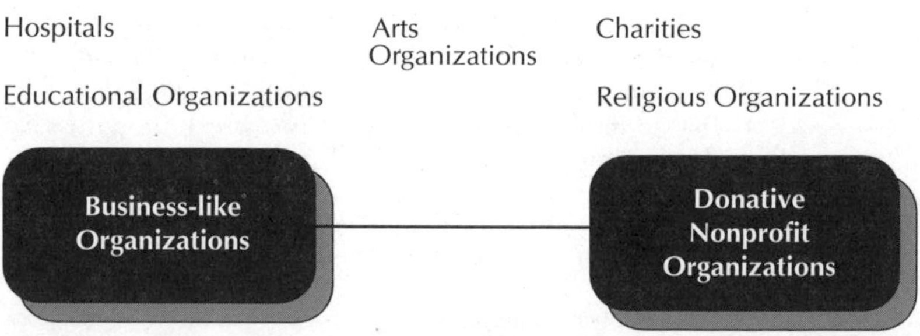

its. Intermediate targets that foster increased profits and stock price are also pursued. These include increasing market share (a company's percent of total industry sales), increasing quality, increasing share of mind (identified by company's target audience), and increasing short-run revenues or reducing short-run costs (or both). Nonprofits that are business-like in nature can adopt many of these same targets. However, donative nonprofits generally do not see their revenues automatically increase when they provide more services. This is significant for two reasons. First, the donative organization is forced to do additional fundraising just to cover the added costs of providing more of the same or new services, instead of simply collecting higher revenues from additional sales, as a business would. Second, the nonprofit that doesn't understand this linkage will find itself in an ever-worsening financial shortfall each period that transpires without new donations. For both reasons, financial management is more challenging for the donative nonprofit.

2. Businesses can price their services, and then use revenues to gauge their marketing success. "Business-like" nonprofit entities, such as hospitals and educational organizations, can do this to some extent, insofar as they do not violate their exempt status and societal role. Revenues do not clearly reflect the quality and quantity of service provided, however.

3. Businesses typically know who their customers and owners are. This may be difficult for nonprofit organizations, particularly donative ones. Are the donors the customers, the owners, both, or neither? Or is the organization tied permanently to the activities specified in the charter and/or articles of incorporation, in a sense owned by society? This is important because to correctly assess tradeoffs when making major programmatic decisions, especially when finances are tight, managers must make the assessment based on the proper criteria. Some organizations have gone overboard with this, defunding or mothballing key programs due to declining financial support, even though those programs were essential to the missions of those organizations.

4. The typical pattern of cash flows often differs, particularly for the donative nonprofit. The fiscal year often begins with a stockpile of financial resources that must cover the shortfall of donations experienced prior to the major inflow around Thanksgiving and Christmas. The stockpile may include one or more of the following: cash on hand, short-term securities, bank loans, soon-due pledges receivable, or salable merchandise. The service effort is typically constant or almost so during the year, and the payroll and supply expenditures continue on a fairly steady basis. Donations tend to cluster around Easter and the period

from Thanksgiving to Christmas. The organization lives off its stockpile, to a large degree, until the heavy inflows materialize, at which time it replenishes its stockpile. This was graphically shown earlier in the chapter when we introduced the cash flow timeline. When face-to-face fundraising is done, and wills and bequests are sought, the organization may use an income stream generated by endowments to partly offset the dry periods. The restricted nature of many of the large gifts and the wills and bequests may preclude interest or principal from being used for operational needs. Consequently, many nonprofits may experience a short-term need for funds during their operating cycles. The need for funds may have resulted from a downward trend in donations, a predictable seasonality in the receipt and disbursement of cash, or an unexpected event affecting costs, such as a strike. The worst case may occur when demand suddenly accelerates: when a *business* experiences higher sales, the sales revenues typically offset the higher costs, but a *charity* has no assurance that donations will increase quickly when more services are provided.

2.4 PREVIEW/PRINCIPLES

The remainder of the handbook provides the foundational principles of proficient financial management. Because much of the material in this book is original, based on an intensive study of religiously based charities, the Lilly-sponsored study has fostered some of our main insights.

(a) The Lilly Study

We have seen much hyperbole about the true state of financial management in nonprofit organizations. This is especially the case regarding perceptions of charities, religious, and art organizations—and all nonprofits outside the health and education sectors. A large group of these donative organizations, which depend on gifts for 60–100 percent of their annual operating revenues, was the focus of a two-phase study completed in 1992–1994. This study was funded by the Lilly Endowment, Inc., which is based in Indianapolis.[5]

More than one thousand religious or religiously based organizations in four categories were selected for study: denominational headquarters, denominational foreign missions (where the

---

[5]This was done as part of a project sponsored by Lilly Endowment, Inc., Indianapolis, IN (1992–1994). The study is entitled "Organizational Goals and Financial Management in Donative Nonprofit Organizations" and was conducted by John Zietlow.

headquarters was separate), independent foreign mission agencies, and localized rescue missions. The latter are often called homeless shelters, but their work goes beyond sheltering.

Treasury management topics were exhaustively studied in Phase 1 of the project. Questions were asked on a 12-page mail survey about organizational and financial goals and all "short-term financial management" (STFM) areas: cash management, cash forecasting, inventory management, accounts receivable and accounts payable management, bank selection and relations, fundraising evaluation, short-term investing, short-term borrowing, risk management, and organizational attributes. Logical organizational characteristics were studied to better understand why certain organizations functioned more effectively or efficiently than others: size, age of the organization, role and interest of the board of directors, and formal training and experience of the Chief Financial Officer.

Completed surveys were received from 288 (29 percent) of the surveyed organizations, a good response rate for a survey that is lengthy and difficult to complete. Based on the survey responses, and with the help of an expert advisory panel, each organization's survey responses were scored based on the STFM sophistication portrayed in the answers provided. For each of the four categories listed above, the "best in class" organization was visited in person, as was an "average-rated" organization. How and why CFOs followed specific approaches and used various financial management techniques was the focus of in-depth interviews and additional decision making and board evaluation questionnaires. Interviews were conducted with the CFO, CEO, and the outside (nonemployee) board member most familiar with that organization's financial management.

The typical organization was small, with an annual revenue of only $800,000. One-half of the CFOs had related business experience, with the one-half having eight years or more. The "best of the best," those organizations having the highest overall STFM score in their respective categories, were: Independent Foreign Mission: Campus Crusade for Christ (Orlando, FL—John Webb, Director of Finance); Denominational Mission: Church of God Missionary Board (Anderson, IN—Darryl Smith, CFO); Southern Baptist Board of Missions (Richmond, VA—Carl Johnson, CFO); Rescue Mission: Peoria Rescue Ministries (Peoria, IL—Rev. Jerry Trecek, CEO and CFO); and Denominational Headquarters: Church of the Brethren (Elgin, IL—Darryl Deardorff, CFO).

The pointers provided in the next section are mostly linked to survey results. Throughout the remainder of the handbook, concepts and techniques are illustrated using field study examples of real organizations. In some cases, the name of the organization is changed to honor confidentiality promises.

(b) Keep the Mission First!

The first principle cannot be emphasized strongly enough: Mission first! Nonprofit organizations do not answer to stockholder owners, but instead must adhere to the charter and mission of the organization. Finance sustains mission. Sadly, some organizations allow that new Program Z to take precedence over existing programs, simply because corporate or foundation or government grant money is easier to get for Program Z (which is not closely linked to the charter or mission of the organization).

(c) Management and Financial Objectives

(i) *Management Objectives.* Maximizing the quality and quantity of service was selected by most respondents, followed by maximize quality. Mission-minded organizations are service-minded, as one would expect.

(ii) *Financial Objectives.* Breakeven was dominant (111 of the 288 respondents), followed by maximize net revenue (59 respondents). As secondary objective, respondents indicated a concern for cost minimization (34 respondents), avoiding financial risk (25 respondents), and maximizing net donations (20 respondents). The main observation is that financial risk avoidance is justifiably gaining attention by religious nonprofit organizations. Breakeven and cost minimization are inadequate as primary financial objectives, in our view. It would be much better to focus on net revenue, financial risk, and net donations—all of which represent more focused attention to the positive contribution the finance function can make to mission achievement. Recognize the overlap between the breakeven and cost minimization and maximizing net revenue, as shown in Exhibit 2.5. Maximizing net revenue or attempting to breakeven will force attention on cost control. Accordingly, net revenue may retain the best of the other two objectives while adding to them. This in no way negates the importance of program outreach and quality attainment, but indicates ways in which resources will be allocated to carry out the mission. (See Exhibit 2.5.)

(iii) *Achievement of Financial Objective—How Well Are You Doing, Regardless of Objectives Pursued?* Self-ratings on the achievement of the stated financial objective were: excellent (14 percent of respondents), very good (43 percent), good (30 percent), fair (10 percent), and poor (4 percent). This self-rating was one of the best indicators of the organization's overall "Short-Term Financial Management (STFM) Score." This score was based on a careful evaluation of each question in terms of its ability to indicate proficient financial management. An expert advisory panel, assembled under

Exhibit 2.5. Overlap of Several Popular Financial Objectives

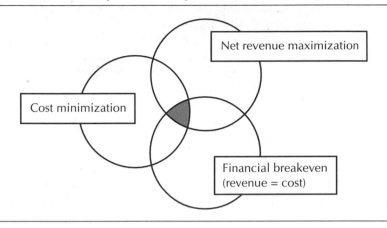

guidance of the Lilly Endowment, assisted in this process. Primitive financial management process and techniques are unlikely to achieve effectiveness in an organization's financial management outcomes. Individual questions within the survey were differentially rated, based on appropriateness for the size and type of organizations studied. Most respondents had a fairly accurate idea of how effective their financial management process was, and the tabulated results indicate that sophistication (what the questionnaire was really measuring) had a strong correlation with perceived effectiveness (as measured by the respondent's self assessment).

(iv) Is the Indicated Financial Objective Really Operational? A hypothetical decision was posed to the respondent to find out whether the financial objective was actually operating, or was merely a stated objective. A new or expanded program recommended by the CEO or board clearly conflicts with the financial objective—what would most likely be done? In 46 (17 percent) organizations, the program would be fully implemented anyway, in 68 (24 percent) organizations it would be scaled down somewhat, but the financial objective would still be violated, and in 166 (59 percent) organizations the objective would be met by scaling down the program adequately or not implementing it at all. Interpreting, 46 organizations have essentially no discipline imposed by the finance function, and in an additional 68 organizations that discipline is weak. Possibly this is due to ignorance among the officers regarding either the proper role of finance or the importance of sound financial management.

Some executives would object to our conclusion that this implies poor management because faith must be exercised. For organizations with a religious orientation, this may be a legitimate response. Finance staff would carefully monitor such program initiatives to ensure that additional funds are ultimately raised to vindicate that faith. Where sufficient funds do not materialize during program implementation, this fact should be made apparent to the CEO and board in order to (1) inform decision-makers of the types of situations to be more cautious about in the future, and (2) ensure that the organization does not unduly expand those programs (draining resources from other important program areas) or add new ones until cost coverage is attained.

(v) Hindrance to Achievement of Financial Objective. Because 44 percent of respondents rated their achievement of the financial objective as either good, fair, or poor, you should know the reason indicated for hindering better achievement of that objective. Insufficient and/or ineffective fundraising was singled out by 120 respondents, followed by no long-range financial planning (49 respondents). A smaller number of organizations mentioned that their impediments were inadequate budgeting (19 respondents), cost control (15 respondents), or staffing (14 respondents). Regarding staffing, we found that 57 percent of the responding organizations have two or fewer individuals "mainly performing the finance function." Only 6 percent of the organizations had 11 or more finance staffers. Knowing this, one might have expected staffing to be the major hindrance, but this was evidently not the case. Better financial performance is an achievable goal for most organizations. Increased fundraising (especially for deferred gifts) and implementation of long-range planning are the first priorities.

2.5 HOW CAN NONPROFIT TREASURY MANAGEMENT BE IMPROVED?

Effective cash management is often evidenced by a shortened cash conversion cycle, as depicted in Exhibit 2.2. In its simplest form, the cash conversion cycle represents the time that it takes a firm to move from an outlay of cash to purchase the needed factors of production, such as labor and supplies, to the actual collection of cash for the produced product or service, such as a completed treatment for a given client. A donative nonprofit faces an additional level of complexity, in that its gifts and grants may be received sporadically and in unpredictable amounts.

Usually the objectives in cash management are to minimize the length of time it takes to bring in cash (the collection period) and to maximize the length of time before we have to pay out cash (the payment period). Tradeoffs often exist; for example, accelerating receivables collection may result in lost sales, accelerating pledge receivables may result in lost pledges, and delaying payments to vendors could result in increased prices or interest charges. Furthermore, from an ethical vantage point, it is considered wrong to "stretch payables" beyond the payment date, unless the invoice was sent late or the shipment was in error, and certain issues must be reconciled.

Working capital may be defined as the difference between current assets and current liabilities. Treasury management includes all decisions that have an impact on these working capital accounts. This includes bank selection and relationship management, risk management, and for the donative nonprofit, fundraising evaluation. Health care organizations typically have amounts reported for the following line items:

- Current assets
  - Cash and short-term investments
  - Accounts receivable
  - Pledges receivable
  - Inventories
  - Other current assets
- Current liabilities
  - Accounts payable
  - Accrued salaries and wages
  - Other accrued expenses
  - Notes payable
  - Current portion of long-term debt

Many charities have very little in inventories, notes payable, and current portion of long-term debt. Exhibit 2.6 illustrates a donative nonprofit's accounts with the 1992–1994 balance sheets for Africa Inter-Mennonite Mission, Inc. This organization functions as a sending agency, placing missionary personnel abroad for several Mennonite denominations. As such, it fits the conduit model. For 1994, ($307 + $147)/$803 or fully 56.5 percent of assets were in the form of cash and short-term investments. Proficiency in bank relations and short-term investments will obviously greatly enhance Africa Inter-Mennonite's financial position. The only other significant working capital accounts are accounts receivable and payable. Note also that its risk management policy, to self-ensure death benefits, gives rise to its long-term liability.

To better understand current asset and liability management and opportunity areas for your organization, distinct categories will

Exhibit 2.6.   Balance Sheets for a Donative Nonprofit Organization (1992–1994)

Assets	12/31/94	12/31/93	12/31/92
Current assets			
Cash and cash equivalents	$307	$268	$210
Investments	147	105	90
Accounts receivable	50	64	113
Notes receivable	4	16	16
Subtotal: current assets	508	453	429
Long-term assets			
Property and equipment—net	271	283	294
Insurance deposit and other	24	28	28
Total assets	$803	$764	$751
Liabilities and net assets	**12/31/94**	**12/31/93**	**12/31/92**
Current liabilities			
Accounts payable	$41	$23	$31
Long-term liabilities			
Death benefits payable	80	75	75
Total liabilities	121	98	106
Net assets			
Unrestricted:			
Undesignated	(17)	(25)	(50)
Board designated	283	300	302
Equity in property and equipment	271	283	294
Temporarily restricted	145	108	99
Total net assets	682	666	645
Total liabilities and net assets	$803	$764	$751

Source: Africa Inter-Mennonite Mission, Inc.

be introduced within short-term finance, followed by profiling and rating donative nonprofits' actual performance within these categories.

(a) Scoring in the Short-Term Financial Management Categories

Nonprofit organizations often get a bad rap when it comes to financial management, especially in the treasury management areas of financial forecasting and analysis, cash management, banking, investing and borrowing, and fundraising evaluation. Original research from the Lilly study will help to better evaluate this perception and understand the relative performance of the surveyed organizations in the various areas of short-term financial management: budgeting and financial analysis, payables, receivables, cash management, banking relations, inventories, short-term investing and borrowing, fundraising evaluation, and risk management. Weaknesses as well as proficiencies are documented followed by some basic steps to improvement linked to a statistical analysis of the survey results.

*Step 1. Budgeting and Financial Analysis: Plan, Evaluate, Revise
If Necessary*

Rating: **Fair/Good**
While 85 percent of respondents develop and use an operating
budget (showing revenues and expenses), one has to wonder about
the ability to manage the affairs of the 15 percent that do not. Budget revisions occur within the fiscal year by 60 percent of the organizations. This is good practice when uncontrollable external
events make previously budgeted amounts useless as standards.
The use of financial data other than "budget versus actual" variances is seriously lacking. Only 53 percent monitor their current
asset amount on a monthly basis (and only 12 percent have a target
for their current assets), and 41 percent evaluate financial ratios periodically. This is inexcusable in an era of personal computer availability.

Step 2. Cash Management: Control and Pool Cash Balances

Rating: **Good**
Cash management, which is a core area of treasury management
and which constitutes a major section of this handbook, consists of
the following:

- Forecasting cash flow and cash position
- Configuring the banking system
- Raising the cash
- Collecting the cash
- Protecting and pooling the cash
- Disbursing the cash
- Investing surplus cash
- Borrowing more cash

Our brief summary of the state of current practice in nonprofits'
cash management starts with the objective of organizations' liquidity management, then moves to actual techniques used, cash forecasting, bank relationship management, receivables (including
cash collection) management, and payables (including cash disbursement) management.

Step 3. Cash Management and Short-Term Finance Objective

Rating: **Fair**
Interestingly, 78 percent of respondents indicated their primary
objective when managing cash and other current assets is to support
operations. This underscores our earlier point that proficiency in

financial management can (at least potentially) aid mission attainment. In some areas, utilization of cash management techniques is commendable: pooling balances into one account (58 percent), wire transfers (42 percent), and direct deposit (30 percent). Inability to access bank balances by personal computer or touch-tone phone hinders 86 percent of the organizations. Being small precludes many organizations from making use of certain cash management techniques which are only cost-effective for large organizations. However, when asked whether the bank with which they made most of their deposits would agree that the organization used the most advanced and appropriate techniques for their size and type, only 48 percent indicated that they could "agree or strongly agree." The validity of this prognosis is confirmed in our overall results—roughly one-half of the organizations can make significant improvement in their cash management.

Step 4. Cash Forecasting: Anticipate Position Changes and Act Accordingly

Rating: Fair

The most reliable indicator of how an organization rated overall (in all STFM areas) was whether the organization used a computer to monitor or forecast its cash position. Seventy-eight percent did use the computer for one or both of these purposes. This may or may not be a cause of high performance. At a minimum, it indicates the following about an organization:

1. It is willing to harness technology, investing the dollars and time necessary which is an indicator of a "learning organization."

2. Its cash forecasting is facilitated, which is one of the ways to implement daily active cash management—practiced by most of the Fortune 500 corporations. Short-term investing and borrowing decisions are improved because of a better understanding of how much excess cash exists now and in the future. With longer maturities yielding higher interest rates, the organization is rewarded for knowing how long it can tie excess funds up.

3. Its cash control is facilitated, because now it can tie its records via personal computer to its bank(s), regularly updating balances—at a minimum, being able to check yesterday's closing balances at the beginning of business today.

Only eight organizations developed daily cash forecasts, whereas 22 projected cash with weekly intervals and 94 developed monthly forecasts. Begin today to attempt a weekly forecast, and if your organization is sizable, make a daily forecast of your ultimate goal.

As interest rates spike upward, you will see greater rewards for your effort.

Step 5. Banking Relations: Rebid and Negotiate Every Three Years

Rating: **Fair**
While 37 percent of the respondents rebid their bank relationships periodically, 52 percent never or almost never do. When reviewing bank relations, only 25 percent compare the banks' availability schedules—which indicate when deposited checks become "good" funds. Less than 40 percent of all organizations receive account analysis statements and alter bank balances in light of those statements. Review your bank relations and opportunities now.

Step 6. Payables Management: Pay on Time but Not Early

Rating: **Fair/Good**
Four out of ten organizations regularly pay invoices early. This is inappropriate except when cash discounts are offered—at other times, the checking account is unnecessarily depleted, reducing interest income. Two-thirds of the organizations are able to and do take advantage of cash discounts, meaning that about one-third should revise their payables policy or gain additional liquidity in order to take offered discounts. Missing a 2 percent cash discount to pay 20 days later is equivalent to borrowing at a 37 percent interest rate. Finally, only 5 percent of organizations are paying bills electronically—which is much less expensive than paying by check if you use the automated clearinghouse (ACH) system. Larger organizations should move immediately to electronic direct deposit of payroll payments.

Step 7. Receivables Management: Collect All, on Time, Deposit Immediately

Rating: **Fair**
Accounts receivables are negligible in many nonprofit organizations, but pledges receivable (whether booked as such or not) may be substantial. On average, there is a two-day delay between receiving a mailed check and deposit at the bank. Only 18 percent of respondents use any technique to speed deposit of checks in excess of $500. Only 8 percent use lockboxes to expedite collection and deposit of mailed checks, which can be cost-effective for

larger organizations. Organizations should move immediately to same-day deposit of checks, at least on larger items.

Step 8. Inventory Management: Keep at Right Levels

Rating: **Good**
Because of insubstantial inventory levels, this is not a problem area for many nonprofit organizations. Few organizations use sophisticated inventory management techniques such as "economic order quantity" or "just-in-time" systems, suggesting that there may be some improvements available here. At a minimum, track your inventory positions for high-value or heavy-stock items. Money tied up in inventory is not available to collect interest or invest in program achievement.

Step 9. Short-Term Investing: Pool Funds, Know Size of Permanent Balances, Take Prudent Risks with the Permanent Balances but Preserve Capital on All Other Balances

Rating: **Fair**
Balances are not pooled by 42 percent of organizations, as noted earlier. High marks are earned by the attention to risk as well as return, particularly for preservation of capital ("default risk"). Greater attention to reinvestment rate risk (only reported by 24 percent of respondents) is advisable. Organizations which have not monitored this have been caught with financial shortfalls, particularly if they partly fund the costs of headquarters operations from investment interest. There are other types of risks (liquidity, interest rate) that are also being overlooked. A few organizations still do not have interest-bearing checking accounts. Minimizing bank balances, even if those balances are in a NOW account (interest bearing checking account), is also advisable. For comparison, the Dreyfus U.S. Government Money Market Fund was yielding 3.26 percent at year-end 1993, versus 2.0 to 2.5 percent for most NOW accounts. On a $500,000 average balance, the extra 1 percent adds up to a $5,000 gain in interest per year. Risk is roughly equivalent; the government guarantees standing behind Treasury and agency securities, in general, is as good as the deposit insurance backing your bank account.

Step 10. Short-Term Borrowing: If Borrowing, Negotiate, Do Not Become Dependent, Pay Back Quickly

Rating: **Good/Excellent**
Many religiously based nonprofits are aware of the biblical teaching not to leave debt outstanding (the biblical reference is Romans

13:8). Many of the surveyed organizations do no short-term borrowing from external sources at all. Only 13 percent use short-term loans each year, and two-thirds never borrow from a bank for short-term needs. Internal borrowing is another matter: 56 percent do some interfund borrowing. To better reflect the degree of self-support for your program or fund experiencing shortfalls, consider charging an interest rate to borrowing funds or programs.

Step 11. Fund-Raising Management and Evaluation: Have Adequate Records, Compute Effectiveness As Well As Efficiency, Raise Funds in Anticipation of Need (Not after the Fact)

Rating: **Good**

Fundraising is a vital part of corporate finance and is taken seriously as part of the treasurer's function, yet it appears as though fundraising management and evaluation is overlooked many times by nonprofit or treasurers. The good news is that 88 percent of the organizations reported having donation records somewhere in the organization. Evaluation is possible. Another positive is that, on average, respondents report a 95 percent fulfillment of pledged donations. Unfortunately, many organizations are underinvesting in fundraising: 55 percent of the organizations indicated that the major reason they do not spend more on fundraising is a shortage of funds. Recall our earlier finding that insufficient or ineffective fundraising is the main reason why organizations do not experience greater achievement of their chief financial objective. Your finance staff should begin now to champion the fundraising cause, debunk the myths surrounding the false guilt over legitimate fundraising, and most importantly begin to calculate a return on investment for your fundraising expenditures. Revise your organization's thinking away from fundraising as an expense and toward its real nature: an investment in your organization's future. Finally, raise funds prospectively instead of reactively: one-half of the respondents agreed with the view that a well-managed organization raises money this year for next year's programs, instead of this year's. Wouldn't it be nice to avoid your annual crisis when the "summer slump" hits?

Step 12. Risk Management: Conceive of Risks That Threaten Financial Viability, Take Steps to Moderate Their Potential Impact

Rating: **Fair**

Only 52 percent of organizations monitor interest rates. Similarly, only 62 percent of organizations having foreign exchange exposure monitor that exposure. Monitoring is obviously only the first step to managing risk, but sampled organizations have a long way to go in this area. Computer models can be developed without too much trouble to show the effect on your organization's operating statement if interest rate change by one percent, two percent, or more. Treasury professionals should begin now to develop such a model. Consider whether a local university has an internship program in its finance major in which a student can get academic credit for helping you develop such a model—at little or no cost to your organization.

(i) Performance Improvement Measures. Statistical work done on the composite score indicates the following uncontrollable indicators of excellence:

- Larger organizations achieve at a higher level—with size opening up opportunities for greater specialization and larger staffs.
- Holding revenue constant, organizations with larger staffs achieve at a higher level.
- The self-rating by the CFO of the degree of achievement of the chief financial objective was also linked to composite score.

Other than merging with other organizations or joining in joint ventures (e.g., a partnership of short-wave radio broadcasters called *World By 2000*), these items are outside the control of the executive staff. Fortunately, there are other proficiency indicators, which are controllable such as follows:

- Use of a computer for cash monitoring or cash forecasting
- The degree to which the present and anticipated financial position of the organization impacts new program adoption or existing program expansion
- The degree of involvement and interest of the board of directors in financial affairs

On the basis of these findings:

1. Begin to use the computer to keep records of your cash position (start with your ending daily bank balance), and start developing at least a crude cash forecasting model.
2. Introduce a financial "feasibility evaluation" into every executive-level and board-level consideration of new programs or program expansion.
3. Introduce new financial reporting formats, additional financial data, and new recommended board policies (e.g., a marketable securities investment policy) into your board communications. Ideally, the CFO should be present at quarterly or annual board meetings, making a brief presentation at each. Recruitment of

dedicated board members with interest and expertise in financial affairs might also prove fruitful.

(b) A Useful Framework for Treasury Diagnosis

At several points later in this book, two tools to diagnose an organization's financial position and the likely effect of financial policy changes will be discussed. These tools are the cash conversion cycle and the cash budget.

   (i) Cash Conversion Cycle.   The *cash conversion cycle* was introduced in Exhibit 2.2. The cash conversion cycle is the time that elapses from the time cash flows out to prepare for and deliver services, until cash comes back to the organization from billing or donations. Cash inflows, particularly for organizations receiving tuition, donations, or grants, are lumpy and episodic, while cash expenses continue at a fairly steady rate. Nonprofit financial executives in the health and human services fields traditionally think of cash management in terms of receivables control. They often believe that better cash management will result if accounts receivable can be reduced or the collection cycle shortened. While accounts receivable management in health-related nonprofit organizations is clearly important, limiting attention to this one area is myopic. Good cash management should focus not only on the acceleration of receivables, but also on the complete cash conversion cycle. Reduction of the cash conversion cycle along with the related investment of surplus funds should be a critical objective of financial managers.

   Many nonprofit organizations are willing to let their banks handle most of their cash management decisions. While this strategy is acceptable in some situations, it often produces less than optimal performance. Risks are sometimes unnecessarily increased or yields on investments sacrificed. Real or perceived conflicts of interest also exist when the bank is represented on the organization's governing board.

   (ii) Cash Budget.   Another key tool used in this handbook is the cash forecast, also known as the *cash budget*. The cash budget focuses on four major activities that may affect the cash position, not necessarily in this order:

1. Purchasing of resources
2. Production/sale of service
3. Billing or fundraising
4. Collection of paid bills or donations

These activities represent time intervals in the cash conversion cycle. The purchasing of resources relates to the acquisition of supplies and labor, such as the level of inventory necessary to maintain realistic production schedules and the staff required to ensure adequate provision of services. Production and sale are virtually the same in the nonprofit industry; there is no inventory of products or services. However, there is often a delay between the production of service and final delivery. Health or human service organizations may hold a patient for 10 or 15 days before discharge, which could be regarded as the final point of sale. Billing represents the interval between the service delivery and the generation of a bill. Collection in this case represents the time interval between the generation of a bill to the actual collection of the cash from the client or the client's third-party payor. Similar delays occur for donative nonprofits, who often invest large sums in direct mail fundraising and then await an influx of mailed cash donations.

This book uses both the cash conversion cycle and the cash budget to demonstrate the squeeze on an organization's cash position that comes about in the normal course of operations, as well as to test the financial effects of financial management policy changes. Before doing so, it is important to understand financial integrity and health and financial planning and strategy—the subjects of our next two chapters.

CHAPTER THREE

Financial Roles and Responsibilities

3.1 Responsibility for Financial Health and Integrity   68
   (a) Board of Trustees   68
   (b) Board Support for Its Financial Responsibilities   70
       (i) Finance Committee   70
       (ii) Investment Committee   71
       (iii) Audit Committee   71
   (c) Chief Executive Officer/President/Executive Director/ Chair   71
   (d) Chief Financial Officer/Controller/Treasurer   71
   (e) Staff Support for Financial Management Responsibilities   73
       (i) Program/Fund Managers   73
       (ii) Financial Tools and Support Structure   75
       (iii) Importance of Financial Structure   75
       (iv) Development of Financial Structure   76
       (v) Financial Structure Soundness   76
3.2 Checklist for Assigning Responsibility   77
3.3 Structure of the Finance Organization   79
   (a) Organization   81
   (b) Financial Function: Service Center or Profit Center?   84
       (i) Focus on Activities   87
       (ii) Is Your Cost Analysis Correct?   88
       (iii) How Can Finance and Accounting Activities Be Evaluated?   88
   (c) Controls   89
   (d) Principles of Effective Control   89
3.4 Accountability Structure   91
   (a) Definition   91
   (b) Purpose   91
   (c) Establishing an Accountability Policy   91
       (i) A General Policy Statement   91
       (ii) Interpretation of Policy   92

(d) Ethics 94
(e) Ethics Check 94
(f) Making Ethical Decisions 95
(g) Designing an Accountability Structure 96
  (i) Monitoring an Accountability Structure 99
  (ii) Schedule of Reviews 99
Appendix 3A: Case Study 101

3.1 RESPONSIBILITY FOR FINANCIAL HEALTH AND INTEGRITY

One person should be placed in charge of the financial health and integrity of a nonprofit organization. However, financial responsibility is ultimately shared by everyone in the organization with decision-making responsibilities: the Board of Trustees, Councils and Committees, Chief Executive Officer (CEO), and other managerial and program staff. According to Internal Revenue Service (IRS) laws governing nonprofit organizations, any of the above-mentioned persons can be held *liable* for financial errors as long as there is sufficient evidence to presume that they should have known about the errors and could have acted to avoid them. It is therefore important to have a clear definition of responsibilities for different roles in the organization, with an accompanying set of checks and balances.

(a) Board of Trustees

Accountability is an important concept for members of nonprofit Boards of Trustees to understand, and they should be well informed about the full extent of the liability, both personal and organizational, resulting from their service. Since accountability laws vary from state to state, legal advice should be sought by all Boards of Trustees to insure that they have the correct information for their organization in their particular state. Some general guidelines are provided below.

1. The standards established for the conduct of Trustees of nonprofit organizations are found in corporate law rather than trust law and are therefore less strict than those governing other types of trustees. Because nonprofit boards do not have the wide range of delegation powers and outside resources found on corporate boards, they are required to exhibit "prudent man" behavior in carrying out their responsibilities and are only liable for gross negligence.

2. Trustees are not likely to be held liable for business or financial decisions, provided they are made through informed judg-

ments. However, they can be found liable if they never attend meetings, approve financial or business transactions with no background information, or engage in illegal financial or business activity.

3. Liability claims can be filed against Trustees who place their personal financial interest above that of the nonprofit corporation, use corporate property for personal gain, take advantage of a financial opportunity at the expense of the nonprofit corporation, or self-deal without appropriate disclosure.

4. Trustees are liable for insuring that the corporation is carrying out its mission, as documented by federal and state law. Trustees are accountable for ensuring that donors' funds are used for the purposes of the organization, as prescribed by the donor.

5. Liability for ensuring that their nonprofit organizations comply with the rules and regulations set by federal, state, and local governments which have jurisdiction over them rests with the Board of Trustees. These organizations must file tax returns with the IRS and applicable state agencies. Fulfilling legal requirements as an employer, including the payment of payroll taxes for the organization's employees, is the ultimate responsibility of the Board of Trustees.

6. The financial health of a nonprofit organization also rests with its Board of Trustees, but it can best be achieved when all stakeholders are assigned some segment of responsibility and accountability. The Trustees fulfill this obligation within the context of their broader set of responsibilities which include:

   - Determine and guard the organization's mission
   - Set policies for ensuring that the organization operates according to its bylaws, the law, and ethical standards while pursuing its mission
   - Develop the organization's overall program, and engage in long-range strategic planning to establish its general course for the future
   - Establish fiscal policy and boundaries, with budgets and financial controls
   - Provide adequate resources for the activities of the organization through direct financial contributions and a commitment to fund raising
   - Select and evaluate the performance of the CEO
   - Develop and maintain a communication link with the organization and the community in promoting the work of the nonprofit

- Monitor the performance of the organization to maximize the welfare of the public, not individuals
- Raise funds for the organization

7. Trustees should avoid the following type of activities:
   - Engage in the day-to-day operations of the organization
   - Hire staff other than the CEO
   - Make detailed programmatic decisions without staff consultation

8. The financial plan of an organization must be properly aligned with the organizational structure and program needs in order to be meaningful and useful. Since all organizations require resources to operate, it is critical for the financial development, implementation, monitoring, and reporting activities to involve the program stakeholders.

9. In the process of addressing its financial responsibilities to the nonprofit organization, the Board should pursue the following tasks:
   - Create a vision
   - Raise funds
   - Communicate
   - Set policy and include the rationale
   - Assign responsibility
   - Establish a budget
   - Project cash flow
   - Monitor and amend the budget
   - Review financial statements
   - Report results
   - Watch the trends
   - Develop long-range plans
   - Evaluate results
   - Ensure internal control

(b) Board Support for Its Financial Responsibilities

If the Board has a committee structure, it is likely to have some of the committees listed below.

(i) *Finance Committee.* The finance committee is responsible for providing a detailed review of financial statements and audit reports, internal as well as external, and reporting the results to the Board of Trustees. The Committee also makes recommenda- tions to the Board on policy matters and issues related to the financial management functions of the organization.

(ii) Investment Committee. The investment committee is responsible for reviewing and managing all the organization's investments, ensuring full compliance with policies and guidelines applying to nonprofit organizations, and reporting its findings to the Board.

(iii) Audit Committee. The audit committee is responsible for overseeing audit functions of the nonprofit organization. Responsibilities include overseeing regular audits of financial activities, adhering to laws and regulations, and monitoring the organization's conflict of interest policies.

(c) Chief Executive Officer/President/Executive Director/Chair

The CEO/president is charged with reviewing and understanding the financial operations of the nonprofit organization as part of his/her overall responsibility for day-to-day operations.

The CEO should appoint individuals who are responsible for various components of financial management like internal control, review the financial statements, and monitor all of the financial details in the organization to ensure their accuracy and integrity. She or he should ask questions until satisfied that answers make sense and are in sync with the mission and related activities of the organization. Individuals with these responsibilities will be held accountable.

(d) Chief Financial Officer/Controller/Treasurer

The chief financial officer (CFO) is typically responsible for selection of those assigned responsibility for the day-to-day financial operations. The CFO of the organization has training and experience in financial management, generally accepted accounting principles, internal control systems, knowledge about the organization's mission and programs and their relationship to the financial requirements and components, and technical expertise and procedures for developing budgets and preparing financial statements.

1. The role of the CFO in nonprofits is to:
    - Safeguard the financial assets
    - Raise funds

- Optimize the use of cash
- Report financial results[1]

2. The CFO is traditionally responsible for
   - Maintaining financial records
   - Preparing timely and meaningful financial statements
   - Budgeting
   - Safeguarding organizational assets
   - Complying with external reporting requirements
   - Anticipating financial needs
   - Reacting to operational changes that affect finances

3. In the small- to medium-sized organization, these roles are often expanded to include
   - Fundraising
   - Management of physical plant
   - Technology
   - Food service
   - Theater
   - Personnel

4. All these functions, and more, have impacts on the finances of the institution and are required to meet its volunteers' expectations and its mission. A lot depends on the size of the nonprofit organization and on the skills of the incumbent in the position. There is no right or wrong way to distribute functions to individuals. These assignments should be constantly evaluated and changed when it makes sense for the organization. In large organizations, many of the responsibilities are delegated to a controller or accountant.

5. The role of a CFO in today's nonprofit corporations is in a constant state of flux. Some current trends for this position are as follows:
   - Operational expertise is one of the primary criteria in the selection process.
   - Skills in interpersonal communication, influencing others, and related areas have become as important as technical skills.
   - Principles and values are used to define appropriate standards of behavior and the finance function in the organization.
   - While numerical integrity and the corporate audit process remain a priority, there is an increased emphasis on employee

[1]Malvern Gross, Richard F. Larkin, Roger S. Bruttomesso, and John J. McNally, *Financial and Accounting Guide for Not-for-Profit Organizations* (New York: Wiley, 1995).

empowerment and softer controls as long as employees understand that a level of control is needed and does not constitute a negative reflection on their integrity or capabilities.

- Empowerment has implicit boundaries and demands greater responsibility and accountability.

- Finance people transcend their functional identities within the organization by serving as key participants in teams engaged in addressing multifaceted organizational problems.

- Remaining competitive in today's global market requires internal and external information sharing and the development of systems to empower people with the information they need.

- While cultural change is most effective when it begins at the top of the organization, the finance function may serve as a catalyst because it interacts with every other function. The finance function may also initiate cultural change in companies experiencing financial difficulty.

- Finance people play an integral role in organizational decision making and focus their efforts on finding creative solutions to issues and problems.

- Organizations depend on finance people to clarify the business impacts during every step of the planning and budgeting process and to act as advocates rather than naysayers. Their early involvement in the decision-making process prevents unnecessary surprises.

- Beyond providing financial reports, the Treasurer should present a balanced picture of what is happening, where the problems lie, and what actions need to be taken to the CEO and Board. The person in this position is also responsible for working with program heads in order to represent their interests and explain the story behind the numbers.

- The finance function is largely decentralized and matrix managed.[2]

(e) Staff Support for Financial Management Responsibilities

In addition to financial support functions for the Board, support for the financial functions are needed to support the program managers and operations in their financial responsibilities.

(i) Program/Fund Managers.   Program managers and fund managers are responsible for the financial management functions of

[2]Henry A. Davis and Frederick C. Militello, *The Empowered Organization: Redefining the Roles and Practice of Finance,* Financial Executives Research Foundation (FERF), (1994).

their programs including budgeting and expending resources and raising funds for their programmatic activities as well as the delivery of the program as a whole within the organization.

The Treasurer/CFO helps Program Managers by providing the financial and nonfinancial information needed to develop and maintain their programs. The Treasurer is also responsible for sharing interrelated program information that can be used to benefit the entire organization.

Financial operations and expertise play an integral role in a number of other critical functions within the organization. Some of these contributions and interrelationships are discussed below.

Marketing (from financial and strategic management for nonprofit organizations).   The financial and marketing functions of an organization are separate and distinct. According to a leading scholar in marketing, "The marketer knows how to research and understand the needs of the other party; to design a valued offering to meet these needs; to communicate the offer effectively; and to present it at the right time and place."

An essential rule of marketing is for the marketer to know both the product and the organization. In the financial arena, marketing involves knowing the various ways in which gifts can be made and selecting the best alternative for each potential donor.

The main marketing function of the CFO is to make a convincing presentation on the best vehicle for making a gift. The Marketing Director is concerned with making the products of the nonprofit organization attractive to the customer, developing client awareness, distributing information to stimulate new customers and contributions, and designing programs to attract new constituencies. The financial function is responsible for money management.

The financial function serves the marketing function by providing information and services needed to determine a final marketing budget. Finance also assists in pricing programs, products, services, and proposals to be marketed and in developing effective fund-raising strategies.

Strategic management/long-range planning.   Planning for the future is critical to the success of a nonprofit corporation. According to Bryce in *Financial and Strategic Management in Nonprofit Organizations*, "strategic management refers to the:

- Determination of the organization's mission and value system
- Setting of long-range targets, the identification of the organization's niche
- Charting of the course that will be followed in fulfilling the organization's mission

Every organization needs to be financed before it can accomplish its mission, and nonprofits are no exception. Programs have short-, mid-, and long-range financial needs to be used for salaries, benefits, supplies, travel, space, furniture, buildings, and other resources. Nonprofit organizations raise the money to support their activities through strategic, financial, and programmatic planning.

Constituents.   Constituents are responsible for requiring and reviewing financial reports and asking the right questions. They also have a fund-raising role which includes making contributions of time and money as well as using their networks to provide additional support of all kinds to the organization.

(ii) Financial Tools and Support Structure.   In order to be useful, the financial structure of both nonprofit and for-profit organizations must reflect the nature and needs of the organization. It consists of the following components:

- Organizational structure it is established to support
- Financial component of the organizational structure
- Chart of accounts created to record financial transactions
- Financial plan
- Fund-raising plan
- Cash-flow plan
- Systems to support the processing of financial transactions and internal controls
- Financial reporting system
- Distribution system for financial reports
- System for producing all financial and management reports
- System for reviewing financial results
- Communication of roles, responsibilities, and accountabilities related to the financial activity
- System for evaluating and adjusting the system to coincide with organizational goals and objectives
- External reporting and relations

(iii) Importance of Financial Structure.   Financial resources allow organizations to accomplish their missions and achieve their goals. They are needed to raise funds, hire and reward people, acquire property and equipment, and fund many types of expenses incurred in pursuit of the organization's mission.

Resources can be maximized by planning, recording, and reporting the financial activity in a manner that is meaningful and useful to the organization. Technical expertise as well as managerial and communication skills are required to design a financial system which serves all the organization's constituents.

(iv) Development of Financial Structure. The Board of Directors of a nonprofit organization is responsible for ensuring that its financial structure is appropriate and meets the organization's needs. Specifically, the CFO develops a proposed structure and presents it to the Board for review and approval. After this occurs, the financial structure is periodically reviewed to ensure its continued ability to meet the internal and external requirements of the organization. It is the responsibility of the Board to ensure that these periodic reviews are conducted.

(v) Financial Structure Soundness. A financial structure is sound when it serves the needs of all internal and external constituents of the organization, who include:

- Board of Directors
- Program Directors
- Fund Managers
- Staff
- Volunteers
- Internal Revenue Service
- Banks
- Auditors
- Investment services
- Donors
- Independent contractors
- Suppliers

Internal controls. It is essential for the financial structure of the nonprofit organization to be safeguarded by a system of internal controls, which requires the delegation of roles and responsibilities in such a way that no one person has control over more than one function.

Financial policy. Every nonprofit organization which raises and expends financial resources should have written financial policies readily available to those who carry out roles and responsibilities on behalf of the organization and its mission. These policies are determined by the Board of Trustees or its designee and are statements of the nonprofit organization's requirements in the financial areas of managing cash, investing, fund raising, budgeting, expending, and reporting financial results.

Financial procedures. The financial structure of the nonprofit organization should be supported by written financial procedures that provide detailed descriptions of how financial transactions are to be processed to ensure compliance with the organization's financial policy. Examples are documented procedures for handling cash, making deposits, managing funds, and developing budgets.

Financial procedures provide information on what is required to process various types of financial transactions successfully within the financial structure and system of the specific nonprofit organization. They contribute to the ongoing integrity of financial data and reports and ensure the correct processing of financial transactions with existing and/or new staff, volunteers, Boards, Committees, and other constituents.

3.2 CHECKLIST FOR ASSIGNING RESPONSIBILITY

The following list details the tasks and responsibilities in the financial arena. Each item on the list is performed at your organization, needs to be assigned to a specific individual.

Task or Responsibility	Performed By:
Collect past-due accounts	
Design and maintain cash management systems	
Determine appropriate financing vehicles and techniques	
Determine return on investment (ROI) on technology	
Develop and train staff	
Develop long-term organizational financial strategies	
Distribute expenses to subsidiaries and other units	
Establish and monitor service provider performance standards	
Establish borrowing policies and strategies	
Establish communication strategy	
Establish contingency plans	
Establish corporate objectives and strategies	
Establish credit policies of the organization	

Task or Responsibility	Performed By:

Establish employee benefit, pension, and other funds

Establish financial policies

Establish investment policies

Establish lending limits of the organization

Establish policies and standards for technology

Establish pricing and compensation

Establish reporting standards

Establish risk-management policies

Establish service quality of the organization

Establish technology policies with respect to security and standards

Evaluate industry standards/benchmarks

Evaluate outsourcing opportunities

Evaluate technological solutions

Evaluate the financial strength of the organization

Forecast cash flows

Forecast international cash flows

Implement security and fraud prevention programs

Implement technological plans

Implement technological solutions

Initiate fund transfers

Initiate loans

Maintain relationships with creditors

Manage accounts payable

Manage accounts receivable

Manage bank balances

Manage brokerage relationships

Manage cash

Manage collections

Manage common stock

Manage compliance with audit requests and recommendations

Manage corporate liquidity

Manage daily cash position

Manage disbursements

Manage equity insurance

Manage foreign exchange

Task or Responsibility	Performed By:
Manage fund assets	
Manage general ledger	
Manage interest rates	
Manage international financial institution relationships	
Manage international investments	
Manage lease requirements	
Manage leases	
Manage long-term investments	
Manage mergers, acquisitions, and divestitures	
Manage property	
Manage relationships with analysts and investors	
Manage risks	
Manage tax and legal issues	
Manage trade financing	
Mentor donor relationships	
Monitor compliance with financial policies	
Monitor compliance with corporate objectives and strategies	
Monitor compliance with risk management policies	
Monitor compliance with technology policies	
Monitor employee benefit payments	
Negotiate acquisitions and mergers	
Negotiate credit arrangements	
Perform float analysis/cash optimization reviews	
Prepare financial reports	
Reconcile and submit corrections for errors	
Report on significant industry changes and directions	
Select technology vendors	

3.3 STRUCTURE OF THE FINANCE ORGANIZATION

To gain proficiency in financial management, there must be a financial structure in place to provide information, coordination, and control. The financial structure consists of the finance organization, centers of responsibility, and financial controls. This chapter focuses on the ways to organize, assign responsibility, and either prevent or correct undesirable financial outcomes for an organization.

Financial managers find their position increasingly important and more complex in today's nonprofit environment. Several developments explain why:

- Increased role for the CFO in strategic initiative evaluations
- Reduced governmental grant or aid provision, necessitating alternative revenue development and/or cost reduction
- "Donor fatigue" and increasing competition for donor dollars, accompanied by increasing demands for accountability regarding efficiency and effectiveness
- Availability of new financial instruments, enabling risk management to better contribute to fiscal stability
- Rapid developments in information technology and automation, such as electronic information and cash management systems, with a proper emphasis on using these developments to make better decisions on a timely basis—with many nonprofits housing (locating) the management information systems (MIS) function in the finance office
- Related to the information technology revolution, the harnessing of information to create and maintain competitive advantage and further mission accomplishment for the nonprofit

Notice the common thread running through each of these forces: information. Information about the impact of proposed strategic initiatives on the organization, information about the decline of traditional revenue sources and the availability of alternative revenue sources, information about cost-reduction opportunities, information provided to present and potential donors, information-producing and processing technologies, information provided to program directors and senior management, and the harnessing of information to expand the organization's programs, flexibility, and resourcefulness. Information gathering and dissemination must be coordinated, and the financial and accountability structures enable the nonprofit to do just that. In other words, these structures are not only for cash-flow management, but for information-flow management as well. Using computers enables one to meet both objectives simultaneously.

Information management is also a cornerstone of a turnaround strategy in struggling organizations. Business turnarounds have CFOs engage in the following practices, which can be adapted to the nonprofit situation.

- *Shift the Information Mode.* Involve operating managers in financial analysis and reporting so that they will acknowledge financial problems usually brought to their attention by the CFO and so that they have a better feel for the implications of the financial information.

- *Improve the Reporting System.* Making small, hardly noticeable changes to the information system may conserve financial resources at this critical time, while providing faster and more accurate operating and financial data.

- *Communicate with Candor.* Since employees, donors, clients, and suppliers will learn the truth sooner or later anyway, gain support of the stakeholders by publicly working through the difficulties, enhancing your chances of success as you gain support of critical constituencies.

- *Form a "Tiger Team" in Larger Organizations.* This small, motivated group of middle managers can make suggestions and help implement them; it should focus on major plans and permanent solutions, not quick fixes.

- *Be Creative in Tapping Sources of Cash.* Tax refunds, restructuring of bank debt, asset-based financing (selling receivables, for example), negotiating with suppliers, aligning with sympathetic donors or customers, and selling off idle assets are all sources of cash in tight times.

- *Enlist Employees' Aid.* In difficult times, employees may be enlisted to accept work rule changes, temporary compensation reductions or deferrals, or benefit reductions.

- *Protect Earned Income, Grant, and Fund-Raising Sources.* It is tempting to engage in across-the-board spending reductions, but this may be tantamount to a high-tech company eliminating their research and development budget: maintain or even increase your investment in revenue-augmenting activities.

- *Eliminate or Automate Administrative Functions.* Assuming you have already done everything possible to reduce overhead expenses, look for administrative functions that may be trimmed or eliminated: using outside fundraising counsel and outsourcing payroll are two examples. A key question is whether volunteer resources are already doing some of these tasks, or whether they are required.[3]

(a) Organization

The financial manager the title "Finance Director" is often a part-time position, sometimes voluntary. In larger organizations, the Finance Director or Treasurer may make many of the financial

[3]Adapted from John S. Purtill and Robert L. Caggiano, "How the CFO Can Lead a Business Turnaround." *Journal of Accounting* (June 1986), 108–113.

policy decisions, with Executive Director and Board Committee or entire Board approval.

In larger organizations, separation of controllership and treasury functions is possible. The structure might result in the organizational chart in Exhibit 3-1.

Some of these areas, such as capital budgeting or MIS, can be found in either the Controller's office or treasurer's office, depending on the organization's preferences. There are two noteworthy differences in the focuses of the two offices: (1) the Controller's office assumes responsibility for most of the bookkeeping, reporting, and compliance issues; and (2) the Treasurer's office handles most of the areas requiring management decisions such as when and how much money must be raised (this may be delegated to and surely is executed by the development office); how to invest pension fund management (or who will do the investing, if outsourced); whether to self-insure risks, which bank(s) to use and how to compensate the bank(s); which capital projects to accept; whether to hedge foreign exchange exposure; and whether a fundraising event provides enough additional revenue to repeat it, even when taxes must be paid on the net revenue. Our useful oversimplification is then:

- *Controller's focus:* Get the financial numbers right and conserve the organization's resources
- *Treasurer's focus:* Increase financial resources and manage financial resources

Many organizations deviate from the above organizational structure in two significant ways:

Exhibit 3.1. Controller's Function versus Treasurer's Function

Controller's Office	Treasurer's Office
Financial Accounting	Long-Term Financial Planning
Operational Budgeting (shared)	Cash Management (including
Financial Reporting	forecasting)
Payroll	Bank Selection and Relationship
MIS	Management
Payables	Tax Management
Receivables	Fund-raising
Audit and Internal Control	Employee Benefits
Regulatory Compliance	Pension Fund Management
	Insurance and Risk Management
	Foreign Exchange
	Investing
	Borrowing
	Capital Budgeting
	Strategy Involvement

1. The organization tries to combine the Controller and Treasury functions into one office.
2. The organization divorces fund-raising from the finance function altogether. Apparently, organizations view fund-raising vis-à-vis finance in the same way a business would view market and finance.

Why not consolidate the Controller's and Treasurer's offices? In small organizations (up to $1 million in annual revenues), it is necessary to combine the Controller's office and Treasurer's office. However, larger organizations that keep the offices together often end up with a "second best" setup that does not allow the organization to work at its full capacity. There are a number of reasons that the organization is placed at a disadvantage:

1. The control focus ends up dominating, lending to ever-stronger financial reporting and internal control (e.g., use of internal auditors), and more detailed financial reports.
2. The "reports in search of a user" phenomenon may surface, conciseness is sacrificed for level of detail, with no improvement in usefulness. Very few of the reports are true management accounting outputs, such as break-even analyses. Operating personnel may receive larger and more frequent requests for data and explanations to feed the exception reporting (variance analysis) process. On the positive side, management may gain a better idea of corrective actions to take, and there may be more protection against employee fraud.
3. The Treasury function invariably suffers, as financial management tasks are important but less urgent than getting the monthly, quarterly, and annual statements compiled, and keeping up with recurring payroll and payables tasks.
4. Capital projects placing ruinous financial burdens on the organization are approved.
5. Planning is sacrificed in favor of over-emphasis on financial reporting and auditing. The problem area is not budget development, except to the extent budgets are not linked to carefully-developed long-range strategies and plans. What suffers is long-range financial planning.[4]
6. Short-term financial management areas suffer from benign neglect: cash management procedures are archaic, bank relationships are never re-evaluated and rebid (costing anywhere from $2,000 to $200,000 in unnecessary fees annually), idle funds are left in low-interest or noninterest bearing accounts.

[4]*See* Chapter 4.

7. Risk management is not considered due to inadequate time and expertise: interest rate and exchange rate exposures go unhedged, the organization overpays for or has inadequate insurance coverage.

8. Financial investments are made in inferior or inappropriate vehicles: some organizations invest in overly conservative vehicles (such as the State of Indiana until the 1996 ballot proposition was passed, allowing stock investments), short-changing employees due to underfunded and/or inadequate pension fund coverage for its employees. Other organizations invested in highly risky mortgage-backed securities because they did not have the in-house expertise to evaluate these investments and have not retained outside counsel.

Why do so many nonprofits suffer from these easily avoidable predicaments? One of the main reasons for the consolidation of controller and treasury functions is the selection of accountants for the CFO position. The emphasis in academic accounting programs at colleges and universities in the United States is financial reporting. Ironically, due to separation of accounting and finance in the academic world, accounting students get very little financial management training. The result? The graduates of these types of programs rarely get any training in the financial aspects of cash management, banking selection and relationship management, receivables management, investments, borrowing, or pension or endowment fund management.

Because of the historical inattention to treasury, additional guidance will be provided regarding what treasurers can contribute. Birkett and Sharpe have identified five treasurer competencies in the corporate sector, which provides a checklist for you to evaluate your own organization. Added commentary for nonprofits' unique situations is provided in Exhibit 3.2.

(b) Financial Function: Service Center or Profit Center?

Traditionally, departmental or other units in the organization have been identified as responsibility centers. Managers are then held responsible for the results of their units. This generally meant that departments were considered cost centers or service centers, although some organizations also designated some units as profit centers or investment centers. The distinction has to do with what the unit has control over and responsibility for. Cost or service centers cannot generate revenue directly, so they are held responsible for the level of cost they incurred. They are doing something necessary for the organization's survival, but are consuming scarce resources which must be conserved. A print shop or telecommunications area in a

Exhibit 3.2. Treasury Professional Competencies

Competencies	Nonprofit Implementation
1. Must understand domestic and international financial market institutions, processes, linkage to governmental economic policies, and the legal/ regulatory environment	1. Engage in a study of interest rates and foreign exchange rates (if have global operations), and how changes in them affect your organization's statement of activity and statement of cash flows. Recognize the linkage of gross domestic product (GDP) and your donors' local economies with your donations and earned income.
2. Must understand how financial instruments and financial markets are shaped by the legal environment	2. Study the trends in nationwide banking and electronic payment methods. Project their impact on your cash collections (e.g., of mailed donor checks) and your methods of paying bills and collecting funds. Conduct a feasibility study of electronic debits for donor remittances and as a means of stimulating donor retention and upgrading.
3. Must understand how investment and financing interrelate	3. Projected financial statements are the key here. Your financial needs are closely linked to program expansion, and the projected statements will depict this clearly. Statements to forecast: the statement of activity and statement of net assets to start with then add the statement of cash flows. The cash flow statement will show to what degree operational surpluses fund investment needs, negating the need to borrow money.
4. Must understand the strategic aspects of the organization's activity, and how strategy links to the organizational structure and management processes	4. Revisit your organization's mission statement to start with. Is it still applicable? If not, revise it. Then, convene the board and top management to detail strategies (see presentation in Chapter 4). Consider how to build organizational structure to facilitate the implementation of your strategies. Is bureaucracy the best approach, or should participative decision making be facilitated with a flat organization?

Exhibit 3.2.   Treasury Professional Competencies (*continued*)

Competencies	Nonprofit Implementation
5. Must possess the necessary intellectual and instrumental skills for carrying out treasury activities.	5. Hire carefully for both top-level and support staff. Then, train and empower, providing resources necessary to carry out the responsibilities professionally and efficiently. Provide training at local or national Treasury Management Association or American Management Association conferences. Provide the technology infrastructure (primarily PCs and local area networks) to financial personnel.

Source: W.P. Birkett and Ian G. Sharpe, "Professional Specialisation in Accounting VIII: Treasury," *Australian Accountant,* February 1997, 49–52.

private school or college would be a cost center. "Physical plant" or "buildings and grounds" activities function as cost centers in most organizations.

To control costs, manufacturing businesses determine benchmarks (standard costs) for labor and material, which indicate costs on a per unit basis. The benchmark cost of a unit of output is often based on time studies or engineering estimates. It represents what the cost of production should be under attainable good performance, and thus serves as a basis for measurement or comparison.[5] Cost overruns are then identified, the cost or service center made aware of them, and the manager of the cost or service center is expected to implement corrective action(s).

If the unit also generates revenues, and has a high degree of control over the amount of revenue generated, it may be treated as a *profit center*. Net revenues are then the focus of periodic evaluations. An *investment center* is held responsible for net revenues *and* the amount of resources (usually measured as assets) used by the area. Think of its results as "return on investment."

Why discuss profit centers in a book about nonprofits? Because there is significant disagreement over whether the treasury area in either a company or nonprofit should be treated as a profit center. Advocates argue that it is legitimate to assume that the treasury department can be held responsible for net interest revenue. First, note the calculation of net interest revenue:

Net interest revenue = (interest revenue − interest expense)

[5]L. Gayle Rayburn, *Principles of Cost Accounting Using a Cost-Management Approach,* 4th Edition (Homewood, IL: Irwin, 1989).

Investments generate interest revenues, while amounts borrowed result in interest expense. The Treasury area controls interest revenue by choices on short-term versus long-term investments, the instruments chosen for investment, and the interest rates earned. Treasury controls interest expenses by their choices on amounts of short-term versus long-term borrowing, the degree of utilization of credit lines, and the interest rates negotiated when borrowing money. Therefore, the argument is to hold the treasurer's office responsible for net interest revenue.

The counterargument is that Treasury should be a service center. Proponents of this idea are concerned that the Treasurer will take undue risks by investing in inappropriate instruments (such as the Orange County debacle), or simply not arrange enough financing. Second, it is argued that Treasurers cannot control the overall level of interest rates earned or paid.

Profit center advocates' rejoinder is that (1) the investment policy controls risk, and (2) the absolute level of net interest revenue may not change much because investment and borrowing rates move up and down together. There are reasons for and against the profit center approach to treasury management. As a profit center or a service center, the function should maintain accountability so that idle funds are invested and prudent risks are taken to enhance returns.

(i) *Focus on Activities.* Nonprofit organizations may not be able to develop standard costs, but they may still *estimate* what good cost performance on an *activity* should be. Using a three-pronged approach, your organization can find innovative ways to increase contributions and accomplish its mission for less cost instead of using the current period's performance as a barometer of success.

1. Tackle the fundamental problems and eliminate "nonproductive structured cost."
2. Redesign services, activities, and business processes to reduce cost.
3. Make major improvements in effectiveness.[6]

Organizations should focus on streamlining business processes and activities, and managing and reducing the *workload*, not just the workforce. Other fundamental activities include asking clients' and donors' advice, continually improving every process (e.g., donor communications), eliminating wasteful activities, reducing workload in each area where feasible, classifying items as utilized or unutilized (as opposed to fixed and variable splits), and controlling the process instead of the results. Involving the individual who

[6]James A. Brimson and John Antos, *Activity-Based Management for Service Industries, Governmental Entities, and Nonprofit Organizations,* (New York: Wiley, 1994).

performs the activity means tapping that person's expertise. Wherever possible, set a target as a minimum level of performance. What may be the most important idea, and most radical, is to focus on outputs and outcomes, not inputs. While outputs and outcomes are difficult to measure and quality is complex, effort should be made to quantify outputs and outcomes where possible. Automate, simplify, and computerize processes wherever possible to reduce human error and mistakes.

(ii) Is Your Cost Analysis Correct? Evaluating cost center performance depends closely on a correct appraisal of costs. An example of mistaken cost analysis is the evaluation of fundraising events. Are all of the costs incorporated into the evaluation? Quite often, even in organizations that computed and reported the event's net revenue (revenue less expenses), the cost of staff time and services necessary to put the event on was not included in the expense total. Instead, only rent, music, food, and prize expenses were considered.

Let's consider another activity: paying a supplier's invoice. The activity cost includes all resources used (e.g., people, equipment, travel, supplies, computer systems) in paying that invoice. The cost of the process of "payables" would be narrowed down to the cost per invoice paid. Quality, cost, and time would be looked at jointly, so as to prevent a myopic "cost only" approach to managing the payables function. Always look for a measure that should capture costs directly for the particular activity you are studying. "Per invoice" works well as the key measure for payables. The activity focus enables one to spot "cost drivers," in which you identify a root cause or an earlier activity that has a great impact on an important activity's cost—such as the processing through and payment of an incorrect invoice. Identification of these cost drivers can lead to prevention rather than costly rework. One is always on the lookout for "non-value-added cost," which means some amount above the minimum amount of time, supplies, or space absolutely essential to add value to the organization.

So how does this "activity management" approach differ from traditional cost accounting? When each organizational unit accumulates costs by cost category, and controls costs on this basis, we have traditional cost accounting. When costs are accumulated and controlled by activity, we have progressed to activity-based management. Partially processed "works-in-progress" such as opened but undeposited donation checks tie up funds that would otherwise be available.

(iii) How Can Finance and Accounting Activities Be Evaluated? Consider the finance and accounting function and the activities it is involved in. Effective organization of that function can reduce waste and provide impetus to the rest of the organization to

engage in activity analysis. For example, the accounts payable area engages in these activities: answer inquiries, receive invoices, pay vendors. Calculating a cost per activity for each of these is a logical starting point for more effective management of the payables area. "Cost per bill paid" is one such measure. Similarly, the payroll area collects/maintains employee data and issues checks. Those two activities provide a logical focus for cost analysis and cost management.

(c) Controls

It was noted in our second chapter that nonprofit administrators have difficulty maintaining strong financial control. To review briefly, this is due to the characteristics of nonprofit organizations that may hinder an effective internal control structure:[7]

- A volunteer governing board, many of whose members serve for limited terms
- A limited number of staff personnel, sometimes too few to provide the appropriate segregation of duties
- A mixture of volunteers and employees participating in operations (Depending on the size and other features of the organization, day-to-day operations sometimes are conducted by volunteers instead of employees. The manner in which responsibility and authority are delegated varies among organizations. This may affect control over financial transactions, particularly with respect to authorization.)
- A budget approved by the governing board (The budget may serve as authorization for the activities to be carried out by management in attaining the organizations' program objectives. Many nonprofit organizations prepare budgets for both operating and capital expenditures.)

(d) Principles of Effective Control

There are several principles of effective control.

1. *Separate key financial activities and establish checks and balances.* The individual counting church collections should not be the same person depositing the money at the bank. More than one individual should count, or at least have a second individual verify the original count. Have a different person reconcile the checking account that the person writing the checks. Require two signatories for checks. Keep check stock locked away in a place that is limited in access. Have a different person handling petty cash than the one doing the bookkeeping. Limit access to any credit cards held in the organization's name. Also limit access to the checking

[7]See footnote 1.

account through withdrawal authorization and ATM card limitations. Talk to your bank about further precautions that can be taken.

2. *Have outside audits done of the books.* Make sure that the bookkeeper takes vacations periodically, when someone else fulfills the accounting responsibility. Even if you cannot afford to hire an outside auditor (even for a review or compilation), form an audit committee of board members or even qualified volunteers who can administer consistency checks and watch for irregularities. This underscores the importance of having at least one individual on your board who possesses a strong understanding of accounting or finance. Insurance or investment professionals, while helpful on risk management or investment issues, are often poorly equipped to carry out this important task.

3. *Pay the modest premiums necessary to have all financial personnel bonded.* A fidelity bond covers your organization against embezzlement, and is surprisingly inexpensive. Watch the fine print to see what the policy does and does not cover.

4. *Network with other organizations similar to your own to see what safeguards they adhere to.* At a minimum, have an investment policy and a general financial policy covering some of the items just mentioned. Volunteers pose an interesting dilemma to many organizations, because of the fine line between requiring them to adhere to control policies and the concern about offending them and losing their devotion to your organization and its mission.

It is strongly recommended that you study the findings and recommendations of the "Treadway Commission" regarding internal controls. This was a congressional study which resulted in the formation of an organization called COSO (Committee on Sponsoring Organizations) to define internal control. In 1992, a report entitled "Internal Control-Integrated Framework" was issued and it has become the standard for internal control. COSO views internal control as a process, affected by an entity's board of directors, management and other personnel, designed to provide reasonable assurance regarding the objective accomplishment in the following three categories:

1. Effectiveness and efficiency of operations
2. Reliability of financial reporting
3. Compliance with applicable laws and regulations

When the Treadway Commission looked at failures in the savings and loan industries, they found that the failures did not result from lower level personnel, but rather at a senior level with unethical business conduct. An integrated framework consisting of the five components of internal control (control environment, risk assessment, control activities, information/communication, and monitoring) should be established by your organization. Preferably, leadership will be taken in this area by your Board.

This concludes our discussion of financial structure and begins a discussion of accountability structure, in which individuals are held accountable for their duties and responsibilities.

3.4   ACCOUNTABILITY STRUCTURE

The many changes in progress in business today, transforming the way in which we do business, require new financial policies, procedures, and techniques. An accountability structure is a way of documenting and clarifying the responsibilities everyone has in this new environment.

(a) Definition

An accountability structure details each of the tasks or processes within a unit and identifies the roles of each person in accomplishing the task or process.

(b) Purpose

Businesses are reviewing how they give authority to their units and their staff, with an eye to empowering and streamlining operations. One important aspect of an accountability structure enables the movement towards giving a unit full responsibility and accountability for their business transactions, by removing the "middle man" as much as possible. In addition, it:

1. Eliminates any confusion about roles and responsibilities
2. Details for all parties within the unit on how the work is performed
3. Verifies compliance with company, government, and any other regulatory agency regulations and guidelines
4. Provides a method of reviewing the accountabilities in the unit to ensure they are kept current and accurate
5. Serves as a guide for measuring performance

(c) Establishing an Accountability Policy

To set up an accountability structure, you first need to be clear about your objectives and goals, and have a method of sharing and conveying those goals to the company, staff, donors, customers, regulatory agencies, and others. Developing a formal policy about accountability can achieve this objective. As with any policy, your policy on accountability should include:

(i) *A General Policy Statement.*   A policy statement presents a brief description of the goal of the policy, such as the following:

The President/CEO delegates the accountability for the financial management of resources to functional units. Consequently, each unit is responsible for properly managing the financial resources of the COMPANY for which they have been provided jurisdiction to include identifying a designee (normally the Chief Administrative Officer) responsible for formulating an accountability structure for each area. This structure depicts the delegation to initiate, process, and review business transactions by only qualified individuals in accordance with the guidelines put forth by the President/CEO and monitored for compliance by various other units (to be specified).

Core principles. Core principles further define the policy statement. They are the rules or practices adhered to in order to comply with the policy statement, such as:

Setting the appropriate accountability delegations to conduct business transactions affecting nonprofit organization funds begins with the core principles listed below.

(ii) Interpretation of Policy. Policy is often written in a language that is technical and not easy for everyone to understand. Policy is a legal document; however, an interpretation of the policy can assist others in applying the policy properly, such as:

A. Individuals delegating accountability can only do so to the extent that this same accountability has been delegated to them.

B. Individuals delegating accountability are responsible for ensuring the qualifications of the individuals to whom they delegate as well as the proper fulfillment of their responsibilities.

C. Qualified individuals are those who:

 1. Are actively involved with the activities being conducted

 2. Possess a working knowledge of the budget, an adequate level of technical skills required to use the various application systems involved, and an awareness of policies, rules, laws, regulations or other restrictions on the use of funds sufficient to either ascertain compliance or seek additional assistance

 3. Have sufficient authority to fulfill their responsibilities so they can disallow a transaction without being countermanded or subjected to disciplinary action

---

The Chief Administrative Officer is responsible for the financial resources within his or her operating unit. They may delegate their responsibility to others. These delegations must be recorded in a document that specifies:

- The kind or type of work the employee performs (e.g., purchasing, accounts payable, payroll, personnel)

- The qualifications, training, and/or credentials of the individual that justified the assignment of their duties

- The individuals responsible for reviewing work (including type and conditions) performed by others (e.g., review all Purchasing transactions performed by the department, or all Purchasing transactions for a specific account)

- An alternate to serve when an individual normally assigned to perform this work is not available (vacation or other absences)

- The accountability structure must reflect universally accepted business practices:
  - Separation of duties (the person who receives cash should not also deposit it or reconcile the transaction)
  - No conflict of interest

- Individuals must understand to whom and where they go when they suspect irregularities. In addition, management must set a tone that encourages and supports individuals

---

D. Each organizational head must officially record all accountability delegations as well as any cancellations or modifications of such delegations, once established.

E. Each business transaction (including commitments) must be reviewed on a timely basis by the individual accountable for the affected accounting unit(s). In instances where this individual prepared the transaction, a second qualified individual must review that transaction and, in so doing, accepts responsibility for the accuracy of the transaction and compliance with all applicable policies, rules, and regulations.

G. Each organizational head (or designee) must regularly review its official record of accountability delegations and related maintenance procedures, to ensure that it remains secure, accurate, and current.

H. Each organizational head (or designee) must monitor the effectiveness of the accountability delegations to ensure that all accountable individuals are performing their functions in accordance with all policies, guidelines, laws, regulations, and related training instructions.

contacting superiors and others when suspicious of irregularities.

(d) Ethics

A discussion of business ethics is beyond the scope of this book. However, since business ethics is always included as a topic in seminars, a section is included on the subject in our book.

Business decisions are often subject to interpretation. Consequently, a decision maker may often find himself or herself in a quandry over how to ensure compliance. Our best advice is that to do your best to thoroughly understand the rules and regulations which apply to the particular issue at hand. Use this information, along with your best judgment, to make your decision.

A simple example to illustrate the point:

> A problem is discovered in the way the organization is accounting for planned gifts. The Chief Administrative Officer must determine how broadly to make adjustments without impacting future gifts or embarrassing people and/or the institution. Questions that must be answered in the process of determining corrective action are: what is the responsible person's duty to inform, to fix, to improve, and to control? The ability to make these hard calls comes from a strong base of experience.

Another challenge is red-tape because bureaucracies are inherently complex and confusing. When faced with the realities of the red-tape effecting the ability to get things done, individuals may feel it is their ethical responsibility to cut-through-it. This places the individual in a gray area between the ethical responsibilities of complying with the regulation or law and our society's push to cut through red-tape.

(e) Ethics Check

As indicated in the audit section of this book, audit as a means of assuring compliance is necessary when reviewing all business

Exhibit 3.3. Range of Ethics

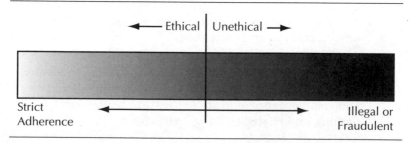

transactions (see Exhibit 3.3). It is also necessary to perform an audit of decision making within your organization.

It is important to constantly review and monitor the interpretations of regulations and laws and assist individuals forced to make these difficult ethical decisions with the stress that it creates; further, to be certain that individuals have not determined they can decide arbitrarily to ignore all laws, rules, and regulations out of habit without regard for special circumstances. Once an individual has crossed this ethical line, how far can he or she go before it becomes immoral or illegal?

Discussions about ethics frequently do not occur. The ethics issue is often ignored for fear that even broaching the subject might cause or raise suspicion. Certainly formal, established policy on how unethical an individual can be without breaking the rules would be unreasonable, but a discussion or pamphlet outlining the company's attitude towards compliance is certainly advisable. It is also possible to teach or monitor company ethics using analogies. Most importantly, individuals within the company must understand the basic assumption that all rules, laws, and regulations must be adhered to and that only when the situation or task makes it absolutely necessary to deviate from the strict interpretation are individuals to consider such an option and to seek the advice of the department head, CFO, or president when making these decisions.

(f) Making Ethical Decisions

It is very tempting to "break the rules" when the organization is financially strapped. One recurring problem for businesses and nonprofits alike is "stretching payables" beyond their due date. How can Boards and top management instill a culture dedicated to integrity in the organization? A starting point is instruction on the three tiers of ethical standards by which employees and volunteers can judge their actions, as shown in Exhibit 3.4.

In the first tier, the concern is whether the action is legal or at least consistent with the relevant law's intent. This would be the minimal requirement of all employees and volunteers. The middle tier moves beyond this to ask whether an impartial observer would judge the organization's decisions, way of conducting business, and reasons for its actions to be both prudent and mutually beneficial to all parties. The Golden Rule applies here. It is clear that stretching payables violates the middle tier standard. Going beyond this, the top tier requires a commitment to enhancing the well-being of the people with whom business is conducted, even if there is a cost to the organization. As one moves from lower to higher tiers, a greater commitment to relationship enhancement is

Exhibit 3.4. Tiers of Ethical Standards

Top Tier
Make a commitment to enhance the well-being of our neighbors, even when this requires some self-sacrifice.

Middle Tier
Subject all decisions and actions to the "sunlight test" and ask, would both interested and impartial observers of the decisions and actions find them to be mutually beneficial to all affected parties; and prudent, practical, sound, discreet, circumspect, wise, informed, etc.?

Lower Tier
Does this decision obey the intent and letter of the law and respect the cultural mores that bear on this action?

Source: Adapted from Richard Chewning, *Biblical Principles and Economics: The Foundations* (Colorado Springs, CO: Navpress, 1989), p. 278.

necessitated. Summarizing, do what is legal, but always strive to make decisions that build and strengthen relationships rather than tear them down.[8]

Individuals within the organization need to be reminded constantly that compliance with regulations, rules, and laws (*Lower Tier*) is consistent with the mission of the company. The development and periodic review of an accountability structure, as a regular, integral part of day-to-day business, provides a mechanism for accomplishing this.

(g) Designing an Accountability Structure

There are six steps to designing a structure:

Step 1: Determine which tasks or processes are performed in your unit.

To determine which tasks or processes are performed in your unit, you may need to survey the staff concerning what they do. Other potential resources are job descriptions, job cards, products, and reports.

[8]See Mary L. Woodell, "Fraud? Imagine You're in the Spotlight," *New York Times* (November 24, 1991), F11. Woodell offers three tests to help make the right decisions: the "smell" test, the "what would your parents say" test, and the "deposition" test. The Treasury Management Association, Bethesda, MD has a code of ethics that applies equally well to financial staffers in businesses and nonprofits.

These major categories might include:

- Purchasing
- Accounts payable
- Payroll
- Personnel
- Accounts receivable

Step 2: Determine where and how these tasks or processes can be divided into steps, amongst individuals to enable appropriate separation of duties.

- Purchasing
  - Price quotations/bids
  - Order placement
  - Document preparation
  - Receiving
- Accounts payable
  - Document preparation
  - Document review
  - Invoice matching
  - Reconciliation
- Accounts receivable
  - Receipt of cash or other monies
  - Tally sheets
  - Document preparation
  - Transport to bank
  - Reconciliation

Step 3: Determine which staff members have the skills necessary to perform the tasks, processes, or steps.

An example of this process is presented in Exhibit 3.5.

Step 4: Determine which role the individual will perform as well as the preparer/performer or reviewer/auditor of the action or process.

When determining the role an individual will play in a process or action, the person with the most knowledge should generally be given the responsibility to review the entire action. The decision is

Exhibit 3.5. Determining Staff Members' Strengths and Weaknesses

	Jeff	Michael	Tricia	Jenny	Nancy
Purchasing					
Price quotations/bids	X	X			
Order placement	X	X	X	X	X
Document preparation	X			X	X
Receiving	X	X	X	X	X
Accounts payable					
Document preparation		X		X	
Document review		X		X	
Invoice matching		X	X		
Reconciliation		X	X		
Accounts receivable					
Receipt of cash or other monies			X	X	X
Tally sheets/counting					X
Document preparation		X			X
Transport to bank	X	X	X	X	X
Reconciliation				X	X

often based on the supervisory or management position the individual holds. While it may appear contrary to tradition, the best reviewer of an action is the person with the most knowledge, regardless of their ranking within the area.

Establish guidelines or rules that each role requires. After establishing these rules and guidelines, detail how individuals should properly perform their functions, to whom they go for advice or training, and how they can properly question a transaction, process, or action without fear of reprimand. A primary and a backup should be assigned to each step (see Exhibit 3.6).

Step 5: Determine whether the workload is distributed appropriately or reasonably.

After determining who has primary responsibilities and back-up responsibilities, review the structure to assure that work is distributed evenly across the unit and make adjustments as necessary. Be sure to factor in work schedules, seasonal fluctuations, and attrition (impacts of retraining and cross-training).

Step 6: Review the structure for accuracy.

Before implementing your accountability structure, review it carefully to make certain that all tasks or processes have been included and that the staff assignments are consistent with the individual's abilities (cross-training may be necessary).

Exhibit 3.6. Determining Preparer and Auditory

	Jeff	Michael	Tricia	Jenny	Nancy
Purchasing (review)	PP			PB	
Price quotations/bids		PP		PB	
Order placement			PP		PB
Document preparation			PP		PB
Receiving		PP		PB	
Accounts payable (review)		PP	PB		
Document preparation				PP	
Document review				PP	
Invoice matching			PB		
Reconciliation			PB		
Accounts receivable (review)				PB	PP
Receipt of cash or other monies			PP	PB	
Tally sheets/counting				PB	PP
Document preparation		PP			PB
Transport to bank	PP		PB		
Reconciliation				PP	PB

(i) Monitoring an Accountability Structure. After developing an accountability structure, its effectiveness should be monitored. Initially the structure will need to be monitored closely to determine that the initial design works in principle. Adjustments may need to be made to the initial design.

After the basic structure has been implemented and determined to be reasonably accurate and functional, periodic reviews of the structure should be performed. There are several types of reviews or factors that should be performed or included:

1. Determine whether additional processes or tasks have been added to the units' responsibilities.
2. Determine whether changes in work load have affected the quality of the work performed.
3. Determine whether individuals are performing their role and responsibilities as intended.
4. Determine that policies and procedures are being followed.

(ii) Schedule of Reviews. The accountability structure should be reviewed at regular timed intervals and as necessary. The uniqueness of your organization will determine how often changes in workload or responsibilities occur. The following guidelines may be used:

• *Monthly:* Review or scan products, reports, output to determine that all tasks and processes are being performed.

- *Quarterly:* Review or scan products, reports, output for quality, accuracy, and compliance with policy.
- *Annually:* Provide performance reviews to all staff members detailing how effective their work has been during the previous year. Where necessary, make changes to the individual's performance objectives and responsibilities, and provide counsel and training where needed.

See Appendix 3A for a case study.

APPENDIX 3A

CASE STUDY

Mr. Jones must be in Japan for a conference next week. This conference is critical to the organization. There is a regulation requiring that domestic carriers be used, unless one is not available. There is also a regulation that requires all expenses to be reasonable. An individual is given the assignment to make the airline reservations for Mr. Jones. After discussing the possibilities with the travel agent, the staff person determines that the airfare on the domestic carrier is $1,500 and the airfare on a nondomestic carrier is $500.

Since the regulations seem to conflict in this situation, the individual is now required to make a more complex ethical judgment trading off multiple requirements to determine which regulation is more important.

- One interpretation of the regulations would require that the domestic carrier be used, assuming that this was the most reasonable fare amongst all the domestic carriers. The regulation specified that a domestic carrier must be used unless one is not available and in this case, there is a domestic carrier available.
- Another consideration is that the reasonableness of the expenditure would be in violation unless the nondomestic carrier is used. Since the difference between these two amounts is so great ($1,000), it would be reasonable to assume that the less expensive airfare is the most important factor in this decision.

What tools are necessary for the individual to make this decision? First, the individual needs to understand the intent of a regulation. Regulations are interpretations of general guidelines or policies. An understanding of the policy underlying this regulation may assist the individual in choosing which guideline should apply. The policy may be "in an effort to assure a constant and steady tax base, thus ensuring continued revenue from which to draw, business should be conducted with domestic businesses, where reasonable."

The individual now has a better understanding of the intent of the regulation, but also understands that a reasonableness criterion can be applied. The "where reasonable" text at the end of the policy statement admits that there will be situations when strict adherence to the policy is in conflict with other policies and goals and allows "reasonable tolerance" to be applied on a case-by-case basis.

In this scenario, it would be reasonable, and in compliance with all regulations to choose the nondomestic carrier.

Consider another scenario with differing amounts. In this scenario, the domestic carrier charges $800 and that nondomestic carrier charges $825. The question put before the individual in this scenario is: "Is the $25 important to my company and is a $25 difference reasonable?"

Let us examine the core policy again: "In an effort to assure a constant and steady tax base, thus ensuring continued revenue from which to draw, business should be conducted with domestic businesses, where reasonable." Now we can focus on another aspect of the policy, "a constant and steady tax base." To simplify the example, assume that the corporate taxes in your state are 10 percent, and that the corporation pays that average. Thus, this business transaction to the domestic business would generate $80 for the state, not to mention the percentage applied at the federal level. Using this as a guide, you can interpret that it is reasonable to pay the higher fare because the long-term impacts of the transaction, the more global impacts, provide more revenue and resources when the domestic carrier is used.

Now consider another possible factor. The budget for this trip is $800. Choosing the domestic carrier would exceed the budget allowance for this trip.

When evaluating business decisions, regardless of interpretation of the regulations and laws, what takes precedence, the law or the budget? This is where the not-for-profit business has special moral obligations that may not apply to for-profit businesses. It would be reasonable for a for-profit business to always choose the lowest reasonable cost when choosing between vendors. This, however, may not apply to a not-for-profit business because the motive of the business is not profit but the accomplishment of its mission, within the guidelines of their operating budget. It is also necessary for the not-for-profit business to be more open with its business transactions and justify each expenditure in a more global way, as a constituent, and as a member of the community.

To finish these scenarios, let us complicate this example one more time by assuming that the domestic carrier is also a major potential donor to the not-for-profit business.

Regardless of the amounts used, is there a long-term impact, or are other issues to be considered which are more important: the community as a whole or the appearance of supporting the donors of the not-for-profit business, and thus support the community? Is there a reasonableness that should be applied? Many could argue that a $25 difference is not sufficient to raise a question of impropriety, combined with the policy regarding the use of domestic carriers. But if the first scenario amounts are used ($1,000 difference in fares), which factors should be given the most weight?

1. Compliance with policy

2. Budget

3. Appearance to donors

4. Appearance to the community

These are the general guidelines that the individual needs to understand, as well as which of the above factors should be given the most weight in all situations. Determining this will enable all employees to evaluate their decisions and be certain that they are in compliance and consistent with the company's position and philosophies.

CHAPTER FOUR

Long-Range Financial Planning and Strategy

4.1 What Is Strategic Planning?   105
4.2 What Are the Organization's Mission and Goals?   108
    (a) Strategy and the "Bottom Line"   108
    (b) What Are Strategic Decisions?   110
4.3 Strategic Management Process—Three Steps   111
4.4 The Strategic Decision-Making Process   113
    (a) What Are Internal Strengths and Weaknesses?   113
4.5 Planning for Change   115
    (a) The Long-Range Financial Planning Process   116
    (b) Financial Planning Basics   117
4.6 Financial Evaluation of Projects That Arise
    from Existing Programs   120
    (a) Example 1: Youthsave, Inc.   121
        (i) Approaching a Capital Expenditure Analysis   121
    (b) Example 2: Equivalent Annual Cost Illustrated   123
    (c) How to Manage the Total Capital Budget   125
    (d) The Capital Budget and Capital Rationing   125
    (e) Rationing the Capital   126
4.7 Financial Evaluation of Program Alternatives   128
    (a) Service Portfolio   130
    (b) Annual Necessary Investment   130
    (c) Mergers and Acquisitions   132
    (d) Motives for Mergers and Acquisitions   132
        (i) Programmatic Synergy   132
        (ii) Financial Synergy   132
    (e) Partnerships, Joint Ventures,
        and Strategic Alliances   137
        (i) Partnerships and Joint Ventures   137
    (f) Strategic Alliances   139
        (i) Motives for Strategic Alliances   139
        (ii) Financial Aspects of Strategic Alliances   141

(iii) Financial Projections of Mergers, Acquisitions,
           or Joint Ventures   142
     (g)   Implementing the Strategic Plan   142
4.8 Conclusion   144

This chapter outlines the financial manager's role in the strategic planning process. The chapter begins by developing the financial plan for existing and already approved programs; then shows how to evaluate individual capital expenditures made as part of program implementation; finally, the financial evaluation of program alternatives such as new ventures, mergers and acquisitions, partnerships, joint ventures, and strategic alliances is explained. Before explaining the financial side of planning, this chapter provides an overview of strategic planning from some of the best available sources.

The benefits of the planning process for a nonprofit organization include the following:

- It forces the management team to look ahead as a built-in, ongoing process that is done in a systematic fashion.
- It sharpens guiding objectives and policies.
- It leads to a better coordination of the organization's efforts.
- It brings a clearer picture of how responsibilities interact for participants.
- It fosters development of performance standards control.
- It makes the organization better prepared for sudden new developments.[1]

Planners, for the most part, seem to be mired in the budgeting process. This is not strategic thinking, but merely bean counting. To plan successfully, a business must have a strategic thinker at its helm and an environment in which it infuses strategic thinking into all of its endeavors. Regardless of line and staff relations, everyone from the executive director down must adopt a planning philosophy. Planning is not just an extension of the budgeting process: good planning identifies the key issues to which the appropriate numbers can later be attached.

4.1   WHAT IS STRATEGIC PLANNING?

Strategy is "the process of deciding on the goals of the organization and on the broad strategies that are to be used in attaining these

---

[1]Melville Branch, *The Corporate Planning Process* (New York: American Management Association, 1962).

goals."[2] It involves deciding how to combine and employ resources. It is not a one-time exercise, but rather an ongoing process. Other aspects pertaining to strategic planning include the following:[3]

- It usually relates to some part of the organization, not the totality (life is too complicated).

- Some elements of strategic planning are essentially *irregular* because problems, opportunities, and bright ideas do not arise according to some set timetable; rather, they are dealt with whenever they happen to be perceived; an overemphasis on some systematic approach (or analytical techniques) could stifle creativity—so the process is essentially unsystematic.

- Estimates used in strategic plans are intended to show the *expected* results of the plan (by contrast management control process and the data used in it are intended to influence managers to take actions that will lead to *desired* results)—for the figures, "Are these the most reasonable estimates that can be made?"

- It relies heavily on external information (e.g., market analyses, estimates of costs and other factors involved in building a plant in a new locality, technological developments).

- Much of the relevant information is imprecise (what will probably happen over a relatively long period of time).

- Communication is simpler and involves relatively few persons (the need for secrecy often dictates that steps be taken to inhibit communication), but then wide communication of the decisions that result from strategic planning is obviously important—this is part of the management control process, however.

- It essentially consists of applied economics and financial analysis.

- It involves top management much more than it does middle management—many operating executives are by temperament not very good at strategic planning, and pressures of current activities preclude allotment of necessary time to such work, and they usually are knowledgeable only about their part of the organization, and strategic planning requires a broader background.

Exhibit 4.1 highlights the differences between strategic planning and management control in for-profit organizations. However, strategic planning differs in nonprofit organizations. Why do nonprofit organizations present unique managerial problems? Six

---

[2]Robert Anthony and John Dearden, *Management Control Systems*, 4th edition (Homewood, IL: Richard Irwin, 1980).
[3]*Id.*, 10.

Exhibit 4.1.   Differences between Strategic Planning
and Management Control

Characteristic	Strategic Planning	Management Control
Focus of plans	On one aspect at a time	On whole organization
Complexities	Many variables	Less complex
Degree of structure	Unstructured and irregular; each problem different	Rhythmic; prescribed procedures
Nature of information	Tailor-made for problem; more external and predictive; less accurate	Integrated; more internal and historical; more accurate
Communication of information	Relatively simple	Relatively difficult
Purpose of estimates	Show expected results	Lead to desired results
Persons primarily involved	Staff and top management	Line and top management
Number of persons involved	Small	Large
Mental activity	Creative; analytical	Administrative; persuasive
Source discipline	Economics	Economics and social psychology
Planning and control	Planning dominant, but some control	Emphasis on both planning and control
Time horizon	Tends to be long	Tends to be short
End result	Policies and precedents	Action within policies and precedents
Appraisal of the job done	Extremely difficult	Much less difficult

Source: Reprinted with permission of The McGraw-Hill Companies and Anthony R. Deatden, et al, from *Management Control Systems, Seventh Edition,* © 1992.

complex factors affecting decision making in nonprofit organizations are as follows:

1. Intangibility of services
2. Weak customer influence
3. Strong professional versus organizational commitment by employees
4. Management intrusion by resource contributors
5. Restraints on the use of rewards and punishments
6. The influence of a charismatic leader and/or organizational mystique on choices[4]

Some nonprofits lose their program focus and overemphasize revenue generation. The joint effect of (1) constantly needing to seek resources, (2) not having a profit motive, and (3) not being able

[4]William H. Newman and Harvey W. Wallender, III, "Managing Not-For-Profit Enterprises," *Academy of Management Review* 3 (January 1978): 24–31.

to accurately measure service quality is to make nonprofit organization managers concentrate more on fund-raising than on the needs of service users.[5] It's a struggle that the organization will constantly have to grapple with, and it often happens when the vision and mission of the organization are unclear, unfocused, or forgotten.

4.2 WHAT ARE THE ORGANIZATION'S MISSION AND GOALS?

Peter Drucker indicates that there are three "musts" to the development of a successful mission:

1. Study your organization's strengths and its past performance. The idea is to do better those things you already do well—if it's the right thing to do. The belief that your organization can do *everything* is just plain wrong. When you violate your organization's values, you are likely to do a poor job.

2. Look outside at the opportunities and needs. With the limited resources you have (including people, money, and competence), where can you really make a difference? Once you know, create a high level of performance in that arena.

3. Determine what your organization really believes in. Drucker notes that he has never seen anything being done well unless people were committed. One reason why the Edsel failed was that nobody at Ford believed in it.[6]

Recapping, there are several questions you should ask when viewing possible activities and programs to get involved with. First, determine what the opportunities and needs are. Then, ask if they fit the organization. Are you likely to do a good job at meeting them? Is there organizational competence in these areas? Do they match the organization's strengths? Does the Board, staff, and volunteer contingent really believe in this?

(a) Strategy and the "Bottom Line"

Nonprofit organizations have no "bottom line." They seem to consider everything they do to be righteous and to serve a cause, so they are not willing to insist, that: if a program doesn't produce results then maybe resources should be redirected. Nonprofits need the discipline of organized abandonment and the critical choices that involves.

[5]Sol Shaviro and Donald Grunewald, "Improving Decision Making in Nonprofit Organizations," *Thought* 63 (March 1988): 52–68.
[6]Peter F. Drucker, *Managing the Non-Profit Organization: Practices and Principles* (New York: Harper Collins, 1992), 56.

In addition to overall strategic direction, functional, *area-specific strategies* are necessary. One critical missing ingredient noted by Drucker in his studies of nonprofit organizations is the lack of a fund development strategy. He notes that the source of its money is probably the greatest single difference between the nonprofit sector and business and government. The nonprofit institution has to raise money from donors. It raises its money—at least, a large portion of it—from people who want to participate in the cause but who are not beneficiaries, or clients. Money is scarce in nonprofits. In fact, many nonprofit managers seem to believe that their difficulties would be solved if only they had more money. He mentions that some of them come close to believing that money-raising is really their mission! As an example, he cites the presidents of private colleges and universities who are so totally preoccupied with money-raising that they have neither the time nor the thought for leading their organizations. What happens then? In his words:

> But a nonprofit institution that becomes a prisoner of money-raising is in serious trouble and in a serious identity crisis. The purpose of a strategy for raising money is precisely to enable the nonprofit institution to carry out its mission without subordinating that mission to fund-raising. This is why nonprofit people have now changed the term they use from "fund-raising" to "fund development." Fund-raising is going around with a begging bowl, asking for money because the *need* is so great. Fund development is creating a constituency which supports the organization because it *deserves* it. It means developing what I call a membership that participates through giving.[6a]

Innovative organizations, both businesses and nonprofits, generally look outside and inside for ideas about new opportunities. A primary example, cited by Drucker, is the megachurch. The pastoral church looks at changes in demographics, at all the young, professional, educated people who have been cut off from their roots and need a community, assistance, encouragement, and spiritual strength. The change seen outside is an opportunity for organizations that are observant. Look *within* the organization and identify the most important clue pointing the way to strategic venturing: generally, it will be the unexpected success. Most organizations feel that they somehow deserve the unforeseen major successes and engage in self-congratulation. What they should be doing is seeing a call to greater outreach and action.

The Girl Scout Association found that the social phenomenon of "latchkey kids" became a tremendous opportunity—which spawned the Daisy Scouts. When doing anything new, don't vault

[6a]See footnote 6.

from "idea stage" to "fully operational stage." Test the idea, possibly with a limited rollout that is often called the pilot stage. A great idea can be labeled a failure when tiny and easily correctable flaws destroy the confidence of your clients, volunteers, or employees.

As a final note, Drucker has noted how persistence can breed improved performance and that sometimes the best thing to do is "cut your losses:"

> When a strategy or an action doesn't seem to be working, the rule is, "If at first you don't succeed, try once more. Then do something else." The first time around, a new strategy very often doesn't work. Then one must sit down and ask what has been learned. "Maybe we pushed too hard when we had success. Or we thought we had won and slackened our efforts." Or maybe the service isn't quite right. Try to improve it, to change it and make another major effort. Maybe, though I am reluctant to encourage that, you should make a third effort. After that, go to work where the results are. There is only so much time and so many resources, and there is so much work to be done.[7]

(b) What Are Strategic Decisions?

Examples of strategic decisions are: deciding to offer a new product line or service; deciding to serve a new clientele. Whenever organizations significantly alter their activities, the strategic management process is at work.

Three factors distinguish strategic decisions:

1. Strategic decisions deal with concerns that are essential to the livelihood and survival of the entire organization and usually involve a major portion of the organization's resources.

2. Strategic decisions involve new initiatives or areas of concern and usually address issues that are unusual for the organization rather than issues that are easily handled with routine decision making.

3. Strategic decisions could have major implications for the way other, lower-level decisions in the organization are made.

Strategic management is used to refer to the entire scope of strategic decision making in an organization; as it can be defined as the "set of managerial decisions that relates the organization to its environment, guides internal activities, and determines the long-term performance of the organization."[8]

---

[7]Id.

[8]Michael J. Stahl and David W. Grigsby, *Strategic Management for Decision Making* (Boston, MA: PWS-Kent Publishing Co., 1992), 20.

Mintzberg, one of the great management thinkers of our day, views strategy as a pattern in a stream of decisions. The ramifications for the organization are recognizing that:

1. Strategy is not one decision, but must be viewed in the context of a number of decisions and the consistency among them.
2. The organization must be constantly aware of decision alternatives.

So, think about strategy as the reasoning that guides the organization's choices among its alternatives.

Is strategy always the result of a planned, conscious effort toward goals that results in a pattern? Not at all. *Deliberate* strategy is what we call this; but *emergent* strategy emerges from the bottom levels of the organization as a result of its activities. Or, it may result from the implementation process—in which changes in goals and "reorienting" may produce strategies that are quite different from what you originally intended. As a starting point in diagnosing the organization, study the decisions themselves and infer strategy from the strategic decisions.[9]

4.3   STRATEGIC MANAGEMENT PROCESS— THREE STEPS

There are three steps in the strategic management process:

1. *Strategy formulation*—the set of decisions that determine the organization's mission and establishes its objectives, strategies, and policies.
2. *Strategy implementation*—decisions that are made to put a new strategy in place or to reinforce an existing strategy; includes motivating people, arranging the right structure and systems, establishing cross-functional teams, establishing policies, and maintaining the right organizational culture to make the strategy work.
3. *Evaluation and control*—activities and decisions that keep the process on track; include following up on goal accomplishment and feeding back the results to decision makers.

In their studies of organizational development, Stahl and Grigsby have found regularities that help us understand the progression of strategic management. The organization will likely have to go through these phases, with each one showing increasing effectiveness, shown in Exhibit 4.2.

[9]This section is based on a presentation in Michael J. Stahl and David W. Grigsby, *Strategic Management for Decision Making* (Boston, MA: PWS-Kent Publishing Co., 1992), 20–24.

Exhibit 4.2. Strategic Management Phases

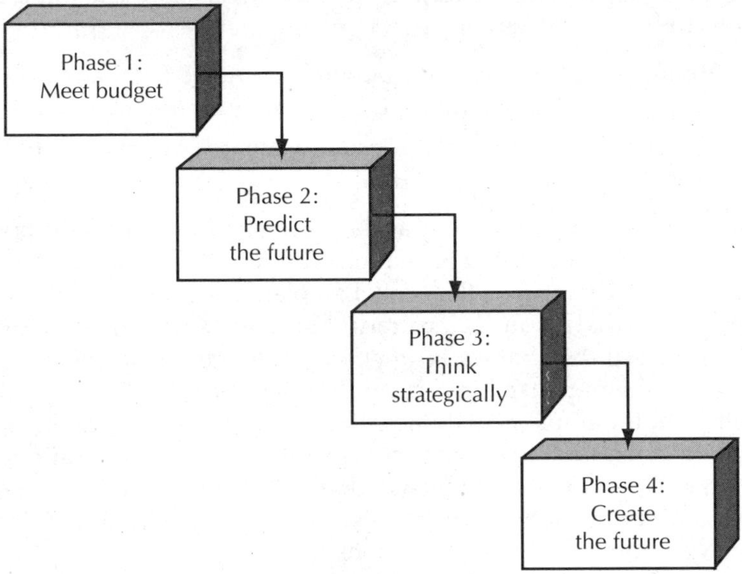

Source: Adapted and reprinted by permission of *Harvard Business Review.* From "Strategic Management for Competitive Advantage" by Frederick Gluck, Stephen Kaufman, and A. Steven Walleck, July–Aug. #58 © 1980 by the President and Fellows of Harvard College, all rights reserved.

- *Phase I:* Basic Financial Planning: Meet Budget
  - Control of operations
  - Setting annual budget
  - Focus is on the various functions
- *Phase 2:* Forecast-Based Planning: Predict the Future
  - Improved planning for growth
  - Environmental analysis
  - Multiyear forecasts
  - Resource allocation is static
- *Phase 3:* Externally Oriented Planning: Think Strategically
  - More responsive to markets and competition
  - Better analysis of situations and assessment of competition
  - Strategic alternatives are evaluated
  - Resource allocation is dynamic
- *Phase 4:* Strategic Management: Create the Future
  - Create competitive advantage using all resources as a group
  - Planning framework is selected strategically
  - Planning process is creative and flexible
  - Value system and culture are supportive of planning and plans

4.4   THE STRATEGIC DECISION-MAKING PROCESS

Common elements of a strategic plan are a mission statement; corporate objectives (including long-, medium-, and short-range objectives); and corporate-level strategies. The strategic plan can be viewed as a framework for strategic decision making. In fact, you may make some of your strategic decisions while you are devising your organization's strategic plan.

When formulating your organization's strategic plan, the manager must analyze conditions inside the organization, as well as conditions in the external environment. This analysis is now so conventional in strategic management that it is referred to as analysis of internal *Strengths* and *Weaknesses* and external *Opportunities* and *Threats*—in a word, *SWOT*. Exhibit 4.3 gives us the worksheet that includes all components of SWOT analysis. You may wish to duplicate it and use it to diagnose your organization's present situation.

(a)   What Are Internal Strengths and Weaknesses?

Issues that are within the organization and usually under your management's control are internal strengths and weaknesses. A strength is anything internal to the company that may lead to an advantage relative to your funding or service competitors and a benefit relative to your clients. A weakness is anything internal that may lead to a disadvantage relative to those competitors and clients. These internal items may have been inherited from past management teams.

A talented and experienced top management team is a great internal asset, especially when the organization is in a rapidly changing or very competitive environment. If your board brings a fresh perspective to strategic issues, instead of rubber-stamping management's ideas as so many boards do, count your board as an internal strength.

Financial management is an area in which strength can advance most decisions management might implement. But a weak financial position (usually signaled by very high levels of debt) weakens the organization. For example, the Chrysler Corporation was in such bad shape financially in the early 1980s that the high hopes of the new Chairman, Lee Iacocca, would have led nowhere if the U.S. government had not provided loan guarantees. A weak financial position can prevent an organization from responding to the wonderful external opportunities.[10]

---

[10]There may be a noneconomic reason why an organization would proceed here, despite the financial shortcomings of the proposal. If the project is implemented, however, the Board should recognize that the project would be a drain on the organization's financial resources.

Exhibit 4.3.   Worksheet for Strength, Weakness, Opportunity, and Threat (SWOT) Analysis

SWOT ANALYSIS WORKSHEET

Directions: In each circle, code the letter S (strength),
W (weakness), O (opportunity), or T (threat),
or leave the item blank if it represents none of these items.

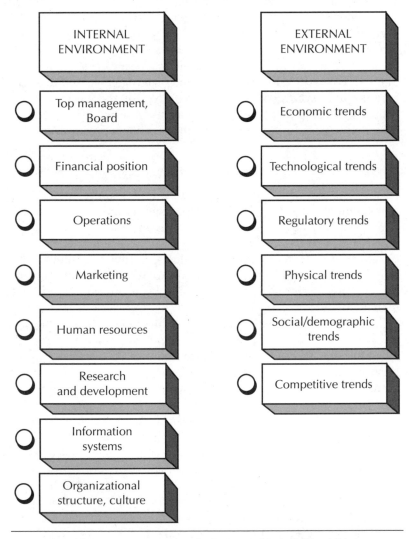

INTERNAL ENVIRONMENT	EXTERNAL ENVIRONMENT
○ Top management, Board	○ Economic trends
○ Financial position	○ Technological trends
○ Operations	○ Regulatory trends
○ Marketing	○ Physical trends
○ Human resources	○ Social/demographic trends
○ Research and development	○ Competitive trends
○ Information systems	
○ Organizational structure, culture	

Source: Adapted from *Strategic Management for Decision Making* by Stahl and Grigsby. Copyright 1992 PWS-Kent Publishing. By permission of South Western College Publishing, a division of International Thomson Publishing, Inc., Cincinnati, OH 45227.

4.5   PLANNING FOR CHANGE

If your nonprofit organization is typical, you are sweating a bunch of changes. It helps to have a framework to help you address change. A formal but simple approach to planning for successful change in a changing environment is the ideal; here we simply provide some key questions to ask in applying an approach which includes the following considerations:[11]

- *What are we?*
  1. Defining the distinct business or service provision areas in which the organization is involved
  2. Identifying the positions of these distinct areas in terms of their product or service life cycles (introduction, growth, maturity, decline)
  3. Characterizing their competitive positions
- *What's our environment? What do we want to be?*
  4. Estimating potential—what can be accomplished with the resources the organization can muster within the limits imposed by our environment
  5. Developing strategic goals and objectives
  6. Analyzing financial and managerial liquidity
- *How do we get there? How do we know when we've arrived?*
  7. Determining strategic risk
  8. Designing a managerial structure
  9. Allocating resources
  10. Measuring progress
- *Further questions to ask:*
  - What are our main strengths and weaknesses?
  - What can we reasonably expect from what we are currently doing?
  - How should we alter what we are doing so that we can do some things better?
  - How are we performing?
  - What do we harvest and what do we continue to expand?

The finance area should particularly assist in steps four, six, seven, and nine.

---

[11]Darryl J. Ellis and Peter P. Pekar, Jr., *Planning for Nonplanners: Planning Basics for Managers* (New York: Amacom, 1980), 33.

The strategic management process is a process, not just a one-shot deal. Yesterday's ideal plan will sometimes become substandard due to some changed or just-discovered internal factor (a strength or weakness, possibly a technological innovation helping you in a key service area) or by a difference in the external environment (such as a new service provider moving into a key service arena). A good manager not only plans, but she or he continually re-assesses those plans while maintaining openness to opportunities. These opportunities are then evaluated against her or his honest appraisal of the company's strengths and weaknesses, resulting in a well-founded decision on whether or not to pursue the opportunity, and if so, in what time span. Don't even begin this procedure until you have asked yourself the basic question, "What is our organization?"

This concludes the discussion of strategic management and strategic planning. Following is an examination of the areas in which you can contribute to the strategic management process, and the long-range planning that must be done in the finance office regardless of what is or isn't being done by top management and the Board.

(a) The Long-Range Financial Planning Process

Financial projections covering the next five years are developed in an exercise called *long-range financial planning*. These projections should be done periodically as part of the organization's strategic planning process. The main financial planning document should be based on all present programs, as well as those future programs already approved. Later planning scenarios can be developed in order to bring possible new programs or ventures into the picture. The purposes of the long-range financial plan are:

- To tie financial resource requirements to the strategic plan
- To identify any future period with fund surpluses, or much more commonly, fund shortfalls
- To determine approximate funding needs for the shortfall periods, which is the essential information the executive needs for planning capital campaigns, other special fund-raising appeals, and endowment building
- To identify the seasonal and cyclical aspects of the organization's cash flows
- To bring together in one place all the interacting sources and uses of funds experienced by the nonprofit organization: operating, investing, and financing

We cannot emphasize the importance of doing a long-range financial plan too strongly. Not only will it help a strong organization to become stronger, but it may spell the difference between survival and bankruptcy for your organization. Frequently, non-profit organizations do a good job of selecting programs, but they often fail to plan for the financial requirements of implementing those programs, leading a number of nonprofit organizations—especially private colleges—to fail.[12] Averting a financial crisis from too-rapid or ill-advised expansion is well worth the expense and effort of long-range financial planning. An example to emulate here is Cedarville College (Cedarville, OH) which uses its strategic planning process to implement "managed growth." Further, where programs are vital to the organization's mission but the financial plan indicates significant shortfalls, the CEO is stimulated to search for other organizations to help share the load. This may take place through a merger, acquisition, joint venture, or strategic alliance.

The degree of sophistication and level of detail in nonprofit organizations' financial planning varies. Many small organizations, and quite a few larger ones, do no formal long-range financial planning—this tends to indicate an organization whose overall financial administration process is poorly managed. The Lilly study found that organizations that did not use "present and anticipated financial positions" to guide programmatic decisions tended to be those deficient in overall financial management.

Some of these organizations may even engage in strategic planning, but are "in the dark" about the funding feasibility of these plans and whether they need to begin arranging financing now or can self-finance the program. Capital campaigns cannot be initiated and executed quickly. Other organizations have sophisticated, computerized financial models. Mostly, these are larger organizations which can afford to devote staff and computer resources to the task, or hire an outside consultant to develop the model. Increasingly, the "Big Four" accounting firms are offering strategic planning services to educational and health care organizations and to a lesser degree charities and other nonprofits.

(b) Financial Planning Basics

Here's a simple approach that can be used to get started in financial planning. It is based on the following three vital inputs:

1. The most recent three years of financial statements.
2. The capital budgets for the next five years, insofar as they are known.
3. Management and board financial policies regarding investments, debt, and minimum necessary liquidity.

[12]Regina E. Herzlinger, "Managing the Finances of Nonprofit Organizations," *California Management Review* 21, no. 3 (spring 1979): 60–69.

Armed with these inputs, the financial analyst can obtain and develop operating forecasts that will enable the formulation of simple long-range financial plans. While the next year may be somewhat detailed (depending on whether the operating budget has been developed yet), years 2–5 will show very little detail—possibly only total revenue and total expense of operations. The following example illustrates the long-range financial plan and the fact that the planning process, when used properly, takes at least two passes or iterations. The first pass takes the strategic plan and pre-existing funding strategies as "givens," and determines each future year's funding surplus or shortfall. The feedback from this exercise provides the organization's managers and board with needed input for possible revisions of the strategic plan and/or the funding strategy—which is the second pass.

To the extent surpluses appear in forward years, the management team can choose whether to

- Develop program initiatives (expand present programs or add new ones)
- Reduce debt
- Increase investment in existing staff or technology
- Build liquidity (if appropriate, based on financial policies)

Where shortfalls appear, organizations can choose whether to

- Have large cash reserves, draw these down
- Reduce discretionary expenses
- Redirect funds from noncore to core (essential to mission) programs
- Sell investment securities from portfolio
- Initiate capital campaign (if capital spending is the reason for the shortfall)
- Increase interest revenue through the use of appropriate investment vehicles and/or building of endowment
- Increase rental and/or unrelated business income revenue
- Increase investment in fund-raising for operations—annual campaign

If there are perpetual problems with shortfalls, initiate or increase investment in planned giving fund-raising.

At a minimum, do a projection of the "statement of cash flows." To keep things even simpler, enter the last 5 or 6 years of "statement of activity" data into a computer spreadsheet. Then, let the spreadsheet program do a straight-line projection of total revenue (income) and expenses. Exhibit 4.4 shows the 1981–1986

Exhibit 4.4. Financial Projection Providing Early Warning of Financial Deterioration

Statements of Activity—Gospel Missionary Union—1981–1986 Expendable Funds	1981	1982	1983	1984	1985	1986	Projected 1987	Projected 1988	Projected 1989	Projected 1990	Projected 1991
Income:											
Contributions	$ 5,121,652	$ 5,088,913	$ 5,721,854	$ 5,725,263	$ 5,852,144	$ 6,618,502	$ 6,665,790	$ 6,945,143	$ 7,224,496	$ 7,503,849	$ 7,783,202
Net gain on disposal of fixed assets	29,733	214,717	85,714	34,816	42,641	78,749					
Investment income	193,319	194,318	227,973	275,187	279,756	364,352					
Sales less cost of goods sold	—	—	—	128,116	142,991	149,530					
Total Income	$ 5,344,704	$ 5,497,948	$ 6,035,541	$ 6,163,382	$ 6,317,532	$ 7,211,133	$ 7,286,914	$ 7,627,449	$ 7,967,985	$ 8,308,520	$ 8,649,055
Expenses:											
Program activities:											
Church growth, evangelism	$ 1,618,616	$ 1,409,014	$ 1,526,571	$ 1,678,493	$ 1,873,124	$ 2,456,467					
Media, translation	548,411	469,713	575,519	697,491	875,791	785,726					
Theological, church leadership training	404,940	356,640	414,600	410,305	360,691	289,019					
Education	272,770	199,141	217,979	246,747	334,175	302,764					
Field administration	207,196	192,317	228,145	297,591	347,325	291,803					
Appointees	206,719	209,831	133,666	108,690	108,726	94,001					
Homeland ministries, furlough	671,830	760,737	726,156	615,136	743,129	866,198					
Relief	96,276	44,915	118,758	192,541	133,910	434,442					
Service to missionaries	71,872	59,049	137,027	135,292	182,386	137,644					
Medical	40,448	41,616	38,114	27,428	57,871	40,639					
Subtotal: program exps.	$ 4,139,078	$ 3,742,973	$ 4,116,535	$ 4,409,714	$ 5,017,128	$ 5,698,703	$ 5,712,065	$ 6,052,459	$ 6,392,852	$ 6,733,246	$7,073,639
Supporting activities:											
Management and general	$ 814,414	$ 996,659	$ 864,530	$ 1,046,032	$ 1,149,552	$ 1,210,873					
Fund raising	81,585	140,880	193,685	188,453	199,089	172,759					
Subtotal: support exps.	$ 895,999	$ 1,137,539	$ 1,058,215	$ 1,234,485	$ 1,348,641	$ 1,383,632	$ 1,501,193	$ 1,593,985	$ 1,686,778	$ 1,779,570	$ 1,872,363
Total expenses	5,035,077	4,880,512	5,174,750	5,644,199	6,365,769	7,082,335	7,213,258	7,646,444	8,079,630	8,512,816	8,946,002
Excess (deficiency) of income over expenses	309,627	617,436	860,791	519,183	–48,237	128,798	73,656	(18,995)	(111,645)	(204,296)	(296,947)
Unadj. fund balance—end of year*	$ 4,388,295	$ 5,005,731	$ 5,866,522	$ 6,385,705	$ 6,337,468	$ 6,466,266	$ 6,539,922	$ 6,520,927	$ 6,409,282	$ 6,204,985	$ 5,908,039

*Shows what fund balance in "Expendable Funds" would have been without adjustments or transfers.

Source: 1981–1986 financial reports used by permission of Gospel Missionary Union, Kansas City, MO. Projections done by author using financial spreadsheet Microsoft Excel™.

financials of Gospel Missionary Union (GMU) (Kansas City, MO). Notice the deteriorating trend; if the trend had continued, the organization would have ended up out of business. Knowing that this is what will occur if corrective action is not taken is well worth the time and effort of the entire planning exercise.

If as CFO of GMU, your organization's financial policies rule out the use of short-term debt, how might you close the gap in 1989–1991? Upon study, the financial manager may note three situational factors which generally act as constraints on his actions:

1. Cannot draw down liquidity without violating the minimum liquidity financial policy

2. Short-term debt forbidden

3. All programs are core

So, the financial manager might recommend the following possible courses of action to the Executive Director and the Board:

• Reduce discretionary expenses

• Increase the investment in fund-raising

• Increase rental and unrelated business income

• To extent possible, build endowment and/or shift investment portfolio to higher-yield investment vehicles (within risk parameters)

The planning exercise is valuable because when shortfalls are projected, it provides early warning of impending financial shortages, and when surpluses are expected, we may consider opportunities to expand or enhance the mission or build endowment.

4.6 FINANCIAL EVALUATION OF PROJECTS THAT ARISE FROM EXISTING PROGRAMS

The next key question to address is "Will the capital expenditure cover all of its costs *and* provide an adequate return on invested capital?" This is a pivotal question for capital expenditures which bring in revenues as well as for selecting between alternative expenditures which involve only costs. Even donative nonprofit organizations may have to consider both capital expenditure types. Any expenditures bringing in multi-year cash revenues should be evaluated in the way we show below. Not doing so could lead to a faulty decision for projects providing cash revenues (revenue would increase, but with an extremely low "return on invested capital" [ROIC]) or when selecting between two or more alternatives which have different up-front costs or different lifespans. Two simplified examples illustrate this point.

(a) Example 1: Youthsave, Inc.

Youthsave, Inc. occupies a building that is much larger than it will need in the foreseeable future. Youthsave has fixed up the part of the building it occupies, but the remaining parts of the building are in of state a disrepair and would need major remodeling in order to be usable. Youthsave has received repeated inquiries from other nonprofit organizations wishing to rent the space if renovated. Several have indicated that Youthsave's prime central business district location would lead them to pay $1,000 per month, payable in a lump sum at the end of each year, for an office area of 2,500 square feet. The prospects would also pay all utilities used by them. Youthsave has received three sealed-bid remodeling estimates from contractors having strong track records of high-quality work. The lowest bid is $95,000. Assuming it would be 15 years both for the lease and before the area would have to be remodeled again, and ignoring any leasehold improvement considerations, should Youthsave engage in the revenue enhancement project? (Assume the organization will not have to pay tax on the rental income.)

   (i) Approaching a Capital Expenditure Analysis. Because the remodeling is an up-front expense and the rent is paid on a monthly basis in the future, it is incorrect to merely multiply the revenue per month by the number of months and then subtract the up-front cost. A dollar received or paid today is worth *more* than a dollar received or paid one, two, or twelve years from now because it can be invested and earn interest. This fact is recognized as the *time value of money*. It implies the need for the following three steps:

1. Specify the project's anticipated cash flows—what cash outflows will result and when, what cash inflows will result and when?
2. Select a discount rate to reflect the time value of money—what rate of return could you have earned per year if you did not tie funds up in this capital project?
3. Apply the discount rate to future cash flows (those anticipated next year and in following years), then subtract any up-front costs to determine the ROIC and project acceptability.

Step 1:

Let's show a cash flow timeline. Cash outflows are shown as spikes below the horizontal axis, cash inflows are represented by spikes above the axis. We have an initial ("period 0") outflow of $95,000 followed by 12 end-of-year inflows of $12,000 (each end-of-year $12,000 is 12 × $1,000):

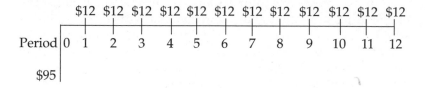

Step 2:

The organization can invest long-term funds at about 10 percent, and the mortgage rate is about 10 percent. So we will use an interest rate of 10 percent to determine the present value (present dollar equivalent) of each of the future cash flows.

Step 3:

We will compute two measures of project acceptability. The first, net present value (NPV), represents the surplus of revenue over expense, if any, after stating all cash flows in today's terms. We "discount" each future cash flow back to today's value by dividing it by (1 + interest rate) raised to a power representing how many years away the flow occurs. Then, we subtract the initial remodeling outlay, which does not need to be adjusted to present value because it occurs at present.

In Youthsave's case, the NPV turns out to be negative:

$$NPV = \underline{-\$21,265.19}$$

What should Youthsave do? The decision rules that tell us what to do after we have calculated NPV are as follows:

- If the NPV is positive, the project more than covers all costs, including financing costs (or foregone investing revenues).
- If the NPV is zero, the project just covers all costs.
- If negative, revenues do not cover all costs. Because the rental contract does not cover all costs in this case, it should be turned down.

Now compute a complementary measure that is easier to interpret. This measure, ROIC, indicates the financial return per year, after adjusting for the timing of project cash flows. Some organizations call it "time-adjusted rate of return." In our example, the ROIC is relatively low:

$$ROIC = \underline{\underline{4.49 \text{ percent}}}$$

This return is clearly less than the 10 percent annual rate Youthsave can earn if they leave that money invested. Additionally, the 4.49 percent return is less than the annual interest rate Youthsave would pay a bank to borrow money for a real estate loan to be able to purchase rental property.

Is it worth the effort to calculate NPV or ROIC? What if Youthsave ignored the time value of money? In that case, the analyst would have multiplied the annual inflow of $12,000 by 10 years to get a revenue of $120,000. Then, she subtracted the initial investment of $95,000 to get a $25,000 net return, and the organization might have made the investment. Properly evaluated, this is *not* a good investment—the ROIC is too low and the investment in remodeling is not cost beneficial.

This same approach of discounting cash flows can be taken when evaluating mergers, joint ventures, strategic alliances, or other strategic investment decisions.

(b) Example 2: Equivalent Annual Cost Illustrated

The Trinova Soup Kitchen is considering which of two commercial stoves to purchase. The first, the Everlast model, costing $41,500, would cost $300 per year to operate (including electricity, cleaning, and maintenance) and would last approximately eight years. The second, the Value Miser, costs only $25,000, would cost $450 per year to operate, and would last only five years. Which should Trinova buy, assuming each is equally reliable within its expected lifespan?

Compared to a business, the nonprofit organization encounters many more capital projects that generate no revenues. Some of these projects are "independent" projects that are undertaken in support of service delivery: buying a new van, adding capacity, buying office furniture, etc. The key here is in getting multiple sealed bids on construction projects or comparing among various vendors for a vehicle or equipment to find the one with the best combination of quality, price, payment terms, warranty, and service after the sale. In some purchasing situations, however, there are two clearly identifiable alternatives, and the analyst must select one from among these alternatives. Assuming quality, service after the sale, and other non-quantifiable factors are roughly the same, the analyst can find the project having the lowest "cost per year" by once again discounting cash flows. The technique is very similar to the discounting we just illustrated, but is a bit more involved. Called *equivalent annual cost* (EAC), it may be applied to alternative projects having different life spans and which will be repeated indefinitely (once a machine wears out, it is replaced with another identical machine).

First, let's see how someone might do a rough analysis in the above example which does not take the time value of money into account.

$$\text{Annual Cost of Everlast} = \frac{\$41,500 + (\$300 \times 8)}{8}$$

$$= \frac{\$43,900}{8} = \$5,487.50$$

$$\text{Annual Cost of Value Miser} = \frac{\$25,000 + (\$450 \times 5)}{5}$$

$$= \frac{\$27,500}{5} = \$5,450$$

Based on this approximation method, which ignores the fact that $1 of cost today is not the same as $1 of cost in later years, Trinova would select Value Miser because its cost per year is $5,450 (compared to Everlast's $5,487.50). Clearly, however, the advantage is almost insignificant—about $48 a year. Let's redo the analysis with a correction: (1) discount the annual operating costs to today's present dollar equivalent, then (2) spread the sum of all acquisition and operating costs over the life span to arrive at a correct cost per year. The appropriate discount rate is again 10 percent.

Step 1:

Calculate each alternative's NPV.

	Everlast		Value Miser	
Year	Cash Flow (CF)	Present Value of CF	Cash Flow (CF)	Present Value of CF
0	$(41,500)	$(41,500.00)	$(25,000)	$(25,000.00)
1	(300)	(272.73)	(450)	(409.09)
2	(300)	(247.93)	(450)	(371.90)
3	(300)	(225.39)	(450)	(338.09)
4	(300)	(204.90)	(450)	(307.36)
5	(300)	(186.28)	(450)	(279.41)
6	(300)	(169.34)	—	—
7	(300)	(153.95)	—	—
8	(300)	(139.95)	—	—
		$(43,100.48)		$(26,705.85)

Step 2:

Convert the NPV into an equivalent "cost per year." The formula used to make this conversion is beyond our scope.

Everlast	Value Miser
Cost per yr. = $8,078.93	Cost per yr. = $7,044.94

Notice the much larger advantage now demonstrated by Value Miser. Taking into account the time value of money—the fact that costs occur in different amounts at different times and the return on investment given up by the much larger (if less frequent) outlay for Everlast—the annual cost savings jump to about $1,000. Much of this comes from the opportunity to repeatedly invest the difference in the two stoves' initial outlays ($41,500 − 25,000 = $16,500) in securities yielding 10 percent, generating investment income (or avoiding interest expense) that would not be received if Trinova buys the Everlast model. The additional funds can be directed into new programs or into existing program expansion.

This completes our presentation on discounted cash flow analysis, a technique used daily in thousands of businesses. Once again you can see the difference that proficient financial management can make in your organization. Even when you are evaluating capital investments that must be made regardless of the financial attractiveness, draw up a cash flow table. This provides the numbers that you will need to do an overall cash budget for your organization, a topic we covered in Chapter 5.

(c) How to Manage the Total Capital Budget

The *capital budget* is the listing of all capital projects which the organization wishes to invest in, typically ranked from best to worst or from most necessary to least necessary. While a business can "in theory" always raise funds when it has a project which will provide an adequate return for shareholders, a nonprofit organization is often limited by the total dollar amount it can invest in capital projects in a given year. This situation, known as *capital rationing*, arises from the inability to raise funds from any kind of stock issue, the unwillingness or inability to borrow funds, and a limited ability to generate funds from revenue-providing activities or capital campaigns. The latter works superbly for periodic building or expansion programs (witness the University of Michigan $1 billion capital campaign which ended in 1996) but cannot be utilized for every year's capital project funding.

(d) The Capital Budget and Capital Rationing

There is $150,000 in funds available for capital projects in 1997. First, list the desired capital expenditures from best (or most necessary) to worst (least necessary). The dollar amount of each investment should be included along with a grand total. Projects which generate revenues should have the computed ROIC number listed next to them. To ensure that later year cash flows are included in the long-range financial plan, another column may be included to signify such flows. Exhibit 4.5 provides a sample listing for an organization.

The total capital budget in Exhibit 4.5, $178,000, is then compared to capital available for projects. The "capital available" amount is based first on cash reserves, which will be listed on the balance sheet as cash.[13] Second, there may well be some short-term marketable securities that are not included in the cash account. However, some of the total in cash and marketable securities is temporarily restricted (for a certain time period or until some action is taken by the organization) or permanently restricted (permanent endowment or revolving loan funds). The temporarily restricted portion may include funds restricted specifically for the purpose of fixed assets, so some or all of this should be included in capital available. Much care must be applied in arriving in the "capital available" figure because, in many organizations, three-fourths of monies raised are restricted as to purpose or time of availability. Let's say that the amount of capital available for Charity First is $150,000. Which project(s) should be funded?

(e) Rationing the Capital

The way to ration scarce capital, assuming the organization cannot free up or raise funds to meet the shortfall, is to consider which set of available projects best utilizes capital available. With the four

Exhibit 4.5.   An Organization's Overall Capital Budget

Charity First Capital Budget			
Project	Cost	ROIC	Future Year Cash Flows?
New central air conditioning unit	$120,000	N/A*	Y
Repair roof	25,000	N/A*	N
Renovate, rent office space	30,000	12 percent	Y
Buy another copier	3,000	N/A*	Y
	Total $178,000		

*N/A means not applicable; usually this means that the project generates no revenue or cost savings.

[13]Refer to discussion of liquidity analysis and how to calculate the appropriate liquid balance for your organization in Chapter 6 (Financial Reporting).

projects in our example (Exhibit 4.5), there are only 10 combinations available:

- 1 only
- 2 only
- 3 only
- 4 only
- 1 and 2
- 1 and 3
- 1 and 4
- 2 and 3
- 2 and 4
- 3 and 4

Taking each of these combinations, the analyst checks to see if the combination's total capital budget would exceed capital available. At the same time, the analyst must make sure donor or fund restrictions are adhered to. This process can be tedious and very time consuming when there are many projects and consequently multiple combinations to evaluate. If one or more of the top-ranked projects are "must haves," the analyst's job is considerably simpler because now only the amount of capital available *after* subtracting the cost(s) of the must-have project(s) need be allocated to remaining project combinations.[14]

Returning to our example, the first two projects might be must haves. Together they would use up $145,000 of the available $150,000. Only the copier purchase could be funded with the remaining $5,000.

One very important caution: there is an assumption in the foregoing analysis that each of the proposed projects has roughly equal program or mission benefits. Each contributes to the organization's mission to roughly the same degree. Looking back at our list of projects, each is a general office-related investment, and it is not necessary to pinpoint the benefits of the various projects. This is so because we are not looking at allocation between various programs, some of which contribute more to mission achievement than others. Guidance on how best to allocate resources (managerial, labor, and financial) to programs is provided next.

---

[14]A mathematical programming computerized worksheet makes the process much simpler. You may do this using the "solver" function built into Microsoft Excel™ or another computer spreadsheet program. If you are unfamiliar with this, you might contact a finance professor at a local college or university; this makes an ideal paid or unpaid internship project.

4.7 FINANCIAL EVALUATION OF PROGRAM ALTERNATIVES

This chapter began by pointing out that the mission, objectives, and strategies of the organization have been revisited, developed, or modified as part of the strategic planning process. The process by which these strategies are implemented by deciding which activities to engage in and how much in resources each activity will receive is called *programming.*

An illustration of this concept is a listing (in Exhibit 4.6) of some of one organization's 158 different human services *program elements,* subactivities within the three similar groups of activities called *programs.*

Four interrelated issues will be highlighted in the remainder of this chapter: (1) how to determine which programs to engage in, (2) how to determine how much in organization resources (if any) to devote to each program on an ongoing basis, (3) how to evaluate the possible addition of new activities (program elements), and (4) how to evaluate the ongoing investment of organizational resources in the various activities. To provide the necessary mindset for our discussion, we begin by analyzing the financial manager's role in strategic planning and programming.

Programming involves four steps:

1. Identification of program alternatives
2. Analysis of program alternatives
3. Actually making the programming decisions
4. Program support development

Exhibit 4.6. Programs and Program Elements for a Social Services Organization

Program Structure (Partial Listing)	
Program	Program Elements
Human services	Adoption agencies Day care centers Food banks Meals-on-wheels services Foster care for abused and neglected children Drug and alcohol recovery
Housing	Apartment complex development for low-income families and the elderly Specialized housing for disabled persons
Health care	Nursing care facilities (4 states)

Earlier in this chapter we introduced the external and internal environment—the financial manager would be the key player in defining the financial environment and he or she would provide input on board goals and policies and have his or her own individual goals as well. Functional strategies related to the finance function are the response of the financial manager, and he or she would want to provide input on the human resources management function, the management information systems (MIS) function, and the fund development function. A very common finance function strategy, and one which once completed tends to raise questions from the public, is to build cash reserves. More appropriately viewed as the overall liquid reserve (by including short-term borrowing capacity), its establishment enables the organization to better assure future mission accomplishment because it provides (1) a safety cushion to weather unexpected developments, or (2) immediate cash with which to respond to drops in donations or urgent program-related developments. Emergency relief organizations are not the only ones that need to be able to respond quickly to human needs.

Turning to programming, some major finance-related responsibilities in both the analysis of program alternatives and programming decisions fall on the financial planner. In analyzing program alternatives, the financial manager might assist in several activities. First, he or she must specify resource (including financial) requirements. Nonfinancial resources include equipment, facilities, materials, and supplies, and staff and professional time. Then, a financial plan should be developed, which provides a summary of all the financial consequences of the programming decisions: sources of funds, costs of resource usage, any surplus or deficits to be expected, and a need for special fund-raising campaigns or borrowing. Third, the financial manager must see that discounted cash flow analysis is conducted when the projects have revenues associated with them. Fourth, the financial manager determines financial feasibility for the organization by projecting cash flows in a long-range planning study. The latter might result in an estimate of the additional grants or donated funds that must be obtained for the organization to remain financially viable if it pursues a given program alternative.

At times the analysis of program alternatives involves consideration of new programs and/or larger resource commitments than usual. The financial manager provides the same kind of assistance as before, but additionally must help the Executive Director and Board see the big picture in financial terms. We need to learn about service portfolios and relative cost coverage to see specifically how the financial professional can contribute to the discussion.

(a) Service Portfolio

Chris Lovelock and Charles Weinberg have taken the concept of business product portfolios and modified them to make them useful for nonprofit strategy evaluation. Every service program can be placed in one of the four following categories:

1. Raise more funds or cut costs to support it
2. Maintain program or spin-off as a for-profit corporation
3. Phase out in total
4. Phase out parts

One factor is "profitability" or cost coverage. Revenues from general fund-raising campaigns are *not* included here, as they help offset nonspecific overhead (fixed) costs. If a cost can be linked to a specific service program, even if it is a fixed cost, it is included in the cost for purposes of this analysis. The other indicator is the extent to which the service offering contributes to the advancement of the organization's mission.

To help classify products or services as to their degree of mission advancement, it is helpful to distinguish between three distinct types. *Core products or services* are those that have been created to advance the organization's mission. *Supplementary products* are often added to either add to the appeal of the core products or to facilitate their use. A restaurant in a children's museum illustrates this. *Resource-attraction products* may be developed to foster the organization's ability to attract added funds, volunteers, and other donated resources. The latter are started and developed to contribute to the organization's financial solvency.

If an organization is operating with persistent deficits, it would try to support the mission at the same time that costs are covered to a greater degree. Quite often, the dual achievement of these objectives is not so easily accomplished.

(b) Annual Necessary Investment

If that program is also growing, but funding resources are not growing more quickly, the manager is faced with the situation in which that program will be draining an ever-increasing share of investable monies over time. The implication is clear: other programs being offered or considered will have to have funding cut over time. Very few nonprofit managers foresee this type of situation, and very few managers study past financials (laid out by program) to even see this in retrospect. This is just the type of contribution the financial manager can make to assist a Board and top-management team in diagnosing and strategically positioning an organization for a desired future in which top-priority programs and mission achievement are secure. Compare the organization's future position to its present position.

Once your management team and board have agreed on a set of programs, conduct a final check on the structure of selected programs before making financial and personnel decisions:[15]

- Are the operating plans well developed?
- Have nonfinancial resources been identified?
- Have financial constraints been considered?
- Are the desired results from the program well defined?
- Does the program have a detailed list of objectives?
- Will the program achieve the organizational goals?

It is at this point that a set of pro forma balance sheets and statement of financial activities should be drawn up for 1–5 years in the future. Possibly a set of four scenarios could be used for each year. Include the status quo (no change in present situation), as well as optimistic, most likely ("base case") and pessimistic scenarios. This will greatly assist in answering the third question ("Have financial constraints been considered?").

The financial manager may also assist in the development of program advocates within the funding sources. The idea here is to procure some stability over the funding source. By demonstrating how the source's funding is critical in a program's long-range financial viability, the organization may be able to gain a deeper, more permanent degree of commitment.

The final duty is budgeting. Financial managers have primary responsibility for the budget process. Our concern here is to ensure that programming decisions are translated into budget line items (the next chapter is dedicated entirely to budgeting). Ideally, as each year progresses, last year's strategic and long-range financial plan becomes the starting point not only for the new strategic and long-range financial plan, but also for the new year's operating and capital budget development. A warning signal emerges when the long-range financial plan is not used to help develop budgets. Possibly it is too inaccurate, or the organization is unaware of the tie between programming and budgeting. Obviously, those organizations updating long-range plans less than annually have less direct correspondence between plans and budgets. Plans are most likely to be implemented when they drive the resource allocation embodied in the annual operating and capital budgets. Finally, the process of planning is invaluable, forcing discussion and resolution of the tradeoffs and prioritization involved in spending decisions.

---

[15]Mary T. Ziebell and Don T. Decoster, *Management Control Systems in Nonprofit Organizations* (Ft. Worth, TX: Harcourt Brace Jovanovich, 1991), 164.

(c) Mergers and Acquisitions

Some, but not all, mergers and acquisitions in the nonprofit sector are financially motivated. In these, the financial manager's role is pivotal. Either he or she must do the financial analysis of the proposal, or locate a consultant or board member who can do it. He or she must translate the financial ramifications of the proposal in either case.

(d) Motives for Mergers and Acquisitions

There are numerous reasons why organizations merge with or acquire other organizations, but most fall into one or more of the following categories:

- Synergy—programmatic
- Synergy—financial
  - Revenue enhancing
  - Cost reducing
- Geographic or service-offering extension
- Competitive threat
- Survival

(i) *Programmatic Synergy.* Synergy is commonly defined as "two plus two equals five," or the whole is greater than the sum of the parts. The combined organizations are in the same or closely related industries. The key in *programmatic synergy* is in program accomplishment—quality and/or quantity. To illustrate, perhaps Alphanumerics has a widespread distribution network and Betaphonics has an advanced and very effective donor acquisition program. Together, the Alphabeta organization can expand the mission achievements beyond what either organization could do on its own.

(ii) *Financial Synergy.* When the efficiency of the combined organizations is such as to reduce costs or increase borrowing power, we have *financial synergy.* The enhanced financial strength that results is what propels the merger or acquisition. Quite often, programmatic synergy and financial synergy go hand in hand because effective service delivery and enhanced program achievements usually result in increased donations and the organization's borrowing power increases correspondingly. The factors that bring about financial synergy may be from revenue enhancement or from cost reduction. Exhibit 4.7 illustrates some of these factors.

Several of these items merit comment. Earned income may be increased not only due to the initiation of ventures related to the core mission of either pre-existing organization, but existing ven-

Exhibit 4.7.   Ways to Bring about Financial Synergy through Combinations

Financial Synergy	
Revenue-Enhancing Factors*	Cost-Reducing Factors
• New fund-raising methods (e.g., face-to-face meetings) • Shared expertise • Larger resource base to invest in fund-raising • Initiation of business ventures • Increasingly risky business ventures can be initiated (due to larger net asset base, less-than-perfectly correlated cash flows) • Initiation or expansion of planned giving • Sale of unneeded assets	• Economies of scale (reduce duplicate staff) • Economies of scope (eliminate overlapping service networks) • Shared expertise • Bring fund-raising in-house if one or both of the organizations formerly relied exclusively on outside fund-raising counsel

*Note: Use "revenue" and "income" interchangeably.

tures may be expanded. Additionally, the new organization may take on riskier program activities and ventures (which typically offer greater revenue–expense differentials) due to the facts that (1) the new organization has a larger net asset base, and (2) the overall cash flows of the merged organization are more stable.[16]

Over on the cost reduction side, we key in on economies of scale and economies of scope. *Economies of scale* refer to lowered costs per unit of service delivered as the service quantity increases. Every organization faces some costs that are fixed (e.g., CEO salary), and the greater the output the less the fixed cost per unit of output (e.g., cost per meal served in a rescue shelter).

Illustrating, let's say salaries are $200,000 at Alphanumerics and $350,000 at Betaphonics; they would not be $550,000 ($200,000 + $350,000) at the combined Alphabeta. Duplicate workers would be let go in some areas, (e.g., you don't need two fund-raising directors), and as Alphabeta grows, the increased volume of service would not necessitate a proportional increase in workers. Specialization and division of labor account for much of the increased efficiency. Similarly, the land and building requirements of the merged organization might be 50 percent or 60 percent of the sum of the separate organizations. One area of savings is in the headquarters facilities. Re-engineering opportunities have larger payoffs in bigger firms, generally. Summarizing, an organization experiences

[16]Statistically this is so because the cash flow streams of the two organizations are less than perfectly correlated. When one organization is experiencing a down year, the other may be neutral or up, or vice versa. In fact, the less closely associated the two organizations' cash flows, the better.

economies of scale whenever costs per unit fall as the scale of options is expanded.[17]

Economies of scope refer to sharing of costs across various programs. Computer resources can be shared by unrelated programs that two merging nonprofit organizations may offer. Fund-raising efforts can be shared. The key is that the costs of producing the products or delivering the services are less when joined in one organization rather than carried out by two separate organizations. Distribution and marketing costs are often given as prime examples of cost elements that can be shared, making the *overall* cost of delivering a given service lower. One example of this, elimination of duplicate service networks, is so important we have pulled it out as a separate item in Exhibit 4.7.

Commercial ventures are appealing not only for the revenues they bring in, but they often share costs with core service programs. Mergers and acquisitions often promise lower costs both because of scale economies and scope economies. However, businesses have tried to exploit these economies much longer than nonprofits. Some of the spectacular failures come from unrelated diversification. We can learn from the lessons learned from the relative success of the many corporate mergers and acquisitions.[18]

1. *Trying to gain stability through a merger with or acquisition of an organization whose cash flows are high when your cash flows are low is extremely difficult:* The goal here is to find an organization whose cash flows follow a different cycle due to economic risks that are quite different from the merger partner. The combined cash flow stream is more predictable, a safety factor that enhances financial viability for both entities when they join together. This is similar to the pooling-of-risks concept that underlies insurance. When one sector is hitting the skids, the story goes, the other should be doing famously well. Why has this concept been so difficult to apply? For one, it is most difficult to find organizations with cash flow streams exactly opposite to each other (see Exhibit 4.8).

   Instead, one may find an industry whose economic cycle turns a little sooner or later than the economy as a whole, or a "defensive" industry such as soft drinks which experiences less cyclicality of sales and cash flows. Graphically, the offsets are not as dramatic (as shown in Exhibit 4.9).

   On top of this, it takes considerable skill to put the right mix of business together to achieve a stable cash flow "portfolio"

---

[17]For more on economies of scale, see Sharon M. Oster, *Strategic Management of Nonprofit Organizations* (New York: Oxford University Press, 1995), 32–34.

[18]*See* Malcolm S. Salter and Wolf A. Weinhold, *Diversification Through Acquisition: Strategies for Creating Economic Value* (New York: The Free Press, 1979), 38–42.

Exhibit 4.8. Perfect Offset for Two Organizations' Cash Flows over Time

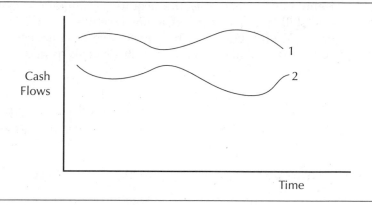

(set of companies or organizations). The ideal merger or acquisition target organization may not be the right size for a match-up with yours, and even if it were, its growth rate may be quite different than your organization's, meaning the combined mix is out of balance in a year or two.

2. *Related mergers or acquisitions may not be safer.* Although it would seem to be less risky to "stick with the knitting," dealing with business and markets you already know, reaping the benefits may be elusive. The quality of the individual entities, how much integration it takes to gain the benefits of synergy (can the cultures be merged, for example), how real the perceived "relatedness" is, and whether the combination provides improved competitive advantage are all key success factors.

Exhibit 4.9. Partial Offset for Two Organizations' Cash Flows over Time

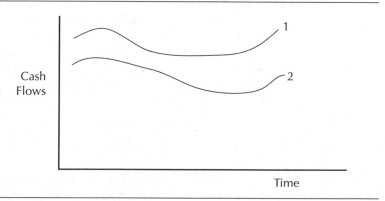

3. *A strong management team at the acquired company.* This may seem important, but in fact it is the acquiring company's management skill and resources that are essential for realizing merger–acquisition benefits. They must have the financial talent and managers that can conduct strategic analysis of diverse industries and markets.

On the positive side, two basic strategies have been found to work for businesses, and these guidelines should prove helpful to nonprofit organizations as well. Under each we see specific road maps.

Strategy 1: Increase the cash flow stream through synergy.

A. Special skills and industrial knowledge of one partner can be used to solve competitive problems and opportunities the other partner is facing.

B. In the long run, cost per unit can be reduced by investing in markets closely related to current markets.

1. Scale effects

2. Rationalizing of product and other important management tasks

3. New opportunities for technical innovation

C. Expanding business in an area of competence can lead to the development of a "critical mass" of resources necessary to do well in a market as a threshold size is reached (e.g., banks must be money centers or superregional banks in order to have the size necessary to offer a broad range of cash management services).

D. Transfer cash from cash-rich to cash-poor units to avert outside borrowing.

1. Some businesses are always cash-rich (Proctor & Gamble); in a nonprofit organization, some programs always need to be subsidized, these may be core programs.

2. Each area may have different cyclical or seasonal patterns of cash surpluses or cash shortages.

E. If a company is diversified, direct cash-rich areas to provide funding to areas that are currently cash-poor, but soon to be cash generators—increasing long-run profitability (cost coverage) for the organization as a whole.

1. Low-growth area sends funds to high-growth area.

2. Internal market intelligence of diversified company can be valuable as information is shared.

F. Through pooling of risks, the diversified company can have lower borrowing costs and do more borrowing, if it so desires.

1. It gains a larger debt capacity.
2. It requires a smaller liquid reserve (not including debt).

Strategy 2: Decrease risk.

A. Reduce variability of the cash flow stream so that it is less than just the average of the variability of the two separate entities. This refers to the offsetting cash flow patterns we graphed in Exhibits 4.8 and 4.9. Down cycles in Organization 1 are partly offset by the up cycles in Organization 2, so that Organization 1 + 2 is on more solid footing than either organization was independently. This feeds back to lower borrowing costs in Strategy 1.F.

What is the bottom line in many business combination failures? Failure comes because companies (1) merge with or acquire what is readily available, not what "meets sound strategic and economic criteria"; (2) pay too high a price for the acquisition; or (3) do not necessarily have the resources and management commitment to exploit the potential advantages.

(e) Partnerships, Joint Ventures, and Strategic Alliances

In 1992, the Partnership for the Homeless brought together New York City religious, governmental, business, and philanthropic leaders in an attempt to fight the growing problem of homelessness. This informal partnership, really a strategic alliance, mobilized 11,000 volunteers who now feed and shelter thousands of people each year and provide permanent housing and employment direction to some clients. More than 400 churches and synagogues joined in this effort.[19] Cross-organizational strategic alliances, partnerships, and joint ventures provide a less costly or significant change than mergers or acquisitions, while enabling some of the same resource-pooling benefits. We begin our discussion with partnerships and joint ventures.

(i) Partnerships and Joint Ventures. A formal *partnership* is defined as an association of two or more entities or persons to carry on a business for profit as co-owners.[20] Because it is looked upon by the IRS as a pass-through entity, a partnership is not taxed. Instead, the partners are liable for income tax.[21] A joint venture does not involve an ongoing relationship among the two parties, but is a

---

[19] "Churches need less parochialism," Letter to the Editor, *The Chronicle of Philanthropy*, (May 30, 1996), 42.

[20] Uniform Partnership Act, Section 6(1); Black's Law Dictionary 1009 (5th Edition, 1979). For more on this topic, *see* Michael I. Sanders, *Partnership and Joint Ventures Involving Tax-Exempt Organizations* (New York: John Wiley & Sons, 1994), on which this section is mainly based.

[21] If income is earned on an unrelated business activity, each member is taxed based on his or her distributive share of income, gain or loss, expenses, or credit.

one-time setup of at least two persons or entities in a business undertaking. However, a joint venture is treated as a partnership when it comes to federal income taxation.

The motives for these combinations are usually to expand and/or diversify program activities. Often, the nonprofit does not have the financial resources. By setting itself up as the sole general partner in a limited partnership, it can tap the limited partners (e.g., cash-rich pension funds or profit-sharing plans) for needed capital. Most joint ventures have involved health care or university organizations. These organizations mostly cite the need to raise capital as the motive for engaging in joint ventures. The primary caution to be noted is that the nonprofit as general partner may jeopardize its Section 501(c)(3) exempt status if the joint venture conducts an activity unrelated to its charitable purpose. The joint venture should be structured to allow the nonprofit to further exclusively its charitable purposes, protect its exempt assets, and not allow for private individuals' benefit and inurement. Instead of being part of a joint venture itself, the nonprofit may form a subsidiary or affiliate to serve as general partner. Another alternative is for the nonprofit to serve as a limited partner in the joint venture when the partnership does not further the organization's exempt purpose.

Another possible setup, having partnerships with other exempt organizations, must further the exempt purpose of *each* organization in order for each organization to be exempted from paying tax on its share of the income earned. Otherwise, the organization must pay UBI tax based on its share of income and expenses.

Why should your organization be interested in partnerships and joint ventures? First, some nonincome-producing informal partnerships (such as the NYC Partnership for the Homeless) can be established that help your organization better achieve its mission without added financial or manpower drains. Second, consider the reasons health care organizations give for engaging in joint ventures.[22]

- Need to raise capital
- Grant service providers (physicians) a stake in a new enterprise or service, thereby increasing physician loyalty and patient referrals
- Bring a new service or facility to a needy area
- New enterprise risk sharing
- Pool various areas of medical competency
- Attract new patients

---

[22]Reasons offered to the IRS when seeking IRS approval for joint venture arrangements; see footnote 21, p. 5.

- Induce physicians not to refer patients elsewhere
- Prevent physicians from establishing a competing health care operation

Some of these motivations will pertain to any nonprofit arena, particularly the need to raise capital, the desire to bring a new service or facility to a needy area, risk sharing on a new enterprise, and competency pooling. The finance office can make a special contribution on the need to raise capital, and in fact may have originally surfaced the need for a joint venture by documenting a funding shortfall in the long-range financial plan. At a minimum, the financial manager can assist in determining the amount of capital that should be raised. Also, regarding risk sharing, through the use of computerized scenarios, the finance staff can show the financial effects of uncertain future outcomes of a proposed new venture, helping top management to see the benefit of engaging in a joint rather than a sole venture. Recall that target liquidity is the primary financial objective of the nonprofit, and evidence that there is a high probability that a "go it alone" venture will financially cripple the organization provides strong impetus to investigate and properly structure a joint venture.

(f) Strategic Alliances

When two or more organizations agree to pool resources and skills in order to achieve common goals, as well as goals specific to each organization, we have a *strategic alliance*. These cooperative arrangements are often multi-year and may encompass from one functional area or activity (e.g., marketing) to all the functional areas. You have heard about the Ford–Mazda alliance, which is actually a joint venture. Strategic alliances encompass these equity joint ventures, but we wish to focus in this section on nonequity ventures such as a joint service development team or a cooperative advertising campaign. The latter are more flexible and can be revised, restructured, or ended more easily. Note the word *strategic*; if a vendor and customer are simply tying their purchasing and supply systems together, this is an operational partnership as opposed to a strategic alliance. The purpose of strategy is to advance mission achievement through selection of markets served, new service development, and similar activities.

(i) *Motives for Strategic Alliances.*   Adapting from the excellent review of business strategic alliances compiled by Varadarajan and Cunningham,[23] nonprofits may benefit because they

---

[23]We draw heavily on the Varadarajan and Cunningham analysis in our discussion of strategic alliances. Refer to P. Rajan Varadarajan and Margaret H. Cunningham, "Strategic Alliances: A Synthesis of Conceptual Foundations," *Journal of the Academy of Marketing Sciences* 23 (Fall 1995): 282–296.

1. Broaden service line/fill service offerings gaps
   - Fill gaps in present service offerings
   - Broaden present line of services
   - Differentiate or add value to the service
2. Enter new services domains/gain a foothold in emerging industries or industry segments
   - Diversify and take advantage of growth opportunities in new services domains (due to traditional market stagnation)
   - Gain foothold in areas where alternative, substitute technologies are developing by allying with organizations already exploiting those technologies
3. Enhance resource use efficiency, lowering costs by taking advantage of:
   - Scale, scope, and experience effects
   - Differential costs of labor, raw materials, or other inputs
4. Extend resources, particularly when a merger (and loss of corporate identity) is unacceptable but the organization cannot manage the internal development or acquisitions
   - Especially for smaller organizations that do not have the resources to invest in research and development (R&D), capital equipment, new products or services, and other activities necessary for meeting the needs of clients

We are most interested in same-industry, or intra-industry strategic alliances. Why would a nonprofit wish to form an alliance with another organization currently competing for resources in the same geographic market(s) or with another organization which constitutes a potential competitor? By pooling R&D, production, and/or marketing resources, the two (or more) organizations may be able to seize new service or market opportunities that neither organization could seize on its own. Many times, however, the perceived competitive threat may not be large because the services provided are geared toward different clienteles or the organizations are separated far enough geographically that their service areas do not (and will not) overlap. Most nonprofits are already members of a trade association (such as the International Union of Gospel Missions [IUGM]) and understand what the benefits are of banding together when there is no competition between the vast majority of the members.

We briefly illustrate the strategic alliance concept before dealing with the financial manager's role in evaluating and implementing an alliance. The Alliance of Ohio Community Arts Organizations (AOCAO) is a multi-year project begun by the state arts agency to bond the state's arts service organizations together.

AOCAO uses a central office in Columbus, and enables sharing of administrative expenses, professional development activities, and many times board members. The director, Susan Banks, indicates that organizations have gotten along well and the services in the respective organizations' fields were increasing as each organization focused on what it did best and took advantage of each other's expertise.[24] AOCAO also is involved in locating common funding. Further, it assists the local arts organizations in finding ways to centralize services, share programming ideas, schedule activities, and become networked with other arts organizations. So some of the activities are operational and others strategic.

(ii) Financial Aspects of Strategic Alliances. Joint fund-raising alliances, such as the new donor development program coordinated for faith-based rescue missions by the IUGM, illustrate that the function that a nonprofit alliance is built around may be fund development. Fund-raising is part of the treasury function in corporations, and is therefore legitimately characterized as a finance function strategic alliance.[25] The financial analyst should be ready to make the argument for cooperative fund-raising, showing the efficiencies (real cost savings) involved as well as the commonly noted potential for more funds to be raised.

Second, the finance office will have to be ready to project the needed financial resources which are the driving force between most strategic alliances (as well as for partnerships, joint ventures, and mergers). Management teams will be naturally reluctant to enter into such arrangements. Management might fear donor attrition, to the extent the alliance partner is either (1) a potential draw to this organization's donors, or (2) viewed negatively by this organization's donors, who will in turn react negatively when hearing of the alliance. Furthermore, management may not want to give up their operating autonomy. Varadarajan and Cunningham make the point that whenever an organization has financial resources to either acquire or internally develop the skills and other resources needed to exploit a market opportunity, they are quite unlikely to enter into a strategic alliance due to a loss of operational control.[26] The desired resources include assets, capabilities, organizational characteristics and processes, information, and expertise. So alliances are not necessarily cost related: business alliances have been predominant for achieving market or sales growth and for gaining access to new markets.

[24]Susan Banks, e-mail posted to talk-amphilrev listserv, December 6, 1995.
[25]See section on finance structure in Chapter 3 for discussion of greater role for the finance area in fund-raising planning, implementation, and evaluation.
[26]See footnote 23, p. 290.

Third, the risks of strategic alliance should be highlighted by the financial manager, in that she or he has ultimate responsibility for asset protection. Two major risks are the possible "stealing" of skills by the alliance partner and the possibility of becoming overly dependent on alliances. Both of these are lesser issues to nonprofit organizations than for businesses trying to protect and build manufacturing and R&D capabilities.

(iii) Financial Projections of Mergers, Acquisitions, or Joint Ventures. Financial spreadsheet software is ideally oriented for projecting the "before and after" financial positions of an organization. The new generation of spreadsheets (Microsoft EXCEL™ version 4.0 or later, LOTUS 1-2-3™ version 4.0 or later, COREL QUATTRO PRO™ version 5.0 or later) have built in scenario (or version) managers to assist the analyst in quickly generating optimistic, most likely, and pessimistic cases for a proposed merger, acquisition, or joint venture. As an example, let's look at the before and after situations for a private school considering a merger with another private school. After projecting combined enrollments and cost savings due to the larger size and the ability to share costs, the analyst ends up with the data shown in Exhibit 4.10.

Why the cost reductions from a merger? Salaries are fixed up to a point, meaning they do not change with small changes in enrollment. Administration costs (principal's salary and benefits) are fixed, and only one principal is needed for the merged institution. Registration and/or certification fees are fixed. Labor, energy, and maintenance expenses are not totally fixed, but "step-function" or "semi-variable" costs. The combined school can order maintenance and office supplies in larger quantities, gaining quantity discounts. Other administrative costs—office related, financing, and purchasing—also decline on a per-student basis as enrollment increases due to the merger. As the number of students increases, these fixed costs, when figured on a per-student basis, decline.

The proposed merger is a winner, financially, from the vantage of the merger partner doing this financial analysis. Using scenario analysis (Exhibit 4.11), even the "worst case" scenario is (1) better than the present situation, and (2) a generator of a fiscal surplus, which can be used to replace aging plant[27] and/or build endowment reserves.

(g) Implementing the Strategic Plan

Many nonprofit organizations plan, but very few excel when it comes to the implementation of those plans. Many times, politics or Board–CEO dynamics, which may be disguised as "organizational

---

[27]Note that depreciation is not included in the expenses listed.

Exhibit 4.10.   Merger Analysis Worksheet

Item	Present Statement of Activity ($)	Proposed Merger Statement of Activity ($)
Revenues:		
Tuition	300,000[a]	920,000[f,g]
Fund-raisers	25,000	65,000
Meal revenue	15,188[b]	32,400[h]
Other	3,200	5,000
Total revenue:	343,388	1,022,400
Expenses:		
Salaries and wages	225,000[c]	325,000[i]
Employee benefits	48,000	7,200
Insurance	30,000	32,000
Materials	35,000	45,000
Rent	20,000[d]	20,000
Utilities	14,400	16,400
Interest	6,000[e]	6,000
Other	3,250	5000
Total expense:	381,650	456,600
Surplus/(Deficit):	(38,263)	565,800

[a]Based on 150 students × $2,000 tuition
[b]Based on $1.25 × 60 students eating on average × 5 days per week × 9 months × 4.5 weeks per month
[c]Based on faculty/administration of eight
[d]The main school building is rented
[e]Offices (with a multipurpose room) constructed with borrowed money
[f]Enrollment projection w/merger: 400
[g]Tuition projection w/merger: $2,300
[h]Meal revenue w/merger: $32,400
[i]Based on faculty/administration of twelve

realities," get in the way. Three vital ingredients increase the likelihood of working the plan:

1. Unqualified and vocal top management and board support
2. Communication
3. Teamwork

Exhibit 4.11.   Scenario Summary

Scenario Summary	Most Likely	Worst Case	Best Case
Changing cells			
Enrollment projection with merger	400	325	500
Tuition projection with merger	$2,300	$2,000	$2,400
Result cells			
Surplus or Deficit	$565,800	$289,725	$853,900

Both top management and the board must continue their overt support of the plan. Change is almost always resisted, so any plan that alters the status quo must be championed.

Communication of the plan and its related program initiatives is also essential. Most important, all volunteers, staff, donors, and regulatory authorities must remain confident that strategic initiatives are consonant with the mission and the organization's tax-exempt purpose. Second, service delivery and staff personnel must be aware of both continuing and new program directives. Gaining a sense of relative importance of the various program activities will enable a concentration of effort on the key areas.

Teamwork is fostered by top management and board support as well as careful and consistent communication. Additionally, teamwork can be bolstered by setting up teams. Quality circles and use of employee suggestions for continuous service delivery improvement are illustrative of what can be done to harness teamwork.

4.8 CONCLUSION

Strategic planning is a vital part of ensuring a prosperous and mission-achieving future for your organization. We have focused on the role of financial staff in the development, evaluation, and implementation of these plans. We have seen that nonprofit organizations are increasingly turning to partnering, strategic alliances, and mergers to leverage scarce resources. The power of PCs and financial spreadsheet software for forecasting and proposal evaluation has also been demonstrated. Informal partnerships, often labeled strategic alliances, abound. These may involve many organizations, such as the Jesus Film Project's involvement with 67 different mission organizations working in India. This underscores the importance of having all organizational personnel work together as team members to communicate and implement the strategic plan. Financial personnel will be the first line of defense to avert financial catastrophes when the organization attempts to move too quickly or necessary funds do not come in on a timely basis. Finally, financial strategies and policies can be developed or revised by the finance staff.

We conclude with a warning about the role of financial position in strategic planning from two students of marketing strategy:

> Nonprofits must resist as much as possible the tendency to make the financial situation the most important determinant of the organization's capabilities. Financial matters are an important element of the strategic plan, but they need to be bal-

anced with other elements. At times, this may mean narrowing the scope of operations. Fulfillment of the mission is of primary importance. If the organization is on a constant treadmill of financial crises, it can easily compromise the mission in the interests of survival. But survival is meaningless if the mission is forgotten. Nonprofits should not hesitate to use the mission to say no.[28]

[28]Katherine Gallagher and Charles B. Weinberg, "Coping with Success: New Challenges for Nonprofit Marketing," *Sloan Management Review* (Fall 1991): 33.

CHAPTER FIVE

Developing and Managing
a Financial Plan

5.1 Introduction   147
5.2 Overview of the Budgeting Process   147
5.3 Are Nonprofit Organizations Doing Their Budgeting
     Properly?   149
     (a) The Lilly Study   149
5.4 Developing and Improving Your Budgeting Process   150
     (a) Preparation for Budgeting (Operations)   150
          (i) The Function of the Budget Director   150
          (ii) Procedural Prerequisites   151
     (b) Step 1: Establish a Budget Policy   152
          (i) Purposes of a Budget   152
          (ii) Uses of the Budget   153
     (c) Budget Preparation Philosophy and Principles   154
          (i) Budget Revisions   157
          (ii) Interim Reports   158
     (d) Step 2: Gather Archival Data   158
     (e) Step 3: Assign or Begin Collection of Other Area Data
          Input or Projections   158
5.5 Setting the Budgetary Amounts   159
     (a) What Do I Need to Know about Forecasting?   159
          (i) Classification of Forecasting Techniques   160
     (b) Revenues   162
     (c) Expenses   162
     (d) Extended Example   163
          (i) Tabular Presentation of Actual Budget
               Development   164
     (e) Budget Approval   164
     (f) Cautions   170
          (i) Budget Ploys   171
          (ii) What Hinders an Effective Budget System?   171
          (iii) Is the Finalized Budget Consistent with Financial
               Targets and Policies?   171

5.6 Budget Technique Refinements   172
  (a) Nonfinancial Targets   172
  (b) Flexible Budgeting   172
  (c) Program Budgeting   175
  (d) Zero-Base Budgeting   175
5.7 Cash Budget   176
  (a) Uses of the Cash Budget   177
  (b) Steps in Cash Budgeting   178
  (c) Forecasting Your Cash Position   178
     (i) Determining Cash Receipts   180
     (ii) Determine Cash Disbursements   180
     (iii) Putting It All Together   180
5.8 Conclusion   181

5.1   INTRODUCTION

At the core of proficient financial management is the budget. A budget is a plan stated in dollar terms. The budgeting process is important because it allocates resources, in turn revealing the programmatic preferences of the parties involved in budgeting. After the budget is developed, a nonprofit organization should use periodic reports to compare budgeted revenues with actual revenues and budgeted expenses with actual expenses.

There are actually three types of budgets: operating budgets, cash budgets, and capital budgets. When we use the word "budget" without stating which type, we are referring to the operating budget. An *operating budget* shows planned revenues and expenses for a period of time, usually one year. Proficient managers manage not only revenues and expenses but also cash flows, so a cash budget is developed. A *cash budget* shows planned cash inflows, cash outflows, and the amount and duration of cash shortages or surpluses for a certain period of time, usually the next 12 months. Its main value is highlighting the periods of imbalance between cash coming in and cash going out, so that the manager can take early action to manage the cash position. As we saw in Chapter 4, a *capital budget* shows planned fixed asset outlays and other large-dollar, long-lived capital acquisitions such as mergers and acquisitions. This chapter will assist you with the key aspects of the operating and cash budgets.

5.2   OVERVIEW OF THE BUDGETING PROCESS

Before any budgeting takes place, your organization should have formulated its mission, objectives, and strategic plan. In Chapter 4, the basics of these processes were presented. Even if your organization does no formal planning, inertia alone engages your organization in a strategic path for specific programs and initiatives. These are translated into operating plans. Those plans, and donors' willingness to support them, give rise to revenues and expenses. The development of the cash budget is a little more complex. Exhibit 5.1 shows that in addition to operating plans and policies and plans arising from liability management (see Chapter 10), current asset management (see Chapters 9 and 11) and fixed asset management (see Chapter 4) are key inputs. These same policies and the just-prepared operating budget and cash budgets, along with the current-period balance sheet, provide the input for projecting the upcoming balance sheet. *There may be feedback to revised operating plans if the projected Statement of Financial Position (balance sheet) is unacceptable based on inadequate liquidity or overly high use of borrowed monies.* This often happens when your organization's capital budget outlays are partly self-financed (reducing cash) and partly financed (increasing

Exhibit 5.1. Budgeting Process

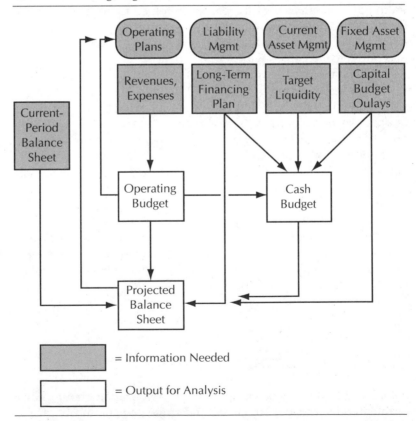

borrowing). In the remainder of this chapter, the context and actual development of the operating and cash budgets is outlined.

5.3 ARE NONPROFIT ORGANIZATIONS DOING THEIR BUDGETING PROPERLY?

There is much room for improvement in nonprofit budgeting. In a study of 17 large nonprofit arts, educational, and health care agencies, the authors concluded:

- Budgets were developed in a very basic, even simplistic, fashion
- Budgets were not used for control
- Very few agencies used newer budgeting techniques such as ZBB or program budgeting effectively

Briefly, the study established that budget development and use were deficient.[1]

(a) The Lilly Study

In Chapter 2, the performance of financial management in faith-based charities was outlined as part of the Lilly study. While 85 percent of responding organizations in the study develop and use an operating budget (showing revenues and expenses), the concern is that 15 percent do not. Budget revisions occur within the fiscal year by 60 percent of the budget-using organizations. This is good practice when uncontrollable external events make previously budgeted amounts useless as standards, but may indicate that budgeting control is largely absent in some organizations. The use of supplemental financial data other than "budget versus actual" variances is seriously lacking. Only 53 percent of budget users monitor their current asset amount on a monthly basis (and merely 12 percent have a target for their current assets), and 41 percent evaluate financial ratios periodically. The fact that roughly 60 percent, or three of five, do not utilize the insights of ratios points to the significant opportunity for improved financial management in the nonprofit sector. There is no excuse for these deficiencies now that personal computers are widely available.

Nonprofit organizations were only rated fair in their cash forecasting. The most reliable indicator of how an organization *rated overall (in all short-term financial management areas)* was whether the organization used a computer to monitor or forecast

---

[1] Anthony J. Gambino and Thomas J. Reardon, *Financial Planning and Evaluation for the Nonprofit Organization* (New York: National Association of Accountants, 1981), 21–35.

its cash position. Seventy-eight percent *did* use the computer for one or both of these purposes. We noted that using a computer facilitates cash forecasting, which is one of the ways to implement daily active cash management—a practice of most of the Fortune 500 corporations. Short-term investing and borrowing decisions are improved because of a better understanding of how much excess cash exists now and in the future. With longer maturities yielding higher interest rates, the organization is rewarded for knowing how long it can tie excess funds up. Furthermore, we noted that the organization's cash control is facilitated, because now it may tie its records via personal computer to its bank(s), regularly updating balances and being able to check yesterday's closing balances at the beginning of today's workday.

Only eight organizations developed daily cash forecasts, whereas 22 projected cash using weekly intervals and 94 developed monthly forecasts. At a minimum, your organization should attempt a weekly forecast, and if your organization is sizable, make a daily forecast your ultimate goal. The higher short-term interest rates go, the greater the rewards for your effort.

5.4 DEVELOPING AND IMPROVING YOUR BUDGETING PROCESS

This part of the chapter provides guidance on how to develop or improve the budgeting process. It starts with what is needed to prepare an organization for budgeting, then moves to actual budget development, and finally concludes with comments about budget refinements such as zero-base budgeting (ZBB) and program budgeting.

(a) Preparation for Budgeting (Operations)

The CFO should attend to the organizational and procedural prerequisites before launching into the actual budget development. The budget director's function shows us what must happen organizationally to ready for the budget process. The procedural prerequisites show us how the organization mobilizes specific information to ensure successful budget development.

(i) The Function of the Budget Director. The individual heading up the budgeting process, whatever his or her title, is generally the chief financial officer of the organization. It is the budget director's responsibility to ensure that a comprehensive oversight system be set up to include each of the following:

- Make sure everyone involved gets the information he or she needs. This includes any and all forecasts, organizational goals and policies, guidelines, performance data and standards, and any organization-unit plans that impinge on budget items.
- Set up and maintain the appropriate planning system. This includes channeling of appropriate information, plan formulation scheduling, and subunit as well as organization-wide checking of adherence to economic and financial guidelines and to organizational goals. Certainly, you would not want one division using an inflation rate of 2 percent for its forecasts, while another assumed a 5 percent rate.
- Set up and oversee use of models. These test for the effect of inside and outside forces on achievement of organizational goals. For example, what would happen if interest rates suddenly went up by 2 percent? Down by 2 percent? One multinational nonprofit had to scale back its headquarters operation by 20 percent in the early 1990s due to an unexpected *decline* in interest rates; it seems that interest revenue earned on cash reserves was funding a significant portion of those operations.
- Make sure performance data are collected. For each organizational responsibility center, data should show how plans are or are not being attained over time, and that analysis is made of variances, especially for large expense overruns or large revenue shortfalls.[2]

Ultimately, the budget director may assume responsibility for each of these four tasks. Indeed, in smaller organizations she may perform each task herself. The organization often suffers as the latter two tasks are often left undone due to time constraints. Furthermore, the department heads may view the budget negatively because it is imposed on them without adequate input on their part.

(ii) Procedural Prerequisites. Before "budget time" rolls around each year, there are three preparatory steps that you may need to take. The first, *establish budget policy*, need not be done annually, but if your organization has never thought these concepts through it is time to do that before setting another budget. The second, *gather archival data*, involves assembling necessary documents from the financial reporting system and fund development office. Finally, we *initiate data collection* to get the appropriate offices working on collecting data that are not normally part of the financial

---

[2]Budget Executives Institute, "Statement of Duties and Responsibilities of the Budget Director," reprinted in *Readings in Cost Accounting, Budgeting and Control*, ed. William E. Thomas, 5th Edition (Cincinnati, OH: South-Western Publishing Company, 1978), 82–83.

reporting process. Please study Exhibit 5.2 to set in your mind the sequence of these activities as a framework for our discussion.

(b) Step 1: Establish a Budget Policy

Every organization should have a budget policy that spells out the purposes of its operating budget, the uses for that budget, guidelines for budget development, revision policy, and the frequency and nature of budgetary reports.

(i) *Purposes of a Budget.* Reviewing the purposes of an operating budget will convince financial and nonfinancial personnel of the indispensability of budgets. Both revenue and expense budgets should be carefully developed and detailed. Some funders will even address budget preparation in their legal contracts. Budgets are also necessary administrative, financial, and program management tools for nonprofit managers. In most cases, there should be individual budgets for each program or separate activity, which fold into a single, consolidated budget for the organization as a whole.[3] In general, the main purposes for operating budgets are:

[3]Most of this section and the next are based on the insights of Gregg Capin, of Capin & Crouse, Inc., Greenwood, IN. (From seminar entitled "Financial Management for Nonprofit Leaders," sponsored by the Christian Management Association, Indianapolis, IN, May 12, 1992.)

Exhibit 5.2.   Steps Prior to Budget Development

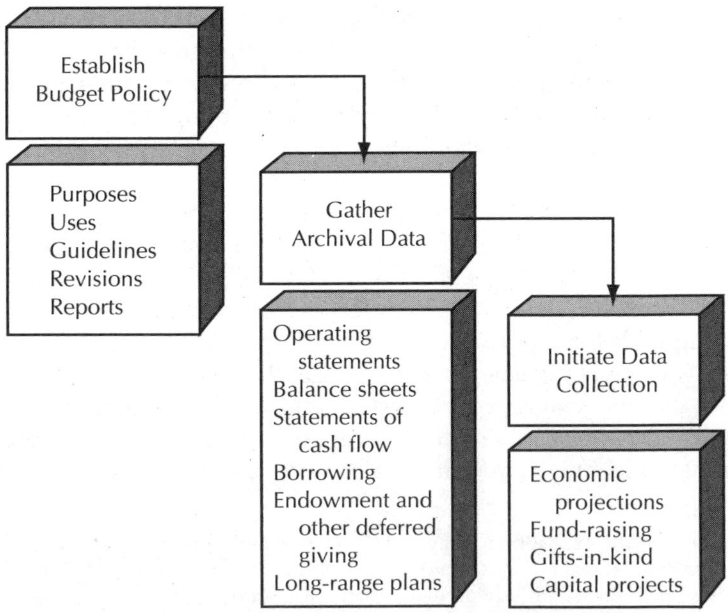

- Priority Control
  - Budget setting should follow mission and program establishment and should not be done simultaneously with those activities.
  - Budgets reveal priorities because they indicate resource allocations and reallocations.
- Fiscal Control
  - Limited funds means need for effective controls over revenue and expenses. Budgets serve this purpose best, in that they allow for regular comparison of budgeted to actual expenditures.
- Administrative Control
  - Nonprofit organizations established to serve public purposes that are often intangible or expensive to measure.
  - Detailed budgets provide administrators with monetary control where traditional for-profit controls (price-versus-cost profit margins) are neither possible or practical.
- Program Control
  - Outside funders may require separate budgets for each program they support.
  - Funding sources may limit spending flexibility by restricting expenditures to specified categories and line items, and they may request that written budget modifications be approved in advance.
- Audit Control
  - Outside funds often have specific expenditure restrictions and compliance requirements.
  - This is the case particularly with government funds, where budgets are utterly essential to ensure that the annual audit will find the nonprofit organization complied with funding-source guidelines.
- Survival
  - If the organization makes unallowable expenditures that must be repaid to the funding source, liquidity problems will ensue.
  - How will you know if expenses are going to be covered until it is too late, if you have no budgetary projection?

(ii) Uses of the Budget. Lack of a budget has several negative repercussions; the organization may face one or more of the following situations:

- *Overspending*—leading to the situation in which the organization is hit with unexpected deficits, as spending quickly outruns incoming revenues

- *Underspending*—resulting in the need to send unspent funds to funding sources

- *Mistimed spending*—the failure to meet required program or activity goals on time, possibly resulting from the fear that revenues are inadequate to cover expenses

- *Misappropriated spending*—spent funds outside allowable cost categories, or when audited it is discovered that questioned costs may have to be repaid to funding sources

(c) Budget Preparation Philosophy and Principles

Several decisions related to budget philosophy and principles are to be used in revising and reporting budget-related data. Budget philosophy involves what approach will be taken, what level of aggregation to use, and the "bottom-line" target to strive for.

The budget approach may be top–down or bottom–up, or a combination of both. The approach used will drive the assignment of budget development responsibilities and level of participation. We advocate the combination approach. When organizations impose budgets on departments, the approach is definitely *top–down*. When department heads submit their budgets, and these are added together to arrive at a consolidated budget, we have a purely *bottom–up* approach. A *combination approach* involves communication of economic and organizational assumptions to be made by all budget participants (to ensure consistency), but department heads have great latitude in establishing budgetary amounts. These are subject to review and mutually agreed adjustment. Participation and involvement of budget managers is essential, and the absence of their involvement leads to budgets that are weak and ineffective as control tools.

The budget's *format and level of aggregation* also must be determined. The minimum requirement here is to have a *consolidated budget* (organization-wide). This budget, sometimes called a *line item budget*, should list the major sources of revenues and the expenses by type. The expenses are listed by what are sometimes called "natural expense elements"—rent, utilities, salaries and wages, insurance, and so forth. Budgets done at this aggregated level of detail help prevent overspending or underspending, and provide the minimal planning, coordination, and control functions. In the revenue and expense budget illustration below, we will show how an organization develops a consolidated budget. As organizations grow and add support staff and accounting and computer systems, they begin to develop a *subunit budget* (for each program, department, or activity). Let's take a look at two logical subunit budgets that you may wish to develop: program budgets and functional budgets.

Program budgets spell out revenues and expenses for each of the organization's major programs. Having information in this format is tremendously helpful for two reasons: first, it makes program allocations and reallocations obvious, and second, it makes cost–benefit comparisons for individual programs much easier. We will return to program budgeting later in the chapter in the section on new budgeting approaches. If each program is operated by a different division or department within the organization, the divisional or departmental budgets accomplish the same thing as program budgets.

Functional budgets show revenues and expenses for each separate functional area. In a business, the major functional areas are marketing, finance, and production. In a nonprofit, these might be development, finance, and services. The services subunit can then be further broken down into program subunits, if desired. The main advantage is that each area can be held responsible for costs, revenues versus costs (net revenue), or net revenue versus investment. After-the-fact comparisons cannot only pinpoint efficiency or inefficiency in areas such as fund-raising, but also provide needed input for redeployment of resources for the following year. Although they are not considered major functional areas, support areas such as human resources and information systems can also be budgeted for separately in the functional budgeting system.

The level of net revenue the organization strives for is the budget's target. On a consolidated budget, should we budget a surplus, breakeven, or deficit? Peoria Rescue Ministries, our highest-rated homeless shelter in the Lilly study, strives for and achieves a budget surplus each year. This provides internal funding for program expansion and related capital projects. Recognize that if your organization includes an expense account for depreciation, that it could be using a balanced budget target, and the amount reported as depreciation expense (which is a noncash charge, merely a bookkeeping adjustment to match the using up of equipment with the revenues it helps generate) could be set aside each year in a special fund. When new capital equipment must be purchased, the monies saved up in the fund can then provide the financing. In some years, you may actually budget a deficit. An organization with long-term financial problems, but which has a significant liquid reserve built up, may continue its essential programs while it repositions itself over a period of several years to break even or even run a surplus.

Anthony and Young (Management Control in Nonprofit Organizations, 1984), in their budgeting presentation, provide some excellent guidance on the subject of how to set a budget target.

They argue that we should plan spending to match the available resources, don't overspend or underspend. Therefore, a balanced budget should be the rule, with some acceptable exceptions (it is assumed that the nonprofit is recognizing the depreciation of fixed assets). They offer five reasons why most organizations *should not* consistently plan a sizable budget *surplus:*

1. This signals that clients are probably not getting the service quality or quantity they might desire.

2. Donors might think they gave too much.

3. This signals a lack of achievement rather than good management—given that most nonprofits have much greater demand on services than they can possibly meet.

4. Charging for services, signals you're pricing too high, perhaps.

5. It may suggest the need for your organization to become a "for-profit" business.

What about consistently projecting a deficit then? On the surface, it appears that many nonprofits are in a perpetual financial squeeze, using their revenue shortfall as an effective fund-raising ploy. This is not advisable, with some years being exceptions. For one thing, you are reducing your endowment, or draining cash from your liquid reserve, which you must replenish (i.e., run a surplus or do extra fund-raising appeals) later. Some faith-based organizations operate under what Peter Drucker terms the "God will provide" mindset. Certainly, God does provide, but as a principle, God can just as easily provide the funds beforehand in response to faith as after/during a certain period. Second, it is interesting that some colleges have had to retrench and even close their doors because of a failure to recognize this. If an organization is impelled to initiate or expand programs that it does not have anticipated revenues to cover, it can build a preventative corrective into place: as the organization moves toward the end of its fiscal year, and it has not received sufficient funds to meet the shortfall, it needs to immediately (1) reduce spending on the new program(s), and (2) recognize that it has suffered from a misdirection. The practical reality for many organizations is that they have not fully exploited their fund-raising ability, either through underinvestment in fund-raising or unfocused fund-raising. This came out loud and clear in the Lilly study. Most organizations indicated that the main reason they do not do better in reaching their financial objective is "insufficient or ineffective fund-raising." As new opportunities arise that match potential donors' desires to help, additional funds can often be raised to cover the added program expenses. This is true, despite the "full mailbox" and "donor fatigue" syndromes.

In technical terms, think about your organization having a "fund-raising net revenue function"—though there are "diminishing returns" to additional expenditures for fund-raising, certainly the funds raised are almost always greater than the costs to raise them. The implication: your organization can often raise more money if particular opportunities present themselves; in particular, one-time "golden opportunities." Fund-raising experience shows that people give more freely to great opportunities than to great needs.

Anthony and Young do recognize the following exceptions to their recommendation that organizations propose a balanced budget:

- Discretionary revenue—basically, this refers to occasions when intensified fund-raising can raise more funds, and the key is to not rely too much on this, or for large amounts (unless we're really thinking about doing this to fund a one-time opportunity).
- "Hard money" versus "soft money"
  - Revenue from annual gifts or short-term grants for research are both considered soft in that onset of recession may cause severe declines.
  - One implication might be to budget surpluses during economic booms.
  - Another implication is to build up loyalty and close relationships with clients and/or donors.
- Short-run fluctuations—count on reserves to tide you through any unexpectedly lean years, in which a proposed deficit might be budgeted; this is why it is not somehow immoral or unethical to run a surplus in some years, as well.
- The promoter—this is the idea of budgeting more expense than revenue, knowing hotshots can make up the difference; probably not wise, as nothing goes up forever!
- Deliberate capital erosion: if overspend versus revenues, part of your permanent capital is being used up by operations; point is, do you want to be doing this? If so, fine (e.g., cure has been found, so this program can be dissolved).

We would add this: if an organization is really program-driven, it might see unfunded needs and foresee anticipated new service delivery several years ahead. It will then build up a "critical mass" of financial resources with which to launch the new service(s). This implies running surpluses for several years.

(i) Budget Revisions. Your organization should have a policy on what circumstances occasion a budget revision. Strike a balance here—don't make it so easy to get a revision approved that

you lose the expense control of a budget, but recognize that environmental changes make some budget plans unreasonable. The budget serves best as a control device when targets are difficult but achievable. We will address using the budget as a management and control tool in the next chapter.

(ii) Interim Reports. Again, you should prescribe what reports will be made to compare actual revenues and costs to budgeted amounts, and with what frequency. Financial reports are also covered in the next chapter.

To recap our discussion of the first step preparatory to budget development, establishing budget policy, we addressed (1) the purposes of its operating budget, (2) the uses for that budget, (3) guidelines for budget development, (4) the budget revision policy, and (5) the frequency and nature of budgetary reports. Not every organization thinks these issues through, but your budgeting process will be more valuable in supporting program delivery and run more smoothly if you have done the groundwork. We move into the data collection phase next.

(d) Step 2: Gather Archival Data

There are a number of data sources you will consult in your budget development. Here are some of the basic ones in an easy-to-use outline format:

- Strategic plan and long-range financial plan
- Operating statements: past budgets and statements of financial activity
  - Revenues
  - Expenses
- Statements of financial position (also called balance sheets)
- Statements of cash flows, if any have been completed
- Mortgage and other borrowing data
- Endowment and deferred giving data
- Previously done projections

(e) Step 3: Assign or Begin Collection of Other Area Data Input or Projections

The degree of delegation possible in getting necessary economic, labor, fund-raising, gifts-in-kind, and capital budget data will depend on the budget approach profiled earlier (top–down, bottom–up, or combination). Allow some lead time for this step in the process—some organizations start this process six months before the budget approval date.

- Economic projections[4]
  - Income and discretionary income, such as local information if your scope is localized (e.g., you operate single local symphony, homeless shelter, retirement center, or "meals on wheels"). Maybe the best you can do is extrapolate, so get recent historical buying power index data from a recent issue of *Sales & Marketing Management* (buying power indexes are published in a special issue once a year).
  - Interest rates, including short-term bank rates, mortgage rates, and charitable gift annuity rates (if applicable)
  - Inflation, such as economy-wide inflation rates and key input (e.g., commodity) price trends
  - Labor cost and productivity, including wages and salaries, nonprofit differentials, local differentials, and productivity
  - Charitable giving (gives check on fund-raising, covered below), including national data, regional or state data (if available), and trends
  - Exchange rates if operate internationally
- Fund-raising
  - Projected annual campaign receipts
  - Projected special appeal receipts
  - Projected capital campaign receipts
  - Projected bequests and other deferred gifts
- Gifts-in-kind
- Capital projects

Once the appropriate assignments for these vital inputs are made, it is important to follow up to ensure that the worksheets are finalized on a timely basis. Once the preparatory work lags, the whole budget process is held up. Budget preparation is stressful enough without having analysts working excessive overtime.

5.5   SETTING THE BUDGETARY AMOUNTS

(a)   What Do I Need to Know about Forecasting?

A budget is a plan, and any plan involves an implicit forecast. How much in donations and other revenues will we take in next year?

[4]Here are some Internet websites to help you gather the economic data: http://www.webcrawler.com/Finance/; http://www.usdata.com/usadata/; and http://204.84.772.5/business/economic.htm and http://www.firstunion.com/reports/.

How much should we project for expenses, given our operating plans? These questions motivate the planner to gain a basic understanding of forecasting techniques. We use Exhibit 5.3 to profile the basic forecasting methods. Space and time do not permit a thorough treatment of these techniques, but we present the basics.[5]

(i) Classification of Forecasting Techniques. Quantitative, or statistical, forecasting methods may be further divided into causal (or regression) methods and time series methods. A *causal method* is one in which the analyst has identified a cause factor for the item he is trying to forecast. In the case of *simple regression*, we have only one causal variable. For example, donations (forecast variable) may be linked to personal income (causal variable). Regression analysis may be used to "fit" an equation to make the relationship precise *and* usable for generating a forecast. In our example, we might find that, if we measure donations and (average household) disposable income in thousands of dollars:[6]

Exhibit 5.3. Forecasting Methods

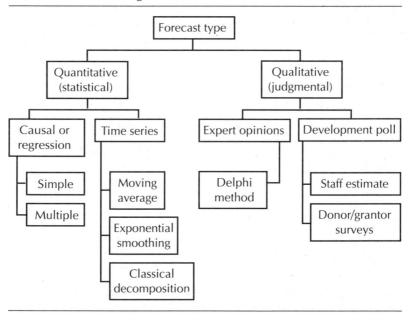

---

[5]Although not tailored to nonprofit applications, an excellent source for more help with forecasting methods is Jae K. Shim and Joel G. Siegel, *Handbook of Financial Analysis, Forecasting, & Modeling* (Englewood Cliffs, NJ: Prentice-Hall, Inc., 1988).
[6]Any financial spreadsheet software will do the trick to analyze the raw data numbers to arrive at an equation of "best fit." Microsoft Excel, Lotus 1-2-3, and Quattro Pro are all very adept, and one does not have to be a "techie type" to cajole the analysis out of the program.

Donations = \$500 + 1.2 (disposable income)

Let's say that disposable income is \$40,000. Donations would then be:

Donations = \$500 + 1.2(40) = \$548

Our forecast for donations would be \$548,000. Notice that because we are forecasting current donations based on current disposable income, the only way to generate a forecast for donations is to get a (hopefully accurate) forecast of disposable income.

A *multiple regression model* illustrates the case of multiple causal factor models. Here, instead of one causal variable, we have two or more. Donations might now be linked to number of individuals in the "empty nest" stage along with our original disposable income variable.

Time series models, in which a pattern from the past is extended into the future, are often more complex. Of the group, a *moving average* is the easiest to understand. A three-day moving average is just the arithmetic average of the most recent three actual values. If your donations for the past three months are \$45,000, \$50,000, and \$60,000, then the moving average would be:

$$\text{3-day moving average} = \left(\frac{\$45,000 + \$50,000 + \$60,000}{3}\right)$$

$$= \underline{\$51,666.67}$$

When the next month's actual value comes in, you update the moving average by adding the new value and dropping the oldest value. In our example, if the new value is \$65,000, the 3-day moving average becomes:

$$\text{3-day moving average} = \left(\frac{\$50,000 + \$60,000 + \$65,000}{3}\right)$$

$$= \underline{\$58,333.33}$$

Exponential smoothing and classical decomposition models are beyond our scope, but information on them may be found in any forecasting book.[7] As with moving average methods, these time series methods basically extrapolate the past into the future. There are three occasions in which to use times series models. One is when you cannot figure out what logical causes affect your forecast variable. Another is when whatever causes your forecast variable to change in value also steadily increases or decreases with the passage of time. The time variable (e.g., 1992 is year 1, 1993 is year

[7]They are also covered in Chapter 12 in a cash forecasting framework in Terry S. Maness and John T. Zietlow, *Short-Term Financial Management: Text and Cases* (Ft. Worth, TX: The Dryden Press, 1998).

2) tends to capture the ongoing effects of the undetected cause variable(s), so go ahead and use a time series model. Finally, time series models make sense when you have many small-dollar items to forecast, making the application of causal or qualitative modeling too time-consuming and expensive.

(b) Revenues

An accounting definition of revenues is "increases in its assets or settlement of its liabilities derived from the activities that constitute the organization's ongoing major or central operations. . . . [Revenues] could result from contributions of cash, other assets, and services from other entities, as well as exchange transactions in which organization provides goods or services to members, clients, students, customers, and other beneficiaries for a fee."[8] Be careful, though, when laying out the revenues for the operating budget. *Excluded* from the Statement of Financial Activity are increases in the entity's net assets that result from "peripheral or incidental transactions." These are considered "gains," not revenues. However, include both revenues and anticipated gains or losses in when estimating budgetary sources of funds to cover expenses. We will reinforce the importance of this in our later section on cash budgeting.

Many organizations budget for revenues and other inflows an amount some percentage above last year's, if that's been the pattern historically. This policy is dangerous in recession or when things change, though. Besides, as we have shown in the forecasting section above, you may gain accuracy with the aid of computer-based statistical forecasting models. This is one of those "ideal for college intern" projects, as most college and university business schools offer business statistics courses to provide basic training to their students in the art and science of forecasting.

(c) Expenses

Technically, "Expenses are outflows or other using up of assets or incurrences of liabilities (or a combination of both) from delivering or producing goods, rendering services, or carrying out other activities that constitute the entity's ongoing major or central operations." (from paragraph 80 of FASB Concepts Statement No. 6, *Elements of Financial Statements*). When arriving at budget amounts: look at inflationary increases, those changes in the environment that you can foresee, program changes you anticipate, additional resources required, and labor cost increases. Remember that labor-related expenses are usually your big-ticket item, and should be estimated carefully.

---

[8]AICPA Audit and Accounting Guide for Not-for-Profit Organizations.

Because the budget may have to be adjusted when significant environmental changes occur within the year, or when establishing flexible budgets (see below), we need to understand variable, semivariable, and fixed costs.

- *Variable costs:* Costs that vary with each unit of activity—labor in manufacturing process (if production increases 10 percent, total labor costs will increase 10 percent because labor cost per unit does not change). Of course, when the cost of the labor increases, total labor costs will rise proportionally.

- *Semivariable costs:* These costs increase as activity increases, but not in direct relationship to it; e.g., maintenance costs—machinery may have some base level of maintenance that must be performed regardless of how intensively it is used, and beyond that maintenance expense varies with machinery usage; the latter component may not be proportional—doubling the usage may only increase the maintenance expense by 1.5 times.

- *Fixed costs:* These costs remain the same regardless of the level of activity; e.g., rent, insurance, top management salaries, property tax for a facility, depreciation expense on previously purchased fixed assets; so, even if service delivery is doubled, the amount of this cost element will not change. It is important to note that fixed costs are fixed within the short term—say, one year. Over the long run, there are no fixed costs. In areas experiencing high inflation rates, even those costs considered to be fixed costs may spiral upward quickly (as in the case of rent or salaries).

What is the relevance of these cost types to expense budgeting? We have already noted that a budget is a plan. When laying out the planned expenses, our method is simple:

- First, state expected level of activity (number of units of items produced or delivered)
- Then, estimate how much costs will be based on this activity level—so that budgeted amount accurately reflects whether this item is a variable, semivariable, or fixed cost
- This whole process takes on added importance when doing *flexible budgeting*, because in that method of budgeting one must calculate the amount of each expense element for various levels of activity—not just the "most likely" or projected level of activity

(d) Extended Example

We use the actual budget development of Peoria Rescue Ministries (PRM) for 1996 to illustrate revenue and expense projections. PRM was one of the top performers identified in the Lilly study.

(i) Tabular Presentation of Actual Budget Development. Exhibit 5.4 shows the capital budget worksheet. Exhibit 5.5, the operating budget, shows the prior year (year-to-date actual plus prior December's actual amount), the current budget, and the projected budget. The "rationale" column gives background or the person responsible for developing the figure, as well as factors considered in developing the budgeted amounts. Also included is a template, Exhibit 5.4, to show how the capital budget is incorporated into the operational budgeting process. Information from both the operating budget and capital budget will be necessary for development of the cash budget. This topic will be discussed next.

Note from our example schedule several things that will help you develop an operating budget. First, some items are *estimated*, others are *calculated*. Estimations involve subjective judgment. Calculations involve (1) finding a historical relationship between one variable (some measure of activity) and the expense element, or (2) simply extrapolating the historic growth rate. Notice second the feedback from this year's year-to-date actual (which is annualized by adding in the month 12 prior year actual amount) to the new year's budget. That is, we don't simply make a mindless adjustment based on a historical growth pattern, but adjust up or down the calculated amount where appropriate. Third, PRM budgets for a surplus. Notice they do not show depreciation expense, so some of this is for plant and equipment replacement. Other portions are for (1) intra-year cash receipts versus cash disbursements imbalance, (2) to offset any negative developments on either the revenue (unfavorable variance being less-than-budgeted amounts) or expense fronts (unfavorable variance begin greater-than-budgeted amounts), and (3) to fund anticipated growth. PRM is growing, in total revenues, at double-digit percentage rates from year to year. PRM also verifies one of our main points in this chapter: the main uses for operating budgets are to anticipate possible problems and then benchmark actual performance.

(e) Budget Approval

Once a budget is agreed upon by all parties, assuming some participation has been allowed, a commitment is fostered. The budget agreement itself signals bilateral commitment. The PRM budget approval process is indicative of good practice. After the initial preliminary budget amounts are determined, a budget meeting is set with the board's Finance Committee. This meeting includes an intensive line-by-line ministry analysis—with input to modify or change programs and budget amounts if warranted. At that meeting, the executive director as well as the business manager are present, and a financial spreadsheet is "live" on a computer screen to

Exhibit 5.4. Sample Budget Worksheet—Peoria Rescue Ministries

Executive Director
Jerry Trecek

Peoria Rescue Ministries

Mailing Address: Post Office Box 822, Peoria, Illinois 61652   /   FAX 309-676-4334   /   Phone 309-676-6416

CAPITAL BUDGET 19XX

MINISTRY MONTH	PURPOSE FOR ITEM	PRIORITY*	AMOUNT

```
*PRIORITY  1= MUST HAVE TO CONTINUE MINISTRY

           2= NOT ESSENTIAL IN THIS YEAR, BUT WILL NEED NEXT YEAR

           3= MINISTRY EXPANSION
```

Rescue Mission: 601 S.W. Adams   /   Peoria, Illinois 61602   /   (309) 676-6416
Victory Acres: 9017 McCullough Rd.   /   Peoria, Illinois 61607   /   (309) 697-1277
Women's Pregnancy Center: 4630 N. Sterling   /   Peoria, Illinois 61615   /   (309) 688-0202
Family Focus U.S.A.: 1125 N. North Street   /   Peoria, Illinois 61606   /   (309) 676-7070

Source: Reprinted, by permission, from David L. McFee for Peoria Rescue Ministries.

immediately adjust the preliminary figures and arrive at a new "bottom line" for the consolidated budget. In this way, the Finance Committee members can conduct "what if" scenarios and see readily how a change to the budget affects the overall budget. At the conclusion of this meeting, each person is given a copy of the proposed budget for further review preparatory to its consideration by the overall Board. Copies are mailed to all Board members who are not on the Finance Committee. The overall Board receives the proposed budget at its December meeting, which is usually at least

Exhibit 5.5. Peoria Rescue Ministries 1996 Budget—Total Ministries Budget 1996

Description	Dec94 Plus Ytd/Nov/95	Rationale	Budget95	Budget96
Income				
Individual Contributions	471099	Development & General Director Plans Based upon Previous Year	500000	480000
Church Contributions	110898	Same as Above	85000	115000
Business Organizations	57237	Dev & Gen Director Plans Based upon Trend and Business Contacts	65000	60000
Restricted Gifts	28230	Spec Projects Planned for Coming Year. Dev Director Input	75000	80000
Gifts in Kind	16624	Past History and Planned or Known Gifts Coming	25000	15000
Misc.	5184	Gifts Too Small to Identify of Unknownd Nature. Past History Guidelines	7000	7000
Education Contribution	450	Based upon Past History and Planned Appeals. Gen Director and Dev Director	10000	500
Internation. Aid Contrib.	11954	Only Budget Known Entities in Next Year and Past Trends	0	15000
Vending	3042	Based upon Our Vending Machines, New Additions, and Projected Prices	3000	3000
Speaking	11064	Gen Director Input Based upon Previous Years and New Contacts for 1996	8000	10000
Evening Offering	5017	Based Entirely on Past History with Alterations for Additional/Fewer Services	5000	5000
Life Ins. Prem	4135	Gen Director Input Based upon Board History and New Projected Policies	4000	4500
Interest	4256	Bank Interest Based upon Projected Rates and Our Cash Flow	3000	4000
Sale of Goods	10889	Dev Director Input and Input from Special Items for Sale	100000	10000
Pallet Sales	43078	Entirely on New Projections—New Contracts for Pallets—History Not Appl	0	50000
Livestock Sales	12546	Farm Director/Gen Director Input on Planned Livestock Sales	13000	5000
Shop Income	2574	Farm Director and Gen Director Plans for Shop Sales	0	2500
Memorials	16834	Past History Guidelines	20000	25000
Special Events	49330	Dev Director. Gen Director 1996 Pland for Spec Events and Proj Income	75000	50000
Book Sales	6473	Dev Director Plans for 1996 Book Sales Based upon His Plan	1000	6000
Consulting Fees	2911	Use History and Known Contracts for 1996	1000	3000
Trusts	3806	Dev Director Known Trust Payouts and New Trusts to Start in 1996	5000	4000
Special Appeals	48523	In House Special Appeals Planned Using Last Year as a Guide for 1996	10000	50000

Item	Actual	Budget	Budget	Basis / Notes
Wills & Estates	35000		35000	Dev Director Known Est for 1996 Plus Est of New Estates Based upon History
Cilco Mailing	1976	5000	20000	Did Not Use in 1996
New Donor Acq.	36198	20000	35000	Planned by Gen & Dev Directors Using Previous Year Plus Special Plans for 1996
Individual Cont. S.A.	45235		45000	Out of House Special Appeals Planned by Development Dir
Sale Wood Prod.	47325		50000	Farm and Gen Director Plans for Wood Chip Promotion and Known Contracts
Sale Wood Chips	9139		20000	Same as Wood Products
Food	7299		7000	Past Trends and Planned Appeals
Meals Thk., Christ	2354		2500	Development Director Plans for Special Thks Christmas Appeal for Dinners
Emergency Assist.	1380		1000	Budgeted Based upon Past History
Total Income	1112060	1060000	1200000	
Expenses				
Salaries & Wages	407513	400000	450000	Gen Director Review Staffing Needs Factors Increases with Consult Directors
Fringe Benefits	61853	96000	68000	Gen Director Reviews Benefit Costs and Sets Budget for 1996
FICA Taxes	30899	32000	34000	Bus Manager Factors Payroll Taxes Based upon Payroll Amounts
Equip Pur. & Rep.	22384	25000	75000	Gen Director with Consultation of Equipment Needs with Ministry Directors
Office Supplies	24937	20000	25000	Gen Director/Bus Manager Review Needs Project 1996 Amount
Program Materials	9593	16000	10000	Ministry Directors Determine Program Consult with Gen Director for 1996 Amt
Travel & Transportation	19467	18000	20000	Gen Director/Bus Manager Budgets Based on Mileage Allow and Vehicle Expense
Professional Expense	13817	13000	15000	Gen Director Based upon Needs of Ministry with Consult of Ministry Directors

Exhibit 5.5.   Peoria Rescue Ministries 1996 Budget—Total Ministries Budget 1996 (*continued*)

Description	Dec94 Plus Ytd/Nov/95	Rationale	Budget95	Budget96
Stipends	9290	Gen Director & Ministry Directors Determine Based on Personnel on Program	10000	10000
Property Tax	1556	N/a Unless We Own Property for Profit Business	1000	
Building Improvement	46	Normally Capital Unless Small in Nature/Gen Director Budgets	20000	
Equipment Repair	0	Gen Director/Ministry Directors Determine Based upon Plan/Needs	4000	
Misc.	25640	Items that Cannot Be Budgeted in Other Areas Bus/Mgr Determines	35000	26000
Insurance	28557	Gen Dir Based on Ins Needs and Projected Ins Coverage—Increases Considered	30000	29000
Building Maintenance	13672	Routine Maint Ministry Directors/Gen Director Projects on Need for 1996	11000	15000
Conferences	7392	Gen Director Projects Based on Ministry Needs	8000	8000
Electric	32806	Gen Director/Bus Mgr Determine Based on Current Amt and Future Rates	35000	30000
Natural Gas	10706	Same as Above	12000	15000
Water	4398	Same as Above	5000	5300
Telephone	11583	Same as Above	10000	12000
Janitorial Supplies	5006	Gen Director and Ministry Directors Based on Square Footage and Each Building	7000	5000
Life Ins. Premium	4109	Correlates with Life Ins Prem in Income Side Should Be Same or Approx Same	4000	4200
Education Fund	3682	Correlates with Life Ins Prem in Income/Gen Director Determines	10000	4000
Vending	1706	Expense of Vending Income. Correlates with Income for Profit	2000	2000
Food	1995	Determined After Income Budgeted. Determined by Gen Director	6000	2000
Livestock Production	1945	Costs Assoc with Farm Directors Assessment of Income	8000	2000
Shop Expense	3335	Farm Director Based upon Shop Income and His Assessment of Needs	10000	4000
Pallet Production	2679	Farm Director/Gen Director Based upon Production Income and Needs	5000	5000
Promotional Material	74806	Newsletters/Ministry Promotion/Ad's/Brochures—Determined Dev Dir & Gen Dir	45000	80000

Item		Description		
Special Events	25889	Dev Director Based upon Events He Planned for Year and Consts Associated	25000	26000
Special Appeals	26125	Dev Director Based upon Special Mailings Planned for 1996	50000	80000
Grain Hay Production	3542	Costs of Grain Hay Prod Budgeted by Farm Director	3000	3000
Fuel at V/A	2500	Fuel Costs for Farm Production Budgeted by Farm Director	3000	3000
Client Expense	5841	Ministry Directors Budgeted for Each Ministry	6000	6000
Mission Support	25614	Gen Director Budgeted for International Mission	0	26000
Mission Staff Support	5576	Gen Director for Staff International Mission	12000	32000
Spec. Appeals External	22316	Dev Director Based upon External Appeals Planned for 1996	0	25000
Wood Chip Prod. Exp.	13367	Farm Director Cost Associated with Wood Chip Project	0	15000
ADP Charge	1002	Bus Mgr Based on Head Count for Payroll Processing	0	
Book Sales Expense	7554	Dev Director Based on Planned Book Prod Costs	0	1000
Medical Client Expense	2963	Gen Director/Ministry Director Based on Client Load	0	3000
Smart Start Expense	826	WPC Ministry Director/Gen Director	0	2000
International Aid	2526	For Special Int Needs Determined by Plan of General Director	0	3000
International Supp.	20941	For Int Ministries Budgeted by Gen Director Based on Proj Needs and Staff	0	
Gift in Kind Expense	2064	For Preparing Merch/Equip Donated for Sale—Projected by General Director	0	21000
Emergency Assistance	1158	Gen Director Based on History and Projected Needs	0	2500
Total Expenses	1005176		1000000	1155000
Net Income/Deficit	106884		60000	45000

Source: Reprinted, by permission, from David L. McFee for Peoria Rescue Ministries.

two weeks after the Finance Committee meeting. PRM also prepares its Capital Budget in conjunction with the Operating Budget,
in order that program personnel think and plan for program needs
as they develop their future programs. A copy of the form PRM
uses is shown in Exhibit 5.4.

(f) Cautions

Anthony and Young note several aspects of budget review that one
should recognize. First, you will face time constraints. Count on it:
you won't have time to go into sophisticated budget procedures, or
be perfectionistic! Second, there are budget review effects on behavior: problems arise because so much of nonprofit spending is
discretionary. This suggests that negotiation be used, and that ability, integrity, and forthrightness is not soon forgotten. Third, politics and gamesmanship often occur. Fourth, watch out for the
"budget ploys."

   (i) *Budget Ploys.*   Four budget ploys are prevalent in the
nonprofits we have observed:

- *Foot in the door:* Here, a modest program is sold initially, but once
  the constituency has been built and the program is underway
  the true magnitude of it is revealed. Sometimes this is triggered
  by "resource hunger"—in which the budgetee's motivation is to
  acquire as many resources as possible, especially when output
  cannot be reliably measured, and the output–input relationship
  is unclear. Your best hope is to detect this up front and disap-
  prove the program; failing that, force the program advocates to
  hold to the original cost estimate.

- *Reverence for the past:* This ploy is used to maintain or increase an
  ongoing program. The argument goes that the amount spent last
  year had to have been necessary to carry out last year's program,
  so the only thing to negotiate is the increment to add to this base
  for this year's program. Time for careful consideration is often
  lacking, so try to implement selective ZBB over a period of several
  years.

- *Make a study:* Users of this ploy are trying to avoid having their
  program's budget slashed. The advocate tries to buy time or
  block the action by demanding that all repercussions of such an
  action be studied. Sometimes the best response is to make the
  study and be persistent in cutting the program, assuming the
  study verifies the original reasoning. Other times, stick with
  your guns and cut the budget without further delay.

- *We are the experts:* Here again, the goal is to forestall cuts. The
  budgetee is arguing that he has superior knowledge which the

supervisor or budget director does not have. Professionals are especially adept at this—teachers, scientists, physicians, and clergy members. The best answer is to insist that the "expert" phrase his reasoning in terminology and expression understandable to all.

(ii) What Hinders an Effective Budget System? Methods and techniques used in the budget system have only limited impact on budget system effectiveness.[9] Of course, methods used should be understood by organization personnel, budgets need to be done on time (and often are not), and variance reports showing actual-versus-budget differences should be prepared regularly, accurately, and on a timely basis. The key determinant of success or failure was the use made *after* the budget is in place. And the use made was primarily aided or hindered by communication. Communication problems arise in several relationships:[10]

- Between the budget department and operating management
- Between the different levels of the management hierarchy (e.g., top and middle management)
- Between the manager responsible for the budget (budgetee) and his or her direct supervisor

Budgets are yardsticks, and sometimes they are taken seriously and operate effectively, other times there is political maneuvering to escape the restraint of the budget. Breakdown in verbal communication was more often the culprit than written communications such as budget variance reports. The way you *use* the budget and the attitudes of top line management are most important. Some of these problems can be prevented by the budget guidelines.

(iii) Is the Finalized Budget Consistent with Financial Targets and Policies? This reality check is essential before publishing the budget. There should be a direct tie between your strategic plan and the budget as well as between your long-range financial plan and your budget. If done at the same time, there should be a very close correspondence between the first year of your five-year financial plan and your operating budget for next year. If the financial policy is to run surpluses for the next three years, obviously your budget should show revenues exceeding expenses.

---

[9]Geert Hofstede, *Uncommon Sense about Organizations: Cases, Studies, and Field Observations* (Thousand Oaks, CA: SAGE Publications, 1994), 140–153.
[10]*Id.*

5.6 BUDGET TECHNIQUE REFINEMENTS

While technique is not the most important indicator of operating budget effectiveness, some organizations have found value in using newer, refined budget techniques, including nonfinancial targets, flexible budgets, program budgets, and ZBB.

(a) Nonfinancial Targets

Many businesses include nonfinancial targets in their annual budget reports. We strongly advocate that you consider doing this, assuming your budget development process is running smoothly. What about nonmonetary budget targets? Anthony and Young recommend the following output measures: (1) workload or process measures, (2) results or "objective achievement" measures, and (3) a framework for the objective achievement measures. The latter framework might be the use of a management philosophy known as "management by objectives" (MBO), which is defined as the use of quantitative measures for measuring planned objectives, possibly including objectives to maintain operations, objectives to strengthen operations, and objectives to improve operations. In this situation, benchmarking and re-engineering studies are helpful.

(b) Flexible Budgeting

Sometimes called variable budgeting, flexible budgeting is particularly useful for organizations operating in an uncertain environment, where you plug in the expense budget when you find out exactly what level of output you're going to be working at. On the expense side, flexible budgeting works well, you might have guessed, only for variable costs. Organizations that do not develop flexible budgets must adapt to changes in the environment "after the fact," scrambling to prepare a revised budget to fit the new realities. You'll live with the original budget? Not if you want the budget to serve as a control and coordinating device, in which managers are held responsible for meeting or exceeding budgetary amounts. Let's use a greatly simplified example, which builds on our earlier classification of variable, semivariable, and fixed costs. Recall that labor expense is the major cost to be managed by nonprofits. This is really a semivariable expense in many organizations: new staff and laborers do not have to be added for each additional client served, but perhaps one laborer must be added for each additional five clients. Salaried workers basically represent a fixed cost. Utilities, insurance, and mortgage payments are fixed costs. And supplies used in client engagements are a variable cost; the more clients served, the more supplies used. Let's start with a base case budget for the year 19XX, based on the "most likely" figure of 1,000 client engagements. We have annotated it to show the cost type for each item in Exhibit 5.6.

To develop a flexible budget, we need to have a way to figure the amount for each variable and semivariable cost expressed as a percent of activity level (services delivered). Recall that the "base case" budget (the one you would have used if you did not go the extra step to develop a flexible budget) was based on 1,000 client engagements. This implies that client supplies are $40 per client engagement:

$$\text{Variable cost per unit} = \text{total cost divided by number of units}$$
$$\$40 = \$40,000 \div 1,000$$

In a formula, we have:

$$\text{Client supplies expense} = \$40 \times (\text{\# of client engagements}).$$

Semivariable costs have both a variable component and a fixed component. To get the fixed component, you need to determine how much of this cost element would be necessary to have a minimal service delivery (say, one or a very few clients). For labor expense, our organization projected $120,000 based on 1,000 client engagements. The staff director suggests that even if the organization had only 20 client engagements (the smallest number it could have and still remain open), the labor expense would be $20,000. What that tells us is that for the remaining 980 clients (1,000 clients assumed in the base case budget, less the 20 "minimal level" clients), there would be $100,000 of labor expense ($120,000 base case budget less the $20,000 minimal level). This implies that the variable component is:

$$\text{Variable cost per unit} = \text{total variable cost}$$
$$\text{divided by number of units}$$
$$\$102.04 = \$100,000 \div 980$$

Exhibit 5.6. Base Case Budget Worksheet

	(1,000 Client Engagements) January 1–December 31, 19XX	
Expense Element		Amount
Variable costs:	Client supplies	$ 40,000
Semivariable costs:	Labor expense	$120,000
Fixed costs:	Salary expense	60,000
	Utilities	5,000
	Insurance	4,000
	Mortgage Payments	15,000
Total Expenses:		$244,000

Let's express the relationship we have just discovered in a format we can use to calculate the semivariable cost for *any* level of clients. We saw that labor expense is $20,000 plus $102.04 per client engagement. Our formula is:

Labor expense = $20,000 + $102.04 × (# of client engagements)

The easy part is estimating the fixed cost. By definition, a fixed cost does not change regardless of the amount of services delivered. So all we have to do is get a total for all fixed costs:

Salary expense	60,000
Utilities	5,000
Insurance	4,000
Mortgage Payments	15,000
Total fixed costs	$84,000

Our formula for fixed costs is very simple:

Total fixed costs = $84,000

And now, the grand finale: let's add the three formulas together to get one overall formula to simplify our flexible budgeting:

Client supplies expense =		$ 40 × (# of client engagements)
Labor expense	=	$20,000 + $102.04 × (# of client engagements)
Total fixed costs	=	$84,000
Total costs	=	$104,000 + $142.04 × (# of client engagements)

Using this formula, we can determine the expense budget for any level of activity we desire. For example, if client engagements double to 2,000, total costs could be:

Total costs = $104,000 + $142.04 × (2,000)
= $104,000 + $284,080
= $388,080

As actual figures for client engagements begin to come in, we can now compare actual amounts to an adjusted "flexible budget" amount, which correctly states what the budget is at that particular activity level. This way, managers are not penalized for expenses that are running higher due to a higher caseload. Further, budget revisions based on environmental changes are no longer needed. The change in caseload due to environmental changes is automatically reflected in budget expense levels. In more technical terms, we no longer have to concern ourselves with a "volume variance"—an actual-versus-budget difference that is strictly due to changes in service activity. We can then limit our concentration on "price variances" that are due to changes in the unit cost of an input, such as a change in the minimum wage, or "mix variances" that are due to a changing composition in the types of clients we serve. One other benefit of doing the extra work involved in flexible budgeting: when cutbacks or expansion of your organization are being considered, you will already be prepared to pinpoint the likely financial effects.

(c) Program Budgeting

Recall that with line-item budgets, the focus is on expense elements. With program budgets, instead of concerning ourselves with the type of expense, we focus on programs and their associated expenses. Essentially, think of it as having subunit budgets, one for each program. By directing our attention to individual programs instead of the overall organization, the manager is aided in allocating the right amount of financial and human resources to each activity. Furthermore, from a control and coordination perspective, program budgeting links spending directly to planned activity levels of the organization's product(s) or service(s). An organization with a well-developed strategic planning process will find that it has already done some of the work necessary to establish the program budgets.[11]

(d) Zero-Base Budgeting

Budgets, whether line-item, flexible, or program, are usually arrived at by changing the past year's budget slightly, perhaps based on new economic assumptions or based on noted actual-versus-budget variances from this year's experience. A more radical, and some would argue superior, approach is to force each program or other subunit to justify its existence and budgetary allocation "from the ground up." This approach to budgeting is known as ZBB. The key components of ZBB are identified as

1. Identify objectives
2. Determine the value of accomplishing each activity or program
3. Evaluate different funding levels

[11]For more information see Robert N. Anthony and David W. Young, *Management Control in Nonprofit Organizations*. 3rd. Edition (Homewood, IL: Richard D. Irwin, Inc., 1984).

4. Establish priorities

5. Evaluate workload and performance measures[12]

The idea here is to look at all the organization's discretionary activities and priorities in a fresh way, and then to redo the budget allocations accordingly. Particularly important is the review of all support allocations. Basic or necessary operations are separated from discretionary or optional tasks. Every dollar of discretionary cost must be justified, and the finalized money allocation based on a cost-benefit comparison of each competing activity's goals, program for attaining those goals, expected benefits and how one will know if they have been attained, alternatives to the program, consequences from *not* approving the activity and its corresponding budgetary allocation, and who will carry out the activity's program(s).

Once the supporting data have been put together, it is time to rank the various activities. This may be done first by program directors for all activities within their programs, then higher-level managers will assemble rankings of organization-wide alternatives. Management must rank order from most beneficial to least beneficial all the alternatives, then decide how to allocate the overall budget to achieve the greatest good. For example, a charity might decide the for the coming year computer software training will do more good than the usual in-service client relations training.

Some proponents of ZBB argue that it can actually simplify the budgeting process and bring about better resource allocation of funds. It does so by making managers consider the various priorities and how funds should be allocated to them. With the list of ranked activities, as the budget year begins managers have an additional tool for augmenting or reducing activities as the allowable expenditure level changes.

Once the operating budget is finalized, it needs to be *calendarized* (distributed across months, as some months are higher revenue or expenditure months than others) and the cash flow ramifications need to be spelled out. The process for showing when cash comes in and goes out is called cash budgeting.

5.7 CASH BUDGET

If your organization's accounting is done on a cash basis, your operating statement provides the input for the cash budget. The cash budget differs in purpose, in that it highlights the cash available to

---

[12]Tom M. Plank, *Accounting Desk Book,* 10th Edition (Englewood Cliffs, NJ: Prentice-Hall, Inc., 1995).

the organization at various points in the future. It is very revealing, especially the first time it is constructed, because nonfinancial managers typically are unaware of just how unsynchronized cash inflows and cash outflows are.

(a) Uses of the Cash Budget

We start our presentation on cash budgeting with a definition: The cash budget shows the timing of cash inflows and outflows, usually on a monthly basis for the next 12 months. It is sometimes called a cash plan or a cash forecast. Exhibit 5.7 shows the value of a cash budget. The cash budget has five major purposes; it shows the:

1. Unsynchronized nature of inflows and outflows (e.g., see October figures in historical cash flow table in Exhibit 5.8)

2. Seasonality of these flows (for example, donations run high around Easter and Christmas)

3. Degree of mismatch (surplus or shortfall)

4. Duration of these surpluses or shortfalls (how long they last, in months)

Exhibit 5.7. Cash Budget: Uses

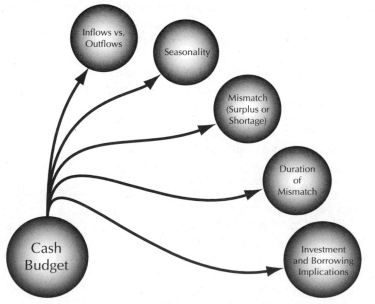

5. Necessary inputs for short-term investment or borrowing plan-ning (together degree and duration of mismatch provide this, with the output being amounts and maturities of short-term in-vestments or borrowing)

(b) Steps in Cash Budgeting

The steps in developing a cash budget are:

1. Determine which measure of cash to manage and forecast
    - General ledger cash balance (checkbook balance if that's your only accounting)
    - Bank balance (preferred)
2. Decide on presentation format
3. Collect historical information (see Exhibit 5.8, for an actual non-profit's prior year cash flows)
4. Develop cash forecast

(c) Forecasting Your Cash Position

When actually laying out your cash budget, you may choose one or more of several formats. Because you already are probably devel-oping a statement of cash flows (SCF), one alternative is to use the SCF format. You would then show projections for cash from/(to) operating activities, cash from/(to) investing activities, and cash from/(to) financing activities. This works well for an annual con-solidated projection but is unnatural for monthly or daily projec-tions. An alternate format, which you may decide to use for your daily or monthly projections, is the following cash receipts and dis-bursements method (see Exhibit 5.9).

To operationalize this method, we would need to provide the necessary detail for each category of cash flow and for the mini-mum necessary cash:

- Categories of cash inflows
- Categories of cash outflows
- Needed minimum cash

See the discussion of how much liquidity an organization should have in Chapter 6.

Basically, all we are doing here is looking back to see what items provided our cash inflows and outflows in the past, and de-ciding how much detail to show for each category. Let's look more closely at projecting our cash receipts, and then we'll comment on cash disbursements.

Exhibit 5.8. Collecting Historical Information

Month Line Item:	Oct.	Nov.	Dec.	Jan.	Feb.	Mar.	Apr.	May	June	July	Aug.	Sep.
Cash Receipts (Total Deposits)	$1,373,317.26	$1,495,458.64	$2,296,298.05	$1,600,345.48	$1,585,682.34	$1,455,742.97	$1,474,501.30	$1,410,048.27	$1,528,613.80	$2,872,784.74	$1,928,010.02	$1,405,515.21
−Cash Disbursements (Total Pymt/withdrawals)	1,866,433.15	1,358,838.60	2,191,922.40	1,826,944.39	1,598,544.96	1,516,459.75	1,417,947.23	1,360,117.18	1,469,020.89	3,064,544.94	1,715,130.63	1,459,922.01
=Net cash Flow	($493,115.89)	$136,620.04	$104,375.65	($226,598.91)	($12,862.62)	($60,716.78)	$56,554.07	$49,931.09	$59,592.91	($191,760.20)	$212,879.39	($54,406.80)
+Beg cash (Beginning Balance)	$626,414.41	$133,298.52	$269,918.56	$374,294.21	$147,695.30	$134,832.68	$74,115.90	$130,669.97	$180,601.06	$240,193.97	$48,433.77	$261,313.16
=Ending Cash (Ending Balance or New Balance)	$133,298.52	$269,918.56	$374,294.21	$147,695.30	$134,832.68	$74,115.90	$130,669.97	$ 80,601.06	$240,193.97	$48,433.77	$261,313.16	$206,906.36

Exhibit 5.9.   Basic Cash Budgeting/Forecasting Template

	January	February
Beginning cash	$250	$ 175
+Cash receipts	100	
−Cash disbursements	175	
=Ending cash	$175	
−Minimum cash	200	
=Cash surplus		
OR		
Cash shortage	($ 25)	

(i) Determine Cash Receipts.   The determination of cash receipts proceeds in a logical and orderly fashion

1. Operating budget is starting point
2. Accrual versus cash basis adjustment (if necessary—if already
    on cash basis, don't worry about adjustments)
3. Watch out for the common oversights
    • Don't forget pre-arranged financing inflows
    • Don't forget (formerly) restricted net assets such as deferred
      giving or time-restricted or purpose-restricted prior gifts that
      will become unrestricted this period
4. Calendarization
    • Study history to see seasonal patterns
5. Anticipate changes in forthcoming 12 months
6. Show quarterly totals to provide one checks-and-balances mon-
    itoring sequence

(ii) Determine Cash Disbursements.   Again, the operating
budget expenses are the starting point. Because of accounts
payable, you may have to make an accrual-to-cash basis adjustment (if necessary). One of the key things to watch out for are the
capital budget outlays—many organizations forget to include
these in the cash budget. Then, calendarize the cash outlays correctly, recognizing seasonal or other ups and downs. Pull together
quarterly subtotals to use down the road for comparisons with actual cash flows.

(iii) Putting It All Together.   Now we are ready to bring the
cash receipts and disbursements together to find the difference
("net cash flow") for each month. Once we have that, we will add it
to beginning cash to arrive at ending cash. We compare ending

cash to minimum cash required (by subtracting the latter), and see if we have a cash surplus anticipated for the month's end, or a cash shortage. This gives a three-step sequence that you should carry out at least monthly and probably weekly or even daily.

- Compute NCF, ending position, cash surplus/(shortfall) for each month.
- Analyze pattern(s)—Are there distinct seasonal highs or lows for either cash receipts or cash disbursements? How will this feed back into our cash planning (i.e., building up larger reserves) or fund-raising appeal timing?
- Make recommendations—with regard to both cash reserve buildup and fund-raising timing or frequency, but also for short-term investments (amount and maturity of securities) and short-term borrowing (amount and anticipated maturity of any short-term borrowing, if your financial policy allows for short-term borrowing).

The chief value of the exercise is in assisting your financial management process.

5.8 CONCLUSION

In this chapter, we have shown how to develop operating and cash budgets. We show the sequence of steps that should be followed, so you can set up the process. We provide warnings of the pitfalls that many nonprofit organizations face along the way. Budget enhancements are also discussed, some of which might merit further study on your part. Budgets are valuable management tools for planning and coordinating your service delivery. Organizations that do not budget are losing financial control of the organization. Organizations that do budget find the budget system most effective when it is tied to the strategic plan. Once in place, the budget may be compared to actual dollar amounts as the budget year progresses, and corrective actions are signaled by the budget variances. We develop budget reports and other financial reports in the next chapter.

CHAPTER SIX

Financial Reports

6.1 Introduction   183
6.2 Major Differences from For-Profit Business Reports   184
   (a) Financial Results Are No Longer the Primary Focus
     in Management Reports   184
   (b) Primary Financial Objective Is Target Liquidity,
     Not Profit   185
   (c) Fewer External Users, with a Different
     Accountability Focus   186
   (d) Different Funds and the (Temporarily or Permanently)
     Restricted versus Unrestricted Net Asset Distinction   190
6.3 Objectives of Financial Reports   193
   (a) Accurate and Timely Representation
     of Financial Situation   194
   (b) Mission Attainment Supportive Role   195
   (c) Evidence of Accountability   196
   (d) Tool for Turnaround Management   197
     (i) Church of the Brethren   199
     (ii) Church of God Missionary Board (Anderson, IN)   199
6.4 Reporting System Design   200
6.5 Major Reports   200
6.6 Internal Reports   201
   (a) Annual   201
   (b) Level 1: Budget Variance Analysis   202
     (i) Operating Budget   202
     (ii) Capital Budget   204
     (iii) Cash Budget   204
     (iv) Supplemental Report: Deferred Giving   206
   (c) Level 2: Annual Financial Statements and Ratios   206
     (i) Statements of Activity, Financial Position,
     and Cash Flows   206
     (ii) Financial Ratio Analysis   209
   (d) Level 3: Fund-Raising Management and Evaluation   219
     (i) Setting the Philosophy and Major Objective
     of Fund-raising   220

(ii) Plan and Then Schedule the Campaign
Expenditures   221

(iii) Assist in the Mid-Campaign Evaluation
and Redirection   222

(iv) Oversee Post-Campaign Effectiveness and Efficiency
Ratio Analysis   222

(e) Level 4: Cash and Liquidity Analysis and Projection   223
(i)   Monthly or Quarterly Reports   226
(ii) Daily or Flash Reports   227

(f) Managing Off the Budget   227
(i)   Budget Variance Analysis Revisited   227
(ii) Cash Position   229
(iii) Responses to Financial Difficulties   229
(iv) Internal Measures   231
(v)   External Measures   232

6.7 External Reports   233
(a) Statements of Activity, Financial Position,
and Cash Flows   233
(i)   Forms 990 and 990-T   233
(ii) Donor Mailings and "Publicly Available"
Reports   233
(iii) State Requirements   234
(iv) Granting Agency Reports   234

6.8 Summary   235

6.1   INTRODUCTION

How are things going with the finances of your organization? Is there enough financial strength to expand or add programs or add new ones? Will there be another cash crisis this year? Can your organization document that you spent the grant money for the purposes for which the money was granted? To provide answers to these questions, whether asked by someone inside or outside your organization, is the role provided by financial reports. It is hard to overemphasize the importance of accurate and timely financial reports for *internal* financial decision making. Additionally, donors, the IRS, and/or charity watchdog groups such as the Council of Better Business Bureaus, the National Charities Information Bureau (NCIB), the American Institute on Philanthropy (and the related Internet Nonprofit Center), and Philanthropic Research, Inc. (a company that publishes a CD-ROM database on nonprofit 990s), will *externally* scrutinize your financial position and policies and judge your organization as to whether it is "support worthy." When you go to the bank for a mortgage or short-term loan, the lending officer will scrutinize your financial reports before making the lending decision. Because both the watchdog bureaus and lenders will be looking at some of the same things you should be looking at periodically in your internal financial process, we will focus almost exclusively on internal reporting in our presentation.

6.2 MAJOR DIFFERENCES FROM FOR-PROFIT BUSINESS REPORTS

Nonprofit financial reports may look much like business reports, but the focus and emphases are different. Business professionals on the board may not be aware of these differences, and it takes some effort on the CFO's part to explain why things are different.

(a) Financial Results Are No Longer the Primary Focus in Management Reports

In businesses, if the stock price is going up and the organization is profitable, the organization is deemed a success. In nonprofits, we no longer have the primacy of financial results, because we no longer have shareholder wealth or profit maximizing as the overarching objectives. In their study of nonprofit effectiveness and excellence, Knauft, Berger, and Gray (1991) surveyed more than 900 staff officers and board chairs from a national sample of nonprofits, and found:

- When asked to list characteristics of an effective organization, most gave an answer that indicated a clear sense of mission accompanied by goals to carry out that mission.

- When asked how a nonprofit can improve, most gave the highest priority to "making mission central."

- A strong mission orientation is the chief criterion used by board chairs to judge the effectiveness of the Chief Executive Officer (CEO).[1]

One of the more interesting interviews conducted in the Lilly study was with Darryl Smith, chief financial officer (CFO) of the Church of God (Anderson, IN) Missionary Board. Prior to coming to the Church of God, Darryl was a plant controller for a chemical company. When asked the difference he noted between the mindset and practices of the charitable organization compared to a corporation, he replied:

> I guess the biggest difference is the mission. Even a corporation has a mission organization—they *should*. I think the mission direction of the not-for-profit, or at least the Church of

[1]E. B. Knauft, Renee A. Berger, and Sandra T. Gray, *Profiles of Excellence: Achieving Success in the Nonprofit Sector* (San Francisco: Jossey-Bass Publishers, 1991).

God board here, is primarily that of trying to have an impact in people's lives around the world almost all times regardless of the cost. I'm not trying to say that we're not concerned about the finances related to that, but that seems to be an area that the church relies on faith and relies on individuals to support that. So it's not necessarily looking at your one-year plan, your three-year plan, your five-year plan and trying to implement that. I think in the private sector without question you've got a shareholder that you've got to relate to, you've got an operating board that is held accountable by the shareholders . . . and many times the primary focus of the private business sector is the operating results related to that. I know in the chemical industry, maximizing your inventories (your turnover rates) your profit and loss statement, those were the biggest areas. . . . So I think the biggest change, the biggest thing I can see is that the mission is not related primarily to the financial strength. I think it's more related to the vision and the direction that the board or any of the staff feels that needs to be done around the world.

The CFO's role: Use the financial reports to show how the financial results facilitated and enhanced present and future mission achievement.

(b) Primary Financial Objective Is Target Liquidity, Not Profit

The very different financial dynamics of businesses and nonprofits are highlighted when their life cycle pattern under financial stringency is viewed:

- Business not making money is closed to conserve shareholder capital; correspondingly the financial reports focus on organization's ability to make a profit and a positive operating cash flow, with stewardship defined as greater profits and cash flow.

- Nonprofit will operate until insolvent, can be in the red for some years without any corrective action being taken; correspondingly the financial reports focus on organization's fund balance (and, ideally, on the amount of that which is spendable in the sense of unrestricted cash and securities balances), with stewardship on maintaining some target level: too little jeopardizes the organization's future both in the sense of limiting its ability to respond quickly to new opportunities and in the sense of providing an insufficient buffer against a bad fiscal year; too much indicates "hoarding," which brings into question both why the organization is not spending more on meeting critical societal needs and whether the organization really merits the same level of donor or grantor support.

CFOs role: Use financial reports to show how the organization uses its financial policies, including the target liquidity level, to add stability and further the organization's potential for future mission achievement. An example from the business community: White Castle ("buy 'em by the sack") states that it intentionally slows its growth rate in order to finance growth only with re-invested profits "so we can provide a stable company for our 9,500-plus employees."

At the program level, for most programs, strive to meet the secondary objective of *cost coverage* (revenues cover cost). A program not raising adequate donor funds within a certain time frame is scaled back or ultimately ended. New programs are always welcome; just make sure to begin building financial support as you move toward implementation. In some cases, as we noted in Chapter 4, programs should be maintained that do not cover their costs, with reliance on earned income or subsidization from other programs that more than cover their costs. The latter has been used unethically by some: monies raised for one purpose are diverted to another purpose.

(c) Fewer External Users, with a Different Accountability Focus

Users have often had a great deal of difficulty in interpreting nonprofit financial statements. Some years ago, a group of Harvard Business School master's degree students were given typical fund accounting-based statements, and after much time and effort the students were unable to analyze and draw correct conclusions from the statements. With the new reporting format, the statements are consolidated and look more like business financials, yet the meaning of such terms as unrestricted general fund, unrestricted investment fund, temporarily restricted, permanently restricted, pledges receivable, and net assets are still confusing.

Despite the difficulties, the general public and present and potential donors want accountability from the nonprofit. As a result, quite often effectiveness and efficiency are judged from the service delivery observed (or read about—press reports such as those in *Money Magazine* are appearing with increasing frequency), or a watchdog agency such as the Better Business Bureau (BBB) or NCIB are relied on by the user. There must be a strong case for your organization's financial position if one of the watchdog agencies rates the organization's cash reserves as "excessive." And be ready to justify administrative expenses if they are thought to be excessive. Not that these external groups are negatives: the perception of an organization through an outside party often conveys valuable information back to your management team and board. And, many times the reports are positive (see Exhibit 6.1 for the NCIB Standards in Philanthropy). Then, take a look at the web page set up by

Exhibit 6.1. NCIB Standards in Philanthropy: Governance, Policy, and Program Fundamentals

1. *Board Governance:* The board is responsible for policy setting, fiscal guidance, and ongoing governance, and should regularly review the organization's policies, programs, and operations. The board should have
   a. An independent, volunteer membership
   b. A minimum of 5 voting members
   c. An individual attendance policy
   d. Specific terms of office for its officers and members
   e. In-person, face-to-face meetings, at least twice a year, evenly spaced, with a majority of voting members in attendance at each meeting
   f. No fees to members for board service, but payments may be made for costs incurred as a result of board participation
   g. No more than one paid staff person member, usually the chief staff officer, who shall not chair the board or serve as treasurer
   h. Policy guidelines to avoid material conflicts of interest involving board or staff
   i. No material conflicts of interest involving board or staff
   j. A policy promoting pluralism and diversity within the organization's board, staff, and constituencies
2. *Purpose:* The organization's purpose, approved by the board, should be formally and specifically stated.
3. *Programs:* The organization's activities should be consistent with its statement of purpose.
4. *Information:* Promotion, fund raising, and public information should describe accurately the organization's identity, purpose, programs, and financial needs.
5. *Financial Support and Related Activities:* The board is accountable for all authorized activities generating financial support on the organization's behalf:
   a. Fundraising practices should encourage voluntary giving and should not apply unwarranted pressure
   b. Descriptive and financial information for all substantial income and for all revenue-generating activities conducted by the organization should be disclosed on request
   c. Basic descriptive and financial information for income derived from authorized commercial activities, involving the organization's name, which are conducted by for-profit organizations, should be available. All public promotion of such commercial activity should either include this information or indicate that it is available from the organization.
6. *Use of Funds:* The organization's use of funds should reflect consideration of current and future needs and resources in planning for program continuity. The organization should:
   a. Spend at least 60 percent of annual expenses for program activities
   b. Ensure that fund-raising expenses, in relation to fund-raising results, are reasonable over time
   c. Have net assets available for the following fiscal year not usually more than twice the current year's expenses or the next year's budget, whichever is higher
   d. Not have a persistent and/or increasing deficit in the unrestricted fund balance

Exhibit 6.1. NCIB Standards in Philanthropy: Governance, Policy, and Program Fundamentals (*continued*)

Reporting and Fiscal Fundamentals
7. *Annual Reporting:* An annual report should be available on request, and should include
    a. An explicit narrative description of the organization's major activities, presented in the same major categories and covering the same fiscal period as the audited financial statements
    b. A list of board members
    c. Audited financial statements or, at a minimum, a comprehensive financial summary that (1) identifies all revenues in significant categories, (2) reports expenses in the same program, management/general, and fund-raising categories as in the audited financial statements, and (3) reports all ending balances. (When the annual report does not include the full audited financial statements, it should indicate that they are available on request.)
8. *Accountability:* An organization should supply on request complete financial statements which
    a. Are prepared in conformity with generally accepted accounting principles (GAAP) accompanied by a report of an independent certified public accountant, and reviewed by the board
    b. Fully disclose economic resources and obligations, including transactions with related parties and affiliated organizations, significant events affecting finances, and significant categories of income and expense—and should also supply
    c. A statement of functional allocation of expenses, in addition to such statements required by GAAP to be included among the financial statements
    d. Combined financial statements for a national organization operating with affiliates prepared in the foregoing manner
9. *Budget:* The organization should prepare a detailed annual budget consistent with the major classifications in the audited financial statements, and approved by the board.

Source: Reprinted, with permission, from the National Charities Information Bureau's *Wise Giving Guide.*

Second Harvest (Exhibit 6.2), the nation's largest food bank, and how the NCIB and BBB reports are incorporated into this communication with donors and other publics.

One other problem: external reporting requirements or needs may dictate internal reporting and budgeting formats, as nonprofits are too hard pressed to do two sets of reports.[2] The NCIB standards will illustrate what we mean. In Exhibit 6.1 you see the standards presently applied. Take some time right now to study them carefully. Note standards 5b, 5c, and 6–9. You can see how important your financial reports and policies are to this evaluating organization. We

[2]Richard S. Wasch, "Budgeting in Nonprofit Organizations," in *Handbook of Budgeting,* 3rd Edition (New York: John Wiley & Sons, 1993).

Exhibit 6.2.   Second Harvest Web Page and Regular Annual Financial Statement

FINANCIAL SUMMARY

Watchdog Report Card

With so many charitable organizations actively seeking your support, where can you turn for help in determining whether or not to support a cause? A number of watchdog organizations have been established to help provide you with the information you need to make informed giving decisions. Two of the more widely recognized organizations are the Better Business Bureau and the National Charities Information Bureau. Both are highly respected organizations that keep a watchful eye on how charities spend your money.

Second Harvest meets all standards set forth by both organizations. Full reports are available free of charge directly from these organizations. A general financial summary is available in this section. In addition, you can obtain printed copies of the latest annual report and the tax form 990 directly from Second Harvest. You can request these materials online through the Getting In Touch section and they will be mailed out to you.

will return to a further discussion of standards related to liquidity (6c) and the unrestricted fund balance (6d) later in this chapter.

Internal users and uses (the reports for which are sometimes called managerial accounting) are in some ways quite different from those outside the organization. Illustrating the difference between planned or budgeted amounts and actual reported results is an important input into whether the organization needs to initiate corrective action and whether it is heading into a financial crisis in the future.

CFO's role: Establish a work-around to provide helpful internal and external reports. Set up a financial spreadsheet in EXCEL or LOTUS 1-2-3 to automatically link your management report form to your external reports.[3] In this way, your management forms are automatically updated each month (quarter or year) as you fill in the board, grant agency, state, IRS or annual financial statement external reports. From there, customize the data into the framework most helpful for your management team.

---

[3]This is easily done using the "cut" and "paste link" (LOTUS 1-2-3) or "paste special" (Microsoft EXCEL) commands in your spreadsheet program. In EXCEL, in the "paste link" dialog box, select the "paste link" option. In LOTUS 1-2-3, click on edit, then on "paste link."

Exhibit 6.2.   Second Harvest Web Page and Regular Annual Financial Statement (*continued*)

FINANCIAL SUMMARY

Financial Summary

Second Harvest is cited as one of the largest and also as one of the most efficient charities in the nation. One of the more widely reported listings comes from the *Chronicle of Philanthropy*, a nonprofit trade publication.

The 1995 listing of the largest charities found Second Harvest in third place, with $425.1 million in private gifts. The figure reflects mostly in-kind donations of food obtained by the national office.

But perhaps a more important number is one relating to efficiency. The *Chronicle of Philanthropy* calculated a highly respectable 99.7% ratio for Second Harvest.

Rank Among National Charities
According to the *Chronicle of Philanthropy*

1.	Salvation Army
2.	American Red Cross
3.	**Second Harvest**
4.	United Jewish Appeal
5.	YMCA of the USA
6.	American Cancer Society
7.	Catholic Charities USA
8.	Harvard University
9.	Boys and Girls Clubs of America
10.	University of Pennsylvania

Efficiency Level
According to the *Chronicle of Philanthropy*

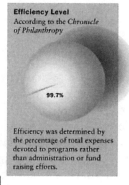

99.7%

Efficiency was determined by the percentage of total expenses devoted to programs rather than administration or fund raising efforts.

(d) Different Funds and the (Temporarily or Permanently) Restricted versus Unrestricted Net Asset Distinction

Fund accounting, by itself, is not a problem. Essentially, it is no different from divisional or department reporting in a business. The problem arises because (1) fund accounting reports are given to external users, who are not accustomed to the format, (2) it is unclear how liquid resources in the plant fund or other funds might be

Exhibit 6.2.   Second Harvest Web Page and Regular Annual Financial Statement (*continued*)

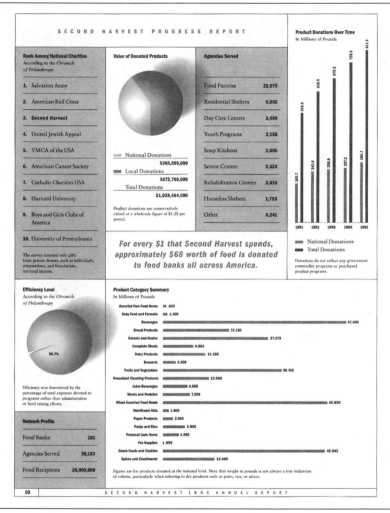

tapped by the organization in an emergency, and (3) there are often inter-fund loans or transfers.

The new distinction between temporarily restricted net assets and permanently restricted net assets should be more helpful than simply reporting items as "restricted." An example, which has been cleared up by moving such items to "unrestricted": in the past some organizations reported board-designated funds as restricted "endowment" funds, when in fact they should have been called "quasi-endowment" as they could be spent at the board's discretion at any

Exhibit 6.2. Second Harvest Web Page and Regular Annual Financial Statement (*continued*)

<table>
<tr><td colspan="3" align="center">BALANCE SHEETS</td></tr>
<tr><td>December 31, 1995 and 1994</td><td colspan="2" align="center">SECOND HARVEST</td></tr>
<tr><td></td><td>1995</td><td>1994</td></tr>
<tr><td>ASSETS</td><td></td><td></td></tr>
<tr><td>Current assets:</td><td></td><td></td></tr>
<tr><td>Cash and cash equivalents</td><td>$ 583,018</td><td>566,842</td></tr>
<tr><td>Pledges receivable</td><td>510,644</td><td>341,266</td></tr>
<tr><td>Other receivables and prepaid expenses</td><td>208,856</td><td>187,612</td></tr>
<tr><td>Total current assets</td><td>1,302,518</td><td>1,095,720</td></tr>
<tr><td>Investments (note 3)</td><td>2,350,815</td><td>2,440,735</td></tr>
<tr><td>Pledges receivable–long term</td><td>40,692</td><td>61,037</td></tr>
<tr><td>Construction in progress</td><td>–</td><td>54,137</td></tr>
<tr><td>Furniture and equipment net of accumulated depreciation of</td><td></td><td></td></tr>
<tr><td>$316,975 and $343,186 in 1995 and 1994, respectively</td><td>327,993</td><td>157,311</td></tr>
<tr><td>Total assets</td><td>$4,022,018</td><td>3,808,940</td></tr>
<tr><td>LIABILITIES AND NET ASSETS</td><td></td><td></td></tr>
<tr><td>Current liabilities:</td><td></td><td></td></tr>
<tr><td>Accounts payable and accrued expenses</td><td>259,289</td><td>238,005</td></tr>
<tr><td>Due to food banks</td><td>179,590</td><td>23,115</td></tr>
<tr><td>Total current liabilities</td><td>438,879</td><td>261,120</td></tr>
<tr><td>Lease payable (note 5)</td><td>126,120</td><td>161,315</td></tr>
<tr><td>Commitments (note 5)</td><td></td><td></td></tr>
<tr><td>Net assets:</td><td></td><td></td></tr>
<tr><td>Unrestricted:</td><td></td><td></td></tr>
<tr><td>Operating</td><td>551,251</td><td>617,063</td></tr>
<tr><td>Designated by Board of Directors as:</td><td></td><td></td></tr>
<tr><td>Reserve Account</td><td>1,529,457</td><td>1,651,130</td></tr>
<tr><td>Endowment</td><td>449,693</td><td>373,446</td></tr>
<tr><td>Investment in property and equipment</td><td>327,993</td><td>211,448</td></tr>
<tr><td>Total unrestricted net assets</td><td>2,858,394</td><td>2,853,087</td></tr>
<tr><td>Temporarily restricted</td><td>561,125</td><td>518,418</td></tr>
<tr><td>Permanently restricted</td><td>37,500</td><td>15,000</td></tr>
<tr><td>Total net assets</td><td>3,457,019</td><td>3,386,505</td></tr>
<tr><td>Total liabilities and net assets</td><td>$4,022,018</td><td>3,808,940</td></tr>
</table>

See accompanying notes to financial statements.

time. Even so, there are questions about how "restricted" these items are or when they will move from the restricted category to unrestricted and become spendable funds. Furthermore, there is an important distinction that may be masked in the classification. Some items are time-restricted, meaning they cannot be spent at the present. Other items are designated for a specific use, and cannot be spent for general operations at any time. The financial manager or outside statement user must determine how much fits either category, and when (if at all) funds will be spendable and can be included in the cash budget to cover needed expenditures.

Exhibit 6.2. Second Harvest Web Page and Regular Annual Financial Statement (*continued*)

STATEMENT OF ACTIVITIES

Year ended December 31, 1995, with comparative totals for 1994   SECOND HARVEST

	Unrestricted	Temporarily Restricted	Permanently Restricted	Total 1995	1994
Public Support and Revenue:					
Public support:					
Individual contributions	$1,752,267	89,506	5,000	1,846,773	1,969,587
Corporate and foundation contributions	663,225	265,600	17,500	946,325	906,317
Corporate promotions	609,477	25,000	–	634,477	433,350
Net assets released from restriction	337,399	(337,399)	–	–	–
Revenue:					
Food bank fees	1,447,347	–	–	1,447,347	1,229,033
Conference fees	193,647	–	–	193,647	164,525
Publications, administrative and materials fees	26,560	–	–	26,560	63,155
Donated services (note 7)	59,792	–	–	59,792	47,140
Investment income	322,230	–	–	322,230	199,667
Total public support and revenue	5,411,944	42,707	22,500	5,477,151	5,012,774
Expenses:					
Program services:					
Network services	1,828,451	–	–	1,828,451	2,002,998
Product distribution	728,237	–	–	728,237	758,719
Product solicitation	663,743	–	–	663,743	660,068
Public education	1,123,857	–	–	1,123,857	698,262
Total program services	4,344,288	–	–	4,344,288	4,120,047
Supporting services:					
General and administrative	420,063	–	–	420,063	449,340
Fund development	642,286	–	–	642,286	788,382
Total supporting services	1,062,349	–	–	1,062,349	1,237,722
Total expenses	5,406,637	–	–	5,406,637	5,357,769
Increase (decrease) in net assets	5,307	42,707	22,500	70,514	(344,995)
Net assets at beginning of year, as restated (note 2(a))	2,853,087	518,418	15,000	3,386,505	3,731,500
Net assets at end of year	$2,858,394	561,125	37,500	3,457,019	3,386,505

See accompanying notes to financial statements.

18   SECOND HARVEST 1995 ANNUAL REPORT

6.3 OBJECTIVES OF FINANCIAL REPORTS

There are four main reasons why the organization puts together financial reports: to represent the organization's financial situation accurately and on a timely basis, to support mission attainment, to evidence accountability, and to facilitate turnaround management. Obviously, these overlap, but each has unique aspects you will want to emphasize.

Exhibit 6.2. Second Harvest Web Page and Regular Annual Financial Statement (*continued*)

STATEMENT OF FUNCTIONAL EXPENSES

Year ended December 31, 1995, with comparative totals for 1994 **SECOND HARVEST**

	Program Services					Supporting Services			Total expenses	
	Network services	Product distribution	Product solicitation	Public education	Total	General and administrative	Fund development	Total	1995	1994
Salaries	$ 527,243	298,219	295,535	204,029	1,325,026	192,085	74,960	267,045	**1,592,071**	1,474,937
Employee benefits	97,743	51,715	52,615	35,516	237,589	30,778	11,409	42,187	**279,776**	271,218
Payroll taxes	44,802	24,987	21,450	17,209	108,448	16,183	6,182	22,365	**130,813**	127,785
Total salaries and related expenses	669,788	374,921	369,600	256,754	1,671,063	239,046	92,551	331,597	**2,002,660**	1,873,940
Travel	139,872	10,323	43,877	23,598	217,670	20,147	9,707	29,854	**247,524**	373,588
Professional services	91,511	25,564	84,104	92,198	293,377	40,652	12,538	53,190	**346,567**	411,272
Occupancy	85,667	51,173	47,118	31,730	215,688	32,709	11,425	44,134	**259,822**	262,527
Telecommunications	40,780	40,814	23,264	33,704	138,562	24,207	5,440	29,647	**168,209**	174,124
Print and production	51,140	19,204	22,252	116,055	208,651	12,537	4,884	17,421	**226,072**	302,096
Postage	29,703	9,596	4,653	22,604	66,556	3,173	1,817	4,990	**71,546**	61,606
Supplies	18,651	10,971	8,780	6,192	44,594	6,624	2,237	8,861	**53,455**	64,443
Equipment maintenance	17,094	10,211	9,402	6,331	43,038	6,527	2,280	8,807	**51,845**	41,348
Fees for service	4,719	2,818	4,315	11,250	23,102	3,183	934	4,117	**27,219**	50,330
Professional development	9,193	6,907	5,014	2,871	23,985	6,496	1,873	8,369	**32,354**	35,704
Publications/memberships	8,960	3,358	5,432	5,743	23,493	2,803	1,679	4,482	**27,975**	18,933
Insurance	2,168	1,295	1,193	803	5,459	828	289	1,117	**6,576**	12,278
Miscellaneous	4,872	405	5,056	3,771	14,104	525	91	616	**14,720**	–
Development campaign efforts	79,248	–	–	98,859	178,107	–	487,344	487,344	**665,451**	713,173
Food bank disbursements	274,619	–	–	–	274,619	–	–	–	**274,619**	91,148
Public service advertising	–	–	–	391,405	391,405	–	–	–	**391,405**	243,669
National conference	164,259	–	–	–	164,259	–	–	–	**164,259**	176,297
Workshops	36,039	–	–	–	36,039	–	–	–	**36,039**	65,419
Transportation	–	128,439	–	–	128,439	–	–	–	**128,439**	110,383
Food bank grants	46,199	–	–	–	46,199	–	–	–	**46,199**	165,295
Donated services (note 7)	19,714	11,776	10,843	7,302	49,635	7,527	2,629	10,156	**59,791**	47,140
Total expenses before depreciation	1,794,196	707,775	644,903	1,111,170	4,258,044	406,984	637,718	1,044,702	**5,302,746**	5,294,713
Depreciation	34,255	20,462	18,840	12,687	86,244	13,079	4,568	17,647	**103,891**	63,056
Total	$1,828,451	728,237	663,743	1,123,857	4,344,288	420,063	642,286	1,062,349	**5,406,637**	5,357,769

See accompanying notes to financial statements.

(a) Accurate and Timely Representation of Financial Situation

Ideally, weekly reports should be available one to two business days after the week's close, and monthly reports within five business days of month-end. If unavailable, issue control totals without the detail in order to speed the information flow. Use "flash reports" to get quick readings of key financial success indicators (KFSIs) such as donations. Use your financial situation analysis of year-to-date and yearly totals to guide new budget development and your long-range financial plans.

Exhibit 6.2.   Second Harvest Web Page and Regular Annual Financial Statement (*continued*)

STATEMENT OF CASH FLOWS

Years ended December 31, 1995 and 1994   SECOND HARVEST

	1995	1994
Cash flows from operating activities:		
Increase (decrease) in net assets	$ 70,514	(344,995)
Adjustments to reconcile increase (decrease) in net assets		
to net cash used in operating activities:		
Depreciation	103,891	63,056
Amortization of lease payable	(35,195)	(35,196)
Net gain on sale of investments	(204,440)	(70,648)
Changes in operating assets and liabilities:		
Pledges receivable	(149,033)	61,879
Other receivables and prepaid expenses	(21,244)	(121,255)
Accounts payable and accrued expenses	21,284	125,103
Due to food banks	156,475	1,611
Net cash used in operating activities	(57,748)	(320,445)
Cash flows from investing activities:		
Purchase of investments	(2,049,882)	(581,726)
Sale of investments	2,344,242	1,091,236
Additions to furniture and equipment	(220,436)	(95,237)
Net cash provided by investing activities	73,924	414,273
Net increase in cash and cash equivalents	16,176	93,828
Cash and cash equivalents at beginning of year	566,842	473,014
Cash and cash equivalents at end of year	$ 583,018	566,842

See accompanying notes to financial statements.

20   SECOND HARVEST 1995 ANNUAL REPORT

(b) Mission Attainment Supportive Role

The financial reports should mirror the role of the finance department: proficient financial management enhances mission attainment. Remember that in striving for your target liquidity level, the end in view is preserving and providing financial resources for the organization to carry out its mission. The fact that financial results are no longer the primary focus in management reports triggers three action points to guide your financial reporting and analysis:

- *Serve the mission achievement end, recognizing that the report is not an end in itself.* Although the usual situation in nonprofits is not to have enough financial analysis, resist the tendency to not only correct the deficiency but to make financial affairs the dominant focus of top management and board attention.

- *Usability should be the guidepost.* Depth interviews and/or focus groups may go a long way to orient you to the informational needs and information processing capabilities of your financial report "customers." Benchmarking, total quality management (TQM), and the new reporting metrics that we discuss later in this chapter have been spawned partly by the viewpoint of seeing through internal customers' eyes.

- *Your reporting and analysis thrust should mainly be internally focused.* Necessary Internal Revenue Service (IRS) and regulatory filings take time and attention from management-oriented and donor-oriented or grantor-oriented financial information. Most nonprofits fall far short of making the necessary managerial information available in the right form on a timely basis. Start where you are in your management reporting, and realize that few businesses in the same size classes as typical nonprofit organizations have strong internal reporting systems either. Focus on a process of continuous improvement. Initially, and at periodic reevaluation points, concentrate on the *process* (procedures and methods) of making decision-making information available, and think through the formats of reports carefully before releasing new or modified reports. One of your first objectives, which we'll help you with later in the chapter, should be to improve on your presentation format (including graphics and annotations attached to the numbers) and variance analysis.

(c) Evidence of Accountability

Organizations must not only be accountable, but increasingly they must persuade skeptical regulators, newspaper reporters, or donors of that accountability. What does it mean to be accountable? Look the word "accountable" up in a dictionary and you will see it is defined as "Liable to being called to account; answerable." The recent scandals with PTL, United Way, Episcopal Church, and New Era Philanthropy have heightened society's calls to account. One group to whom charities are becoming answerable is to the go-between watchdog groups such as the Council of Better Business Bureaus (CBBB) and the NCIB. The NCIB standards that we looked at in Exhibit 6.1 portrayed accountability in philanthropy as providing complete financial statements that are prepared in a stan-

dard format and fully disclose both resources and obligations as
well as the expenses for program as well as administration. This is
an excellent start, and you will notice that some of the other standards, even though not labeled as accountability standards by the
NCIB, bear on the issue. We need a broader framework, though,
and one is outlined in Exhibit 6.3.

Note that accountability starts with staying true to the mission. Then, be able to answer to those asking about effectiveness
(doing the right things and doing them in a way that achieves desired end results) and efficiency (doing those right things with a
minimum of resource consumption). Then, is there a viable risk
management framework in place? Much better to *prevent* scandal,
fraud, and mismanagement than to *control the damage* after the fact.
Donors have needs and desires that your organization is also answerable to: they will wonder why you need their funds if you have
a huge stockpile of cash reserves, for example. They will not comprehend about the funding cycle you face without your explanation
in terms they can understand. What's more, the more involved and
astute donors—present or potential—will watch the operating administration and policy-setting actions for signs of accountability
and proficiency. In the past, the visible nature of and organization's
services and meeting of client needs seemed to cover a multitude of
financial and managerial sins; few organizations have that sort of
community and donor loyalty today. Besides, why wait to be
pressed into accountability when you can enhance your image by
taking the initiative to be in the forefront of organizational stewardship. We saw earlier how Second Harvest does this using their Internet web page. That principle is increasingly evidenced in all sectors of the nonprofit economy. The initiation and rapidly expansion
of an online discussion group dedicated to accountability, called
Cyber-Accountability, points up this trend.[4]

(d) Tool for Turnaround Management

One of the best-kept secrets in the nonprofit financial management
sector is the role financial reporting plays in the financial turnaround of struggling organizations. In the Lilly study, we were
startled to find that two of the four top-performing organizations

---

[4]Started in early 1996 by Harriet Bograd and Peter Swords of the Nonprofit Coordinating Committee (NYC), the group has attracted widespread interest. You may
subscribe by sending an E-mail message to Tim Legg at: tlegg@fcny.org. In the body
of the message, include your full name, organization, and location (city, state,
and country). Send any comments about the listserv to Harriet Bograd at
HBogard@compuserve.com. You may also wish to visit the related web site at
http://www.bway.net/~hbograd/cyb-acc.html

Exhibit 6.3. Accountability and Your Financial Reports

Who are the key stakeholders in your organization? Are you evidencing accountability as a good steward to each of the stakeholder groups? Can you provide a coherent response to a given stakeholder group which contends you are not doing enough for them (and maybe benefiting another stakeholder group to do so)? If so, your organization, speaking generically, is well on the way to being accountable.

Your key accountability, ultimately, is to the mission founders (upon whose vision the organization received approval to exist as a charity) and the present and potential donors. These stakeholders and their requirements are the boundaries structuring your provision of accountability-related information. In developing your reports, consider two things:

1. What information evidences fidelity to and achievement of the original (or revised) mission? If the mission changed, how did the change mesh with the original vision of the founders? Data to include:
   • Program effectiveness
   • Program efficiency
   • Program controls (including financial)
   • Program resource commitment
      In each category, pick one or two key indicators of each area so as not to overwhelm your audience.
2. Are donors' desires being honored? Donors want all of the items just listed, but also want to know:
   • What is your primary financial objective, and how are you doing in reaching it?
   • If you budget for other than break-even, why? Did you make budget this year? If not, why not?
   • How are you rated by CBBB, NCIB, AIP, Philanthropic Research, Inc., etc., and if any of these bodies identifies a "problem area" how are you addressing it (or if you do not see it as a problem, why not)?
   • Designated funds spent as directed
   • Waste eliminated
   • A process of continual improvement (which usually means you admit some areas of weakness)
   • Entrepreneurial and creative initiatives to find new resources and better use existing ones
   • More and better information about your fundraising function:
      • Some key ratios
      • The philosophy and how it was honored
      • Integrity first, last, and in between
      • Evidence that you are not overly dependent on one source of funds, particularly if that source is "expensive" (in terms of costs and in terms of diverting attention from other, preferable sources of funds)

This brief outline gives some ideals that informed donors might hold. They would be delighted to get all of this information, but would not be surprised that you did not provide all of it because at times you do not have the data (yet, anyway) and you realize you don't want to overload them. So parcel the information out over time in your various communications. Perhaps most important is that your attention to detail and to staying in touch shows a professional, dedicated, and informed management approach.

had recruited CFOs from the corporate sector who had radically redesigned financial policies and reporting. Both brought an emphasis on financial control and financial reporting that is rarely seen in
nonprofits. Maybe the situation at your organization is not severe,
but turnaround management is just a special case of transforma-
tional leadership that every organization can adopt. Remember:
the process of continuous improvement is the path to take you to
proficient financial management.

(i) Church of the Brethren.   The Church of the Brethren, in
Elgin, Illinois, had hired their top financial manager from the Day-
ton Press newspaper. Darryl Deardorff, CPA, who was CFO at the
time of the study, had inherited a situation that was almost out of
control. The previous CFO had totally given up on a deteriorating
financial situation, in which expenses consistently outstripped revenues. The first thing Darryl accomplished was convincing the top
management and board of the necessity to maintain a balanced or
surplus budget. Although it took awhile to persuade them, with
the assistance of reports he prepared portrayed the seriousness of
the situation. Then, on an ongoing basis, he used periodic actual-
versus-budget reports to monitor progress toward meeting the
budget goal. In this way, the Church of the Brethren avoided a
much more serious crisis that would have jeopardized the survival
of the headquarters operation and shaken the confidence of members worldwide.

(ii) Church of God Missionary Board (Anderson, IN).   The
transformation at the Church of God Missionary Board is not any
less impressive. The Board had been running deficits for a number
of years, with no sign of improvement. Darryl Smith worked in the
chemical industry for 26 years with various organizations, and at
the time he was recruited by a Church of God board member was
plant controller for Mobay Chemical. Smith, a Certified Management Accountant, had college training in finance and sociology
and an MBA in finance. The competitive, profit-oriented focus on
the chemical industry turned out to be instrumental for Smith
in his work at the Church of God. In our interview with him, he
recounted the relative overemphasis on mission, to the exclusion of
financial affairs, at the time he came to the Missionary Board:

> Q: Why did you pick financial break-even your primary finan-
> cial objective?
>
> A: I think the past has reflected a very difficult financial direc-
> tion for the board because the primary focus has been to maxi-
> mize the ministry opportunities and then to determine methods

of financing those. I think what is happening now with the organization is that we are saying, "Wait a minute, let's not only
maximize our ministry but let's also be able to finance that ministry to a point of break-even." One of the things we don't want
to do is to have a whole bunch of money sitting here to draw interest off of. That's not one of the board's directives. They're
saying we can break even, which means that we are maximizing the use of our resources for the ministry, for the needs of the
people around the world. So, I believe break-even would be the
primary objective.

Interestingly, in the four years Darryl had been in the CFO
position, he still had not seen the achievement of break-even, but
he felt confident that in one or two years the organization would be
there. The moral of the story: be patient in implementing change.
Furthermore, there must be "buy-in" to the mission by the CFO
and other financial professionals. The CEO and board must be assured that the CFO is not in a mindless "shut-the-door" mode. We
will return to this issue in two later sections of this chapter. Having
concluded the main objectives of financial reporting, we will now
comment briefly on reporting system design and then survey the
main financial reports and their frequency.

6.4 REPORTING SYSTEM DESIGN

For those organizations considering reporting system redesign,
here are several developmental principles:

1. Keep the end users in mind, and consider their technical knowledge and time constraints.
2. The accounting system must provide needed data, or revise it.
3. Management information must be provided on an accurate and
   timely basis.
4. Provide two cuts: program-by-program detail and natural expense elements (e.g., salaries in total).
5. Be able to get data *out of* accounting system and other databases
   into financial spreadsheet.
6. Very important: the finance director or board treasurer must be
   able to get liquidity detail and, it is hoped, "almost automatic,"
   if naïve, projection of future liquidity position.

6.5 MAJOR REPORTS

When most people think of nonprofit financial reports, they picture
the statement of activity, the statement of net assets (also known as

the balance sheet or statement of financial position), and the statement of cash flows. Donors may think of the Form 990 submitted to the IRS. These reports do double duty as internal and external users find them helpful for understanding the organization's financial position and how it has changed during the year, as well as the ability to cover costs from all funding sources. However, our focus here is primarily managerial: we emphasize the internal reports that management decisions will be based on. That requires that we talk about variance analysis, in which actual revenues and expenses are compared to budgeted amounts, and corrective action taken when necessary. The next sections are laid out as follows: we begin with internal reports, looking at the annual reports first, then quarterly, monthly, and daily reports that organizations might use. Within that discussion we talk about the CFO's involvement in overseeing fundraising evaluation. Then, we turn to external reports, mentioning these only briefly. Finally, we get into the core of proficient financial management: managing off of the budget and the reports we are learning about in this chapter.

6.6 INTERNAL REPORTS

Because your chief concern should be with management reports, we start with the internal reports. Even small organizations may develop budgets and should do some annual budget comparisons at a minimum. We will start, then, with some of the annual reports you should prepare for the top management team and for the board. We include financial ratios and fundraising evaluation in our annual reporting framework. Then, we move to quarterly reports, monthly reports, and daily reports. Finally, in our internal reporting framework, we turn to the financial management process that we call "managing off of the budget." There our focus is how the manager actually uses the financial ratios and budget variances to trigger organizational responses when the budget situation shows a deteriorating financial picture.

(a) Annual

To set up our annual reporting commentary, study Exhibit 6.4, "Financial Reporting Pyramid." Even the smallest organization should cover the base-level responsibilities, which involve a commentary and possibly graphs explaining why the actual revenues and expenses came in at the levels they did. Included here are highlights of significant dollar and/or percentage differences for the various revenue and expense items. Cause-and-effect discussion is vital, in order that the user can assess the likelihood of recurrence for good

Exhibit 6.4. Financial Reporting Pyramid

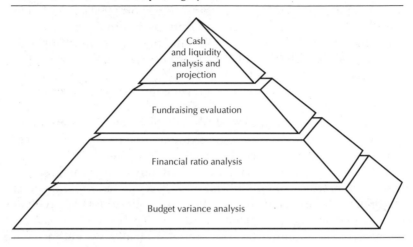

news and bad news. Staff resources and time permitting, then move to the second level of the pyramid, which involves financial ratio analysis. Included here are basic looks at net revenue, liquidity, borrowing, and degree of dependence on funding sources. If this is being done, you are ready for financial input into the fund-raising process, in which you assist and provide accountability to the development office. Finally, and very important for demonstrating the highest level of financial proficiency, conduct refined cash and liquidity analysis. Very few nonprofit organizations have gotten very far with level 3 fundraising evaluation, much less the refined, sophisticated analysis represented by level four. We should also mention here that you have two separate but overlapping audiences: the top management team (other than the CFO) and the board of directors. How will your presentation differ? Show more detail for the top management presentation, but present the cause-and-effect discussion to the board as well. If yours is more than a policy-making board, such as in the case of local rescue missions, share much of the information that goes to the CEO.

Level 1: Budget Variance Analysis

First in importance for managerial usefulness is the budget variance analysis (BVA) report. Typically, the BVA is associated only with the operating budget (see Chapter 5), and we begin our discussion with that budget.

(i) Operating Budget. As we discuss later, this process has been ongoing on a monthly basis during the year, so there should be few surprises at year-end. Variances are the difference between

actual (what happened) and budgeted (what was expected). A variance is a symptom that may be linked to many different problems, some more severe than others. Being alerted to ongoing or emerging *significant* problems enables the manager to initiate corrective action. Sometimes, the cause of the variance implies an obvious correction: uncollected pledges receivable suggests more and firmer follow-up contacts and better front-end donor education. Other times the variance springs from uncontrollable factors, such as a change in exchange rates that was not hedged against or a drop in interest rates earned on cash reserves, and the organization will have to make offsetting adjustments in controllable areas. Of course, information from this year's results feeds back into new budget development even before the year is closed. Generally, the variance reports should conform to the following checklist (Exhibit 6.5), with some pointers applying to monthly variance reports and others applying to weekly, monthly, or annual variance reports.

In some organizations, the budget development and variance analysis processes are highly political. What can be done to eliminate political conflict? Five precautions, some of which must be

Exhibit 6.5. Variance Report Checklist

- Weekly or daily variance reports should be prepared for selected items over which management has control and that are vital to the success of the organization. Waiting until month-end is sometimes too late. For example, radio and TV stations conducting telethons give constantly updated totals for management use and for prompting donor response.
- Show month's variance (both % and $) to the left of the revenue line item, and the year-to-date or full-year variance to the right of the account information. A brief explanation can be included to the right of the tabulated variances if space permits; otherwise provide the information below the table.
- Implement management-by-exception by highlighting variances that pass threshold tests—say, greater than 10 percent of the budgeted amount or greater than $500.
- Highlight positive variances as well as negative ones. Usually, show unfavorable variance numbers (lower revenue or higher expense amounts) within brackets; favorable variances should not be bracketed.
- Include in the written explanations not only variance cause(s), but also what will be done to correct the problem.
- Show enough detail so that offsetting variances within an expense category do not disguise underlying problems. For example, if donations is shown only in total, a mail campaign positive variance may be offset by a negative variance on face-to-face fundraising, and no corrective action gets triggered for the latter.
- Highlight controllable items for special management attention.
- Recognize that a variance may signal a faulty budget or a change in the environment, which should trigger the development of a revised budget to guide the remainder of the fiscal year.

taken at the time the departmental or program budgets are developed; are helpful:

1. Have final budgets prepared by a cross-departmental committee, and then have everyone affected by the budgets review them.
2. Have the manager that prepared the budget explain the variance. Whoever oversees the reporting process should make sure actuals are not "massaged" to hit budgeted amounts.
3. Include and retain budget development assumptions in the final budget documentation.
4. Do not blame departments or individuals for variances, but focus attention on positive ideas for reversing the problems.
5. Find the causes of the variances, and to the extent they are linked to a faulty budget, ensure that the next budget that is developed is done on a more accurate basis. Also, instead of blaming someone for the inaccurate budget, develop a revised budget. Some organizations persist in estimating expenses and then writing down a revenue figure to match total expenses. This makes revenue variance analysis almost useless—unless the organization sets within-year targets that serve as control points if and when the revenue forecast is not realized.[5]

We will return to the specifics of presentation format and what generic actions your organization can take if revenues are below budget, or expenses are running above budget in our section on "managing off of the budget."

(ii) Capital Budget. The capital budget was presented in Chapter 4. Compile a summary report at year-end to show what projects were totally or partly implemented during the year. Compare that to the capital budget(s) approved in the past year(s). Post-audit the actual project expenditures, by project, to find out if they matched anticipated amounts and if not, why not. This will greatly help your organization in future capital project analyses.

(iii) Cash Budget. The cash budget preparation was demonstrated in Chapter 5. How is it be used to do after-the-fact analysis? Quite simply, to check the accuracy of your year-earlier forecast and see if seasonal or trend patterns emerge in the actual cash flows that occurred. Determine in which months your forecast was furthest off, and why. Use that information to guide your development of next year's cash budget. Of chief importance, should the

---

[5]Michael C. Thomsett, *The Little Black Book of Budgets and Forecasts* (New York: AMACOM, 1988).

target liquidity be adjusted based on the past year variance? Let's consider the two cases of positive and negative variances in the net cash flow, which we define as:

Net cash flow = cash receipts − cash disbursements

Case 1: Net cash flow comes in above budget. In this case, the cash position is growing, unless the trend was spotted during the year and additional expenses incurred or assets purchased. Possibly, the liquidity target should be adjusted downward, but whether you do so depends on several considerations. Illustrating, some of the factors you should look at are:

- If the trend is temporary and is about to be reversed (possibly because of special factors such as one-time undesignated gifts to the organization) do not change the liquidity target, because your cash position will return to its normal level in the near future.
- If some of the cash receipts were simply proceeds from borrowing,[6] the amount will be repaid, bringing the cash position back to its normal level.
- If the trend is permanent, and you do not anticipate increasing service provision, you may reduce the amount of liquidity because you have a level of operations that brings in revenues more than covering expenses.
- If you are not sure as to the cause or permanence of the change, gain interest income and retain flexibility by parking some of the cash buildup in longer-term securities, say with one-year or two-year maturities, making sure to choose those that are readily marketable.
- If your organization is growing rapidly, sit tight with the higher level of liquidity until you have a better idea of how much liquidity you need.

Case 2: Net cash flow comes in below budget. In this case, cash expenses are outstripping cash revenues, and you have less cash at the end of the year than you originally anticipated. Possibly, you went out and borrowed some money to meet the shortfall. To the extent possible, you will probably want to rebuild the drained cash reserves. Recognize now that you will need to discuss increased

---

[6]This should not be the case if you followed the recommended format in Chapter 5. In that format, each month gives a cash surplus (if positive) or cash shortage (if negative), with the cash shortage reflecting the *cumulative shortfall* and therefore the borrowed balance at that point in time. So the loan amount does not appear in cash receipts at all.

fundraising activity to meet that target. In some cases, taking the flip side of the list we just looked at, the change is temporary, and possibly self-correcting. More often than not, nonprofit executives and board members blithely assume that such events are self-correcting, but you should take the change seriously. It may be that your organization is heading for chronic deficits and a rapidly eroding cash position. Your organization may also need to change its programming, if fees are part of the revenue base, or engage in earned income ventures to supplement donations. If your organization is growing rapidly, the problem is compounded, because quite often funds are disbursed to finance the growth before the donor base responds to the increased outreach. You will gain additional ideas as we work through Levels 2, 3, and 4 of the annual financial reporting pyramid.

(iv) Supplemental Report: Deferred Giving.   Has the organization ever done a complete report on the status and revised projections of deferred gifts? If not, it's time to start, and your office can give input to the development office, or to the projection in your shop. The idea is to bring all funding sources into the picture as you evaluate the significance of your just-completed budget year. As we did with capital projects, compare gifts received with gifts projected. Recognize that bequests are about the most difficult item to project in the entire spectrum of forecasts, except in the case where an estate is almost settled and you have some basis upon which to project a remittance.

Recap of Level 1 Budget Comparisons.   The budget variance analysis you do is extremely important. Too many organizations either (1) do not conduct these comparisons, or (2) seize upon an asserted explanation, but then do nothing to correct important deficiencies or to build upon unexpected success. Work hard at improving your analysis and the clarity of presentation to the executive team and to the board.

(c) Level 2: Annual Financial Statements and Ratios

We ordinarily think of the annual financial statements as being prepared for external users. However, there are useful insights to be gleaned from them beyond what you found with the budget variance analysis. First, there are comparisons that can be made with the statements themselves or with a restatement of them ("common-size statements"). Second, there are financial ratios that can be calculated from them that will give added insight. Let's begin by looking at the statements themselves and their restatement.

(i) Statements of Activity, Financial Position, and Cash Flows.   The Statement of Activity shows us the degree of cost cov-

erage of the organization's operations during a certain time period. We are interested in the degree to which all costs are covered. If costs are not covered, we find out the shortfall (deficit), and if they are more than covered, the surplus is identified. We want to know whether this was a planned or unplanned outcome, and if unplanned, the reason(s) for the deficit or surplus. Beyond this, we would like to compare this year's results to those of recent years, and we would also prefer to know what percent of revenue is attributable to each cost element. The way to do this is with a "common-size statement of activity." Using the basic functional expense example in Exhibit 6.6, we can readily see how this is done. Simply divide each expense amount by total revenue.

Not only does this reveal the program, management, and fundraising ratios that are closely watched by philanthropic bureaus, but it gives us an idea of relative magnitude for our expenses and can be monitored from year to year and from quarter to quarter.

The Statement of Financial Position (also called the Statement of Net Assets, or Balance Sheet) shows us items owned or over which our organization has control and how they are financed. To the extent we use borrowed funds to finance assets, we are in a riskier position due to the necessity to pay interest and ultimately repay principal. The use of past surpluses reduces risk because this amount represents permanent financing that does not have to be repaid. We will return to these issues in Chapter 10 on liability management. Once again, as we did with the Statement of Activity, we will also prepare a "common-size statement of financial position" to see the relative magnitude of each asset item (divide each line item by the total assets dollar amount) and for each liability or net asset item (again dividing each item by total assets). Compare the percentages over several years to see the trends affecting your organization. Especially note an increasingly reliance on borrowed funds.

The Statement of Cash Flows is still not well understood by most nonprofit managers or board members. It shows how cash was received to support operations, how cash was disbursed to provide programs, and it reconciles the change in cash on the Statement of Financial Position. In our view, it is probably the

Exhibit 6.6.   Common-Size Statement of Activity

Item	Dollar Amount	Percent
Revenue	$450,000	100
Program expense	300,000	66.7
Management and general expense	85,000	18.9
Fund-raising expense	50,000	11.1
Surplus/(Deficit)	$15,000	3.33

most valuable of the three statements for *showing how target liquidity will meet.* Because that is the primary financial objective of the proficient organization, we will want to tap into the usefulness of this statement. Once again, we look at the line items by themselves to observe the big dollar amounts. Beyond that, we look (1) at the sign of each of the three categories (operating, investing, financing), and (2) the operating cash flow dollar amount relative to the investing dollar amount and relative to the financing dollar amount.

If the sign of the operating cash flows is negative, your operations have reduced your cash and liquidity during the year (recall the similar comments we had about the cash budget analysis made at year-end). To meet the reduction, either your organization drained cash and cash equivalents (which you will see at the bottom of the Statement of Cash Flows) or it funded this amount by selling assets (literally liquidating part of the organization's asset base) or taking on additional financing. None of the three mechanisms for covering operating cash deficits is sustainable. Take the negative operating cash flow very seriously if you have one. Be vigilant to eliminate this situation immediately.

Looking at the operating cash flow dollar amount relative to the investing or financing cash flow can also be instructive. A brief discussion will show what we mean. Let's assume that the operating cash flow is zero or positive. If zero, your operations "broke even" on a cash basis. If positive, you will want to compare the operating cash flow to the investing cash flow (simply divide the $ operating cash flow by the $ investing cash flow). For a healthy business, this generally results in a positive numerator divided by a negative denominator, as the growing business uses some of its surplus cash from operations to finance growth in plant and equipment investments. If such is the case for your organization, you might have this situation:

OCF $50
ICF −$25
OCF/ICF = $50 / −$25 = −2.0

What this means is that you generated enough cash to cover the investing needs twice over. We can do a similar analysis by comparing operating cash flow to financing cash flow. Temporary uses of financing to fund deficits is acceptable, which might result in the following situation:

OCF −$25
FCF $25
OCF/FCF = −1.0

The ratio value of -1.0 tells us that the operating cash out-flow was just covered by a financing cash inflow. One year or per-haps two years of this pattern might be acceptable, but we would not want this pattern to persist because we are experiencing ever-greater reliance on restricted gifts (that cannot be tapped to meet cash crisis needs) and/or borrowed money.[7]

(ii) Financial Ratio Analysis. Financial ratios are relative measures of an organization's financial position. We compute a fi-nancial ratio by taking an amount from the statement of activity or statement of financial position and dividing it by a different amount from either of those two statements. Ratios are useful for seeing (1) where our organization has been over time, financially, (2) the financial strength it has at this point in time, and (3) how it com-pares to other organizations in the same industry of the same ap-proximate size. Despite their value, only four of ten organizations use ratios as part of their financial management process (Lilly study). We present basic ratios below. If you've never computed ra-tios before, start with these ratios and work with them until you and your management team and board are comfortable with them.

We will primarily use the set of ratios highlighted by Robin-son (1989), because there are comparison standards presented for those ratios.[8] Robinson focused on a set that includes 11 ratios and one level (dollar amount) measure. To that we will add a target liq-uidity level measure. The basic ratios fall into three categories: liq-uidity, funding, and operating. One of the difficulties in the non-profit sector is the absence of industry standards (average values for other organizations serving the same clientele as your organiza-tion). Robinson calculated standards for faith-based organizations spanning organizations from churches to radio/TV stations, social welfare organizations, colleges and private secondary schools, as-sociations, and camps and conference centers. Arts and health care organizations are advised to check with their trade association or one of the Big Four accounting firms or private debt rating organi-zations in order to get comparative data. Failing that, develop a network with five or six organizations similar to your own and de-velop your own comparative data and standards.

Liquidity ratios. The basic liquidity ratios are cash ratio, cash reserve ratio, current ratio, asset ratio, and target liquidity level.

---

[7]The exception here is the case in which equity is issued for a for-profit subsidiary, which shows up as a financing flow for the consolidated organization.
[8]We advise the interested reader to acquire a copy of this study of 479 audited fi-nancial statements because of its careful study of ratios and their value. The study is available at cost from: Chris Robinson, Controller/Partners International/1470 N. Fourth St./San Jose, CA 95112. An executive summary is available without charge.

Maintaining liquidity is crucial for your organization, because cash is the lifeblood of your organization's finances. Running a donative nonprofit is especially risky, in that you are basically raising your financing from ground zero each and every year. Having liquid resources helps you bridge the dry seasons and to give some breathing room when your fund-raising shows year-over-year declines. These resources also provide the fuel for program expansions and provision of emergency needs such as natural disaster relief aid, one-time or short-term opportunities, and acquisitions or strategic alliances. Each measure we will look at gives us a slightly different perspective on the spendable funds of the organization.

$$\text{Cash ratio} = \frac{\text{cash and cash equivalents}}{\text{current liabilities}}$$

$$\text{Cash reserve ratio} = \frac{\text{cash and cash equivalents}}{\text{total annual expenses}}$$

$$\text{Current ratio} = \frac{\text{current assets}}{\text{current liabilities}}$$

$$\text{Asset ratio} = \frac{\text{current assets}}{\text{total assets}}$$

$$\text{Target liquidity level} = \text{cash and cash equivalents} \\ + \text{short-term investments} \\ - \text{short-term loans}$$

Cash ratio.   The cash ratio shows us the organization's coverage of near-term financial obligations with its cash and near-cash investments. The typical financial obligations are accounts payable, accrued interest, wages, salaries, possibly taxes, and principal repayments due within one year. We usually interpret a ratio value by expressing it per unit of whatever item is in the denominator. For example, if the ratio value is 2.0, and both numerator (let's say, cash and cash equivalents) and denominator (say, current liabilities) are in dollars, we interpret the ratio as $2 of current assets per $1 of current liabilities. Overall, Robinson found organizations had a ratio of about 1.4; this implies that every $1 of near-term obligations were covered by $1.40 of cash or near-cash investments, which is quite good. The mean (average) and median (midpoint value, with one-half of the organizations having values above or below it) were quite different for some industry groups, however: medians ranged from 0.72 for schools and colleges to 2.41 for foreign missions and social/medical agencies. Recognize that your organization is giving something up by having more money in the cash and cash equivalent category. Interest rates on cash (most of this would be in interest-bearing checking accounts) and on cash equivalents (investments purchased with original maturities of three months or less, which would include some Treasury bills, commercial paper, money market mutual funds, and certificates of deposit) are normally lower than on one-year Treasury bills or two-year Treasury notes. This is one reason not to have too much of your liquidity in cash and cash equivalents, and also the reason our target liquidity level will include all short-term investments.

Cash reserve ratio. The cash reserve ratio uses the same numerator as the cash ratio, cash and cash equivalents, but compares it to a year's worth of operating expenses instead of what liabilities happen to be listed as current at this moment of time. Not only does it avert seasonality of liabilities (you may be measuring liabilities at a low point in the year), but it provides a "time to ruin" measure for the organization. It tells us how long the organization could meet operating expenses if revenues were totally shut off and is expressed as a fraction of a year. For example, a ratio value of 0.75 tells me that my organization can operate for 9 months without additional revenues. A very conservative measure of liquidity is provided by this measure, but the key point is that it is giving me another perspective on my organization's liquidity. One organization can compare its figure to past values and to other similar organizations. The median ratio across the groups studied by Robinson was 0.09, which implies that these organizations could last only 33 days (.09 × 365 days) if their revenues were cut off. From this vantage, liquidity is very poor. Only professional associations (0.19, or 69 days) had a median ratio value above 0.13 (47 days). Again, while we would not expect a complete shutdown of the revenue stream, we have evidence here of relatively low levels of liquidity. While you may not experience any month in the year in which you receive *no* revenues, there are months when the donations trickle in, and your organization is plunged into a cash crisis because of the low level of cash as compared to daily expenses. Measure expenses on a cash basis when doing this calculation.

Current ratio. The current ratio measures the coverage of near-term obligations, again, but with a broader measure of "ability to pay." This ratio includes near-term pledges receivable, accounts receivable, inventories, and prepaid expenses in the numerator. The ratio is not as conservative as the cash ratio, but more correctly matches up near-term obligations with the resources that will be available to meet those obligations. The overall average was 4.08, but the overall median value was 3.09 (some high numbers

skewed the average). This means the average organization had between $3 and $4 of cash and other liquid resources with which to
pay its obligations coming due within the next year. Again, this is a
positive sign of strong liquidity. We would want to compare our organization's current ratio against other organizations of the same
type and approximately the same size. The sector is important
here: Church median current ratio was 0.97 but denominations/
denominational groups had a median value of 10.85. Most nonprofit sectors studied had medians of 2 or 3, which corresponds
closely with what we see in business enterprises. A value of 2 or
above is generally thought to signal adequate liquidity in industry.
The very large value for denominations is partly linked to inventory held for churches and outreach ministries, but it also reflects
the pooling of liquid assets as funds are "upstreamed" from member congregations. These funds are held longer than they should
be, in some cases, prior to being disbursed or invested in pensions
or buildings. If funds are being held on a semipermanent basis,
they should be invested in longer-term investments, which are not
accounted for as current assets.

Asset ratio. The asset ratio is not only a liquidity ratio but an
investment strategy ratio as well. It looks at the asset investment as
a whole, and asks what percent of the pie is placed in near-term assets. To the extent that more of the assets are placed in the current
items (cash and cash equivalents, accounts receivable, inventories,
short-term investments, prepaid expenses, contributions receivable), they are nearer to cash; therefore, the organization is more
liquid. Less current assets implies greater long-term assets, such as
plant and equipment or pension assets. These cannot be readily
turned into cash to pay bills that come due or to meet unexpected
emergencies. Beyond the liquidity aspects, though, lies the investment strategy element. As we said a moment ago, short-term investments are sometimes made when longer-term investments are
more appropriate. The organization substitutes liquidity for operating net revenue enhancement linked to the higher interest rates
of the longer-term investments. Furthermore, plant and equipment
can often be rented out or used otherwise to generate earned income that might far exceed the low interest rates paid on interest-
bearing checking accounts or near-term investments. The overall
mean and median were about 0.35, meaning that 35 percent of the
assets of sampled organizations were in the current category, with
the remainder of 65 percent in long-term assets. Again, the sector
matters greatly: churches had a median current asset investment of
only 6 percent and camps and conference centers only 14 percent,
while foreign missions had 51 percent, denominations had 62 percent, and professional associations had 78 percent in short-term as-

sets. The higher values signal greater capital intensity, typically bringing with them higher fixed operating costs and higher debt levels to finance those long-term assets.

Target liquidity level.   The target liquidity level shows us whether we have reached our goal for liquid resources, and may be measured in several ways. Our formula (cash and cash equivalents + short-term investments − short-term loans) is one way of measuring the target liquidity level. An alternate formula would include only the first two terms, leaving short-term loans as one of several ways of providing the liquidity desired. The reason we prefer our approach is that it shows us how much liquidity we have after paying back arranged financing. Let's say that when your liquidity falls short of its target level, you use short-term loans to increase the liquidity—would the two measures give the same number when the amount of arranged financing is held in cash or short-term securities? Let's assume your desired target liquidity level is $300,000, but at present you have $175,000 in cash and cash equivalents, $50,000 in short-term securities, and no short-term loans. If your organization takes a loan out for the $75,000 needed to get liquidity (cash and securities) up to $300,000. Calculating our formula and the alternate measure, we get a different result:

Our measure: Target liquidity level = $175,000 + $50,000
+ $75,000 addition
− $75,000 loan
= $225,000

According to our measure, liquidity has not really increased, because the increase is not permanent. The loan (and interest) will have to be repaid. Short-term borrowing may be fine to provide for *temporary* needs, such as a seasonal buildup in inventories or receivables, but should not be a source of permanent liquidity financing.

Alternate measure: Target liquidity level = $175,000 + $50,000
+ $75,000 addition
= $300,000

According to this alternate measure, liquidity has increased to the organization's predetermined target level. It will have to plan carefully to have enough funds to pay back the loan at maturity, or if it is a credit line, during the bank's "clean-up period," when it must pay the loan down to zero.

For many nonprofit organizations, the two measures would give the same reading because their financial policy is to use no short-term debt. Two-thirds of the organizations in the Lilly study never do any short-term borrowing, and only one in eight have short-term loans each year. If you plug a value of $0 in for short-term loans in our formula, you get the same result as you would with the alternate formula. We will provide more detail on evaluating liquidity when we get to the Level 4 analysis, and we address short-term borrowing do's and don'ts in the liability management chapter (see Chapter 10).

Funding ratios.   The second group of ratios are the funding ratios. This group includes a ratio that indicates the dependence on donated funds (contribution ratio) as well as one that measures the degree to which we use borrowed money to finance assets (debt ratio). Risk is the central focus here. First, using the contribution ratio, how "donation dependent" are we for each year's expenses? Second, based on the debt ratio, are our assets in place funded with borrowed money, which has to be paid back with interest, or net assets which are permanent contributions or earned income retained in the organization? The greater the value of either number, the more risk we have in the organization's structure. In the corporate sector, the first measure would be called operating risk or business risk, and the second measure would be labeled financial risk.

$$\text{Contribution ratio} = \frac{\text{total contributed revenue}}{\text{total revenue}}$$

$$\text{Debt ratio} = \frac{\text{total liabilities}}{\text{total assets}}$$

Contribution ratio.   The median value for the contribution ratio in the Robinson study was 0.84. Fully 84 percent of total revenues were from donated funds, showing a heavy reliance on such funds. Projections of donations drive the financial planning process for these organizations. If donations are expected to taper off, the organization must move quickly to replace the lost funds or face a financial crisis. Schools/colleges and camps/conference centers were the least reliant on donations, with median values of 0.28 and 0.37, respectively. This makes sense given that they can charge for their services. Churches, foreign mission agencies, and social and welfare agencies all had ratios of around 0.90 or above, showing extreme reliance on donated funds. Fund-raising is obviously very critical for these organizations, and we emphasize in the Level 3 discussion below the vitality of having the CFO involved in the fundraising management and evaluation process. Another category of funding that is considered "soft money" is grants. A high degree of reliance on grants also places the organization at risk.

Debt ratio. The median value for the debt ratio across all organizations was 0.24. This indicates that about one-fourth of all assets are funded by borrowed funds. As you would expect, the sector again has much to do with the debt usage: social/medical agencies, camps/conference centers, foreign mission agencies, domestic missions (such as homeless shelters), and schools/colleges all had ratios of 0.17–0.25; publishers and radio/TV organizations had ratio values in the mid-thirties, and churches and denominations had ratios of 0.47. Consider the longer-term asset investment in plant and equipment, which drives the long-term mortgage loans that figure largely in these results. Asset intensity turns into financial leverage risk as the long-term fixed assets are financed with borrowed funds. The borrowing puts a strain on the organization as it has to pay interest and repay principal. We return to this subject in Chapter 10 on liability management.

Operating ratios. Our final category of ratios is a set of six operating ratios. We want to assess the cost coverage, expense composition, and "return on investment" in our operations. We use the return ratio, the net operating ratio, the fund balance reserve ratio, the program expense ratio, the support service expense ratio, and the net surplus level.

$$\text{Return ratio} = \frac{\text{total revenue}}{\text{total assets}}$$

$$\text{Net surplus} = \text{total revenues} - \text{total expenses}$$

$$\text{Net operating ratio} = \frac{\text{net surplus}}{\text{total revenue}}$$

$$\text{Fund balance reserve ratio} = \frac{\text{fund balance}}{\text{total expenses}}$$

$$\text{Program expense ratio} = \frac{\text{program expenses}}{\text{total expenses}}$$

$$\text{Support service expense ratio} = \frac{\text{support service expenses}}{\text{total expenses}}$$

Return ratio. The return ratio is generally considered to be an efficiency measure. Efficiency here is not in the sense of being cost-effective, but in bringing in funds. In a business, it is called "total asset turnover" because it shows how often the investment in total assets "turn over" into sales. For nonprofits, we are measuring the ability of an organization to generate or raise revenue from its asset base. In another sense, it is a "return on investment," where the return is revenues flowing into the organization each year per dollar invested in assets. Another way to view it is a size-adjusted measure of revenue-generating ability, because organizations of different sizes (asset bases) will all be measured on a "per dollar of assets" basis. If the ratio value is 1.25, the organization receives $1.25 in revenue per $1 invested in assets. For donative organizations, you are largely measuring the efficiency of the fundraising function. For schools or health care organizations, you are mainly gauging the efficiency of earned income ventures. In any case, you are also measuring asset intensity—an organization with little fixed asset investment will tend to have a higher ratio. We again emphasize: measure yourself against similar organizations or against your own past values. The median value was 1.34, but here this disguises a great deal of variability. Schools/colleges (0.5), camps/conference centers (0.68), and churches (0.65) were at the low end, and domestic missions (1.99), professional associations (2.38), and foreign missions (2.8) were considerably higher. For further comparison, for the 128 varied nonprofit organizations registered with the State of Oregon in 1993, the average return ratio was 0.89 (1993 fiscal year data, Oregon Department of Justice).

Net Surplus. Net surplus is the "profit" on operations for a given period. For a business, profit is a primary measure of effectiveness and success. Nonprofits don't like to talk about profit, so they call it net revenue. How does the manager view it? As the relative cost coverage by revenues for the period. If positive, then revenues more than covered costs. If zero, the revenues just covered cost, a situation most call "financial break-even." Recall from our Chapter 2 discussion that most respondents in the Lilly study selected this as their primary financial objective, even though we advocate target liquidity level as a better objective, and one that is practiced by the best-managed organizations. Obviously, a negative value suggests that in this period the revenues did not cover costs. The key question to ask: was it planned? If so, no problem. If not, we have to go back to the BVA to find out why not and how to avoid the situation next year. Robinson's data indicate that regardless of espoused objectives, most nonprofits were running surpluses. The median was $16,000, with only one subgroup (professional associations) running a deficit (median loss of $3,000). On the low end of the remainder of the organizations running surpluses were publishers and radio/TV ($2,000), domestic missions ($5,000), foreign missions ($10,000), and churches ($16,000). At the high end, again using median values, were social/medical ($34,000), camps/conference centers ($40,000), denominations ($46,000), and schools/colleges ($75,000). Because many organizations do raise money in advance of planned expansion or to build up to the target liquidity level, running surpluses in some periods may simply show good managerial foresight. On the other hand, persistent surpluses by a no-growth organization may reflect hoarding and inadequate provision of much needed services. Finally, at the time of Robinson's study many organizations were not depreciating assets, and surpluses would be in some cases deficits were restatements made. Yale University became famous for its inability to properly plan for renewal of its crumbling infrastructure, and we again urge you to put into practice the strategic and long-range financial planning tools presented in Chapter 4.

Net operating ratio.   The net operating ratio gives us the same information as the net surplus, except in relative terms. Its analog in business is the net profit margin. For an organization pricing its services, such as schools/colleges and camps/conference centers, we get insight into pricing and its degree of cost coverage. For all organizations, it gives cost coverage feedback as scaled to the total revenue. Again, as we saw with the return ratio, you can view the denominator as a scaling factor to put different-sized organizations on an equal footing. Surplus or deficit is expressed per dollar of revenue. The overall median was 0.02 (a 2 percent surplus), with the same relative ranking as we saw with the net surplus. The differences, though, are not nearly as great. The highest values were achieved by camps/conference centers at 0.05 (5 percent). Schools and colleges (0.03) and social/medical agencies (0.03) are next in line. The "profits" reported above appear to be much more modest when scaled by revenue.

Fund balance ratio.   The fund balance reserve ratio is very similar to the cash reserve ratio we discussed in the liquidity section. The difference is that we are looking at what would be similar to equity in a business, and asking how it compares relative to total yearly expenses. We're not thinking that we would "liquidate" net assets to pay a year's expenses, but instead are wondering how much of a cushion of permanent financing we have built up relative to annual expenses. From the flip side, a combined view of the cash reserve ratio and the fund balance reserve ratio provides us with another view of operating risk. The larger the cash reserve ratio and the fund balance reserve ratio, the less risky the operating posture of the organization. The overall median here was 0.49, meaning one-half a year's expenses are built up as permanent, non-interest-bearing financing. At the low end are professional associations (0.27), domestic and foreign missions (0.34), and publishers (0.35); at the high end we find camps/conference centers (1.24) and schools/colleges (1.27). Robinson (1988, pg. 83) points out that the latter organizations may hold these fund balances in liquid form for capital renovation and construction.

Program expense ratio and support service expense ratio. Program expense ratio and the next ratio, support service expense ratio, show the split of expenses into program and the sum of management/general and fund-raising. We are asking if most of our annual expenses are program-related or is too much of our resource allocation going to "overhead" activities that are necessary but are not providing services to our clientele. Recognizing the arbitrariness of accounting allocations, we still have a valuable indicator when comparing to prior year values, and possibly when comparing to other organizations using similar accounting practices. The overall median is 75 percent for program expenses and 25 percent for support services. The highest program amounts were denominations (81 percent) and foreign missions (79 percent); the lowest were camps/conference centers (71 percent) and social/medical (73 percent). Camps and conference centers battle the limited-year phenomenon, in which they generally receive revenues and provide programs for only part of the year, and yet have administrative and fund-raising expenses pretty much year-around. For reference purposes, for the 128 varied nonprofits registered in Oregon (1993 Oregon Department of Justice figures), the median organization had a program expense ratio of 78.2 percent, with a median management/general expense ratio of 9.5 percent, and a median fund-raising expense ratio of 12.3 percent (making the median support service expense ratio 21.8 percent). Be aware that you may get positive or negative publicity based on your ratios for these categories. *Money Magazine* annually ranks the 100 largest charities in the United States according to program expense ratio, from largest to smallest, and labels the organization with the highest program expense ratio as the "nation's most efficient charity."

As we bring our discussion of ratio analysis to a close, we remind you to always exercise caution when drawing conclusions. Ratios are but one piece in your overall evaluation, and you must look at what is special or unique about your organization or those to whom you are comparing yourself. It is usually safest to begin with a trend analysis of your own organization, which studies how your organization has changed from year to year. Then, find a group of similar organizations to compare yourself to. Ideally, put both comparisons on the same graph, so you have a given ratio for your organization and other organizations plotted for at least three years. Once you get comfortable with that, you are ready to move to Level 3, involvement in fund-raising management and evaluation. Some CFOs must get involved regardless of their mastery of Levels 1 and 2 because of their expanded job responsibilities.

(d) Level 3: Fund-Raising Management and Evaluation

Fund-raising management and evaluation is an area in which non-fund-raising, financial personnel can and should be involved. It is an area in which the organization may be forced to rely on the CFO, because it cannot afford and chooses not to hire a development officer. Or, the CFO may also hold the title of development officer. We contend that it is also an area in which nonprofits can learn from businesses. First, recognize that in businesses, the treasurer is the fundraiser. The treasurer is responsible for arranging funding, typically from leases, debt, and equity. Second, she or he has global view of many interlocked facets of the organization:

- Organizational strategy
- Long-run financial plans
- Present and anticipated financial position
- Cash flow characteristics
- Alternate sources of revenue and liquidity
  - Investments maturing
  - Investments ready for sale
  - Debt financing
  - Grant proposal and status
  - Business income
  - Historical pattern and trends of donation revenue
  - Split of "general fund" restricted and unrestricted funds
  - Split of restricted and unrestricted liquid funds in noncurrent categories

We show the global view of the treasurer in Exhibit 6.7. It is apparent that the financial manager has a bird's eye, integrated perspective that no one else in the organization has—at least at this level of detail and with this degree of comprehension.

Third, we contend that the organization benefits from having the nonprofit CFO increase his involvement in fund-raising objectives, planning, execution, and post-campaign evaluation:

- Better integrates the entire spectrum of financial resource utilization
- Assists fund-raising office in communicating its objectives, methods, and resource needs across the organization
- Provides improved strategic direction and continuous improvement to the fundraising office/function

Exhibit 6.7.   Financial Manager's View of the Cash Position and Revenue Stream

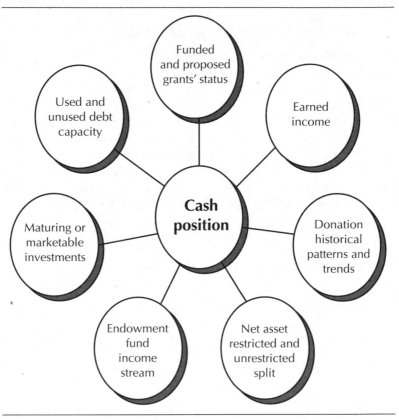

Summarizing, proficient organizations have CFOs with ·hands-on authority and/or oversight over the organization's revenue stream. How can we put these ideals into operation? The CFO should pursue four strategic involvements, in this order of priority: (1) ensure adherence to the correct philosophy and major objective of fundraising, (2) plan and then schedule the campaign expenditures, (3) assist in the mid-campaign evaluation and redirection, and (4) oversee post-campaign effectiveness and efficiency ratio analysis. We will expand on each of these briefly.

(i) Setting the Philosophy and Major Objective of Fundraising.   The fund-raising expenditure must be viewed as an investment, like other capital expenditures, not as an expense. An appropriate philosophy for the annual campaign is to proactively raise money this year for next year's operations, instead of for contemporaneously trying to fund this year's operations; failure to

recognize this explains why so many nonprofits are living hand-to-mouth and experiencing recurrent cash crises. A major objective of fundraising is to do its part to help meet the service provision objective, which has already been spelled out by the proficiently managed organization in the long-range financial plan (see discussion in Chapter 4) and in the annual budgeting process (see Chapter 5); the investment in annual campaign fund raising is derived from the anticipated service provision spelled out in the budget, and is a direct output of the budgeting process.

There is one important modification/amplification: looking back at our hub and spokes diagram (Exhibit 6.7), we must adjust up or down the annual campaign dollar goal based on the relative revenue contributions of those other revenue sources, with the overall objective of hitting a liquidity target that is based on transactions needs for cash (which increase along with service activity); see the cash management discussion elsewhere in this manual of setting the liquidity target for other factors that may reduce the liquidity target, such as re-engineered bank relations and/or using controlled disbursement account, etc.

The organization should have fund raising policies that spell out its philosophy of fundraising to prospective donors. While this is beyond the scope of our presentation, check with other organizations to find out what they are doing. Prison Fellowship, the Washington D.C.–based organization founded by Chuck Colson to provide an outreach to prisoners, has an outstanding set of policies that might serve as a model for you.[9]

(ii) Plan and Then Schedule the Campaign Expenditures. Instead of prolonging the start of the annual campaign or doing it at the development office's convenience, use your knowledge of the organization's cash flow cycle and current cash position to provide direction to the effort. Second, recognize and help others on the management team understand the timing of the underlying cash flow cycle in an annual campaign:

Cash outflow for materials and labor → cash inflow
from campaign

The annual campaign is a cash draining activity for some period. The implications? Expenditures must be anticipated, and enough cash on hand prior to the campaign to fund the campaign. The most important reason for not achieving their organization's financial objective, according to financial officers surveyed in the

---

[9]See the pamphlet "The Ministry of Fund Raising," by Whitney Kuniholm, pp. 39–47, published by Prison Fellowship, P.O. Box 17500, Washington, D.C., 20041-0500.

Lilly study, was inadequate and/or ineffective fund raising. We emphasize: fund raising must be looked at as an investment, not as an expense, regardless of the accounting treatment. It is vital that you work with the development officer to convey this mindset to your CEO and board, and ultimately your donors or grant sources. Some CFOs or board treasurers counter: "But we don't have the cash to do the level of fundraising that we really need to undertake." Bill Levis, a fund-raising expert associated with Baruch College in New York City, recommends that organizations go one step further with the timeline analysis and raise funds this year to fund next year's expenses. Let's think about that. Takes a planning mindset, doesn't it? What are some likely repercussions of such a policy? It results in having the equivalent of one year's operating expenses in unrestricted liquid assets (in addition to the "money for a rainy day" you already hold in cash reserves) by the end of this year.[10] In turn, that may require educating the donors, and it will also in some cases result in a red flag raised by one of the philanthropic oversight bureaus—particularly if you have sizable reserves saved up for planned program expansion or for a merger/acquisition.

(iii) Assist in the Mid-Campaign Evaluation and Redirection. Here is an example of using reports gathered within the year to help guide management for the remainder of the year. As results start coming in, the financial office can work with the development office, where separate, to interpret the results to management and the board. With its global view of the organization, the finance office knows how critical a shortfall is at any given point in time, and can provide guidance as to the best use of a surplus when positive results are achieved.

(iv) Oversee Post-Campaign Effectiveness and Efficiency Ratio Analysis. In the past, it was well nigh impossible to find good information on measuring fund-raising efficiency and effectiveness, but this is changing.[11] Here are some of the general guidelines offered by expert James Greenfield (1996, page 676):

---

[10]Your organization may already be there without consciously planning such a strategy. Do you have both (1) cash reserves significantly greater than next year's anticipated operating expenses (and will you still have it at the end of the fiscal year) and (2) a policy that allows the organization to draw down cash reserves to some minimum level in order to fund operations? If so, you are in the same financial position as an organization which consciously adopts this forward-year annual campaign strategy.

[11]We gratefully acknowledge the assistance of Philip M. Purcell, J.D., Director of Planned Giving and Development Counsel, Rose-Hulman Institute of Technology, Terre Haute, IN. A very helpful resource for those wishing to conduct self-assessment of fundraising is *Fund-Raising Cost Effectiveness: A Self-Assessment Workbook*, by James M. Greenfield (New York: John Wiley & Sons, Inc., 1996).

Activity	Reasonable Cost Guideline
Direct mail acquisition	$1.00 to $1.25 per $1.00 raised
Direct mail renewal	$0.20 per $1.00 raised
Membership organization	$0.25 per $1.00 raised
Donor club program	$0.20 per $1.00 raised
Benefit events	$0.50 per $1.00 raised
Volunteer-led annual giving	$0.10 to $0.20 per $1.00 raised
Individual major gift programs	$0.10 to $0.20 per $1.00 raised
Capital campaigns	$0.10 to $0.20 per $1.00 raised
Planned giving/Estate planning	$0.20 to $0.30 per $1.00 raised

A three-year study of 51 American colleges and universities found that on average it costs 16 cents to raise a dollar, with a median cost of 11 cents and the middle 50 percent of campuses experiencing costs of between 8 and 16 cents.[12] This figure covers all direct fund-raising staff and programs, but does not include any allocation for president or dean's salaries or space or utility overhead costs. The study was conducted by CASE and the National Association of College and University Business Officers, and funded by Lilly Endowment, Inc. It also found that, on average, colleges spend just over 2 percent of their educational and general (E&G) budgets for raising money, with gifts raised for operations meeting 10 percent of that budget. The report made an important observation:[13] "The objective of an institution's program should not be to spend as little as possible each year to raise money, but to maximize the net. A program that annually produces $2 million at a cost of $160,000, or 8 percent, may look good and is indeed efficient, but one that produces $3 million at a cost of $300,000, or 10 percent, is presumably of more help to the institution—it is bringing in $860,000 more."

As a financial officer, offer assistance to the development office in developing cost standards and efficiency and effectiveness reports. Offer assistance to the CEO and board in interpreting those reports and making resource allocation decisions related to fund raising. Above all, help these parties understand the concept of return on fund-raising investment. Once you are there, you are ready to embark on the final achievement: Level 4.

(e) Level 4: Cash and Liquidity Analysis and Projection

Moving to the next level is not too difficult once the financial manager gains the global perspective we viewed in the fund-raising involvement in the third level. The tasks we have in mind here are:

[12]Ellen Ryan, "The Costs of Raising A Dollar," *Case Currents* (September 1990), 58–62.
[13]*Id*. 58.

1. Refine the analysis of cash and liquidity that you did in Levels 1, 2, and 3. Specifically,
   - Look at your historical cash flow patterns to see which months have the highest net cash inflows (cash receipts minus cash disbursements), the lowest net cash inflows, and the longest period within a fiscal year in which you are in a "net borrowed position" (showing a bottom-line cash shortage which persists across several months)
   - List all of the sources of cash your organization has tapped in the past, and to what degree, to weather cash crunches
   - Estimate the variability of net cash flow by statistical estimation of the range and standard deviation of your historical figures[14]

2. Work through the diagnostic questionnaire shown in Exhibit 6.8. Use the diagnostic indicators shown toward the left of the diagram to determine if your target liquidity level is set too low. Reverse the questions to give an assessment of the possibility of having excess liquidity.

3. Develop a refined cash projection model by incorporating your findings from Steps 1 and 2. Begin to use this model alongside your present forecasting method until you gain confidence in it. If funds are available, check into advanced forecasting computer software such as FORECAST PRO FOR WINDOWS (Business Forecast Systems).

4. Once you are comfortable with your model in Step 3, go beyond the "single case" model to develop scenarios. These are built in the newer releases of the financial spreadsheet programs such as Microsoft Excel™ and Lotus 1-2-3.™ If you have the capability, or can arrange a college internship with a business student from a local college or university, utilize simulation analysis to simulate your monthly cash budget.

5. Attempt to redetermine your organization's target liquidity level based on your findings in Steps 1–4 (see below for further guidance).

6. Develop a prioritized listing of cash sources that your organization will tap when it faces its next anticipated or unanticipated cash shortfall. Indicate dollar amounts for your first source, second source, etc. Be sure to contact banks to prescreen them for availability of funds if you intend on using credit lines to cover some or all of a shortfall.

7. Strategize with your CEO and board on potential strategic alliance or merger partners that would be able to provide funding

[14]Once you have your daily cash receipts and cash disbursements in a financial spreadsheet, use the statistics functions to do this for you.

Exhibit 6.8. Determining Whether Your Organization Has Too Little Liquidity

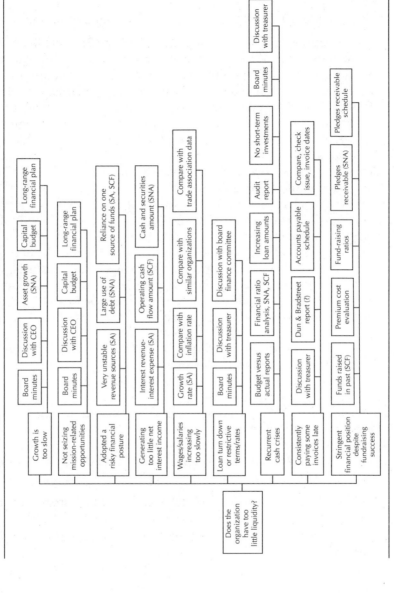

Abbreviations: SA, statement of activity; SNA, statement of net activity; and SCF, statement of cash flow.

for expanded or new program initiatives that are the most "cash-intensive" of all your anticipated program offerings.

As for the optimal level of target liquidity, you will have to do the analysis yourself because the Robinson study did not address this issue. As a starting point, take a look at the low point in your fiscal year, which for many nonprofits is late September or early October. Set a liquidity level for your peak season, probably early January, that is sufficient to cover your organization through the dry season. This is where your annual cash budget re-evaluation, covered as part of Level 1 above, is so helpful. Study past cash flows carefully and note when the cash crunches came as well as how much liquidity would have been necessary earlier in the year to prevent each cash crunch. The degree of flexibility your organization has in "managing off of the budget" (see below) will also help you determine the size of your "safety buffer" of liquidity.

This concludes your guidelines for using the four-level pyramid of annual financial reporting and the associated analysis. We now conclude our internal reporting coverage with brief discussions of monthly or quarterly reporting, daily or flash reporting, and then how to actually use reports to manage off of the budget.

(i) Monthly or Quarterly Reports. Much of what we have to say here is redundant with the annual reporting cycle. Obviously, you will not have as much time to do thorough analysis of the monthly or quarterly data. And, you will not need to do as much thinking about the impact of variances on next year's budget or the long-range financial plan. However, some boards meet monthly, especially for nonprofits with a very localized scope of service provision. Others meet quarterly or semiannually, and they will require a concise and insightful presentation from you on the following:

- At a minimum, provide budget reports (BVA), financial ratio analysis, statement of activity, and updated cash forecast.
- Ideally, same as annual in scope and coverage, but practically more limited in both
- Focus on variance analysis and likelihood of meeting full-year budget target
- Capital campaign and deferred giving reports, if applicable, help give the bigger picture
- Target liquidity scorecard to show how we are doing in maintaining or reaching the target liquidity level

Graphs and explanatory comments are very much appreciated by report users. The CEO may also ask for information regarding nonfinancial data (meals served, persons housed) that you will need to merge or have someone else merge with this financial data.

(ii) Daily or Flash Reports. What kinds of information should be provided to you or others on a daily basis? The following are some reports that would serve a useful purpose on a daily or weekly basis:

- Cash position, including bank deposits and withdrawals
- Donation report
- Ideally, add receivables (accounts receivable and contributions receivable) and payables updates to give a better picture of near-future cash receipts and disbursements

As with the monthly or quarterly reports, the CEO or board may also request information regarding nonfinancial data (meals served, persons housed) that you will need to merge or have someone else merge with this financial data.

(f) Managing Off the Budget

We have provided much information on budgetary reports, but up to this point we have not given very much guidance on what to do when the BVA shows a deteriorating financial position. In this section, we will provide some pointers.

(i) Budget Variance Analysis Revisited. Some organizations either ignore their target liquidity levels or never set them in the first place. Remember the interview with the executive director of the Midwest Finance Association (MFA) that we included in the budget development presentation (see Chapter 5). As the association continued to run deficits, what do you suppose happened to their liquidity? Right! The cash reserves continued to dwindle, until the viability of the organization was in jeopardy. Finally, in late 1996 the president of the association (MFA) wrote the members of the chronic deficits, and notified the membership that the dues were being almost doubled in order to bring the organization back to a break-even or surplus, and more importantly, to preserve and rebuild the cash reserves. In the MFA's case, the corrective action took place after an evaluation of annual results as they fit into the past years' established trend. Most organizations can react more quickly by harnessing their ongoing financial reports.

Three reporting principles will help you manage off the budget:

- An exception reporting focus will help focus attention on the large-dollar or large-percentage items that contribute most to the problems and therefore the likely solutions.

- Inclusion of year-to-date (YTD) variances as well as the last month and/or last quarter will give the needed perspective for decision making.
- If possible, include Actual versus Forecast as well as Actual versus Budget (2 comparisons) in your variance analysis reports.

The latter principle necessitates more management time for preparation, because each month or quarter you not only have to review the past performance, but do a new forecast which possibly varies from the budgeted amounts. Organizations that use flexible budgets, if recalculated, may eliminate the need to do an "Actual versus Forecast" because the revised budget may have been a new forecast based on how things have changed.

Progressive organizations are moving beyond mere financial reporting and including nonfinancial items in their periodic reports. Let's face it: your financial results three or five years from now are going to be closely linked to nonfinancial factors and trends. Accordingly, universities and businesses are adopting a new approach in their monthly or quarterly meetings, in which they highlight KFSIs and possibly cost drivers. The former are things like contacts made by the admissions office, follow-up letters written by academic unit heads, and the like. Indiana State University board members receive a report of KFSIs each board meeting based on consultation provided by business students and a faculty member, as refined by the internal auditor.[15] The focus in a key success indicators report is on selected areas of performance in which satisfactory results will ensure the organization's competitive success, meriting top management time and attention.

Several other success factors seem to enhance the potency of your reporting and its usefulness to the organization. One is the importance of doing your variance analysis and situation analysis in conjunction with ratios and other indicators. As we saw earlier, ratios taken as a group provide a composite picture of the organization's financial health. There are a number of other indicators that can be used beyond what has been presented here, and all the important indicators should be assessed. Gross, Larkin, Bruttomesso, and McNally (1995, pp. 383–386) provide five classes of indicators of impending financial trouble, including community support, financial independence, productivity, deferred current costs, and management practices. A second success factor we noted in the Lilly Study is the importance of the "1,000-word picture."

[15]The key success indicator approach is documented in Mary M. Sapp and M. Lewis Temares, "A Monthly Checkup," *NACUBO Business Officer*, (March 1992), 24–31. We strongly advocate that you evaluate using this approach in your management reporting, regardless of your organizational type.

Board members who work as engineers at Caterpillar in Peoria, Illinois, draw up trend line charts to show revenue and expense trends for the Peoria Rescue Ministries CEO and other board members. Related to this, a third success factor is to include not only trends but also comparative data if available (peer analysis). This gives a more balanced view of the present situation. Fourth, we noted in the Lilly study the importance of the verbal presentation accompanying the reporting of financial results (both by John Webb at Campus Crusade and Darryl Smith at the Church of God Missionary Board). Learn to walk your management team and board through the maze of financials that they might not have the time, energy, or expertise to wade through. Finally, you might be surprised at the importance of annotating the financials with brief interpretive comments (because your listeners will forget the verbal presentation and possibly misinterpret the graphs and ratios). Even though it was part of the external reporting of the organization, we have included below a graphic financial report sent out by HCJB World Radio to its donors (see Exhibit 6.9).

    (ii) Cash Position. As your cash position changes, you will be in the position of advising management and the board of the seriousness of the change and what corrective actions, if any, are needed. You will want to do this each quarter, and if warranted, more often. Some organizations take a new look at the liquidity each week, or even daily. As cash manager of the organization, assuming you have enough cash to make it worth your while, each day you will look at the checking account balance to determine whether and how much to transfer to overnight or longer investments.

    Now that we have an idea of the role of reports in "managing off of the budget," we will look at some of the responses you might consider to cope with financial difficulties. Or, you may wish to look at these as ways to fine-tune your already healthy financial position.

    (iii) Responses to Financial Difficulties. First, many organizations within and outside of the nonprofit sector are engaging in re-engineering. This happens when service delivery and internal management processes are opened up for radical redesign instead of just incremental improvements. The approach is much like zero-based review or zero-base budgeting, except it is applied to *efficiency* of service delivery and internal management *processes.*

    Second, some organizations are noting the difficulties that similar organizations are getting into, and are moving ahead of time to build an endowment or their cash reserves as "money for the rainy days." Related to this, financial analysts are planning ahead for the overhaul of aging plant and equipment so as not to

Exhibit 6.9.   Graphical Financial Report

Financial Report

Unaudited Financial Report for Year Ended September 30, 1995
Donor Support and Revenue

Support:			Revenue:		
Contributions	$12,065,549	62.5%	Hospital and		
Donated Goods			Medical Service	$5,094,955	26.4%
and Services	$229,475	1.2%	Investment	$251,458	1.3%
			Sale of Electric		
			Power	$355,250	1.8%
			Other	$1,312,771	6.8%

Total Donor Support and Revenue: $19,309,458   100.0%

The Mission Dollar

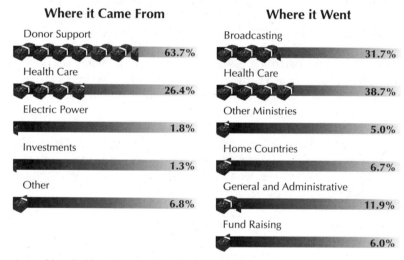

Where it Came From	Where it Went
Donor Support — 63.7%	Broadcasting — 31.7%
Health Care — 26.4%	Health Care — 38.7%
Electric Power — 1.8%	Other Ministries — 5.0%
Investments — 1.3%	Home Countries — 6.7%
Other — 6.8%	General and Administrative — 11.9%
	Fund Raising — 6.0%

A copy of the audited financial statement for the fiscal year ended September 30, 1995, will be sent upon request.

Source: Reprinted, with permission, HCJB World Radio Annual Report, 1996.

be caught short when the time comes for refurbishment or replacement. Organizations such as residential colleges, churches, and museums must be especially careful to plan for the fixed asset needs that they will have to fund or arrange funding for. Other organizations are noting the need for pension funding.

But what if it's too late to plan ahead? Let's profile some responses to financial shortfalls.

• Quickly eliminate deficit spending
• Quickly increase internal control

- Quickly increase the role and prominence of the finance department (OK, it sounds self-serving, but it certainly helped the Church of the Brethren and the Church of God Missionary Board)
- Quickly reorienting the organization to a more deliberate program expansion (whether new programs or expansion of existing ones)
  - "Managed growth" of Cedarville College (Cedarville, OH), which chooses to grow at a manageable pace
  - Sustainable growth rate[16]
  - Internal growth rate

In addition to these stopgap measures, there are some internal and external measures you can take to stem a long-term decline.

(iv) Internal Measures. There are six major financial strategies to embark on within your organization. Briefly, they are as follows:

1. *A New Emphasis on Cash Forecasting,* with Shorter Horizon (Month) and Interval (Weekly). *3M policy:* accurately forecast cash sources and uses and take whatever actions are deemed appropriate so that adequate cash is on hand at all times and so that daily and long-term liquidity needs are met at the best price.
2. *Asset Sales* ("Strategic Disposition," Focus on Core Business[es])
3. *Expansion Strategy:* Land Purchase, Lease to Builder, Leaseback to the nonprofit organization; this strategy enables the builder to utilize the depreciation (40-year) expense deduction whereas the nonprofit would be unable to.
4. *Asset Redeployment:* Put scarce labor and volunteer resources in critical areas.
5. *Cost Reduction / Containment:* This is the "downsizing" we hear so much about.
6. *Treasury Strategies:* Much of what is in mind here involves revising your treasury management approach and operations based on benchmarking. Here are some benchmarks to begin using to gauge your treasury operation by (Exhibit 6.10).

A second set of benchmarks is linked to your internal treasury management *processes:*[17]

---

[16]For information on the sustainable growth rate see Terry S. Maness and John T. Zietlow, *Short-Term Financial Management* (Fort Worth, TX: Dryden Press, 1998), Chapter 2. The internal growth rate is profiled in most introductory corporate finance texts.
[17]*Source:* International Benchmarking Clearing House, "Treasury Benchmarks," *Corporate Cashflow,* October 1992, 30.

Exhibit 6.10. Treasury Performance Benchmarks

Activity	Benchmark	Source
Regular activities		
Short-term investing	90-day T-bill	*The Wall Street Journal*
Short-term bank borrowing	Average prime rate	Bank reports
Short-term nonbank borrowing	Average of Fed composite Commercial Paper rate	Federal Reserve Bank of New York
Foreign exchange	Average spot rate	*The Wall Street Journal*
Special activities		
Lockbox study	Balances reduced	Consulting report
Disbursement study	Float improvements	Consulting report
Electronic payment study	Net cost savings	Consulting report
Treasury review	Net cost savings	Consulting report
New computer system	Reduced operating costs	Internal study
Intercompany activities		
Bank compensation	Average balances and/or fees	Account analyses
Unit's short-term borrowing	Average Commercial Paper or bank rates	Internal reports versus parent's

Source: Reprinted, with permission, of the McGraw-Hill Companies and Jarl Kauberg and Kenneth Parkinson, from *Corporate Liquidity: Management and Measurement,* © 1992.

- How long does it take to reconcile bank accounts?
- What percentage of the time do you hit target balances (as the cash manager)?
- What is your policy on transferring funds from demand deposit account (DDA) to short-term investments? How followed? Tied into Cash Forecast?
- Measure how well any given process succeeds in achieving its stated goal.
- What are your financing expenses as a percentage of sales revenue?

(v) *External Measures.* The external measures that organizations may take to cope with financial problems fall into three major categories:

1. *Fund-raising:* increase the intensity and focus of your fund-raising efforts
2. *Bank borrowing:* document future improvements to merit short-term financing to bridge the gap

3. *Merger/acquisition partner or strategic alliance:* join hands with a partner that has deep (or deeper) pockets

This concludes the major portion of this chapter. We conclude the chapter with a brief portrayal of the external reports your organization will provide.

6.7 EXTERNAL REPORTS

(a) Statements of Activity, Financial Position, and Cash Flows

Organizations are already well aware that they must provide financial reports adhering to the appropriate financial accounting standards. Financial Accounting Standards Board (FASB) Statements 116 and 117 guide the reporting for most of the organizations we are addressing in this book. As discussed above, the three required statements per FASB 117 are the Statement of Activity, the Statement of Financial Position (or Statement of Net Assets), and the Statement of Cash Flows. The intent and purpose of FASB 117 was to bring uniformity to the financial statements of nonprofits, mostly for the benefit of external users. Statement 117 also requires Voluntary Health and Welfare Organizations (and encourages other nonprofits) to prepare an additional financial statement which portrays expenses in natural classifications (e.g., salary expense), as well as the functional (program, etc.) classifications required of all nonprofits. The three classes of contributions recognized in Statements 116 and 117 (permanently restricted net assets, temporarily restricted net assets, unrestricted net assets) should give readers a better idea of the organization's liquidity and financial flexibility.

Briefly, your external reports should be accurate, timely, show the appropriate level of detail, and provide supplemental commentary if done in the context of an "Annual Report." Graphs are also helpful, as we discovered earlier.

(i) Forms 990 and 990-T. In addition to the three reports listed above, most sizable (gross receipts of $25,000 or more) non-church-related nonprofits will be required to file a Form 990 (or if gross receipts during the year are less than $100,000 *and* total assets at year-end are less than $250,000, the Form 990-EZ) with the IRS each year, and if they have unrelated business income (gross income of $1,000 or more), the Form 990-T with accompanying payment of taxes owed. Information on filling these forms out is beyond our scope, but extensive information is now available at the IRS web site on the Internet.

(ii) Donor Mailings and "Publicly Available" Reports. Another outside party which has great interest in your organization is the base of present and potential donors. Accountability is provided

by the organization that provides useful and accurate information to donors on a timely basis. Scandals have had their effect, watchdog bureaus have had their effect, but so have the large number of organizations which have not been forthcoming with their financial reports when requested. Form 990 should be made available freely to anyone interested. *World Magazine* did an exposé in February 1995 in which it revealed that "six out of 10 evangelical [religious] organizations surveyed initially failed to provide the most basic financial information upon request."[18] Clearly, there is room for improvement in reporting to donors.

What should I tell my donors?　Donors want to know about effectiveness (results attained with their money), efficiency (including waste and how you're eliminating it), and steps of progress (innovation, new initiatives, creative approaches). Because the results attained are sometimes difficult to quantify, they may use your financial data to infer effectiveness—much as a stockholder would look at profits.

Annual report.　We already said, in our discussion of graphical portrayal of financial results, how one organization presents its main financial data to its donors. The main idea is to focus on the main ideas, without overwhelming your nontechnical audience.

Mail appeal "stuffer" reports.　Don't overlook the opportunity to use your mail appeals as an opportunity to showcase your main accomplishments and financial results. Radio Bible Class (RBC) in Grand Rapids, Michigan has developed expertise in this area and would be a good model to follow. RBC mails out a pamphlet entitled "Our Support" in which it presents its financial policy, its source of support, its balanced budgeting (with pie charts for both funds received and funds distributed), and its statement of financial accountability.[19]

(iii) State Requirements.　State reporting requirements vary tremendously. Check with your Secretary of State or Attorney General's office for the specific requirements in your state and each state in which you raise funds. At a minimum, raising funds in a state generally requires that you register with the appropriate state agency.

(iv) Granting Agency Reports.　Again, granting agencies have specialized formats that they want to have used for grant re-

[18]"Christian Financial Follies," *World Magazine*, December 23/30 1995, 19.
[19]For more information write to Radio Bible Class, Grand Rapids, MI 49555-0001.

quests and periodic follow-up reports. The key point here is to follow the format and provide the necessary information, just as you would to donors in general.

As a final comment on external reporting, guard against the tendency to evaluate performance based only on easily measured input measures (hours worked) or output measures (clients served). Go the extra mile to define the appropriate measure(s) of effectiveness, then educate donors and grantors on how you will be presenting that information to them.

6.8 SUMMARY

In this chapter, we have presented the major internal financial reports and how they might be compiled. We focused on usefulness and practicality. We recognized that although your reporting might now be geared primarily to the IRS or grantor needs, the greatest benefit comes to the organization that harnesses its financial reporting to management and board decision-making needs. The emphasis should be on budget variance analysis, financial ratio analysis, and constant vigilance over the target liquidity level. Once financial strains begin to appear, take steps to ward off the problems, and use stopgap measures when necessary. Begin benchmarking treasury management performance and processes now.

CHAPTER SEVEN

Technology Tools—
Managing Information

7.1 Introduction   236
7.2 How Much Technology and Which to Choose?   237
   (a)   What Types of Technology Tools Should I Consider?   237
   (b)   Are They Required?   240
   (c)   Do I Need Them?   240
   (d)   What Will They Do for Me?   240
   (e)   What Will They Not Do for Me?   241
   (f)   Can I Afford Them?   241
   (g)   What Changes Will They Introduce
      to My Organization?   241
      (i)   Example 1   242
      (ii) Example 2   243
7.3 What Should I Know/Do before Investing
   in Technology Tools?   244
   (a)   Planning for Growth   244
7.4 Software: Design from New or Purchase?   245
7.5 Disclosure, the Law, and Security   246
7.6 Needs Assessment and Analysis   246
   (a)   Assess   246
   (b)   Analyze   248
   (c)   Critique   249
   (d)   Decide   249
   (e)   The Final Step: Getting People to Use It   250

Appendix 7A: Glossary of Technical Terms   252
Appendix 7B: Framework for an Implementation Strategy   256

7.1   INTRODUCTION

Technology has been the buzz word of the 1980s and 1990s. The rush
to automate and implement new technologies has been seen as the

solution to increase productivity, reduce errors, keep up with the increasing demands for more and more information, and improve performance.

To properly evaluate the need for technology tools and how to implement them, it is necessary to explore what each can offer, and attempt to forecast the future capabilities, direction, and growth of each industry. These tools improve and expand rapidly. They are out of date the moment the purchase order is issued; however, finding some stability in this arena is both possible and necessary before their introduction into the workplace.

When many people hear the term *technology tools*, the computer is the first tool that comes to mind; however, technology tools have been with us in the workplace since the first abacus was introduced to accounting. The typewriter, adding machine, telephone, switchboard, and telex are technology tools that we accept in the workplace as standard. The migration to advanced technology tools—the computer, e-mail, voice mail, fax, and so forth—has been thought to radically alter how we work, when actually, it has simply improved on what is familiar; repackaged to be smarter, faster, and more efficient.

7.2   HOW MUCH TECHNOLOGY AND WHICH TO CHOOSE?

Technology tools can dramatically improve performance if they are used appropriately and wisely. They can also be used inappropriately and damage a smooth-running operation. For example, many companies are opting for the use of electronic receptionists, offering their customers a series of questions to direct their calls. This technology can be very useful in the right environment, such as a highly technical customer base; however, if the customer base is nontechnical (more service based), the selection of this technology may damage customer or client relations.

The same is also true with the use of computers, either personal computers or mainframe. There should be a good, sound reason to automate a task or process, not just a desire to jump on the *technology bandwagon*. To analyze your organization's need for technology, use the checklist in Exhibit 7.1.

(a) What Types of Technology Tools Should I Consider?

During the early 1980s, there was a myriad of personal computer platforms from which to choose. The industry was blossoming, and small computer manufacturers were developing proprietary systems. IBM entered the market strategically in 1984 and has held

Exhibit 7.1.   Technology Checklist

To determine whether a task or process could benefit from automation, use the following checklist:

Why do I want to automate this process?

1. *To handle a redundant process (The same task is repeated over and over.)*
   Any task that is repeated could greatly benefit from automation. Computers are good at doing that same thing repeatedly.
2. *To share or manipulate information*
   If there is a need to share information across departments, divisions, or work groups, or a need to have the same information manipulated for different audiences, then maintaining it in a computer is the best way to accomplish the task.
3. *To enable staff to do more work*
   This is a common reason for the decision to automate. It, in itself, is not a valid reason for automation, nor will automating for this reason yield the desired results. This is the most common erroneous justification for automation. There must be something specific about the task or process that could be streamlined, simplified, or improved on with the use of an automated technology. This reason is sound only if it is followed by a qualifier, such as, "To enable staff to do more work . . . by automating the routine tasks they perform, thus reducing their workload."
4. *To reduce errors*
   There can be a great reduction in errors with the use of technology *if* the systems, processes, and rules can be built; however, if the system design is as freeform as the manual process, those same errors will be introduced into the automated process. In addition, since the automated process will be new, more errors will be made as staff are learning to use the technology.
5. *To produce multiple outputs (e.g., reports, cards, badges, graphs, charts, form letters)*
   This is one of the best reasons for automation (where the same information is used for different reasons). If done well, automating this type of process can dramatically reduce errors and workload, and increase productivity.

that market share with their AT[1] Architecture (despite a temporary foray into their PS/2[2] Architecture). Although other systems have a share of the market (e.g., UNIX, Sun), the standard in the business world has been the IBM/AT technology (roughly 80 percent U.S. market share) and Apple MacIntosh (roughly 20 percent of the U.S. market share).

Before deciding on a specific platform (e.g., PCs or Macs), the following needs to be evaluated:

[1]AT Architecture, copyright © IBM Corporation.
[2]PS/2 Architecture, copyright © IBM Corporation.

1. *What software is available for this system that the business will require?* Traditionally, Macs are used in businesses that produce graphics (e.g., advertising, marketing) and PCs (e.g., accounting, forecasting) are used for number crunching. While the differences between the two platforms are diminishing rapidly, the majority of accounting applications, for example, are available only for the PC, and some design packages are available only on Macs.

2. *Who will need to access the information?* Will a network need to be established linking the computers? If so, there may be a need to standardize around a certain type of architecture and possibly compromise on the financial management needs with that of the rest of the business. If not, a diversity of platforms will not hinder or interfere with your specific needs in the financial management arena. It is also possible to establish two different networks—one for the administrative/business needs of the organization and one for the creative aspects.

3. *Are there sufficient resources (financial and staff) to implement a new technology?* It is easy to budget the costs of the equipment, but the hidden costs of down time, training, installation, maintenance, new supplies, and other factors are not as easy to predict, manage, or forecast.

4. *What does the research of others in a similar industry suggest?* With noncompeting organizations, it is often possible to develop strategic alliances to share expertise and reduce development costs and the risks associated with the implementation of new technologies.

5. *Is there a suitable software product available on the market or will a customized product be required to meet the need?* In the past, organizations designed their own applications from scratch. This was an appropriate strategy for the time, but it is no longer the case, owing mainly to the rapid release of operating system upgrades and the need for systems to work seamlessly with other software programs (e.g., word processing, database, and spreadsheet). Operating system and equipment advancements occur at least, annually. If a nonstandard architecture is selected, these systems will become obsolete (nonupgradable) almost immediately. Most organizations learned this lesson too late and are faced with the task of re-introducing automation. To avoid this obsolescence, an off-the-shelf package, moderately customized to meet the need, should be selected. Selecting the appropriate software package should be done before deciding on an equipment platform.

6. *Have the findings and decisions been reviewed carefully?* All decisions, assumptions, and recommendations should be discussed with peers. If possible, a consultant with expertise in this specific area should be contracted to review the plans.

(b) Are They Required?

If a task or process can be effectively performed manually, technology tools may not be required; however, the ability to converse with other businesses or individuals may require automation or the introduction of technologies. The fax, for example, is a technology that has become a standard for most businesses, even though at first the need to *receive* a fax may have greatly outweighed the need to *send* a fax.

If there is a need to communicate and share information with other businesses, government agencies, bureaus, or the like, technologies should be introduced that will enable compliance with these other demands. If this is the case, implementation strategies should include these immediate needs, as well as long-term strategies for applying new technology in other areas of the organization.

(c) Do I Need Them?

In a nonprofit business technology may not be required for all applications. In the financial arena, however, the capabilities provided by new technologies will dramatically improve the quality of work, or at least, streamline or simplify the process. The migration from "counting beans" to "analyzing trends and forecasting needs" is the major thrust of automating the process of financial management.

The major focus of financial management is the ability to review financial information to make decisions, forecast needs, evaluate performance, and assess progress. The quality of financial management is based on the integrity of the information reviewed and evaluated. The manual process of accounting has provided a level of accuracy and quality that for many years was acceptable. The introduction of technology and the automation of the process does provide a higher quality of data than can be provided by a manual accounting process. The removal of as much human error as possible to the process is the single most important reason to automate. While it is still necessary to have a human contact, to enter the information into a system, to review what is entered, and reconcile the information against other documents, the simple enhancement of the computer over the 10-key adding machine can dramatically reduce errors and speed up the process.

(d) What Will They Do for Me?

Many financial-type software programs on the market resemble checkbooks that are easy to use. While some organization's financial management needs may be much more sophisticated, one of these programs can provide all that is needed to automate the financial operation of many businesses. These software programs, if set up properly, will enable individuals to enter information in a format and style that is easy to understand and use. The ability to produce reports and retrieve information from these systems is quite remarkable. With most of these *off-the-shelf* programs, a balance sheet can be produced as swiftly and easily as a transaction record.

(e) What Will They Not Do for Me?

Technology cannot solve the organization's problems that are caused by human resources conflicts, poor organizational structure, or complex or ineffective policies or procedures. In fact, the introduction of technology will bring these problems to the surface and, in many cases, magnify their impacts on the organization. It is not uncommon, when technology implementations are underway, for the technology to be blamed for crippling the organization, when in fact, the organization was already crippled by these other factors.

It is important to remember that technology tools *automate a predefined task or process.* Technology does not define the process. If there are existing problems with the processes, there will be problems in the automation of the process.

(f) Can I Afford Them?

These new technologies can be expensive. The initial costs of the equipment and software are only the beginning of the expenditure requirements. With any decision to purchase, there must be a justification for the expenditure. Exhibit 7.2 illustrates one method of determining if there is a justification for the introduction of a new technology.

Exhibit 7.2 assumes the cost of a typical PC configuration at $5,250. At Line 3 (Exhibit 7.2), a 15 percent increase in productivity (or elimination of an extra position at that percentage) recovers the costs of the typical configuration in the first year. Each subsequent year, a savings of $4,250 can be achieved.

The chart ends at 35 percent. However, if one staff person or the need to hire an additional staff member can be eliminated, the costs of the technology are assuredly justifiable.

(g) What Changes Will They Introduce to My Organization?

All change is dramatic to an organization. Managing the change is the only way to assure that the introduction of new technologies will provide a desired and positive outcome. Accepting that all change is challenging, the introduction of technology has its own set of issues and concerns. Many of these issues and concerns are

Exhibit 7.2.   Determination of Expenditure Need

One-time costs		
Typical PC configuration	$ 2,500	
Software	$ 1,000	
Printer	$ 500	
Other	$ 250	
Total	$ 4,250	
Annual costs (recurring)		
Training	$ 500	
Supplies	$ 300	
Maintenance	$ 200	
Total	$ 1,000	
	$ 5,250	

Average Annual Staff Salary	Productivity Increases (% of Position Eliminated)	Annual Net Savings
$35,000	5%	$ 1,750
$35,000	10%	$ 3,500
$35,000	15%	$ 5,250
$35,000	20%	$ 7,000
$35,000	25%	$ 8,750
$35,000	30%	$10,500
$35,000	35%	$12,250

unfounded and are based on myths about technology, but they still need to be addressed and discussed.

Assimilating the new technology will not be automatic. Depending on the level of change, new work flows, diagrams, work rules, policies, or procedures will need to be reviewed and, in most cases, revised or rewritten. Putting a computer on someone's desk will not automatically provide increases in productivity. In most cases, the transition process will yield a decrease in productivity until the training and assimilation process is complete. All support systems and processes need to be reviewed, and staff need to be retrained.

(i) *Example 1.*   The use of the computer was widely accepted, and staff learned quickly how to enter the information into the system. Reports were produced, data appeared to be of higher quality, and the staff should have had more time for analysis; however, the support structure for the system had not been redesigned. The staff were still maintaining all of the paper documents in cross-filed indexes and logs, as they always had. The staff had learned to provide others with the information they needed, but had not yet learned how to use the information themselves nor did they believe it was their place to make major changes in the way they maintained their records.

(ii) Example 2. A request was made of one staff member to provide historical information about spending on an item type. The staff member went immediately to her paper files rather than the computer. When questioned about it later, she stated that the individual wanted a specific item that was not one of the categories of expenditures the person had requested. When reminded that this person bought only that item, so that category would have been accurate, she realized she could have retrieved the information from the system.

In many other implementation situations, the biggest problem is the dramatic change on what is valued in the organization. Rules and regulations that had taken decades to learn and memorize were suddenly programmed into the system. Individuals who had spent so much time learning these rules were suddenly no more qualified or valued than the newest person in the organization. So, in addition to new work flows, ways of positively rewarding and recognizing tenure need to be established in the organization.

Another challenge to the introduction of technology is *fear*— fear of a machine, fear of losing one's job, fear of not being able to use the technology. The greatest pacifier is open communication. The following is a strategy for introducing technology into an organization (also refer to Appendix B at the end of this chapter):

1. Determine what impacts the new technology will have on the organization.
2. Develop a strategy for communicating the plan and the change to the staff within the organization. The strategy should include:
   - Why and how the need for technology was determined
   - Management's commitment to the change
   - How the technology will be introduced, who will be affected, what it will do
   - How training will be handled
   - The time line (schedule) for the implementation
   - The support systems that will be available
   - How future communication about this change will be administered
   - How this will be applied within the organization, what it will replace, what policies or procedures will be altered, and so forth

7.3 WHAT SHOULD I KNOW/DO BEFORE INVESTING IN TECHNOLOGY TOOLS?

With the introduction of any new technology, there will be changes and unexpected delays and costs; plan for them. If no other method of allowing for hidden expenditures is possible, an extra line item should be added to the budget of "Unforeseen Expenditures" as a percentage of the total budget. If a vendor or a contractor promises to deliver a product by a certain date, penalties or rewards for meeting or missing the deadline should be included in the contract.

In addition:

- Budget time for planning the implementation.
- Recognize that not all staff will agree with the decisions and some will try to stop or sabotage the implementation, either directly or indirectly.
- Accept that some staff may not be able to deal with the changes and may leave on their own, or they may need to be removed from the organization or retrained for other positions.
- Seek advice from colleagues and peers from other organizations. Careful attention should be paid to their experiences and any problems or obstacles they faced should be assumed to re-occur, no matter how well the implementation plans and strategies are carried out.
- Realize that mistakes will be made along the way.

(a) Planning for Growth

The biggest challenge of any new venture is predicting future needs. With technology, this can be especially critical. Many technologies are sold in blocks, accommodating a specific number of users, telephones, connections, etc. While it is never wise to over purchase, it is also imprudent to replace existing equipment unnecessarily or too quickly.

Predicting future growth doesn't have to be as unscientific as reading a crystal ball; however, an accurate prediction of future needs should not be expected. Projections should be conservative, either in terms of growth or investment. The best measurements begin with an analysis of historical growth, plus or minus contributing factors.

Exhibit 7.3 lists the total number of employees for a given organization over the last ten years, with an average number of employees of 61. Predicting that the organization will have an average of 61 employees per year would be a misinterpretation of the data. Examining the data more closely (Exhibit 7.4) shows that a greater

Exhibit 7.3.   Growth Analysis

	No. of Employees
1987	15
1988	30
1989	45
1990	47
1991	49
1992	55
1993	89
1994	92
1995	92
1996	97
Average:	61

pattern of growth occurred during the first five years, and a steady but slower growth in the second five years.

7.4   SOFTWARE: DESIGN FROM NEW OR PURCHASE?

Many software companies are now working with clients to lease/finance software. Leasing costs more but is often worth it in the longer term. A typical approach in many organizations who need to purchase computer technology (hardware and software) is to engage in a lengthy process of identifying needs, shopping vendors, and so forth. After identifying the needs, they prepare a Request for Proposal including all the specifications they want and need.

A short cut many take is to network with other similar organizations and approach a vendor to design a system that works for

Exhibit 7.4.   Expanded Growth Analysis

	No. of Employees	Growth from Previous Year	Average Growth	Five-Year Average
1987	15	0	0	
1988	30	15	50%	
1989	45	15	33%	
1990	47	2	4%	
1991	49	2	4%	21%
1992	55	6	11%	
1993	89	34	38%	
1994	92	3	3%	
1995	92	0	0%	
1996	97	5	5%	12%
Average:	61	8.2	13%	

everyone. The vendor maintains the right to sell the product to similar organizations. The end result is that the development costs are spread among a greater number of users.

As discussed earlier, during the 1980s, organizations generally designed their own software. The latest trend is to purchase existing software and *tweak* it to meet unique needs. In most cases, at least three major vendors, in any given area, provide software for a specific task or process. It is easier, cheaper, and safer to purchase one of these products than to design a new one. In addition, these vendors will also provide (generally free of charge) hardware specifications for the application.

Changing technology requires the technology manager to constantly review what the organization's systems do and do not do, and to modify needs based on current procedures and task flows.

7.5 DISCLOSURE, THE LAW, AND SECURITY

There are many laws regarding the disclosure of information. A public institution's financial records may be public record; however, in many instances a portion of the data does not need to be disclosed, and in some cases, disclosure of certain pieces of information is illegal. It is imperative that a thorough investigation of the laws and policies pertaining to the types of data maintained be reviewed (see Chapter 15 for additional resources on maintaining data).

Establishing a policy regarding the use of company data will also provide a mechanism for training staff about the security requirements of the data. Exhibit 7.5 provides a sample policy that pertains to maintaining sensitive and/or confidential information.

7.6 NEEDS ASSESSMENT AND ANALYSIS

Before deciding on the type of technology, needs and requirements must be determined. The tool the *experts* use for seeking out this information is a *needs assessment*. There are as many ways to conduct a needs assessment as there are technologies from which to choose. After completion of the assessment, an analysis of the information is performed to evaluate the results. The steps involved in conducting a needs assessment are shown in Exhibit 7.6.

(a) Assess

In the first portion of the process, after determining what information is needed and choosing a method for gathering the information, the assessment is conducted. The broader the sampling (meaning,

Exhibit 7.5.   Guidelines for Using Personal Information on Individuals

You as volunteers and staff are involved extensively in fund-raising, governmental relations, and public communications programs. You are acting as agents of <Company Name> and have been chosen for your abilities to be representatives of <Company Name>.

In this capacity, you are often provided with personal information on individuals (e.g., name, address, telephone number, employer). This information is maintained on the <System Name> database and its auxiliary systems. We consider the information on these databases protected information that should be handled with appropriate care. Use of this information should be guided by the following policies:

Under the 1977 Information Practices Act, <Company Name> is able to retain personal information on individuals upon informing them of their rights, that our use of the information will be limited to the furtherance of the <Company>'s business, and that the information will not be disseminated to others except as required by law. It is proper for <Company Name> to share with our volunteers and staff a certain degree of personal information on individuals to enable them to carry out their respective assignments. However, we have an obligation both to the volunteers, staff, and individuals on whom we retain information to inform them that this is: (1) personal and confidential information which we are allowed to retain under the Information Practices Act; (2) only to be used to carry out the <Company>'s work; and (3) not for dissemination to third parties.

It is our policy not to release address and telephone information for any records to a third party either over the phone or in person. When asked to verify a individuals involvement with <Company Name>, you can transfer the request to the <individual/department>.

Information in the form of lists, labels, computer tapes, diskettes, downloads, and reports is available only to authorized <Company> representatives in support of approved activities and authorized <Company> business. It is the responsibility of the unit requesting information to maintain the confidentiality of that information.

---

the greater number of people contacted for the assessment), the more accurate the results. Methods of assessment include:

1. *One-on-one interview:* The most effective method of gathering information is using an interview technique. The most important steps with this technique are to develop a pre-established list of questions and to conduct the interview without judgment. The art of interviewing for a needs assessment is not dissimilar to playing poker: wearing a poker face, never letting on what information the interviewer hopes to prove or disprove.

Exhibit 7.6.   Needs Assessment Flow Chart

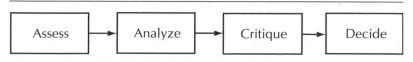

2. *Telephone interview:* This method can be very successful, especially if the questions asked are of a personal nature. The lack of face-to-face contact with individuals may make it easier to ask personal questions. However, it also precludes the interviewer from reading facial clues or gestures that are very valuable in changing the interview's tone to probe further on a particular question.

3. *Meeting:* A meeting can be a very effective forum for gathering information for an assessment, although extremely challenging and taxing for the facilitator. Often, a round-table discussion will develop as attendees hear how other people answer the questions. This method is also useful in that it immediately identifies where there is consensus and where there will be conflict.

4. *Questionnaire:* The least effective of the four methods, this is the most commonly used because it efficiently allows a broader audience to be contacted. The ability to survey a larger group can often outweigh the benefits of the time-consuming task of one-on-one interviews.

(b) Analyze

This is the portion of the process where the information collected is evaluated, tabulated, and summarized. Weighting the questions for relevance and applicability to a specific respondent can be very important. For example, if an assessment was conducted with order takers, the response of a person who takes many orders each day or whose only responsibility is to take orders, as opposed to someone who took fewer orders would have greater relevance. This person's opinions would be more valuable than another's.

When using the weighting table (Exhibit 7.7), answers given by someone who took 1 to 10 orders per day would count one time, whereas the answers of someone who took 51 to 60 orders per day would be counted six times (as if six people had taken the survey).

Another set of criteria is to weight the answers based on the relevancy of the question itself. Some questions may be much more critical than others. A similar weighting method should be used for each question.

Finally, there may be questions that need to be evaluated against another question, or a combination of questions. For example, if one was asked, "How proficient are you with Microsoft Windows: Excellent, Good, Fair, or Novice," the question should be balanced with a series of questions specific to Microsoft Windows (e.g., asking specific questions of skills or tasks the person could

Exhibit 7.7. Weighting Table to Determine Relevancy of Answers

No. of Orders Taken Per Day	Weight Factor
1–10	1
11–20	2
21–30	3
31–40	4
41–50	5
51–60	6

perform in the program, such as saving a file, opening a file, cutting and pasting). If an individual stated that he or she had excellent skills with Microsoft Windows but answered "no" to the question "Can you open a file in Microsoft Windows?," one could logically assume that the person inaccurately answered the question about their proficiency with Microsoft Windows.

(c) Critique

After analyzing the information, it should be determined whether there are results that may be in conflict. In this step, an evaluation of the results is made to verify whether they are as expected or completely off the scale as compared to the original assumptions. It should not be assumed that the original assumptions were incorrect, but also, it should not be assumed that the results of the survey are correct. Following up with a few respondents may determine that they misunderstood the question or had other reasons (sometimes personal or political) for answering in the manner they did. As a general rule, obscure or irregular results may be disregarded. Obscure survey answers should be investigated vigorously. It is possible that the person being surveyed misunderstood the question, but that should never be assumed. It is more likely that there is something unique about the individual's work or assignments that caused their obscure answer. It is just these types of issues that the needs assessment attempt to flesh out. The individuals who provided the answers (if possible) should be contacted for a follow-up assessment to gather more information to clarify the issue.

(d) Decide

The last step is to make a decision by reviewing the information collected, so an educated nonbiased decision can be made.

(e) The Final Step: Getting People to Use It

It does not matter how wisely the information was evaluated, how successfully the purchase contract was negotiated, or how accurately the needs of the organization were determined, if the staff cannot be motivated to use the tool. If it is not used, the implementation and the tool is a failure. Before making the final decision to purchase or implement, the purpose of the new tool and the willingness or ability of the staff to use it need to be re-evaluated.

There can be hundreds of reasons why staff in an organization will refuse to use a new tool. Each person may have his or her own specific reasons; however, in general, the reasons a new tool is not used fall into one of the categories described in Exhibit 7.8.

Exhibit 7.8. Reason/Solution for Refusal to Use the New Tool

Reason	Description	Solution
"I don't know how to use it."	The biggest reason why people will not use a new tool is the most obvious one: they just don't know how to use it.	Provide training in the new tool or system.
"I went to the training, but I still don't know how to use it."	After training is conducted, it is likely that staff will not immediately begin using the system, unless, a schedule or an assimilation plan for each individual or group has been created. So often in organizations, staff learn to ignore change as a way of making it go away.	Develop an implementation strategy that includes post-training follow-up. Monitor the progress of each individual or group, setting goals or milestones that need to be achieved by a specific time. Establish rewards (or punishments, if necessary) to meeting these targets.
"Training was bad."	A common complaint about any new system or tool not being used is that the training was ineffective. While it may be considered as a viable reason, it is more likely that there are other causes or reasons besides the training the individual received.	Evaluate the effectiveness of the training as part of the training process. Avoid the use of "smile sheets" (measurement tools that evaluate only how some liked or felt about the training) as opposed to good measurements that evaluate what they knew before they attended training and what they knew immediately after training. Another important factor in the training program is the relevance to the person's job. If the training examples used are too vague or general, the individual will not

Exhibit 7.8. Reason/Solution for refusal to use new tool (*continued*)

Reason	Description	Solution
		be able to assimilate the information. The closer the examples are to the real-life situations or tasks the individual will perform, the more likely the individual will be able to remember (assimilate) the information.
"I forgot what I learned."	Individuals may report that they found the training useful, but it was so long ago that they forgot what they learned.	It is possible that the training was ineffective and the step above should be employed in this example as well. More likely the reason will be that the training occurred too early, before the tool was available. Training should occur no earlier than one month before the tool is available. It is best if the tool is in place before the training is received.
"This isn't as good as the old way."	Looking at information or performing a task in a new way may cause some individuals to judge the process as ineffective. This comment should be interpreted not as a judgment but as a request for clarity about why things needed to change.	Communicate throughout the implementation process. Staff need to be told what will be different about the new process or tool, and why and how the decision was made to change from one to another.
"The system (or tool) is too hard to use." "The training was too hard."	This is a very powerful comment and may not be heard often. If it is heard, it should be taken to heart. The individual is stating what is true for him or her, not necessarily what is true about the system or the training.	Make sure that staff have the prerequisite knowledge to successfully use the new tool or complete the training course. If a new computer system is being introduced, and staff have never used a computer before, basic computer training must be provided *before* beginning training on a specific application or system. This prerequisite training does not need to be time consuming or detailed, but provide a basic level of understanding from which the individual can build his or her knowledge of the new tool.

GLOSSARY OF TECHNICAL TERMS

All disciplines have a vocabulary spoken by the experts. In the technology arena, the explosion of terms and acronyms, *tech speak*, leaves many feeling that it is a language they can never understand.

Communication Technologies	The explosion of technologies enhancing or replacing the capabilities of the phone line has seen the greatest increase in the 1990s. These technologies have literally revolutionized the way in which we communicate and have completely changed the dynamic of time and distance.
E-mail	Electronic-mail, *e-mail*, replaces or enhances a myriad of business communications. First and foremost, electronic mail is used to write and distribute letters or notes. It is also used to deliver phone messages; schedule meetings; and send files, pictures, sounds clips, and so forth to co-workers across the desk or across the globe in seconds.
FAX	Paper facsimiles, *fax*, provide a method of sending a copy of a document to another location. In combination with electronic mail, the fax has in many cases replaced the need for telex or wires in the workplace.
Internet	The *Internet* is a series of connected computers. The Internet began as a way of connecting government, research institutions, and colleges and universities, but has exploded into the new communication medium. By searching the "net," one can find and retrieve information on just about any topic around the globe. A presence on the net, usually in the form of what is called a "home page," is becoming a standard for all businesses.
Voice Mail	*Voice mail* has provided a personal receptionist for its users. Rather than talking with a person to leave a message, voice mail enables callers to record a message—similar to phone answering machines.
Hardware	*Hardware* is the term used to describe any tangible piece of computer equipment; meaning, it can be touched or felt. Printers, computers,

diskettes, computer boards, chips, and monitors are all examples of computer hardware.

PC

Personal computer (PC) is the term used to describe any desktop or laptop computer; however, for many, the term PC is used to describe the IBM/AT technology. Conversely, the term "Mac" is used to describe the MacIntosh technology from Apple. Both Macs and PCs are personal computers, but the term PC generally applies to the IBM/AT platform.

Mainframe

Mainframes are high-capacity computers that have terminals connected to them. The terminals themselves are not computers, just a mechanism to converse with the mainframe. Although many businesses are opting for local area networks (LANs) to replace mainframes, the mainframe continues and will continue to be a viable tool in many industries.

Network

Network is the term used to describe computers that are connected to one another. A network can be as small as two computers connected by a single wire, or as large as a major network linking thousands of machines through a variety of technologies, including wire, telephone, and cellular or satellite.

Client/Server

Client/Server technology has made it possible to replace or enhance mainframes or minis in a way that peer-to-peer or traditional server-based networks have not. While the increase in PC capabilities has been enormous, the size and requirements of data-processing needs of many businesses cannot be handled on a PC and still requires the speed and magnitude of a mainframe or mini computer to store and process their central data. Mainframe technologies have not been as user friendly as PC technologies, so a bridge between the two, Client/Server, has enabled the two technologies to merge.

Peer-to-peer

Peer-to-peer is a type of network that connects a series of computers in a continuous chain, rather than a central network server. Each computer can perform its own singular function or can be accessed by others on the chain.

Server

Server networks use one or more computers, as the center of its network, similar to the center of a wheel with each of the connected computers as the spokes. All the other computers are connected to it to, allowing communication back and forth from the server. Each computer connected to the server can perform singularly, but access to other computers connected to the server is not possible.

Operating System (OS)

The *Operating System (OS)* constitutes the basic instructions a computer uses to communicate with the user and how it stores, retrieves, and structures data. Software programs use these common instructions for a variety of functions including how data are stored on disk, how documents are printed, and how files are viewed, MSDOS (Microsoft Disk Operating System) was the most commonly used platform for the AT Architecture. MS Windows 95, MS Windows NT, MacIntosh, and UNIX, are all examples of standard operating systems. It is important to know that certain hardware systems and software programs may be available for a limited number of operating systems.

Software

Software is the term used to describe programming instructions to a computer. Any set of instructions that cause the computer to carry out a set of instructions or commands is software; however, most commonly, software is used to describe major sets of programs, such as word processing, and database.

Accounting

Accounting programs perform all the routine and complicated tasks of accounting. Many programs are sold in modules such as: General Ledger, Accounts Payable, Accounts Receivable, Payroll, while others for home or small business are available as a complete package. Most businesses, when performing their accounting functions manually, had to choose single-entry accounting as their method of recording transactions. With the use of computers, double-entry accounting is the standard.

Graphics   *Graphics* programs replace the paintbrush, pen, chalk, and easel of the art world. In addition, other graphics packages allow the manipulation of photographs, pictures, and any other graphic media.

Database   *Databases* are collections of information in a structured format. Phone books, rolodex cards, member lists, and date books are examples of databases used everyday. The computer handles databases exceptionally well.

Desktop Publishing   *Desktop publishing* programs automate the manual task of paste-up. What was once performed with typesetting machines, photographs, razor blades, glue, and tape is now performed electronically with desktop publishing software.

OLE   *OLE* is the acronym for Object Linking and Embedding, meaning, an object from one software application (such as a spreadsheet) is embedded (copied) into another application (such as a memo in a word processing application). Optionally, linking is when the applications are instructed to keep track of the status of each of the documents and to automatically (or with warnings) update the embedded object when the source object is modified or changed. More simply, a spreadsheet can be produced and included (embedded) in a memo or report. If the spreadsheet is changed, it will automatically be updated in the memo (linking).

Word Processing   *Word processing* programs allow the manipulation and storage of text for the production of any printed media. There is a wide diversity of products on the market, ranging from simple to complex. The word processing programs on the market today, averaging about $250, are more powerful than the dedicated word processing machines sold in the late 1970s and 1980s costing over $100,000.

FRAMEWORK FOR AN IMPLEMENTATION STRATEGY

The following information should be contained in a communication/implementation strategy provided to all employees affected by the new system or process:

I.   How did we get here?

    A. What is the time line?

    B. What are the current conditions?

    C. What has historically occurred?

II. What were we looking for?

    A. Is this a new way of doing business?

    B. Is this a new venture?

    C. Was this caused by growth?

    D. What is the strategy?

III. Who was involved?

    A. Was this a partnership among units or unit involved (departments)?

    B. Who were the individuals?

    C. Who is affected?

IV. What did they do?

    A. Did they conduct a series of interviews?

    B. Did they hold meetings and discussions?

    C. What were the results?

    D. What conclusions were drawn?

V.   What were the guidelines?

    A. How did they select appropriate technology?

    B. Which requirements were targeted?

    C. How will infrastructure be built?

    D. Will implementation teams be created?

VI. What are we going to have when we're done?

    A. What will the system do?

    B. What will it provide?

    C. What will it replace?

    D. How long will it last?

VII. How are we going to do it?

    A. How will it be introduced?

B. What support will be available?

C. What training will be available?

D. How will individual needs and requirements be dealt with?

VIII. When will the system be available?

    A. What will the system do for me?

    B. What will I see?

    C. What can I view?

    D. What can I produce?

IX. What is it?

    A. What will it look like?

    B. How will it perform?

    C. How will I use it?

X. Who will use it?

    A. In the long term?

    B. In the short term?

XI. What is my role and responsibility?

XII. How do I protect the information?

XIII. What support will be available?

    A. User guides

    B. Reference materials

    C. Glossaries

    D. On-line help

    E. Labs to practice using the system

    F. One-on-one follow-up

    G. Support assistance

        1. Help desk

        2. Training classes

        3. Refresher sessions

        4. One-on-one support on-call

CHAPTER EIGHT

Types and Sources of
Funding for Your Program

8.1 Introduction 259
8.2 Basic Fund-Raising 260
8.3 Contracts and Grants 260
    (a) Locating Potential Awards 261
    (b) Managing Contracts and Grants 261
    (c) Financial Reports 269
8.4 Summary of Types of Gifts 269
8.5 General Fund-Raising 272
8.6 Your Role as Financial Educator 273
    (a) Developing a Simplified Set of Policies or a Guidebook
        for Volunteers and New Hires 273
8.7 The Role of the Development Officer 276
    (a) Prospecting, Cultivating, and Solicitation 276
8.8 The CFO's Role in Support of the Development Officer 276
    (a) Fund-Raising Management and Evaluation 276
    (b) Cash and Liquidity Analysis and Projection 281
8.9 Types of Fund Raising 281
    (a) Promotions/Special Events 281
        (i) Description 281
        (ii) Financial Considerations 282
    (b) Pledge Drives 283
        (i) Description 283
        (ii) Financial Considerations 283
    (c) General Mailings/Telemarketing Campaigns 283
        (i) Description 283
        (ii) Financial Considerations 284
8.10 Charitable Giving—Planned and Outright 284
8.11 Roles and Responsibilities for Planned-Giving Programs 285
    (a) Role of the Governing Board 285
    (b) Role of the Nonprofit Financial Manager 285
    (c) Organizational Fit 286

8.12 Donor Motivation   286
    (a) Planned Giving   286
    (b) Wills   287
    (c) Marketing Charitable Planned Giving   287
    (d) Taxes   288
8.13 Outright Gifts   288
    (a) Securities   288
    (b) Real Estate   289
    (c) Tangible Property   289
    (d) Life Insurance   289
8.14 Deferred Gifts   289
    (a) Life Income Gifts   289
    (b) Pooled Income Fund   290
    (c) Charitable Remainder Trusts   290
    (d) Annuity Trust   296
    (e) Charitable Gift Annuity   296
    (f) Charitable Lead Trusts   296
    (g) Trusts   296
    (h) Testamentary Gifts   297
    (i) Restricted and Unrestricted Bequests   297
    (j) Restricted and Unrestricted Endowments   297
    (k) Retirement Plans   298
    (l) Special Considerations Surrounding Planned Gifts   298
    (m) Valuation of the Charitable Deductions   298
    (n) Administration   298
    (o) Services Offered   299
Appendix 8A: A Donor Bill of Rights   301

8.1   INTRODUCTION

This chapter discusses a variety of funding types, as well as their unique requirements and the responsibilities required by the Chief Financial Officer (CFO).

The funding of many nonprofit organizations comes from a variety of sources, both public and private. Some nonprofits rely strictly on donations or contributions from the private sector while others receive much of their support from the government from distribution of tax revenues (in the case of schools, colleges, or universities, for example) or in the form of contracts and grants. In general, there are two types of funding:

Unrestricted funds[1] are those that may be used at the discretion of the Board (or a particular individual within the organization).

[1] Regardless of the restrictions or lack of restrictions on funding types, all funds used by a nonprofit must comply with the rules, regulations, and policies required by law.

Unrestricted funds are commonly received as a result of a capital campaign or other general fund-raising effort. It is critical for a nonprofit to have a portion of its funding in unrestricted funds. This gives the Board the flexibility to direct funds and efforts toward the greatest need.

Restricted funds are those that must be used for a specific purpose or project. Much of restricted funds are received through government contracts or grants, but restricted funds may also be received from nongovernmental sources.

It is not uncommon for many funding types to fall somewhere between the two definitions above.

8.2 BASIC FUND-RAISING

Nonprofit organizations rely on contributions to support their operations. These contributions are raised for nonprofit organizations from a combination of individuals, foundations and organizations, and the government.

There are a myriad of approaches to raising money for your organization. The approach chosen will be greatly determined by the type of service provided. Your organization and your financial needs will impact how you set about raising funds: from bake sales to planned giving arrangements or contracts and grants.

There are dozens of books on the subject of marketing, public relations, and donor relations. This chapter is not intended as the know-all, tell-all, of raising money in nonprofit organizations; however, we attempt to provide a general overview of the fund-raising activities, and what is unique or significant from your perspective: the financial manager.

8.3 CONTRACTS AND GRANTS

Contracts and grants may be received from a variety of sources: private or public. Generally, these types of funds are restrictive; meaning, the funds must be used for a specific purpose.

A *contract* involves an agreement between two parties. The contractor provides resources (e.g., money, staff, space) with the understanding that he or she will receive something in return (e.g., a research paper, a tangible product, clinical evidence). For example, pharmaceutical companies enter into contracts with research institutions (both non- and for-profit) to perform clinical trials of new drugs. The pharmaceutical company receives, at the completion of

the project, the results of the trial (generally in the form of a research paper). The pharmaceutical company may hope that these
trials are positive (meaning that the new drug produces the anticipated benefit) but it is not the responsibility of the recipient of the
funds to sway the outcome. The only *product* the company will receive as a result of the contract is the findings, either positive or
negative.

Grants are typically awarded for a specific project or individual's efforts (such as a scientific research project). Unlike a contract, a grant does not require that the grantor receive anything in
return.

There is no difference in how the CFO manages a contract or
a grant, with the exception of assuring that the *product*, promised in
a contract, is delivered within the terms and conditions defined in
the contract. The funds themselves are managed identically.

(a) Locating Potential Awards

There are a variety of ways of locating sources for contracts and
grants. Within the academic and research communities the U.S.
government and various foundations and organizations which
award funds often announce a new research project in the form of
a request for proposal (RFP). Although these agencies widely distribute the RFP requests, it is also wise to verify that your organization is on their mailing lists.

In addition to the list of foundations shown in Exhibit 8.1, information may be found on the Internet at Foundations On-Line
(http://www.foundations.org/).[2] Exhibit 8.1 lists some of the major
awarding organizations.

(b) Managing Contracts and Grants

The financial-management requirements for contracts and grants
are based on a combination of the awarding entities' policies and
those of the receiving nonprofit organization. Often, as part of the
negotiation process, the nonprofit organization may be required to
deliver a copy of its financial policies. These policies are the template for the award.

> <Nonprofit Organization> agrees to adhere to the following
> policies: <Nonprofit Organization> Standard Policies and
> Procedures dated <date> and <Giving Entity>'s Standard
> Policies and Procedures dated <date>.

---

[2]Foundations.org is a service of the Northern California Community Foundation, Inc.

Exhibit 8.1.   Listing of Foreign and U.S. Foundations

Foundation	Organization Mission
Abell Foundation	Private foundation whose mission is to effect positive change focusing on education, economic development, health, and human services
Amateur Athletic Foundation of Los Angeles	Awards grants to youth sport organizations within Southern California and manages the largest sports research library in North America
Amy Foundation	Offers cash awards and support materials for those who wish to communicate Biblical truth to our nation through popular media
Annie E. Casey Foundation	Private charitable organization dedicated to helping build better futures for disadvantaged children in the United States
Asia Foundation	A private American grant-making organization that makes more than 1,500 grants each year to government agencies and nongovernmental organizations in 31 Asian and Pacific Island nations
Associated Grantmakers of Massachusetts	Statewide association of corporate and foundation grantmakers. Support and advance effective and responsible philanthropy throughout the Commonwealth of Massachusetts
AT&T Foundation	Overview of programs and guidelines for grant applications
Ben & Jerry's Foundation	Offers competitive grants to not-for-profit organizations throughout the United States that facilitate progressive social change, by addressing the underlying conditions of societal or environmental problems
Benton Foundation	Promotes public interest values and noncommercial services for the National Information Infrastructure through research and policy analysis, outreach to nonprofits and foundations, and print, video, and on-line publishing
Bertelsmann Foundation	German Foundation working to solve social problems by carrying out projects with partners in scientific, public, and private institutions (in German and English)
The Big Ben Foundation	Cooperative between members of the Allentown, Bethlehem, and Easton communities and the students of Lehigh University distributing funds to nonprofit community-based organizations or individuals with specific economic hardships
Carnegie Corporation of New York	

Foundation	Organization Mission
Charles A. and Anne Morrow Lindbergh Foundation	Dedicated to furthering the Lindbergh's shared vision of a balance between technological advancement and environmental preservation
Chiang Ching-kuo Foundation for International Scholarly Exchange	Awards grants to promote the study of Chinese culture and society
China Youth Development Foundation	
Coleman Foundation	Offering grants to any university, college, or community college establishing an entrepreneurship program, course, or community outreach program focusing on self-employment and/or business ownership
The Commonwealth Foundation	Intergovernmental grant-giving organization distributing funds to nongovernmental organizations in Commonwealth countries
The Commonwealth Fund	Supports independent research on health and social policy issues
Community Foundation of Santa Clara County	Creates charitable funds with donors and makes grants to nonprofit organizations in the Silicon Valley area
Council on Foundations	An association of foundations and corporations, serves the public good by promoting and enhancing effective and responsible philanthropy
David and Lucile Packard Foundation	
Directory of Texas Foundations	On-line listings and statistics on grant amounts and assets
Do Right Foundation	Seeks to fund pilot programs addressing violence prevention, joblessness, justice system productivity, welfare, government efficiency, and parenting skills
The Ewing Marion Kauffman Foundation	An operating and grant-making foundation that works toward the vision of self-sufficient people in healthy communities
The Ford Foundation	Providing grants and loans to projects that strengthen democratic values, reduce poverty and injustice, promote international cooperation, and advance human achievement
Foundation Center	Independent nonprofit organization established by foundations to increase public understanding of the foundation field

Exhibit 8.1. Listing of Foreign and U.S. Foundations (*continued*)

Foundation	Organization Mission
Foundation for the Mid South	Nonprofit organization that seeks to help Arkansas, Louisiana, and Mississippi share resources and leadership across geographic, political, and provincial boundaries
Fundacion Pedro Barrie de la Maza	Private foundation devoted to promoting the development of Galicia from a global perspective (in Galician, Spanish, and English)
Gary Payton Foundation	Benefits underprivileged youths
Gates Library Foundation	Founded by Bill Gates and Melinda French Gates, and dedicated to partnering with U.S. and Canadian public libraries to bring computers and digital information to the communities they serve
George Gund Foundation	Making grants quarterly in areas of education, economic development and community revitalization, human services, arts, environment, and civic affairs
Hartford Foundation for Public Giving	A foundation that forms an endowment for the community, the income from which provides a source of charitable support for numerous local organizations
Houston Endowment Inc.	A private foundation dedicated to the support of charitable undertakings
Jackie Robinson Foundation	Nurtures scholars who are the living legacy of his dedication to improving America for everyone
Japan Foundation	
John D. and Catherine T. MacArthur Foundation	Information about programs, how to apply, recent grants listing, and more
John Simon Guggenheim Memorial Foundation	Provides fellowships for advanced professionals in all fields (natural sciences, social sciences, humanities, creative arts), except for the performing arts
Knut och Alice Wallenbergs Stiftelse (Knut and Alice Wallenberg Foundation)	Promotes scientific research and educational activities that benefit Sweden (site in Swedish and English)
Lila Wallace-Reader's Digest Fund	Private grant-making foundation making grants to enhance the cultural life of communities through arts and culture, adult literacy, and urban parks programs
Lymphoma Research Foundation of America, Inc.	Funding research and providing patient resources, including support groups, educational materials, clinical trials, information, and a periodic newsletter

Foundation	Organization Mission
Marion Foundation	
Markle Foundation	Provides funding in the development and use of the technologies of communication and information to enhance lifelong learning and promote an informed citizenry
Medina Foundation	Aids in improving the human condition in the greater Puget Sound community by making grants to selected qualified charitable organizations
Meredith Miller Foundation	Addresses issues important to women and children, particularly involving violence, in memory of Meredith Miller, a student who was murdered in 1994
Milken Family Foundation	Has worked with more than one thousand organizations which share its purpose of discovering inventive ways of helping people help themselves to lead productive and satisfying lives
Nathan Cummings Foundation	Private grant-making foundation focusing on arts, environment, health, Jewish life, spirituality, and democratic values
National Heritage Foundation	Resources and services you need to set up your charitable foundation
National Hospice Foundation	Devoted exclusively to increasing awareness of and access to hospice care through the financial support of education and research
Near East Cultural and Educational Foundation of Canada	
Nelson Mandela Children's Fund	
New England Biolabs Foundation	Private foundation supporting grassroots organizations working with the environment, social change, the arts, elementary education, and scientific research; site includes grant application guidelines
New York Regional Association of Grantmakers	Nonprofit membership association of donors in the tristate area
Nobel Foundation	
Our Kids Foundation	Volunteers working toward improving life for our children; we fund various projects in the Ottawa–Carleton region
Peace Development Fund	Nonprofit foundation supporting progressive grassroots movements through grants and training

Exhibit 8.1. Listing of Foreign and U.S. Foundations (*continued*)

Foundation	Organization Mission
Peter F. Drucker Canadian Foundation	Finds, celebrates, and inspires innovation in the nonprofit sector in Canada
Peter F. Drucker Foundation for Nonprofit Management	
Pew Charitable Trusts	Private philanthropies supporting nonprofit activities in the arts and culture, education, the environment, health and human services, public policy, and religion
Philanthrofund	Dedicated to funding community organizations that serve the lesbian, gay, bisexual, and allied communities of the upper Midwest
Puerto Rico Community Foundation	Nonprofit philanthropic organization supported by community resources, whose mission is to help community groups solve pressing socio-economic problems
Rex Foundation	Embodying the spirit of altruism in the Grateful Dead Community by supporting groups engaged in environmental, social and community services, the arts, and cultural preservation
Rockefeller Brothers Fund	Private, grant-making foundation
The Rockefeller Foundation	Committed to helping to define and pursue a path toward environmentally sustainable development consistent with individual rights
Rotary Foundation	Not-for-profit corporation that supports the efforts of Rotary International to achieve world understanding and peace through international humanitarian, educational, and cultural exchange programs
Sasakawa Peace Foundation	Dedicated to fostering world peace and prosperity by supporting nonprofit activities with a global perspective and a global impact
Sega Foundation	Offers funding for education and health projects
Sloan Foundation	Philanthropic nonprofit institution established by Alfred P. Sloan, Jr. in 1934
Spain '92 Foundation	Chartered to promote, support, and develop a variety of cultural and educational programs between Spain and the United States
Stockholm Water Foundation	Founded in 1990 to encourage research and development of the world's water by awarding the Stockholm Water Prize

Foundation	Organization Mission
A Territory Resource	Public foundation funding northwest organizations working to create a more equitable society; donation and volunteer opportunities available
The Virtual Foundation	Consortium of not-for-profit organizations that fund small, international, grass-roots grants
W. Alton Jones Foundation	Private grant-making foundation focusing on global environmental protection and the prevention of nuclear war or other massive release of radioactive material
W.K. Kellogg Foundation	Focusing on building the capacity of individuals, communities, and institutions to solve their own problems
Weingart Foundation	Making grants to a wide range of human service organizations, educational and health institutions, and cultural centers throughout Southern California
Windham Foundation	Established to restore buildings and to provide financial support for education and private charities in Vermont
The Winston Foundation	Dedicated to the prevention of conflict worldwide
Z. Smith Reynolds Foundation	Private, charitable family foundation created to serve the people of North Carolina. Information on grant application procedures and special programs

Source: Reprinted, with permission, Northern California Community Foundation, Inc.

The negotiation and the resulting contract or grant award will include language which identifies the policy requirements *and* exceptions and/or additional requirements beyond those defined in the standard policies of each party. (Refer to the Financial Policy chapter for more information.)

Ultimately, it is the responsibility of the contract or grant recipient (generally the principal investigator) to appropriately manage and monitor the funds; however, it is common practice for these individuals to *delegate* all or part of these responsibilities to the CFO or fund manager. Therefore, the CFO or fund manager must assure that all expenditures made against a contract or a grant are appropriate and directly applicable to the specific project and purpose of the funding. In addition, expenditures must be reasonable and customary.

Reasonable and customary are common terms found in most contract and grant awards. The inclusion of these terms will demand that a protocol for the acquisition of supplies and services be followed. It is not sufficient that each expenditure acquisition follow a standard protocol, but that the adherence to the protocol be documented sufficiently to withstand an audit.

The minimum policy requirements for any U.S. government award are compliance with Office of Management and Budget (OMB) Circular A21 and OMB Circular A110. The U.S. Department of Health and Human Services, the umbrella organization for a variety of other U.S. government departments, provides a variety of publications which specify the policy requirements for each award (see Exhibit 8.2 for information on contacting the United States Health and Human Services [USHHS]).

Exhibit 8.2. How to Fund Information about Health and Human Services Grant Programs

The Department of Health and Human Services (HHS) has approximately 300 grant programs, most of which are administered in a decentralized manner by five agencies. HHS does not have a single publication that describes all HHS grant programs. Instead, we use the Catalog of Federal Domestic Assistance (CFDA). The Catalog profiles all Federal grant programs, including HHS programs. It also includes a helpful section on writing grant applications.

The CFDA is published annually and updated mid-year. It is available for reference in the government documents section of most major libraries and in the offices of state and local governments. And, more recently, it is now available on-line through GrantsNet. There are various ways to obtain your copy of the Catalog:

1. An on-line electronic text version is available for keyword searching and downloading to your own PC from the GrantsNet (http://hhs-custos.dhhs.gov/progorg/grantsnet/) information service.
2. A diskette electronic text version can be purchased from the General Services Administration (202-708-5126) for a basic purchase price of $60.
3. An on-line electronic database version is available through the Federal Assistance Programs Retrieval System (FAPRS). To access this system, you must have communication software and a modem in addition to a personal computer and printer. For an annual fee of $50, you will be able to access this electronic database to search and retrieve information from the Catalog. Contact the General Services Administration (202-708-5126) for more information.
4. A hardcopy version of the Catalog may be purchased for $50 from the Superintendent of Documents, U.S. Government Printing Office (202-783-3238).

(c) Financial Reports

Financial reports may be required by the provider of either a contract or a grant. The type and frequency of the reports will vary, even with government agencies. Commonly, monthly, quarterly, or annual reports are required that, at minimum, provide a summary of expenditures by budgetary or cost category. In addition, detailed transaction level reports may also be required at regular intervals either along with or in addition to the summary report.

With rare exception, the awarding organization (e.g., agency, foundation, corporation) has the right to audit the financial records which pertain to the contract or grant. If, during the audit process, the awarding organization determines that some or all of the expenditures were not "reasonable or customary," they may be disallowed. If disallowances occur, it is the responsibility of the nonprofit to reimburse the awarding agency for those expenditures. These reimbursements are required to be expended from unrestricted funds (meaning they cannot be reimbursed from another contract or grant).

8.4 SUMMARY OF TYPES OF GIFTS

In addition to various types of ways for raising money, there are also various types of gifts your organization may receive:

Cash and currency	These will come in the form of checks, cash, or credit card transactions (normally less a 3 percent transaction fee from the involved financial institution)
Gifts	
• Securities	Stocks bonds, Treasury bills, etc.
• Personal property	Real estate, etc.
• In-Kind	Tangible items, such as computers, printing, and food
• Services	Consulting services, marketing services, etc.

Each of these types of gifts requires a unique set of methods for tracking and managing their use, as well as different benefits to your organization and the donor. Tax law varies widely and in most cases the donor will be required to complete an itemized form in order to claim any charitable gift. The donor should seek the advice of his or her personal accountant or financial manager to determine how best to donate the gift to your organization.

WHAT IS PLANNED GIVING?[a]

The term planned giving refers to charitable gifts that require some planning before they are made. Planned gifts are popular because they can provide valuable tax benefits and/or income for life.

Whether a donor uses cash or other assets, such as real estate, artwork, or partnership interests, the benefits of funding a planned gift can make this type of charitable giving very attractive to both the donor and charity.

POTENTIAL BENEFITS OF PLANNED GIFTS TO DONOR

- Increase current income to yourself or others
- Reduce your income tax
- Avoid capital gains tax
- Pass assets to your family at a reduced tax cost
- Make significant donations to charity

With the assistance of a well-informed development officer and/or financial advisor, anyone can create a planned gift to meet his or her charitable and financial goals.

Planned gifts include bequests, trusts, and contracts between a donor and a charity. Basic descriptions of the most popular types of planned gifts follow.

BEQUEST

When a donor decides to leave some assets to charity in her will, she is making a bequest. The donor's estate will receive a charitable estate tax deduction at her death, when the gift is made to charity.

GIFT ANNUITY

A gift annuity is a contract between a charity and a donor. In return for a donation of cash or other assets, the charity agrees to pay the donor, or a friend or family member the

[a]Provided by PG Calc Incorporated, a leading supplier of planned giving software and services to the nonprofit community

donor chooses, a fixed payment for life. The donor can also claim a charitable tax deduction. If long-term capital gain property is used to fund a gift annuity, the donor may avoid some capital gains tax.

Income from a gift annuity can be deferred for a period of years. Deferred gift annuities are often set up by younger donors to supplement retirement income.

POOLED-INCOME FUND

The name describes this planned gift well—a charity accepts gifts from many donors into a fund and distributes the income of the fund to each donor or recipient of the donor's choosing according to the donor's share of the fund. For making a gift to a pooled fund, a donor receives a charitable income tax deduction and may avoid capital gains tax. When an income beneficiary dies, the charity gets the donor's portion of the fund.

CHARITABLE REMAINDER TRUST

This trust makes payments, either a fixed amount (annuity trust) or a percentage of trust principal (unitrust), to whomever the donor chooses to receive income. The donor may claim a charitable income-tax deduction and may avoid capital gains tax. At the end of the trust term, the charity receives whatever amount is left in the trust.

Charitable remainder unitrusts provide some flexibility in the distribution of income, and thus can be helpful in retirement planning.

CHARITABLE LEAD TRUST

This trust makes payments to charity for a number of years. At the end of the trust term, the principal goes to heirs named by the donor. The donor may claim a charitable-gift tax deduction for making a lead trust gift.

RETAINED LIFE ESTATE

A donor may make a gift of his house to charity and retain the right to live in the house for the remainder of his life. The donor receives an immediate income tax deduction for the gift. At the donor's death, the house goes to charity.

8.5   GENERAL FUND-RAISING

The least restrictive type of fund-raising is money that is not ear-marked for a specific purpose, but the marketing of this type of drive does not often carry the benefit of the urgency of a specific funding drive. For example, if your ceiling was to collapse during a flood and you created a specific fund-raising drive to collect monies to repair the ceiling, you have created a sense of need, an urgency, and a finite amount of money is needed. All monies collected for this purpose would need to be used for that purpose. This creates special challenges for the financial manager.

It is critical that the financial manager communicate her needs to the individuals responsible for creating a marketing campaign or fund-raising effort so as to not create unnecessary restrictions in the use of contributed funds. The individuals responsible for the fund-raising effort are not always aware of the fiduciary responsibilities of your organization, nor are they aware of the flexibility required in cash or fund management. Very minor changes on designation or contribution forms can mean the difference between restricted monies and those than can be used freely (Exhibit 8.3).

The most ideal situation would be for the financial manager and fund-raising manager to meet to discuss any new campaigns, and to review any literature that may be distributed to potential donors. As shown in the right-hand side of Exhibit 8.3, a minor change in designation, offering the donor a choice in how the funds may be administered, may make a tremendous difference in how the monies may be used.

Exhibit 8.3.   Restricted versus Unrestricted Donations

Help Us Raise the Roof

Enclosed is my check in the amount of $ _____ for the new ceiling.

Restrictive Before

Help Us Raise the Roof

Enclosed is my check in the amount of $ _____ :

☐ Please use my contribution as needed, including the repair of the new ceiling. I place no limits on how best this contribution may be used.
☐ Please use my contribution solely for the new ceiling. I limit the use of my contribution for this purpose.

Restrictive and
Unrestrictive After

8.6   YOUR ROLE AS FINANCIAL EDUCATOR

In any organization, there is always a potential conflict between the individuals who spend the money and the individuals who pay the bills. The leaders, who set the vision and the goals in your organization, may not have the technical financial knowledge necessary to accurately understand the financial reports or details provided to them. As the financial manager of your organization, one of your responsibilities is to educate the leadership about matters relating to finance.

In addition, volunteers, public relations staff, or marketing specialists may also be unfamiliar with financial matters. The best approach may be to assume that individuals outside the financial arena do not understand the information contained on standard reports, such as balance sheets and profit and loss statements, nor will they understand the restrictive nature of fund accounting. This does not mean, however, that you should not distribute financial reports; rather, you should be available as an educator or mentor to everyone in your organization who may need a quick lesson in accounting terms or how to read a financial report.

The volunteers or individuals who raise money for your organization will be instructed on how to raise money. Or, they may come to your organization with this skill set. This special set of skills in negotiating, dealing with people, and so forth, should be highly valued. Individuals involved in these kinds of pursuits are often very creative and dedicated to the mission of your organization. Any activity that they believe interferes with their mission of raising funds may be viewed as restrictive or bureaucratic. It is the responsibility of the financial manager to assume responsibility for those activities that do not require input from your fund-raisers and to educate them on why certain activities must be performed.

While it is true that it is your responsibility to turn vision and goal into a financial reality, there are limits on what you will be able to do. Your willingness to be flexible and to investigate options will help a great deal in bridging any gaps and demonstrating to others that you share their vision. The more you are able to communicate your special requirements and responsibilities, without burdening others with the specific details of your work, the more willing they will be to comply with the rules and regulations to which you must adhere.

(a) Developing a Simplified Set of Policies or a Guidebook for Volunteers and New Hires

As part of the ongoing process to educate and communicate your needs to others in the organization, the following is a sample of a simplified-procedures document that may be used as a template to develop your own set of procedures. This type of document can be distributed to individuals in your organization as part of a new-hire or assimilation document created for new staff.

The document you create and distribute to staff and volunteers does not take the place of a standard set of policies and procedures. The purpose of a simplified procedure document is to provide information in an easy-to-follow format. Your standard policies will be used most specifically by fund and project managers whose roles and responsibilities require strict adherence to policy. Staff and volunteers who do not work directly with the fiscal affairs will benefit greatly from a streamlined procedural document, as shown in Exhibit 8.4.

Exhibit 8.4. Simplified Financial Policy

INTRODUCTION

The following process applies to the set of funds listed below. As of <DATE>, these include:

- General fund
- Designated fund
- Capital fund
- Other

All other funds are managed "externally," that is, by volunteers, or paid staff. These programs submit quarterly financial statements to the Board of Directors.

BUDGET PROCESS

1. The Board of Directors makes the call to Program Directors/Fund Managers for annual budget requests.
2. Board reviews budget requests and makes recommendations/adjustments.
3. Board notifies Program Directors/Fund Managers of approved budget.
4. Program Director/Fund Manager conducts program.
5. CFO provides monthly detailed reports of activity (budget and actual) to Program Directors for review. Directors notify CFO of any questions or changes that need to be made.
6. CFO keeps all directors apprised of total financial picture on a monthly basis as well as the details of their own activities per financial statements.
7. Final monthly reports are distributed to Board of Directors and Program Directors/Fund Managers.

FINANCIAL MANAGEMENT PROCESS CASH RECEIPTS

1. Income comes into the organization through mail, hand delivery, and various other methods.
2. Office staff, with volunteer(s), prepares cash receipt reports and deposit slips and takes cash to the bank.
3. Office staff notifies CFO of cash receipts by copy of reports.
4. CFO enters into the accounting system for financial statement purposes. Verifies entries with receipts and notifications sent from bank.
5. Bank sends statements and reconciliations are performed manually by CFO and with the system data.

Exhibit 8.4. (*continued*)

6. CFO prepares financial statements. These statements include the details of all income. These reports are distributed monthly to Board of Directors, Program Directors/Fund Managers, etc.
7. All discrepancies are reported to the CFO, Board of Directors, etc., and corrections are made, as necessary.

APPROVING EXPENDITURES
Assumptions

Program Director/Fund Manager has approved budget (per budget process) to work within. Program Director/Fund manager authorizes expenditures related to their program.

Process

1. Program Director/Office Staff prepare a form (check request) to cover the amount of the expenditure and obtains the Program Director/Fund Manager approval signature on the form.
2. Program Director/Fund manager authorizes invoices for payment.
3. After Program Director/Fund Manager approves for payment, the CFO reviews for accounting correctness (e.g., in budget, correct account number, money in bank).
4. The check request form, with all approval signatures is delivered to the CFO who enters it into accounting system for issuance of the check as designated.
5. Office Staff verifies backup documents, audits check and documentation, obtains signature on check, sends check, with appropriate backup, to the vendor.
6. Office Staff file copy of payments and paid invoices in central office files for review and audit as necessary.

Financial Statements and Reports

1. At month end, the CFO produces financial statements from the Power Church Fund Accounting system and distributes them to the Program Directors, Council of Finance, and Board of Directors.
2. The CFO also distributes copy of the financial statement to each of the Program Directors/Fund Managers, along with the detailed general ledgers related to the accounts for which they have jurisdiction. The CFO also distributes budget versus actual reports.
3. Program Managers notify the CFO if they have questions or if changes are necessary.
4. System produces check registers which are available to Board, Councils, and others for review.

Payroll

1. The Staff Committee recommends all salary and fees and submits them to the Board of Directors for approval.
2. Upon approval, the Committee notifies all staff and contractors of their compensation package.
3. Staff Committee notifies the CFO, who gets payroll implemented.
4. Monthly, the CFO provides reports of same to the Chair of the Staff Committee for review, to insure that approved activities are occurring.
5. Year-end 1099s and W2s prepared, distributed, as required by law.

Note: This is the annual process. Mid-year hiring, contract negotiations, and wage adjustments are handled in a similar manner on an as needed basis.

8.7 THE ROLE OF THE DEVELOPMENT OFFICER

Donors make contributions to help "the public" upon receipt of factual information and trust in the nonprofit organization. Solicitation of funds is done by the nonprofit organization using various fund-raising methods.

(a) Prospecting, Cultivating, and Solicitation

Asking for a gift is the culmination of the fund-raising process. Before asking for contributions, the following steps should be taken by the organization.

1. *Identification of priorities*
2. *Prospecting:*
   - Know everything possible about prospective donor(s)—it is critical to match donor interest and dollars with priorities.
   - Ask within a range that makes it possible for the prospective donor to give.
3. *Cultivation:* Take time to help potential donors understand the needs of the organization. This may involve inviting the prospect to activities, following up with phone calls and visits.
4. *Solicitation:* Making the "ask:" The ask is described as giving the donor the opportunity to make a gift that makes him or her *feel good*, while at the same time, allows the organization to accomplish its mission.

8.8 THE CFO'S ROLE IN SUPPORT OF THE DEVELOPMENT OFFICER

(a) Fund-Raising Management and Evaluation

Fund-raising management and evaluation is an area in which non-fund-raising, financial personnel can and should be involved. It is an area in which the organization may be forced to rely on the CFO, because it cannot afford and chooses not to hire a development officer. Or, the CFO may also hold the title of development officer. We contend that it is also an area in which nonprofit organizations can learn from businesses. First, recognize that in businesses, the treasurer is the fund-raiser. The treasurer is responsible for arranging funding, typically from leases, debt, and equity. Second, she or he has global view of many interlocked facets of the organization:

- Organization strategy
- Long-range financial plans

- Present and anticipated financial position
- Cash flow characteristics
- Alternate sources of revenue and liquidity
  - Investments maturing
  - Investments ready for sale
  - Debt financing
  - Grant proposal and status
  - Business income
  - Historical pattern and trends of donation revenue
  - Split of "general fund" restricted and unrestricted funds
  - Split of restricted and unrestricted liquid funds in concurrent categories

Exhibit 6.7 presents the global view of the treasurer. It is apparent that the financial manager has a bird's eye, integrated perspective that no one else in the organization has—at least at this level of detail and with this degree of comprehension.

Third, we contend that the organization benefits from having the nonprofit CFO increase his involvement in fund-raising objectives, planning, execution, and post-campaign evaluation:

- Better integration of entire spectrum of financial resource utilization
- Assists fund-raising office in communicating its objectives, methods, and resource needs across the organization
- Provides improved strategic direction and continuous improvement to the fund-raising office/function

Summarizing, proficient organizations have CFOs with hands-on authority and/or oversight over the organization's revenue stream. How can we put these ideals into operation? The CFO should pursue four strategic involvements, in order of priority: (1) ensure adherence to the correct philosophy and major objective of fund raising (other involvements are more self-explanatory); (2) plan and then schedule the campaign expenditures; (3) assist in the mid-campaign evaluation and redirection; and (4) oversee post-campaign effectiveness and efficiency ration analysis. We will expand on each of these briefly.

1. *Setting the philosophy and major objective of fund-raising:* The fund-raising expenditure must be viewed as an investment, like other capital expenditures, not as an expense. An appropriate philosophy for the annual campaign is to raise money proactively this year for next year's operations, instead of for contemporaneously trying to fund this year's operations; failure to recognize

this explains why so many nonprofits are living hand-to-mouth and experiencing recurrent cash crises. A major objective of fund-raising is to do its part to help meet the service provision objective, which has already been spelled out by proficiently managed organization in the long-range financial plan (see discussion in Chapter 4) and in the annual budgeting process (see Chapter 5); the investment in annual campaign fund-raising is derived from the anticipated service provision spelled out in the budget, and is a direct output of the budgeting process.

There is one important modification/amplification: looking back at our hub and spokes diagram (Exhibit 6.7), we must adjust up or down the annual campaign dollar goal based on the relative revenue contributions of those other revenue sources, with the overall objective of hitting a liquidity target that is based on transaction needs for cash, which increase along with service activity (see the cash management discussion on setting the liquidity target and other factors that may reduce the liquidity target, such as re-engineered bank relations and/or using controlled disbursement account).

The organization should have fund-raising policies that spell out its philosophy of fund-raising to prospective donors. While this is beyond the scope of our presentation, check with other organizations to find out what they are doing. Prison Fellowship, the Washington, D.C.-based organization founded by Chuck Colson to provide an outreach to prisoners, has an outstanding set of policies that might serve as a model for you.[3]

2. *Plan and then schedule the campaign expenditures:* Instead of prolonging the start of the annual campaign or doing it at the development office's convenience, use your knowledge of the organization's cash-flow cycle and current cash position to provide direction to the effort. Second, recognize and help others on the management team understand the timing of the underlying cash flow cycle in an annual campaign:

Cash outflow for materials and labor → cash inflow from campaigns

The annual campaign is a cash-draining activity for some period. The implications? Expenditures must be anticipated, and enough cash must be on hand prior to the campaign to fund the campaign. The most important reason for not achieving their financial objective, according to financial officers surveyed in the Lilly study, was inadequate and/or ineffective fund-raising. We

---

[3]*See* the pamphlet by Whitney Kuniholm, "The Ministry of Fund-raising," Prison Fellowship, P.O. Box 17500, Washington, D.C., 20041-0500, 39–42.

emphasize: fund-raising must be looked at as an investment, not as an expense, regardless of the accounting treatment. It is vital that you work with the development officer to convey this mind-set to your Chief Executive Officer (CEO) and Board, and ultimately your donors or grant sources. Some CFOs or Board Treasurers counter: "We don't have the cash to do the level of fund-raising we really need to undertake." Bill Levis, a fund-raising expert associated with Baruch College in New York City, recommends that organizations go one step further with the timeline analysis and raise funds this year to fund next year's expenses. Let's think about that. It entails a planning mindset, doesn't it? What are some likely repercussions of such a policy? It results in having the equivalent of one year's operating expenses in unrestricted liquid assets (in addition to the "money for a rainy day" you already hold in cash reserves) by the end of this year?[4] In turn, it may require educating the donors, and it will also in some cases result in a red flag raised by one of the philanthropic oversight bureaus—particularly if you have sizable reserves saved for planned program expansion for a merger/acquisition.

3. *Assist in the mid-campaign evaluation and redirection:* Here is an example of using reports gathered within the year to help guide management for the remainder of the year. As results start coming in, the financial office can work with the development office, where separate, to interpret the results to management and the Board. With its global view of the organization, the finance office knows how critical a shortfall is at any given point in time, and can provide guidance as to the best use of a surplus when positive results are achieved.

4. *Oversee post-campaign effectiveness and efficiency ratio analysis:* In the past, it was well nigh impossible to find good information on measuring fund-raising efficiency and effectiveness, but this is changing.[5] Here are some of the general guidelines offered by expert James Greenfield:

---

[4]Your organization may already be there without consciously planning such a strategy. Do you have both (1) cash reserves significantly greater than next year's anticipated operating expenses (and will you still have it at the end of the fiscal year) and (2) a policy that allows the organization to draw down cash reserves to some minimum level in order to fund operations? If so, you are in the same financial position as an organization which consciously adopts this forward-year annual campaign strategy.

[5]We gratefully acknowledge the assistance of Philip M. Purcell, J.D., Director of Planned Giving and Development Counsel, Rose-Hulman Institute of Technology, Terre Haute, IN. A very helpful resource for those wishing to conduct self-assessment of fund-raising is James M. Greenfield, *Fund-Raising Cost Effectiveness: A Self-Assessment Workbook,* (New York: John Wiley & Sons, 1996), 676.

Activity	Reasonable Cost Guideline
Direct mail acquisition	$1.00 to $1.25 per $1.00 raised
Direct mail renewal	$0.20 per $1.00 raised
Membership organization	$0.25 per $1.00 raised
Donor club program	$0.20 per $1.00 raised
Benefit events	$0.50 per $1.00 raised
Volunteer-led annual giving	$0.10 to $0.20 per $1.00 raised
Individual major gift programs	$0.10 to $0.20 per $1.00 raised
Capital campaigns	$0.10 to $0.20 per $1.00 raised
Planned giving/estate planning	$0.20 to $0.30 per $1.00 raised

A three-year study of 51 U.S. colleges and universities found that, on average, it costs 16 cents to raise a dollar, with a median cost of 11 cents and the middle 50 percent of campuses experiencing costs of between 8 and 10 cents.[6]

This figure covers all direct fund-raising staff and programs, but does not include any allocation for president or dean's salaries, space, or utility overhead costs. The study was conducted by CASE and the National Association of College and University Business Officers, and funded by Lilly Endowment, Inc. It also found that, on average, colleges spend just over 2 percent of their educational and general (E&G) budgets for raising money, with gifts raised for operations meeting 10 percent of that budget. The report made an important observation:[7] "The objective of an institution's program should not be to spend as little as possible each year to make money, but to maximize the net. A program that annually produces $2 million at a cost of $160,000, or 8 percent, may look good and is indeed efficient, but one that produces $3 million at a cost of $300,000 or 10 percent, is presumably of more help to the institution—it is bringing in $860,000 more.

As a financial officer, offer assistance to the development office in developing costs standards and efficiency and effectiveness reports. Offer assistance to the CEO and Board in interpreting those reports and making resource-allocation decisions related to fund raising. Above all, help these parties understand the concept of return on fund-raising investment. Once you are there, you are ready to embark on the final achievement: Level 4.

[6]Ellen Ryan, "The Cost of Raising a Dollar," *Case Currents* (September 1990), 58–62.
[7]*Id.* 58.

(b) Cash and Liquidity Analysis and Projection

Moving to the next level is not too difficult once the financial manager gains the global perspective we viewed in the fund-raising involvement in the third level. The tasks we have in mind here are:

1. Refine the analysis of cash and liquidity from Levels 1, 2, and 3:[8]
   - Look at your historical cash flow patterns to see which months have the highest net cash inflows (cash receipts minus cash disbursements), the lowest net cash inflows, and the longest period within a fiscal year in which you are in a "net borrowed position" (showing a bottom-line cash shortage which persists across several months).
   - List all the sources of cash your organization has tapped in the past, and to what degree, to weather cash crises.
   - Estimate the variability of net cash flow by statistical estimation of the range and standard deviation of your historical figures.
2. Work through the diagnostic questionnaire shown in Exhibit 6.5. Use the diagnostic questions shown toward the left of the diagram to determine if your target liquidity level is set too low. Reverse the questions to give an assessment of the possibility of having excess liquidity.

8.9 TYPES OF FUND RAISING

There is a myriad of approaches to raising money for your organization. The approach you choose will be greatly determined by the type of service you provide. Your organization and your financial needs will greatly impact how you set about raising funds.

(a) Promotions/Special Events

(i) Description. Promotions range from give-aways to the sale of merchandise. Public television uses promotions as their primary means of raising money from public sources. Thousands of vendors supply merchandise specifically targeted to nonprofit organizations. Examples include candy or cookie manufacturers (Girl Scout Cookies), pen manufacturers, wrapping paper, catering services, and household items such as bric-a-brac. There are currently hundreds of thousands of reference listings for these types of

---

[8]Once you have your daily cash receipts and cash disbursements in a financial spreadsheet, use the statistics functions to do this for you.

promotional activities listed on the Internet as well as other sources. It is possible to have businesses donate items to promote; however, in most cases, your organization will be purchasing goods and services for this purpose. In order for this type of fund-raising effort to be successful, at minimum, the costs of the goods or service must be covered completely by the donation. The purpose of this type of drive is to raise funds in excess of the total cost of the promotional item.

(ii) Financial considerations. When calculating the cost for the promotional item, the following needs to be considered as the total cost of the item (Exhibit 8.5). Many of the vendors that provide this type of service may also provide "drop shipments." Drop shipments are deliveries made directly from the manufacturer or distributor and include all the costs shown in Exhibit 8.5. Careful consideration should be given to this type of service as the vendor will be given the list of names and addresses of your donors. If this type of option is chosen, part of the purchase contract should include the confidentiality (or lack of) for this information.

Exhibit 8.5. Calculating the Minimum Donation Costs

	Total	Qty	Per Unit	Considerations
Base cost	$ 500.00	200	$ 2.50	Factor total cost divided by quantity
Receipt—shipping and delivery	$ 55.00	200	$ 0.28	Factor total cost divided by quantity
Distribution—shipping and delivery Postage			$ 0.55	Postal Service rate per item
Packaging			$ 0.75	Envelope/box and tape, staples, labels
Labor	$ 8.25	15	$ 0.55	Total hourly rate (including benefits and taxes) divided by the number of packages produced per hour
Storage	$ 155.00	200	$ 0.78	Factor total cost divided by quantity
Subtotal:			$ 5.40	
Damage allowance	$ 5.40	10%	$ 0.54	Percentage of total
Minimum donation rate:			$ 5.94	

When ordering, the most challenging decision is determining the quantity. Many vendors that specialize in these types of promotional goods have buy-back plans: they agree to buy back, at a predetermined rate, merchandise that is not distributed. This may be at a pre-negotiated price per item or the original cost of the item less a restocking fee, generally 15 to 20 percent. When negotiating the contract, be sure their buy back policy is clearly stated in the purchase contract.

(b) Pledge Drives

(i) Description. Pledges are gifts of money or other assets at set intervals. This method of fund-raising is commonly used with religious organizations. Members are asked to commit to a set pattern of giving, or a target of giving for a specific time period (such as within a year).

(ii) Financial considerations. The major benefit of pledges is that they produce a regular cash flow. After several years, your organization will have historical data on which to base estimates of "defaults" on pledge commitments. Beyond factors unique to your organization, such as bad publicity, or a perception of lack of need, there are economic factors which may cause your pledges to vary from year-to-year:

- Inflation, general health of the economy
- Unemployment rates in your area (if a large employer suddenly lays off workers)
- Natural disasters in your area (e.g., fire, flood, earthquake)

A method of recording pledges and payments needs to be established. In addition, annual statements, monthly statements, or reminders may need to be produced. A common method of tracking pledges is to assign each donor a pledge number. Each contribution (often a contribution envelope) has a space for this pledge number. By assigning a number to each donor:

- Confidentiality of the donor is maintained, regardless of who is tallying payments.
- Accurate posting to the proper donor account is more likely.

A variety of pledge management software programs is available as well as member tracking software.

(c) General Mailings/Telemarketing Campaigns

(i) Description. General mailings and telemarketing campaigns ask donors for contributions for general or specific purposes.

(ii) Financial considerations. General mailings are popular because they have the lowest initial fund-raising costs; however, they may also prove to have the lowest percentage of return. A 5 percent response rate to a general mailing is generally considered a good response. Combining this type of activity with a follow-up phone drive or visit may yield higher returns.

The initial audience for general mailings would include constituents, members, or friends of your organization. There are a variety of methods for seeking additional addresses.

- Direct marketing consultants provide mailing and phone lists for specific regions, buying or purchasing trends, community affluence, and so forth.

- Telephone book software is a new boost to organizations and companies seeking a relatively inexpensive way of searching out new contributors. These software packages may include both "white and yellow pages." It is important to select a package that matches the need. For example, some have limitations on the number of times a name may be used. Also to be considered is the flexibility for selecting addresses by various demographic groupings.

- Reference books available through book or software stores or local libraries can provide addresses for a specific individual or groups of individuals. Examples include *Who's Who in America* and Almanacs.

8.10 CHARITABLE GIVING—PLANNED AND OUTRIGHT

At a time when nonprofit organizations are struggling to maintain the financial status quo, they would be wise to encourage their members and constituents to consider alternative forms of contributing, especially when donors could substantially and personally benefit from such transactions. It has been long recognized that more and more charities are chasing less and less money. Many of these charities have successfully encouraged individuals and companies to consider noncash gifts or planned gifts at a time when cash is in short supply. The response to this call for nontraditional gifts has been unprecedented and has substantially exceeded traditional giving. Thus, nonprofit organizations should direct their Treasurers or CFOs to explore these opportunities to the greatest extent possible.

While this chapter provides some very basic, general information on charitable planned giving to those responsible for monitoring funds for the organization, it is recommended that this information be used in conjunction with professional legal and financial-planning advice.

The financial management responsibility for managing planned gifts is complex. Recently, more and more professional help in this arena is available from banks and specialized companies. For small- to medium-size nonprofit organizations, it would be cost-effective to hire the experts rather than try to build in-house expertise in this field.

8.11 ROLES AND RESPONSIBILITIES FOR PLANNED-GIVING PROGRAMS

(a) Role of the Governing Board

An organization's success in planned giving demands a high level of commitment on the part of its Board that includes:

- Accepting the fiduciary role required for planned giving
- Setting a variety of policies related to planned giving
- Developing procedures to be used in the planned-giving process
- Assigning specific roles and responsibilities to all parties involved in the process
- Holding responsible parties accountable for their actions in the program
- Understanding the liabilities, as well as the advantages, of engaging in a planned-giving program for the organization
- Providing education and communication to everyone involved in the planned-giving program

(b) Role of the Nonprofit Financial Manager

Since one of the primary roles of the nonprofit financial manager is to raise funds, he or she should be well informed about planned-giving opportunities for donors and the nonprofit organization. The level of information and technical expertise required of the financial manager may depend on the size and staffing of the nonprofit organization and the resulting levels of technical expertise available on the staff. One would expect this expertise to be more readily available in the form of in-house staff specialists or independent consultants in a large nonprofit than in a small one. Nonetheless, it is essential for the financial manager to deliver the necessary information and technical expertise on planned giving to the nonprofit organization's constituents.

(c) Organizational Fit

Before developing a planned-giving program, the charitable non-profit organization should assess its fund-raising program to determine whether such a strategy is compatible with the organization. Not all organizations are suited for this type of contribution program; however, an organization is remiss if it fails to educate itself about, and assess its potential use of, these contribution vehicles.

An organization that is considering the adoption of a planned giving program should address the following baseline questions:

- Does planned giving fit with the overall fund-raising program of the organization?
- Do the contribution history and donor base lend themselves to this type of program?
- Are professional and technical resources available to support this type of giving program?

8.12 DONOR MOTIVATION

Individuals and organizations make charitable contributions for a variety of reasons. Some donors are motivated by an income-tax deduction in which the government shares in the cost of the contribution. For example, if a person in the 40 percent tax bracket makes a gift of $10,000, the contribution actually costs the donor only $6,000 because his/her tax liability has been reduced by $4,000. The higher the income tax bracket, the more savings and lower cost to the donor. This same motive exists with estate planning, providing significant tax and other benefits to the donor.

Nontax motives for nonprofit contributions include furthering a particular mission, investing in the future, improving the community, expressing gratitude, or simply feeling good about helping others. Various marketing, educational, and donor solicitation techniques, used in conjunction with a strategy to maximize income tax benefits, often produce a substantial increase in fund-raising revenue for the organization.

(a) Planned Giving

Planned giving is the term given to the process of planning the ultimate distribution of an estate upon death. Internal Revenue Service (IRS) laws provide certain benefits to those who include a charitable contribution to a qualified nonprofit organization in their estate planning. A number of planned-giving vehicles are available to help donors accomplish their goals in this area.

An individual can dictate the distribution of his or her assets by executing a will that may include a contribution to a qualified nonprofit organization. A number of techniques are available for facilitating such a contribution through a will, most of which include important tax advantages for the donor.

The three basic categories of charitable planned gifts are: life income gifts, outright gifts, and testamentary gifts.

(b) Wills

A will can be defined as a vehicle used to dictate the distribution of an estate upon death. Some basic facts about wills are as follows:

- Anyone of sound mind and over the age of 18 can make a will.
- Everyone over 18 years of age should have a will, regardless of the size of their estate.
- A will can be revoked or changed at any time by destroying it or writing a new will that explicitly revokes the old one.
- Wills often specify who assumes responsibility for minor children, if any, and how the estate is to be distributed.
- Wills allow you to leave your assets to anyone, not just family members. However, most states will not permit you to disinherit your spouse, and some will not allow you to disinherit your children.
- Both spouses in a family need wills.
- Wills do not expire but should be reviewed periodically to ensure that they are current, reflect your wishes, and employ current state and federal tax laws; reflect the current value of your estate, current structure of your family (e.g., marriages, divorces, births, deaths), ever-changing tax laws, personal interests, and relocation from one state to another since estate tax laws vary in different parts of the country.

(c) Marketing Charitable Planned Giving

In order to benefit from charitable planned giving opportunities, the nonprofit organization and its constituents should expect the financial manager to do the following:

- Communicate on the subject of charitable planned giving (either to the Development Officer or to the donor, as needed):
  - What is charitable planned giving?
  - What benefits can it provide to the donor?
  - What benefits can it provide to the recipient nonprofit organization?
  - Where can donors obtain assistance?

- Provide access to expertise (legal, estate planning, accounting) for both the nonprofit organization and the donor.
- Furnish services to facilitate the process, and ensure that both the donor and the recipient have adhered to all laws regulating charitable planned giving.
- Identify what the donor is contributing to the nonprofit when making a planned gift.
- Explain why your nonprofit organization needs planned gifts.

(d) Taxes

Upon death, an estate may be subject to state and/or federal taxes, depending on its size. Since state taxes vary from place to place, only federal taxes are discussed here. Estate tax is an excise tax on your right to pass on your assets to someone upon your death. It is assessed on the fair market value of those assets at the time of your death, with some exceptions, and applies only to taxable estates larger than $600,000.

There are several ways to reduce or eliminate taxation on your estate. The marital tax deduction is one such tool which allows you and your spouse to make unlimited, tax-free transfers of assets to each other, either during your lifetime or at the time of death. Specific trusts can be used to take full advantage of the marital deduction.

Estate taxes can also be reduced by specifying charitable deductions in your will to qualified organizations operated for religious, charitable, educational, scientific, or literary purposes. Charitable contributions reduce the value of your taxable estate, dollar for dollar. A will can be used to make outright gifts of money, securities, or property, or to establish trusts.

8.13 OUTRIGHT GIFTS

A donor can make an outright charitable gift of cash, appreciated securities, real estate, and other tangible property. Gifts of appreciated securities and property often provide additional tax savings to donors due to potential savings in capital gains taxes.

(a) Securities

Publicly traded and closely held stocks and bonds can be donated to a qualified nonprofit organization, entitling the donor to a charitable tax deduction equal to the value of the securities on the date of the gift. The charitable organization can then sell the securities and use the proceeds without paying capital gains tax, due to its nonprofit status. Gifts of closely held stock require careful planning but can deliver significant benefits to the donor.

(b) Real Estate

Real estate gifts can include a full or partial interest in a principal or vacation residence, farm, commercial building, subdivided lot, or unimproved land. The benefits applying to gifts of securities also apply to gifts of real estate. The primary methods of making charitable contributions in the form of real estate are: outright gifts, fractional interest, residence, or farm with retained life estate.

(c) Tangible Property

All tangible property, including art, jewelry, and other valuable personal belongings, is subject to estate taxes upon death. Gifts of tangible property related to the mission of the charitable nonprofit organization are deductible at fair market value; other gifts not so related may generate a lower tax deduction. It is not uncommon for an organization to receive a gift of this type that is not useful to the organization. This may pose special tax implications.

(d) Life Insurance

Gifts of life insurance can be made in the form of the following:

- A fully-paid life insurance policy
- A new policy designating the nonprofit organization as the beneficiary and owner of the policy

8.14   DEFERRED GIFTS

(a) Life Income Gifts

Charitable gifts may be structured so that an individual makes a donation, receives a charitable income tax deduction, and benefits from the income generated from the gift for life. These types of gifts are referred to as "deferred giving" and are arranged through charitable trusts, pooled income funds, and charitable gift annuities. Such charitable gifts often produce income for the donor or his beneficiaries and may also reap the following benefits:

- Current charitable income-tax deduction
- Protection of capital gain in the appreciated property used to make the gift

- Reduction in estate and inheritance taxes
- Professional management of the gift
- Tax-free income
- Satisfaction of making a significant contribution to the charity of one's choice

Life income gifts in the form of charitable remainder trusts, charitable lead trusts, pooled income fund gifts, and charitable gift annuities all may be established through a donor's will. These types of gifts will not provide tax savings during the donor's lifetime but may reduce estate taxes, provide life income for a loved one, and offer a new estate-planning option.

(b) Pooled Income Fund

A pooled income fund (PIF) is a specific kind of trust that operates, in concept, like a mutual fund. It differs from other planned gift arrangements because many gifts from separate donors are commingled or "pooled" together. The donor transfers property, retains a life income interest in the property for one or more individuals (beneficiaries), and contributes the irrevocable remainder interest in the property to the charitable organization. The property (or gift) consists of cash or marketable securities and is combined with gifts from other donors into a fund for investment purposes. The fund can neither receive as a contribution nor invest in tax-exempt securities. PIFs are not exempt from taxation; although a PIF ordinarily does not pay income tax because (1) the fund is required to distribute its net income each year to its beneficiaries and is allowed a deduction for such distribution, and (2) the fund is allowed a deduction for long-term capital gains. Short-term capital gains are taxed to the PIF unless such gains are allocated to income and thus distributed to the income beneficiaries.

The primary objective of the PIF is to produce a reasonable level of current income (exclusive of capital gains and losses) for the income beneficiaries consistent with the current interest rate environment. Long-term appreciation of the fund is secondary, but an important component, so that the value of the gift is maintained. Each donor is assigned units of participation at the time of their contribution. Income is usually distributed on a quarterly basis according to each beneficiary's units of participation. The remainder interest cannot be split among unrelated charities. See Exhibit 8.6 for additional characteristics.

(c) Charitable Remainder Trusts

A charitable remainder trust distributes income to a donor or other beneficiaries for their lifetimes or a specified period of years, with

Exhibit 8.6. Checklist—Pooled Income Fund

Gift Document	• Gift minimum: The charity sets the minimum. A modest initial investment is usually one of the fund's most appealing features (e.g., $5,000 first gift, $1,000 thereafter).
Investment Requirements	• Primary investment objective: Income [provides variable income for life to beneficiary(s)]. • Fund may not invest in tax-exempt securities. • Securities transferred to the fund by a donor may be sold or retained as part of the investment for the pool. • More than one pooled income fund can be created to offer range of investment options
Trustee	• No donor may serve as a trustee. • No beneficiary may serve as a trustee, however, if the charity is also an income beneficiary it may serve as a trustee.
Capital Gains	• Short-term gains are taxable to the fund or distributable to the beneficiary. • Long-term capital gains are to be added to principal. *Note:* Do not distribute long-term capital gains since even the inadvertent distribution of these gains can disqualify the fund.
Income Distribution	• Must be distributed to beneficiaries in accordance with trust document • Must be distributed within 65 days after the close of the fund's year • At the time a donor transfers cash or securities to the fund, the income interest retained by the donor is assigned units of participation in the fund. The number of units assigned depends both on the fair market value of the property transferred by the donor and on the fair market value of an outstanding unit on the transfer date. Thus, the number of units assigned to the income interest is determined by dividing the fair market value of the property transferred by the fair market value of one outstanding unit. The fair market value of that one unit is determined by dividing the fair market value of the fund's assets immediately before the transfer by the number of units outstanding immediately before the transfer. • To determine the allocation of fund income each year to the income beneficiaries, the fund's income for the year is divided by the number of units outstanding at the end of the year. The income allocable to a

Exhibit 8.6. Checklist—Pooled Income Fund (*continued*)

	particular beneficiary is then determined by multiplying the income per unit by the number of units assigned to the beneficiary. • Adjustment must be made for the units held by a beneficiary for only a portion of the year.
Determining Unit/ Unit Value	• Transfers to a pooled income fund may be made throughout the year, and it may be impractical to value the fund's assets each time a transfer is made. In such cases, the units assigned to a beneficiary may be based on the value of the fund's assets on the "determination date" immediately preceding the transfer and the one immediately succeeding it. A fund's determination date is the date on which the fund's assets are valued during the year. There must be at least four such dates during the year. The first such date must be on the first day of the fund's tax year; succeeding dates cannot be more than three calendar months apart. • It should be practical, however, to at least do monthly valuations and this would be the preferred approach.
Beneficiaries Payments (Income Interest)	• Beneficiaries are to be identified in the gift document. • Donor may retain the right to receive an income interest. • Income paid quarterly unless donor specifically requests annual or semi-annual payment dates. Monthly payments are permitted but discouraged. Estimated quarterly payments can be made each quarter with the final payment being adjusted within 65 days after the close of the calendar year. • Payments to beneficiaries are fully taxable as ordinary income.

Death of a Beneficiary	• Severance of property from a pooled income fund upon the termination of an income interest can be done in either of two ways. The regulations provide that the value of the remainder interest may be either:
	  • Its value as of the determination (valuation) date next succeeding the termination of the income interest, or
	  • Its value as of the date on which the last regular payment was made before the death of the beneficiary if the income interest is terminated on such payment date.

- The amount that is severed from a pooled income fund upon the termination of a life income interest either must be paid to, or must be retained for the use of, the public charity/remainderman. Which of these courses is followed is determined by the governing instrument.

Accounting
Requirements

- Accrual basis of accounting is required.
- Trustee has discretion not to amortize bond premiums on bonds acquired by fund.

Action Items
(Review Pooled Income
Fund Documents)

I.   Review gift document for content and completeness:
   A.   Date
   B.   Fair Market Value (FMV) of securities
II.   Document the applicable items below:
   A.   Date of birth (proof)
   B.   Social Security Number(s) of each beneficiary
III.   Documentation on gift:
   A.   Fund's highest yearly rate of return (preceding 3 years)
   B.   Beneficiaries (other than donor)
   C.   Identify and list the beneficiary(s)
   D.   Identify method of payment (direct deposit, checks)
   E.   Identify payment schedule
IV.   Calculate value of remainder interest (amount of charitable deduction)
   A.   A donor to a pooled income fund realizes a deduction for the present value of the charitable remainder. The present value of the income interest depends both on the age of the income beneficiary and on the rate of return earned by the fund. The rate of return used in valuing the income interest is the highest yearly rate of return earned by the fund for the three tax years immediately preceding the year in which the transfer is made. If the fund has been in existence for less than three tax years preceding the year of the transfer, the highest yearly rate of return is deemed to be one percentage point less than the highest annual average of the monthly rates used for valuing charitable gifts (120 percent of the applicable federal midterm rate) for the three calendar years immediately preceding the year in which the fund was created.

Exhibit 8.6. Checklist—Pooled Income Fund (*continued*)

	V.	IRS Publication 1457 provides tables of valuation factors for use in determining the present value of the remainder interest in the property transferred to pooled income funds. The higher the rate of return, the lower the charitable deduction. Our planned gift software should be used. (Planned Giving consultant)
	VI.	Review and file all related correspondence for future reference.
Calculate Unit Valuation	VII.	Determine by dividing the fair market value of the fund's assets by the number of units outstanding
	VIII.	Record FMV of property transferred and the pre-transfer value of a unit.
Plan to Obtain and Maintain Information	IX.	For each asset transferred to pooled income fund, record: A. Date of gift B. Fair market value on date of gift C. Cost basis
	X.	Holding Period A. Prepare Form 8283 B. Record number of units assigned to each donor's gift
	XI.	Record FMV of the fund on each valuation date
	XII.	Calculate income earned by fund for each quarterly income period
	XIII.	Record date income paid to each beneficiary
	XIV.	Record amount of income paid to each beneficiary
	XV.	For each asset purchased by the fund, record: A. Cost basis B. Date of purchase
	XVI.	For each asset sold by the fund, record: A. Date of sale B. Sales price C. Amount of gain or loss and whether short-term or long-term gain or loss
	XVII.	Calculate fund's rate of return for each taxable year computed under method prescribed in Treasury Regulations
Make Payments to Income Beneficiaries	XVIII.	Distribute 90 percent of the estimated income of the fund to the PIF participants in four equal payments during the year (March, June, September, December)
	XIX.	Make 10 percent adjustment by the 30th date following the close of the fund's year (must make within 65 days.)

Prepare Tax Reporting	XX.	Copy of each new pooled income fund agreement (together with copy of pooled income plan) should be attached to Form 1041.
	XXI.	Prepare statement detailing fund's method of calculating its yearly rate of return and attach tax return each year
Prepare: Accounting Statements (Income)	XXII.	Annual Report to income beneficiaries (courtesy report—by March 15)
	XXIII.	Calculate I.R.S. rate of return (aim for January 31)
Tax Statements	XXIV.	Prepare and distribute the following tax statements: *Federal:* A. 5227 (split-interest Trust Information) due to IRS April 15 B. 1041 (Income Tax Return for Estate & Trusts) due to IRS April 15 C. 1041-A (Trust Accumulation of Charitable Account) due to IRS on April 15 D. Schedule K-1 due IRS April 15 (mail to beneficiary by 2/28 as a courtesy) *State:* as required
Charge Fees	I.	Charge administrative fees, if applicable.

the balance of the trust assets available for the use of the charitable nonprofit organization at the end of the trust. Charitable remainder trusts provide donors with many opportunities to reach specific individualized goals and situations. They take two forms: the charitable remainder unitrust, and the charitable remainder annuity trust.

Benefits of a charitable remainder trust include the following:

- Appreciated assets are converted into lifetime income
- Capital gains taxes are not paid when the asset is sold
- Estate taxes are reduced or eliminated
- Current income taxes are reduced through a charitable income tax deduction
- One or more charities reap the benefits of the trust
- Donors receive more income over their lifetimes than if their assets had been sold
- Donors leave more to their children or others by using a life insurance trust to replace gifted assets

A charitable remainder unitrust pays income based on a percentage of the fair market value of the trust assets, as determined once per year. The payout rate is negotiated by the donor and the recipient charitable nonprofit organization. Because a unitrust pays a variable amount of income based on the market value of trust assets, this form of charitable remainder trust can be an effective hedge against inflation. As the value of the trust principal increases, the income stream to the donor will also grow.

(d) Annuity Trust

A charitable remainder annuity trust pays income based on a percentage of the initial value of the trust and does not change. The payout rate is negotiated by the donor and the benefiting charitable nonprofit organization when the annuity trust is established. Since the payout on an annuity trust does not change during the term of the trust, an annuity trust provides a fixed income stream to the donor regardless of fluctuations in the value of the trust assets.

(e) Charitable Gift Annuity

A charitable annuity is a simple agreement between a donor and charitable nonprofit organization to pay a lifetime annuity in exchange for a charitable gift. The amount of the annuity payment is fixed and is usually determined by the age of the beneficiary of the annuity. Charitable gift annuities can also be structured to defer income until a future date. These types of annuities are called deferred charitable gift annuities, which are considered a prime retirement income vehicle because the income is deferred and, consequently, provides a larger income stream to the donor. This technique also provides the donor with a larger tax deduction.

(f) Charitable Lead Trusts

Charitable lead trusts are the mirror image of the charitable remainder trust. The "lead" or initial interest of the trust is to benefit the charitable nonprofit organization. Upon termination of the trust, the assets are transferred to other beneficiaries, who may include other family members. The primary benefits of this donor vehicle are the reduction or elimination of the tax imposed on the transfer or gift of assets to children or others at the end of the trust, and the ability to make a current gift to a charitable nonprofit without giving away your property. This form of gift has highly complex technical requirements but provides a very useful estate planning tool when they are met.

(g) Trusts

A trust is an excellent mechanism for transferring assets to individuals or charities. They are also useful in providing for the care of minor children or "infirm" adults because they enable the cash flow to an individual or a charitable organization to be monitored and reduce or eliminate estate and inheritance taxes. Trusts are simple to create. A "trustee" is identified, and assets are transferred to that individual who assumes responsibility for managing and investing the funds. The two types are: living trusts and testamentary trusts. Living trusts are created during one's lifetime; testamentary trusts are created through one's will.

(h) Testamentary Gifts

Some individuals choose to make their charitable gifts at the time of their death. This is accomplished by bequest through a will. A contingent trust is one type of testamentary trust. Contingent is defined by Webster as "intended for use in circumstances not completely foreseen." For example, a contingent trust may dictate that a spouse receive all assets upon your death; however, if the spouse dies, the children will each receive an equal portion of the estate assets to be placed in a trust until they reach a specified age.

Another type of testamentary trust is a family trust, which can specify that one's assets will be held in trust and used to support all of the children until the youngest comes of age. When the children all reach the specified age, the trust can be terminated and the assets distributed equally among them. A charitable trust is a trust created through one's will. This vehicle is used to take care of loved ones as well as contribute to a favorite charity.

The different types of charitable trusts are: charitable remainder annuity trusts, charitable remainder unitrusts, charitable lead annuity trusts, and charitable lead trusts. The annuity trust and unitrust are designed to make payouts to named beneficiaries for a term of years or for life. At the end of the trust period, the charity can use the trust principal for the purpose designed by the donor. On the other hand, the lead trust makes payments to one or more charities for a term of years prior to the time when the principal is passed on to a named beneficiary. Each of these trust vehicles may significantly reduce estate taxes.

(i) Restricted and Unrestricted Bequests

Bequests can be restricted or unrestricted. Restricted bequests detail the purpose for which the bequest may be used. Unrestricted bequests are not limited to specific use or purpose.

(j) Restricted and Unrestricted Endowments

Endowments can be restricted or unrestricted. Restricted endowments detail the purpose for which the endowment may be used.

Unrestricted endowments are not limited to specific use or purpose.

(k) Retirement Plans

Retirement plans and vehicles such as IRAs, tax-sheltered annuities, self-employed plans (SEPs), 401 (k) plans, 403(b) plans, and other qualified pension plans can provide support to nonprofit charities. In order to make a gift from one of these fund sources, the donor should include the nonprofit organization as a beneficiary on the documents related to the plan.

(l) Special Considerations Surrounding Planned Gifts

Some of the special considerations that are important to donors making deferred gifts are briefly discussed below.

(m) Valuation of the Charitable Deductions

The valuation, for tax purposes, of gifts of property donated to charity must be in accordance with IRS requirements. Professional assistance from legal or accounting professionals is recommended.

(n) Administration

The administration of a planned-giving program is complex, and its success rests on the following key provisions:

- Recommendation of a policy to trustees
- Technical support for those responsible for implementing the program
- Information requirements to ensure that the gift-related documents are completed accurately
- Custodial services for the gifts
- Investment strategy for the gift assets
- Implementation of an investment strategy for the gift assets
- Legal and financial planning, and tax advice
- Reports and payouts
- Communication with all stakeholders in the program transactions

The duties associated with the administration of gift property are:

1. Assist in the analysis and development of major or planned gifts that involve the acquisition of property

2. Inspect and analyze the proffered real property for its acceptability, including review of:
   - Title
   - Appraisal of value
   - Environmental and hazardous conditions
   - Other potential liability issues
   - Condition of property (especially to assess potential expenses to upgrade and provide the level of project oversight necessary)
   - Ongoing management requirements
   - Other potential or actual expenses
   - Marketability and potential sale time frame including any financing required to expedite the sale

3. Transfer of real property upon acceptance of the gift, including:
   - Title services coordination
   - Gift document preparation and review
   - Escrow services
   - Closing including the recording of deed(s)
   - Insurance and other liability coordination
   - Transfer of utilities and other services

4. Management services for real property acquired by gift pending its final disposition, including:
   - Collection of rents
   - Maintenance oversight, gardening, etc.
   - Coordination of all repairs
   - Arrangement of security
   - Payment of expenses
   - Visitation of properties to monitor their condition

5. Facilitating the ultimate disposition of owned real-property gifts, including:
   - Listing with real estate brokers
   - Oversight of marketing efforts including advertising
   - Review of purchase offers and development of counter-offers
   - Closure of sales (by overseeing escrow proceedings)

(o) Services Offered

Many nonprofit organizations offer complementary services related to planned gifts of appreciated assets such as stock, real estate, and income property. Examples of the services provided are:

- Educational seminars on how to sell stock without paying capital gains tax, increase the rate of return, and receive annuity income for life
- Computer services illustrating how to increase the estate for heirs
- Informative materials that are easy to understand
- Planning strategies customized to specific individual needs
- Educational seminars on how to sell a principal residence without paying capital gains tax, purchase a retirement home, and receive an annuity income for life
- A referral service to highly qualified professionals who are available to assist with all estate-planning needs
- Asset preservation and retirement planning oriented to the concerns of physicians and the lifestyle needs of seniors
- Personalized planning tailored to unique goals and concerns

APPENDIX 8A

A DONOR BILL OF RIGHTS

Philanthropy is based on voluntary action for the common good. It is a tradition of giving and sharing that is primary to the quality of life. To assure that philanthropy merits the respect and trust of the general public, and that donors and prospective donors can have full confidence in the not-for-profit organizations and causes they are asked to support, we declare that all donors have these rights.

1. To be informed of the organization's mission, of the way the organization intends to use donated resources, and of its capacity to use donations effectively for their intended purposes

2. To be informed of the identity of those serving on the organization's governing board, and to expect the board to exercise prudent judgment in its stewardship responsibilities

3. To have access to the organization's most recent financial statements

4. To be assured their gifts will be used for the purposes for which they were given

5. To receive appropriate acknowledgment and recognition

6. To be assured that information about their donations is handled with respect and with confidentiality to the extent provided by law

7. To expect that all relationships with individuals representing organizations of interest to the donor will be professional in nature

8. To be informed whether those seeking donations are volunteers, employees of the organizations, or hired solicitors

9. To have the opportunity for their names to be deleted from mailing lists that an organization may intend to share

10. To feel free to ask questions when making a donation and to receive prompt, truthful, and forthright answers

Developed by:
    American Association of Fundraising Counsel (AAFRC)
    Association For Healthcare Philanthropy (AHP)
    Council for Advancement and Support of Education (CASE)
    National Society of Fundraising Executives (NSFRE)

Endorsed by (information):
    National Catholic Development Conference (NCDC)
    National Committee on Planned Giving (NCPG)
    National Council for Resource Development (NCRD)
    United Way of America

Please Distribute "A Donor Bill of Rights" Widely.

CHAPTER NINE

Cash Management
and Banking Relations

9.1 Introduction   303
9.2 What Is Cash Management?   305
   (a)   Banking Environment   305
   (b)   Purchasing Bank Services   307
   (c)   Managing Bank Service Charges   311
9.3 Collections Systems: Managing and Accelerating Receipt
   of Funds   314
   (a)   Lockbox Processing   316
   (b)   Disbursements   318
   (c)   Structuring a Funds Management System   319
   (d)   Monitoring Bank Balances and Transactions   320
   (e)   Cash Forecasting   321
   (f)   Data Elements for Cash-Flow Estimates   321
   (g)   Account Reconciliation   322
   (h)   Short-Term Borrowing   323
   (i)   Short-Term Investing   324
   (j)   Bank Sweep Accounts/Investment Services   325
   (k)   Benchmarking Treasury Functions   327
   (l)   Upgrading the Caliber of Treasury Professionals   328
   (m) Security and Risk Management Issues   329
      (i) Types of Financial Risk   329
      (ii) Fraud   329
9.4 Future Trends   330
Appendix 9A: Nonprofit Organization Guide to Direct
              Payment   332
Suggested Readings   335

9.1   INTRODUCTION

Fund-raising is central to many nonprofit organizations. For most,
the treasury function revolves primarily on collecting, handling

and managing cash gifts. For others, managing liquidity to support borrowing and investing decisions is also vital to ensure funding for the nonprofit's varied activities. Today, it has become increasingly important for these functions to be carried out efficiently to maximize resources and control costs. Treasury responsibilities have evolved from paper-based, manual processes to highly automated and sophisticated systems that interface seamlessly with banks, service providers, and other internal operating units.

Cash management is a subset of treasury management and it involves the collection and disbursement of cash within a business enterprise. Moving funds and managing the information related to the funds' flows and balances are fundamental to good cash management. With a strong understanding of the banking system and the products and services offered by banks, the cash manager can achieve effective mobilization of funds, prudent investing of these funds, and cost-effectiveness in services used.

Depending on its size and scope of activities, a nonprofit's financial structure may range from simple to highly sophisticated. In any case, a system needs to be designed to monitor the cash flow time line that links the revenue/cash receipts and purchasing/cash disbursements. For some, transactions can be more complex when cash flows cover large payrolls, sizable inventories, vehicle fleets, and other supplies for an organization like the Red Cross or a major health care facility with heavy financing and working capital needs.

A comprehensive understanding of an institution's operational processes is basic to structuring a sound cash management program. Identifying and quantifying the activities, interfaces, and resources that make up the collective cash flow lead to a better assessment of service requirements for banks or other financial service providers. Significant advances in technology have impacted the delivery of cash-management services and offered numerous opportunities for managing deposits, funds concentration, disbursements, and information and control. As new applications have emerged, real processing capabilities have replaced paper-based information and inquiry systems. Cash managers now use computerized workstations to execute transactions and gather information ranging from bank balances, investment transactions, and other financial activities. Processes that required manual intervention are now routinely handled by innovative electronic collection, concentration, and disbursement applications. Cash management activities are being carried out better, faster, and cheaper. With increased productivity through automation and "smart systems," there are many opportunities for cash managers to add value and enhance service support to other parts of the organization. With nonprofits expected to do more with less, re-engineering and outsourcing possibilities should be considered alongside traditional approaches.

The primary goal of this section is to identify the trends and opportunities that nonprofits should consider to enhance treasury functions relating to cash management. Collection and disbursement mechanics which have benefited from technological advances will be highlighted along with regulatory and banking developments. Identifying electronic systems for accelerating the collection of remittances and controlling disbursements to ensure timely and orderly outflows will be explored. Lastly, the strategy for identifying, selecting, and working with the right bank or financial service provider will be addressed. What is the bank's breadth of product, systems, and service levels? How committed is the bank to maintaining and improving its product and service offerings? How important is this account to the bank? What is the financial strength of the bank? With the right bank(s) as a partner(s) and the appropriate technology to support operations, many benefits and opportunities can be maximized. References are provided for cash management applications and other technical material that may not be covered in-depth in this chapter.

9.2 WHAT IS CASH MANAGEMENT?

Cash management encompasses a number of activities within the following primary functions:

- Cash collection
- Cash concentration
- Disbursements
- Investment of surplus cash, if any
- Financing or borrowing
- Forecasting "cash flows"
- Managing bank relations

The fiduciary responsibility of nonprofits must be balanced in the way business is conducted. Financial risks should be recognized and appropriate measures taken to safeguard assets. In designing and structuring a good cash-management program, distinguishing day-to-day functions from strategic objectives is important. At the same time, focusing on efficiency must take into account control and flexibility in managing cash, based on a strong understanding of organizational cash flows (Exhibit 9.1).

(a) Banking Environment

Commercial banks serve as depositories for cash and also act as paying and receiving agents for checks and other fund transfers.

Exhibit 9.1. Comprehensive Cash Flow Management

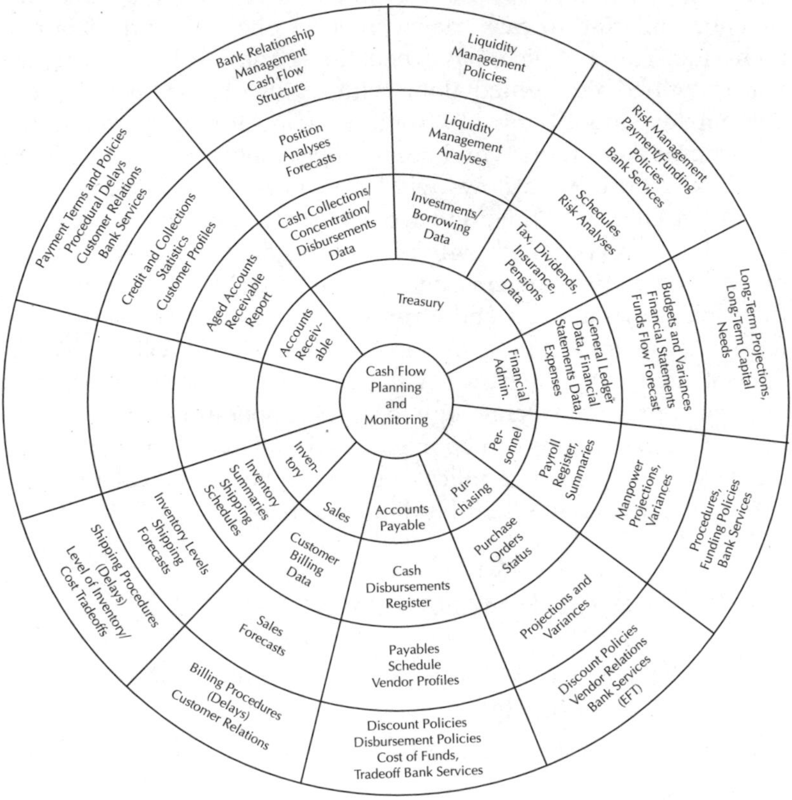

Source: Aviva Rice, "Improving Cash Flow Control Throughout the Corporation." ©1997 by the Treasury Management Association, all rights reserved. Used with permission of the Treasury Management Association.

Banks have been a traditional source of financing for short- and medium-term needs, a provider of investment services, fiduciary/ trust services, and global custody. The latter services are covered in more detail in Chapters 8, 11, 12, and 13 when emerging trends are discussed for investment and planned-giving programs.

With few exceptions, a full-service commercial bank can offer a range of cash-management services that will meet all the requirements of a nonprofit institution. Building a good relationship and partnership with the right bank offers many advantages. A growing nonprofit organization will benefit from the right association and could leverage such a relationship to integrate services such as cash management, trust, capital markets, and credit. In certain situations, "unbundling" services and seeking out multi-bank relationships may be appropriate where services are required in different geographic regions of the country or even overseas. International banking is offered by many major banks, and specialized needs for foreign exchange, letters of credit, and other international transactions are easily met. Pricing, quality of service, support, and technology are factors that must be considered in deciding on a single or multi-bank setup. Nowadays, technology for cash concentration can link multiple accounts in different banking relationships without slowing cash transfers or incurring added expense. What value-added benefits can be realized in a single or multi-bank relationship is a question that needs to be explored.

Services Provided by Treasury Management Banks

Account Reconciliation	Information Reporting
Automated Clearing House (ACH) Services	Retail Lockbox
Check Clearing	Sweep Accounts
Controlled Disbursement	Treasury Management Software
Demand Deposit Accounts	Wire Transfers
Electronic Data Interchange (EDI)	Zero Balance Account

(b) Purchasing Bank Services

When purchasing bank services, a formalized approach will help ensure that important decision factors are not overlooked in the evaluation and purchase of cash management services. In certain situations, an informal or partial request for a product or service may be conducted. However, there are potential disadvantages to such a process that can be eliminated through the use of two suggested critical steps: a request for information (RFI) and a request for proposal (RFP).

The RFI is part of a structured information gathering effort to identify potential vendors and their product offerings. Through trade directories, publications, and referrals,[1] this informal process can provide data on banks and vendors which will include such information as experience, technological capabilities, and creditworthiness. This process could potentially eliminate the need for an RFP when there is clearly one superior vendor, or specific service requirements can only be met by one or two vendors. While not optimal, this approach provides a basis for a more informed decision than one based solely on previous relationships and price. At least once every few years, an RFI is helpful in comparing capabilities outside of an existing relationship and staying current with changes in the industry.

[1]Treasury Management Association Annual Directory of Cash Management Services.

An RFP is the next step to take when soliciting bids for several cash services and a comprehensive search is warranted. The process can be fairly involved and time consuming. Key to an RFP would be a statement of the nonprofit's objective in soliciting the proposal. This would include:

- A description of the service sought
- The preferred location
- The volume of transaction by service (measure costs under various activity volumes)

Exhibit 9.2 provides an outline of a sample RFP for lockbox processing.

In addition, specific service requirements should also be addressed:

- Any special features or customization required
- The level of support service expected (who, hours, level of authority)
- Problem-resolution procedures
- Automation capabilities
- Mechanisms for funds transfer
- Availability of information (cutoff times, cost)
- Level of quality expected
- Pricing information; pro forma account analysis
- Questions relating to product-specific issues and buyer requirements for special transaction requirements
- Deadline for response
- References (do a thorough check)
- Contact person

Spelling out both general and specific qualifications and requirements will provide a more objective approach and meaningful comparison of service levels. When the best vendor is identified, the next step is to secure a commitment in writing and document the details and fees involved. This should also include deviations from the RFP, specific computations, price commitment, change notification periods, cost of uncollected funds, overdrafts, and daylight overdraft provisions. Use of a matrix that scores the responses from banks or vendors is recommended.

In putting together an RFP, questions can be organized from the general to the specific. Exhibit 9.3 contains examples of methods that may be used.

For assistance in preparing RFPs for banking services, the Treasury Management Association (TMA) and the Bank Administration

Exhibit 9.2. Sample RFP: Lockbox Processing

GENERAL QUALIFICATIONS

1. Monthly volume in total and for the three largest customers
2. General work flow description
3. Equipment used in processing
4. Problem-resolution procedures
5. Bank/vendor output records for receivable/payables accounting
6. Methods and timing of data transmission
7. Mechanisms for funds transfer
8. Timing of balance report on daily activity, etc.

PRODUCT-SPECIFIC ISSUES

1. Flow of mail through bidder's postal facility
2. Zip code arrangements (unique, zip + 4, other)
3. Schedule of daily and weekend post office collections
4. Delivery site and resulting delay of mail distribution within bidder's premises
5. Staffing and experience of lockbox operation
6. Maximum daily volumes that can be processed for same-day ledger credit
7. Timing/security for transmission of lockbox data, including remittance media
8. Error rate in lockbox processing, etc.

BUYER'S PROCESSING REQUIREMENTS

1. Specific volume projections, now and in three years, at peak and average
2. Geographic distribution of customers
3. Processing exceptions as to payee, check date, nonmatching dollar amounts, missing check signature, and foreign items
4. Handling of customer correspondence
5. Anticipated data-capture requirements from scanline or from remittance documents
6. Procedures for charging nonsufficient funds items
7. Delivery procedures for remittance advices, deposit slips, and other materials
8. Data transmission baud rates, timing and security, etc.

SUPPLEMENTAL INFORMATION

1. Product brochures
2. Sample contract or agreement of service
3. Phoenix-Hecht Postal Survey data on mail and availability times
4. Sample output from bank or vendor processing
5. Customer references
6. Complete product pricing schedule
7. Chart of service area organization
8. Implementation checklist, etc.

Source: From James S. Sagner and Larry A. Marks, "A Formalized Approach to Purchasing Cash Management Services." Sagner/Marks, Inc., *Journal of Cash Management* 13, No. 6.

Exhibit 9.3.   RFP Questions

LIST 1   ORGANIZING QUESTIONS BY FUNCTIONAL OR ORGANIZATIONAL AREAS

1. Accounting
   - Reconciliation
   - Reporting
2. Cash management
   - Balance reporting
   - Funds transfer: wire transfers, ACH
3. Control
   - Security
   - Audit trail

LIST 2   ORGANIZING QUESTIONS BY PRODUCT LINE, INCLUDING CURRENT AND FUTURE NEEDS

1. Controlled disbursement
   - Current needs
   - Future needs
2. Lockbox
   - Current needs
   - Future needs
3. Funds transfer
   - Current needs
   - Future needs

Source: From James S. Sagner and Larry A. Marks, "A Formalized Approach to Purchasing Cash Management Services." Sagner/Marks, Inc., *Journal of Cash Management,* 13, No. 6.

Institute have developed a publication to help in selecting cash management banks. Standardized RFP provide a comprehensive list of questions on all aspects of bank services. Detailed RFPs are available for the following cash-management services:

- ACH
- Controlled disbursement, account reconciliation, and positive pay
- Depository services
- EDI services
- Information reporting
- Wholesale lockbox, including electronic lockbox and network services
- Wire transfer

Once a vendor is selected and a contract signed, steps should be taken to build and strengthen the relationship. Keeping the account officer well informed of activities, changing requirements, operational processes, policies, and future plans is fundamental. Giving honest feedback also ensures a productive partnership. In the long run, negotiations are made easier, and the account officer becomes very knowledgeable of the nonprofit's operations. The account officer's input can be a resource in identifying opportunities for improvement. Developing a consultative partnership can be useful in analyzing treasury functions and getting valuable suggestions for process improvement. An annual review between banker and client completes the process toward constructive relationship building.

What can the cash manager and banker do to get the most from a bank relationship? What are each other's expectations, objectives? Are they attainable and reasonable? Building a relationship requires a real investment of time for all parties involved. Strategies for relationship building are premised largely on trust, open communications, honest feedback, and team building. Setting realistic objectives is fundamental and provides the framework for implementing agreed-upon procedures and service requirements. When a client calls a banker only when a problem arises, the relationship stands on shaky ground. Regular meetings and follow-ups are healthy to ensure open communication. With the rise in bank mergers, take overs, and consolidations, managing a relationship has become increasingly challenging. The consistency in quality, service, and price that a client seeks in a bank tends to be disrupted as bank cultures change and personnel turnover creates dislocations. When a strong relationship has been cultivated, problems and uncertainties will be more manageable and less stressful to handle. A win-win situation is a likely by-product of a healthy relationship.

(c) Managing Bank Service Charges

What does it cost to do business with your bank? How are balances determined? What are the reserve requirements? What is the basis for calculating the earnings credit rate? Are all the services needed? How should the services be paid—by fees, balances, or a combination of both? Answers to these questions can be gathered from an account-analysis statement; which presents a clear picture of bank services and account status. The monthly statement contains two separate sections on balance and service information. It is critical to understand the account analysis statement, and its terms, and components to verify the accuracy and level of charges. Understanding the activities and relating this to the pattern of collections and disbursements could lead to potential cost savings. When multiple banks are used, comparisons using spreadsheets would be necessary on a monthly basis. Basic to the analysis are the following:

- Cutoff, preparation, and timing of analysis statement by bank
- Bank service charges organized by type of service: depository, remittance banking, reporting, disbursement, lending

The balance section should be reviewed in terms of where the information comes from, the type of activity and the service charge associated with each activity. Reconciliation helps ensure accurate and timely assessment of balances. How best to compensate the bank can also be answered when investment alternatives offer higher rates of return than the earnings credit rate (ECR) banks allow against collected balances. In such a scenario, paying by fees may be more advantageous when one can invest collected balances and earn a higher interest income.

Computation of the ECR may be tied to a market rate, such as the 90-day treasury bill rate or a managed rate determined by the bank based on factors such as cost of funds and competitive pressures. The formula for calculating an ECR must consider the impact of the reserve requirement on bank charges. Until recently, deposit insurance was also charged and when added together, both costs drastically lowered balance levels. In considering payment by fees or balances, compensation to banks must be analyzed and negotiated to understand which arrangement is cost effective. A clear agreement must be in place to identify the method and timing of compensation, especially if a method other than monthly settlement is preferable. Banks prefer monthly settlement, but when balances are used for compensation, quarterly, semi-annual, or annual settlements may be appropriate to maximize use of excess balances that occur within the settlement cycle. Carrying forward excess balances must be negotiated, and the time period should be stated. Whenever settlement occurs, deficiencies should be billed and may be debited directly from the checking account.

Auditing and reviewing the account analysis statement could spot price changes and potentially identify cost-cutting opportunities. Working together with the bank relationship manager, a review may suggest ways to cut bank costs that are more directly tied to how the cash-management system operates. Examples would include:

- *Payment alternatives*—(paying by ACH is cheaper than Fed wire transfers; using terminal-initiated wire transfers is cheaper than manual transfers)
- *Account maintenance*—combine or eliminate checking accounts, since $25 to $50 can be charged per account
- *Checks deposited*—consider encoding or sorting checks
- *Stop payments*—use an automated system
- *Account reconciliation*—use a paid-only (partial) reconciliation service instead of a full account reconciliation program

Refer to Exhibit 9.4 for definitions of terms used in an account analysis statement and Exhibit 9.5 for a description of the components of the account analysis statement.

Exhibit 9.4. Definition of Terms Used in an Account Analysis Statement

Average ledger balance	The sum of the daily, end-of-day gross balances on deposit divided by the number of days in the period
Average float	The sum of the daily amount of deposited items that were in the process of collection divided by the number of days in the period
Average collected balance	The sum of the daily ledger balances less "uncollected" balances (float) divided by the number of days in the period
Reserve requirement	The amount that a bank is required to leave on deposit with the Federal Reserve; currently, 10 percent of checking balances
FDIC	Federal Deposit Insurance Corporation—assesses bank's premiums to federally insure deposits
ECR	The rate established by a bank, adjusted for the reserve requirement—applied to collected balances to derive the fee equivalent of balances maintained
Earnings allowance	The amount available to support services—calculated by multiplying the ECR times collected balances
Service description	Description of the services used
Unit price	The bank pricing for each transaction—unit price may or may not be the banks standard price
Volume	The number of transactions for each service
Service charge	The results of the calculation of unit price times volume
Collected balance required	The balances needed to compensate a bank for services rendered

Exhibit 9.5.   Components of the Account Analysis Statement

Customer information	General customer information such as name and address, account title and number, period covered, and bank contact
Current/historical balance and compensation information	Section containing current and historical ledger, collected and uncollected balances and any adjustments for the period, and current and historical excess/deficit balance positions. The current and subsequent months ECRs displayed, along with the earnings allowance and total monthly service charge and, in many instances, the multiplier (collected balance required to support $1 of fees)
Adjustment detail	Any adjustment for a prior period is included in this section, which indicates description, transaction date, date of adjustment, amount, and the number of days included in the adjustment
Summary of accounts	This section shows all of the accounts included in the account analysis statement, along with selected summary information (e.g., average balances, float, total service charge)
Service description "and cost" information	This section is usually grouped into categories, and shows services used, monthly volume, unit and total price, and collected balance equivalents which requires close scrutiny and can often result in cost savings.

9.3   COLLECTION SYSTEMS: MANAGING AND ACCELERATING RECEIPT OF FUNDS

Electronic collection is slowly replacing checks as the payment of choice. Although donations are still collected largely from checks mailed by donors, electronic payment options are gaining acceptance. This has been influenced by factors such as an increase in comfort with electronic products, personal convenience, and an increased sense of security about the medium. Cash substitutes in the form of debit and pre-paid cards, direct deposits through the ACH and ACH debits are growing. The ACH is basically a computerized network for processing electronic debits and credits between banks for its customers through the Federal Reserve system. Appendix 9A provides a Nonprofit Organization Guide to Direct Payment.

Credit-card payments are also increasingly used but may cost more than checks or ACH payments, depending on the transaction size. Electronic transmittal of credit-card transactions offers cost advantages over paper-based processing with the potential for a reduced discount rate and direct credit. Upon transmission, notification is immediately provided on any discrepancy in account information by a payor or disallowed transaction (e.g., credit limit exceeded). As the volume of credit-card payments increases, an annual review should be conducted. Keeping track of credit-card amounts and activity will be helpful in negotiating a lower discount rate since merchant banks base their pricing on average ticket size and volume.

When agreements are in place to collect pledges using an ACH or other electronic payments, the cash forecast is significantly improved. Money becomes available at the monthly or quarterly interval agreed upon. Within 48 hours from initiation of an ACH debit, funds will be credited to the checking account or swept to a concentration account. Credit-card transactions can be collected within two or three days. The percentage of collections handled through check substitutes is still low but is gaining acceptance. The experience of nonprofits that have used ACH debits suggests that a pilot test and survey must first be conducted to gauge the willingness of donors to participate in such a program. One foundation has been using ACH debits for quarterly payment of its annual-fund pledge payments. Specifying a cutoff amount that will be cost effective to handle is also recommended, and it is available to start with a focus group or payment type. The process saves staff time, postage costs, and other expenses associated with issuing pledge reminders and invoices.

An ACH credit is a payment choice for more and more corporations that have matching gift programs for their employees. The ABC Educational Foundation signed up for Upjohn Corporation's matching gift program and now receives a direct deposit to its bank checking account. Like any other deposit transaction, the payment is clearly identified and shows up in the bank balance report. For beneficiary distributions to planned-giving donors, The ABC Educational Foundation makes monthly or quarterly payments by ACH. This replaced check payments that required more staff time to process. A donor's financial institution or bank does not charge for ACH remittances, unlike a wire transfer which could cost $10 to receive. The only drawback encountered with ACH payments occurs when a donor designates a non-bank account to receive the deposit. For example, a deposit to a brokerage money-market account cannot be accommodated with the limited message field that shows further credit instruction. The transfer may end up in a suspense account or the brokerage firm's depository account, and a trace would be needed to ensure further credit to the beneficiary account.

Check collections can also be accelerated through pre-encoding of the amount in the magnetic ink character recognition line or "presorting" by drawee bank locally, by city or region. Depositors can avail of preferential pricing and better availability from their banks using these two options. Costs for check processing are also decreasing as a result of regulatory edicts and improved processing capabilities. The Federal Reserve's Same Day Settlement (SDS) initiative permits a collecting bank to present items to any paying bank directly, without establishing a relationship with that bank or paying presentment fees. SDS will spur more efficient clearing mechanisms by eliminating intermediary check "clearers" and ultimately decrease clearing float and costs.

Electronic check presentment promises to revolutionize check collection by clearing checks and identifying return items using data transmissions rather than moving paper checks. Combined with image processing, information on returned checks and access to gift data can be gathered sooner and at less cost.

(a) Lockbox Processing

The lockbox system was developed to accelerate check collection and expedite deposit of accounts receivable. The concept began in 1947 with the recommendation to use a post office box (lockbox) to collect large dollar remittances. A corporation, through an authorization letter to the postmaster, permits a designated bank to extract mail from the corporation's box around the clock. With frequent pickups throughout the day, a bank can process remittances faster compared to directing mail to company premises. The objective is to minimize mail and processing time so that checks are converted into available funds more rapidly.

Many nonprofits today use lockbox services to process gift checks, membership dues, and other receivables associated with marketing and merchandising activities. In addition to banks, other service providers now offer lockbox processing. Current generations of lockbox services employs automated production interfaces, including bar code technology to receive and sort the mail; automation to encode, endorse, and photocopy checks; high-speed capture of payor bank routing information; and PC terminal access to confirm balance and receivables information.

If outsourcing collection processing makes sense, a lockbox service should be evaluated. In selecting a vendor, the following factors must be considered:

- Types of plans offered
- Vendor's operational capability
- Automation
- Professional staff (years experience, turnover)
- Quality-control checkpoints (low error rates)
- Availability schedule
- Support and problem-resolution responsiveness
- Cutoff times and weekend processing
- Pricing
- Reporting capabilities
- Interface with accounts-receivable system or an integrated accounting software

In using a lockbox service, the cash manager should coordinate with other departments' specifications relating to invoices and other remittance material. This may include image-ready invoice redesign, proper ink colors, background print elimination, proper specifications for window envelopes, use of bar coding, and strategic location of key pieces of information (donor identification numbers, mail zip codes, return address). The cash-management account officer of the bank or vendor should be consulted for assistance in designing the remittance document to providing more efficient processing and data capture in an electronic format. Reporting can also be streamlined so that the appropriate service plan can be identified and the pertinent information can be captured. Otherwise, the cost can be high.

Advances in imaging technology may replace costly printouts for lockbox remittance information that take longer to produce and deliver. Image technology can capture details on invoice data, donor name, address, or dollar amount, and eliminate the need for stapling the invoice, envelope, and check photocopy. Information can be captured electronically and the image transmitted by modem or disk. Data can be sorted and users can store large volumes of data. Storage media are optical disk, CD-ROM, tape, or magnetic storage. Paper documents are replaced by images warehoused in a relational database-management system. The database is accessible from multiple locations and can automatically route information to various points within an organization. A development officer inquiring about a donor's gift can access a file containing the image of the check and the solicitation document. Both can be transmitted through e-mail or accessed through a network database. Where marketing is involved, inventory tracking is also enhanced and payment information is readily accessible.

Outsourcing through a lockbox service has its advantages. It is an option that merits comparison against internal processing. The cash manager must evaluate the cost and staffing associated with internal processing, notably peak-period demands as well as the break-even receivable size. If check or receivables processing is close to full capacity, this limits flexibility in bringing in trained personnel at peak periods and outsourcing may be worth considering.

(b) Disbursements

Just as speeding collections is a recognized cash-management tool, so is the control of disbursements. Disbursements in the form of checks and drafts typically include all payments a nonprofit makes in the course of doing business. This may include payroll, vendor payments, grants, and distributions, to name a few.

A well-planned disbursing system includes well-defined, systematic, and accurate procedures for authorizing, generating, and accounting for payments. Whether a system is paper based, as with the use of checks, or electronic wire transfers and ACH, the cash manager's task is to orchestrate all the elements of checks, bank services, and the check-clearing process to monitor and control the outflow of funds. A sound disbursement system will help maximize the working capital funds available and enhance overall liquidity.

The disbursement function is handled primarily through bank checking accounts. In the past, delaying payments has been a technique employed to maximize float—the amount of time that elapses from the moment a check is released to the moment a check is charged to the issuer's account. This consists of the aggregate of mail float, processing float, and clearing float. Managing float is becoming less relevant in today's low-interest rate environment. With electronic payment mechanisms, float has been practically eliminated.

Effective check disbursement practices are important for all organizations since many rely on checks as a payment mechanism. The treasury professional will be well served to have check disbursement controls in place to avoid fraud and potential losses. The following recommendations for internal control should be built into treasury operations:

- Implement stringent disbursement approval, release, and stop-pay procedures. Ensure that only authorized personnel are performing these functions and that all procedures are documented and kept up-to-date.

- Secure check stock and facsimile signature plates. Remove check stock from printing equipment and store in a locked location when not in use.

- Maintain current signature card and bank agreement files. Update authorized signatories for all organizational and bank network changes. Notify bank of approved signatories on a periodic basis to ensure accuracy of records. Conduct periodic reviews to verify that currently used bank services and all applicable laws are reflected in bank agreements.

- Segregate the disbursement and account reconciliation duties of staff.

- Perform timely checking account reconciliations, preferably before the next month-end.

- Implement stringent voided check procedures. Punch out the signature on the voided check and promptly void the check in the Accounts Payable system.

- Consider using bank or internal automated account reconciliation and positive pay services.

- Conduct periodic treasury/internal audit reviews.

(c) Structuring a Funds Management System

The use of a general bank account or a set of accounts for deposits and disbursements is a decision that varies from one nonprofit to another. The choice is largely dictated by the type, size, and complexity of transactions associated with the nonprofit organization's activities. A well-designed bank account configuration is needed to maximize flow of funds, enhance earnings, improve efficiency, and facilitate better control of financial resources.

Cash concentration and controlled disbursement accounts are two cash-management structures which separate the collection and disbursement of funds. If multiple locations deposit funds, cash concentration can be accomplished electronically through the ACH or by depository transfer checks through the national clearing system. A cash concentration service will transfer funds from any financial institution in the country to a designated bank where the concentration is centralized. Transfers can be prepared at specified cutoff times each day, and funds will be available in one business day. This service offers a number of benefits: it eliminates idle funds in local depository accounts; speeds up identification of available cash; provides the potential for increased earnings on investments or reduced interest costs on debt as a result of funds centralization; enhances control over funds; facilitates quick decision making through timely receipt of deposit information; and provides data for monitoring deposits and balances.

Controlled disbursement eliminates guesswork from daily funding requirements on checks presented for payment. Through a controlled disbursement account, checks are paid through one or more disbursement accounts. Information on checks presented for payment is reported daily, and automatic transfers are made from a checking account to cover the day's disbursement activity. This service can reduce overdrafts and the use of credit lines. With computerized reporting, accurate data collection is possible and clerical workload can be reduced through automatic funding and reporting.

Another cash-management tool for disbursement and concentration is an automated zero balance account. The process links any number of disbursement or depository accounts. At the end of business each day, all balances over designated cash levels are transferred to a concentration account. Conversely, all balances below the designated level are automatically covered by transfers from a concentration account. Funds transfers from and to a single concentration account are handled automatically, and balances in disbursement and depository accounts can be set at a target amount or at zero. By eliminating idle balances in accounts and centralizing cash, better control will reduce overdrafts and increase efficiency in managing cash.

(d) Monitoring Bank Balances and Transactions

Accurate and timely information on cash balances is essential to managing liquidity and making critical financial decisions about the use of funds. Today information on bank transactions, deposits, payments, return items, and other activities are readily accessible through a wide variety of mechanisms. These range from manual reporting by voice operator and touch-tone devices to highly automated computer transmissions.

Bank-balance reporting is a product which conveniently provides the cash manager access to bank account activity and information. Using a computer and modem, dial-ups can be automatically programmed to gather balance information from as many banks as required or manually initiated. Balance reports include current ledger and collected balances, deposits subject to one- and two-day availability, error adjustments and resolutions, balance history, and average balance over previous time periods. Details of debits and credits, lockbox transactions, borrowing and investments, concentration reports, and other transactions can also be downloaded.

In addition to information retrieval, initiation of transactions such as wire transfers and ACH payments is now possible using cash-management software. Services can be customized and expanded as needs change. Security features include passwords and multiple levels of identification codes. The use of cash-management and information systems offers many benefits in terms of monitoring and controlling account activity, locating cash surpluses or shortages for more productive use of funds, enhancing cash forecasting, allowing stop payments, and reducing clerical time and expense in tracking cash positions. Investment activity and foreign exchange reporting can also be downloaded using bank information systems.

Automated information systems are widely available and competitively priced. They offer convenience and efficiency in cash management, and nonprofits are well served to use them. Information gathering is significantly enhanced, and the demand for timely information by management and trustees can be satisfied.

(e) Cash Forecasting

Cash forecasting is a valuable treasury tool. It begins with a definition of objectives for the forecast and a realistic assessment of the structure and activities of an organization. Forecasting allows management to evaluate changing conditions and formulate appropriate financial strategies. As a planning tool, cash forecasts have to be monitored and updated to reflect both short- and long-term variables.

Depending on a nonprofit's funding and operational needs, cash forecasts can determine optimal borrowing and investment strategies. Many nonprofits rely on gift contributions for funding, and their timing is difficult to project. Accordingly, gathering information from internal sources is more predictable, particularly with the expense side of the equation. Common sources are a nonprofit's accounts-payable and accounts-receivable departments. Purchasing and sales units are also good sources of information.

For some institutions, cash scheduling may be a more relevant technique in determining short-term cash position (one day to six weeks). The process begins with a forecast of deposits to plan the timing and amount of funds for cash concentration. Simultaneously, estimates are made on when checks will be presented. When concentration and disbursement accounts are used, cash scheduling will help the cash manager to mobilize funds without giving up the opportunity costs associated with excess and idle balances. Ideally, balances can be maintained at target levels in the appropriate concentration or disbursement account.

(f) Data Elements for Cash-Flow Estimates

Receipt and disbursement items vary among nonprofits but mirror treasury transactions in a typical corporate environment. In a broad sense, projecting collections and payables is necessary to determine the timing of each cash flow component although there may be little control over certain inflows associated with fund-raising. Trends and patterns over certain time periods can provide a good basis for arranging financing alternatives during slow months or investing surplus cash longer without risking penalty for "pre-termination." Statistical methods of analysis and qualitative techniques may be combined to arrive at a reasonable cash forecast.

Receipts	Disbursements
Lockbox collections	Vendor payments
Deposits	Payroll, benefits
Loans/credit lines	Programmatic expenses
Pledge payments	Grants and allocations
Debt proceeds	Debt repayments and interest expense
Maturing investments	Insurance payments
Income from investments	Distributions for planned gifts
Endowment fund distributions	
Stock gift proceeds	

Estimating the amount and timing of various receipts and disbursements can be time consuming. However, with coordination from various units that have an input to the process, a reasonable forecast can bridge gaps and improve financial planning. Management and marketing issues must be considered along with payment policies on early-payment discounts and costs that may be unnecessarily incurred due to overdrafts.

(g) Account Reconciliation

Timely and accurate reconciliation of check payments is now effectively handled through account reconciliation services. Many banks offer a full or partial plan to provide accounting on the status of checks issued. This can include paid, outstanding, exception, stopped, voided, or canceled items. Use of the service helps to balance an account faster, improves audit control, and provides protection against unauthorized, altered, and stopped checks. This service is most advantageous when a significant number of checks is written each month. It can simplify bookkeeping procedures and reduce staff time in balancing accounts.

Deposit reconciliation is another application suited to nonprofits with multiple locations depositing into a single account. The service segregates deposits by location and lists nonreporting locations. Through special serial-number groupings, daily report-ing, and comprehensive monthly reports, the service facilitates au-diting and enhances control over local depository activity. At the same time, the convenience and economy of a single depository ac-count can be retained.

Another service now offered by banks is positive pay. This option provides daily access for authenticating check payment by comparing checks issued to checks paid. A bank provides a daily list of nonmatching checks paid, and the exception is submitted to the institution. Instruction for payment or return of checks on the list can be given to ensure payment of legitimate checks only. This service is another tool for controlling fraud and is accessible online with the bank.

Overdrafts are likely to occur without a reliable cash forecast-ing and balance reporting system. Timely information on the status of disbursing accounts will enable a cash manager to move funds and avoid overdrafts. Monitoring funds availability is also impor-tant to minimize ledger overdrafts. When overdrafts occur, there are costs incurred aside from the interest expense charge. Opportunity costs arise in terms of income lost from foregone investments, costs associated with transferring funds, and costs of delayed payments on bills (lost discounts, ill will, and other related costs). For a non-profit institution making distributions to planned-giving donors, donor relation issues are very sensitive, and accuracy is critical. Arrangements for overdraft protection or a line of credit would be advisable.

Aside from normal overdrafts, daylight overdrafts occur when funds are not sufficient to cover a transfer although the negative balance is covered by the end of the day. With Federal Reserve policy discouraging daylight overdrafts, banks pass charges to their customers. To avoid daylight overdrafts, accounts should be monitored intraday. Fed-wire payment outflows can be timed to correspond with the availability of Fed funds from in-coming transactions. Another technique is to match the method of payment with the source of covering funds. For example, Fed wires and ACH payments settle differently, and it would be costly to rely on ACH deposits that may not be available to cover Fed wires.

(h) Short-Term Borrowing

External financing is an alternative source of funds when no sur-plus cash is available to meet working capital shortfalls. To account for both short- and long-term financing needs, it is necessary to have a complete picture of the sources and uses of funds, linked to both operational and strategic plans of the organization. Major capital and program expenditures would require a different type of financing, and, typically, loans have to be collateralized.

For liquidity purposes, a bank credit line may be sufficient to fill temporary or seasonal financing needs. This is generally an unsecured loan made on the basis of the borrower's financial strength. Borrowing against a line of credit is usually in the form of specific notes for set maturities, such as overnight, 7 days, 14 days, or 60 days. The cost to borrow varies and is usually negotiated or reconfirmed annually. Most credit lines carry a variable interest rate based upon an agreed base rate. Depending on the perceived risk and the negotiating position of the organization, the interest rate may include a specified spread over the base rate. Interest payments are frequently made monthly or at the maturity of the loan.

Banks usually require compensation for offering a credit line in the form of balances and/or fees. The interest rate on a loan may be negotiated depending upon the level of balances held at the bank. Likewise, other activities in the relationship and the overall profitability of the nonprofit's account will affect pricing.

In addition to a bank line of credit, deferring payment on disbursements can be a temporary source of liquidity applying to vendors and other suppliers. However, this should not be pursued without taking into account the cost of missed discounts in the terms of sale or a penalty fee for late payment. Implicit costs associated with loss of goodwill and damaged credit rating should not be overlooked.

In certain situations, internal financing may also be an option. For example, borrowing against an endowment portfolio may be possible on an arms-length basis. For such transactions, careful attention must be given to the terms and conditions of the loan to avoid any potential conflict of interest.

(i) Short-Term Investing

Chapters 11 through 13 discuss portfolio-management techniques and strategies for investing. However, this section will address some basic considerations. When surplus cash is available, it can be managed to meet liquidity needs or invested. The first step is to determine whether funds are cash reserves solely for operating purpose or available over a longer time frame. This would enable the cash manager to develop an appropriate strategy to maximize earnings and satisfy liquidity requirements.

With funds managed in a fiduciary capacity, the cash manager's foremost investment objective is safety of principal. Many investment instruments are available, and it is important to understand the market and the types of securities that are bought and sold. Whatever the reason for short-term investing, specific policies and guidelines should be defined prior to making any investment. Investment policies and guidelines should state investment objectives, define tolerance for risk, address liquidity factors, identify the level of return or yield acceptable for different instruments, and identify personnel roles and responsibilities regarding the implementation and monitoring of an investment program. Poor investment judgment, assumption of imprudent risks, assignment of responsibilities to unqualified personnel, and fraud can lead to opportunity costs and loss of principal.

From a cash-management perspective, the following suggestions are offered:

- Provide copies of investment guidelines to your banker, money manager, or broker with whom you will trade; this will be a good basis for developing appropriate investment strategies and identifying suitable financial instruments.

- Arrange for safekeeping of securities; this offers added security and control and facilitates the audit of securities held. If safekeeping is maintained with the relationship bank, include cost of service in bank account analysis.

- In the absence of a custody or safekeeping account, document instructions for transfer of funds and designate specific accounts for payment of trade proceeds.

- Institute proper operational procedures and controls for investment activities.

- Provide a list of authorized personnel and their specimen signatures.

- Review all portfolio holdings for compliance with credit quality ratings.

- Determine the value of portfolio holding and market-to-market securities.

- Assimilate investment activities into funds-flow forecasts to manage liquidity.

(j) Bank Sweep Accounts/Investment Services

One way to handle short-term investing is through *sweep accounts*. It is natural for banks, the location where your surplus funds build up, to offer fee-based investment services. Banks offer their own securities as well as serve as brokers for other institutions' securities. The bank offers investors its own instruments, or those of its parent holding company, as a means of purchasing funds that the bank can loan out or invest. In addition to offering investment securities, many banks offer corporate agency services to safeguard the company's investments, manage trusts and pensions, and handle record keeping related to bonds your organization has issued.

Popular investments your organization can buy through a bank include repurchase agreements (often as part of a sweep agreement), commercial paper, certificates of deposit, and treasury bills. We will discuss only repurchase agreements and sweep accounts here.

A repurchase agreement, or "repo" as it is often called, involves the bank selling the investor a portfolio of securities, then agreeing to buy the securities back (repurchase) at an agreed-upon future date. The securities act as collateral for the investor, to protect against the possibility that the bank will default on the repurchase. The difference between the selling price and the repurchase price constitutes the interest.

Quite often, banks will set up a sweep arrangement to automate the repurchase decision-making process, sparing the treasurer daily investment evaluations. All balances above those necessary to compensate the bank for services or to fund disbursements are swept nightly into repos. The bank may also impose a $1,000 minimum to eliminate small-dollar transfers, which is accomplished by a set of bookkeeping entries at the bank. Excess balances are invested for one business day, with the principal amount credited to the checking account the following day. An investment report is produced daily, indicating the amount of the daily investment, the interest rate, the amount of interest earned, and what investment security stands behind (is collateralizing) the investment. This type of arrangement is one of the fastest growing cash management-related services (see the survey done by Treasury Strategies, Inc., in Exhibit 9.6). As an added advantage of such arrangements, some banks will not charge the company for an

Exhibit 9.6.   Examples of Interest Earned on Repos

	Bank A	Bank B
Amount Invested	Annualized Interest Rate * (%)	Annualized Interest Rate (%)
$0–$999,999	4.00	4.85
$1–$2M	4.25	4.90
$2–$5M	4.25	4.95
$5–$10M	4.45	5.05
$10M +	4.45	5.15

*Bank A does not have a minimum transfer amount, and calculates yield using a formula based on the amount invested each day.

overdraft if the sum of the available balance and the repurchased amounts is sufficient to cover presentments, choosing instead to cover the checks with the bank's funds.

You may wonder what interest rate you can receive on such a short-term investment. Exhibit 9.6 shows the rate structures for two large Midwestern banks.

- up to $1 million, Fed funds rate, minus 1.3 percent
- from $1 million to $5 million, Fed funds rate, minus 1 percent
- over $5 million, Fed funds rate, minus 0.6 percent

The message is clear: if you still have a Negotiable Order for Withdrawal account, you are better off transferring your money into an overnight investment because the yield pickup is significant. Finally, you will be charged a monthly fee plus a daily transfer fee for the sweep account, and the automated sweep-account fee is slightly higher than a manually operated sweep. These fees must be weighed against the increased interest revenue to determine if your organization would profit from establishing a sweep account.

If you have operations abroad, the availability of bank-provided overnight investing varies considerably. For example, a survey by academics Luc Soenen and Raj Aggarwal found that in Europe, 78 percent of British banks, 44 percent of Dutch banks, and only 26 percent of Belgian banks offered the service. Exhibit 9.7 shows growth in overnight sweep accounts.

(k) Benchmarking Treasury Functions

Benchmarking is a process through which an organization compares its internal performance to external standards of excellence. The objective of benchmarking is to achieve and sustain optimum performance through continual process improvement. Unless an effort is

Exhibit 9.7.   Growth in Overnight Sweep Accounts

Category	1993	1994	1995	1993–1995 Growth (%)
Sweep Assets ($B)	25.9	32.8	46.8	81
Sweep Accounts (000)	30.7	40.3	54.5	78
Avg. Assets/Acct. ($000)	844	814	858	2
No. of Sweep Banks	246	288	312	27
Avg. Assets/Bank ($M)	105	114	150	12
Avg. Accts./Bank	125	140	174	40

Source: Reprinted, with permission, from Treasury Strategies, Inc. For more information, visit their website at www.treasurystrat.com.

made to clearly understand the mission, operations, staffing and services provided as well as its customers, improvement will be slow.

Total quality management (TQM) is a process that has been applied to treasury functions. Creating a vision and mission statement; understanding suppliers, customers, and the "big picture;" encouraging cross-functional collaboration; and focusing problem solving on removing root causes can produce significant gains. Involving the bank relationship manager and other vendors in assessments will provide valuable feedback to internal staff. Strengths and weaknesses are addressed for various types of processes. TQM also relies on quantitative measures and statistical data gathering to evaluate results and monitor process improvement. Through regular reviews/audits, fine-tuning can be pursued and changes can be instituted in an organized manner. Nonprofits must approach their business in the same way as for-profit corporations. In so doing, they will be more proactive than reactive, and, ultimately, better efficiency will result in cost savings.

The account-analysis statement is a useful source of information for evaluating the quality and cost of various bank services. Transaction volumes can be plotted and analyzed to gauge patterns in lockbox collections, wire transfers, and return items, to name a few examples. Benchmarking can be valuable and should encompass a broad range of activities to provide a meaningful basis for improvement.

(l) Upgrading the Caliber of Treasury Professionals

Cash managers of nonprofits must stay abreast of regulatory, service, and product changes. Many major cities have regional treasury associations that provide extensive educational opportunities for practitioners. Participation in treasury conferences such as the Treasury Management Association or other forums on financial electronic data interchange (FEDI) will provide tremendous exposure to current and emerging technologies and information. Industry publications, bank newsletters, and technical books are additional sources of information.

Likewise, networking with peers and corporate treasury professionals should be pursued to accelerate learning opportunities and implement changes that can be applied in a nonprofit organization's treasury department. An enlightened treasury professional is an asset to every nonprofit, and management must invest in staff advancement opportunities.

To ensure continuity in operations, cross-training of staff should be supported. Ongoing training is recommended with backup personnel assigned to critical treasury functions. As advances in technology lead to changes in how tasks are performed, it is advisable to document procedures. A manual should be maintained and updated to reflect any organizational, bank, and system changes that may occur in procedures for initiating wire transfers and ACH transactions. Documentation pertaining to banking resolutions, authorized signatories, and investment guidelines should also be included. Centralized record keeping will ensure continuity and minimize disruptions in operations.

(m) Security and Risk Management Issues

Nonprofit organizations have a fiduciary responsibility for the gifts and donations that constitute a large percentage of their revenues. Recent events associated with fraud, failed investments, rogue brokers, and other financial losses have created concerns beyond risks normally associated with financial instrument quality or creditworthiness. There are various types of financial risk, and a prudent risk-management program is relevant not only for treasury functions, but also throughout the entire organization.

(i) Types of Financial Risk

- *Market risk:* risk of change in market price of an underlying instrument which may be due to adverse movements in currency exchange rates, interest rates, commodity and equity markets, as well as time value of money
- *Liquidity:* risk associated with illiquidity which can adversely affect pricing of a security
- *Credit risk:* risk of counterparty default on an obligation
- *Legal risk:* loss exposure due to unenforceable contracts caused by documentation deficiencies
- *Funding risk:* risk from internal cash flow deficiencies
- *Operational risk:* risk of unexpected loss due to system malfunction, inaccurate accounting and record keeping, settlement failure, human errors, incorrect market valuation, and fraud

An effective risk-management program begins with identifying and understanding risk. Top management must be knowledgeable about the types of risk that could potentially threaten financial and operational stability. Once identified, appropriate measures can be instituted and tolerance levels defined. This will have a bearing on the limits set for transactional volumes, avoiding fraud, and ensuring proper checks and balances in operating setups. Protection against certain risks may translate into higher insurance premiums or added to the costs of doing business. Hedging strategies using derivatives are helpful in protecting investments or loans against adverse interest rate movement. However, the use of derivatives must be fully understood, and investment guidelines should clearly state which specific transactions are allowed or disallowed.

The most common financial risk for nonprofits may be related to market exposure and volatility for investment assets. Investment guidelines must be formulated to clearly define permitted transactions, credit quality, exposure limits, maturity or duration parameters, safekeeping, and trading authority.

(ii) Fraud. Fraud is another type of risk that confronts many organizations. Check fraud has led to mounting losses with illegal check schemes on the rise. The increase in check fraud is attributed primarily to the widespread availability of inexpensive desktop publishing software and laser printing equipment. The section on Disbursements discusses, in detail, ways to counteract check fraud.

Natural disasters, fires, and other force majeure have to be anticipated. Contingency plans for business resumption should be drawn, and recovery measures should be well communicated throughout the organization. Ongoing review and testing are imperative to cover changes in operations, personnel, and procedures. Off-site storage of critical documents, backup procedures for computer applications, emergency banking arrangements, and other key operations must be covered and priorities set. It is also worth looking at out-of-state banking alternatives and utilizing those accounts for emergencies. However, proper authorizations and procedures have to be spelled out. Nowadays, heavy reliance on electronic processing and initiation of transactions using computer terminals can lead to paralysis in the event of a power failure. Nonautomated alternatives should be explored particularly with funds transfer mechanisms (e.g., voice or phone transfers with callback procedures). Another measure includes documenting all account information, contact persons, telephone numbers, and other essential data in both hard copy and disk or other media. All should be housed in a separate but secure location. Redundant systems may save tremendous time and expense in the event of a disaster. Being without a contingency plan is risky, and adequate preparation is essential to every treasury operation.

9.4 FUTURE TRENDS

Nonprofit organizations are faced with increasing cost pressures and competition for donated funds. In such an environment, eliminating inefficiencies and maximizing cost savings have become imperative. Total quality and re-engineering processes are providing opportunities and solutions. Outsourcing is another option that has been gaining acceptance. It is best that treasury practitioners focus their resources on their core competencies and outsource tasks that can be handled effectively by external service providers.

Technology is replacing many paper-based applications as it becomes more affordable and accessible. However, technology leads to the need for greater security, fraud control, and regulatory requirement. In implementing new processes driven by technological advances, nonprofits should not cut costs at the expense of flexibility and control.

Increased integration of business systems is another trend made possible by advances in technology. Functions such as accounting, accounts payable, accounts receivable, purchasing, and inventory can now be linked. Related financial services, such as cash management, securities, trust, and custody products, are available through computer interfaces and provide significant enhancement to information reporting. Fully integrated systems will serve as a cornerstone of the financial function of a nonprofit organization, providing control, decision support, and audit trails. Linking systems not only enhances productivity, but also minimizes input errors when rekeying information. Faster availability of financial information is helpful in analyzing and re-engineering work flow.

Partnerships with banks or service providers should be explored. Changes that can benefit treasury practices are oftentimes known in advance by bank officers. A good relationship can be a worthwhile investment.

NONPROFIT ORGANIZATION GUIDE TO DIRECT PAYMENT[a]

In the donor relations game, you and your donor win with direct payment.

Excellent donor relations are good business. An easy way to sustain donor giving is to offer donors several payment alternatives for making their gifts. Win over your donors by adding direct payment to your menu of gift payment options.

What is direct payment?

Direct payment is a method of electronically collecting regular financial gifts from your donors. With the help of your financial institution, you can collect donations through the Automated Clearing House (ACH), the same system used for the direct deposit of payroll. Donors who choose direct payment for regular financial gifts (monthly, quarterly or annually) will authorize you to electronically debit their bank account on a regular basis for a predetermined amount. Direct payment provides you and your donors with an efficient electronic alternative to paper checks.

Winning is easy with direct payment.

Whether you're collecting alumni association dues, annual subscription/membership renewals or fund raiser pledges, direct payment will help you by:

- *Increasing fulfillment rates.* With direct payment, pledge amounts and payment dates are set up in advance, and funds are collected automatically. You're assured that donor pledges will be received, as promised.

- *Improving donor retention.* Once your donors experience the ease of direct payment, they're more likely to continue giving. Collecting annual renewals is as simple as sending your donors a reminder.

- *Increasing pledge amounts.* Breaking up a single donation into smaller monthly or quarterly payments helps donors budget their gift dollars. Repeat donors tend to increase their donations with direct payment.

- *Enhancing your image.* Direct payment shows your donors that you're donor-oriented and cost-conscious. You'll also be offering your donors a way to customize their payment method.

- *Improving your cash flow.* With direct payment, the timing of donations is more predictable and reliable. Your cash flow will be more manageable with stable donor gifts each month.
- *Lowering your costs.* Direct payment will reduce both the number of pledge reminders to be sent and low-dollar checks to be processed. By eliminating the manual, labor-intensive process of handling check payments, you can improve the cost effectiveness of your payment operations.

Win over your donors with direct payment.
In addition to providing you with many benefits, direct payment helps your donors by:

- *Saving time preparing payments.* All your donors need to do is enter the amount of their gift in their checkbook. No writing checks, addressing envelopes or running to the mailbox. What could be more convenient?
- *Improving budgeting.* Donors who aren't able to give a large lump sum will appreciate the option of small, regular gifts. Budgeting for a smaller gift often allows donors to give a larger amount during the course of a year.
- *Saving money.* Your donors will eliminate postage costs and reduce checking account fees (if they're charged for each check) and check-printing costs.
- *Contributing more to your cause and less to your overhead.* As you are able to reduce your costs for collecting donations, your donors' gifts will go further to help achieve your organizations' goals.
- *Receiving fewer gift requests.* Once donors are set up with direct payment, there is no need to send them multiple gift requests throughout the year.

Who's winning with direct payment?
Charitable organizations of all sizes are winning with direct payment. The following types of organizations and their donors enjoy the many benefits of direct payment:

- Public television
- Public radio
- Colleges and universities
- Religious organizations
- Cultural/arts organizations
- Humanitarian organizations

To learn more about how you and your donors can win with direct payment, call the National Automated Clearing House Association, toll-free, at 1-800-467-2329, extension 590, or the nearest Federal Reserve Bank. Become a champion with direct payment today!

A few nonprofits successfully using direct payment:

> "For us, Direct Payment is a win-win service. The university benefits through higher donor retention and gifts, and lower processing costs, and donors benefit through increased convenience. A high percentage of donors who give automatically through direct payment continue giving year after year. And many of them increase their contributions each year."
>
> *Jann Cutcher—Ohio State University*

> "Some alumni who were giving $25 a year are now giving up to $100 a year because they're able to spread their donations out over the course of the year."
>
> *Laura Scarlett—Massachusetts Institute of Technology*

> "The ACH (direct payment) has been our saving grace in terms of cash flow and processing efficiency."
>
> *Rafia Siddiqui—The Columbia Association*

> "EasyGift (direct payment) means automatic money for us every month—guaranteed."
>
> *Chris Prukop—WGBH Educational Foundation*
> *Public Radio and Television*

[a]*Source:* Reprinted, with permission, from Federal Reserve Bank of St. Louis. For more information, visit their website at www.stls.Frb.org/epaymnts/nonprofit.htm/.

SUGGESTED READINGS

Bort, Richard. *Corporate Cash Management.* Boston: Warren, Gorham & Lamont, Inc., 1993.

Essentials of Cash Management. Bethesda, Maryland: Treasury Management Association. Various Editions.

Eklund, Diane. "Dealing with the Forces of Financial Risks in the 21st Century." *TMA Journal* 15, No. 6 (Nov/Dec 1995).

Gergern, Mark J. "Image Technology for Cash Management." *TMA Journal* 15, No. 6 (Nov/Dec 1995).

Clark, James. "Taking Positive Steps Against Check Fraud." *TMA Journal* 15, No. 2 (March/April 1995).

Karkazis, Dean. "Using Technology Enhancements to Fight Check Fraud." *TMA Journal* 15, No. 2 (March/April 1995).

Spanard, Karan. "Harnessing the Latest Developments in Deposit Concentration." *TMA Journal* 15, No. 2 (March/April 1995).

Burger, Catherine. "RFPs Re-Defined." *Journal of Cash Management* 12, No. 6. (Nov/Dec 1992).

McDonough, Stephen G., Schieffer, Michael P. "Cash Management Process Review: Bridging Theory to Reality." *TMA Journal* 14, No. 5 (Sept/Oct 1994).

"Directory of International Treasury Management Banks." *TMA Journal* 16, No. 3 (May/June 1996).

Stewart, Barry. "Sharpening the Focus on Payment Security and Control." *TMA Journal* 16, No. 3 (May/June 1996).

Page, Robert. "Understanding the Account Analysis Statement." *TMA Journal* 14, No. 2 (March/April 1994).

Manthey, Stephen. "Cash Forecasting: Fictional Facts and Factual Fiction." *TMA Journal* 16, No. 3 (May/June 1996).

Barta, Patricia O. "Best Practices in Treasury Controls." *TMA Journal* 16, No. 3 (May/June 1996).

Sagner, James S., Marks Larry A. "A Formalized Approach to Purchasing Cash Management Services." *Journal of Cash Management* 13, No. 6 (Nov/Dec 1993).

O'Donnell, Patrick. "Bank Relations: Five Steps to Championship Management." *Journal of Cash Management* 13, No. 6 (Nov/Dec 1993).

Barta, Patricia O. "Risk Benchmarking: Assessing Your Treasury Risk." *Journal of Cash Management* 13, No. 6 (Nov/Dec 1993).

Hart, Ronald. "Creating an Effective Investment Policy." *Journal of Cash Management* 13, No. 6 (Nov/Dec 1993).

Kluesner, Margaret. "Balance or Fees—How to Compensate the Bank." *Journal of Cash Management* 13, No. 1 (Jan/Feb 1993).

CHAPTER TEN

Managing Your Organization's Liabilities

10.1   Payables   337
10.2   Short-Term Borrowing   338
10.3   The Strategic Financial Plan   340
    (a)   Borrower's Strategic Financial Objectives   341
    (b)   Borrowing Requirements   342
10.4   Steps to Successful Borrowing   342
    (a)   Understanding Debt   343
        (i)   Risk-Reward Tradeoffs   343
        (ii) Leverage   344
    (b)   The Loan Approval Process   344
        (i)   Basic Preparation for a Loan Presentation   344
        (ii) Reasons for Borrowing   345
        (iii) Immediate Concerns of Lenders   345
        (iv) Evaluating the Application   346
        (v) How Lenders Are Repaid   346
        (vi) Refinancing   346
    (c)   Alternative Sources of Short-Term Funds   347
10.5   Matching Financial Sources to Strategic Objectives   348
10.6   Preparing the Financing Proposal   349
    (a)   Term Sheet   349
    (b)   Plan Overview   349
    (c)   Presentation Contents   350
10.7   Making the Presentation   350
    (a)   The Importance of Questions   351
    (b)   Answering Objections   351
    (c)   Personalizing the Presentation   352
10.8   Other Factors in Borrowing/Lending Decisions   352
    (a)   Borrowing from the Bank   353
    (b)   Domestic Short-Term Bank Loans   353
    (c)   International Short-Term Bank Loans   355
    (d)   Trends in Short-Term Lending   357

10.9 Municipal and Taxable Bonds 358
    (a) Municipal Bonds 358
10.10 Selection of an Underwriting Firm 358
10.11 Preparation of Bond Documents 359
    (a) Who Issues Municipals and for What Purpose? 361
    (b) Taxable Bonds 362
        (i) How Can My Organization Use Taxable Bonds? 362
        (ii) Can I Get Short-Term Financing through Taxable
           Bonds? 363
        (iii) What Qualifies My Organization to Issue Bonds? 363
10.12 Leasing and Nontraditional Financing Sources 364
    (a) Why Lease Instead of Borrow? 364
10.13 Summary 365

The nonprofit landscape is littered with failed organizations that presumed on their financial futures by taking on too much debt. This chapter provides guidance for an organization that chooses to borrow with short-term loans, long-term municipal bonds, or mortgage loans. This chapter outlines the lender's view on a borrower's creditworthiness. Recall from the Lilly study that two of three of the organizations surveyed never do short-term borrowing, and only one in eight are perennial short-term borrowers.[1] Many of these same organizations do have mortgage loans, however. This chapter also discusses different liability, or borrowed fund, accounts. A liability that gets little attention but that can provide an organization much-needed and interest-free financing is discussed first—accounts payable.

10.1 PAYABLES

Think of the accounts payable function as interest-free financing from suppliers. True, the cost of this credit extension is built into the price of the supplies you are buying. Correspondingly, the seller expects you to take advantage of the credit period offered. Common terms are "net 30," meaning the full amount of the invoice is due and payable 30 days after the date of the invoice. The Lilly study unearthed a minority of nonprofits who still think it is commendable if they "pay the invoice the day it hits our desk." Such a policy is simply an unwise use of scarce cash resources. Pay on time, but not early.

---

[1]See Chapter 2.

Some credit terms are stated like this: "2/10, net 30." This means a 2 percent cash discount is being offered if the bill is paid within 10 days of the invoice date, or the full amount of the invoice may be paid in 30 days. Should you take the cash discount, paying $98 per $100 invoice amount in 10 days? Almost invariably, the answer is "yes." You are giving up a 37 percent rate of return by foregoing the cash discount. This is demonstrated in the following formula:

$$\text{Cost of foregone discount} = \frac{\text{cash discount \%}}{(100 - \text{cash discount \%})}$$

$$\times \frac{365}{(\text{normal credit period} - \text{cash discount period})}$$

This formula is used to estimate the cost of a foregone discount (the rate of return you could have had if the cash discount was taken) with 2/10, net 30 terms:

$$\text{Cost of foregone discount} = \frac{2}{100 - 2} \times \frac{365}{30 - 10} = \frac{2}{98} \times \frac{365}{20}$$

$$= 0.3724 \text{ or } 37.24\%$$

Surprisingly, many of the nonprofits surveyed in the Lilly study indicated they either chose to or had to forego cash discounts some or most of the time. Such as policy is unwise—one would be better off using some of her short-term credit line, if necessary, to have the funds take the discount.

10.2 SHORT-TERM BORROWING

Why might a nonprofit borrow money?

1. Borrowing is much faster than grants or fund raising for bringing money into the organization, with funds made available within days or a few weeks.

2. Borrowing can stabilize the organization's cash flow and compensate for temporary revenue shortfalls. Meeting payroll when in a temporary cash crisis is one use that may be made of borrowed funds.

3. Borrowing can prevent costly delays in starting new projects. This "bridge financing" is an important role for borrowing. Government agencies at the state and local level issue "bond anticipation notes" for this purpose.

4. Borrowing can increase earned income by speeding up the start of a revenue-generating project. Getting income-producing ventures off the ground may necessitate start-up financing or financing to fund the expansion of the new venture.

5. Borrowing can help consolidate bills. The idea here is to enable the organization to take cash discounts or maintain good supplier relationships.

6. Borrowing can initiate or build on long-term relationships with financial institutions. Individuals know the value of an established credit history, and the same holds true for a nonprofit organization.

7. Borrowing can help improve the organization's financial management. Financial institutions will require financial reports with a fair amount of detail and the calculation of key financial ratios. Organizations which previously managed without key financial data will be pressed to improve their financial and accountability structures.

8. Borrowing can help the organization achieve independence. By replacing restrictive donations or grants/contracts, the organization may be freed to pursue the mission it is called to accomplish. The flip side is that your organization may be limited via restrictive "loan covenants" placed on you by the financial institution. Limiting the borrowing and keeping the loan payments current will enable the organization to avoid becoming the "servant to the lender."[2]

Furthermore, there is a cost to raising funds through donations and grants. Let's say that $100 is raised for every $10 spent. That amounts to a 10 percent interest rate if $10 is taken as "interest" and $100 as principal. The main difference, of course, is that the donation funding stream must be renewed every year, while the borrowed funds are there until "maturity"—which is when the organization must make the principal repayment on the borrowed funds. Our point is that there is a cost of funds, regardless of how you acquire them.

Planning for short-term borrowing must take place within the context of the organization's overall strategic planning process (see Chapter 4). Otherwise, borrowings may cost more than they should or funds will be borrowed on the wrong terms, or both.

Financial managers have two different ways with which to plan and manage an organization's debt and capital structure: (1) the at-whatever-price theory, and (2) the strategic planning theory. The at-whatever-price theory is related to the traditional

---

[2]Adapted from Edward Skloot, *Smart Borrowing: A Nonprofit's Guide to Working With Banks*. (New York: The New York Community Trust, n.d.), 3–4.

supply-and-demand concept and is based on the belief that any financial manager can raise enough capital to do business if there is sufficient pressure.

Under the at-whatever-price theory, capital is like any other commodity: the greater the need, the higher the cost. Unfortunately, the at-whatever-price theory suggests that the most advantageous time for an organization to borrow money is when it does not need to borrow money, the most advantageous time being when borrowing is least expensive. In some cases, such blind financing can be attractive. It can be less expensive and less restrictive than financing under more pressing circumstances, for instance, when the organization has an acquisition target in mind or has committed to a major construction project or needs to purchase a major piece of equipment. Bankers are then aware of the urgency of the need to obtain money and may be inclined to dictate stiffer terms.

The more advantageous financial approach is to make capital and debt management crucial parts of the organization's strategic planning process. In fact, capital and debt management should be accorded as important a place in strategic planning as revenue projections, cost containment programs, community marketing programs, and expansion plans. If capital and debt management is part of an organization's strategic planning process, its long-range goals and objectives can be considered under all types of financing options.

10.3　THE STRATEGIC FINANCIAL PLAN

A strategic plan for financing should be a specific statement of an organization's financing goals. A debt manager must become a team member when it is time to establish a plan for the organization's capital and debt strategy. By assisting in this aspect of the strategic plan in advance, a financial manager can ensure that the organization obtains financing on the most favorable terms.

Most importantly, when setting a strategic plan, the organization must ensure that the plan dictates financing requirements; financing requirements should not determine the plan. The plan must include considerations of the organization's present assets and debt, internal funding sources, and management's expansion goals. Other pertinent factors to consider regarding the organization are the following:

- Mission or charter
- Financial and operational goals
- Market and competitive analyses
- Strategies for achieving goals and objectives

No financial plan can answer every question. There is always uncertainty about future business conditions, government regulations, information technology and other technological advances, and new service delivery techniques. A good strategic plan, however, will include various scenarios, thus adding a degree of flexibility.

(a) Borrower's Strategic Financial Objectives

Answers to the following questions will begin the process of identifying the institution's strategic financial objectives:

- Is the institution public or private?
- How much risk is management willing to take for various financing alternatives?
- How much interest can the institution afford?
- Does the institution intend to provide collateral to the lender, such as assets or stock?
- If privately owned, will the institution's principals sign a personal guarantee to secure a loan?
- What type of covenants and restrictions is management willing to allow?
- How much control does management want to retain?
- What limitations in other agreements must the institution consider when pledging assets?

By answering these questions, a financial manager can help to clarify the organization's current financial status and to determine the direction in which management is moving or wants to move the organization. The answers also help specify financing sources and keep short-term strategy consistent with long-term capital management objectives. For instance, in a publicly owned for-profit company, the interests of shareholders must be treated with the highest priority. Consequently, there will be an emphasis on consistent growth, no matter how small.

In a privately held business, by contrast, strategic objectives can be more flexible and include nonfinancial and charitable goals, if desired. The primary shareholders may be willing to forgo the reassurance of consistent growth in favor of a long-term payoff of their investment.

Even the nonprofit organization must develop a strategic financial plan to assure its long-term fiscal health. The absence of identifiable shareholders does not relieve the financial manager from operating the organization as a business and strategically planning the fiscal health of the organization. A nonprofit organization exists to serve members of the public, who are its very real, although anonymous, shareholders. Failure to maintain fiscal health over the long term is the death knell of all organizations, public or private.

(b) Borrowing Requirements

A strategic plan should evaluate short-term borrowing requirements. Lean periods never can be fully anticipated, so an institution always requires a contingency plan that may include short-term borrowing to tide it over until cash flow resumes. Before a plan can be developed, however, the financial manager must monitor and understand the elements of the institution's cash flow. Cash flow should be forecasted and monitored on monthly, weekly, and daily bases.[3] When studying cash flow, the following factors should be considered:

- Seasonality of revenues
- Collection periods and timeliness of disbursements
- Regulatory changes and economic trends
- Contingency plans

Seasonality of revenues can have a tremendous impact on a nonprofit organization's short-term borrowing requirements. By looking at historic seasonal revenue patterns, a financial manager can obtain part of the picture needed to plan borrowing strategy. In other words, the financial manager must monitor and measure the lag time between the provision of services and the collection of revenues (whether from donations, grants, or fees charged), as well as predict the amount to be collected. Fewer receivables and more payables may dictate that the institution borrow money to see it through the lean months. By analyzing the institution's cash flow, the financial manager can anticipate this situation and plan accordingly.

10.4 STEPS TO SUCCESSFUL BORROWING

Management will be ready to approach potential financing sources after determining strategic objectives and developing a cash flow forecast that indicates the amount of money needed, when it must be borrowed, and when it can be repaid. Before any financial source is approached, however, financial managers must understand:

1. Debt and what borrowing involves for the organization
2. The loan approval process

[3]See Chapter 5.

3. The various short-term borrowing alternatives
4. The suitability of financing sources versus strategic objectives
5. The preparation and presentation of a loan request

(a) Understanding Debt

Debt is a way of life for most consumers and business organizations. It is interesting to note that borrowing and investing are two sides of the same coin. "Capital" can be defined as the resources that an organization needs to attain a financial objective. There are two broad categories of capital: (1) equity, and (2) debt. Equity is money belonging to the business owner, and debt is money belonging to another person or organization. Because borrowed funds carry the borrower's obligation to repay the debt and lenders furnish money for the sole purpose of earning more money, the only differences between debt and equity appear to rest with the person who provides the capital and the return that person seeks.

(i) Risk–Reward Tradeoffs.   Although similarities between debt and equity capital exist, the returns that accrue on each type of funding are very different. Debt capital, in the form of financing received from a lender, generally is priced in terms of an interest rate. Equity capital is "priced" in terms of appreciation of a organization's stock or assets. For example, small business entrepreneurs often are willing to receive little monetary return in the short run in order to develop a business idea. A lender financing the entrepreneur's dream, however, sees the opportunity quite differently. As a financing source for a risky venture, the lender will expect a large return to compensate for the risk.

An important element in the pricing of debt and equity is the relationship between risk and reward: the greater the risk, the greater the reward. Whether that reward is garnered in terms of equity or in terms of debt depends on the perspective of the person providing the funds. The entrepreneur is willing to risk his or her time in return for a high-equity reward, while the lender is willing to risk only money in return for monetary rewards. The "junk," or high-yield, bond market that developed during the 1980s illustrates the lender's perspective. An organization that wants to issue long-term bonds, but that does not have an investment grade rating, must issue noninvestment grade bonds and pay a higher return to attract the needed funds than would an investment grade company. When managing debt, a financial manager must assess the level of risk that the firm presents to a financing source, the resulting availability of financing, and the cost that the financing will carry.

(ii) Leverage.   Leverage is defined as the use of another person's or organization's financial resources. The more leverage, that is, the greater the proportion of debt to equity that an organization has, the greater the risk to the organization and to the lender that the organization will be vulnerable to the impact of external factors. The effects of external factors, such as business conditions and interest rates, are magnified by leverage, sometimes positively and sometimes negatively.

The amount of leverage varies that a nonprofit organization can take on without risking future loss of control to the institution's lenders. Illustrating, in the nursing home and home health care industries, markets must be served; lenders can be instrumental in forcing changes where existing management demonstrates lack of ability. Where the market already is well served, lenders are usually inclined to limit their losses by simply closing down an inefficient or ineffective business. Financial managers can get a good idea of where they stand in the eyes of a lender familiar with the nonprofit industry by studying the financial statements of other nonprofit organizations in similar service arenas. This will also assist financial managers in determining the financial alternatives available.

(b) The Loan Approval Process

It is essential that financial managers understand what lenders and bankers consider important in making decisions to provide financing. The decision to lend capital may be an emotional one based on the personalities of the lender and the borrowing organization's officers. Before the financial manager attempts to make a presentation to a lender, he or she should have some idea of the type of personality that will be sitting across the table. Although the stereotype of the banker-lender is not a totally accurate gauge, it does point out some common traits that lenders share. Lenders tend to be conservative, cautious, and pessimistic. They will look at what is wrong with a borrowing proposal and appear to exclude what is right.

(i) Basic Preparation for a Loan Presentation.   In order to be successful in obtaining financing, a financial manager must distinguish the institution's presentation from all others that lenders evaluate. The financial manager also should try to discern what the lender already emotionally believes about the deal. The financial manager must attempt to reinforce a positive belief and reverse a negative one. To be effective, a financial manager should be aware that lenders, too, think in stereotypes about nonprofit organizations that seek financing. They perceive nonprofit officers who make financial presentations as generally unprepared, hopelessly

optimistic, and out of touch with economic reality. When presenting a loan proposal, therefore, the successful financial manager will demonstrate better preparation, greater knowledge about the organization and its financial prospects, and better capability of repayment than any other customer that approaches the lender.

The financial manager can assess the level of preparedness to make a loan proposal by addressing the following questions:

- Why would a nonprofit organization borrow money?
- What does a lender want to know immediately?
- How does a lender evaluate a loan proposal?
- How does a borrower generate funds to repay a loan?
- Under what reasonable circumstances would a lender agree to refinance a loan?

None of these questions are particularly easy, but the right answers may very well predict the success of a loan proposal.

(ii) Reasons for Borrowing. The reasons why a person or organization does something are important. Knowing the reasons and, more importantly, explaining them quickly are crucial when a financial manager must persuade a lender that the nonprofit organization deserves a loan. The three essential reasons for borrowing are

1. To buy an asset
2. To pay an expense
3. To make an acquisition

Knowing those reasons, however, is not sufficient. Financial managers also must know how different lenders view these reasons. For instance, leasing firms financing equipment purchases have no interest in funding other investments. Banks are more interested in providing short-term working capital financing for seasonal needs and modest longer-term financing for equipment and construction.

(iii) Immediate Concerns of Lenders. The immediate concerns of a lender are important because they generally dictate the terms and conditions of the loan:

1. How much money do you need to borrow?
2. How long do you need to keep the money?
3. What do you need the money for?
4. How do you plan to repay both the principal and the interest?
5. What contingency plans do you have in case your intended source of repayment does not work?

The most important of these questions, of course, are the last two, the repayment method and the contingency plan. Above all, a financial manager must be able to show a lender how the loan will be paid back, in scenarios of both expected conditions and unexpectedly negative circumstances.

(iv) Evaluating the Application.　All lending decisions are based on the same classic set of factors known as the "5 C's of credit":

1. Character of management
2. Capital available to the organization
3. Capacity to earn cash flow to repay the loan
4. Conditions of the market
5. Collateral that the borrower has available to pledge

Of these factors, the two more critical are the character of management, which may account for as much as 80 percent of a lender's evaluation, and cash flow. If one of the other factors is inadequate, a borrower can usually obtain the loan, although the source of financing, the approach to obtaining it, and its interest rate may be altered. The borrower will not be able to raise external capital, however, if the character of management or cash flow are deficient.

(v) How Lenders Are Repaid.　There are four ways to repay lenders:

1. Use earnings and cash flow
2. Borrow more money
3. Find another lender
4. Sell existing assets

Borrowing more to repay a loan is often acceptable, but it can be an expensive proposition. Selling assets also can be acceptable, especially as part of a contingency plan, but the best way to repay a loan is to generate cash flow. Consequently, a financial manager is wise to keep borrowing plans confined to the capacity of the organization to generate sufficient cash flow to repay the loan within a reasonable period. Lenders much prefer this method of repayment, even when they tell you they insist on having collateral to back up their loans. They would much rather not have to think about seizing and selling that collateral, especially given the public relations problems that action can cause the lender when foreclosing on a charitable institution.

(vi) Refinancing.　Barring a decision to restructure a borrower's total debt, a borrower seeks to refinance loans for either of

two reasons: (1) the original plan did not work, or (2) the borrower did not use the money for the intended purpose. No lender is sympathetic to a borrower who did not use the money for the purpose stated in the loan proposal. Most lenders, however, understand that not all business plans work as intended. The fact is that most business plans do not work as originally intended, but they do work after they have been modified. Lenders understand that planning is a dynamic process and flexibility is part of it. Therefore, business plans that do not work are generally considered valid reasons for lending more capital.

(c) Alternative Sources of Short-Term Funds

Before a nonprofit organization commits itself to borrowing money, it should look within. Often there are internal sources of funding that are not immediately apparent. Indeed, one of the objectives of making debt and capital management part of the institution's strategic plan is to identify such internal sources of funds before management seeks funding from outside. Four primary internal financing sources, along with methods to use them, are listed below.

1. Aggressive working capital management:
    - Improve collection practices
    - Extend terms of payables[4]
    - Reduce idle cash
    - Sell nonproductive assets
2. Existing operations:
    - Increase service fees
    - Charge for services previously provided free
    - Increase marketing effort for donations and grants
    - Reduce operating costs
3. Overfunded pension plans:
    - Seek to recapture assets in the plans for the institution's use
4. Change in business structure:
    - Seek strategic alliance partnerships and joint ventures with other service providers
    - Establish employee participation programs

These internal alternatives will not meet the needs of all organizations. The financial manager is then faced with a long list of prosaic and creative financing alternatives. Consider, for instance,

---

[4]This may be by negotiating with the supplier, or it may simply mean only paying invoices early when there is a cash discount offered.

the following financing possibilities. A nursing home or home health care agency could:

- Obtain a bank loan, either secured by assets or unsecured
- Sell accounts receivable without recourse (nonprofit does not have to stand behind sold accounts that prove to be uncollectible)
- Sell accounts receivable with recourse
- Securitize accounts receivable for offering in public or private markets

The differences among these short-term financing alternatives lie in the source rather than the particular use of the funds, and they are based on the criteria that a lender considers when making a loan decision. There are three basic criteria:

1. How much debt capital must be raised?
2. How long a term does the borrower need to repay the loan?
3. What return will the lender receive for the loan?

10.5 MATCHING FINANCIAL SOURCES TO STRATEGIC OBJECTIVES

It is difficult to match the best capital source to the strategic objectives of a nonprofit organization; few financial alternatives provide perfect matches. When attempting to match financial sources to strategic objectives, however, financial managers should

- List the strategic objectives in the order of their apparent levels of priority
- Summarize in writing the alternative choices
- Seek advice from consultants or others who are involved in matching strategic planning and financial sources
- Consider the decision carefully and preferably without pressure of time

The first two items listed force the financial manager to focus on the organization's critical issues, because they involve ranking objectives. By reducing these issues to a one-page summary, the financial manager can identify the major financing alternatives. This requires that the major advantages and disadvantages of each alternative be considered. It can be helpful to develop a scoring system to rate financial alternatives, although a scoring system is only as good as the thought that conceived it.

The time criterion is also particularly important. Making a final decision a day or a week after completing the list of alternatives is generally a good idea. This provides the financial manager time to reflect on the institution's strategic objectives and whether the alternative choices meet them. All alternatives should be thoroughly evaluated before a decision is made. On the other hand, delay in the name of perfection can be counterproductive. A financial manager can delay a deal so long that interest rates rise before a choice is made. Financial markets also lose interest when they believe that management is only shopping around and is not serious about a deal. It is good to generate competition among financing sources, but not to the point that it paralyzes the borrower and prevents it from meeting its objectives in the most effective manner.

10.6 PREPARING THE FINANCING PROPOSAL

After the financial manager has determined what type of financial source is best to meet the institution's particular short-term capital needs, it is time to obtain the financing. The basic tool for this task is the financing proposal package. The financial manager uses this document to present the institution's "story" as well as to anticipate and answer all questions posed by the lender. Of utmost importance in telling that story are the five criteria essential to all lenders, beginning with the character of organization management (see the previous section, "Steps to Successful Borrowing").

(a) Term Sheet

One of the most important parts of the proposal is called the term sheet. In this part of the plan, the financial manager must answer the five basic questions a lender will ask: how much, how long, what for, repayment plan, and contingent repayment plan.

(b) Plan Overview

A financing proposal must contain a brief overview of the plan. Bankers and other lenders tend to make decisions quickly. Review committees, for instance, generally rely on a subordinate's summary and recommendation when evaluating loan requests. A review committee may spend only two or three minutes looking at what took weeks, even months, for a financial manager to assemble. As a result, when a business plan is turned into a proposal, it must include an "executive summary." This should be the most sparkling part of the package.

The overview must describe the essential nature of the organization's service offerings, list its major services, and characterize its management people. The overview focuses on facts, but the facts should be presented in such a way that a potential investor—and that is, after all, what a lender is—gets a positive emotional feeling about the institution.

(c) Presentation Contents

The overview can be supplemented with marketing brochures, testimonials, and perhaps even a video presentation to enhance the written word. A full set of financial statements for three years is essential. The financial statements will be used to evaluate the risk of the proposed loan and determine the terms and conditions of any financing deal. The statements should be supplemented with explanations wherever appropriate. For example, the statements of some care providers contain quirks that may confuse a lender unless they are explained. When dealing with a lender who is basically unfamiliar with the health care field, some explanation of reimbursement methods and the handling of unreimbursed charges is desirable so the lender can understand the inevitable write-offs of receivables. This explanation should extend to both the balance sheet and the income statement.

Nonprofit business plans also need to cover the basics of an organization's business: delivery of service, marketing, and accounting/finance. The plan should show how the desired financing will enhance these areas. However, the projections should be realistic. Lenders often believe that a borrower is hopelessly optimistic, and aggressive revenue projections will make the lender even more skeptical. In fact, it is always better for management's position if actual operating results turn out to be higher than anticipated by the projections, rather than using forecast figures that are too rosy. If management really does believe that revenues will grow by 200 percent, however, then substantiating information should be included in the plan along with documentation showing why the projections are realistic. Detail is crucial in a business plan. Any error in calculations, for instance, can threaten a plan's credibility; it gives the impression of sloppy management.

10.7 MAKING THE PRESENTATION

Even more important than a detailed business plan is the ability to communicate it with confidence and forcefulness to potential investors. Financial managers may not think of themselves as salespeople, but that is exactly what they are when they represent the institution that requires financing. They must sell the entire organization, its business, plans, and creditworthiness. Asking questions throughout the presentation is an excellent technique as it focuses the presentation on the needs of the audience. A pointed presentation is important, because it shows that the organization has thought out its financing needs. This distinguishes it from other organizations competing for the same scarce financing dollars.

(a) The Importance of Questions

Questions can be the most effective tool for the financial manager in preparing and making the presentation. They provide valuable information and allow the financial manager to focus the presentation. Close scrutiny is avoided until the financial manager has all the necessary information to test assumptions regarding the audience, confirm suspicions, and figure out what the lender considers important, before making the actual request for financing. Consequently, the financial manager is better able to handle objections. It is surprising how good questions will keep the mood relaxed and the conversation flowing.

Financial managers should not feel inadequate when they ask about the lending and loan approval process. Each lender does things a little differently. A financial manager should also ask for a copy of the financial analysis the lender performed on the institution. The analysis can provide valuable information the next time financing must be sought. Asking questions about the process will also show that the borrower is more sophisticated and thus a better credit risk.

(b) Answering Objections

No matter how controlled and tightly organized the presentation may be, objections will arise and the financial manager will have to answer the lender's questions. Further questions by the borrower can be excellent answers to lender questions. For instance, if the lender's major objection focuses on collateral, the financial manager might ask, "Isn't it the case in bankruptcy that legal fees cause liabilities to increase while the value of collateral generally decreases?" The financial manager might further ask, "Doesn't the organization's real value lie in its ability to generate cash flow rather than its present holdings of assets?" And, "In a bad loan situation, does the amount of collateral really make much of a difference?" Almost any objection can be handled by turning it around with a simple question. By understanding the motive of the investor in making an objection, the financial manager can gauge what response will be most appropriate.

The importance of questions does not end with the presentation and objections. Questions are even more important when a loan has been turned down; they may even be able to salvage a rejection or make it easier to obtain financing from the same source the next time around. Potential questions should be designed to discover why the proposal was declined, where such financing could be obtained, what would make this financing more attractive, and how would the lender who turned down the proposal respond to inquiries from other lenders. As with the other questions, this information can provide feedback that will help in the next presentation.

(c) Personalizing the Presentation

Finally, anything that will personalize the presentation will usually work to a borrower's benefit. It is also helpful for the financial manager to invite a representative of the potential lender to tour the nonprofit institution's facilities before the presentation. This will get the lender more emotionally involved with the institution and more concerned about its future success. It also provides a more personal and relaxed atmosphere to make initial contact with a lender. The key to obtaining a loan is to connect emotionally with the lender, to persuade the lender that the institution's success is the lender's success as well.

10.8 OTHER FACTORS IN BORROWING/LENDING DECISIONS

Borrowing and lending decisions would be easy if the loan criteria listed above were as straightforward as they sound. A financial manager would then choose the alternative that raises the most capital at the least cost over the longest term. Unfortunately, however, one alternative generally raises the most funds, while another has the longest term, and yet a third costs the least. The lender's decisions also would be more mechanical if each element to be considered were based merely on its own merits. Intangible factors, however, often complicate borrowing and lending decisions. These factors include the following questions involved in loan evaluation:

- Is the transaction flexible enough to be structured to meet the institution's financial needs?
- Does the borrower have confidence that the lender will be able to complete the transaction?
- Can the deal be documented and negotiated within the borrower's time frame?

- How complex is the legal documentation?
- Can the borrower afford the front-end fees associated with the transaction?
- Will the borrower be able to cancel the deal if circumstances dictate, and how much it will cost to do so?
- What requirements does the investor have for credit support?

(a) Borrowing from the Bank

Nonprofits borrow short-term for seasonal working capital, to cover abrupt changes in payment patterns or unexpected expenses, and when net revenue is not adequate to support continued operations. Banks traditionally have provided most of the short-term and medium-term loans for nonprofits.

About one-half of short-term bank loans are unsecured (usually in the form of a line of credit) and the other half are secured (where collateral is required to ensure an adequate secondary source of repayment). We will survey bank credit and credit-related services by noting the major domestic and international services offered, and we conclude the short-term lending discussion by talking about some lending trends.

(b) Domestic Short-Term Bank Loans

Bank lending alternatives are best described in terms of their maturities, or how long they allow borrowers to use the money. The shortest-term lending generally takes the form of a line of credit, which allows the organization to borrow up to a pre-arranged dollar amount during the one-year term. Credit lines may be established on an uncommitted or committed basis, and they sometimes have the added feature of overdraft protection.

An uncommitted line of credit is technically not binding on the bank, although it is almost always honored.[5] Uncommitted lines are usually renewable annually if both parties are agreeable. These informal arrangements are appealing to organizations who only rarely need to draw down the credit line, who maintain a consistently strong financial position, and who like the fact that uncommitted credit lines do not require a fee to be paid on unused balances. The only charges are interest on amounts borrowed. Banks like the flexibility offered by such arrangements, which free

---

[5]The banks give themselves the flexibility to deny some borrowers credit if many requests are received at the same time. Thus, total credit lines for a given bank exceed its ability to finance them simultaneously. Furthermore, material changes in the potential borrower's financial condition might result in the bank's denial of credit for an uncommitted line, although this also is rare.

the bank from providing funds in the event of deterioration by the borrower or due to capital restrictions being imposed on the bank by federal regulators.

A committed line of credit is a formal, written agreement contractually binding the bank to provide the funds when requested. Committed lines usually involve commitment fees of up to 1 percent of unused balances. Whether uncommitted or committed, an overdraft credit line has the added feature of being automatically drawn down whenever the organization writes a check for which it does not have sufficient funds. The treasurer is thereby delegating to the bank the need to carefully monitor disbursement account balances and to fund it when necessary.

A noteworthy trend regarding credit lines is the rapid growth of the standby letter of credit, which guarantees that the bank will make funds available if the organization cannot or does not wish to meet a major financial obligation.

The second type of bank financing is intermediate term. The two major forms of this are revolving credit agreements and term loans. A revolving credit agreement, or "revolver," allows the borrower to continually borrow and repay amounts up to an agreed-upon limit. The agreement is annually renewable at a variable interest rate during an interim period of anywhere from one to five years. At the end of the interim period, the agreement generally is converted to a term loan for a period of years. The key advantage to the borrower is assured credit availability for the life of the agreement, regardless of overall economic conditions and credit availability. Like on a committed credit line, the bank will charge a commitment fee on unused amounts of revolvers, along with interest on drawn-down amounts. Revolving credit agreements are usually unsecured.

A term loan is simply a loan made with an initial maturity of more than one year. Maturities for bank-originated term loans range from over one year to ten years. Like revolving credit agreements, they involve an extensive written loan agreement and an in-depth "due diligence" analysis of the organization's management and financial position. Term loans are generally repaid in equal monthly or quarterly payments and may be fixed or variable rate. Nonprofit organizations use term loans to replace other loans or to finance ongoing investments in working capital, equipment, and machinery. The main advantage is that they provide a stable source of funds.

Some secured bank loans are a form of asset-based lending. Like any collateralized lending, such lending has a claim on an asset or group of assets, ordinarily receivables or inventory that could be easily sold if the borrower defaults on the loan. The difference is that while most conventional lending relies on the cash flows from the overall business for repayment, asset-based loans are offered based on anticipated cash flows arising from the sale or conversion of a specific asset or group of assets, such as inventories. These loans are especially attractive to small, growing organizations that may only qualify for this form of borrowing and whose management are willing to pay the higher interest rate necessary to compensate the bank for continuous monitoring of the asset serving as collateral.

One final borrowing-related service that more banks are beginning to offer is a swap. In its simplest form, an organization engaging in a swap exchanges a fixed interest rate obligation for one that has a variable, or floating interest rate. Nonprofit organizations that qualify for a lower variable rate spread (the amount of extra interest the organization must pay over and above the bank's cost of funds is lower on variable rate loans than on fixed rate loans, or perhaps the bank does not wish to make a fixed rate loan) might enter into a variable-to-fixed rate swap to eliminate the risk of rising interest rates and the resulting higher monthly payments. Banks usually serve as the opposite side on the swap, called the counterparty, but they may later find another counterparty who wants to make the opposite exchange.

(c) International Short-Term Bank Loans

The nonprofit organization operating in multiple countries must consider a more complex set of bank lending services. This is so because operating abroad introduces the treasurer to different economic and banking regulations, the uncertainty about how exchange rates will change in the future, and new customs and cultures. U.S.-headquartered banks provide a valuable service simply by introducing the treasurer to foreign banking officers and to the different payment systems that will be encountered. In addition, three major lending services are offered internationally.

First, banks doing business abroad, whether United States or foreign banks, offer various forms of documentary credit. Included here are sight and time drafts, bankers' acceptances, and letters of credit. The sight draft is a formal, written agreement whereby an importer (drawee) contracts to pay a certain amount on demand ("at sight") to the exporter. The bank is not extending credit, but simply helping in the payment process by receiving the draft and presenting it to the drawee. A time draft does involve a credit element, because the payment obligation agreed to by the drawee is designated as due at a specified future date. A bankers' acceptance is a time draft drawn on the buyer, whose bank agrees to pay (accepts) the amount if the buyer does not. In essence, the bank's creditworthiness is exchanged for the buyer's, and there is an active secondary market where these acceptances are traded. The bank charges the buyer a fee for this service. Related to this, a short-term acceptance facility allows the selling firm to initiate drafts (called bills of exchange) against the buyer's bank instead of against the buyer, which can be discounted at the bank.[6] This facilitates foreign trade, but in the United States and United Kingdom it also is used to finance working capital needed to conduct domestic trade. A commercial letter of credit is a guarantee of payment by an importer, made by its bank, which becomes binding when the shipping and other documents related to the goods sold are presented to the bank.[7] Exporters appreciate the bank guarantees involved in acceptances and letters of credit due to the lack of information about foreign customers, as well as the shifting of the complexities and costs that might be involved in collecting on unpaid accounts. Note that most letters of credit used in international business are unconditional, differing from the standby letters of credit we discussed earlier.

Second, banks increasingly are getting involved in international asset-based lending. As with domestic asset-based lending, lending is done mainly by banks and commercial finance, companies, with the collateral and source of the cash flows counted on for debt service usually being inventories or accounts receivable. Asset-based lending has been utilized in the United States for some time, but is in its infancy in the United Kingdom, Japan, and Hong Kong, and has not been used in other European countries. With the growing unification of European economies, most observers anticipate asset-based lending to expand rapidly in Europe. Banks based in the United States hope to capture a large share of the European secured lending volume.

Third, there are several traditional forms of bank lending. Nonprofit organizations operating abroad are offered overdraft services that are renegotiable each year, may be secured, and are generally based on some percent above the bank's base rate. For example, a strong organization might be charged 1 percent above the base rate, which is often the London Interbank Offered Rate, or LIBOR. Whether the bank uses LIBOR or not, the base rate is reflective of that bank's cost of funds. Organizations are prohibited

[6]When drawn against the buyer, these drafts are called bills of exchange, but when a bank sets up an acceptance facility, the seller draws against the bank, and the resulting instrument is called an acceptance credit. The bank will pay the seller the discounted value of the acceptance's face value, with the amount of the discount based on prevailing money market rates.

[7]The same transaction often has both a commercial letter of credit and banker's acceptance involved: The letter of credit may be sent to the exporter's bank, which in turn draws up a time draft and shipment documents, and sends those back to the importer's bank. If the importer's bank accepts the draft, guaranteeing the payment of the draft at the due date, a banker's acceptance is created.

by law from overdrafting demand deposit accounts in the United States, although banks have permitted intraday ("daylight") overdrafting.

Another standard lending service seen abroad is an advised line, which is very similar to a credit line in the United States. This involves unsecured lending of up to one year in maturity, available on short notice to the borrower. The rate is somewhat less than would be the case for overdraft services, but is still calculated from the base rate.

The foreign parallel to the term loan is called a committed facility. The bank charges a fee to compensate it for agreeing to lend upon request for a period of five to seven years. Loan terms and conditions, including whether the funds made available will be in the home currency or some other currency, and the formula for calculating the interest rate are described in a written agreement.

Our discussion of international bank services up to this point fits the major industrial economies of the world, but not developing countries. Recent survey evidence suggests that most undeveloped countries do not yet have connections to the major global cable and payment settlement mechanisms, making it almost impossible for nonprofit organizations operating in those countries to tap international financial lending sources for domestic borrowing.

(d) Trends in Short-Term Lending

More and more banks are going after smaller businesses and nonprofit organizations as part of their client base. For example, Wells Fargo has begun offering small businesses a credit card that acts as a committed line of credit.[8]

Banks' reliance on asset-based lending, term loans, and revolving credit agreements (especially to smaller businesses) has grown largely because of the lack of competition from the commercial paper and participation markets. The extent of nonbank penetration into lending is illustrated by the fact that total debt held outside the banking industry is about equal to that held by banks ($4 trillion), whereas in 1970 banks held about $700 billion in debt versus approximately $300 billion outside the banking system. Finally, globalization is occurring in lending services.

---

[8]Two surveys conducted in 1990 found that only 10 percent to 13 percent of all banks offer credit lines to small businesses. As nonprofits are generally the same size as small businesses, it is likely that about the same percentage offer credit lines to nonprofits. Three examples of banks that have actively solicited loans to religious organizations are First Atlanta, Third National Bank (Nashville, TN) and First American National Bank (Nashville, TN). See Tim Loughran, "Heavenly Profits From Church Lending," *Bankers Monthly*, (November 1989), 66–67.

10.9 MUNICIPAL AND TAXABLE BONDS

(a) Municipal Bonds

In the fall of 1987, many large municipal bond underwriting firms either curtailed or completely eliminated their activities in the municipal bond market. Salomon Brothers, Kidder Peabody, L. F. Rothchild, and E. F. Hutton (now part of Smith Barney) were among these firms. The turmoil occurred as a result of two specific changes in the municipal bond market during the preceding two years:

1. Fewer municipal bonds could be issued due to recent tax law changes. Therefore, municipal bond firms had much less "product" to sell and the reduced volume made dealing in municipal bonds less profitable. Tax law changes[9] included the following:

   • The loss of "arbitrage" profit opportunities

   • A limit of 2 percent on the cost of issuance related to initiating new bond issues

2. Most securities dealers, in addition to carrying an inventory of bonds that they sell to investors, trade or speculate in bonds for their own profit. Many dealers had misjudged the market and consequently suffered substantial losses from their speculative trading. These losses added to their desire to leave the municipal bond area.

These changes were rather substantial and obvious, but there have been other, more subtle effects on the municipal bond market. However, this brief section of the chapter will discuss primarily the impact of the changes mentioned above on nonprofits that borrow in the debt markets through the issuance of municipal bonds.

10.10 SELECTION OF AN UNDERWRITING FIRM

Because of the limited choice available, a nonprofit organization must be particularly careful in its selection of a capable and experienced underwriting firm. The nonprofit financial manager must first determine that the underwriting firm plans to continue in the municipal bond business for at least a sufficient period of time to market the bond issue. A firm that knows its bond operations soon will be terminating is simply interested in getting the issue sold as quickly as possible without the attention necessary to present it in the market in a proper and competitive fashion, and make a market (buy and sell the bonds) in the bond issue until it becomes seasoned.

[9]Readers should verify current laws with their tax or bond counsel.

If the bond issue is a floating rate, put-option bond (investors can cash out by "putting" the bond back to the issuer) and the investor has the right to redeem it for the return of principal on a one-day or one-week notice, what is known as a "remarketing agent" is required. This agent provides the vital function of accepting bonds tendered, or put, by investors and immediately finding other investors to purchase the bonds. A continuing underwriting responsibility exists to accommodate both investors and the borrower, whose interest it is to see that the issue continually remains in the hands of investors. The remarketing responsibility is usually assumed quickly and efficiently by other institutions.

Although most issues, once sold, do not trade actively in the secondary market, it is important to the nonprofit organization that its bonds receive reasonable secondary market activity, particularly if it expects to sell bond issues in the future. The institution does not want to lose potential investors because they had purchased its previous bonds and had been unable to sell them due to a weak or, worse yet, "no bid" situation.

After a municipal bond issue has been sold, securities dealers frequently buy the bonds from investors who sell them before maturity or sell them to investors who are looking for secondary (or already-issued) bonds. It is important to maintain a relatively stable market price for the bond issue after its initial sale to the public. Therefore, the underwriting firm or group of firms that brought the issue to the public market should continue to participate actively in buying and selling the bonds in the secondary or resale market.

10.11   PREPARATION OF BOND DOCUMENTS

After selecting a bond underwriter and other professionals necessary to complete the financing task, including bond counsel, the actual indenture or disclosure statement is one of several documents that must be prepared. Of particular importance is the segment of the borrowing indenture that lists the instruments considered acceptable for investment of the bond issue proceeds prior to their disbursement or ultimate use. In the case of rated nursing home and educational facility debt, the credit rating agencies, such as Moody's Investors Service and Standard & Poor's Inc., have their own rating criteria that include specific information about the instruments in which bond proceeds may be invested. However, very often the bond counsel for the underwriters uses a file form for the compilation of indenture clauses, including one listing acceptable investments. This file is often outdated and inappropriate for the listing of acceptable investment instruments.

It is very important for the nonprofit financial manager to submit to the underwriter a list of investments that the nonprofit institution considers safe and appropriate. The list should be broad enough in scope to meet the bond's indenture requirements. Typical instruments that can be listed are U.S. Treasury securities, government agency securities, certificates of deposit and banker's acceptances issued by major creditworthy banks, commercial paper, and other corporate obligations rated in one of the top rating categories by the credit-rating agencies (Moody's, Standard & Poor's, Duff & Phelps, Fitch). If others involved in the borrowing process disagree with this list they should make it known, so that the list can be negotiated to one that is acceptable to all parties. However, the financial manager, after researching the appropriate investments to be included, should initiate a list of acceptable investments and not wait until the indenture is essentially complete before submitting it to the underwriter.

Another area of concern, with respect to the process of investing bond proceeds, is the specific approach of actually implementing these investments within the approved list of instruments included in the indenture. In considering the question of investing the proceeds from a bond issue pending their final disbursement, it is important to recognize the arbitrage provisions of the tax code. Briefly stated, these provisions will not allow the borrowing institution to benefit from any profit received on the investment of funds from a bond issue. Specifically, if the interest earned on the funds from a bond issue exceeds the cost of the interest on the money borrowed by the bond issue, that excess must be returned to the federal government. The intent of the provisions is to discourage entities from borrowing at a low interest cost through the sale of municipal bonds and investing the proceeds at a higher return, if the primary goal is to capture a profit from the privilege of being able to use municipal bonds as a borrowing vehicle.[10]

Most municipal bond issues are subject to the arbitrage provisions of the tax code. In this context, arbitrage refers to borrowing at a relatively low interest rate and then investing the proceeds in a higher-rate investment security. It is obvious that an issuing organization will not benefit from any interest earned that is in excess of interest cost unless interest rates fall sharply during the five-year period during which the yield is averaged. This situation certainly will not provide an incentive to earn maximum interest on the proceeds of the bond issue until such time as the funds are finally disbursed. Therefore, it is important that under no circumstances should aggressive investment techniques be used or higher risks taken simply to earn additional interest income. It takes a substantial amount of additional interest income to equal principal lost through unwise investment of bond proceeds.

---

[10]Readers should verify current laws with their tax or bond counsel.

These limitations on earned interest are referred to as "permitted yield." Although they provide no incentive to earn yield in excess of interest cost, there are other situations that must be considered. The institution may find itself in a low-interest rate environment and need to be a competitive investor simply to earn the level of return to equal the cost of money borrowed. In this situation, it is extremely important that investment yields be taken seriously to minimize the interest cost incurred on municipal bond borrowing.

Whatever interest conditions prevail at the time the municipal bond issue is brought to market, it is important to be a prudent and efficient investor. There are many alternatives available for the investment of proceeds from the bond issue. In examining these alternatives, the financial manager should be aware of the institution's needs, not only with respect to arbitrage provisions, but also as to internal management capabilities, proper compliance with indenture investment limitations, and sound overall financial practices.

(a) Who Issues Municipals and for What Purpose?

Increasingly, public universities and private colleges and even some religious organizations are issuing taxable municipals or tax-exempt municipal bonds. When tax exempt, the interest paid to investors is exempt from federal income taxation and may also be tax exempt for state or local income tax purposes if the investor lives in the issuer's state. Most municipals, or munis, as they are called, are tax exempt. Because of the tax-exempt feature, the yields on munis are lower than those on comparably rated (equally risky) taxable securities. Much of the issuance goes to pay for building refurbishment or new construction to keep the institution competitive from a physical facilities standpoint. Many of these colleges would rather leave investment funds in their endowments, gaining interest and building larger principal amounts, instead of spending these monies on buildings. Private institutions face a limit of $150 million in tax-exempt securities they may issue, but public institutions face no such limits. Some securities are short-term notes, but these are quite often issued by municipalities awaiting funds forthcoming from taxes or the sale of a bond issue.

Let's illustrate how your organization can use tax-exempt bonds. In the 1995–1997 period, four private nonprofit organizations issued tax-exempt bonds in central Indiana. The following are some features of those bonds:

- Pleasant Run Children's Home issued bonds "induced" by the city of Indianapolis—meaning that they were issued in the name of Indianapolis but are not a direct obligation of the city.

These bonds were 7-day variable rate bonds, or "low floaters" as they are called, and paid between 3.75 percent and 4.25 percent during 1996. The bonds were used to raise funds for facilities. The organization's foundation guaranteed payment on the bonds, and the issue was backed by a letter of credit from Fifth Third Bank of Central Indiana. For a fee of just over 1 percent of the amount of the issue, the bank stands ready to make interest payments or principal repayment if the issuer cannot.

- Archdiocese of Indianapolis issued $48 million in bonds to finance facilities and construction of private schools and cemeteries. The Archdiocese did not need a letter of credit and took 18 months to close the deal from start to finish. This issue was the first of its kind in the United States.

- Lutheran Child & Family Services issued bonds to finance a treatment facility for children, also structured as a 7-day low floater, with a letter of credit backing the issue.

- Goodwill Industries issued bonds to pay for construction costs for new thrift stores, instead of getting a ten- or fifteen-year commercial mortgage on each new store that it opened. The $8.5 million issue refinanced existing mortgages and funded several new retail stores. Again, this issue was backed by a bank letter of credit.

To get these issues induced by the municipality, discussions and presentations were held with the mayor's office and appropriate city offices.

(b) Taxable Bonds

Many bonds issued by nonprofit organizations are not tax exempt in that the bond investor must pay income tax on the interest received. Church bonds, bonds issued to pay for private schools, and nursing home bonds illustrate the taxable bonds issued by nonprofits. The flexibility of the investment banker structuring the borrowing allows these to be used for bridge financing, working capital loans, or construction. Sometimes, the state or city in which the nonprofit operates can lend its tax-exempt status to allow what would normally be fully taxable bonds to be issued as a tax-exempt bonds, as noted earlier.

(i) How Can My Organization Use Taxable Bonds? Let's illustrate the use of taxable bonds. Alanar, Inc. (Sullivan, IN),[11] is an investment banker whose slogan is "Financing America's Churches."

---

[11]Information regarding Alanar was provided by Vaughn Reeves, president, Bob Bontrager, investment banker, and Jody Thomas, analyst.

Alanar arranges the public sale and distribution of first mortgage bonds, which are secured by a mortgage on the property. These bonds are certificates of indebtedness issued by churches, private schools, and other nonprofit organizations to provide funds for:

- Acquisition of property
- Building expansion
- Debt retirement

Many of the organizations issuing bonds through Alanar did so because financing from banks was not available, or not available at acceptable terms (interest rate, down payment, or maturity). Many of the bond investors are members or friends of the borrowing organization. The bond issue is normally structured so that some of the bonds mature each six months, with the final set maturing in 15 years. The bonds are taxable, meaning that investors will have to pay tax at the ordinary income tax rate on interest received. Bonds are usually sold in denominations of $250 or any multiple thereof.

(ii) Can I Get Short-Term Financing through Taxable Bonds? Although banks are the primary lenders for short-term funding needs, if a need is construction related you might use an organization such as Alanar to help you raise the funds via a bond issue. Let's say you need some money up front to build part of a project. You might do a 36-month revenue bond if your long-term financial track record shows you are reliable in paying your bills on a timely basis. As of this writing, the interest rate on such an issue would be between 8 percent and 9 percent. In evaluating your suitability for issuing such bonds, the investment banker will look at

- *Purpose*—what you want the money for
- *Timing*—how soon you need the money
- *Insufficiency of other sources*—why you need bond financing

(iii) What Qualifies My Organization to Issue Bonds? Investment bankers will look for the following on mortgage bonds:

- Borrowing amount not to exceed 3.5 times annual gross revenues
- Projected cash flows showing enough excess cash inflow to make interest payments and principal repayment (or a realignment of cash uses to free up necessary cash flows)
- The total amount financed not to exceed 70 percent or 75 percent of the property's appraised value.

Credit checks will also be performed on the borrower's chief administrators, and the investment banker will look for evidence that the organization will stand behind the bonds, even if the administrators depart.

Organizations that have defaulted on their bonds are characterized by one or both of the following:

- Lack of understanding about what they are getting into
- Lack of resolve about debt repayment

One must understand that interest payments cannot be "laid off" like employees when times get tough. Furthermore, one must realize that the organization will lose the property if it does make debt payments. Out of this understanding, and based on members' integrity, should come the resolve to stay current on debt repayment.

10.12 LEASING AND NONTRADITIONAL FINANCING SOURCES

A broad definition of leasing is the use of equipment for money. The process you would follow to get lease financing from a lease finance company entails the following steps:

1. Fill out a lease application and mail or fax it to the lease financing company (lessor).
2. Within 24 hours, the lessor will accept or deny the application.
3. Lease documents are prepared (assuming your application was accepted).
4. Documents are then properly executed by your organization (lessee), and equipment or vehicle is acquired.
5. You return the documents, along with the equipment or vehicle invoice, to lessor.
6. You are contacted by lessor via phone to provide verbal acceptance (which authenticates the mailed documents).
7. Lessor pays vendor within 24 hours.

(a) Why Lease Instead of Borrow?

There are several advantages to using lease financing, several of which result from the fact that you are not buying the equipment or vehicles as you would under a loan arrangement:

- You may get longer-term, and therefore, lower monthly cost, financing due to the two- to five-year lease terms, possibly longer than what a bank would allow.
- You may get almost 100 percent financing, as opposed to 20 percent down or a compensating balance requirement when using bank financing.

- When squeezed for liquidity, you will appreciate having both your cash and your machines or vehicles for use, as opposed to outright purchase of the items.

- Capital project restrictions on outright purchases (whether using cash or bank borrowing), perhaps due to delays in getting a capital campaign off the ground, will not impede critical purchases that can be made with lease financing.

- It protects your organization against owning computers or other equipment that rapidly become obsolete.

- You may gain flexibility, both on the lease terms and on what your options are at the end of the lease: renewal, purchase, or return of equipment.

These advantages come at a cost, as you well know if you have considered a personal lease on a car purchase. And, unless you are using the leased items in a for-profit enterprise, you will not get the tax advantage that motivates some businesses to lease (lease expense is tax-deductible, and if the lease period is shorter than the depreciation schedule that would apply to a purchase, the lease can lower your tax bill). However, a lease may fit your organization's need to finance copiers, computers, computer software, construction equipment, or an entire office. And, as is true of so many other business transactions, you can now apply for a lease right from your computer![12]

10.13 SUMMARY

Borrowers come in all shapes and sizes, and the astute lender must seek a way to differentiate between good loans and potentially unsuccessful loans. The financial manager must assist the lender to discern the differences between the good loan represented by the financial manager's organization and all others.

The process begins with the preparation of a strategic financing plan that is part of the institution's overall strategic business plan. Then, the financial manager must garner all the relevant facts and information that the lender will require, anticipate the lender's questions, and assemble a presentation to the lender. The presentation is a combination of written information and oral discussion, often including an on-site tour of the nonprofit's facilities.

To be successful in the borrowing process, the financial manager must ensure that the selected lender matches the intended use

[12]As best we can determine, the first leasing company to offer "lease by Internet application" was First Credit Corporation. Their web address at the time of this writing was: http://www.firstcredit.com/.

of the funds and the duration of the loan. Banks, leasing companies, and insurance companies all have different objectives. The financial manager must recognize these differences and position itself toward the lender's interests.

Proficient financial managers with funding needs investigate bond financing as well as bank or insurance lease financing companies. They ensure that the organization pays its bills on time and makes interest payments and principal repayments as required. Because the worst time to contact a lender is when you finally really need them, they plan liquidity and capital project needs well in advance.

CHAPTER ELEVEN

Investment Policy
and Guidelines

11.1   Investment Policy   368
        (a) Short-Term Investment Policy   369
        (b) Long-Term Investment Policy   370
11.2   Investment Guidelines   371
        (a) Who Is Responsible for the Investing Program?   371
        (b) Who Does the Investing?   372
        (c) How Are Assets to Be Allocated?   372
             (i) Investment Instruments 373
             (ii) Fixed-Income Instruments   373
             (iii) Equity Instruments   374
             (iv) Alternative Investments   374
             (v) Socially Conscious Investing   374
        (d) How Is Performance Measured and Reported?   376
             (i) Measurement   376
             (ii) Reporting   376
        (e) What Level of Risk Is to Be Assumed?   377
             (i) Limitations on Maturity   377
             (ii) Currency Denomination   378
        (f) Review and Modification of the Investment Guidelines:
             Who Is Responsible for What?   378
11.3   Checklist of Elements for Long-Term Endowment
        Investment Policy and Guidelines   379
        (a) Investment Policy Summary   379
Appendix 11A   Sample of Short-Term Investment Policy
               and Guidelines   381
Appendix 11B   ABC Foundation Unendowed Short-Term
               Investment Pool Policy   385
Appendix 11C   Short-Term Investment Policy for HIJ
               Foundation   388
Appendix 11D   Sample of Investment Policy Statement
               for the ABC Foundation's Long-Term
               Endowment Fund   390

■   367   ■

Appendix 11E   Definitions of Fixed-Income Instruments   396
Appendix 11F   Definitions of Equity Instruments   404
Appendix 11G   Glossary   405

11.1   INVESTMENT POLICY

A written document containing a statement of investment policy and a set of guidelines—a framework for achieving the investment goals—is absolutely essential for the success of both the short-term and long-term investing of an institution's funds. Individuals who function as fiduciaries to both the donors and the Board have ultimate responsibility for investments for the nonprofit organization. The written investment policy and guidelines document forms the bridge of understanding between the Board and the person(s) executing the investment program. In a very real sense, the policy and guidelines document is an agreement between the Board and the investment manager and should describe the parameters of that agreement.

Definition of Terms:

Although these terms are used differently among users, the following are typical definitions used within the investment policy area discussed in this chapter.

- Liquidity (new cash)   Period of up to 180 days

- Short-term   Period of up to 2 years

- Intermediate term   Period of 3–5 years

- Long-term   Period of 5 years or longer

- Endowment   A fund invested to produce a steady flow of income, both now and in the future.

The investment objectives of an organization should be the first element(s) contained in a written investment policy. The importance of having a written investment policy in your organization cannot be understated. The current trend toward engaging external professional money managers to provide investment management advice to the Board, or its designee, makes this requirement more important than ever.

Without a well-defined investment policy, the *in-house* investment manager will make your organization's investments the way that he or she believes they should be made. An *external* investment manager, in the absence of written policy, will probably make your investments in the same way he or she does for other clients. In order to ensure that investments are made to meet your organization's requirements, investment goals and objectives must be documented in a written investment policy; otherwise, the investment manager may make investment decisions which exceed your comfort zone.

To provide clarity and avoid confusion, it is recommended that the short-term investment policy of the institution be separate and distinct from the long-term investment policy. One reason is that short-term and long-term investment goals and instruments are clearly separate and distinct; however, intermediate goals and instruments can fall into either the short-term or long-term policy, depending upon the organization. In any case, the investment policy or policies must include a written statement of the investment objectives. These objectives should be stated clearly and concisely and should set forth the order of priorities if there are multiple objectives.

In a short-term investment policy, investors typically have three objectives:

1. Preservation of principal
2. Maintenance of liquidity
3. Yield

It is important for your organization's policy to state these goals and place them in priority order. In a short-term portfolio, most nonprofit organizations' investment requirements would fall in this order. Preservation of principal and maintenance of liquidity often both take precedence over yield.

(a) Short-Term Investment Policy

A typical investment policy statement for a short-term portfolio might read:

> It shall be the policy of this organization to invest its temporary surplus cash in short-term and intermediate-term, fixed-income instruments to earn a market rate of interest without assuming undue risk to principal. The primary objectives of making such investments shall be, in their order of importance, preservation of capital, maintenance of liquidity, and yield.

These two sentences clearly lay out the organization's objectives in priority order.

(b) Long-Term Investment Policy

After the short-term cash needs of the organization are met, the growing nonprofit organization will reach a level of maturity and financial condition where capital is available to invest for the long term. A nonprofit organization will likely have the assets to invest for the long term in the form of endowment, which by its nature is invested for the long term to provide funds to support the intended programs in perpetuity. Typically, the larger a long-term endowment fund becomes, the more complex the investment decisions become.

A typical endowment investment policy is concerned with:

1. Preservation of principal
2. Provision of a reliable source of funds for current and future use
3. A rate of return which maintains or enhances the purchasing power of the endowment over time (growth of principal)
4. Prudent levels of risk

Often the terms "long term" and "endowment" are used interchangeably. For purposes of ease in this chapter, we will use "endowment," which has the most stringent objectives in terms of protecting principal and providing an income stream in perpetuity.

Surplus assets (e.g., accumulated funds being held to fund the future construction of a building), which are *not* endowment, can be invested for the long term. Generally, funds of long-term investment pools and endowment pools follow the same investing parameters.

As with short-term investment policies, the long-term endowment policy must state the return objective in very clear terms. Since endowments are intended to exist in perpetuity, a typical return objective seeks to hedge against inflation. The goal is to maintain or enhance the purchasing power of the endowment to maintain the activities it supports. This objective should be stated in terms of the "real rate of return," defined as total return less inflation. Real rate of return is more meaningful since inflation changes from period to period. A spending target stated in terms of fixed return, rather than real return, can be misleading.

Essential elements of both short-term and long-term investment policy include the following:

1. Who is responsible for the investing program?
2. Who does the investing?
3. How are assets to be allocated?
4. How is performance to be measured and reported?
5. What are the maximum risks to be assumed?

6. Who is responsible for the review and modification of the investment guidelines?

See Exhibit 11.1 for an additional checklist of essential elements.

11.2 INVESTMENT GUIDELINES

(a) Who Is Responsible for the Investing Program?

In a nonprofit organization, the Board of Directors is ultimately responsible for the investment program. In keeping with its fiduciary responsibility, the Board sets policy, selects managers, oversees investment activities, reviews performance, and monitors compliance to guidelines.

In creating and managing an investing program, it is necessary for the Board to place continuing responsibility and authority for the conduct of the program with a particular person or a specific committee. Actual investment management may be delegated to a particular person or external manager(s).

It is customary to establish an *Investment Committee* and to charge that committee with responsibility for managing all aspects of the investing program. The Committee is normally made up of senior financial and administrative executives of the organization and may include representation from the Board and other individuals with extensive financial or business expertise.

The Investment Committee normally drafts the policy and guidelines for Board approval. However, the board may also delegate authority and responsibility for implementation to the Investment Committee.

Exhibit 11.1. Example of Asset Allocation

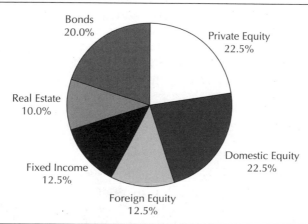

Bonds 20.0%

Private Equity 22.5%

Real Estate 10.0%

Domestic Equity 22.5%

Fixed Income 12.5%

Foreign Equity 12.5%

Responsibilities of the investment committee include:

- Set policy determining how investments are to be managed
- Make asset allocation decisions; determine a spending policy
- Select investment manager(s)
- Review the portfolio's performance
- Provide reports to the Board of Trustees on investment results and operations

The investment guidelines should clearly identify individuals responsible for managing the investing program and their respective levels of authority. The opening of accounts with brokers, dealers, and banks; the establishment of safekeeping accounts; arrangements for ongoing securities safekeeping; and authority to execute documents and agreements needed to implement the program may be delegated. The guidelines should also provide for the Investment Committee to select and employ independent investment advisors, if deemed advisable.

(b) Who Does the Investing?

The guidelines should clearly delegate operating authority and responsibility to the financial officers who will actually execute transactions, if an external investment manager is not contracted. Commonly, such authority for entering into agreements is granted to the financial manager, or Chief Financial Officer (CFO), the Treasurer or Controller, and the Assistant Treasurer or Assistant Controller. For example, it may provide for the CFO to act together with either the Treasurer or Assistant Treasurer, but neither of the latter two individuals may operate alone.

It is essential, however, for one qualified individual to be available at all times to execute investment transactions. That authority should be strictly and clearly delegated within the limitations defined in the investing guidelines. Typically, such authority is granted to the CFO, who, in turn, may redelegate the authority to subordinates within the treasury function. It is usually required, through copies of corporate resolutions, to notify banks and securities dealers in writing of the scope of authority granted to each authorized person.

(c) How Are Assets to Be Allocated?

Asset allocation (also known as strategic asset allocation) is one of the primary responsibilities of the Investment Committee. How you allocate your assets mainly determines your return. Asset allocation has two major components: selection of assets in which to invest, and assignment of those assets to investment managers with delegated responsibility for them.

Asset allocation is the division of your total assets (e.g., cash, stocks, bonds, real estate) among the best mix of investments in ideal proportions. Asset allocation includes estimating expected returns on investment, risks, and price movements among the various asset classes. Asset allocation is the most successful investment technique available to investment portfolio managers today.

Asset allocation can be active or passive. Active allocation allows a money manager to shift monies from one asset class to another within prescribed limits. For example, if it is determined that the optimum strategy to obtain the best investment performance results entails this mix of assets—35 percent bonds, 45 percent stocks, 10 percent cash, and 10 percent other—an active allocator could adjust (on a daily basis, if necessary) the mix of assets owned in these and the other categories to try to achieve maximum performance. This would be done as the outlook for the performance of the asset classes changed.

A passive allocator, on the other hand, would typically invest the portfolio in a mix of assets (cash, bonds, equities, other) and rebalance the portfolio once a year. Exhibit 11.1 shows an example of one organization's asset allocation target for a long-term endowment portfolio.

(i) Investment Instruments. The investing guidelines must describe the instruments in which the company will invest. The guidelines should further state that unless specifically permitted under the guidelines, all other investment instruments are prohibited. (A good reason to require an annual review of the guidelines is because new instruments may be introduced in which the organization is prohibited from investing. The guidelines should be modified to permit such new instruments, if and when warranted.)

Appendix 11.E presents a brief summary description of the most common investment instruments that should be provided to those who must approve the policy. This will be useful in creating or revising investment guidelines. The allocation of dollars between these various instruments is called *asset allocation* or *strategic asset allocation*. Short-term and long-term policies usually call for the inclusion of some element of fixed-income instruments in the investment portfolio. Short-term investment portfolios do not include equities. Investing guidelines typically permit several kinds of investment instruments.

(ii) Fixed-Income Instruments. Fixed-income instruments include the following:

- U.S. Treasury securities
- U.S. government agency obligations
- Municipal securities
- Bank obligations
- Certificates of deposit (CDs)
- Fixed-time deposits
- Banker's acceptances (BAs)
- Commercial paper
- Loan participations
- Corporate notes and bonds
- Repurchase agreements involving permitted securities
- Money-market mutual funds

(iii) Equity Instruments. The list of equity instruments includes:

- Common stocks
- Convertible securities
- Preferred stocks
- Index funds
- Warrants
- Rights (corporate action)
- Rule 144a stock
- American depository receipts (ADRs)

(iv) Alternative Investments. Alternatives to fixed-income and equity instruments are:

- Private investments
- Hedge funds
- Event-driven investment instruments
- Market-neutral instruments

(v) Socially Conscious Investing. In short-term and long-term investment programs, investable funds offer an organization certain choices and considerations, including using funds to achieve nonfinancial goals. One specific nonfinancial consideration is to lend support to a social cause through the types of investments that are made or not made.

Causes to Consider. When making investment decisions, many investors avoid providing indirect support to the alcohol or tobacco industries because of their link to many diseases. Also, most socially-conscious investment programs for years have refused to invest in companies that conduct business with various oppressive governments.

Many corporations believe that doing business in such countries provides support for the economic strength and authority of the nation's government.

Other social concerns often prompt institutional investors to use their dollars in promoting a better international society. They exclude companies that pollute the environment or disregard the ecology of areas where they do business.

Developing a socially conscious policy. When an organization has identified the social issues its investment program should or should not support, a method for efficiently implementing an investment policy is needed. If funds will be managed by an external adviser, the investing organization should provide specific instructions. Similarly, if funds will be internally managed, an organization's financial staff should be given a written investment policy reflecting management's views on social issues.

The following actions should be included when developing an investment policy with socially conscious objectives:

- Develop a comprehensive set of investment guidelines with a statement of social objectives.
- Provide direction on types of investments to be excluded from the investment program.
- Review investment and social goals of the investment policy and adopt guidelines to validate their accuracy and timeliness on an annual basis.

Taking these steps will help to maintain a socially-conscious program and to adjust the direction of investment activities as circumstances warrant.

For organizations which internally managing their investments, information will be needed on which investments to avoid. A list should be compiled of corporations that act in a manner contrary to the organization's socially conscious investment objectives. After a list is established, investment staff members should be instructed not to purchase obligations issued by particular organizations.

Before deciding on an investment program that includes socially-conscious objectives, an organization's managers should remember that a degree of yield or return on investment may be sacrificed by such a program. Internally maintaining an investment program also may require additional time to complete investments, including record-keeping responsibilities.

The benefits and costs of a socially-conscious investment policy must be weighed by an organization's managers—and its course must be set accordingly.

Once the asset allocation decision has been made, diversification strategies should be employed to further enhance the success potential for the long-term investment portfolio. Some strategies to be considered are diversification by:

- Investment type
- Manager style
- Type of issuer
- Industry sector
- Geography
- Time
- Foreign versus domestic
- Category

These and other techniques for diversifying the investment portfolio are discussed in Chapter 13.

(d) How Is Performance Measured and Reported?

(i) Measurement. Measurement of investment performance is essential to the investment process. Furthermore, performance measurement criteria are key to the investment policy and guidelines of the institution.

Some elements of investment performance to be measured are:

- Overall results
- Return on investment
- Comparison to historical performance
- Comparison to performance by style
- Effectiveness of communication
- Cost of investing services

(ii) Reporting. Operating an investing program can create a nightmare of reports and paperwork. Therefore, it is essential for the Investment Committee, if not the Board, to specify the type and frequency of reports needed. Otherwise, the financial manager who actually executes the transactions may feel compelled to furnish too much information to too many people.

A practical approach is to establish tiers of reports, as in a pyramid. Proceeding upward in an organization, the volume of reported data gets smaller. The financial manager who executes the transactions maintains the bottom tier and must be responsible for total detail concerning these transactions. The financial manager also must be responsible for ensuring that appropriate information is fed to the accounting department to record the transactions properly in the company's books and records.

For the financial manager's own use, it is generally necessary to have a daily or weekly report of securities held and the instruments listed in maturity date order, with the earliest maturity listed first. The manager may also need to have the same information sorted: (1) by issuer, to ensure that there is no undue concentration of funds invested in any one issuer; (2) by type of issuer, such as bank holding company, industrial company, finance company, domestic issuer, and foreign issuer by country; and (3) by safekeeping agent or other location where the securities are held in custody. All information is needed by the investment manager in order to conduct the day-to-day investing operations.

The level of detail that the financial manager needs is not necessary for his or her immediate superior, other senior management, and members of the Investment Committee. Thus, the Investment Committee and the Board should specify the level of detail and the frequency of reports they require. Typically, these reports contain a listing of all securities held, including maturity dates and yields, as well as a weighted-average yield of the entire portfolio. The reports are often produced on a monthly basis and may be accompanied by a schedule of transactions conducted since the last report.

By using microcomputers, database management software, and electronic spreadsheets, much of the report data can be handled easily and sorted by different fields to produce the desired results. Microcomputer-based programs are also available to handle short-term investment portfolio reporting. If an outside investment manager is used, the reports they provide should be adequate for your internal reporting needs.

(e) What Level of Risk Is to Be Assumed?

Investment guidelines should include a statement about the safeguards required by the investment program of your institution. Risk avoidance techniques should be explained.

(i) Limitations on Maturity. Because the short-term investment portfolio has primary objectives of preservation of capital and maintenance of liquidity, the investing guidelines should contain a statement that limits the maturity of the portfolio to avoid interest-rate risk. The limitations can relate to both the weighted average maturity of the entire portfolio and maximum limitations on maturity of any one instrument. For example, the guidelines might restrict the maturity of any one instrument to "not more than five

years from the date of purchase," and the weighted average maturity of the entire portfolio may be no more than three years.

Two dimensions of maturity limitation working together can prevent the occurrence of several interesting, but potentially detrimental, activities. For example, if the guidelines address only the weighted average maturity of the portfolio, the financial manager may use a "barbell" strategy. One half of the portfolio could be invested in very short-term instruments, such as 30- and 60-day maturities, and the other half in relatively long-term instruments maturing in eight to ten years. Mathematically, the weighted average maturity of the portfolio could be within the three-year limitation. Clearly, however, the actual deployment of funds does not meet the safety of principal and liquidity goals that management had set due to the inclusion of longer-term securities.

On the other hand, simply limiting the length of maturity of any one instrument may be inadequate. If the guidelines restrict the maturity of any one instrument to two years, for example, the financial manager may feel at liberty to invest virtually all of the portfolio in instruments maturing in about two years. This, too, could work in opposition to the stated objectives of preservation of capital and maintenance of liquidity.

(ii) Currency Denomination. The institution's investing guidelines should clearly stipulate that securities must be denominated in U.S. dollars or in currencies other than U.S. dollars, if permitted. This is an important distinction because investments in securities denominated in foreign currencies introduce a new element of foreign-exchange risk. Unless an organization understands and accepts that risk, the guidelines should stipulate that all investments be denominated in U.S. dollars.

It is also important for the amount of the investment, including principal and total interest due at maturity, to be hedged with a foreign exchange forward or futures contract. Even though the security is denominated in a foreign currency, this will help ensure that the ultimate proceeds will be converted into a known quantity of U.S. dollars at maturity. The institution's guidelines should specifically require that all investments be made in U.S. dollars or be fully hedged into U.S. dollars if made in foreign currencies.

Investments in foreign instruments can be done on a hedged or unhedged basis, both of which have risk/cost implications.

(f) Review and Modification of the Investment Guidelines: Who Is Responsible for What?

Even the best-designed investing guidelines must be periodically reviewed and modified to accommodate changes in the organization's own situation and in conditions prevailing in the securities markets. The guidelines themselves should contain provision for their review and modification.

The Investment Committee should have the responsibility of initiating additional reviews and modifications and perhaps delegating the responsibility to the CFO for making recommendations for modification as conditions warrant. Many organizations require an annual review of the guidelines. The Investment Committee also often delegates authority to the CFO who may, in turn, redelegate it to the Vice President of Finance to make the current investing program more restrictive than defined by the guidelines. For example, the guidelines may permit investment of funds in a particular area, such as obligations of foreign banks. It may come to the attention of the Vice President of Finance that the economy of a particular country has suddenly weakened. The Vice President may choose to restrict investment in obligations of banks domiciled in that country as a temporary measure (see Appendix 11.A).

11.3   CHECKLIST OF ELEMENTS FOR LONG-TERM ENDOWMENT INVESTMENT POLICY AND GUIDELINES

Does your long-term endowment policy include clear, concise statements? (See Exhibit 11.2)

(a) Investment Policy Summary

A written investing policy and set of investing guidelines are essential elements in both the successful short-term (liquidity) and long-term (endowment) investing program of a nonprofit institution. The document is a contract between the Board of Directors or Trustees and the financial manager. The policy statement describes the parameters within which the financial manager shall perform the tasks of investment management. The guidelines can be simple or complex, they can be restrictive or liberal, and they can cover a liquidity portfolio or dedicated proceeds of a bond issue or endowment fund within a single document or multiple documents.

A well-structured investment policy and guidelines document clearly places authority and responsibility for management of the investing program and enables modifications to the guidelines within reasonable bounds. The guidelines further set forth the requirements for reporting the investment activities and portfolio condition, and they clearly describe the types of securities that are acceptable for investment. They also address the operational issues

Exhibit 11.2. Checklist of Elements for Long-Term Endowment Investment Policy and Guidelines

Element	Location in Appendix 11.D Sample of Investment Policy for Long-Term Endowment Pool	✔ Done
• Purpose of the endowment	Opening paragraph	
• Responsibilities assignment	Opening paragraph	
• Investment objectives	I	
• Reference to endowment spending policy	I, Paragraph 2	
• Asset allocation	II	
• Minimums, targets, maximums		
• Fixed income vs equities		
• Guidelines for selection of fixed-income securities	III	
• Diversification	III.A	
• Quality	III.B	
• Duration	III.C	
• Guidelines for selection of equities	IV	
• Diversification of manager	IV.A	
• Performance	V	
• Permissible and nonpermissible assets	VI	
• Selection of investment managers	VII	
• Responsibilities of the investment manager	VIII	

of executing and verifying transactions and of holding the investment instruments in safekeeping for maintenance of appropriate security.

The financial manager should never invest in an instrument that he or she does not understand. It is essential for the financial manager to understand the risk/reward relationship and be comfortable with the level of risk assumed when making investment decisions for the nonprofit organization.

SAMPLE OF SHORT-TERM INVESTMENT POLICY
AND GUIDELINES

This example may be best suited for a large organization and may be compared and used in the development of organizational policies.

Investment Committee

Within the spectrum of activities of this organization, it is necessary to provide a framework for the regular and continuous management of investment funds. Because there is currently no formal Investment Committee, the Directors will assume this responsibility.

Investment Policy

The policy shall be to invest excess cash in short-term and intermediate-term fixed-income instruments, earning a market rate of interest without assuming undue risk to principal. The primary objectives of such investments in order of importance shall be preservation of capital, maintenance of liquidity, and yield.

Investment Responsibility

Investments are the responsibility of the Vice President of Finance. This responsibility includes the authority to select an investment adviser, open three accounts with brokers, establish safekeeping accounts or other arrangements for the custody of securities, and execute such documents as necessary.

Those authorized to execute transactions include: (1) Vice President of Finance, (2) Director of Accounting, and (3) cash manager. The Vice President of Finance shall ensure that one qualified individual is always available to execute the organization's investments.

Reporting

The Treasurer shall be responsible for reporting the status of investments to the Directors on a quarterly basis. Those reports should include a complete listing of securities held, verified (audited) by parties either inside or outside this organization who have no connection with the investment activities.

Investments

A. Obligations of the U.S. Government or Its Agencies

Specifically, these refer to the U.S. Treasury, Federal Home Loan Bank, Federal Home Loan Mortgage Corporation, Federal National Mortgage Association, Federal Farm Credit Bank, Student Loan Marketing Association, and Government National Mortgage Association. Note: When-issued items must be paid for *before* they may be sold.

B. Banks—Domestic

The organization may invest in negotiable CDs (including Eurodollar denominated deposits), Eurodollar time deposits (with branches domiciled in Cayman, Nassau, or London), and BAs of the 50 largest U.S. banks ranked by deposit size. Thrift institutions whose parent has long-term debt rated A by Moody's or Standard & Poor's are acceptable. Exceptions may be local banks or thrift institutions that have lent the corporation money or that would be appropriate to use for some other reason. (These banks and institutions should be listed, along with the maximum dollar amount of exposure allowable for each.)

C. Banks—Foreign

The organization may invest in negotiable CDs (including Eurodollar denominated deposits), Eurodollar time deposits (with branches domiciled in Cayman, Nassau, or London), and BAs of the 50 largest foreign banks ranked by deposit size. However, the issuing institution's parent must have a Moody's or Standard & Poor's rating of at least A.

Limitations

(1) The organization's aggregate investments with foreign entities shall not exceed 50 percent of total investments, and

(2) No more than 10 percent of total investments shall be exposed to any one foreign country's obligations, or $X million per country, whichever is greater.

D. Commercial Paper

All commercial paper must be prime quality by both Standard & Poor's and Moody's standards (i.e., A- by Standard & Poor's and P1 by Moody's).

E. Corporate Notes and Bonds

Instruments of this type are acceptable if rated at least A by both Moody's and Standard & Poor's credit rating services.

F. Municipal

Municipal or tax-exempt instruments (suitable only if your organization pays federal income tax). Only tax-exempt notes with a Moody's Investment Grade One rating, or bonds that are rated by both Moody's Investor Service, Inc., and Standard & Poor's as A, may be purchased. Not more than 15 percent of the total issue size should be purchased, and issues of at least $20 million in total size must be selected.

G. Repurchase Agreements

Repurchase agreements (repos) are acceptable, using any of the securities listed above, as long as such instruments are negotiable/marketable and do not exceed other limitations as to exposure per issuer. The firm with whom the repo is executed must be a credit-acceptable bank or a primary dealer (reporting to the Federal Reserve). Collateral must equal 102 percent of the dollars invested, and the collateral must be delivered to the organization's safekeeping bank and priced to market weekly (to ensure correct collateral value coverage) if the repo has longer than a seven-day maturity.

H. Money Market Funds

Acceptable funds are those whose asset size place them among the 30 largest cording to the Morning Star Report and that are in the TUP rating or Standard & Poor's Corporation.

I. Safekeeping Accounts

Securities purchased should be delivered against or held in a custodian safekeeping account at the organization's safekeeping bank. An exception shall be: (1) repos made with approved (see above) banks or dealers for one week or less, and (2) Eurodollar time deposits, for which no instruments are created. This safekeeping account will be audited quarterly by an entity that is not related to the investment function of this organization and the results of that audit shall be provided to the Vice President of Finance.

J. Denomination

All investments shall be in U. S. dollars.

K. Diversification of Investments

In no case shall more than 15 percent of the total portfolio be invested in obligations of any particular issuer except the U.S. Treasury.

Maturity Limitations

Overall, maximum weighted average maturity shall be three years. However, on "put" instruments, which may be redeemed (or put) at par, the put date shall be the maturity date.

Review and/or Modification

The Vice President of Finance shall be responsible for reviewing and modifying investment guidelines as conditions warrant, subject to approval by the Directors at least on an annual basis. However, the Vice President of Finance may at any time further restrict the items approved for purchase when appropriate.

Source: Seidner & Company, Pasadena, California.

ABC FOUNDATION UNENDOWED
SHORT-TERM INVESTMENT POOL POLICY

This example might be more easily adaptable to small- or medium-sized organizations.

General Policy

The basic objective of the Unendowed Investment Pool is to maximize returns consistent with safety of principal, liquidity, and cash flow requirements. The maximum maturity shall be five years except for mortgage notes related to ABC Foundation property transactions, the XYZ Department Loan Program, and mortgage-backed securities with an average life not to exceed five years. The portfolio shall be invested at no less than 20 percent for under one year. The Vice President-Finance is responsible for arranging the actual investments pursuant to this policy. All investment activity shall be under the general jurisdiction of the Investment Committee.

Authorized Investments

The following categories of investments shall be authorized as indicated:

A. Commercial Paper—Rated A-1 (Standard & Poor's) and P-1 (Moody's)

B. Bankers Acceptances—Any bank rated A or better by Standard & Poor's or Moody's

C. Eurodollars—An amount not to exceed 10 percent in banks or subsidiaries of banks rated B/C or better by Thompson Bankwatch Service. (No Eurodollars shall be purchased with a term greater than one year.)

D. Certificates of Deposits—Not to exceed 10 percent in any bank whose parent rated A or better by Standard & Poor's or Moody's. (For banks not rated, investments shall be limited to amounts within FDIC's insurance limit.)

E. U.S. Treasury Bills, Notes, and Bonds—No limitation on amount invested

F. U.S. Government Agencies—No limitation on amount invested

G. Repurchase Agreements—There shall be no limitation on the amount invested, provided the vehicle is collateralized by U.S. government securities

H. Corporate Bonds and Medium Term Notes—Rated investment grade BBB/Baa by Standard & Poor's Corporation or Moody's Investor Services

I. Master Participation Notes—Notes of issuer shall be rated A1/P1 for its commercial paper or BBB/Baa or better for its long-term debt

J. Mortgage-backed Pass Through Securities—Rated AAA and an average life not to exceed five years

K. Floating Rate Securities—Debt of issuers with maturities not to exceed five years, provided interest rates reset at least every 90 days to reflect changing market conditions

L. Bargain Sale Investments—Not to exceed $500,000 per individual transaction, as authorized by the Planned Gifts Committee unless approved by the Board of Directors

M. Mortgage Notes—Related to ABC Foundation property transactions and second trust-deed program for the Athletic Department and Coaches Loans

N. Mutual Funds—Domestic or global funds invested in a portfolio of high quality debt securities (Funds must have a reasonable performance record and net asset value in excess of $100 million.)

O. Equity Securities—Limited to investment grade, high yielding equities (When such equities are in a managed portfolio, a proven hedging strategy must be in place to significantly reduce exposure to principal erosion caused by changing market conditions.)

P. Other Investments—Between meetings of the Investment Committee, if deemed advisable, other investments not specifically authorized by this policy may be made if approved by both the Vice President—Finance and Investment Committee Chairman (Any such action shall be taken to the Investment Committee at its next meeting for approval.)

Investment Procedures:

Selection of the appropriate investment from among the approved alternatives shall be determined by relative availability and maturities required. All other things being equal, the investment providing the highest return will be preferred.

Diversification:

Securities purchased shall be diversified in terms of industry concentration as well as type of investment instrument.

Quality Ratings:

Quality rating is defined in terms of the underlying credit of an issuer in a particular transaction. For maturities over one year, the minimum acceptable rating is BBB or Baa based on Standard & Poor's and Moody's ratings. For short-term securities, the equivalent commercial paper rating of A-1/P-1 is the minimum acceptable. If a security has a Letter of Credit (LOC)/guarantee supporting it, then the issuer is the entity providing the LOC/guarantee.

The quality rating guidelines to be used shall be the ratings as of the date of purchase of the security. If a rating change occurs which disqualifies a security that is already held in the Pool, the security must be reviewed for determination of possible sale.

Ratings on securities purchased shall be, as indicated in this policy or in its absence, an equivalent rating as appropriate in keeping with ABC Foundation guidelines on quality.

Marketability:

Securities purchased should be readily marketable and should meet the quality guidelines of this policy.

Safekeeping:

Securities purchased shall be held in the ABC Foundation safekeeping account at its principal banks except for Repurchase Agreements and Branch Certificates of Deposit, which shall be held by the branch bank.

APPENDIX 11C

SHORT-TERM INVESTMENT POLICY FOR HIJ FOUNDATION

This example of a short-term investment policy is concise and includes all the necessary components that may be used for any size organization. The undersigned hereby certify that the following investment policy was duly adopted and approved by the act of a majority of the Directors of the Foundation present at a meeting of the Board of Directors held on the 14th day of March, 1995, at which a quorum was present.

RESOLVED, that the purpose of this policy is to define the criteria to be followed by the HIJ Foundation for investment of surplus cash. All investments are to be made in conformance with the following criteria listed in the order of importance.

1. Safety of principal
2. Liquidity
3. Yield

Surplus funds, in excess of short-term future needs, may be invested in the following:

(a) Short-term CDs, U.S. or Eurodollar time deposits, or BAs having maturities not exceeding six months with any commercial bank having a combined capital and surplus of not less than $500 million, not to exceed 10 percent in any bank rated A by Standard & Poor's Corporation and Moody's Investor Service, Inc.

(b) Commercial paper of U.S. industrial issuers maturing no more than 270 days from the date of acquisition thereof and, at the time of acquisition, having a rating of A-1 (or better) by Standard & Poor's Corporation or P-1 by Moody's Investor Service, Inc.

(c) Repurchase agreements entered into with investment banks having shareholders' equity of at least $500 million; such repurchase agreements to be collateralized at least 100 percent by negotiable securities of a type described in (d) below.

(d) U.S. Treasury bills, notes, and bonds and other marketable direct obligations insured or unconditionally guaranteed by the United States of America or issued by any sponsored agency thereof and having a remaining maturity of five years or less.

(e) U.S. corporate bonds and medium term notes having a remaining maturity of five years or less and rated A or better by Standard & Poor's Corporation and Moody's Investor Services, Inc., with diversification in terms of industry concentration.

(f) Any mutual fund with a net asset value in excess of $100 million that invests solely in U.S. treasury bills, notes, and bonds (or agencies backed by the U.S. government) and such securities have a remaining life of 13 months or less and the fund maintains a net asset value of $1.00 per share.

The adoption and approval of the foregoing resolution constitutes the act of the Board of Directors of the HIJ Foundation pursuant to Article II, Section 5, of the Restated Bylaws of the HIC Foundation.

APPENDIX 11D

SAMPLE OF INVESTMENT POLICY STATEMENT
FOR THE ABC FOUNDATION'S
LONG-TERM ENDOWMENT POOL

The purpose of the ABC Foundation's endowment is to support the educational mission of the ABC University by providing a reliable source of funds for current and future use. Investment of the endowment is the responsibility of the Investment Committee (Committee). The Committee establishes investment objectives, defines policies, sets asset allocation, selects managers, and monitors the implementation and performance of the Foundation's investment program. The Committee is supported by the office of the Vice President—Finance, which analyzes investment policies and management strategies, makes recommendations to the Investment Committee, and supervises day-to-day operations and investment activities.

I. Statement of Investment Objectives

The endowment will seek to maximize long-term total returns consistent with prudent levels of risk. Investment returns are expected to preserve or enhance the real value of the endowment to provide adequate funds to sufficiently support designated University activities. The endowment's portfolio is expected to generate a total annualized rate of return, net of fees, 5 percent greater than the rate of inflation over a rolling 5-year period.

The Foundation's spending policy governs the rate at which funds are released to fund-holders for their current spending. The Foundation's spending policy will be based on a target rate set as a percentage of market value. This rate will be reviewed annually by the Investment Committee. The spending target rate is 5 percent for Fiscal Year 1995–1996.

II. Asset Allocation

To ensure real returns sufficient to meet the investment objectives, the endowment portfolio will be invested with the following target allocations in either domestic or global securities:

	Minimum (%)	Target (%)	Maximum (%)
Fixed-income	30	35	40
Equities	60	65	70

The Investment Committee may appoint equity and fixed-income managers, or select pooled investments, when appropriate. It is the overall objective to be 100 percent invested in equities and fixed income. If at any time the equity manager determines it is prudent to be invested at less than 80 percent, the Committee shall be notified. Equity managers may invest cash positions in marketable, fixed-income securities with maturities not to exceed one year. Quality rating should be prime or investment grade, as rated by Standard & Poor's and Moody's for commercial paper, and for certificates of deposit, a B/C rating by Thompson Bank Watch Services. The managers are expected to reasonably diversify holdings consistent with prudent levels of risk.

At the discretion of the Committee, the endowment portfolio will be rebalanced annually to target allocations as opportunities permit.

III. Guidelines for the Selection of Fixed-Income Securities

A. Diversification

Except for the U.S. government, its agencies or instrumentalities, no more than 5 percent of the fixed-income portfolio at cost, or 8 percent at market value, shall be invested in any one single guarantor, issuer, or pool of assets. In addition, managers are expected to exercise prudence in diversifying by sector or industry.

B. Quality

All bonds must be rated investment grade (BBB/Baa or better) by at least one of the following rating services: Standard & Poor's or Moody's, except that bonds not receiving a rating may be purchased under the following circumstances:

- The issue is guaranteed by the U.S. government, its agencies or instrumentalities.
- Other comparable debt of the issuer is rated investment grade by Standard & Poor's or Moody's.

The average quality rating of the total fixed-income portfolio must be AA or better. Securities downgraded in credit-quality rating subsequent to purchase, resulting in the violation of the policy guidelines, may be held at the manager's discretion. This is subject to immediate notification to the Investment Committee of such a change in rating.

C. Duration

At the time of purchase, the average duration of the bond pool should be no longer than the average duration of the current Merrill Lynch 3–5 Year Treasury Index plus one year.

IV. Guidelines for Selection of Equities

A. Diversification for Each Manager

No more than 5 percent at cost, and 10 percent at market value, shall be invested in any one company. In addition, managers are expected to exercise prudence in diversifying by sector or industry.

V. Performance

Performance of the endowment and its component asset classes will be measured against benchmark returns of comparable portfolios as follows:

Total Endowment	SEI Balanced Median Plan Median Plan, Merrill Lynch Balanced Universe
Domestic Equities	S&P 500 Index; Russell 2000 Index Top third of the Merrill Lynch Equity Specialty Universe
Global Equities	MSCI World Index
Fixed-Income	Merrill Lynch 3–5 Year Treasury Index

At least annually, the Investment Committee will conduct performance evaluations at the total endowment, asset class, and individual manager levels. At the total endowment level, the Committee will analyze results relative to the objectives, the real rate of return and composite indices. Further, investment results will be reviewed relative to the effects of policy decisions and the impact of deviations from policy allocations.

On the asset class and individual manager levels, results will be evaluated relative to benchmarks assigned to investment managers or pooled investments selected. These benchmarks are a vital element in the evaluation of individual and aggregate manager performance within each asset class.

The Committee may utilize the services of performance measurement consultants to evaluate investment results, examine performance attribution relative to target asset classes, and other functions as it deems necessary.

VI. Permissible and Nonpermissible Assets

All assets selected for the endowment must have a readily ascertainable market value and must be readily marketable. The following types of assets are permitted:

Equities	Fixed-Income
Common stocks	U.S. Treasury and agency obligations
Convertible securities	Mortgage-backed securities of U.S. government
Preferred stocks	Money-market funds
Index funds	Short-term investment fund accounts
Warrants	Certificates of deposit
Rights (corporate action)	Bankers acceptances
Rule 144a stock	Commercial paper
American depository	Repurchase agreements
Receipts (ADRs)	Asset-backed securities/ Collateralized bond obligations
Corporate securities	
Collateralized mortgage obligations	
ABC Shared Appreciation Mortgage Program	
First trust deeds of gift properties	
Index funds	

Within the mortgage-backed securities and collateralized mortgage obligations sector, investments in CMO tranches with reasonably predictable average lives are permitted, provided at time of purchase the security does not exceed the average duration of the current Merrill Lynch 3–5 Treasury Index plus one year. Interest-only and principal-only (PO) securities—or other derivatives based on them—are prohibited, as are securities with very limited liquidity.

Emerging market investments are permitted within the global equity manager's portfolio, subject to a maximum of 10 percent. Likewise, currency hedging as a defensive strategy is permitted in the global portfolio.

The following types of assets or transactions are expressly prohibited without prior written approval from the Investment Committee:

Equities	**Fixed-Income**
Commodities	Unregistered securities, except rule futures 144-A securities
Margin purchases	Tax-exempt securities
Short selling	Any asset not specifically permitted
Put and call options	
Direct oil and gas participations	
Direct investments in real estate	

VII. Selection of Investment Managers

The Investment Committee may choose to select and appoint managers for a specific investment style or strategy, provided that the overall objectives of the endowment are satisfied.

VIII. Responsibilities of the Investment Manager

A. Adherence to Statement of Investment Objectives and Policy Guidelines

1. The manager is expected to observe the specific limitations, guidelines, and philosophies stated herein or as expressed in any written amendments or instructions.

2. The manager's acceptance of the responsibility of managing these funds will constitute a ratification of this statement, affirming his or her be-

lief that it is realistically capable of achieving the endowment's investment objectives within the guidelines and limitations stated herein.

B. Discretionary Authority

The Manager will be responsible for making all investment decisions for all assets placed under its management and will be held accountable for achieving the investment objectives stated herein. Such "discretion" includes decisions to buy, hold, and sell securities (including cash and equivalents) in amounts and proportions that are reflective of the manager's current investment strategy and that are compatible with the endowment's investment guidelines.

APPENDIX 11E

DEFINITIONS OF FIXED-INCOME INSTRUMENTS

U.S. TREASURY SECURITIES

The U.S. Treasury finances federal deficits by issuing debt instruments called Treasury bills, notes, and bonds. The credit standing of each is the same, and the sole difference is the length of maturity. Treasury bills are issued for periods of one year or less, notes are issued to mature from more than one year but less than 10 years, and bonds are issued to mature from more than 10 years up to 30 years. Because of the credit quality of U.S. Treasury securities, investors from all over the world with all forms of investment needs are attracted to these instruments. As a result, the market for these securities enjoys a depth that provides for substantial liquidity.

U.S. GOVERNMENT AGENCY OBLIGATIONS

Various agencies of the U.S. government issue debt securities to finance various types of public operations. The agencies that issue the most popular securities, and probably issue the largest volume of government agency securities, are the Government National Mortgage Association (GNMA, commonly referred to as Ginnie Mae), Federal National Mortgage Association (FNMA, commonly known as Fannie Mae), Federal Home Loan Mortgage Corporation (FHLMC, commonly known as Freddie Mac), Federal Farm Credit Banks (FFCB), and Student Loan Marketing Association (called Sallie Mae).

With the exception of the Farm Credit Banks and Sallie Mae, debt instruments issued by the agencies are often in the form of certificates of participation in the ownership of pools of mortgage loans. While the certificates of participation themselves are not obligations of the U.S. government, the underlying mortgages owned by the pools usually are guaranteed by an agency of the government, such as the Federal Housing Administration (FHA) or the Veterans Administration (VA) in the case of Ginnie Mae.

Both FNMA and FFCB are privately owned organizations that perform specific functions in the public interest. They have strong ties to the federal government; however, there is only implied federal responsibility for the financial health of the institutions and protection of investors in the debt instruments issued by these institutions.

When an investor is considering a certificate of participation or a debt obligation of a federal agency, the investor should make a diligent investigation into the adequacy of the instrument for its purposes. In some cases, the cash flow emanating from certificates of participation is very good; the certificates provide current income and repayment of principal to the investor. At the same time, however, accounting considerations are complicated because of the combination of both principal and interest in the cash stream. Moreover, before making the investment, the investor in certificates of participation should understand the nature and long maturity of the mortgages or other debt contained in the investment pool.

For example, a GNMA pool of FHA mortgages may have an average maturity of 17 years, but in a period of declining interest rates, many of these loans in the pool may be prepaid by their respective homeowners/obligors as they refinance their home mortgages at lower interest rates. As a result, the investor in the GNMA pool will realize a more rapid return of capital and a smaller total income figure than had been anticipated. This situation may not fit into the investor's plans for providing cash flow over a budgeted period, or the heavier than anticipated stream of cash flow may cause the investor problems in reinvesting the excess funds.

MUNICIPAL SECURITIES

These are instruments issued by various nonfederal government political entities, such as states, counties, water district, etc. They provide, in most cases, tax-exempt income to investors who pay taxes. However, increasingly, they are appropriate for investors who have no tax liability. Municipal securities come in a variety of types and maturities, often providing a yield advantage over government securities or corporate instruments of similar credit ratings.

BANK OBLIGATIONS

Bank obligations are evidenced either in the form of deposits in the bank or instruments that have been guaranteed or endorsed by a bank and offered in the secondary (resale) markets, such as banker's acceptances.

There are two basic forms of interest-bearing bank deposits: (1) negotiable time certificates of deposit, known as certificates of deposit (CDs) and (2) fixed-time deposits.

Certificates of Deposit

CDs maturing in a year or less are payable to the "bearer" and therefore, if properly held by a New York custodian, are liquid in the hands of the holder, if the CD is issued for at least $1 million. Many banks and investment dealers establish markets in CDs of the leading banks of the world and offer to buy and sell CDs for their own account. This is known as the secondary market. An investor can purchase a CD from one of these banks or dealers in the secondary market. Alternatively, an investor may initiate the bank deposit directly, in which case the CD is known as a primary certificate of deposit. If the investor chooses to sell the primary CD prior to maturity to recoup its cash funds early, it may sell it in the secondary market to another bank or dealer. A bank is not permitted to repurchase its own CDs; this would be tantamount to early redemption of the deposit and subject to penalties. It is critical to note that a secondary market exists only for CDs issued by better-known banks and savings and loan institutions. Also, the instrument itself must be in correct negotiable form and available for prompt delivery in New York. A CD issued by a bank located offshore—usually London, Cayman Islands, Nassau—is called a Eurodollar CD.

Fixed-Time Deposits

Fixed-time deposits are similar to negotiable CDs except that a bearer certificate is not issued. Fixed-time deposits often are issued domestically for amounts a bank wishes to accept. However, amounts of $1 million and more are usually required in London branches of major banks located in London, Nassau, the Bahamas, and the Cayman Islands. These are called Eurodollar time deposits since they are placed in offshore branches. Because these deposits are not represented by negotiable certificates, they are not liquid. Therefore, they often carry a higher yield to the investor than CDs.

Banker's Acceptances

BA is a draft drawn by a bank customer against the bank; the instrument is then "accepted" by the bank for the purpose of extending financing to the customer. The bank's acceptance of the draft means that the bank plans to sell the instrument in the secondary market, and it also indicates the bank's unconditional willingness to pay the instrument at maturity. A BA often originates as the result of a merchandise transaction (often in international trade) when an importer requires financing.

As an investment instrument, a BA of a particular bank carries higher credit quality than the same bank's CD, because it is not only a direct obligation of the bank, like a CD, but is also an obligation of an importer and usually collateralized by the merchandise itself. However, BAs are not deposits and do not carry the $100,000 insurance coverage of the Federal Deposit Insurance Corporation. Often BAs can be purchased at a few basis points' higher yield than a CD from the same issuing bank, because many investors are not as familiar with BAs as they are with CDs.

ASSET-BACKED SECURITIES

These are securities where some type of collateral, or pool of assets, serves as the basis for the credit worthiness of the security. Earlier in this section were reference government National Mortgage Association Securities whose underlying collateral was a "pool" of mortgages. Also, many other nongovernment securities are issued with collateral such as auto loans or credit-card loan receivables.

COMMERCIAL PAPER

Commercial paper is an unsecured promissory note issued by a corporation. The issuer may be an industrial corporation, the holding company parent of a bank, or a finance company that is often a captive finance company owned by an industrial corporation. Commercial paper is issued to mature for periods ranging from one to 270 days. Corporate obligations issued for longer than 270 days must be registered with the Securities and Exchange Commission; therefore, companies needing short-term financing typically restrict the maturities of this debt to 270 days or less. Commercial paper is available to the investor through many major banks, that issue the bank's holding company commercial paper or act as an agent for other issuers, and through investment bankers and dealers who may underwrite the commercial paper for their clients.

LOAN PARTICIPATIONS

A loan participation as an investment medium is attractive to an investor, because it presents an opportunity to invest in a corporate obligation that is similar to commercial paper but normally carries a somewhat higher yield. Banks have invested in loan participations of other banks for decades as a means of diversifying loan portfolios. However, the use of loan participations as an investment medium for corporations was a new development during the late 1980s.

The loan participation investment medium begins when a bank makes a loan to a corporation using standardized loan documentation. After the loan has been made, the bank seeks investors to buy "participations" in the loan. The investor in the loan participation has the obligation to investigate the credit of the obligor, since the bank selling the participation offers no guarantee or endorsement, implied or otherwise. Many companies that are obligors of these loans are rated by the commercial paper rating agencies, such as Standard & Poor's and Moody's Investors Service. In some cases, the entire short-term debt of the issuer is rated, while in other cases only the commercial paper of the company is rated. However, if the short-term debt or commercial paper is unrated and an investor must rely on his or her own credit analysis, the investor must use extreme caution due to the difficulty in ascertaining the credit soundness of the investment. Loan participations may have maturities ranging from one day to several months. Occasionally, the investor may be able to obtain a loan participation to suit its precise maturity requirements, particularly when large amounts (in excess of $1 million) are available for investment.

The investor should be aware that a loan participation is not a negotiable instrument and, therefore, is not a liquid investment. It does not constitute good collateral for the investor who needs to pledge part or all of his or her investment portfolio to secure certain obligations. A loan participation, however, may be a good investment from the standpoint of yield, subject to appropriate credit investigation by the investor.

CORPORATE NOTES AND BONDS

Corporate debt instruments with maturities longer than 270 days are considered notes if they mature within 10 years from their original issue date. The instruments are considered bonds if they mature more then 10 years from the original issue date. Notes with maturities up to approximately three to five years can play an important role in portfolios where the objective is to increase yield over what is available from strictly short-term portfolios, and where nearly perfect liquidity is not necessarily required. Because they have a longer maturity than money market instruments, corporate notes are subject to greater market risk due to changes in interest rates. However, because the maturities may be only three to five years, the instruments are not subject to swings in market values as much as bonds.

Corporate bonds are often included in investment portfolios in which the time horizon is much longer than liquidity portfolios. Bonds are seldom included in liquidity portfolios unless they will mature in one year or less.

REPURCHASE AGREEMENTS

A repurchase agreement is an investment transaction between an investor and a bank or securities dealer, in which the bank or dealer agrees to sell a particular instrument to the investor and simultaneously agrees to repurchase that instrument at a certain date in the future. The repurchase price is designed to give the investor a yield equivalent to a rate of interest that both parties negotiate at the time the transaction is initiated.

On its face, a repurchase agreement transaction, commonly referred to as a "repo," appears to place full and complete ownership of the underlying securities in the hands of the investor. However, a number of incidents of default by dealers occurred during the 1980s, resulting in court rulings that brought the fundamental nature of repos into question. Those rulings implied very strongly that a repo was not, in fact, a purchase with a simultaneous agreement to repurchase the underlying securities, but rather a loan made by the investor to the dealer secured by the pledge of the underlying instruments as collateral to the loan. This viewpoint was bolstered by the fact that in the repo business, the underlying instruments always have been called "collateral." Investors who were previously authorized to invest instruments subject to repurchase were now faced with making secured loans to banks and brokers.

Because repos traditionally have been a fundamental investment medium used by institutions to invest temporarily surplus funds overnight and for periods of approximately one week, the court rulings seriously undermined the viability of the repo for this important purpose. It was not until Congress adopted the Government Securities Act of 1986 (as supplemented by regulations issued by the Treasury Department early in 1988) that the investment community regained its confidence in the repo as an investment medium. That act, however, addressed only part of the issue. It laid out very clearly the rights, duties, and obligations of the dealer in a repurchase agreement as long as the dealer is not a bank. However, it left hanging in the wind the relationship of the dealer if the dealer is a bank. This void continues to exist.

In order to fill the void, the investor should enter into an underlying written agreement with the dealer or bank as the counterparty to the transaction. The agreement should spell out very clearly the rights, duties, and obligations of each of the parties, particularly in the event of the default of one of them. The agreement should also state clearly that the transaction is intended to be a purchase/repurchase transaction and explicitly is not a loan by the investor to the dealer or bank. The agreement should further provide that in the event of the default of the dealer, the investor has the right to take possession of the collateral, if the investor does not already have such possession, and to dispose of that collateral in order to recover its investment.

The Public Securities Association, an organization of securities dealers, prepared a model agreement in 1986 that many banks and securities dealers have adopted and which they require their repo customers to execute. This model agreement appears to have been drafted in an even-handed manner and supports the interests of both counterparties in the repurchase transaction. Therefore, if the bank or securities dealer does not offer such an agreement, the investor should ask for the agreement from the bank or dealer.

Because of past history involving the collapse of some investment houses that were heavily involved in repos, an investor should be forewarned that the real risk in entering into a repo is the risk of failure of the counterparty (i.e., either a dealer or a bank) to perform under the agreement. Before the spate of failures during the 1980s, the investor typically looked only to the collateral for safety of principal. The investor, however, should recognize that the success of the transaction actually depends on the viability and willingness of the dealer or bank to repurchase the securities at maturity of the transaction. Accordingly, the investor must be diligent to investigate the credit standing of the counterparty to the transaction.

As an additional protection, the investor should specify to the dealer or bank those securities that are acceptable as underlying collateral. Investing guidelines should specify that such underlying collateral may consist of only investment instruments permitted by the guidelines. Moreover, the guidelines should require that in a repo transaction, the value of the underlying collateral should exceed the .3 amount of the investment transaction by some small increment, usually stated in terms of 102 percent of the amount of the transaction. This should be monitored by the investor on a regular basis to keep current on the market value of securities used as collateral. One final point to be considered is whether the collateral is set aside for the investor and does actually exist. This point is fully covered in the repurchase agreement section in Chapter 13 (13.13).

MONEY-MARKET MUTUAL FUNDS

A money-market mutual fund is itself a portfolio of money market instruments. It provides a reasonable vehicle for investing modest sums where the amount may be too small to manage an effective investing program. For example, in managing amounts of less than $3 million, an investor is hard-pressed to meet the objectives of preservation of capital, maintenance of liquidity, and yield because money-market instruments normally trade in $1 million pieces. The portfolio loses some diversification because of the large size required. If diversification is necessary, it forces the size of any one investment to be less than $1 million, and the company will sacrifice liquidity.

One solution to this dilemma is to invest in a money-market mutual fund where the amounts invested may range from a minimum of perhaps $2,000 (in a retail oriented money-market fund) to many millions of dollars. Various kinds of money-market mutual funds exist. The more popular funds cater to consumers and businesses with modest amounts available, and others serve institutional investors with large amounts of investable funds. Generally, both categories of funds operate similarly, with the institutional funds requiring larger minimum investments and often taking smaller management fees.

The mutual fund affords the investor the opportunity to meet its investment objectives of safety of principal, maintenance of liquidity, and yield provided that the investor carefully selects the particular fund. Fund selection should be based on a thorough review of the prospectus, with particular attention paid to the investment objectives of the fund, the experience and investment record of the fund's management, and the quality and liquidity of the investment instruments that the fund maintains in its portfolio.

The investor should inquire about redemption privileges and requirements of the fund and the fund's "pain threshold" for withdrawals. Most money-market mutual funds allow withdrawal virtually on demand either by check (which is actually a draft drawn against the fund) or by electronic funds transfer to the investor's bank account. Electronic funds transfer may be either a wire transfer for value the same day as the withdrawal, or it may be an automated clearinghouse transfer with settlement the following day. The pain threshold refers to the size of withdrawal that the fund can tolerate without incurring its own liquidity problems. For some of the very large money-market mutual funds, an immediate withdrawal of $50 million can be tolerated with little pain because of the fund's size. On the other hand, a small fund of less than $500 million may have a problem meeting a withdrawal request for $5 million. The size factor should be seriously considered when selecting a money-market mutual fund.

APPENDIX 11F

DEFINITIONS OF EQUITY INSTRUMENTS

American Depository Receipts American brokers function as intermediaries in the purchase and sale of foreign issues by acting as a conduit for shares which are listed on international exchanges. A broker retains shares in a pool, which are represented by salable depository receipts (ADRs).

Common stocks Securities that represent an ownership interest in a corporation.

Convertible Securities A bond, debenture, or preferred share of stock that may be exchanged by the owner for common stock or another security of the issuing firm. These issues are particularly useful in new ventures when the founders are seeking capital and include several types of both convertible equity and convertible bond issues.

Index Funds A mutual fund whose portfolio matches that of a broad-based index such as Standard & Poor's Index and whose performance, therefore, mirrors the market as a whole.

Preferred Stock A class of stock with a claim on the company's earnings before payment may be made on the common stock which is usually entitled to priority over common stock if the company liquidates it is usually entitled to dividends at a specific rate when declared by the Board of Directors and before payment of a dividend on the common stock and depending on the terms of the issue.

Rights (Corporate Action) Rights offerings entitle owners of common stock to purchase shares of new stock issuance at a price somewhat below the current market price; usually the right has a duration of 90 days following the issuance of new common stock.

Rule 144a Stock A pool of common shares that has been authorized by a corporation's Board of Directors is usually not entirely disbursed or marketed for sale, but is held in an internal pool known as treasury stock. A certain number of shares from this pool is often set aside for internal distribution, and hence is never registered with the Securities and Exchange Commission. Prior to registration, these Rule 144 shares are not used in calculations of a company's worth such as P/E ratios or book value.

Warrants A certificate giving the holder the right to purchase a fixed number of common stock securities at a stipulated price within a specified time limit or perpetually. Warrants are created by a corporation to facilitate the sale of debot or preferred stock.

APPENDIX 11G

GLOSSARY

American Depository Receipts (ADRs) American brokers function as intermediaries in the purchase and sale of foreign issues by acting as a conduit for shares which are listed on international exchanges. A broker retains shares in a pool, which are represented by salable depository receipts (ADRs).

Asset-Backed Securities (ABSs) Mostly AAA-rated securities secured by consumer credit card receivables. These issues are credit-enhanced by overcollateralization, letters of credit, and subordination of portions of cash flow to cushion against any losses is the underlying receivables.

Collateralized Mortgage Obligations (CMOs) A multiclass bond backed by a pool of mortgage pass-through securities or mortgage loans.

Common Stock Represents equity ownership in a corporation, though the right to residual claims on corporate assets is subordinated to the rights of debt holders, in the event of liquidation. Further rights guaranteed by common stock ownership can generate entitlements that have intrinsic marketable value. These include *rights offerings,* or *pre-emptive rights,* which entitle the holder to purchase shares of a new stock issuance at a price somewhat below the current market price; usually the right has a duration of ninety days following the issuance of new common stock. *Warrants* provide the holder the right to purchase a fixed number of shares of common stock at a predetermined price during a specific period, though some warrants are perpetual. Warrants are created by a corporation to facilitate the sale of debt or preferred stock.

Convertible Debt Instruments These securities act like convertible equity issues, but have fundamental pricing differences. Usually, the conversion on bonds is expressed as a conversion price rather than as a ratio, as is the case with convertible equity issues.

Convertible Preferred Equity Issues The convertible preferred equity issue can be exchanged, at the shareholder's option and at any pre-specified ratio or at a pre-established conversion price, for shares of a company's common stock. The conversion ratio is the par or stated value of the preferred stock divided by the purchase price; conversions of equity issues usually occur at a conversion ratio as opposed to a particular price.

Convertible Securities Debt instruments and equity securities that are convertible into forms of common stock. These issues are particularly useful in new ventures when the founders are seeking capital, and include several types of both convertible equity and convertible bond issues.

Index Fund Mutual fund whose portfolio matches that of a broad-based index such as Standard & Poor's Index and whose performance, therefore, mirrors the market as a whole.

Investment Grade Various ratings services publish analyses on the array of investment instruments currently available on the markets. Among the most widely-known fixed-income ratings services are Moody's and Standard & Poor's (S&P). Their investment grades are as follows:

Company	High Quality	Quality	Below Investment Grade	Very Poor Quality
S&P	AAA-AA	A-BBB	BB-B	CCC-D
Moody's	Aaa-Aa	A-Baa	Ba-B	Caa-C

Preferred Equity Redemption Cumulative Stock (PERCs) A type of convertible preferred stock first brought to the market in 1991, PERCs automatically convert to common stock at the termination of a three-year period, unless called prior to that by the issuer. A cap is set on the conversion value, generally at about 30 percent above the common stock price at the time the preferred stock is issued. If at the end of the three-year period the stock is trading at or below the common stock price, holders receive one share of common stock for each PERC share. PERCs are marketable, though as with all equity securities, a market is never guaranteed.

Preferred Stock An equity issue that has fixed-income characteristics; preferred shares have a fixed dividend, which is stated as a percentage of par value. These shares usually do not have preemptive rights or voting rights, though they are senior to common shares in terms of liquidation claims.

Real Estate Mortgage Investment Conduits (REMICs) Various mortgage tranches, or classes of bonds, are offered (e.g., planned amortization class, inverse floaters, sequential pay, etc).

Rule 144 Stock A pool of common shares that has been authorized by a corporation's Board of Directors is usually not entirely disbursed or marketed for sale, but is held in an internal pool known as treasury stock. A certain number of shares from this pool is often set aside for internal distribution, and hence is never registered with the Securities and Exchange Commission. Prior to registration, these *Rule 144* shares are not used in calculations of a company's worth such as P/E ratios or book value.

CHAPTER TWELVE

Investing Principles, Procedures, and Operations for Short-Term and Long-Term Endowment

12.1   Introduction   409
12.2   Managing Liquidity Funds and Optimizing Return
       on Excess Short-Term Working Capital   410
       (a) Cash-Flow Forecasting   410
       (b) Developing an Investing Strategy   411
12.3   Criteria for Investing   411
       (a) Safety of Principal   412
       (b) Liquidity   412
       (c) Risk   414
            (i)   Credit Risk   414
            (ii) Market Risk   416
       (d) Timing of Funds Usage   419
       (e) Re-investment Requirements   420
       (f) Money-Market Instruments—An Overview   420
       (g) Case Study of Risk Tasking Resulting in Loss   422
       (h) Yield Improvement by Pooling of Funds   424
12.4   Investor or Speculator?   425
12.5   Standard Operating Investment Procedures   426
       (a) Portfolio Review   426
            (i)   Unrealized Gains and Losses   427
            (ii) Trading Activity   427
12.6   Investment Operations—An Introduction   427
       (a) Selecting a Custodian   428
       (b) Bearer versus Registered (and Book Entry) Form   430
       (c) Securities Safekeeping   431

(d) Operating an Investment Program   432
    (i)   Executing Transactions   433
    (ii) Transaction Memos   433
    (iii) Maturity Ticklers   435
    (iv) Transaction Log   435
    (v)   Technology Tools   435
    (vi) Verifying Transactions   437
    (vii) Reporting Transactions   437
(e) Operations Using an Outside Investment
    Manager   437
(f) Investment Operations Summary   438
12.7 Endowment Management   439
(a) What Is Endowment?   439
(b) Why Is Endowment Important to Nonprofit
    Organizations?   440
    (i)   Stability   440
    (ii) Reduced Pressure on Public   440
    (iii) Endowed Programs Are Important   440
    (iv) Flexibility   441
    (v)   Long-Term Relationship   441
(c) How Is an Endowment Created?   441
(d) How Can Endowments Be Directed?   441
(e) Who Is Responsible for the Endowment?   442
    (i)   Board of Trustees   442
    (ii) Investment Committee   443
(f) How Are Endowments Managed?   443
(g) What Is UMIFA?   444
(h) Modern Portfolio Theory   445
12.8 Characteristics of Endowment   445
(a) Withdrawals from Endowment   445
(b) Endowment Asset Allocation   446
(c) Endowment Assets   446
12.9 Endowment Investment   449
(a) Endowment Investment Policy   449
(b) Investment Philosophy   449
(c) Endowment Growth   449
(d) Endowment Investment Return   449
12.10 Principles of Endowment Management   450
(a) Asset Allocation   450
(b) Spending Rate   451
(c) Bonds   455
(d) Equities Investment (Stocks)   455
(e) Diversification   456
    (i)   Diversification by Investment Type
          or Asset Class   456
    (ii) Diversification by Manager (Styles
          and Single Versus Multi-Manager)   457

(iii) Diversification by Type of Issuer 457
(iv) Diversification by Industry Sector 458
(v) Diversification by Geography 458
(vi) Diversification by Global (Foreign) Investing 458
(f) Investment Time Horizon 458
(i) Risk Tolerance 458
(ii) Volatility 459
(iii) Duration 459
(g) Managing Risk 459
(h) Monitoring Performance 460
12.11 Endowment Spending Policy 460
(a) Endowment Investment Strategy—A Discussion 462
(b) Investment Policy 462
(c) Spending Policy 463
(d) Total Return Spending 463
(e) Spending Rates 464
(f) Effect of Inflation 465
(g) Implementation Issues When Spending Policy Is Set or Changed 465
(h) Endowment Spending Policy Summary 467
(i) Definition of Terms Used in Endowment Management 468
12.12 Investment Advisers 470
(a) Professional Investment Advisers 470
(b) Reasons for Using Outside Investment Advisers 470
(c) Types of Outside Investment Advisers 471
(d) Selecting an Outside Investment Manager 474
(e) Compensating Outside Investment Advisers 476
(f) Working with an Investment Manager 478
(g) Investment Advisers Summary 478
Appendix 12A: Uniform Management of Institutional Funds Act 480
Appendix 12B: West's Annotated California Codes 481

12.1 INTRODUCTION

The principles of investing are the same, whether one is investing the liquidity or strategic reserves of an organization or its long-term endowment funds. Sound investing requires setting clear investment objectives and guidelines appropriate to each organization's situation.

Investing opportunities occur when the institution operates with a residual of surplus cash flow or long-term capital, or when it has segregated funds earmarked for investment in longer-term assets. In order to invest appropriately, management should develop an investing strategy that recognizes both the source of the funds and their use. For example, endowment funds are invested very differently from liquidity reserves and working capital needs. The source and use of funds dictate whether surplus cash is to be invested over a short- or long-term horizon.

Endowment funds are expected to be permanently employed to augment the capital structure of the organization and are invested with growth of principal and income in mind. The first part of this section will deal with investments which are part of the organization's treasury management, or short-term financial function, rather than that of long-term type investing, which will be discussed later. There may be situations where a portion of an endowment needs to be available to meet institutional or donor requirements in a shorter term. In these instances, the strategies for both long- and short-term investing will be employed with an endowment. Conversely, there may be situations that will allow the investment of nonendowed funds in longer-term strategies.

The investment program of the nonprofit organization is the fiduciary responsibility of the Board of Trustees, and it is an integral part of the Board's responsibility to be good stewards of the organization's assets. In this chapter, investing objectives and guidelines will be referred to as "investment policy." In written form, the policy defines the allocation of investable funds across asset classes, based on short- and/or long-term objectives and risk tolerances. An institution's governing board approves the policy statement. The policy serves as a guide to the Investment or Finance Committee in the implementation of investing programs. A comprehensive policy includes several components: return objective, time horizon, long-term asset allocation guidelines, short-term asset allocation guidelines, manager selection, and evaluation criteria.

In the absence of a written and approved policy document, the financial or investment manager may find it difficult, if not impossible, to invest funds confidently. Without a written policy, the financial or investment manager also risks his or her job every time an investment is made, because senior officials or members of the Board have the opportunity to second-guess the investment action if there are no accepted investing standards. Accordingly, in the absence of an existing written policy statement and guidelines, the financial manager should initiate the development of such a document.

12.2 MANAGING LIQUIDITY FUNDS AND OPTIMIZING RETURN ON EXCESS SHORT-TERM WORKING CAPITAL

(a) Cash-Flow Forecasting

The manager of a successful investing program must have an effective cash-flow forecasting system in place. The forecasting system is necessary to give the manager an idea of the amount of liquidity funds available for investment and the time period that the funds will be available. Liquidity refers to the capability of an investment instrument to be converted into cash prior to maturity without the investor suffering an unacceptable loss of principal.

(b) Developing an Investing Strategy

The financial manager is ready to begin development of a strategic plan for investing liquidity funds after the necessary tools are in place for producing forecasts. These include a short-term cash flow forecast and an intermediate-term forecast for several months. A long-range forecast is also helpful in determining the amount and duration, if any, of funds available for longer-term investing. The strategic plan should be established in concert with development of the investing policy and guidelines to ensure that the guidelines are compatible with, and indeed support, the investing strategy.

At this point, the financial manager may begin to think in terms of managing two different segments of portfolios. One segment would be the liquidity portfolio containing only short-term, fixed-income securities with high-grade credit quality and liquidity. It is this portion that will be used tactically on a daily basis to absorb temporarily excess funds generated from operations and to provide liquidity to the institution when there is a shortfall of funds. The other portion of the portfolio, for longer-term strategic use, such as an endowment, could be invested in intermediate-term, fixed-income securities or stocks.

Before investing any funds, however, the financial manager will want to assess the institution's tolerance for risk. Typically, when asked about tolerance for risk, management will say that it has absolutely no tolerance for it. However, when faced with the low yields of risk-free, short-term Treasury bills, management will frequently inquire about other securities that offer a higher yield.

12.3   CRITERIA FOR INVESTING

In evaluating the various avenues used to approach the investment of a particular pool of funds, the financial manager must consider a number of criteria and alternatives available with respect to each criterion. The criteria to be evaluated include:

- Safety of principal
- Liquidity
- Risk
- Timing of the use of funds

- Re-investment requirements
- Management's (directors or trustees) special attitude toward such items as supporting local banks with deposits, risk sensitivity, and degree of participation in investment activities (which should be addressed in the investing guidelines)

(a) Safety of Principal

This point cannot be overemphasized. Ask a business executive or administrative manager about his or her tolerance for risk in making investments, and the response undoubtedly will be that there is no tolerance for risk. Then ask that same person whether he or she finds short-term U.S. Treasury bills to have an acceptable rate of return, and the response undoubtedly will be negative as well. Obviously, there is a conflict in these responses, because one cannot have a total absence of risk and reap high returns at the same time. The earning of a "normal rate of return" is related to the acceptance of a level of risk. Every investment policy must address and specify that level of risk the organization is willing to accept. The statement of risk tolerance is the number one element in a written set of investing policy and guidelines. There are essentially two forms of risks: (1) credit risk and (2) market or interest-rate risk.

(b) Liquidity

Liquidity refers to the capability of an investment instrument to be converted into cash prior to maturity without the investor suffering an unacceptable loss of principal. A portfolio is said to have near-perfect liquidity when it consists of extremely high-credit quality instruments and it matures entirely in one day. In that case, interest rates could change overnight but would not affect the market value of the portfolio. However, if maturity of the instruments in the portfolio extends beyond overnight, there is the possibility of the introduction of market risk and therefore the introduction of some illiquidity.

Primary goals of managing liquidity funds usually are the preservation of principal and the maintenance of liquidity (convertibility to cash). Generating a competitive yield on the funds is often a third objective. In managing an organization, whether a religious institution or a manufacturer, the maintenance of the organization's liquidity is crucial to its short- and long-term success. Even in financially successful organizations, there are periods in which disbursements exceed receipts, and the well-managed organization must be prepared for this occurrence. An entity that manages its cash properly will not maintain sufficient cash in its checking account to clear short-term hurdles. Rather, it will keep all excess cash in the form of liquid investments composed almost exclusively of short-term, fixed-income money market instruments that are convertible to cash on virtually a moment's notice with no risk to principal.

Another, perhaps more obvious dimension of liquidity, relates to the depth and breadth of the market itself for the particular security involved. The good news about the huge size of the national debt is that it provides the broadest and deepest market dimensions for the debt instruments of the U.S. government. The vast breadth and depth of the market enable any investor to buy or sell virtually any amount of current actively traded U.S. Treasury securities at virtually any moment with a minimum search for buyers and sellers.

At the opposite extreme of this dimension of liquidity are debt obligations of obscure banks and corporations whose creditworthiness is not investment grade and for which there are not many ready buyers or sellers in the marketplace. It would not be unusual for the holder of an instrument of an obscure company to encounter delays of days or even a week while a broker searched for a potential buyer, if one exists. It is important to note that even unusual U.S. Government Agency (not Treasury) securities can be quite illiquid, if the structure of the instrument is particularly unusual.

It is said that every asset has its price and that no matter how poor a credit risk or how long the instrument's maturity, there is always an investor somewhere in the marketplace who will buy that instrument. However, the question is, "At what price?" Even for 30-year U.S. government bonds, the market price is determined by literally thousands of active buyers and sellers at any moment. This depth of the market provides the seller the ability to convert a government obligation into cash on a moment's notice. Meanwhile, the free-flowing market mechanism of continuing transactions between buyers and sellers provides constant adjustment to the market price, based on current interest rates and expectations. This is the traditional concept of liquidity. The holder of the debt instrument of the obscure corporation may also find a willing buyer. In the absence of other potential buyers, however, the one buyer who is interested can probably dictate the price to the seller and that price may very well represent a huge loss. Therefore, while the seller can indeed convert the security to cash, he or she may have to suffer a loss in order to do so prior to maturity.

Liquidity is also an issue when funds are placed into instruments that are legally unredeemable until maturity. These include, for example, fixed-time deposits of banks or savings and loans where the amount is small or the investor has no legal or market ability to sell or transfer the deposit to a subsequent party. In the case of certificates of deposit of well-known and high-credit rated institutions where the investor has the legal right to sell the instrument, liquidity is considerably improved. Interest-rate risk, however, may reduce the market value of the instrument if interest rates have risen since the instrument was acquired.

Accordingly, the financial manager who seeks to ensure a high level of liquidity for the institution's portfolio should focus on investing in instruments of the highest possible credit quality and of relatively short maturities. On the other hand, where liquidity is not a large factor in the objectives of the funds, the financial manager may consider matching the maturity of the investment to a particular date when the funds are known to be needed. For example, in managing an endowment fund portfolio, the investment manager may elect to invest in an instrument maturing when a grant is expected to be made. In this case, the possibility of realized loss due to market risk would be diminished because the instrument would likely mature (at face value) in time to be used for the intended purpose. The only risk would be credit risk.

(c) Risk

(i) Credit Risk. Credit risk, also known as default risk, refers to the possibility that the obligor of a debt instrument will fail to repay principal or pay interest on a timely basis in accordance with the terms of the instrument. Credit risk can be analyzed and measured by the investor prior to investing in a particular debt instrument, or the investor can rely on a credit analysis performed for a fee, by a credit-rating agency (Exhibit 12.1). It is generally assumed that the credit risk represented by debt of the government of the United States is the highest form of credit and that all other issuers' credit ratings are measured against the benchmark of the U.S. government.

Many investors mistakenly believe that the debt markets are rational and that differences in credit risk are quickly reflected in differences of yield among similar instruments of different issuers. For example, a commercial paper note due in 90 days issued by a corporation of medium creditworthiness will yield the investor a greater return than will a 90-day U.S. Treasury bill. Similarly, the yield on commercial paper issued by a very creditworthy corporation will yield somewhat less return than the rate of return on commercial paper of a medium-quality issuer.

This dilemma between no tolerance for risk and a desire for high yield should be explored and defined in the investment guidelines. If they are unwilling to accept any risk greater than short-term U.S. Treasury bills, they must be willing to accept the rock-bottom yields that Treasury bills offer. On the other hand, if

Exhibit 12.1. Several Major Credit-Rating Firms

Rating Service	Address and Phone Number
Moody's Investors Service	99 Church Street New York, NY 10007 (212) 553-1658
Standard & Poor's Corporation	25 Broadway New York, NY 10004 (212) 208-1146
Duff & Phelps, Credit Ratings	55 East Monroe Street Suite 3500 Chicago, IL 60603 (312) 368-3198
Fitch Investors Service, Inc.	1 State Street Plaza New York, NY 10004 (212) 908-0900
Sheshunoff and Co., Inc.	P.O. Box 13203 Capital Station Austin, TX 78711-3208 (512) 472-2244

they wish to obtain higher yields, they must be willing to accept the reasonable credit risk of top credit-rated U.S. and foreign banks and top credit-rated industrial corporations and their captive finance company subsidiaries. This decision addresses only the question of credit risk; the issue of market risk which is determined by length of maturity still must be considered.

If management really wishes to have yield take a front seat, it should be willing to accept other investing possibilities. These include banks of less than top quality (although many are nevertheless sound), and commercial paper of industrial and financial companies that are rated in the second tier of credit ratings. The matter of market risk, or the risk that interest rates will rise, thereby forcing a decline in the market value of fixed-income securities, also must be considered. This is particularly important in a liquidity portfolio where safety of principal is of paramount importance. Management must be willing to accept market risk, even from Treasury bills, unless it is prepared to keep maturities as short as 90 days or less.

However, markets are imperfect and sometimes very much so. It is important for the financial manager to be aware of the respective "normal" relative levels of credit quality and yields among the issuers in whose securities and instruments the organization is investing. To do this, the financial manager must maintain current information about issuers and changes in their credit ratings.

In the management of pools of funds held for liquidity and intermediate-term purposes, investors tend to demand credit quality of the highest order; that is, they will generally invest only in instruments issued by companies of the highest-credit quality or by the U.S. government. This is to ensure the greatest degree of market "salability" or liquidity. However, the risk of such investments still must be carefully examined.

Some investors take a higher-risk approach, and apply the theory of portfolio management that expects some investments in a portfolio to pay off while others actually incur capital losses. Other investors use a more conservative approach and plan to have the bulk of the investments in a portfolio generate normal yields of approximately the average market rate of return. The hope, of course, is to manage a broad optimum portfolio of investments where winners will exceed the losers, as to yield, with the result that the portfolio as a whole realizes a minimal amount of risk and an optimal amount of return and growth. However, this approach is suited only to highly skilled investors who can afford a higher degree of risk.

(ii) Market Risk. Market risk, or the risk of loss to principal due to changes in interest rates, is a subtle but very real form of risk and can be equally as devastating as credit risk. Interest rates affect the market value of a debt instrument when the interest rate, or coupon, of the instrument is fixed (nonfloating or nonmarket rate adjusting). When yields in the marketplace change, either the market value of existing instruments must change or the rate of return paid on that instrument must change in order to adjust an instrument's market yield to current market yield. If a bond has a fixed-rate coupon and interest rates in the marketplace rise, then the market value of that bond must decline to a point where the fixed-rate coupon and a change in its market value combine to reflect current market yield. Likewise, when interest rates decline, the market value of the bond must rise. When this bond is purchased by an investor, the combination of the bond's coupon rate and principal cost will put the net yield, based on the price paid versus interest received, where comparable instruments are now offered.

When investing in a fixed-rate coupon instrument, the investor realizes that the longer the term until maturity, the greater the possibility for fluctuation in market value due to interest rate changes and, therefore, the greater the market risk (see Exhibit 12.2). Conversely, an instrument that matures in a relatively short period of time will be somewhat insulated from changes in market interest rates; the investor will need only to hold the instrument until maturity to receive 100 cents on the dollar.

Different types of instruments bear different levels of sensitivity to the volatility of interest rates in the marketplace. Zero coupon bonds, for example, typically carry the highest level of volatility, or market risk, because there is no current income to cushion the investor's return. Consequently, a change in market interest rate lev-

Exhibit 12.2. How Changes in Interest Rates Affect Market Prices

Maturity	1 percent Rise in Interest Rates Equals Approximately this Amount of Dollar Market Value Decline (Per $1,000,000 of Par Value)
1 month	$ 734
3 months	2,500
6 months	4,699
1 year	8,681
2 years	23,212
5 years	43,414
10 years	70,728
20 years	113,194
30 years	129,645

els impacts immediately, directly, and to the fullest extent the market value of a zero coupon bond. At the other end of the volatility spectrum are floating-rate instruments where the coupon yields are not fixed but are reset periodically to reflect changes in market interest rates. Because the coupon on these instruments changes with the market, their market value is rather stable.

High-quality credit ratings also tend to insulate a security from market volatility to some degree. It has been shown empirically that in times of stress or increasing interest rates, investors begin a "flight to quality" by buying higher-credit quality instruments. It creates a demand for the instruments, thereby further forcing their prices further up and yields down. This was amply demonstrated in the well-documented stock market crash of October 19, 1987, when equity prices went into a free-fall and there was complete turmoil in both the equity and credit markets. Investors fled stocks in droves, and many placed their funds temporarily into U.S. government obligations. The yields on U.S. government securities remained inordinately low during the weeks immediately following the crash. Investors had bid up the prices as they purchased these instruments to obtain high-credit quality investments.

Loss of principal due to market risk is *realized* only when the security must be sold prior to maturity. At that time, the market value of the instrument may be above or below what the investor paid for it and also may be different from the maturity value of the instrument. Market risk does not result in a loss if the investor holds the instrument until maturity, because at that time the investor will realize the return of 100 percent of the face value of the instrument. Market risk exists not only for corporate and bank securities, but also for U.S. government securities. Therefore, it is incorrect for an investor to say that he or she demands that funds be invested only in U.S. government securities in order to avoid risk to principal. Indeed, credit risk can be avoided or at least minimized, but market risk cannot be unless the securities are held until maturity, even for Treasury instruments.

Recognition by the financial manager of the existence of market risk, in addition to credit risk, is critically important to the management of an investment portfolio, particularly a pool of funds whose use is not anticipated for several years. The temptation in managing these funds is to invest in long-term securities and collect a possibly higher income, while knowing that the securities are sufficiently liquid to be sold on very short notice. The financial manager must recognize, however, that while the liquidity and current income will remain constant, a change in interest rates may cause the market value of the portfolio to decline. Losses could be realized if it were necessary to convert the portfolio to cash prior to maturity of the instruments. Therefore, in addition to analyzing and monitoring credit risk as represented by the potential for default by issuers of securities, the investment manager also must be cognizant of market risk and its potential capability to erode the market value of a portfolio.

Because of the potentially devastating effects of both credit risk and market risk, the institution's investment policy must be clear about how these two forms of risk are to be handled. This must be done before establishing an approach to investing and before discussing the particular issues and forms of investments that are acceptable. The decisions with regard to the level of tolerance for credit risk and market risk should be made by the most senior officials in management, if not by the Directors or Trustees themselves. The considerations should be made consciously and the results communicated in writing to the financial manager in such a way that there could be no mistaking the intentions of senior management.

There are two ways to protect against market risk. The customary method most companies use is simply to maintain short maturities ranging between 30 and 60 days. If interest rates rise (causing the value of the instrument to fall), the investor has to wait only a short period until maturity. The other method, which is far from perfect, is to invest in interest rate futures contracts and options as hedges. When interest rates move upward, a hedge position should generate a profit to offset the loss in the value of the investment instrument.

The use of futures and options, however, is a very sophisticated practice. It should be used only by investors with very large portfolios, who can observe all the markets virtually on a full-time basis. Futures and options could be equally beneficial for the investor with a modest-sized portfolio, but these investors typically do not have the time or expertise to become involved with the sophisticated hedging techniques that futures and options represent.

Another strategy for managing short-term investment funds exists where the funds have been earmarked for a specific project, such as construction of a building. In this type of situation, market risk impact can be reduced by purchasing investment instruments with maturities that coincide with the projected need dates for the funds. For example, if construction plans call for a payment on a certain date four months from now, the financial manager can invest in an instrument maturing just prior to the payment date. The institution will be assured of receiving 100 cents on the invested dollar, plus interest, at maturity, rather than risking possible loss in a sale prior to maturity. The entire investment portfolio for the project can be assembled with maturities to coincide with estimated payment dates and amounts required for the project, thereby largely immunizing the portfolio from any market value changes due to interest rate swings. However, if construction is ahead of schedule and funds are required sooner than expected, an instrument may have to be sold prior to maturity. This may result in possible loss of principal.

(d) Timing of Funds Usage

The financial manager must know the intended use of investment funds in order to manage maturities properly. Maturity and liquidity objectives should correspond with the purpose of the specific funds, whether it is to make a grant, repay bank debt, meet expenses, or be used as contributions to an employee benefit plan.

Grant payments, for example, can occur on fairly short notice and require relatively large amounts of funds. Long-term illiquid investment instruments may be inappropriate if the pool of invested funds will be used for daily expenses. Bank debt repayments are usually scheduled and known well in advance. Bank loans that are revolving credits, however, are subject to being repaid and reborrowed at the borrower's discretion. Therefore, repayments can occur virtually at any time the borrower has sufficient funds available. Most large payment requirements also are known well in advance. Employee benefit plans, such as pension plans, are subject to contributions with fairly regular and defined payment dates, but the amounts may or may not be known.

Accordingly, the financial manager must plan the maturity dates of the investment instruments in the pool to coincide with the funding dates of the various uses of the funds. The manager must also obtain the highest possible market yield on the pool of funds and attempt to schedule the maturities so as to optimize the yield along the yield curve. The challenge occurs when the investment manager must seek the optimal tradeoff between safety and liquidity of principal and rate of return on the investment.

(e) Re-investment Requirements

In order to operate an investment program properly, management must decide how to use the income earned on the pool of investments. Options include incorporating the income stream from investments with the other revenue streams of the institution or retaining the income stream in the investment pool where it is re-invested. This is a policy decision and its implications may be relatively important if investment income is substantial and becomes a large source of "budgeted" revenue. Another consideration involves funds invested in long-term instruments where the income is not used. The financial manager may have difficulty re-investing the income proceeds in similar long-term investments when the amount of the income stream is small.

(f) Money-Market Instruments—An Overview

The ideal money-market investment medium is a debt instrument that does not fluctuate substantially in value, that carries no risk of default by the issuer, and that may be converted to cash at any time without loss of principal. The instrument that most closely approaches this standard is a short-maturity (90 days or less) U.S. Treasury bill; a short-term debt obligation of the U.S. government. In this imperfect world, the U.S. government is considered to carry the highest domestic credit rating, which means that the risk of default on its debt obligations is the lowest in the United States. As a result, credit ratings as well as yields of all other domestic instruments of any maturity are based on spreads (yield variations) from U.S. government securities.

Risk of loss in short-term investing is not confined to credit risk alone. Loss of principal can also occur by investing in an instrument that must be sold prior to maturity, if interest rates have risen before the instrument matures. This phenomenon is usually referred to as "market risk" or "interest rate risk," and it can result in loss to investors, even to those who invest only in U.S. Treasury bills.

Because of market risk, the financial manager should purchase instruments with maturities that closely match the need for the funds. If the cash-flow forecast indicates that the funds should be available in 45 days, for example, the financial manager is well advised to purchase instruments maturing in approximately 45 days. Purchasing a six-month security under these circumstances could result in loss of principal if interest rates rise, thereby forcing value of the instrument down and having to sell the instrument to raise funds for an unexpected cash need. Of course, the opposite situation may occur. Declining interest rates during the period could result in a gain on the early sale of the instrument. However, most prudent financial managers primarily will look at avoiding risk to their liquidity funds.

Other short-term debt instruments commonly used as money-market investments are the negotiable bank certificate of deposit, the time draft called a banker's acceptance (the payment of which is an obligation of a bank), and the short-term promissory note of a corporation known as commercial paper.

The latter half of the 1980s saw many significant changes in the marketplace for money-market instruments. During the same period, the nature of commercial banking changed significantly as well, and this contributed to the alteration of the money markets. Historically, when a firm needed to borrow for its short-term working capital needs, it went to a bank and borrowed on a 90-day promissory note that the bank traditionally held until maturity. In the 1980s, however, the banking industry encountered its own liquidity crisis as well as an industry-wide shortage of permanent capital in relation to assets. When these elements were combined with the severe economic stresses resulting from the collapse of the energy, real estate, and agriculture industries, in addition to loans to less developed countries that went sour, banks became pressed to find methods of improving their ratio of permanent capital to total assets. In fact, the regulatory authorities mandated higher capital levels for banks that had to be met by the end of 1992.

There are two ways to improve a capital ratio: (1) increase the amount of capital or (2) reduce the amount of assets. Because the cost of capital was exceptionally expensive for banks during this period, many banks took the easier path and sought ways to reduce their assets without impairing earning capacity. It was not long before banks discovered that they could originate loans and sell them to investors, reducing their assets while retaining an interest rate spread for servicing the loan. This device of selling loans helped the banks to restore their own capital ratios for regulatory purposes, but it had a direct impact on borrowers. Many borrowers now were required to execute standardized loan documentation and to face the possibility that someone other than their bank—even perhaps a competitor—would be the holder of the borrower's debt.

Very large companies in the United States have been borrowing in the public money markets for many years via commercial paper, but companies smaller than Fortune 500 firms were not accustomed to this kind of treatment. During the late 1980s and early 1990s, it became increasingly customary for companies of even modest size to be required to borrow under documentation, hinting that the bank might not hold the debt until maturity. Perhaps the most significant effect of these developments was the recognition that an investment instrument was merely the reverse side of the borrowing instrument. In the latter half of the 1980s, it became obvious to commercial bankers and investment bankers that their respective pools of borrowers and investors had interests in common. Consequently, the bankers designed new instruments that simultaneously serve the needs of both the borrower and the investor. This brought some very creative thinking to the game. The traditional short-term investment instruments—certificates of deposit, commercial paper, bankers' acceptances, and treasury bills—became rather pedestrian.

With the proliferation of new deritive instruments in the money markets, the typical investor is hard-pressed to discern between instruments that are truly safe and liquid and those that present hidden risks. While there have been no major disasters in this regard yet, many investors of institutional liquidity funds remain somewhat skeptical about instruments with names such as DARTS, CATS, and Low Floaters. Other investors, often seeking new, more unusual investments, forge ahead and usually enjoy a somewhat higher yield than their friends who remain with the traditional money-market investment instruments. It is questionable, however, whether these more adventuresome investors truly understand the issues surrounding potential liquidity and credit problems, even though there is little or no documented evidence of failures in these areas to date.

One can wonder what would have happened if the economy had entered a severe recession during this time instead of an almost continuous growth pattern since about 1983. If a financial manager knowingly enters into a risky investment transaction and that risk is realized with loss of principal, the loss can be much more acceptable if the manager's actions have been in accordance with Board-approved policy and guidelines. Along with the variety of new instruments, the mine fields also have expanded to the potential detriment of the well-being and job security of financial managers responsible for investing their institutions' liquidity funds without Board direction.

(g) Case Study of Risk Taking Resulting in Loss

ABC Foundation was a large organization with more than 26 employees, serving an economically expanding middle-class (and higher) geographic area. The Foundation had accumulated funds of approximately $40 million that were managed by a business manager reporting to the Board of Trustees. The cash flow to the Foundation was more than adequate to cover expenses with no immediate need forecasted for the use of any funds; the business manager had relatively few constraints and little direction to keep cash available for immediate needs. Furthermore, no comprehensive written investment policy was in place to specifically limit ABC Foundation's investment activities.

Within this loose framework, the business manager began to purchase longer-maturity (10 through 30 years) U.S. Treasury securities for the following reasons:

- The longer maturities presented a higher yield and would improve the rate of return on the organization's investment portfolio.

- There were no immediate plans to utilize the funds; therefore, short-maturity dates appeared to be inappropriate for the investment.

- Because the instruments were issued and guaranteed by the U.S. Treasury, there appeared to be no risk to principal.

As the rate of return on the foundation's portfolio was better than the yield available on shorter-term investments, such as local bank certificates of deposit, the trustees complimented the business manager on his ability to achieve an attractive rate of return. Furthermore, during this investment period, interest rates began to decline, causing the market value of the long-term securities to increase. This situation led the foundation's business manager to become more active in trading (actively buying and selling) these securities to capture a capital gain from their improvement in price. As interest rates continued to decline, the prices of these instruments continued to go up, and capital gains were realized from the transactions. Combined with their higher interest (accrual) rate, the gains substantially enhanced the foundation's investment return and brought further praise to the business manager from the Trustees.

Soon, the reality of interest-rate fluctuations began to set in as financial market conditions changed. Interest rates stopped going down and, in fact, began to rise quite rapidly. By this time, the Foundation's bond portfolio consisted entirely of long-maturity U.S. Treasury bonds. Just as these instruments had gone up in price as interest rates were declining, they were now going down in price as interest rates were increasing. Accordingly, the business manager was no longer able to sell the instruments in his portfolio at prices higher than he had paid. Therefore, unrealized capital gains quickly turned into unrealized capital losses. Recently, the government began using a single-price system in which notes are awarded at the highest yield needed to sell the securities.

Compounding this situation was a substantial slowdown in cash flow to the foundation. Now there was a need to rely on funds from its excess cash investments, all of which were in the investment fund. This need for cash necessitated the sale of several investments which resulted in substantial realized losses to the Foundation. At this time, the losses were noted by the Foundation's auditors who discovered additional unrealized losses in the Foundation's investment portfolio.

As a result of the speculation engaged in by ABC Foundation's business manager, the Foundation realized approximately $2.5 million in losses. Its remaining investment portfolio, with an initial value of $40 million, had declined in value approximately 10 percent from the original principal investment.

This information contained in the audit report was made available to the Trustees, who immediately demanded the situation be remedied. Unfortunately, with the losses in place and more cash needs ahead, the opportunities to remedy the situation were limited simply to establishing procedures to avoid a repetition in the future.

The following procedures should have been set in place before this situation developed:

- Comprehensive investment guidelines should have been established with specific limitations on risk, including maturities.
- Maturities should have been limited to conform strictly with the estimated cash needs at that time or limited to a maximum maturity date, as stated in the guidelines, to avoid excessive interest rate or market risk.
- The business manager responsible for the investment portfolio should have been trained more thoroughly, or outside professional assistance should have been contracted.
- Frequent (quarterly) review or audit of investment activities should have been instituted to ensure that investment activities conformed with investment guidelines and to discover any unusual situations.

(h) Yield Improvement by Pooling of Funds

Another technique that can effectively increase investment yields for the institution is consolidation of all available funds into one pool. Many medium and large institutions, particularly, operate their cash systems in a fragmented manner with collection points and disbursement points scattered throughout their organizational structures. By centralizing cash flows and cash management, an institution can create a larger pool of investable funds. This gives the institution's financial manager greater bargaining power and the ability to invest more money in "round lots" in the money markets. In addition, the cash-flow imbalances of various operating units in a large organization tend to average out and offset one another. The organization as a whole typically can operate on a smaller working cash balance than can the sum of its parts. The centralized liquidity pool usually can be invested for a longer duration than its separate components, which enhances the overall yield obtainable on the institution's invested funds.

Another frequent benefit of fund consolidation and a larger investment portfolio is a higher level of professionalism can be supported in the investment process. An internal professional funds manager or outside investment management firm using proper cash forecasting and cash management techniques may often bring about higher returns on available funds. The use of investment professionals also tends to reduce the institution's exposure to credit risk because they are familiar with debt issuers and instruments and can give constant attention to the market.

12.4 INVESTOR OR SPECULATOR?

Even in his prime, Babe Ruth struck out much more often than he hit home runs. The financial manager who seeks to hit home runs in managing the investment portfolio will undoubtedly find that the strikeout percentage is too high to be acceptable to senior management and the Board of Directors or Trustees. Instead, the acceptable method of operation is to be a "singles hitter" with a very high batting average and probably never any home runs. After all, the financial manager who hits only singles has a certain degree of job security, while the financial manager who loses principal due to speculative investments may be frequently searching for a new job.

Professional institutional speculators in the investment profession are paid to risk capital in order to make considerable profits, or suffer losses, by participating continuously and aggressively in the marketplace. However, financial managers of nonprofit institutions are, in effect, part-time investors who are involved in the investment markets only occasionally. The part-time investor is at a severe disadvantage against a speculative marketplace. Even full-time investment speculators strike out with a good degree of frequency. The part-time investor, however, never can be expected to hit a prodigious home run. On the other hand, the institution's senior management will not likely forget the strikeouts.

The cardinal rule for the small or part-time investor, therefore, is: Be an investor and not a speculator. When the financial manager encounters an apparently attractive instrument not normally included in the institution's portfolio, he or she should seek specific management approval of the instrument before executing the transaction. This requires thorough research and preparation of a recommendation by the financial manager for senior management to review so it can determine suitability of the instruments. If management supports the investment after examining all aspects of the recommendation, the financial manager cannot be criticized later for imprudence.

12.5 STANDARD OPERATING INVESTMENT PROCEDURES

The financial manager faces credit risk and market risk daily in the management of the investment portfolio. Additional risk from other quarters certainly is not welcome. However, insidious forms of risk exist within the financial manager's own office. These include fraud, malfeasance, and repeated errors. Fraud is the intentional misrepresentation of facts for the personal benefit of the financial manager or a staff member. By contrast, malfeasance is the failure to conduct business affairs properly, resulting in poor performance. Repeated errors are usually the result of incompetence or poor training.

To avoid these forms of internal risk, the financial manager is well advised to document fully all operating procedures relating to the management and operations of the investment process. Documentation of procedures is vital to the success of the internal control system. However, it is a time-consuming process, and too few firms actually get around to writing the procedure documents. A single instance of fraud or malfeasance, or repeated errors, however, can readily demonstrate the value of written procedure manuals and system documentation.

The procedure documents should include:

- A description of the operating structure
- Job descriptions and statements of responsibility
- Detailed descriptions of the processing of investment transactions, related funds transfers, and securities safekeeping requirements
- Valuation and mark to market of holdings
- A description of all forms used to execute and confirm transactions
- A description of limitations on the authority of each employee
- A clear delineation of the duties and responsibilities of each employee involved in the investing process to report any perceived impropriety or errors

(a) Portfolio Review

As part of the standard operating procedures in the management of an investment portfolio, senior management should review the portfolio periodically, at least quarterly or perhaps monthly, and attempt to discover any potential problems. There are several elements that should be examined by senior management, including an analysis of unrealized gains and losses and a trading analysis.

(i) Unrealized Gains and Losses. An excellent way to discover potential problems in a portfolio is to analyze the gains and losses that exist on paper among the securities held in the portfolio. An accumulation of unrealized or "paper," losses must be recognized in the operating income statement even though the securities may not have been sold, according to the accounting standards. Conversely, an increasing amount of unrealized gains in the portfolio may indicate success in the investing operations. Management may wish to realize these gains by selling the instruments and re-investing the proceeds in other instruments with perhaps less future market price movement potential. Also to consider large gains today can signal speculative trading which, in the future, can result in large losses.

(ii) Trading Activity. An additional, effective way to monitor the performance of the financial manager is to review the number of transactions taking place during a one week or one month period. If new money is being added to the portfolio, or if there are significant numbers of maturing instruments, a higher than normal level of trading activity, particularly on the purchasing side, would be expected. On the other hand, if there is no unusual inflow of funds but a high level of buying and selling, the financial manager may be trading for speculative profit. The unusual activity in buying and selling should be cause to ask the financial manager to explain this action in light of the institution's investing policies.

12.6 INVESTMENT OPERATIONS—AN INTRODUCTION

Managing an investing program has many facets and considerations, but the financial manager should have three key elements in place before embarking on an investing program:

1. Written investing policy and set of guidelines
2. Safekeeping arrangements for the securities
3. Defined operating procedures

The first element, the written investing policy and guidelines, is discussed in Chapter 11. Custody arrangements for safekeeping of securities and appropriate operating procedures are explained in this chapter. A well-defined operating procedure is a key component of an institution's investment program.

(a) Selecting a Custodian

Traditional custom and practice dictate that settlement of money market securities transactions occurs by delivery of the securities in New York City against payment to the seller of the amount due. Therefore, it behooves the investor organization to maintain a custodian account in New York for the clearance and safekeeping of its portfolio of securities. An investor organization that does not have a banking relationship in New York usually can work through a local or regional bank's New York correspondent bank to provide the custodian service. Many banks throughout the United States offer custodial and safekeeping services, but they typically act as investors' agents and make arrangements with New York City banks to handle the actual securities clearance and safekeeping operations.

It is not a good idea for delivery to occur outside of New York City. Taking delivery of securities in another city entails additional costs for delivery as well as additional costs for redelivery upon redemption or early sale. Also, it is unwise for an investor to accept physical delivery of investment instruments because of security considerations.

Selection of the securities clearance/custodian bank may be as simple as merely approving the use of the correspondent bank of the organization's principal depository bank or as complicated as an elaborate selection process that includes requests for proposals and personal visits. In any event, the investor's fundamental interest is to ensure: (1) safety of the portfolio holdings, (2) integrity of information concerning the investment instruments, (3) accuracy and accountability of the custodian, and (4) reliability of the custodian to execute instructions concerning receipt and delivery of securities in settlement of investment transactions.

Using a New York correspondent bank introduces an extra layer of administrative bureaucracy into the picture, and the financial manager should be satisfied that this extra layer provides value. The financial manager also should inquire as to where in the New York bank and the local bank the securities clearance and safekeeping services are performed. For example, many banks offer similar services out of both their trust and investment departments. Experience has shown that securities clearance services provided by an investment department tend to be expedited because of that department's own requirement for handling transactions swiftly and accurately.

The securities clearance service offered by a trust department, on the other hand, is not often geared to the fast-paced settlements required in money-market securities transactions. This difference simply reflects the nature of the business handled by the respective departments. Trust department investments are more heavily weighted toward equity securities that settle in five business days rather than same- or next-day settlements of most money-market transactions. Consequently, trust departments tend not to function with the speed and cost-effectiveness required when dealing with money-market instruments.

Banks that offer custody services are willing to hold in safe-keeping virtually all types of fixed or variable income or equity securities for the customer regardless of where they were purchased. Banks usually base their charges for the service on the volume of transactions conducted in an account; however, some banks base charges on the value of the portfolio held in safekeeping or a combination of the two bases.

The concept of delivery versus payment (DVP) is fundamental to the operation of an investment portfolio because it is an important safeguard against the risk of loss for the nonprofit institution. The alternative to DVP is to pay for the purchase of securities by wire transfer and to allow the selling investment dealer to retain possession of the instruments. This presents a risk, however, that the selling dealer may fail to segregate properly the customer's securities from the dealer's own inventory of securities, or fail to segregate the securities owned by each customer. Securities dealers, of course, welcome the opportunity to hold customers' securities free of charge, while banks charge fees for this service. However, an independent custodian does add value in the form of assurance that the specific asset actually exists.

The use of an independent custodian is very important in the investing process for the following five reasons:

1. It provides securities clearance service in New York City that makes it possible for the investing organization to deal with virtually all brokers and dealers in the country.

2. It eliminates the possible co-mingling of securities owned by multiple clients and the investment dealer itself.

3. It provides independent verification of the receipt and holding of securities and facilitates the investor's audit process.

4. It ensures the safety of the investing organization's funds in the event of the failure of a dealer from which the investor has purchased securities, because the DVP method of settlement involves an independent third-party safekeeping agent.

The importance of the last point is illustrated by the failure of ESM Government Securities, Inc. as well as several other securities dealers that failed during the mid-1980s. While ESM's failure was caused by a number of factors, not the least of which were alleged mismanagement and fraud, dozens of investing institutions lost hundreds of millions of dollars because they had not insisted on delivery against payment of the purchased securities to an independent custodian. Therefore, ESM was able to resell the securities, or borrow further, by using their customers' securities as collateral.

One investor, a municipality, initially lost more than $14 million (before recovering $10 million after spending $1 million in legal fees) when ESM failed. In the aftermath of this debacle, auditors discovered that ESM apparently had sold the same securities not only to the municipality, but to other investors as well. Had the municipality insisted that ESM deliver the securities to an independent custodian against payment, there would have been no question about the safety of the municipality's funds and the integrity of its investment portfolio. The municipality would have had either the funds or the investment securities; however, in the absence of actual delivery, the municipality had neither the funds nor the investment instruments.

(b) Bearer Versus Registered (and Book Entry) Form

Many years ago, all securities were issued in physical form as certificates. The burden of storing and moving all of this paper became too great, however, and a number of securities markets changed their method of operation to maintenance of ownership records in electronic form. When a security changes ownership, the transaction and resulting ownership registration records are changed in the central computer. Today, most markets utilize the electronic "book-entry" form of registration; some markets offer a combination of physical and book-entry forms. Stocks listed on the New York Stock Exchange, for example, are generally held in book entry form at a central depository, but any investor who wishes to hold a physical stock certificate may do so upon request.

The U.S. Treasury, on the other hand, has been phasing out physical certificates completely. Since 1987, all T-bills have been issued in book-entry form. The T-bill investor maintains an account with the Treasury at the Federal Reserve Bank, and all transactions involving Treasury securities are handled through this account.

To accommodate the use of book-entry delivery through independent bank custodians, settlement systems have been developed that enable the electronic delivery of a security against electronic payment. The accuracy of using an electronic system is at least as great as the accuracy of the clerk reviewing the physical characteristics of the paper certificate and authorizing the issuance of a paper check for payment. Moreover, the maintenance of inventory and transaction records is greatly enhanced by the use of the book-entry form of transactions. Finally, institutions are able to retard the escalating costs of manually handling these transactions and can pass along savings in administrative costs to their investing clients.

The paper certificate is negotiable only when payable to "bearer" or when payable to an individual whose signature accompanies the certificate on a separate form, called a "Bond Power," and has been guaranteed by a bank, trust company, or stockbroker. To negotiate or transfer a certificate registered in the name of a corporation, on the other hand, requires that a certified copy of a corporate resolution authorizing the transfer of the security be attached to the certificate. This process is cumbersome and subject to legal review. Consequently, delivery of a security registered to a corporation is viewed with caution. Accordingly, corporate investors are encouraged to accept physical delivery of securities payable to "bearer" or, if registration is required for some reason, to accept delivery in negotiable form and to reregister the security in the name of a nominee of the custodian. A nominee is a fictitious name properly and appropriately registered for use by the custodian whereby the custodian is able to execute transfers without the necessity of obtaining corporate board resolutions.

(c) Securities Safekeeping

The prudent investor will not take delivery of securities from a dealer or bank. There is the risk of loss due to theft or damage, and it is not practical to make physical delivery upon the maturity or sale of securities.

An investor will usually select a bank to safekeep securities. Most New York City banks function as securities custodians and clearance agents for investors all over the country, either directly or through a network of correspondent banks. The investor establishes a safekeeping account either with a New York bank or one of its correspondent banks, and delivery of securities is accomplished through the account.

When the investor purchases a security from a dealer, it instructs the dealer to deliver the instrument to the safekeeping bank against payment of the amount of money due on the purchase. This ensures that the purchased instrument will be delivered exactly as ordered, because the safekeeping agent should reject the delivery if there is any discrepancy. The funds remain in the investor's account until the security is delivered. If, for some reason, the selling dealer is unable to make delivery, the funds do not leave the investor's account. The safekeeping bank renders a periodic statement showing all of the securities in the safekeeping account, which is an excellent audit tool.

Another very significant advantage of the DVP system is the investor's ability to deal with any securities dealer, wherever it may be located. The transaction is agreed to by the dealer and investor over the telephone, and the dealer then makes delivery in New York as described above. The need for wire transfers of funds is eliminated because the New York agent is able to charge the investor's account directly or charge its correspondent bank who charges the investor's account. This system eliminates the control problems associated with wire transfers and allows the investor to deal with more than just one or two investment dealers.

Bank safekeeping agents charge for their services. These charges may be based on the dollar value of the portfolio held by the agent or, more likely, on the basis of a price per transaction. Generally, all securities movements incur charges. Upon the purchase of an instrument, there is a charge for accepting it and lodging it in the inventory. At its sale prior to maturity, there is also a charge for delivering the instrument. These charges apply whether the instrument requires physical delivery of a piece of paper or only book-entry delivery.

An increasing number of securities are being made subject to book-entry delivery, including virtually all U.S. government securities. Book-entry delivery involves the maintenance of accounts with the Treasury. The Federal Reserve acts as the clearing agent for U.S. government securities and credits the delivery of securities to the investor by credit to the investor's account. Certain other securities also settle through the Federal Reserve account. Other clearing entities, such as Depository Trust Company, handle stocks and certain other corporate securities.

The importance of using an independent safekeeping agent cannot be overemphasized. This was demonstrated during the early 1980s when many securities dealers failed. Investors who had taken delivery of securities used as collateral for repurchase agreements or other securities purchased outright from these dealers generally did not lose any of their funds. The investors who were burned had left their securities in the custody of the dealers. Auditors discovered that many of these dealers, through either sloppy bookkeeping or outright fraud, had sold and resold securities owned by one investor to other investors simultaneously. This situation created multiple claims on the same securities and was common to virtually all of the failed investment banking houses. It makes the best case for taking possession of one's own securities through the use of a safekeeping agent.

(d) Operating an Investment Program

Having selected a custodian to hold the portfolio of securities in safekeeping and become familiar with the registration requirements of particular securities, the nonprofit financial manager still must establish the operating procedures for the execution of transactions. In this connection, certain documentation needs to be created or borrowed from other sources. These documents are designed to: (1) record the transactions as they are made, (2) control those transactions for research and follow-up, (3) provide the means by which an investment manager is reminded of the maturing securities in the portfolio, and (4) provide an audit trail.

The financial manager requires a systematic approach to investing. The basic elements of the system include:

- Execution of transactions
- Verification of transactions
- Delivery and safekeeping of instruments (previously discussed in this chapter)
- Reporting of transactions, portfolio inventory, and yield earned

A properly constructed set of documentation and procedures will facilitate the swift verification of transactions and the maintenance of appropriate records for reporting and research. The discussion below describes many details of the procedures and documents that are used in some well-designed investing programs.

(i) Executing Transactions.   It is very important for the person authorized to execute investment transactions to be fully aware of the internal rules and regulations contained in the written investing policy and guidelines. This document constitutes the "contract" between the manager who handles the investing program and the organization's senior management and Board of Directors or trustees.

Money-market investment transactions are executed on the telephone between the financial manager (or other authorized person) of the investor organization and the salesperson of the securities dealer. The financial manager may talk with salespeople of several dealers before agreeing to buy or sell a particular instrument at a certain price. Although the aggregate dollar volume of money market transactions each day is huge, there is no central marketplace and each dealer quotes his or her own prices to buy and sell particular securities. Therefore, financial managers should shop among several dealers for a competitive price (yield) value on their investment.

(ii) Transaction Memos.   The financial manager generally uses a form, called a transaction memo or ticket, that indicates the basic information, as depicted in Exhibit 12.3. Upon completing a transaction on the telephone, the financial manager fills out the transaction memo and sends a copy to the accounting department.

Another copy should be sent to a person responsible for independently verifying the transaction.

A description of each numbered component of the transaction memo illustrated in Exhibit 12.3:

1. *Transaction number:* a unique internal trace number assigned to each trade that identifies the particular transaction
2. *Name of issuer:* party whose indebtedness is evidenced by the investment instrument
3. *Par value:* stated value of the instrument; the amount that will be paid at maturity
4. *Type:* type of security (e.g., T-bills, CDs, BAs, commercial paper)
5. *Cost:* the amount paid by the investor to acquire the instrument
6. *Purchase date:* date on which the investor and dealer agree to make the transaction
7. *Settlement date:* date on which ownership of the instrument and payment will change hands
8. *Maturity date:* date on which the instrument is scheduled to be paid
9. *Coupon:* rate of interest paid on the instrument, as stated on the face of the instrument

Exhibit 12.3. Transaction Memo

Transaction no.: (1)	Name of issuer: (2)		Par value: (3)
Type: (4)	Cost: (5)	Purchase date: (6)	Settlement date: (7)
Maturity date: (8)	Coupon: (9)	Yield: (10)	Guarantor: (11):
Rating: (12)	Custodian: (13)	Delivery: (14)	Call provisions: (15):

Executed by: _____ Dealer: _____

Sales representative: _____

10. *Yield:* rate of return to the investor, based on the coupon as well as the cost

11. *Guarantor (if not the issuer):* name and form of guaranty (e.g., letter of credit) attached to the instrument, if any

12. *Rating:* rating assigned by a credit rating agency that predicts the degree of certainty applicable to the full and timely payment of principal and interest on the instrument

13. *Custodian:* name of the safekeeping custodian

14. *Delivery:* description of method of delivery (e.g., DVP, dealer hold)

15. *Call provisions:* date and price at which the instrument may be prepaid by the issuer, if any

(iii) Maturity Ticklers. A cardinal error in managing an investment portfolio is to lose track of maturing investments and unintentionally to leave the proceeds uninvested, even for a day. The financial manager, therefore, needs a foolproof system to signal maturing investments. If the portfolio inventory is maintained in a database, the database usually can be sorted by maturity date showing the earliest maturities first. As a backup procedure, the financial manager may also maintain a file of transaction memos in maturity date order and have an assistant check the file daily. It is a good idea to mark on the maturity file copy the ultimate disposition of the instrument, such as "matured" or "sold on (date) to (name of dealer)."

(iv) Transaction Log. To facilitate the tracking of inventory and the conduct of audits, each security purchase should be assigned a unique identification number. The simplest method is to assign consecutive transaction numbers by prenumbering the transaction memos in serial order. Another method is to incorporate the Gregorian or Julian date of the transaction together with a one- or two-digit number that recycles each day. As transactions are executed, they are recorded in a log, either paper or electronic, to show at a glance the transactions that have been conducted. Exhibit 12.4 depicts a sample transaction log sheet.

(v) Technology Tools. There are a number of important technology tools in the marketplace about which the financial management responsible for investment should be knowledgeable about. These tools include the Bloomberg, Reuters, or Quotron systems, provide essential information for investors. The Internet also provides other sources of financial information, including news groups, and discussion forums, as well as services which allow for the trading of stocks and bonds.

Exhibit 12.4. Transaction Log

Transaction no.	Cost	Issuer	Type	Settlement date	Maturity	Yield	Dealer

(vi) Verifying Transactions. To ensure the integrity of the investment operation, each transaction should be verified soon after execution by someone other than the person who executed the transaction. Verification takes the form of both verbal (immediately after the trade) and subsequently written confirmation from the broker or dealer and from the custodian. The verifications are matched to the transaction memo (see Exhibit 12.4) prepared by the financial manager prepared at the time of executing the transaction. If the three "tickets" (dealer, custodian, and the financial manager's transaction memo) match in all respects, they are then marked with the transaction number, stapled together, and filed, usually by transaction number. If there are any discrepancies, the verifier should be instructed to bring them to the attention of either the financial manager or that person's immediate superior, who should discuss the situation promptly with the financial manager. Responsibility for resolution of the discrepancy usually lies with the financial manager.

(vii) Reporting Transactions. The financial manager is responsible for reporting transactions, the inventory, and yield of the portfolio. Management should determine the frequency and extent to which reports are prepared and the distribution of these reports; however, the financial manager needs most of these reports for the internal operations and management of the portfolio.

The financial manager must have a continually updated listing of the inventory of investment instruments in order to conduct portfolio transactions. The inventory listing is often maintained in a database or electronic spreadsheet system. It should have the capability to sort by various data fields in order to give the financial manager immediate access to the portfolio on the basis of maturity date, issuer, type of security, yield, investment dealer, or custodian (if there is more than one).

Incorporated into the inventory listing can be a program that calculates and reports the weighted average maturity and the weighted average yield of the portfolio as of any moment in time. These two characteristics, maturity and yield, can be plotted periodically to show trends in yield and maturity length. In the management of the portfolio, there should be a close correlation between changes in cash need forecasts and average maturity of the portfolio. Again, it is important to remember that maturity date decisions should not be made on the basis of anticipated changes in interest rates, since this is sheer speculation by the financial manager.

(e) Operations Using an Outside Investment Manager

Use of an outside investment manager need not compromise the security of an investor's system. There are many ways in which outside investment managers operate, ranging from the mutual fund approach, to investors' separate accounts under complete control of the investment manager, to investors' separate funds with no access by the investment manager. Each outside manager has its own preference for the method of operation, and the investor's management should determine for itself the degree of control, if any, that it is willing to relinquish to an outside investment manager.

If management prefers not to relinquish control over its assets, then the investor's bank account configuration can include a separate "investments" bank account. The investment manager would be authorized to operate this account for DVP transactions only. An important advantage of this method is that all investment transactions, including purchases, sales, maturing investments, and dividend and interest collections, are run through this account and can be easily audited. Further, by isolating only investment transactions in the account, the investment manager can be in control of the full balance without that balance being disturbed by other noninvestment transactions. This permits re-investment of income, as well as principal, and places the burden on the investment manager to remain as fully invested as possible.

In addition, the institution authorizes the investment manager to give DVP instructions to the custodian. In this way, the investor's assets are protected; they are always in the form of either funds in the bank account or securities in the custodian account. They can never be used for other purposes.

(f) Investment Operations Summary

Initiation of an investment management program for a nonprofit institution requires careful planning well in advance of making the first investment. The institution's tolerance for investment risk must be assessed, the sources and ultimate uses for the investment funds must be examined and documented, and a written set of investing objectives and guidelines must be drafted and approved by senior management.

The financial manager should not embark on an investment program until these elements have been crafted. Otherwise, the institution may incur undue risk to principal, either through unwise credit exposure or excessive exposure to the vagaries of interest rates; or it may unwittingly invest in maturities that do not suit the liquidity or income requirements of the institution.

A nonprofit institution typically manages several forms of investment funds. These range from a pool of liquid investments used in the daily management of its receipts and disbursements streams, to grants awaiting payment, to fixed giving programs, to endowment funds, and to employee benefit and retirement funds. Each type of fund has its unique purpose and application, which the financial manager must recognize and invest accordingly.

Operation of an investment portfolio requires careful attention to the details of executing investment transactions and monitoring the resulting inventories. Systems and procedures must be established to ensure that all necessary information about transactions and inventories is readily available and that controls are in place to highlight promptly any errors that occur. The system also must be capable of producing reports of inventory and transactions in multiple versions to enable management to monitor compliance with guidelines and to audit the portfolio holdings.

Whether the portfolio is large or small, appropriate procedures and controls must be in place and made effective. The required procedures and controls include, but are not limited to, a system of checks and balances, reconciliation of records, written assignment of accountability to designated person(s), and written audit procedures and risk standards. Otherwise, the financial manager may jeopardize the safety and liquidity of the investment portfolio.

12.7 ENDOWMENT MANAGEMENT

(a) What Is Endowment?

An endowment is a fund donated to a tax-exempt (nonprofit) organization with a donor-imposed restriction that the funds not be expended but rather invested for the purpose of producing income. The earnings on the fund(s) can be used to advance its charitable, religious, or educational mission as long as the organization exists. It allows donors to transfer private dollars to the ongoing support of public purposes.

The function and purpose of an endowed fund is to provide monies through investment to be spent for a specific purpose today, while ensuring that the fund will exist in perpetuity. The overall management of an endowment must assure that adequate monies exist today to fund the named activity, as well as maintenance of comparable purchasing power in the future. An endowment investment policy that provides inadequate income for current needs while emphasizing long-term fund growth is as inflexible and constraining as a policy that spends too much on current programs and erodes the purchasing power of the endowment in the future.

There are three types of endowment:

- *True endowment:* contains donor provisions prohibiting the spending of principal

- *Quasi endowment:* does not carry the same legal prohibitions against spending principal, sometimes referred to as funds functioning as endowment
- *Term endowment:* allows the principal to be spent at a pre-specified date

(b) Why Is Endowment Important to Nonprofit Organizations?

Endowment is important to nonprofit organizations because it:

- Provides stability
  - Provides the ability to plan
  - Reduces pressures on the public for funds
  - Provides independence from economic and political forces
  - Subsidizes the organization's operating budget
  - Underscores the importance of the programs which they support
  - Provides flexibility
- Guarantees a long-term relationship between the donor and the institution

    All of the above factors improve the nonprofit organization's ability to carry out its mission. In today's world of reduced funding and competition for financial resources, most nonprofit organizations are looking more and more toward building their endowment so that endowment income is increased to support the annual spending for their programs. Exhibit 12.5 explains why the college and university sector is significantly referenced in the endowment management area.

    (i) Stability. Endowment provides stability to an organization because the principal of the endowment is not spent and generates earnings year after year to support the programs of the institution. This financial stability is important for all programs, especially those that cannot be easily stopped and restarted. Fluctuations in support can be costly and debilitating to programs.

    (ii) Reduced Pressure on Public. An endowment allows an organization to provide a higher level of service at a lower cost. Without endowments and other private gifts, nonprofit organizations would be forced to reduce their programs and services to the public and/or obtain additional public funding for their programs.

    (iii) Endowed Programs Are Important. The importance of programs that are supported by endowed funds is clearly stated by virtue of the endowment.

Exhibit 12.5. College and University Endowment Examples

Throughout this chapter, the college and university sector will be referenced in examples and trends in the endowment management area. Therefore, references are cited from National Association of College and University Business Officer (NACUBO) surveys as well as those of The Common Fund, which is a nonprofit, membership organization dedicated to educational institutions. The mission of The Common Fund is "to enhance substantially the financial resources of educational institutions through superior fund management and investment advice." The Common Fund has helped shape endowment management for more than 25 years."

Source: Reprinted, with permission, from The Common Fund's, *Principles and Objectives: The Common Fund Perspective,* 1997.

(iv) Flexibility. Endowed funds provide important flexibility to the nonprofit organization. Unrestricted endowed funds create additional flexibility because their use is unrestricted and can be determined by the organization's leadership to help meet its unfunded needs.

(v) Long-Term Relationship. A long-term relationship between the donor and the recipient of endowed funds is guaranteed because the endowed gift continues to give year after year in perpetuity. This continued giving encourages the ongoing relationship between the donor and the nonprofit organization. A donor who creates an endowment is assured that the gift will continue to support his or her vision in the future.

(c) How Is an Endowment Created?

As provided for in state trust and probate law, an endowment is created by donated funds where the donor stipulates that the income, but not the principal, may be spent. The income generated from the gift is used to support the program designated by the donor.

(d) How Can Endowments Be Directed?

Nonprofit organizations usually have many opportunities for endowed gifts. The nature of the opportunities depends upon the mission of the organization and the organization's unmet needs. In general, endowed funds can be earmarked for a special purpose, program, or area of interest. The direction of endowed gifts varies among nonprofit organizations and depends on the mission of the organization.

Examples of directed endowments in a college or university include endowed professorships in specific academic discipline, undergraduate scholarships, graduate fellowships, faculty research, teaching support, or community service.

Endowments can also be undesignated or unrestricted by the donor, so that the Board of Directors or President of the organization can use the income from endowment to meet the high-priority needs of the institutions, as determined by them.

At a large university, the following are some examples of how some endowments are directed:

- *Faculty Chair:* provides the resources to award a distinguished faculty member for academic achievement; income from the endowment provides funds for the chairholder to pursue new research, teaching, and other scholarly initiatives

- *Faculty Research Fund:* Supports the vital research of a renowned faculty member

- *Graduate Student Fellowship:* Enables the university to attract the best advanced degree candidates (helping to support future scholars and leaders in their special area of expertise)

- *Undergraduate Scholarships:* Provides support to an exceptionally talented student

- *Endowed Lecture Series:* Supports a lecture series allows the university to bring distinguished speakers to share their research with the campus and community at large

(e) Who Is Responsible for the Endowment?

(i) Board of Trustees. The Board of Trustees of the nonprofit organization has ultimate management and oversight responsibility for the endowment management functions of the organization. The Board is charged with the fiduciary responsibility of preserving and augmenting the value of the endowment. It is one of the Board's responsibilities to set the investment policy for the organization. Through its investment policy, investment objectives for the institution are spelled out to maximize total return. In organizations where size and resources allow, the Board often delegates responsibility for implementation of the investment objectives to a Board Committee.

An investment policy set by the Board of Trustees will address the following objectives:

- Support the current needs of the institution

- Preserve or enhance the purchasing power of the endowment

- Strike the appropriate balance between current and future interests

In larger nonprofit organizations, the Board committee structure includes an Investment Committee that is charged with managing the organizations investments, including endowment.

(ii) Investment Committee. The Investment Committee of the Board has fiduciary responsibility for the management of endowment assets. The Investment Committee may include members who are not on the Board of Trustees, although the Investment Committee Chair should be a Trustee.

In today's environment, the Investment Committee should be a small group that seeks professional investment advice from consultants and external investment managers. It is critical that the advice sought is relative to the needs of the organization and the size of its portfolio.

It is unusual in today's world for an Investment Committee to make its own direct investments, although the Committee can reserve the right to do so in certain circumstances. Today's role for members of the Investment Committee requires good judgment and the ability to work with other Investment Committee members and external money managers. It does not require the technical knowledge necessary to buy and sell securities.

The Investment Committee is responsible for developing the strategies and guidelines required by the nonprofit organization to meet the investment objectives set by the Board of Trustees.

Responsibilities of the Investment Committee include:

- Determining how to manage the investments of the organization
- Making asset allocation decisions
- Setting endowment spending rate targets
- Defining permitted and excluded investments
- Selecting, reviewing, and/or replacing investment managers
- Reviewing the performance of the endowment portfolio
- Monitoring compliance with endowment investment and management guidelines
- Providing periodic reports of investment operations and results to the Board of Trustees

(f) How Are Endowments Managed?

Each nonprofit organization determines its own strategies and rules for the management of its endowment funds. These strategies and rules are meant to maximize the endowment's ability to support both current spending and future needs without using principal.

Some institutions manage their endowment with internal staff; others rely on Trustees, external investment counselors, or some combination (multi-manager) of all these approaches. Some organizations manage their endowment investments to maximize annual income stream (interest and dividends); others manage to achieve total return (income plus capital appreciation) and set an annual spending rate to determine the amount of annual income devoted to programs.

(g) What Is UMIFA?

The Uniform Management of Institutional Funds Act (UMIFA) is a Federal law introduced in 1972 and immediately adopted by approximately 25 states, followed by a number of others up to the present day. UMIFA changed the complexity of endowment management from the simple practice of collecting and spending income from donated funds to many investment alternatives and spending options regulated by trust and corporation law. UMIFA opened up a number of investment opportunities to endowment managers.

UMIFA established five provisions:

1. Endowment funds can be pooled for purposes of investment, as in a mutual fund.

2. The "prudent man" standard can be applied to the endowment as a whole, and not necessarily to each separate investment. The "prudent man" requirement is rooted in trust law, which holds that Trustees can be held personally liable for investment losses if they do not act according to appropriate standards. Further, the "prudent man" might be described as an individual who makes his investments in a way that maximizes income and protects principal. The "prudent man" is not a speculator; he is prudent and discrete.

3. Endowment funds can be invested in the full range of investment vehicles, including new ones.

4. Capital appreciation may, under general circumstances, be spent without violating the prohibition against spending principal.

5. Trustees may delegate investment-management responsibilities.

The original UMIFA legislation is provided in Appendix 12A. Since 1974, 25 states have adopted a version of this law. The actual documents are quite lengthy and cannot be included in this publication. Additional information may be found in your local law library or university, or at various sites on the Internet (http://www.wfu.edu/~peilma/vol7).

(h) Modern Portfolio Theory

Modern portfolio theory (MPT), developed by Harry Markowitz during the 1950s, brings probability theory to investment management. Based on statistical analysis, MPT projects investment performance based on investments of different types in order to achieve optimal investment results. Markowitz and Sharpe received the Nobel Prize in 1990 for their work in this field. All large endowment, pension, and foundation funds use these MPT models to make their investment decisions.

12.8   CHARACTERISTICS OF ENDOWMENT

The characteristics of endowment in 1996, according to information provided by the National Association of College and University Business Officers (NACUBO) are as follows.

(a) Withdrawals from Endowment (Exhibit 12.6)

- On average, total withdrawals from endowment amount to 5.7 percent in fiscal 1996. Of this, 4.3 percent consisted of endowment payout, which corresponds to what most institutions label as "spending." Of the remainder, 0.5 percent went to pay investment management and custody fees, and 0.8 percent to "other distributions" that include nonrecurring capital expenditures funded from the endowment.

Exhibit 12.6.   Mean Withdrawals from Endowment

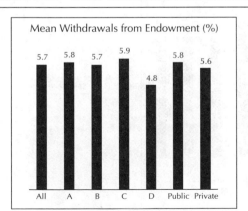

Source: Reproduced, with permission, *1996 NES Executive Summary,* © 1996 by National Association of Colleges and University Offices.

- On average, endowments over $100 million to $400 million report the highest rate of withdrawals (5.9 percent), while endowments over $400 million report the lowest (4.8 percent). Public institutions report a higher rate (5.8 percent) than those in the private sector (5.6 percent).

(b) Endowment Asset Allocation (Exhibit 12.7 and 12.8)

- Endowment holdings are classified into five broad asset categories: marketable securities, nonmarketable securities, noncampus real estate, campus real estate, and other miscellaneous assets.
- As of fiscal 1996 year-end, 89.1 percent of the assets of responding institutions was invested in marketable securities, 5.1 percent in nonmarketable securities, 3.6 percent in noncampus real estate, 0.6 percent in campus real estate, and the remaining 1.6 percent in other miscellaneous assets.
- On average, the largest endowments (greater than $400 million) have a significantly larger percentage of their portfolios committed to nonmarketable securities than the smaller institutions.

(c) Endowment Assets (Exhibits 12.9 and 12.10)

- 472 institutions participated in the 1996 NACUBO Endowment Study (NES), and 467 reported endowment assets totaling $123.2 billion.

Exhibit 12.7.   Endowment Asset Allocation

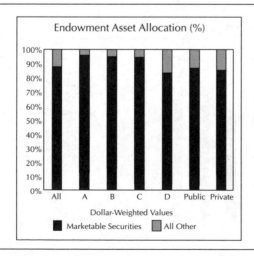

Source: Reproduced, with permission, *1996 NES Executive Summary,* © 1996 by National Association of College and University Business Officers.

Exhibit 12.8.   Endowment Asset Allocation: Nonmarketable Securities, Real Estate, and Other

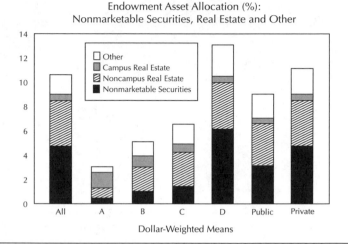

Source: Reproduced, with permission, *1996 NES Executive Summary,* © 1996 by National Association of College and University Business Officers.

Exhibit 12.9.   Total Reported Assets by Endowment Size

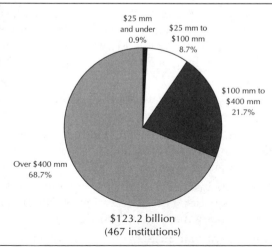

Source: Reproduced, with permission, *1996 NES Executive Summary,* © 1996 by National Association of College and University Business Officers.

Exhibit 12.10.   Total Reported Assets by Institution Type

Public
26.3%

Private
73.7%

$123.2 billion
(467 institutions)

Source: Reproduced, with permission, *1996 NES Executive Summary,* © by National Association of College and University Business Officers.

- This wealth remains highly concentrated; only 68 of these 467 schools have assets in excess of $400 million, yet they control 69 percent of the total.
- The largest endowment among all participating institutions continues to be that of Harvard University ($8.8 billion).
- The participating public institution with the greatest endowment assets per FTE student is the Virginia Military Institute Foundation ($131,357 per FTE student). Among private institutions, the highest ranking is Princeton University ($701,146 per FTE student).
- The study includes 326 private and 141 public institutions providing 1996 endowment market values.
- Slightly more than one-half of the public institutions in this year's NES are research universities, and they hold 86 percent of the public sector endowment assets.
- Among the private institutions participating, only 40 (12 percent) are research universities, but their portion of the private institutions' aggregate endowment assets is 63 percent.
- 46 percent of the private institutions included in the study are baccalaureate schools (i.e., liberal arts), and these control 22 percent of the private institutions' aggregate endowment assets.

12.9 ENDOWMENT INVESTMENT

(a) Endowment Investment Policy

Investment policy sets in writing the investment objectives of the endowed fund. Endowment investment policy is made up of two major components:

- Investment strategy
- Spending and accumulation policy

(b) Investment Philosophy

The key elements of any investment philosophy and objectives for endowment investing are:

- Maximization of real long-term total return within prudent levels of risk
- Safety of principal and liquidity
- Preservation of purchasing power by achieving returns which are equal or greater than the rate of inflation
- Increased income to support designated activities

Chapter 11 provides a more detailed discussion on investment policy and guidelines.

(c) Endowment Growth

Several factors contribute to endowment growth:

- Gift contributions
- Investment return
- Spending rate

Of the three factors that affect endowment growth, investment return and spending policy (which determine spending rates) are discussed in some detail in this chapter. Gift contributions are not discussed in detail. However, the combination of good management, accountability, investment returns, policies and procedures, performance review, and communication of all the above with donors and prospective donors will enhance the potential gift contributions for the future.

(d) Endowment Investment Return

Investment return is a key component of successful endowment management. Coupled with the endowment spending rate, it determines whether or not the endowment requirements of preserving principal, maintaining purchasing power, and funding the current program supported by the endowment can be achieved. An endowment investment strategy must be developed, implemented, monitored, and rebalanced in order to achieve the investment returns required to meet the endowment goal.

12.10 PRINCIPLES OF ENDOWMENT MANAGEMENT

The principles of endowment management include:

- Asset allocation
- Spending rate
- Equities investment
- Diversification
- Investment horizon
- Review of performance, including costs
- Risk tolerance

(a) Asset Allocation

Asset allocation decisions result in the mix of investments made with endowed funds. Asset allocation determines which assets are held and in what proportions, and it is a significant determinant of investment performance for the endowment. Many studies validate that asset allocation (in combination with spending decisions) far outweighs the contribution to return that investment managers make through selection of securities. Two landmark studies have confirmed this:

- "93 percent of long-term portfolio return is the result of asset allocation"[1]
- "90 percent of equity portfolio return is the result of equity style (growth, value) selection"[2]

Typically, endowments are invested in a mix of asset classes such as domestic equities, fixed-income securities, foreign equities, real estate, and private equities.

Once the organization sets its investment goals, the next and most important step is to make the asset-allocation and spending-policy decisions. These policy decisions determine whether or not an endowment accomplishes its goals.

Exhibits 12.11 and 12.12 display three asset allocation alternatives and the results.

[1]Gary P. Brinson, Randolph L. Hood, and Gilbert L. Beebower, "Determinants of Portfolio Performance," *Financial Analysts Journal*, (July–August 1986).
[2]William F. Sharpe, "Asset Allocation: Management Style and Performance Measurement," *The Journal of Portfolio Management*, (winter 1992).

Exhibit 12.11. Three Asset Allocation Alternatives

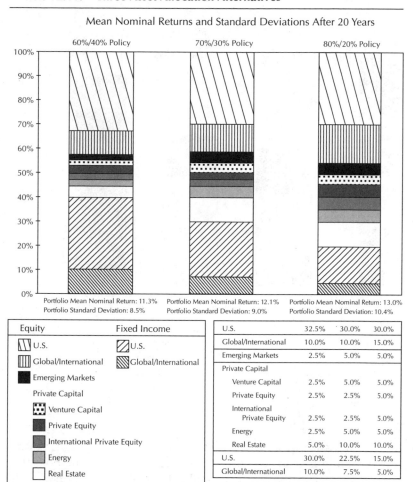

Mean Nominal Returns and Standard Deviations After 20 Years

Equity	Fixed Income		60%/40%	70%/30%	80%/20%
U.S.	U.S.	U.S.	32.5%	30.0%	30.0%
Global/International	Global/International	Global/International	10.0%	10.0%	15.0%
Emerging Markets		Emerging Markets	2.5%	5.0%	5.0%
Private Capital		Private Capital			
Venture Capital		Venture Capital	2.5%	5.0%	5.0%
Private Equity		Private Equity	2.5%	2.5%	5.0%
International Private Equity		International Private Equity	2.5%	2.5%	5.0%
Energy		Energy	2.5%	5.0%	5.0%
Real Estate		Real Estate	5.0%	10.0%	10.0%
		U.S.	30.0%	22.5%	15.0%
		Global/International	10.0%	7.5%	5.0%

Portfolio Mean Nominal Return: 11.3% (60%/40%), 12.1% (70%/30%), 13.0% (80%/20%)
Portfolio Standard Deviation: 8.5% (60%/40%), 9.0% (70%/30%), 10.4% (80%/20%)

Source: Reprinted, with permission, from The Common Fund's *Endowment Planning Model.*

(b) Spending Rate

The spending rate is inextricably linked to achieving the investment objectives of endowment investing. This is the case because endowment growth is significantly affected by the amount of endowment funds spent to support the ongoing program on an annual basis. As described by The Common Fund, Trustees are required to "maintain generational neutrality" to protect the purchasing power of the endowment in perpetuity. In order to accomplish this objective and achieve stability over time, spending must remain steady (net of inflation), and the principal must not be

Exhibit 12.12.   Endowment Planning Results from Three Asset Allocation Alternatives

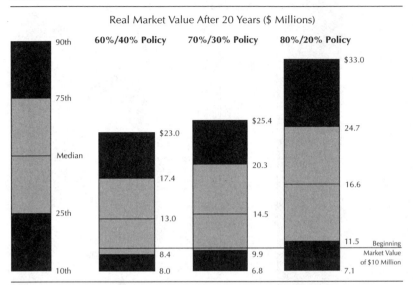

Real Market Value After 20 Years ($ Millions)

This chart represents the Endowment Planning Model results from three asset allocation alternatives based on a beginning market value of $10 million and a spending policy of 5 percent of a three-year moving average of market value. It shows graphically that by increasing the endowment's exposure to equities there is a greater probability of exceeding the original market value and experiencing real (net of inflation) growth in the endowment.

Source: Reprinted, with permission, from The Common Fund's *Endowment Planning Model.*

eroded. Further described by The Common Fund, these requirements "should lead Trustees to a specific investment objective, which is to earn a total return equal to the sum of inflation plus the spending rate and the costs associated with investing." Stated another way, a sustainable spending rate is total investment return minus inflation. Because asset allocation is the chief determinant of total return, asset allocation and spending are inexorably linked.

Exhibit 12.13 makes these points.

Since asset allocation and spending rates are inexorably linked, Exhibit 12.14 provides some useful calculations to help choose asset mixes and spending rates which are compatible.

Institutions have adopted a wide variety of spending policies, rates, rules, and practices. Exhibits 12.15 and 12.16 show existing trends in this area in the college and university setting.

Stock prices fluctuate widely, so different stock allocations are appropriate for different investors. Past stock performance is not indicative of future returns.

Exhibit 12.13.   Stocks, Bonds, Cash Equivalents, and Inflation Average Annual Compound Returns

	1935–1995 (60 Years)	1975–1995 (20 Years)	1985–1995 (10 Years)
Nominal Returns			
Stocks	11.6%	13.6%	14.7%
Bonds	5.0	10.1	12.2
Cash	4.0	7.3	5.7
Inflation	4.1%	5.4%	3.6%
Real Returns			
(Nominal Returns Adjusted for Inflation)			
Stocks	7.3%	7.8%	10.7%
Bonds	0.9	4.5	8.4
Cash	0.1	1.8	2.0

Stocks = S&P 500 Index = U.S. Long-Term Gov.t Bonds, Cash = U.S. 30-day T-Bill, Inflation = CP

Source: Used with permission. ©1997 Ibbotson Associates, Inc. All rights reserved. (Certain portions of this work were derived from copyrighted works of Roger G. Ibbotson and Rex Sinquefield.)

Exhibit 12.14.   Calculating Compatible Asset Mixes and Spending Rates

A quick calculation can help you match various asset mixes and spending levels:

- Total Return − Inflation = Real Return
- Real Return = Spending
- Assume Real Return Stocks = 7.3% and on Bonds = 0.9%

In order to determine the asset mix consistent with a 5 percent spending rate, solve the following equation: $7.3x + 0.9 (1 − x) = 5$, where x equals the proportion invested in stocks and $1 − x$ equals the proportion invested in bonds. Answer: 60 percent stocks/40 percent bonds.

How much can you spend without depleting the purchasing power of the endowment?

Equity/Fixed-Income Asset Mix	Spending
80%/20%	6.0%
70%/30%	5.5%
60%/40%	5.0%
50%/50%	4.0%
40%/60%	3.5%

Source: Used with permission. ©1997 Ibbotson Associates, Inc. All rights reserved. (Certain portions of this work were derived from copyrighted works of Roger G. Ibbotson and Rex Sinquefield.)

Exhibit 12.15.   Median Expected Real Endowment Value Assuming 80 percent/20 percent Policy and Different Spending Rates

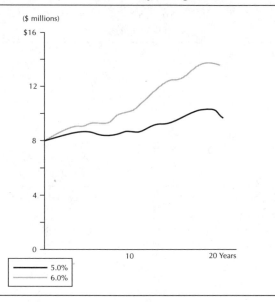

Source: Reprinted, with permission, from The Common Fund's *Endowment Planning Model.*

Exhibit 12.16.   Median Expected Real Spending from Endowment Assuming 80 percent/20 percent Policy and Different Spending Rates

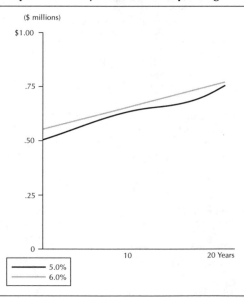

These graphs show that spending a lower percentage of market value results in a higher dollar level of spending over the long term. After 20 years, schools spending 5 percent will be able to spend more than those spending 6 percent.

Source: Reprinted, with permission, from The Common Fund's *Endowment Planning Model.*

(c) Bonds

Bonds can provide income and the potential for capital appreciation to your portfolio. Complementing a stock portfolio with bonds helps diversify the total investment because bonds often do well when stocks do not.

Bond prices depend on several factors, the most important of which is the level of interest rates. In general, bond prices appreciate as interest rates fall, and vice versa. Generally, when the economy is improving, inflation tends to rise and interest rates tend to follow. As a result, bonds often do not appreciate significantly in price and will probably fall. Conversely, when the economy is not doing well, rates tend to fall and prices tend to rise.

A bond's income or yield changes with interest rates and is also affected by many other factors. Bonds are issued by many countries, states, localities, and corporations. They come in various qualities and have different maturity periods that may be 30 years or longer. Bond selection should be determined by your investing time frame, risk tolerance, and need for current income.

(d) Equities Investment (Stocks)

History shows that over time, stocks have a greater return than bonds and short-term securities (see Exhibit 12.17).

Exhibit 12.17.   Historical Return by Asset Class

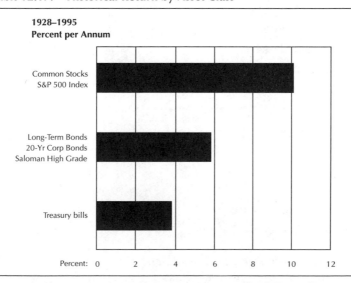

1928–1995
Percent per Annum

Source: Used with permission. ©1997 Ibbotson Associates, Inc. All rights reserved. (Certain portions of this work were derived from copyrighted works of Roger G. Ibbotson and Rex Sinquefield.)

A stock's return on investment is determined by many factors including the company's management, industry, country or region, and the economy. Stocks of small, cutting-edge companies (small-cap stocks), for example, do not perform the same during various market cycles as the stocks of large, well-established companies (large-cap stocks). The style of investing in equities is also a significant determinant of portfolio performance. Two well-known styles of stock investing are "value" and "growth". Each style is successful at various times. Value managers seek stocks of established companies that are currently undervalued. These stocks pay high dividends and feature low selling prices compared to their earnings and book values. Growth managers focus on the future and buy stocks of fast-growing companies exhibiting accelerated earnings and increasing market share. Growth managers believe that rapidly growing sales and earnings will benefit stockholders. The stock of growth companies can be very volatile.

(e) Diversification

After asset allocation decisions are made for the organization, these assets can be spread to achieve greater investment diversity. The goal of diversification is to increase the probability that your investment portfolio will achieve or exceed the earning goals.

Many techniques are used to diversify, and the list grows each day. Some of the ways in which an investment portfolio can be diversified are by:

- Investment type
- Investment class
- Manager style
- Single vs. multi-manager
- Type of issues
- Industry sector
- Geography
- Time
- Domestic vs. global
- Small cap vs. large cap
- Emerging markets

(i) *Diversification by Investment Type or Asset Class.* Diversification by type or asset class refers to investing in stocks, bonds, and short-term securities. Investment managers choose to invest in assets from different classes, based on their style. Examples of current asset classes are: cash, equities, bonds, real estate, and venture capital.

It is important for the financial manager in the nonprofit organization to be aware that these various aspects of the professional investment discipline exist and are considered in the development and implementation of an investment program for the nonprofit organization.

(ii) Diversification by Manager (Styles and Single Versus Multi-Manager). Professional investment managers have different styles. In this context, style refers to the approach used by the investment manager to select securities for investment. Style refers to the stocks that an investor picks and the process by which he or she decides to choose specific stocks. Two important but different styles of management are "value" and "growth." Each style is successful at various times and tends to move in and out of favor. Subcategories of these two major styles further describe how the manager makes investment choices.

The investment policy and guidelines should spell out who will manage the investment portfolio. Will the portfolio be managed in house, by external professional money managers, or by a combination of both? If external money managers are engaged, will there be one or more than one? Generally, the multiple-manager approach is the most effective because it provides a number of investment-style options. However, too many managers and duplication of styles should be avoided because they are difficult to administer and expensive. One advantage of a single manager is that the Investment Committee can delegate asset allocation decisions. The multiple-manager approach is more demanding on the Investment Committee. If more than one professional manager is hired, it must be determined what style of manager is to be hired. Consultants are available to assist in identifying styles and to report historical performance of the manager.

(iii) Diversification by Type of Issuer. Four basic forms of debt issuers are: (1) governments, (2) banks, (3) industrial companies, and (4) finance companies. Presumably, the banking industry could become severely stressed, with all banks as a group suffering in credit quality. This condition probably would affect other companies functioning in the economy, but it can be assumed that the other companies would not be as directly affected as the banks. Industrial companies as a group could be impacted by a recession; the finance companies that support their sales would not be as affected, because their portfolios of receivables are very broadly based. These examples indicate that diversification by type of issuer makes sense. However, some companies erroneously believe

in diversification by type of instrument. The instruments are irrelevant if they are all guaranteed by the same type of issuer.

(iv) Diversification by Industry Sector. Industry is divided into sectors such as utilities, technology, and manufacturing.

(v) Diversification by Geography. Most investors attempt to maintain a geographical dimension to their portfolio diversification. Many factors influence the world's economies, including economic mismanagement and differentials in interest rates between countries. Investments of nonprofit institutions in debt instruments issued by both U.S. and foreign companies and banks should not present a problem. However, quite often, debt instruments issued by a particular bank or company will offer both higher yields and very good credit quality. The institution should exercise care in preventing its portfolio from being dominated by instruments of one country or one industry, or of several countries closely related to each other. Events could occur within a country or industry that would adversely affect investments. Civil war, severe inflation resulting in economic chaos, a natural disaster, or sudden political instability can wreak havoc on an institution's portfolio that is not well diversified. Investing guidelines should place a dollar or percentage limit, or both, on the portion of a portfolio that may be invested in the securities of any one country, region, or industry.

(vi) Diversification by Global (Foreign) Investing. We are living in an increasingly global society, and new markets are rapidly evolving around the world. In 1980, the U.S. stock market represented more than one-half of the world's stock market value; now it represents less than 40 percent as foreign stocks outperform U.S. stocks and as new markets emerge around the world.

Global investing allows access to these growth and income prospects. When the U.S. economy is struggling, the foreign markets in England, Japan, Germany, and other countries may provide good investment opportunities. Foreign stocks and bonds provide a way to further diversify your investment portfolio.

(f) Investment Time Horizon

A long-term investment perspective tends to reduce investment risk. Volatility is reduced when assets are held over longer time periods and yet returns can be enhanced. How is performance measured and reported?

(i) Risk Tolerance. Risk management involves assessing the potential for loss under any circumstances. Risk is managed by

implementing sound internal controls and procedures as well as monitoring external managers controls, monitoring compliance with the investment guidelines for the organization, engaging in due diligence and manager oversight, and reviewing performance.

Controlling the risk of an investment portfolio involves allocating the investment among small and large company stock and domestic and foreign company stock to participate in both the "growth" and "value" styles of investing.

Asset quality can be determined by consulting asset quality ratings assigned by well-respected agencies such as Standard and Poor's, Moody's, and others. A list of generally accepted rating agencies is provided in Exhibit 12.1. Two measures of risk are volatility and duration.

(ii) Volatility.   Volatility is the characteristic of a security or market to rise or fall sharply in price within a short period of time.

(iii) Duration.   Duration is a concept that measures bond price volatility by the length or time period of a bond.

(g) Managing Risk

Managing risk means assessing the loss under any circumstances, risk tolerance. Managing risk is a critical factor in endowment management programs. A number of risk elements are involved in any endowment management program. Some key areas of internal and external risk, to be managed and monitored, include:

- People
- Partnership
- Financial
- Manager oversight
- Compliance with investment and guidelines
- Performance review
- Due diligence
- Communications risk
- Technology
- Operations
- Policy and procedures
- Credit
- Interest rate
- Volatility

- Currency
- Legal
- Liquidity
- Accounting
- Concentration
- Capital

The successful nonprofit organization will perform a risk-assessment survey in its own endowment management program to identify and reduce those risks before significant losses are incurred.

(h) Monitoring Performance

Monitoring performance of the organization's endowment management program is essential. The checklist provided below will be useful in the development of such a performance monitoring program.

Your investment performance review program should:

- Compare the performance of your investment portfolio to comparable, acceptable benchmarks (see Exhibit 12.18)
- Compare investment returns with inflation rates
- Compare investment return with investment returns of the market in general
- Compare your investment returns with investment returns of similar investments
- Compare your investment return with investment returns of competing investments
- Compare your investment return with historical comparisons
- Compare the cost of your investing to industry standards
- Obtain an independent analysis of your program's investment performance
- Quantify level of risk assumed relative to return

12.11 ENDOWMENT SPENDING POLICY

Endowment spending policy is a unique component of endowment management that does not come into play in other long-term investing programs in the nonprofit organization. Endowment spending policy should not be confused with endowment investment policy. However, endowment investment policy includes endowment spending policy since the two are integrally related and must be compatible.

Endowment investment policy deals with issues related to how the investments are made, and spending policy addresses

Exhibit 12.18.   Indices Used as Benchmarks for Comparing Investment Performance

Equity

- DJIA
- DJ Global—U.S.
- DJ Global—world
- S&P 500
- Nasdaq Comp.
- London (FT 100)
- Tokyo (Nikkei 225)
- Small-Co., Index Fund
- Lipper Index: Europe
- Barra
- Russell 1000, 2000, 3000
- Morgan Stanley World Index
- MSCI EAFE (Europe, Asia, and the Far East)

Fixed Income

- Lehman Brothers
- Aggregate Bond Index, Corporate/Government Bond Index
- Salomon Mortgage-Backed
- Bond Buyer Municipal (tax-exempt clients)
- Merrill Lynch Corporate and Government Bond Indices
- Lipper L-T Government
- Consumer Price Index (Inflation measure to compare or measure objective of preserving purchasing power)

Others

- Commodity Research Bureau (CRB) Index
- Goldman Sachs Commodity Index

Source: Reproduced, with permission, *1996 NES Executive Summary,* © 1996 by National Association of College and University Business Officers.

how much of the endowment income or return can be spent to support programs on an annual basis.

Spending policy deals with issues such as:

- How should the current needs of the institution be weighed against its future needs?
- How much of the return from endowment funds should be spent and how much saved?

Examples of spending policy rates are:

- *Spend income only:* Spending only the current income (dividends and interest) earned on the endowed investment.

- *Spend total return:* The total return of a portfolio is the combination of interest, dividends, and other current earnings, plus capital appreciation (or less capital depreciation) for the period. Thus, a fund utilizing the total-return approach may spend not only current investment income, but also may use a portion of capital appreciation over time as part of its spending rate.

(a) Endowment Investment Strategy—A Discussion

The determination of investment strategy for endowment funds can be viewed as the resolution of creative tension existing between the demand for immediate income and the need for a growing stream of income to meet future needs.

Investment policy deals with issues such as: How to diversify? What level of risk is to be assumed in the investment portfolio? How can the investment focus from income to total return? How can the focus be shifted from the performance of the individual investment to the performance of the total portfolio? How can new investment opportunities, like venture capital and emerging markets, be incorporated into the portfolio? How can new delegations of authority and responsibility be used in managing the endowment investment portfolio?

Spending policy deals with issues such as: How should the current needs of the nonprofit organization be weighed against its needs in the future? How much of the return from endowment funds should be spent and how much saved?

(b) Investment Policy

The current investment policy of some nonprofit organizations is one of total return; specifically, to maximize real, long-term total return and to preserve capital and the purchasing power of endowed projects. The spending policy, however, is to spend income only. Thus, the investment policy is to invest for total return (income plus capital appreciation), with the spending policy being to pay only current income earned (excluding any realized capital gain) during the period.

The investment management world has changed dramatically in the past few decades. The UMIFA allows governing boards to operate according to principles which take full advantage of available investment vehicles. Important developments in the field include expansion of the "prudent man rule," introduction of portfolio theory, new investment opportunities, and delegation of investment decisions.

Current investment strategy generally indicates that diversification pays, risk should be judged in the context of the total portfolio, and investment performance should be judged over the long term, not the short term.

Increasingly diverse asset classes are emerging that pay few or no dividends. The prospect for lower yields on fixed-income investments remains for the foreseeable future. Both of these trends mean that it will be difficult to maintain the income streams at their historic or current levels without change asset mix or putting unnecessary constraints on investment selection.

This points to the need for endowment funds to have highly qualified and skilled professional managers who are not overly constrained. It is likewise important to develop a clearly defined plan of long-term investment strategy and to retain it despite other variable factors as long as the fundamental assumptions on which it is based can be shown to have continuing validity.

(c) Spending Policy

Existing endowment funds are invested to return current income or yield (interest, dividends, and rents) and, usually, capital gains. A critical question is whether an institution contributes only its endowment yield, or a combination of its yield and gain, to the operating budget.

If the decision is to contribute only endowment yield, spendable income becomes a by-product of the investment policy. If an institution opts for the latter, it must adopt a "spending rule" that determines how yield and gain totals are allocated between the operating budget and endowment. The "spending rule" approach requires a considered choice between spending and saving.

Adoption of a total-return spending policy with a spending rule decouples investment decisions from spendable income decisions. On the other hand, spending rules add complexity and require strong discipline.

(d) Total Return Spending

Many endowments have adopted a total-return approach to their spending policies. The total return of a portfolio is the combination of interest, dividends, and other current earnings, plus capital appreciation (or less capital depreciation) for the period. Thus, a fund utilizing the total-return approach may not only spend current investment income, but also may use a portion of capital appreciation over time as a part of its spending rate.

The investment community is aware of the Ford Foundation study on the total return spending approach during the late 1960s and the fact that many concepts introduced in that study have proven to be sound over time. This is evidenced by the results of the

1996 NACUBO study of trends in endowment management spending rules in colleges and universities, as cited in Exhibit 12.19.

Today many endowment governing boards use various approaches to setting investment policies, establishing a meaningful spending rate, and using a variety of formulas to incorporate these factors into a total rate of return approach. Funds using these techniques have benefited from the achievement of consistently above-average returns over time. In terms of the real objectives (inflation adjusted) of these funds, risk has been modified rather than significantly increased.

(e) Spending Rates

A number of formulas have been developed by different endowments to establish their total return objective, generally inclusive of the rate of inflation and a compatible maximum spending rate. Such formulas indicate how much of the total return may be used for the endowment's current needs as opposed to being re-invested. The spending rate can be viewed as a specific portion of the total return (e.g., 5 percentage points) applied to a moving average of asset values over any period desired (e.g., the past three years or five years).

The desired rate of return and spending rate require careful consideration and thought, although many endowments tend to pick these rates somewhat arbitrarily and to set them at levels too high to be justified by historical experience. Over long periods of

Exhibit 12.19. Endowment Spending Rules

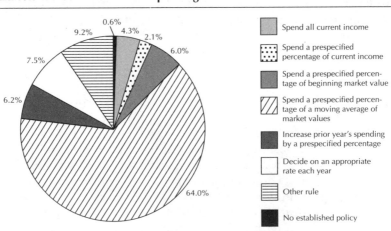

Source: Reproduced, with permission, *1995 NACUBO Endowment Study,* © 1995 by National Association of College and University Business Officers.

time, spending rates exceeding 5 percent ultimately result in erosion of the purchasing power of the principal, as the spending rate plus inflation begins to exceed actual rates of return.

Endowments with higher proportions invested in common stock have less risk in this regard because equities have historically provided higher returns than fixed-income securities over longer periods of time, but they also pay less current income.

Exhibit 12.20 shows the current trends in this area for colleges and universities.

(f) Effect of Inflation

One problem facing all endowment fund managers is the requirement that funds must grow to compensate for inflation. Endowment funds depend upon their returns on an ongoing, continuous basis. As seen in Exhibit 12.21, in endowment funds, fluctuation in principal can be tolerated, but fluctuation of income generally cannot.

(g) Implementation Issues
When Spending Policy Is Set or Changed

If your nonprofit organization changes its spending policy from income only to total return, the checklist below will help ensure that all related changes are also part of the implementation.

Exhibit 12.20. Spending Rules for 1996

Spending Rule	Participating Institutions	
	Number	Percentage
Spend all current income	20	4.3%
Spend a prespecified percentage of current income	10	2.1%
Spend a prespecified percentage of beginning market value	28	6.0%
Spend a prespecified percentage of a moving average of market values	299	64.0%
Increase prior year's spending by a prespecified percentage	29	6.2%
Decide on an appropriate rate each year	35	7.5%
Other rule	43	9.2%
No established policy	3	0.6%
Total	467	100.0%

Source: Reproduced, with permission, *1995 NACUBO Endowment Study,* © 1995 by National Association of College and University Business Officers.

Exhibit 12.21. Correlations among Selected Asset Classes and Inflation

	S&P 500	U.S. Small Cap	Venture Capital	International Equity	Real Estate	U.S. Treasuries	U.S. Treasuries	U.S. Treasuries	International Bonds
S&P 500	1.00								
U.S. Small Cap	0.76	1.00							
Venture Capital	0.28	0.22	1.00						
International Equity	0.55	0.43	0.19	1.00					
Real Estate	0.24	−0.20	−0.04	−0.12	1.00				
1-Year U.S. Treasuries	0.07	−0.09	0.02	−0.01	0.38	1.00			
5-Year U.S. Treasuries	0.13	0.12	0.04	0.06	−0.23	−0.14	1.00		
20-Year U.S. Treasuries	0.06	0.06	0.00	0.01	−0.25	−0.32	0.88	1.00	
International Bonds	0.09	0.07	0.05	0.42	−0.12	−0.07	0.50	0.45	1.00
Inflation	−0.32	−0.26	−0.07	−0.19	0.52	0.42	−0.06	−0.02	−0.05

Source: Reprinted, with permission, from the Common Funds' *Endowment Planning Model.*

This change presented a number of other challenges including:

- Review individual fund terms for all true endowments to determine spending requirements
- Determine how much to spend, and establish a formula
- Evaluate economic conditions, levels of risk, price-level trends, expected total return
- Invest in more than just fixed-income securities
- Set spending rules and rates
- Make related policy changes
- Review and respond to all legal and accounting issues
- Change related procedures
- Attend to detail of ongoing processing
- Track the addition of new funds and contributions to existing funds to determine the base to be used for calculating total return
- Increase levels of education, communication, and training for everyone involved

(h) Endowment Spending Policy Summary

Endowment funds are a critical source of funding for nonprofit organizations. They are given by donors for a specific purpose and invested by the nonprofit organization through prudent investment policy to ensure that the purchasing power of the funds will exist in perpetuity. This responsibility is achieved by setting comprehensive investment strategy to govern the investment of endowment for the institution.

Two of the most important components of this investment strategy are investment policy and spending policy. Investment policy deals with issues such as diversification, level of risk, and investment focus. Spending policy deals with weighing present needs against future needs and determining how much endowment return should be spent and how much saved.

Some nonprofit organizations have a total-return investment policy and an income-only spending policy. This means that investments are made with a total-return objective (the sum of income earned, and realized and unrealized appreciation), while spending is limited to income only.

The policy to spend income only has been very successful to date for some organizations, but like all policies, it should be periodically reviewed to make sure it is the best policy for the future. In the university setting, 86 percent of the 440 institutions responding to the 1993 NACUBO study have adopted a spending policy other than to spend income only. Today many endowment boards use a total return investment approach and a pre-set spendable income target. Many of these funds have achieved consistently above-average rates of return over time and are well positioned for the future.

Some organizations have adopted a total-return spending policy with a spending rule to mitigate the effects of short-term market volatility on spending from endowment.

This policy change should be considered by nonprofit organizations, in part, to make it easier to fulfill their investment strategy for the endowment pool of total return through principal growth and consistent growth in income. With increasingly diverse asset classes developing in the market, it is more difficult to obtain both objectives. Equity investments that often have the best potential for principal growth may pay few or no dividends, making income growth difficult. In a falling or stable interest rate environment, fixed income instruments may not provide any significant level of income growth. In an endowment with 2.3 percent of the pool invested in emerging-market equities and venture-capital partnerships, two areas where the potential for significant principal growth is very high, the current income generated is 0.18 percent of market value (as compared to 2.66 percent of market value for domestic equities). A spendable income policy that spends a pre-set amount from income or capital appreciation should eliminate any potential conflict or impede the investment strategy for the endowment pool.

Adoption of a total-return spending policy will increase flexibility for the nonprofit organization through the provision of:

- A stable and easily predictable source of funds to support its mission and programs
- Flexibility for the investment committee to consider a variety of investment vehicles without the consideration of current yields or interest rates

(i) Definitions of Terms Used in Endowment Management

- *Alternative equities:* investments in emerging markets and venture capital partnerships, which are included in equity holdings
- *Asset allocation:* the distribution of endowment or investment pool assets among various asset classes (e.g., cash, equities, bonds, real estate, venture capital)
- *Average annual total return:* a hypothetical rate of return that, if achieved annually, would have produced the same cumulative total return if performance had been constant over the entire period
- *Inflation rate:* measured in terms of the Consumer Price Index (CPI) to reflect changes in the price of goods and services (the rate of inflation affects the purchasing power of endowments)

- *Investment management fees:* charges incurred for the external or internal management of assets

- *Quasi-Endowment:* a type of endowment treated as permanent capital that functions like a true endowment and permits spending of principal and income as provided in the gift agreement

- *Spending rate:* expressed as a percentage of market value, it represents amounts withdrawn from an investment pool or endowment; distribution calculated as an annual rate and may include earned income as well as net realized or unrealized gains

- *Spending policy:* the guideline used by an institution to determine annual distributions from its endowment

- *Investment policy:* the goal set by the Board of Trustees for its organization's investment return

- *Total return:* gain or loss plus income generated

- *True endowment:* assets donated to provide permanent financial support to designated activities of the nonprofit organization; consists of permanent capital and an ongoing stream of current cash; intended to support a program or activity in perpetuity

- *Yield:* the rate of income earned on invested assets calculated as a percentage of total market value; consists of interest and dividend income earned from cash, money market, bond, stock, or mutual fund holdings

- *Diversification:* participation in different asset classes in domestic and global financial markets

- *Specialty-managers approach:* use of multiple specialized investment managers to access different investment styles and varied investment strategies

- *Endowment pool:* a group of endowment funds consolidated into one pool for purposes of investment

- *Hedging:* strategy used to offset an investment risk—a perfect hedge is one eliminating the possibility of a gain or loss

- *Small-cap stocks:* small-capitalization stocks—usually have a market capitalization (number of shares outstanding multiplied by the stock price) of $500 million or less

- *Large-cap stocks:* large-capitalization stocks—usually have a market capitalization of $1 billion or more

- *Liquidity:* ability to buy or sell an asset quickly, and in large volume, without affecting the asset's price

- *Efficient markets:* a theory that states that the market prices reflect the knowledge and expectation of all investors

- *Maintain purchasing power:* to maintain the purchasing power of endowment funds, the long-term total return of the invested endowment portfolio must be equal to, or greater than, the rate of inflation

12.12 INVESTMENT ADVISERS

(a) Professional Investment Advisers

The nonprofit organization's financial manager, because of other duties, may find the operation, supervision, and management of the institution's investment portfolio unduly burdensome. Proper investment management requires hands-on experience in the securities marketplace. It is also necessary to maintain complete records that account for portfolio transactions, provide reports, stay abreast of changes and trends in the securities markets, and continually remain within the bounds prescribed by the firm's investing guidelines and the overall context of an investing strategy.

These responsibilities, further explained in subsequent chapters, may be impossible for the nonprofit organization's financial manager to handle along with other duties. Therefore, many financial managers turn to outside professional investment advisers for assistance in managing their organizations' investment portfolios. Professional advisers with the necessary qualifications and investment expertise constitute a useful resource for the institution.

(b) Reasons for Using Outside Investment Advisers

Outside investment advisers are used by organizations with portfolios of all sizes. One major reason for employing an outside investment adviser is the organization's lack of a sufficiently large portfolio to support a full-time, in-house investment manager and the research and information services needed for an in-house investment manager to function properly. Often, institutions with small portfolios are in the greatest need of outside advisers. With the small portfolio, the financial manager probably is not attuned to the fast-paced securities markets. Consequently, the overall knowledge of markets and investment securities is at a relatively low level, and the financial manager can easily make a mistake that would cost the organization dearly.

Another reason for using an outside investment adviser is a large portfolio that is not permanent. This effectively prevents the investor from hiring permanent staff to manage the portfolio and makes it desirable to retain outside professional investment management. When the investment funds are no longer available, the relationship with the investment adviser can be terminated.

Professional investment advisers outside the institution can be particularly helpful in monitoring investment changes and trends in the marketplace. A competent adviser usually can enhance the profitability of the institution's portfolio sufficiently to offset their fee. The adviser provides an additional service by reducing the risk of loss due to inadequate evaluation of risk, as well as reducing the risk of loss of employment by the financial manager when principal losses occur. The financial manager also has more time available for other responsibilities.

(c) Types of Outside Investment Advisers

Two types of outside professional investment advisers work with financial managers in handling investment portfolios: investment managers and investment consultants. Investment manager services range from simple advisory consultation (with no authority to manage investments) to full management control over investment activities. The latter use their own discretion in the selection of particular instruments within client-approved guidelines. Investment managers often specialize in one investment area, such as stocks or fixed-income instruments, as well as other specifics, such as in equities emerging growth-type issues, global, and capitalization (see Exhibits 12.22 and 12.23). Within the fixed-income arena, they may specialize in short-, intermediate-, or long-term maturities. Generally, institutions seek investment managers who specialize in short- to intermediate-term maturities of fixed-income securities for their working cash investments and stock, and long-term bond managers for their endowment or growth-type portfolios.

Investment consultants (see Exhibit 12.24), on the other hand, do not manage funds; rather, they assist the financial manager by

Exhibit 12.22. Traditional Asset Classes—Examples of Various General Investment Manager Specialties by Investment Objective

Equity	*Balanced*
• Capital Appreciation	• Stock/Bond Blend
• Growth	
• Small-Company	*Fixed Income*
• Mid-Cap Stock	• Short-Term Debt
• Growth & Income	• Intermediate Corp. Debt
• Equity Income	• Intermediate Government
• Global (including U.S.)	• Long-Term Corp.
• International (non-U.S.)	• High Yield Taxable
	• Mortgage Bond
	• World Income

Exhibit 12.23. Nontraditional Asset Classes

Market Neutral

- U.S. Convertible/Warrant Hedging
- Japanese Convertible/Warrant Hedging
- European Convertible/Warrant Hedging
- Statistical Arbitrage—Global
- Fixed-Income Arbitrage—Global
- Long/Short
- Long/Short Japan
- Long/Short Utilities
- Closed-End Fund Arbitrage
- Pairs Trading
- Emerging Market Debt

Event Drivers

- Distressed Debt
- Capital Structure Arbitrage
- Merger Arbitrage
- Distressed Mortgages
- Niche Financing
- Mezzanine
- Bank Debt

Hedge Funds

- Global Long/Short
- Regional and Country Funds
- Sector Funds
  - Technology
  - Energy
  - Banking
  - Healthcare
  - Natural Resources
- Macro Trading
- Day Trading
- Commodities
- Emerging-Market Equities
- Emerging-Market Debt

Private Investments

- Venture Capital
- Buyout Funds
- Real Estate
- Distressed
- Sector Funds
- Emerging Markets
- International
- Regulation D
- SBIC/Mezzanine

Exhibit 12.24.   Representative List of Investment Consulting Firms

Asset Strategy Consulting	11766 Wilshire Boulevard 12th Floor Los Angeles, CA 90025
Callan Associates Inc.	Ms. Martha Spano 71 Stevenson Street Suite 1300 San Francisco, CA 94105 (415) 974-5060
Cambridge Associates	Bert Whitehead Detroit (Franklin) Office 2611 W. 14 Mile Road Suite #100 Franklin, MI 48025 (810) 737-7094
	Savvas Giannakopoulos Ann Arbor Office 5340 Plymouth Road Suite #200 Ann Arbor, MI 48105 (313) 741-8191
	Bert Whitehead Arizona Office (also Services CA of FL) 6700 N. Oracle Road Ste. 409 Tucson, AZ 85704
Canterbury Consulting	Mr. D. Robinson Cluck 660 Newport Center Drive Newport Beach, CA 92660 (714) 721-9580
Frank Russell Company	Mr. George Oberhofer 909 A Street Tacoma, WA 98402 (253) 572-9500
Hewitt Associates	Mr. Timothy G. Solberg 100 Half Day Road Lincolnshire, IL 60069 (847) 295-5000
Paine Webber	Mr. Joseph W. Martin Jr. 2800 Sand Hill Road Menlo Park, CA 94025 (415) 233-7049

(continues)

Exhibit 12.24.   Representative List of Investment Consulting Firms (*continued*)

SEI Investments	Mr. James Woods SEI Investments Oaks, PA 19456 (610) 676-2264
Watson Wyatt Investment Consulting	Ms. Adrian P. Anderson 345 California Street Suite 1400 San Francisco, CA 94104 (415) 986-6668
Willshire Associates	1299 Ocean Avenue Suite 700 Santa Monica, CA 90401-1085
Wurts & Associates	Mr. Victor Lee 999 Third Avenue Suite 3650 Seattle, WA 98104 (206) 622-3700
Yanni-Bilkey	Mr. James E. Yanni 2500 Grant Building Pittsburgh, PA 15219 (412) 232-1000

reviewing the institution's investment objectives and other investment needs and searching for a suitable investment adviser/manager in the marketplace who appears qualified to fill those needs. Investment consultants are not only instrumental in selecting an outside investment manager, but they also may help to develop the investing guidelines, monitor the investment adviser's performance, periodically review current strategies, and make recommendations for adjustments in any of the above.

(d) Selecting an Outside Investment Manager

The selection process for an investment manager should include careful attention to all appropriate details. Frequently, an investment consultant is enlisted to assist in the selection, as referenced above. The process begins with the consultant's review of existing guidelines to ensure that they adequately address the client's investing objectives and provide the necessary amount of flexibility. For example, it hardly would be worthwhile to retain an investment manager if the guidelines restricted the portfolio to U.S. Treasury bills maturing in 90 days or less.

When a well-crafted set of investing guidelines is in hand, the consultant searches a proprietary database of investment managers to identify those who appear to meet the criteria for the type of investments, credit quality, and maturity required by the investor. After reviewing the results of the initial search, the consultant identifies three to five of the most attractive candidates. If a consultant is not used, the institution's financial manager prepares a request for proposal (RFP) describing the nature and size of the portfolio, the investment objectives and existing guidelines, and the requirements for the investment manager. The RFP should also describe any unusual features or requirements pertaining to operation of the portfolio. Investment managers have widely varying approaches to the management of funds; the institution's financial manager will want assurance that the investment manager will use compatible methods of operation, goals, and objectives. These candidates are then brought to the investor's designated representative to make the final selection. These representatives are usually a committee of the Board of Trustees, such as the Investment Subcommittee or the Finance Committee.

After receiving written proposals from the top candidates, the consultant and the financial manager, as representatives of the investor, conduct in-person interviews. Each candidate is given an opportunity to discuss past performance and method of operation, and to respond directly to the investor's questions. The interview process should include discussion of investing goals and differing assumptions and criteria on which they are based. There usually is more than one way to state an investing goal; experienced investment managers often provide guidance in this area. In any event, the investment manager must fully understand and accept the investor's goals before a meeting of the minds can occur.

Other important considerations are brought to the surface through the candidates' formal proposals and the interviews:

- The candidate's willingness to engage in discussion, to demonstrate flexibility regarding the client's investing program, and to use the client's own investing guidelines
- Other clients of the investment manager with similar investing goals and guidelines
- The investor's portfolio size in comparison with the portfolios of the investment manager's other clients
- The registration of the investment manager with the U.S. Securities and Exchange Commission (SEC), under the Investment Advisors Act of 1940, and with the state of the investment manager's domicile

- Performance history of the manager, calculated in compliance with AIMR rules, over at least the past three years, which should then be compared to a benchmark, such as an index (see Exhibit 12.13), for a comparable period
- Any past censures by the SEC or other regulatory authority of the investment management firm or its principals for misconduct
- The turnover rate among the investment management firm's portfolio managers, key support staff, and supervisory personnel
- The experience and background of the investment management firm's principals and portfolio managers
- The ease with which the client may communicate directly with the investment management firm's portfolio manager
- The use of a written investment management contract and the inclusion of the following four elements:
    1. Clear description of how fees are calculated
    2. Additional charges above the basic fee
    3. Reasons for termination of the contract by either the client or the investment manager
    4. Capabilities of the investment manager to handle the type of portfolio involved
- Computerized information and analytical resources, and the specific credit review services that are used
- The format and frequency of reports, and the investment manager's ability to customize reports to meet the investor's particular needs

When the investment manager is selected, the institution may retain the consultant to provide assistance in reviewing the manager's performance.

(e) Compensating Outside Investment Advisers

Investment managers usually receive compensation based on the size of the portfolio that they manage. Investment consultants typically are compensated with a flat fee which may be made in either soft dollars or hard dollars.

Soft-dollar compensation is when the investment adviser directs the commissions generated by the execution of investment transactions to the consultant. Payment via soft dollars superficially saves the investor from paying the additional consultant's fee; however, the use of soft-dollar compensation can discourage the investment manager from seeking the most competitive prices

SUMMARY OF CRITERIA FOR REVIEWING INVESTMENT MANAGERS

Organization

- Experience of firm
- Assets under management
- Ownership
- Number of professionals; turnover
- Fee and minimum account size

Performance

- One-, three-, or five-year comparisons
- Up/down market comparisons
- Risk/return graphs

Skill set analysis

- Sector diversification
- Security selection
- Security consideration
- Market timing

Securities Summary

- Equities
- Stocks

on the execution of transactions. Instead, the investment manager may seek to execute transactions where soft-dollar compensation is available rather than where the best prices are obtainable. The investor may wish to confirm the investment manager is obtaining a competitive execution, thereby minimizing transaction costs.

There are two principal aspects to the evaluation of an investment manager's fee: (1) the fee should be competitive with those of other qualified investment managers dealing with similar investment instruments and maturities, and (2) the fee should not exceed the cost of establishing the investment management function internally with an acceptable level of sophistication and quality.

(f) Working with an Investment Manager

The investment manager should become familiar with the objectives, liquidity requirements, and relative risk-aversion tendencies of the institution's financial and administrative managers. After meeting with the institution's managers, the investment manager should review the existing investing guidelines. If they do not appear adequate or sufficiently comprehensive, the investment manager should propose revisions.

In addition to refining the investing guidelines, the investment manager should assist in developing operating arrangements necessary to execute investment transactions and facilitate delivery of investment management and advisory services to the client. In this process, the investment custodian must be selected for the safekeeping of securities, and appropriate documentation must be executed authorizing the investment manager to conduct business with securities dealers and the custodian. Finally, regular contacts with the client institution's financial staff must be established, including a meeting schedule for regular review of the investment manager's performance, usually quarterly.

With all these details handled, the nonprofit organization's financial manager will be able to use a structured, methodical, fulltime, and professional approach to the task of managing the institution's investment portfolio. The financial manager thereby assumes the role of overseeing the investment manager and becomes insulated from the minutiae of daily investment tasks.

(g) Investment Advisers Summary

Developing an investment program for the short- and long-term portfolios of an institution has many facets. These include managing the funds to meet their respective objectives and purposes and providing a meaningful forecast of receipts and disbursements of funds. The latter enables estimations regarding the size of the remaining pool of funds and the time horizon for its usefulness. When the physical aspects of the investment portfolio are determined, management can begin to develop a strategy for investing the funds to meet goals and maintain appropriate levels of liquidity and risk/return. Finally, the organization must develop an operating plan for executing, verifying, and settling transactions and ensuring the safety of instruments held in the portfolio.

Unfortunately, many financial managers begin investing surplus funds without giving conscious thought to each of these elements. Too often the absence of a well-thought-out and structured program leads to losses caused by either acute sloppiness or by working with unscrupulous investment dealers who take advantage of an unsuspecting investor.

Many sources of investment advice, advisers, and managers are available to assist financial managers in developing an informed approach to investing. Operation of an investment portfolio requires careful attention to the details of executing investment transactions and monitoring the resulting inventories. A feasible approach may use the services of an outside professional investment adviser to guide the institution through the thicket of details or to manage the investments according to the institution's investing policy and guidelines. After a review of the investment information, discussed in subsequent chapters, the financial manager will be better able to decide whether to manage funds internally or to seek the assistance of an outside professional.

One of the jobs performed by investment bankers and securities underwriters is devising new and different investment instruments in response to changing investor needs and demands. In many cases, the creativity of investment bankers has worked to the benefit of institutional investors. At the same time, however, many innovative instruments have caused more problems than they have solved. Collateralized mortgage obligations (CMOS), for example, were designed to solve the problems inherent in the repayment of principal and interest in mortgage-backed securities. However, CMOS have their own set of disadvantages. A well-informed, educated investor should be aware of the characteristics and risks of an instrument before a purchase is made.

Accordingly, financial managers must weigh all the possible problems of new and unusual securities. Such securities often have yield advantages over other types, but frequently the yield advantages are compromised for the following three reasons:

1. The accounting effort to maintain the securities in an investment portfolio is costly.
2. Interest income is lost because principal is not paid on time.
3. Most new instrument types have limited initial market activity. Therefore, a weak market can destroy the liquidity and further adversely affect the market price of the instruments, reducing the additional income paid if they must be sold.

Financial managers should examine all the consequences of investing in new and exotic instruments, estimate any yield problems, and evaluate the problems against the benefits before buying the instruments.

APPENDIX 12A

UNIFORM MANAGEMENT OF INSTITUTIONAL FUNDS ACT

Bill Summary & Status for the 93rd Congress
H.R. 12196
SPONSOR: Rep Fauntroy, (introduced 1/22/74)

- SHORT TITLE(S) AS INTRODUCED:
Uniform Management of Institutional Funds Act

- OFFICIAL TITLE AS INTRODUCED:
A bill to adopt for the District of Columbia the Uniform Management of Institutional Funds Act, and for other purposes.

STATUS: Floor Actions
1/22/74 Referred to House Committee on the District of Columbia

- COMMITTEE(S) OF REFERRAL:
House District of Columbia

- INDEX TERMS:
District of Columbia

DIGEST:
(AS INTRODUCED)
Uniform Management of Institutional Funds Act—States that the governing board may appropriate for expenditure for the uses and purposes for which an endowment fund is established so much of the net appreciation, realized and unrealized, in the fair value of the assets of an endowment fund over the historic dollar value of the fund as is prudent under the standard established by this Act, except when the applicable gift instrument indicates the donor's intention that net appreciation shall not be expended.

Provides that the governing board, subject to any specific limitations set forth in the applicable gift instrument or law, may (1) invest and re-invest an institutional fund in any real or personal property deemed advisable by the governing board; (2) retain property contributed by a donor to an institutional fund for as long as the governing board deems advisable; (3) include all or any part of an institutional fund in any pooled or common fund maintained by the institution; and (4) invest all or any part of an institutional fund in any other pooled or common fund available for investment.

States that, with the written consent of the donor, the governing board may release, in whole or in part, a restriction imposed by the applicable gift instrument on the use or investment of an institutional fund.

PROBATE CODE DIVISION 9. TRUST LAW PART 4. TRUST ADMINISTRATION CHAPTER 1. DUTIES OF TRUSTEES ARTICLE 2.5—UNIFORM PRUDENT INVESTOR ACT

Current through end of 1995–1996 Regular Session and 1st–4th Executive Session 16047. Standard of Care: Investments and management; considerations

(a) A trustee shall invest and manage trust assets as a prudent investor would, by considering the purposes, terms, distribution requirements, and other circumstances of the trust. In satisfying this standard, the trustee shall exercise reasonable care, skill, and caution.

(b) A trustee's investment and management decisions respecting individual assets and courses of action must be evaluated not in isolation, but in the context of the trust portfolio as a whole and as a part of an overall investment strategy having risk and return objectives reasonably suited to the trust.

(c) Among circumstances that are appropriate to consider in investing and managing trust assets are the following, to the extent relevant to the trust or its beneficiaries:

(1) General economic conditions.

(2) The possible effect of inflation or deflation.

(3) The expected tax consequences of investment decisions or strategies.

(4) The role that each investment or course of action plays within the overall trust portfolio.

(5) The expected total return from income and the appreciation of capital.

(6) Other resources of the beneficiaries known to the trustee as determined from information provided by the beneficiaries.

(7) Needs for liquidity, regularity of income, and preservation or appreciation of capital.

(8) An asset's special relationship or special value, if any, to the purposes of the trust or to one or more of the beneficiaries.

(d) A trustee shall make a reasonable effort to ascertain facts relevant to the investment and management of trust assets.

(e) A trustee may invest in any kind of property or type of investment or engage in any course of action or investment strategy consistent with the standards of this chapter.

CREDITS
1997 Electronic Update

CHAPTER THIRTEEN

Fixed-Income Securities Portfolio Management and Investment Operations

13.1 Introduction   485

13.2 Yield Curve Analysis   485
- (a) Factors Influencing the Yield Curve   486
- (b) Using the Yield Curve   488
- (c) Riding the Yield Curve   488

13.3 Yield Spread Analysis   490

13.4 Price Movement of Fixed-Income Securities   492
- (a) Rise in Interest Rates   493
- (b) Decline in Interest Rates   493
- (c) Calculating Yield   494
  - (i) Current Yield   494
  - (ii) Yield to Maturity   495
  - (iii) Yield to Discounted Cash Flow   496
  - (iv) Yield to Call   496
  - (v) Total Realized Compound Yield   496

13.5 Effect of Changing Interest Rates on Longer Maturities   497

13.6 Summary of Yield Curves   497

13.7 Fixed-Income Investment Instruments: An Introduction   498

13.8 U.S. Treasury Securities   498
- (a) Background   498
- (b) Liquidity and the Market   499
  - (i) Treasury Bills   500
  - (ii) Treasury Notes   500
  - (iii) Treasury Bonds   501

13.9 U.S. Government Agency Securities   501
- (a) Credit Quality   501
- (b) Advantages   502
- (c) Methods of Sale   502
- (d) "When Issued" Trading   503

(e) Types of Government Agency Securities 503
  (i) Farm Credit System Securities 503
  (ii) Federal Home Loan Bank Securities 504
  (iii) Federal Home Loan Mortgage Corporation 505
  (iv) Federal National Mortgage Association 505
  (v) Student Loan Marketing Association 505
  (vi) Governmental National Mortgage Association 505
  (vii) Adverse Features of GNMA Investments 506
  (viii) Mortgage Pass-Through Securities 507
  (ix) · Collateralized Mortgage Obligations 508
  (x) Asset-Backed Securities 508
  (xi) Municipal Debt Instruments 509
  (xii) Municipal Bond Insurance 509
  (xiii) Types of Municipal Bonds 510
  (xiv) General Obligation Bonds 510
  (xv) Revenue Bonds 510
  (xvi) Refunding Bonds 510
  (xvii) Pre-refunded Bonds 511
  (xviii) Certificates of Participation 511
  (xix) Zero Coupon Municipal Bonds 512
  (xx) Municipal Notes 513
  (xxi) Tax Anticipation Notes 513
  (xxii) Revenue Anticipation Notes 513
  (xxiii) Bond Anticipation Notes 513
  (xxiv) Floating-Rate Notes with Put Option Futures 513
13.10 Municipal Floating-Rate Instrument Problems 513
13.11 Corporate Debt Instruments 514
  (a) Commercial Paper 514
    (i) Issuing Formats 515
    (ii) Types of Commercial Paper 515
  (b) Loan Participations 517
  (c) Corporate Notes 517
  (d) Corporate Bonds 518
  (e) High-Yield (Junk) Bonds 518
  (f) Master Notes 519
13.12 Money Market Instruments Issued by Banks 520
  (a) Banker's Acceptances 520
  (b) Negotiable Certificates of Deposit and Time Deposits 521
    (i) Variable-Rate CDs 522
    (ii) Eurodollar Time Deposits 522
    (iii) Eurodollar CDs 523
    (iv) Yankee CDs 523
  (c) Money Market Mutual Funds 523
  (d) Bond Funds 524

13.13 Repurchase Agreements   525
    (a)   Introduction   525
    (b)   Definitions   526
         (i)   Reverse Repurchase Agreements   527
         (ii)   Brokered or Matched Repurchase
                Agreements   528
    (c)   Risks of Repo Transactions   528
    (d)   Reducing Repo Risk   530
         (i)   Custodial Arrangements   530
         (ii)   Delivery Repo   530
         (iii)   Three-Party Repo   531
         (iv)   Letter Repo   531
    (e)   Alternatives to Repos   531
13.14 Summary   531
Appendix 13A   Derivatives Checklist   533

13.1 INTRODUCTION

Many nonprofit organizations have a substantial commitment to fixed-income securities. This is often due to their need for a large current income to sustain original expenses. Also, many elect to manage internally (i.e., not use an investment manager) for their shorter-term, liquidity funds. It is for these reasons this section deals in depth with management of a fixed-income securities portfolio. One enduring characteristic of investment markets is price volatility. Like any other activity within the U.S. economy, the market for fixed-income investments is subject to the laws of supply and demand. And like any other shopper, a financial manager seeks to make these laws work to the advantage of the institution. To do so, the financial manager must seek specific instruments that provide the best relative value among different securities with different maturities while meeting the institution's needs for safety and liquidity. Consequently, the financial manager must have tools and techniques with which to compare the various types of instruments and their differences in credit quality and maturity.

The financial manager can use two analytical tools to judge relative value, a yield curve analysis and yield spread analysis. By using a yield spread analysis, the financial manager can evaluate a fixed-income security in relation to others by comparing the yields of different securities having different risk characteristics but similar maturities. By using yield curve analysis, the financial manager can judge the best relative value of a maturity length in relation to other maturity lengths, because the analysis compares yields and maturities relative to market risk and reward. Combining yield spread and yield curve analyses should improve a financial manager's selection process and therefore, the institution's overall yield.

13.2 YIELD CURVE ANALYSIS

Yield curve analysis provides a method for a financial manager to determine how changes in interest rates are likely to affect the value of the institution's investment portfolio. The yield curve shows the relationship between yield to maturity and time to maturity. It allows an investor to compare the returns of different types of fixed-income instruments, evaluate possible changes in interest rates, and gauge potential price movements. Yield curve analysis allows a financial manager to estimate the rates of return an investment will produce as interest rates change.

(a) Factors Influencing the Yield Curve

Yield curves allow comparison if the securities they compare are identical in all respects except length of maturity. Yield data and yield curves are often published in *The Wall Street Journal*, most major newspapers, and publications issued by securities dealers. Each type of investment security, such as U.S. Treasury bills (T-bills), has a unique yield curve. The horizontal axis plots the security's maturity, expressed in months or years. The vertical axis plots yield levels. The yield curves in Exhibit 13.1 show how different economic conditions can affect the instrument's yield.

The positively sloped and the negatively sloped curves in Exhibit 13.1 illustrate an important generalization about yield curves. In periods of economic expansion, with positively sloped yield curves, investors find long-term rates more attractive. In a slow economy, with negatively sloped yield curves, investors are wary of tying up funds at low interest rates for long periods of time. One of the factors that influences the shape of the yield curve is interest rate,

Exhibit 13.1.　Yield Curves

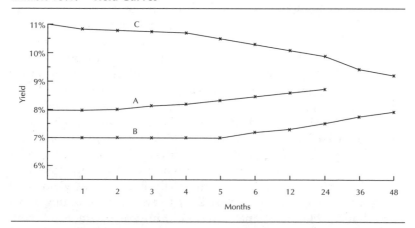

or market, risk. Investors are exposed to market risk in any investment, and market risk tends to be greater as the maturity of an instrument lengthens. As a result, yield curves tend to curve upward; that is, yields are higher at longer maturities. In curve A, a relatively flat yield curve, economic expectations may be described as stable to uncertain. There is not much reward for investing in longer maturities, so most investors will remain with short-term instruments.

Curve B, on the other hand, rewards the investor for taking on longer-term maturities and is more nearly like the classic positive (upward) sloping yield curve. In this scenario, the yield curve rises sharply with yields increasing as maturities lengthen. Curves such as this one typically occur when business conditions are beginning to improve after a recession and interest rates are expected to increase even further. This causes investors to be reluctant to tie up their money for long periods of time. Consequently, rates for long-term securities are relatively higher to reflect the increased risk of a long-term investment under these economic conditions.

Curve C, an inverted or negative (downward) sloping yield curve, is characteristic of interest rates in a recession, where short-term interest rates are high and the market anticipates that interest rates may soon fall. As a result, borrowers are willing to pay high interest rates to cover their short-term requirements, but they will only pay lower rates for longer-term debt.

The shape of the yield curve is influenced by factors other than the present health of the economy. Such factors include the expectations of investors (affecting demand) and a heavy or light calendar of new issues (affecting supply). For instance, if investors believe that interest rates are going to rise, they will seek to keep funds invested in short-term maturities. At the same time, borrowers seek to lengthen maturities on their debt in order to lock in low interest rates before rates rise. Both responses force short-term interest rates down and long-term interest rates up. Consequently, the upward slope of the yield curve is heightened.

Conversely, if investors expect interest rates to fall, they often invest in longer-term instruments (causing demand for these maturities that forces prices to rise and yields to fall), because they want to lock in high yields for as long as possible. At the same time, borrowers are paying high short-term interest rates while they wait for interest rates to decline. As a result, the yield curve could be inverted, such as curve C in Exhibit 13.1.

Large sales of new issues also can skew the shape of a yield curve. Such sales would be reflected in the yield curve by a large upward bulge in the maturity range of the new security.

In general, then, the shape of the yield curve is influenced by the supply and demand for short-term investment maturities in relation to the supply and demand for long-term investment maturities.

A pitfall to avoid when calculating the yield curve is the different methods used to measure the yield on discount securities and interest-bearing securities. For instance, interest on Treasury notes is calculated on the basis of an actual day year, while interest on certificates of deposit (CDs) is calculated on the basis of a 360-day year. Consequently, a one-year Treasury note at 8 percent, using the par value of $1,000,000, produces a return of $80,000, compared with a one-year CD, where interest is calculated on a 360-day year, that yields $81,111. Of course, the difference is partially offset because the CD pays interest only at maturity while the Treasury note pays interest twice a year.

(b) Using the Yield Curve

There are two basic ways a financial manager can use yield curves. First, yield curves allow the investor to judge whether the price of a new issue is in line with current market trends. Second, yield curves allow a financial manager to compare securities of different maturities. Even so, it can be difficult to predict normal spreads between securities with different maturities, because the slope and shape of yield curves vary over time.

Despite this uncertainty, yield curve analysis can be helpful in the management of an institution's investment portfolio. Yield curves are useful in determining whether yields are more attractive in short-term or long-term instruments. The duration for which an institution wants its funds invested, however, should be spelled out in a written investing policy and comprehensive set of investing guidelines and not rest solely on yield curve analysis.

Yield curve analysis also enables a financial manager to assess market risk. The yield curve can help determine whether the potential market risk of loss on an investment is outweighed by its yield. It can also assess the effect of rising interest rates as they relate to the investor having to sell the instrument at a loss. For instance, the yield curve may shift upward as the economy heats up, with the potential increase in return outweighing the decline in value of certain securities.

(c) Riding the Yield Curve

A financial manager can receive yield on the sales of securities before they mature, and indeed in some cases the best investment strategy is to sell securities before that time. When a financial manager buys one-year Treasury bills at 7 percent and holds them for a year, they earn 7 percent. If the bills are sold before the date of maturity, the earned rate will, of course, depend on the market rate prevailing when the bills are sold. If that rate is higher than 7 percent, the return will be less than if the bills had been held to maturity, but the proceeds can be reinvested in higher-yield securities.

As a result, it is possible for the financial manager to use yield curve analysis to time buying and selling opportunities in order to reap unanticipated profits. Using the yield curve to help determine the timing of investments is called riding the yield curve. The following example, depicted in Exhibit 13.2, illustrates how financial managers can ride the yield curve to profits.

Assume that an institution has $1 million that it can invest for three months. Its financial manager observes that six-month T-bills are trading at 7.5 percent and three-month T-bills are trading at 7.1 percent. The financial manager can buy either the three-month T-bills and hold them to maturity or the six-month T-bills and sell them after three months. To determine which strategy will work best, the financial manager uses break-even analysis.

The six-month T-bill would yield an additional 80 basis points, or $2,000, compared to the three-month T-bill (over three months, one basis point is worth $25). The gain is 80 basis points because the financial manager accrues interest at 40 basis points above the three-month T-bills (7.50 − 7.10 = .40). The other 40 basis points arise because, assuming the yield curve remains unchanged, the financial manager will sell the six-month bill at the 7.10 level and realize a gain of 40 more basis points, bringing the total return to 80 basis points. Of course, the risk involved in this strategy lies in whether the yield curve will remain constant. If the yield curve rises during the three-month period, the investor may find that three-month T-bills yield 7.50 percent, and there would be no gain on their sale at that time.

In fact, the rate on three-month T-bills would have to rise above 7.90 percent before it would be advisable for the financial manager to buy three-month bills and hold them to maturity, assuming that interest rates remain the same. The slope of the yield curve shows that six-month T-bills should trade at 7.10 percent in

Exhibit 13.2. Riding the Yield Curve

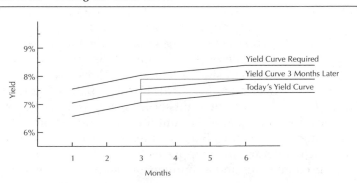

three months if the yield curve remains the same. The financial manager thus has an 80 basis point cushion against increased interest rates. If he or she believes that it is unlikely that the yield curve for T-bills will rise that much, then the best bet is to buy the six-month T-bills and ride the yield curve.

13.3 YIELD SPREAD ANALYSIS

A financial manager uses yield spread analysis to ensure that the institution's investment portfolio is generating maximum profits. The yield spread is the difference between yields of various investment instruments of similar maturities. Like the yield curve, the yield spread is affected by market conditions and thus changes constantly. A financial manager should stay abreast of the spreads between different investment instruments. In fixed-income instruments, the benchmark for comparison is Treasury securities, because their liquidity and credit quality are consistently high. In general, as a security's credit risk increases and its liquidity decreases, its yield in relation to Treasury securities increases.

Yield spreads are measured in basis points, which are equal to one-one hundredth of a percentage point. For example, if six-month Treasury bills are quoted at 6.45 percent and six-month commercial paper is quoted at 6.65 percent, the spread between the two types of instruments is 20 basis points. By studying the spreads between different types of securities with similar maturities, a financial manager can decide whether a riskier security carries a sufficiently larger return to justify the investment, as long as the choice is consistent with investment guidelines. Exhibit 13.3 shows the yield spreads that generally exist among common investment instruments.

The yield spreads in Exhibit 13.3 are estimates as of a specific moment and under specific economic conditions. These spreads change continuously, requiring constant monitoring, and do not always follow a normal pattern. Abnormal spread relationships occur frequently, and such spreads can provide investment managers with profit-making opportunities.

The two bars on the left of the graph in Exhibit 13.4 show the normal relationship between Treasury bills and government agency discount notes of similar maturities. Normally, the government agency discount notes yield 12 basis points higher than T-bills. The two bars on the right show an abnormal yield spread, where government agency discount notes are more than 100 basis points higher than T-bills. Such a difference may be possible because of a temporary oversupply in the market for government agency discount notes and a simultaneous shortage of Treasury se-

Exhibit 13.3.   Approximate Yield Spreads of Various Instruments in Relation to U.S. Treasury Bills

Type	Quality	Yield (%)
Government agencies	Discount notes	0.12
CDs	Prime quality U.S. banks	0.30
Commercial paper	Prime rated (A1-P1)	0.40
Euro CDs	Prime quality U.S. banks	0.55
Time deposits, Eurodollars	Prime quality U.S. banks	0.50
Banker's acceptances	Prime foreign banks	0.30
Yankee CDs	Prime foreign banks	0.40
Time deposits, Eurodollars	Prime foreign banks	0.70

curities. A financial manager who monitors market conditions can use some of the institution's excess cash to make a short-term investment in the government agency notes, thus reaping an unexpected profit, in this type of situation.

Time constraints and limited personnel often prevent financial managers at nonprofit institutions from checking yields on every investment vehicle suited to the institution's portfolio. They can obtain daily yield spread information easily, however, by developing strong relationships with securities dealers and bank investment departments. These organizations keep abreast of the

Exhibit 13.4.   Normal and Abnormal Yield Spread Variations (Six-Month Maturities)

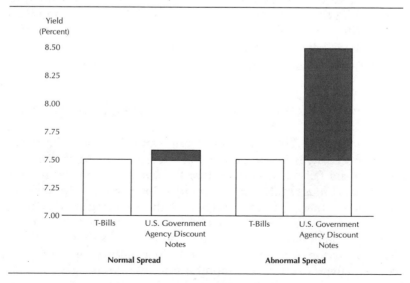

markets and can be valuable sources of current information. Financial managers can obtain market information over the telephone. Many organizations distribute market information gratis through printed newsletters. By the time the newsletters reach the desks of financial managers, however, much of the information may be obsolete.

Securities dealers are happy to provide information to investors with whom they have done business before. Accordingly, it is of the utmost importance that financial managers carefully select their securities dealers, especially if they make only a limited number of transactions. (Dealers eagerly offer market information to investors with a large number of transactions.) The difference between valuable market information and market gossip is often difficult to discern, so financial managers, as buyers, must beware.

Finding an attractive value among a morning's investment opportunities requires a financial manager to obtain yield and maturity information quickly on an array of securities and to compare yield spread and yield curve data. Dealers and brokers readily provide this basic information for T-bills, government agency securities, bank instruments, and commercial paper. Rates gathered from dealers then can be plotted so that yield spreads and curves become clear. To highlight yield spreads and curves, the financial manager can use color-coded graphics to chart the yields of several instruments at various maturities. The chart should reveal the similarities and demonstrate the differences among instruments.

For instance, a financial manager may learn from yield spread analysis that T-bills are presently at yields close to those of instruments of lower credit quality. Because the lower-quality instruments are riskier than T-bills and because yield spread analysis shows that the yields are similar, the financial manager can invest the institution's money in T-bills. He or she does so knowing that T-bills have better credit quality and liquidity at a yield similar to lesser-quality instruments and therefore present a better value.

13.4 PRICE MOVEMENT OF FIXED-INCOME SECURITIES

The relationship between interest rates and the price of a fixed-income security is inverse; that is, as interest rates rise, the price of the security falls. This ensures that the value of the fixed-income security is brought into line with market interest rates. To compensate for fluctuating interest rates and the resulting market price risk, yields on fixed-income securities are adjusted to prevailing rates after they are issued through the market price mechanism. For that reason, it is important that a financial manager use yield curve analysis to attempt to monitor interest rate changes.

As the institution's funds are invested, the financial manager must know how the investments will introduce market risk into the portfolio. A simple approach is to examine the yield curve to predict how returns may increase as maturities are extended. In that way, the financial manager can ascertain the point on the curve where rates provide the greatest return consistent with the market risk appropriate to the portfolio. The following examples illustrate how changes in interest rates affect the prices of investments.

(a) Rise in Interest Rates

In the first example, the financial manager for Organization A buys a new six-month CD with a par value of $1 million, bearing interest at 10 percent. At the time the investment is made, other instruments of similar credit quality and maturity are also trading at 10 percent. One month after the purchase, however, interest rates increase. As a result, CDs maturing in five months (the term remaining on the six-month CD one month after purchase) are now yielding 11 percent. Because interest rates have increased, the value of the 10 percent CD declines so that its yield is in line with the increased market rate.

After one month, the CD has accrued interest (at 10 percent) of $8,333.33 and therefore a book value to the investor of $1,008,333.33. If the investor wants to sell the CD, the CD must fetch a price calculated to provide the new investor with a prevailing market interest rate. As a result, the financial manager must sell the CD at a loss. The buyer will pay only the amount calculated to yield an 11 percent return over the remaining five months. That amount is only $1,003,984.06, leaving the selling investor with a discount (or loss) from the accrued basis of $4,349.27. When the instrument reaches its maturity value of $1,050,000 ($1,000,000 plus interest at 10 percent for six months), the new investor will realize a return of $45,650.73 on its investment of $1,003,984.06. This results in a yield of 11 percent over the five months that the second investor owns the CD.

(b) Decline in Interest Rates

In the second example, the financial manager at Organization B buys a six-month CD bearing interest at 10 percent. One month later, interest rates fall to 9 percent. This increases the market value of the CD so that a new buyer must pay more than par to purchase the CD. The premium, however, will be lost at maturity when the CD is redeemed at par value plus interest; the CD thus costs the second buyer more than par. In this case, the new investor is willing to pay as much as $1,012,048.19 (compared to the first buyer's book value of $1,008,333.33) for the instrument that has a maturity value of $1,050,000 in five months. The amount of income earned, $37,951.90, represents a yield to the new investor of 9 percent over that period.

(c) Calculating Yield

Financial managers can receive information that will lead to beneficial investments by analyzing and anticipating changes in yield. Calculating yield, however, can be difficult. The most widely used methods of calculating the yield of fixed-income securities are:

- Current yield
- Yield to maturity
- Yield to discounted cash flow
- Yield to call
- Total realized compound yield

Each of these methods has specific uses for different investments, so financial managers must know which analysis is best suited to the instrument at hand and the available information.

(i) *Current Yield.* Current yield relates an investment instrument's annual interest payment to its current market price. It is the rate of return (annual interest payments) divided by the current market value of the instrument. As such, current yield does not take into account other possible sources of income, including reinvestment of interest income during the life of the security, an important consideration when an investment's market price is at either a premium or discount in relation to par. Calculation of the current yield on an instrument involves multiplying its coupon rate by its face value, then dividing that by the instrument's market price, and multiplying by 100. The current yield on a note with a $1,000 face value that sells at $985.13 (a discount) and has an 8 percent coupon is thus 8.12 percent:

$$[(.08 \times 1,000) \div 985.13] \times 100 = 8.12 \text{ percent}$$

On a discount note or bond, the current yield always will be less than its yield to maturity. This is because the current yield does not include the instrument's capital gain. Conversely, the current yield on a note or bond selling at a premium always will be greater than its yield to maturity. For instance, a $1,000 instrument with an 8 percent coupon selling at $1,014.73, a premium, to yield 7.5 percent has a current yield of 7.88 percent. Because current yield does not take into account capital gain (or loss in the case of instruments

selling at a premium), yield to maturity or call is the most prevalent calculation of an instrument's yield.

(ii) Yield to Maturity.   The calculation of yield to maturity
(YTM) takes into account the capital appreciation and depreciation of a fixed-income instrument. It also takes into account reinvestment of interest. However, the calculation assumes that the
rate at which interest payments are reinvested is equal to the YTM
existing at the instrument's purchase date, which may or may not
be the case.

Calculation of YTM for nondiscounted format instruments includes two components. First, the calculation includes the coupon
rate, the maturity date (to determine the holding period), and any
discount or premium resulting from changes in market interest
rates. Second, the yield calculation includes the accrued interest that
has accumulated from the time the instrument was issued. It is important for financial managers to understand that YTM is based on
total dollars invested. Because that total figure includes the premium or discount plus any accrued interest, the instrument's return
at maturity is a net return based on the total dollars returned and
total dollars invested in the instrument.

For example, a new six-year note with an 8 percent coupon is
issued at par. Six months later, the Federal Reserve tightens the
money supply causing yields on comparable securities to increase
to 8.5 percent. The security must now sell at less than its par value;
a new investor who buys this "seasoned," or secondary issue will
receive only the maturity value based on the 8 percent coupon and
will want to be compensated for buying the instrument at a time
when 8.5 percent returns are now available in other similar instruments. Consequently, the new investor will want to pay less than
par value for it.

It is necessary to understand the concept of YTM as an effective yield in order to determine how much less than par the instrument should be priced. Again, there are two parts to the return an
investor receives on a security that is bought at a discount and held
to maturity. Return consists of the periodic interest payment plus a
capital gain. The capital gain is the difference between the instrument's purchase price and its par or face value. Investors who buy
instruments at a premium and hold them to maturity also receive a
two-part return. In this case, the return consists of interest payments plus a capital loss, which is equal to the dollar value of the
premium. An investment instrument's overall or effective yield
takes into account both interest and capital gains or losses. When
financial managers choose between securities of comparable risk
and maturity, they do not make their decisions on the basis of
coupon rate but on the basis of effective yield.

In the above example, then, once market interest rates increase to 8.5 percent, a security bearing interest at 8 percent must be priced at a discount if a buyer is to be found. The discount, of course, must be large enough to make the instrument's YTM equal to 8.5 percent. The calculations involved in putting a dollar figure to that difference are complex. Using a bond calculator, a dealer can determine that a $1,000 note with an 8 percent coupon and three and one-half years to maturity must sell at $985.32 in order to yield 8.5 percent at maturity. The dollar discount is thus $14.68.

(iii) Yield to Discounted Cash Flow. The yield to discounted cash flow calculation allows financial managers to relate the current value of future cash flows expected from an instrument, such as periodic coupon and principal payments, to the instrument's current market price. In short, the calculation discounts each interest and principal payment and, consequently, allows cash flows from both interest and principal to be predicted and discounted back to a present value.

(iv) Yield to Call. Some fixed-income investments contain provisions that allow the issuer to redeem ("call") the issue before it matures at a predetermined price. Financial managers can calculate the yields on such issues in two ways. First, yields can be calculated by using the yield-to-maturity method; this assumes that the instrument will remain outstanding until maturity. Alternatively, the yield-to-call method can be used. This method assumes that the investment is called by the issuer at the earliest possible date, as specified in the bond's indenture. Financial managers often use both methods and base their evaluation of the investment's attractiveness on the method that provides the lower yield, thus providing a measure of conservatism to the consideration.

Like YTM, the yield to call calculation assumes that all investment payments will be reinvested at a rate equal to the YTM that existed at the time the instrument was purchased. Yield to call disregards how the proceeds will be invested after the investment is called.

(v) Total Realized Compound Yield. Total realized compound yield measures the underlying fully compounded growth or accumulation rate relating to a fixed-income instrument. The measure takes varying reinvestment rates into account. Because the rate at which coupon payments will be reinvested is uncertain, the financial manager can only estimate a range of rates. Varying assumptions on interest rates determine the range used in the calculation.

13.5   EFFECT OF CHANGING INTEREST RATES ON LONGER MATURITIES

As maturity lengthens, risk increases and long-term investments thus should be compensated for the risk. The compensation is reflected in the upward sloping yield curve that says, in effect, that yield increases as maturity increases. Exhibit 13.5 illustrates how changes in interest rates affect the market value of Treasury securities.

Although a positive yield curve suggests that yields rise steadily as maturities lengthen, this is an arguable assumption when it comes to developing an investment strategy for a nonprofit institution. A financial manager who chooses investments of long maturities must always assume that they are putting the institution's principal at a greater risk. The financial manager cannot assume that the additional yield will compensate for the increased risk.

13.6   SUMMARY OF YIELD CURVES

A yield curve can be used to monitor future interest rates. If the yield curve has a sharp upward slope, it often reflects the aggregate perceptions of investors that interest rates will continue to rise. As a result, investors will demand higher rates for investments with longer maturities.

The best protection against fluctuating interest rates is to distribute maturities in the institution's portfolio among short-, intermediate-, and long-term maturities. This strategy will ensure that the institution's portfolio is protected even against rates dictated by a positive yield curve.

Exhibit 13.5.   Effect of Interest Rates on Market Value of Fixed-Income Securities

Maturity	Approximate change in market value after a 1 percent change in interest rates per$1 million par value
1 month	$ 734
3 months	2,500
6 months	4,699
1 year	8,681
2 years	23,212
5 years	43,414
10 years	70,728
20 years	113,194
30 years	129,645

13.7 FIXED-INCOME INVESTMENT INSTRUMENTS: AN INTRODUCTION

One of the more important jobs a financial manager performs is to ensure that the institution's cash is always working. Cash that lies in a checking account when it is not needed to pay bills is not working. Rather than leave cash in checking accounts, a financial manager invests it; the institution derives financial benefits from its cash surplus. Hundreds of investment vehicles may be used for excess cash, some with long terms and some with short terms, some extremely safe and some quite risky. A financial manager must match the yield objectives, level of risk, and liquidity tolerances of the institution, as stated in the investment guidelines, before making investments. As an aid in that decision-making process, this chapter describes the most common types of investment vehicles: U.S. Treasury and government agency instruments, corporate and money market instruments, and repurchase agreements.

It is apparent that many of these instruments are quite similar. In many cases, the only difference is in the length of maturity. Therefore, it is important for a financial manager to understand the importance of managing maturities in an investment program. The longer the instrument's maturity, the greater the possibility that its market value will fluctuate as interest rates change. In choosing securities for investment, a financial manager must examine and be satisfied with each of the following aspects of an investment instrument besides its maturity:

- Issuer's credit quality
- Instrument's liquidity
- Instrument's complexity
- Ease of obtaining an instrument's credit rating
- Instrument's sensitivity to market risk
- Flexibility of the instrument's maturity ranges
- Yield of the instrument
- Investor's potential tax exemption
- Structure of the instrument's principal and interest payments
- Financial manager's ability to actively manage a portfolio containing that particular instrument

13.8 U.S. TREASURY SECURITIES

(a) Background

The U.S. government is one of the largest economic organizations in the world; it is also one of the most indebted. In fact, the U.S. Department of the Treasury is the largest issuer of debt instruments in the world. Even so, debt instruments issued by the U.S. Treasury are considered to be the safest investments available. They are used as a means to reap investment returns from surplus cash by financial managers from all types of businesses, including nonprofit institutions, that seek to put this cash to work. U.S. Treasury debt instruments meet their requirements of high liquidity and low credit risk and make perfect investments for this purpose. The strength of the U.S. economy, for instance, prompts dealers and investment analysts to grade Treasury securities as virtually free of credit or default risk.

(b) Liquidity and the Market

One of the criteria for high liquidity is the existence of a large market for an investment instrument. Liquidity refers to the ability to convert a security into cash quickly and without loss of principal. Because the volume of debt issued by the Treasury is so great, the market for government securities is one of the most active and thus most liquid of investment markets. There is a tremendous amount of participation by both foreign and domestic investors in this market. Liquidity is further increased by the existence of a core of primary dealers that buy and sell huge quantities of government securities, both among themselves and with other investors. It is a highly competitive market, with prices varying between dealers by only one or two thirty-seconds of a point (on a par value of $1,000,000, one thirty-second of a point is $312.50). Liquidity is also increased by the existence of a huge resale market, where dealers and investors who bought securities at issuance sell them before maturity.

Treasury securities are initially sold at auctions that are conducted through regional Federal Reserve Bank offices. Dates for those auctions are announced in newspaper notices well beforehand. There are two types of bidding at Treasury auctions: (1) competitive bids for certain quantities of securities at a certain price, and (2) noncompetitive bids submitted by an investor or institution that simply agrees to buy a certain amount of the security and pay a price equal to the weighted-average price of all competitive bids accepted by the Treasury. The difference between competitive and noncompetitive bids involves risk. When financial managers submit competitive bids, they take the risk of paying more than the average noncompetitive price or of bidding too low to obtain the desired securities. (After the auction's deadline, the Treasury reviews all bids and establishes the minimum price at which bids will be accepted.)

Individual and institutional investors may bid on Treasury securities at a Federal Reserve Bank or have major banks or securities dealers submit bids on their behalf. Investors may also, of course, buy Treasury securities from the many resale markets through banks or securities dealers.

Before considering Treasury securities as an investment, financial managers must be familiar with the different types of Treasury securities and their characteristics. Treasury securities fall into three categories: bills, notes, and bonds.

(i) Treasury Bills. T-bills are short-term debt instruments that are issued at a discount and repaid at full value, called par value, upon maturity. The amount of interest on a T-bill is thus the difference between the purchase price and the value of the bill's par value. T-bills are issued with maturities of three months, six months, and one year. Also, when the Treasury needs funds to finance operations before a tax receipt date, it will issue "cash management bills" having odd maturities ranging from a few days to 60 days.

The advantages of T-bills for the institutional investor are the wide range of short-term maturities, their high liquidity, and an active secondary market for most denominations. The minimum denomination of a T-bill is $10,000; additional amounts are available in increments of $5,000. T-bills are sold only in book entry form (by credit to the investor's account with the Treasury).

(ii) Treasury Notes. Treasury notes (T-notes) (also called coupon notes) are instruments that mature from more than one year up to 10 years and bear interest. They are issued at or near face value and are redeemed at par value upon maturity. Original maturities for T-notes are two, three, four, five, and 10 years. Notes with a two-year maturity are issued each month, while notes of three years and longer are issued quarterly. The Treasury issues notes of other maturities if it needs to balance its maturity schedule. Like T-bills, T-notes are issued in various denominations. The minimum denomination of two- and three-year notes is $5,000, and the size increases in $5,000 increments. Notes with maturities of longer than three years are issued in minimum size of $1,000, with larger amounts in $1,000 increments. Interest on T-notes is paid semiannually and at maturity together with par value of the notes.

T-notes, like T-bills, are initially sold to investors at auctions conducted by the Federal Reserve. Investors bid on the basis of YTM, and the Treasury accepts the bids that result in the lowest cost to the Treasury. Accordingly, the market itself generally determines the interest rate of T-notes. Also like T-bills, T-notes are highly liquid because of the existence of a vast secondary market, especially for notes in denominations of $1 million and more. The secondary market also provides a wide range of maturities and prices. T-notes, like all direct obligations of the U.S. government, carry no credit risk.

(iii) Treasury Bonds.   Treasury bonds (T-bonds) are interest-bearing debt instruments with original maturities longer than 10 years; most original maturities are 20 or 30 years. T-bonds do not have a call feature that allows the Treasury to pay off the bonds. Like T-notes, the bonds pay interest income semiannually. These long-term Treasury securities are issued in $1,000 denominations and are sold quarterly at auctions. They have the same liquidity and credit risk characteristics as T-bills and T-notes.

13.9   U.S. GOVERNMENT AGENCY SECURITIES

Most of the departments and agencies of the U.S. government, as well as organizations and corporations chartered by Congress, issue debt securities. They are referred to collectively as government agency securities. Like Treasury securities, they are either issued at a discount and redeemed at par upon maturity, or they pay a fixed rate of interest until maturity.

(a) Credit Quality

All agencies of the federal government are considered to be more creditworthy than private organizations. However, some government agencies are more creditworthy than others. The liquidity of government agency securities also varies by issuer. Most investors consider government agency securities to have little default risk. Even so, financial managers investing an institution's funds should keep three points in mind:

1. Not every government agency security carries the full faith and credit of the U.S. government; many actively traded government agency securities must maintain their own financial strength and security.

2. Of the major credit-rating agencies, only Moody's rates most government agency debt. Securities that carry a direct government guarantee or are backed by collateral generally receive an AAA rating. Because the rating agencies tend not to rate government agencies, however, it is difficult to find information on the financial strength and stability of many agencies.

3. Government agencies can experience financial difficulties; some so substantial that the agency must apply to the federal government for assistance. In 1986, for instance, earnings and assets of the Federal Farm Credit Banks (FFCB) began to suffer as a result

of the deteriorating agricultural sector of the country's economy. The FFCB had to ask Congress for financial aid while the agency strengthened its financial position. While Congress was considering aid, the uncertain status of the FFCB's creditworthiness caused its debt instruments to trade at much higher yields than those of other government agencies.

(b) Advantages

Safety, liquidity, and yield are the main advantages of government agency securities. Despite some credit concerns, these securities are still among the safest instruments available to an investor. In most instances, government agency debt is considered second only to Treasury securities in terms of safety. Although few agencies besides the Treasury are backed by the full faith and credit of the U.S. government, many experts contend that Congress has a "moral obligation" to bail out an agency that finds itself in fiscally dangerous waters. Indeed, Congress approved a form of aid for the FFCB when it was having loan problems. It ruled that the government could buy FFCB securities to provide the agency with a temporary source of funding, under the condition that the agency institute fiscal reforms.

The liquidity factor of most government agency securities, although generally not as high as Treasury securities, is still a major advantage. Many of these securities are more liquid than other types of financial instruments, because there is active secondary-market trading in most government agency securities. A financial manager should look carefully at liquidity, however, as not all government agency securities have active markets. Those that are not very liquid have been omitted from descriptions of government agency securities in the next section of this chapter.

The differences between government agency securities and Treasury securities regarding safety and liquidity lead to yet another major advantage of agency securities; yield. Because most government agency securities are not backed by a Treasury guarantee and are slightly less liquid, they generally trade at higher yields than Treasury securities. The amount of the yield spread for any given maturity between Treasury securities and government agency securities depends on market conditions, but the yield spread is always present. This spread is usually $\frac{3}{8}$ percent for maturities under one year and $\frac{1}{4}$ percent beyond one year.

(c) Methods of Sale

Government agency securities are not sold at auction like Treasury securities. They are issued through an underwriting syndicate composed of a select group of securities dealers and banks. Every dealer in the group underwrites a specific portion of the total issue. Consequently, the interest rate for government agency securities is not determined in the same manner as the rate for Treasury securities, as there is no auction in which the market can determine the rate. Instead, the coupon yield of each issue is set by the underwriting syndicate and the agency's fiscal manager on the morning of the sale date.

Before setting the interest rate, the syndicate must obtain instructions from the agency as to the amount of money it needs and the length of maturity it prefers. If the money needs of the agency are less demanding, the security will carry a rate that is below the prevailing market rate. If the agency needs money for a particular date, however, a higher rate will be set to attract investors. Yields on government agency securities thus reflect both market conditions and the needs of the borrower, much like commercial paper rates. The public learns of the amount, maturity date, and settlement date for government agency securities through the news media. Most daily newspapers carry "pre-sale" announcements of these securities. Syndicate members then take orders from investors.

(d) "When Issued" Trading

Dealers begin to make markets to buy and sell new securities when an issue is announced, even if that instrument has not yet been issued. The period of time between announcement of a security issue and when it is paid for and delivered is called the "when issued" (WI) period. To trade in securities on a "when issued" basis requires little or no principal investment during the WI period, because payment is not due until the settlement date. This enables speculation during the WI period; both Treasury and agency securities are heavily traded during this period. Conservative financial managers, however, should avoid the temptation to speculate by committing only to securities on a WI basis when they intend to take delivery of the securities on the settlement date.

(e) Types of Government Agency Securities

Certain government agencies that are in the business of lending funds generally issue debt to fund lending activities. The following sections provide descriptions of the more actively traded government agency debt obligations.

(i) *Farm Credit System Securities.* The nation's farmers require an enormous amount of credit and financial assistance. A constant supply of funds is maintained to meet farmers' credit needs through the Farm Credit Administration, which oversees the Federal Farm Credit System. The system, which contains 12 farm credit districts each having a Farm Credit Bank, raises funds to lend to farmers by selling notes and bonds to the public. The FFCB securities, called Consolidated Systemwide discount notes and bonds, are backed by the assets of the Farm Credit Banks. The securities are not guaranteed by the U.S. government, so their market value is subject to the credit soundness of the farm loan market. In the mid-1980s, for instance, the Farm Credit Administration suffered substantial losses as a result of the collapse of the agricultural markets. Congress temporarily bailed the system out in January 1988, but whether the reforms mandated by Congress will keep the agency solvent remains to be seen.

Consolidated Systemwide short-term debentures are issued monthly and have maturities of 180 and 270 days. They are issued at par and pay principal and interest at maturity. The system also frequently issues medium-term notes, with maturities up to five years and longer-term notes, approximately six times a year, with maturities of up to 30 years with interest payable semiannually. Debentures with maturities of less than 13 months are issued in increments of $5,000, and those with longer maturities are issued in $1,000 increments. All of these securities are issued in book-entry form. Under a special program, dealers can issue Consolidated Systemwide notes with maturities ranging from five days to a year. These notes trade at a discount from face value and are repaid at par upon maturity. They are issued in $500,000 denominations and in book-entry form only.

(ii) Federal Home Loan Bank Securities. The Federal Home Loan Act of 1932 created the Federal Home Loan Bank (FHLB) system. The system's two primary responsibilities are to (1) oversee its member savings and loan institutions and savings banks, and (2) lend money and provide liquidity to its members. To obtain the money that the FHLB lends to its members, it borrows money from the public by issuing bonds and notes. Debt is issued by a credit system operated by the FHLB system's 12 district banks under the supervision of a central board based in Washington, D.C.

Three types of securities are issued by the FHLB, consolidated bonds, medium-term notes, and consolidated discount notes. The debt is called "consolidated" because it is the joint obligation of all 12 FHLBs. These banks operate under a federal charter and are supervised by the government, but their securities do not carry a government guarantee. The banks, however, are required to maintain assets at least equal to the amount of debt that has been issued. Such assets include guaranteed mortgages, U.S. government securities, and cash.

(iii) Federal Home Loan Mortgage Corporation. Called "Freddie Mac," the Federal Home Loan Mortgage Corporation (FHLMC) is a government-sponsored enterprise. Established in 1970, the FHLMC is charged with maintaining mortgage credit for residential housing development and promoting a nationwide secondary market for conventional residential mortgages. The agency accomplishes these goals by buying mortgages from individual lenders. The mortgage purchases are financed by marketing mortgage participation certificates (PCs).

(iv) Federal National Mortgage Association. Called "Fannie Mae," the Federal National Mortgage Association (FNMA) is a public corporation owned by nongovernment stockholders. (It was originally a government-chartered corporation that did not issue stock.) The FNMA's primary goal is to provide funding for conventional mortgages, which it finances by selling debentures and short-term securities.

FNMA debentures have maturities of up to several years and its short-term securities have up to one year. The FNMA issues a large volume of short-term securities, thereby fueling a strong secondary market that provides a good deal of liquidity to its securities. FNMA notes are unsecured obligations of the issuer and are not backed by government guarantees. As a result, they often provide high yields in relation to Treasury securities.

(v) Student Loan Marketing Association. Called "Sallie Mae," the Student Loan Marketing Association is a private, nonprofit corporation that was created to encourage lending for higher education by guaranteeing student loans and financing the Federal Guaranteed Student Loan Program. Sallie Mae buys loans made by financial institutions under various federal and state student loan programs. Securities issued by the agency include discount notes that carry maturities ranging from a few days to one year. The agency also issues floating-rate obligations and fixed-term debentures that carry maturities of several years. (Rates on floating-rate securities vary on the basis of changes in market rates.) The federal government oversees the operations of Sallie Mae but does not guarantee its securities.

(vi) Government National Mortgage Association. Called "Ginnie Mae," the Government National Mortgage Association (GNMA) supervises and sponsors support programs for mortgages that do not qualify for private mortgage insurance and therefore cannot be sold in normal non-federally guaranteed mortgage markets. Ginnie Mae also funds and provides liquidity for conventional mortgages. GNMA securities are called PCs, and they provide a

pass-through (or pay out) of the interest and principal on pools of mortgages. The underlying mortgages are guaranteed by the Federal Housing Administration or the Veterans Administration. As a result, Ginnie Mae securities are considered to be backed by the full faith and credit of the U.S. government. This makes Ginnie Mae securities one of the few government agency securities carrying that high guarantee.

Because Ginnie Mae PCs have competitive yields and are backed by a government guarantee, many investors consider them to be an attractive investment in the intermediate- and long-term maturity areas. Maturities on Ginnie Mae pass-through certificates are 30 years. Homeowners whose mortgages have been sold to Ginnie Mae, however, may refinance them or sell their homes and repay the mortgage loans underlying the certificates. For that reason, Ginnie Mae mortgage pools actually have a much shorter average life than 30 years. Calculating the exact length of that average life is not easy; in fact, experts disagree over what method produces the most accurate results. Such disagreements are not academic, especially to investors who intend to hold Ginnie Mae or other mortgage-backed securities until maturity so that they can receive a stream of cash over the security's life.

For example, if the aggregate yield for mortgages in the pool is higher than current mortgage rates, the homeowners who are obligated on these mortgages will refinance the mortgages or repay the mortgages faster than scheduled. Homeowners have demonstrated a propensity to refinance mortgage loans as interest rates decline, with such refinancing representing repayment of the original mortgage and creation of a new mortgage. The new mortgage will not be part of the same Ginnie Mae pool as the original mortgage. On the other hand, mortgages in a Ginnie Mae pool with rates lower than the prevailing rate for mortgage financing will be paid off slower than the expected payment rate. Despite such uncertainties, a generally accepted estimate for the average life of a Ginnie Mae pool is about 12 years from its original creation.

(vii) Adverse Features of GNMA Investments. Mortgage-backed (MB) securities and PCs carry several potentially adverse features of which investors should be aware. Prices for these types of securities tend to be more volatile than prices of other government securities with similar maturities. GNMA prices tend to fall faster with rising interest rates than other 12-year government agency securities and T-bonds. Ginnie Maes tend to trade in a manner similar to 30-year bonds (the stated maturity of Ginnie Mae certificates is 30 years). As a result, an investor who sells Ginnie Maes in a market with higher interest rates than those prevail-

ing at the time the certificates were purchased may have to take a loss.

It also can be difficult to reinvest interest proceeds on Ginnie Mae certificates (or other pass-through securities) unless the investor holds a large portfolio of Ginnie Mae securities providing several hundreds of thousands of dollars in monthly cash flow. One problem with reinvesting the proceeds of a portfolio providing less than $100,000 in monthly cash flow is the difficulty in finding instruments that have yield, portfolio compatibility, and liquidity characteristics suitable for proper investment. A financial manager may end up with a portfolio consisting of small amounts of various instruments, rather than large blocks of securities. A large block of a security tends to be more liquid than a small block.

A second problem with these securities is the possibility of an accounting nightmare. Because the cash flow of the securities combines both principal and interest payments, delays and accounting errors can occur. It takes time to verify payment amounts and to file claims on incorrect amounts, both of which result in lost interest on funds received past their due dates. The yield advantage of the securities is thus diminished. Many investors think these securities are exempt from state income taxes, as Treasury securities are. In an increasing number of states, they are not tax exempt, however. It is important to have a tax adviser review state tax exemptions on government agency securities. It is also important to check into guarantees on the securities because not all of them carry a government guarantee.

Another potential problem with Ginnie Mae securities results from yield volatility. When interest rates drop and homeowners pay off mortgages faster than anticipated, the remaining life of the mortgage pool declines rapidly. An investor who bought a security with a high yield will find that the period of time the high yield continues to accrue shortens with falling interest rates. If the investor paid a premium to obtain the above-market yield, the income stream that was to amortize the premium could be prematurely eroded. Accordingly, market prices on the securities do not rise as fast as prices on other investments when interest rates fall.

(viii) Mortgage Pass-Through Securities. During the past several years, financial innovations have been responsible for the creation of many types of securities based on pools of home mortgages. Mortgage pass-through securities guaranteed by GNMA have been quite popular, because they typically provide greater yields than Treasury securities. Some studies even suggest that GNMA pass-through securities provide higher returns than many other fixed-income securities, but those returns are partly the result of some investors' resistance to the complexity of the instruments.

Before investing in mortgage pass-through securities, the financial manager must study all of the characteristics of the underlying mortgage pool, especially if the securities will be sold before maturity. Again, the guarantee status of the securities is important; those issued by Freddie Mac, for instance, do not carry a government guarantee.

(ix) Collateralized Mortgage Obligations. Collateralized mortgage obligations (CMOs) are bonds backed, or collateralized, by instruments such as GNMA or FHLMC pass-through securities. They were designed to improve on simple mortgage-backed securities and provide more predictable returns by taking specific characteristics of MB securities and solving the problems of receiving repayments that combine principal and interest. In essence, investment bankers have developed computer models that estimate the payback dates of a mortgage pool. Based on this analysis, specific durations, or ranches, are created. As mortgages backing the CMO pay back principal, the cash is set aside to pay off the first maturity, or tranche, on a quarterly basis. This process continues until all of the tranches are paid off. A more predictable maturity duration is thus established.

Because the actual duration of the underlying pool is not certain, however, CMOs still suffer some of the same payment problems as other MB securities. Despite the yield advantages CMOs have over other securities of comparable credit quality, financial managers should beware of the following four disadvantages:

1. CMOs have very complicated payback formulas, like other mortgage-backed securities, when interest rates are volatile.
2. Accounting is difficult because flows of principal and interest are uneven.
3. Incorrect and late payments can result from problems in bank and dealer offices.
4. Market prices are more volatile on CMOs than other fixed-income securities as a result of such problems.

(x) Asset-Backed Securities. Asset-backed securities are instruments who's credit worthiness is usually established by a pool of assets serving as collateral for security. Many U.S. government agencies sell securities that are asset banked (i.e., Student Loan Marketing Association uses student loans, GNMA uses mortgages). However, these securities carry certain guarantees, special or implied, by the U.S. government to assure investors of their credit quality. However, there are many other types of asset backed securities that are not government released and have collateral

pools consisting of auto loans and credit card receivables. The credit worthiness of these instruments by (credit rating firms) advisory based on the typed of loans or assets their default history, reserves set aside for losses, and other factors. Overall, with some cautions, asset backed securities are viable in most fixed-income securities portfolios.

(xi) Municipal Debt Instruments. Municipal securities are debt obligations paying a fixed or floating rate of interest as designated for a specified period of time (with principal and interest payable at maturity) that are issued by state and local governments and their agencies. Usually, the interest paid on them is exempt from federal income taxes and often from state and local taxes within the state in which they are issued. However, many municipal securities pay non-tax-exempt interest and are therefore suitable for nonprofit organizations. The proceeds from municipal securities provide working capital or fulfill interim or seasonal funding needs for the issuing entity. They are grouped into two categories: general obligation securities (GOs) and revenue bonds. With revenue securities, payment of interest and principal is made from revenues received, including tolls, user charges, rents paid by those who use the facilities financed by the security issue, or other revenue tied specifically to the security.

Municipal instruments are available with maturities from 7 days to 30 years, providing investors with flexibility in fulfilling their time-structured investment needs with adequate liquidity. Also, the municipal instrument market has a good overall record of safety. Municipals, in fact, are often considered second in safety only to government agency issues.

(xii) Municipal Bond Insurance. [Note: The author highly recommends that unsophisticated investors purchase *only* insured or pre-refunded (discussed later) municipal obligations.] In an attempt to provide additional security to a bond issue, some municipal investors have incorporated third-party guarantees or insured their municipal bonds. Many institutions insure municipal bonds. The major groups, consisting of large insurance companies and banks, that have formed associations to provide insurance to issuers of municipal bonds are Municipal Bond Investors Assurance Corporation (MBIA), Financial Guarantee Insurance Company (FGIC), Bond Investor Guarantee (BIG), and the AMBAC Indemnity Corporation. These associations guarantee the timely payment of interest and principal to municipal bond investors. This type of insurance normally elicits an AAA rating from credit rating agencies, as it greatly increases the credit quality of the municipal bonds to which it is attached.

Other types of guarantees are provided by insurance companies and banks; they also bring an AAA credit rating. When selecting an instrument with a guarantee, the investor should be aware that the credit quality of the municipal issue is only as good as the credit quality of the insuring institution. Generally, AMBAC and MBIA are thought to provide better quality insurance than banks, groups of banks, or other small institutions do.

Issuers of municipal bonds pay a fee to obtain this insurance or a letter of credit (LOC) from a major bank, either foreign or domestic, to add the element of credit quality to the municipal instruments they will issue. This LOC, depending upon the creditworthiness of the bank that provides it, often gives the investor an additional assurance of safety to principal if the bank providing the guarantee is sound. However, the investor should remember that if the quality and creditworthiness of the institution that provides the LOC deteriorate, the quality of the guarantee on the municipal bond will also decline.

Furthermore, the investor should investigate whether the insurance guarantee or LOC guarantee covers natural disasters, including earthquakes. If this type of insurance is not provided, the municipal bond insurance may turn out to be inadequate in the event of a financially devastating natural disaster. Also, it is important to verify that the insurance will be in force for the life of the bond and covers the entire amount of the issue.

(xiii) Types of Municipal Bonds. The municipal security market contains a myriad of distinct instruments, including general obligation bonds, revenue bonds, and refunding bonds.

(xiv) General Obligation Bonds. This type of instrument is considered one of the most credit secure of all municipal bonds, assuming that the issuing municipality is of sound credit. Payment of principal and coupon interest is secured by the state or local government's full faith and credit and the timely payment of principal and interest by the limited or unlimited taxing power of the municipality.

(xv) Revenue Bonds. Revenue bonds are bonds issued to fund a project. When the project is completed, the revenue it produces is used to pay the principal and interest on the bond issue. It is important to be sure that completion risk is assessed and that the project will be completed. This type of financing is often used by the government entities to fund the building of bridges, tollways, and housing facilities.

(xvi) Refunding Bonds. Refunding bonds are bonds issued to replace an outstanding issue of instruments that is being called

redeemed, or refunded because more favorable interest rates are now available in the market. If an institution has bonds outstanding, it becomes economical after interest rates drop, perhaps 2 percent or more, to consider coming to market with a new bond issue and using the proceeds of that new bond issue, which would be sold at a lower interest rate cost or accrual cost factor, to pay off the older issue and therefore create a savings in future interest expense.

There are different types of refunding bond issues. Principal and interest from some issues are called or paid off immediately with the proceeds from a new bond.

(xvii) Pre-refunded Bonds. Pre-refunded bonds are bonds that have been called and have a stipulated remaining life of one to several years. In other words, because of the initial terms of the bond indenture, the proceeds from the refunding issue are put into an escrow account and those funds are invested in a particular type of security as stipulated under the terms of the refunding. These bonds have unusually high credit ratings since the money to pay them at maturity has been placed in an escrow account and invested in a particular security that will be available to pay the interest and principal on the pre-refunded bonds on the date stipulated for their early payment. The securities purchased and held in the escrow account may vary from Treasury securities to instruments issued by a variety of institutions, including bank CDs. If the securities deposited in the escrow account are Treasuries (zero credit risk), refunded bonds possess little, if any, credit risk themselves. (Note: this type of municipal is the most appropriate type for investors who wish to avoid default risk.) Generally, such Treasury-backed refunded bonds are given AAA/Aaa ratings by Moody's and Standard & Poor's. If the escrow account contains Treasury or governments however, the investor should be careful to verify that there is no possibility the pre-refunded bonds will be called prior to their pre-refunded payment date. Their specific call or maturity must be ascertained by the investor.

(xviii) Certificates of Participation. Over the past two decades, a tax limitation mood has swept the United States, leading voters in a number of states to limit the taxing authority of their municipalities. These tax limitation initiatives require the governing bodies of their states to obtain approval by one-half to two-thirds of the voters, before initiating new or higher taxes. To get around this, new instruments, such as the certificate of participation (COP) were created to allow municipalities to meet the tax limitation initiative requirements.

COPs are bonds issued to pay for a particular project whereby a share of the revenues from the project—that is, a particular portion of the income—is used to repay the principal debt and the income expense. COPs have become particularly common in California, which was one of the first states to approve tax limitation legislation.

(xix) Zero Coupon Municipal Bonds. Zero coupon municipal bonds are issued at a large discount from their maturity value. When they mature, the difference between the investor's cost and the maturity value is their interest. However, zero coupon bonds, like longer-term notes and bonds, have call features that allow the issuer to redeem, or pay off, the bond issue before its maturity date. (This is often done if interest rates go down substantially from the date the bond was issued, enabling the bond issuer to pay off an older, high-interest bond and issue a newer one at a much lower interest cost.) Although Treasury zero coupon bonds have call features, they are not usually callable until close to maturity. Consequently, unlike many other zero coupon bonds issues, they do not present this problem. In particular, zero coupon municipal bonds with a long maturity have call provisions that, if not carefully tended to at the time of purchase, can be extremely costly to an investor.

Specifically, many zero coupon municipal bonds are issued with a call provision stating that when the bonds are called, the call price will be equal to the initial issuer price plus whatever interest they accumulate, or accrue, at the initial interest rate at time of issue until called. This is referred to as their accreted value. If the investor buys a zero coupon municipal bond at a time other than its initial issue date and the bond goes up in market price so that he pays an amount of principal above its initial issue price and that bond is then called, he may receive substantially less for it than his purchase price. So before buying a zero coupon municipal bond, the Chief Investment Officer should ask the following questions and be certain he has the right answers.

- How much over its original price am I paying for this bond and how does the price relate to its accreted value?
- What are the call features of this bond?

Also, the investor should be sure to have his municipal zero coupon bonds registered with the issuer's paying agent. Otherwise, he may not know when these bonds are called. For example, if he held them for 10 years to their maturity date, he might find that as he presented them for payment they were called eight years earlier and he was not notified because the paying agent, or registrar, had no record of his purchase. Accordingly, he would receive his invested principal and only two years' interest.

(xx) Municipal Notes. Municipal notes have a shorter maturity than municipal bonds, ranging from a few months to five years. They include tax anticipation notes, revenue anticipation notes, bond anticipation notes, tax-exempt commercial paper, and floating-rate notes.

(xxi) Tax Anticipation Notes. Tax anticipation notes are issued by municipalities to finance their operations in anticipation of future tax receipts. They are usually GOs.

(xxii) Revenue Anticipation Notes. Revenue anticipation notes are issued by municipalities to finance their operations, although the revenues anticipated are not always tax receipts. These are usually GOs.

(xxiii) Bond Anticipation Notes. Bond anticipation notes are issued by municipalities to finance projects that will later be funded by the sale of long-term bonds. These are usually GOs. Care must be used to select issues for which bonds will actually be issued to pay off the notes. Also, if a project is the purpose of this type of issue, it is important to verify that the project will be completed.

(xxiv) Floating-Rate Notes with Put Option Futures. The rates of a number of tax-exempt notes are set weekly or daily on the basis of an index established by the issuer. Usually an investor may redeem or put these notes at par with either one day or one week's notice, depending on their issuer format. Interest on these instruments is paid monthly. This category of municipal has become a widely accepted money market, short-term investment because of the flexibility. Although the instruments are issued with a long maturity date, the put feature of the one- or seven-days, which is usually secured by an LOC or other guarantee, is the critical feature.

13.10 MUNICIPAL FLOATING-RATE INSTRUMENT PROBLEMS

The following steps should be taken by an investor who buys municipal floating-rate instruments.

1. Check the accuracy of each new reset rate and date (based on the terms of the instrument), as they can be set in error. He should not assume that they will always be set as they should be. These instruments are all a little different and must be followed closely to verify proper rates at reset dates.
2. Check the dollar amount of each interest payment. He should not assume that they will always be correct.

3. Check the date on which the interest payment is received to be sure it is on time.

4. Since these instruments mature beyond one year, they must be registered with a transfer agent and may not be held in bearer form. Therefore, the investor should make sure a safekeeping agent holds these securities in their "nominee name" to facilitate the transfer if a put may occur. Furthermore, the investor should realize that any transfer of title on a security may take a few days to five weeks—or even longer. Accordingly, if the investor plans to redeem or put these bonds shortly (in less than three months) after he purchases them, a problem could arise if the bonds are out for re-registration into his bank safekeeping unit's nominee name. The only way to avoid this problem is to leave the put bonds with the dealer from whom they were purchased since the dealer can easily put them on his behalf. Accordingly, investors should not have these instruments registered in their own name, but rather in their safekeeping agent's nominee name. Again, because paperwork to transfer ownership causes some delay, it may prevent a timely put exercise shortly after the purchase date.

5. Should the investor purchase a floating-rate municipal, he should be aware that portfolio records will need to be updated regularly to reflect each new interest reset rate, i.e., each new weekly or daily reset rate. Should several issues of this type be purchased, much time and attention will be needed to keep records current.

13.11 CORPORATE DEBT INSTRUMENTS

Corporate debt is issued by industrial corporations, utility companies, finance companies, bank holding companies, domestic facilities of foreign institutions, and other private-sector organizations. All corporate debt is subject to default risk. Therefore, financial managers should examine the credit ratings of the organization issuing corporate debt instruments. In general, corporate debt falls into three categories: (1) commercial paper, (2) medium-term corporate notes, and (3) long-term bonds. The differences among these categories, of course, lie in varying maturity lengths.

(a) Commercial Paper

Many large corporations in recent years have eschewed bank loans in favor of financing obtained from less expensive sources. For a large corporation with an excellent credit rating, the least expensive source of financing is to issue its own debt in the form of commercial paper that is sold to investors through the capital markets. Domestic and foreign manufacturing and industrial companies issue commercial paper, as do finance companies and bank holding companies. Paper issued by finance companies is called direct finance paper; it is generally sold directly to investors through banks acting as agents for the issuers. Paper issued by industrial companies is called dealer paper; it is usually sold through dealers who have purchased the paper themselves. Commercial paper is a promissory note, usually unsecured, maturing on a specific date. In most cases, it is issued in bearer form in minimum denominations of $100,000. Commercial paper is liquid, because a secondary market exists. However, investors generally hold commercial paper to maturity. Issuers and dealers often will buy paper back if an investor needs cash.

Maturities on most commercial paper run from 1 to 180 days. The longest maturity that commercial paper carries is 270 days, as debt issues with longer maturities must be registered with the Securities and Exchange Commission (SEC). Registration is expensive. Commercial paper provides investors with an efficient short-term investment instrument that matures on a specific date.

The yield on commercial paper depends on the issuer's credit rating, its need for money, maturity of the paper, its face value, and general money market rates. Most companies that issue commercial paper are rated by agencies such as Moody's, Standard & Poor's, Fitch, and Duff and Phelps. Commercial paper that falls into the highest rating class is called "top tier." Investing in top tier paper entails minimal credit risk, though risk is still present. Commercial paper, therefore, provides higher yields than Treasury and government agency securities of the same maturities.

(i) Issuing Formats. In addition to the flexibility and efficiency of its maturity dates, commercial paper offers a choice of two formats, interest-bearing or discounted. An investor buying $1 million in interest-bearing commercial paper pays the $1 million face value and collects interest upon maturity. Not much interest-bearing commercial paper is issued, however, except in very short maturities. Because most interest-bearing commercial paper is held to maturity, its liquidity is decreased. Discount commercial paper, which is more common, works like U.S. T-bills, where an investor buys the note at a discount and receives its face value at maturity.

(ii) Types of Commercial Paper. Commercial paper is a flexible investment vehicle available in eight types:

1. Bank holding company commercial paper is issued by the parent companies of commercial banks.

2. Industrial commercial paper is issued by major industrial companies to provide short-term working capital.

3. Finance company commercial paper is issued by captive finance companies of major industrial corporations. The finance companies use the money generated by commercial paper programs to provide financing to buyers of the parent corporation's products.

4. Dealer commercial paper is issued by corporations through securities dealers, rather than through banks or the company itself. A dealer generally underwrites an issue, which means that the dealer buys the paper and resells it to investors.

5. Direct or finance commercial paper is paper distributed by banks. Until recently, banks could not act as dealers; they could act only as agents for commercial paper issuers, generally finance companies. The bank would take orders from investors but would not invest any of its own money to maintain its own inventory of an issue.

6. Foreign commercial paper is issued in the United States by domestic subsidiaries of foreign industrial and financial organizations. The paper generally is guaranteed by the foreign parent.

7. Collateralized commercial paper is usually issued to generate funds to purchase loans from an affiliated savings and loan. The collateral often takes the form of Treasury or government agency securities pledged by the institution's parent. Many investors consider collateralized commercial paper to be a secure short-term investment.

8. LOC commercial paper (also called "commercial paper LOC") is, as its name suggests, supported by a bank LOC. A major bank or insurance company backs the credit quality of LOC commercial paper for a fee. Companies that issue LOC commercial paper tend to be smaller, are less well-known, and have less than the highest credit rating. These issuers use the LOC guarantee to enhance their credit standing to raise short-term borrowings at a lower interest cost. The credit strength behind the paper is not the issuing company but the institution that provides the LOC.

This commercial paper comes in the following varieties:

- *Full-and-direct pay paper.* The institution backing the issue with its LOC will pay upon maturity if the issuer cannot pay the full amount directly to the investor.

- *Standby LOC commercial paper.* This variety does not carry as strong a guarantee as full-and-direct pay LOC commercial paper. A standby LOC, for instance, may cover only partial payments and various types of delayed payments. This is acceptable but not preferable in the opinion of many investors.

- *Irrevocable LOC commercial paper.* The LOC cannot be revoked or canceled.

(b) Loan Participations

Major money center banks developed loan participations as a means of providing financing to bank customers in lieu of the customers issuing commercial paper. Because it had been illegal for commercial banks to underwrite commercial paper, several banks developed loan participations as a way of keeping customers from going to other institutions for financing. Under a loan participation arrangement, a bank creates a loan to one of its customers, then sells pieces of the loan to investors. It is similar to a securities dealer selling commercial paper to investors in order to provide funds for a corporate borrower.

Investors find loan participations attractive because their yields are higher than CDs and commercial paper. Yields on loan participations can be as much as 15 basis points greater than comparable investment instruments, depending on the creditworthiness of the borrower. Loan participations are attractive borrowing vehicles because they carry low administrative charges. Accordingly, finance managers can look upon loan participations as good investment alternatives, though they should be used selectively. Loan participations are not liquid investments. Before investing in a loan participation, an investor should examine the borrowing company's credit ratings.

(c) Corporate Notes

Medium-term notes are promissory notes that pay either a fixed- or variable-rate of interest, with principal payable at maturity. As the name suggests, these instruments lie in the middle ranges of the yield curve. Corporate notes carry maturities ranging between nine months and 10 years; their maturities thus begin where commercial paper maturities end. Issued in much the same way as commercial paper, corporate notes are available either through underwriting or ongoing issuance programs called "medium-term notes" or shelf registrations. Under a shelf registration, an issuer maintains a continuing registration statement with the SEC and posts rates daily for a range of maturities. This allows the issuer to control both maturity length and the overall distribution of securities. The ability to offer medium-term notes whose rates fluctuate for different maturity periods allows large corporations to plan borrowing better based on corporate needs and market rates. (Shelf registrations were made possible by changes to SEC Rule 415 that allow corporations to make certain types of amendments to debt documents without SEC review.)

For investors, on the other hand, medium-term notes allow financial managers to choose the exact maturities they need and to base investment decisions on the yield curve. Medium-term notes offer four basic advantages to institutional investors:

1. Medium-term notes are issued with a range of maturities. By choosing any maturity date within that range, financial managers can tailor the instruments somewhat to fit into a portfolio.

2. The primary and secondary market availability of medium-term notes allows investment managers to satisfy maturity, yield, and duration needs of a portfolio.

3. Yield spreads on medium-term notes are relatively stable under most market conditions, because many different issuers and maturities are available on any given day.

4. Growth in the medium-term market, since it first appeared in 1982, has resulted in excellent liquidity for the instruments. This allows financial managers to use active investment management techniques.

(d) Corporate Bonds

Corporations seeking to borrow large sums of money over a period of time longer than 10 years issue corporate bonds. A corporate bond is essentially an IOU under which the borrower (bond issuer) agrees to pay the investor a fixed amount of interest in return for the use of the investor's money over the period of the loan (the bond's maturity). There is an active secondary market for corporate bonds of many large companies, and this enhances their liquidity. When an investor wants to sell bonds before maturity, the bond's value becomes critical, especially because the long-term bond market can fluctuate widely. Bonds offer the important advantage of high return to financial managers who can invest in longer maturities. Because an investor takes on more risk when investing in instruments with long maturities, fixed returns are greater. Bond investors also stand to gain if interest rates decline, though bonds often have call features, allowing the issuer to redeem them prior to maturity without penalty.

(e) High-Yield (Junk) Bonds

High-yield bonds, commonly called junk bonds, are bonds that have a high default risk. They are issued by unrated borrowers or borrowers with low credit ratings. Because bonds issued by these borrowers have low perceived credit quality that portends a high default risk, they offer a high yield. In terms of credit ratings, junk bonds carry a rating of Ba and below when rated by Moody's Investors Service and BB or less when rated by Standard & Poor's, assuming they are rated at all. According to Moody's *Bond Record,* "Bonds which are rated Ba are judged to have speculative elements; their future cannot be considered as well assured. Often the protection of interest and principal payments may be very moderate and thereby not well safeguarded . . ."

(f) Master Notes

Master notes are variable-rate demand notes that are used in ongoing borrowing programs of large companies. Master notes are made available to investors through bank trust departments by some of the same companies that issue commercial paper and medium-term notes. Master notes are generally issued in denominations of between $5 million and $10 million. They are flexible instruments that allow an investor to determine the terms under which funds are invested. Investors can stipulate such requirements as:

- The amount of money the investor wants to invest initially and the ability to add or withdraw from that investment on short notice
- The length of maturity that the investor wants, as an investor can withdraw funds on short notice
- The times at which the investor wants to receive interest payments, whether monthly, quarterly, or semiannually

Accordingly, each master note has its own terms and conditions that can be discussed and set through negotiations with the dealer. The ability to deposit and withdraw funds on short notice is the primary advantage of a master note.

A master note is generally issued in two parts: (1) "A Note," a variable-term note, and (2) "B Note," a fixed-term note. The note is divided because master note investors usually keep their balances at a certain level. The bottom half of the master note (the B Note) is the half in which funds are maintained. The investor often is required to give notice of up to 12 to 15 months to withdraw funds from the B Note. Investors can withdraw funds from the top half of the master note (the A note) on demand. A master note structured in two parts should pay a higher yield than a regular master note because the borrower is able to lock up a portion of the funds for a fixed term.

Yields on master notes are generally set in relation to a well-established base rate. For instance, daily floating yields may be set on the basis of the Federal Reserve's daily Fed funds rate. Yields on master notes are about the same or slightly less than those of other money market instruments. The reason for the lower rate is that master note investments are highly liquid and flexible, as they essentially allow financial managers to determine maturities and investment amounts.

13.12 MONEY MARKET INSTRUMENTS ISSUED BY BANKS

The term "money market," as distinguished from the term "capital market," refers to borrowing and lending for periods of a year or less. Organizations issue money market instruments for a variety of reasons, one of the most common of which is the mismatched timing of their cash receipts and cash disbursements. They need financing in the short run and can obtain it by borrowing from a lender or issuing short-term, or money market, instruments. From the investor's point of view, the money market affords a way to earn interest on excess capital without tying it up for long periods of time. The more common money market instruments used by financial managers for short-term investing are discussed below.

(a) Banker's Acceptances

Banker's acceptances (BAs) are short-term drafts whose drawee bank has accepted the obligation to pay the instrument at maturity. BAs are used primarily to finance trade transactions, frequently in international trade, and are similar to commercial paper except they entail less risk to investors. A BA is drawn on and accepted by a domestic bank and sold to an investor at a discount. The bank agrees to redeem the note at maturity for full face value. Most BAs have maturities of three months, though they can be as long as six months, and are sold in denominations of $500,000, $1,000,000, and multiples of $1,000,000. BA investments offer the following advantages:

- Yield spread advantage ranging between 25 and 75 basis points higher than T-bills
- Smaller capital investments that produce yields similar to CDs
- Full negotiability
- Active secondary market for BAs of $500,000 or more

The following example illustrates how BAs work to finance international trade transactions. Company A, a U.S. company, plans to import optical lenses from Company B, a West German company. Company A wants to pay for the lenses six months after shipment, hoping that the lenses will have been sold and the proceeds collected by that time. Company A is too small to issue debt in the open market, so it seeks financing from its bank. The company uses BA financing, because it is less expensive than a normal business loan. For its part, the bank issues a LOC to Company B on behalf of Company A for the purpose of importing and paying for the lenses. When the lenses are shipped, Company B draws a time draft due in six months on Company A's bank that issued that LOC, discounts the draft at its own West German bank, and receives payment. The West German bank then sends the time draft to Company A's bank, which "accepts" the draft, indicating acceptance of the liability to pay the instrument when it matures.

Company A's bank is obliged to pay the draft at maturity. Meanwhile, Company B's bank may hold the draft until maturity or sell it in the money market to investors. Ultimately, it is the responsibility of Company A's bank to pay off the acceptance at maturity even if Company A cannot. As a result, BAs are direct obligations of both the accepting bank and issuing company, and usually the goods underlying the transaction are pledged to secure the obligation. Investors have very little risk if the draft is accepted by a bank with a top credit rating. Very large banks long have been active in BA financing. In 73 years, no investor has lost principal except on counterfeit BAs. There are three additional varieties of BAs.

(b) Negotiable Certificates of Deposit and Time Deposits

The removal by the Federal Reserve system of interest rate restrictions on time deposits during the early 1980s has led to increased competition among banks. Banks now attract deposits by offering higher interest rates than their competitors, especially for deposits of more than $100,000. The result has been an active resale market for CDs in amounts exceeding $1 million.

Corporations and other investors with large sums to invest had not used fixed time deposits because they lacked liquidity. Consequently, negotiable time CDs were invented in 1961. Negotiable CDs thus provide institutional financial managers with the advantages of flexible maturities, an active secondary market, and some collateralization of deposits.

Marketable CDs are generally sold in units of $1 million or more. They are issued at face value and generally pay interest semiannually if issued for maturities of one year or more. Maturities on CDs range between a few days and several years, but most are less than a year. Yields on CDs are greater than Treasury and government agency securities, as investors are exposed to some credit risk. Liquidity depends on the credit quality of the issuing bank and the size of the instrument. An excellent secondary market for CDs issued by major banks does exist.

There are four sources for negotiable CDs: (1) domestic banks (Domestic CDs); (2) U.S. branches of foreign banks (Yankee CDs); (3) thrift institutions (Thrift CDs); and (4) Foreign issued CDs, in Eurodollars. Thrift institutions include savings banks and savings and loan associations. There is an active secondary market for Domestic CDs; Yankee CDs; and, to a somewhat lesser degree, major thrift CDs. Domestic and Yankee CDs are sold directly to investors by banks or through dealers. These dealers also contribute to the activity of secondary CD markets. Since CDs have federal deposit insurance (FDIC or FSLIC) only up to $100,000, an investor must check the credit quality of the issuing entity for amounts over $100,000.

(i) Variable-Rate CDs. Variable-rate CDs are a relatively new type of negotiable CD. Two types of variable-rate CDs dominate the market: (1) six-month CDs with a 30-day roll, and (2) one-and-a-half year or longer CDs with a three-month roll. Interest is paid upon each roll and a new coupon set. Coupons established at issue, as well as those set on roll dates, are set at some increment above a benchmark interest rate that often is the average rate banks pay on new CDs with similar maturities. Rates range from 12.5 to 30 basis points above the benchmark, depending on the credit of the issuer and the maturity of the note. Benchmark rates are published by the Federal Reserve System. Financial managers must examine variable-rate CDs closely because of their unique features. Variable-rate CDs provide investors with some rate protection against increasing interest rates. They tend to be less liquid than other CDs, however, until their last roll period when they trade like regular CDs of similar maturity.

(ii) Eurodollar Time Deposits. Eurodollar time deposits are non-negotiable deposits made in an offshore branch of a foreign or domestic bank. They have all the protection afforded to any domestic deposit except Federal Deposit Insurance Corporation (FDIC) insurance. As their name suggests, Eurodollar time deposits are deposits; hence, no financial instrument is created. Because the deposits are not traded, they are illiquid. Some banks, however, will allow depositors to withdraw their money early with no interest penalty, although investors interested in liquidity should use Eurodollar time deposits only as short-term investments (one to 90 days).

A unique risk element of Eurodollar time deposits is sovereign or country risk. This refers to an investor's exposure when money falls under the control of the country in which it is deposited. If the foreign government decides that funds will not be transferred out of the country, investors may find their money tied up for longer periods than they had planned. Investors can minimize sovereign risk by selecting offshore sites carefully. Professional investors consider the branches of major banks in London, the Cayman Islands, and Nassau to be relatively safe locations for depositing investment dollars.

(iii) Eurodollar CDs.   Because Eurodollar time deposits are not liquid and many investors desire liquidity, banks that had accepted Eurodollar time deposits in London and Nassau began to issue Eurodollar CDs. A Eurodollar CD is similar to a domestic CD, except that the liability resides with the bank's offshore branch rather than its domestic branch. Any domestic or foreign bank can issue Eurodollar CDs, though Eurodollar CDs issued in London and Nassau are the most common.

The primary advantage of Eurodollar CDs to a financial manager is their rate of return, which is higher than for most domestic CDs. However, they are also susceptible to sovereign risk and are slightly less liquid than domestic CDs. Many Eurodollar CDs are issued through dealers that maintain an active secondary market in the instruments. If the instrument is denominated in U.S. dollars, domestic investors have no foreign exchange exposure.

(iv) Yankee CDs.   When foreign banks issue U.S. dollar-denominated CDs through their domestic U.S. branches, the instruments are called Yankee CDs, in contrast to Eurodollar CDs that are issued through offshore branches. Yankee CDs are not as liquid as domestic CDs, so their rates are closer to those of Eurodollar CDs and a little higher than domestic CDs but not substantially. Most of the institutional investors that buy Yankee CDs are interested primarily in yield. Changes in Federal Reserve regulations that make it more expensive for foreign banks to raise money by issuing Yankee CDs account for less attractive rates on Yankee CDs.

(c) Money Market Mutual Funds

Pools of money invested in particular categories of instruments (i.e., stocks, 4 bonds, and short-term money market instruments) and managed by professionals are called mutual funds. Money market funds, of course, are a type of mutual fund that invests solely in short-term, fixed-income instruments. In return for investing money in a mutual fund, an investor receives shares and becomes a part owner of the mutual fund. The original purpose behind mutual funds was to allow individual investors to earn the same returns as large institutional investors. However, large institutional investors are now investing in mutual funds because they are easier to manage than some other forms of investment.

In fact, a money market mutual fund can occasionally provide higher yields than direct investments made by an experienced money market investor. When interest rates are falling, for instance, yields on money market mutual funds are slow to fall, because of the time it takes for instruments to mature and be replaced with new instruments that carry the lower rate. Money market mutual funds generally invest in instruments with maturities of 60 days or less, and they generally do not penalize investors for early withdrawal.

However, there are risks associated with money market mutual funds. The primary risk is mismanagement, though the investment manager is required to keep any promises made in the prospectus. The other risk is poor investing. The fund must invest in instruments that have risk characteristics acceptable to the institution and that have performed well over time.

There are advantages to money market mutual funds as well. Some funds allow investors to write checks or otherwise transfer money invested in the fund. Many money market mutual funds invest in municipal instruments that provide tax-exempt returns to investors in high tax brackets. These funds also may limit market risk, as most instruments carry maturities of less than 60 days and do not tend to fluctuate in price. Many newspapers carry listings of current yields and weighted average maturities on a variety of money market mutual funds. It is easy to compare yields and lengths of maturity, because most funds use standard formulas in reporting them.

(d) Bond Funds

During the past ten years, bond funds have grown in relation to the number of funds offered and the number of investors attracted to them. Marketing of all types of bond funds, from those investing in municipal bonds to those investing in government securities, has been heavy. The major advantages of bond funds are (1) reduced administrative expenses, (2) reduced research and management costs, and (3) yields equal to a broad market index for government, corporate mortgage, or municipal securities.

However, it is recommended that institutional financial managers take particular care when investing in bond funds for the following five reasons:

1. Until recent Federal Regulations were imposed, advertisements often did not state fund income accurately. The advertised yield was the current yield of the items in the fund, not the fund's

total return. The total return may have been substantially lower because of the effect of market prices on yields. Investors should make sure that fund yields, as advertised, comply with the new standards for accurate comparison.

2. Bond funds, in order to present more attractive yields to investors, often buy bonds with the longest maturities available, and these usually have the highest yields. At the same time, however, long-term bonds decline in price faster than other instruments when interest rates increase, and they are difficult to sell in unsettled markets. Bond funds, therefore, can decline in value relatively fast.

3. Investors are often under the impression that no-load funds allow them to buy shares without paying a sales charge (called a load). Fund managers can, however, charge a redemption fee that reduces an investor's total yield.

4. Bond funds sometimes have difficulty changing investment strategies to reflect changes in the bond market. This is especially true of funds that specialize in municipal bonds, Ginnie Mae securities, and junk corporate bonds. Their markets may not be highly liquid or stable; indeed, in the highly unstable markets of May and October 1987, for example, massive redemptions by municipal bond funds contributed to market instability.

5. A bond fund can receive permission from the U.S. SEC to stop redeeming its shares in situations such as panic selling a fact not many investors know. Such situations are rare, however.

When these five factors are considered, along with sales charges and management fees, it is often less expensive to retain a professional fixed-income investment adviser than to buy into a bond fund. This decision, however, depends on the amount of money the institution has invested in fixed-income securities.

13.13 REPURCHASE AGREEMENTS

(a) Introduction

For many institutional financial managers, repurchase agreements, or repos, are one of the most common fixed-income investment media. Repos are short-term investments, often for one day only, that supplement a cash management or liquidity portfolio. Securities dealers use repos to finance their inventories of U.S. Treasury government agency, and other securities. The dealer puts its inventory of securities up as collateral (see Exhibit 13.6). The repos allow the dealer to finance its inventory at a lower interest rate than other

Exhibit 13.6.   Repurchase Agreements

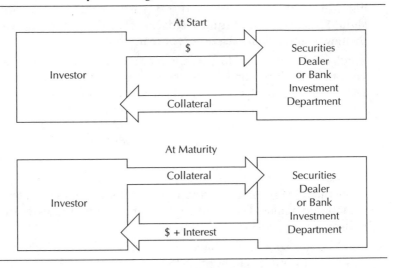

sources of short-term capital. The Federal Reserve System also uses repos to manage the nation's money supply. It initiates repos to add money and reverses repos to decrease the money supply. For the investor, repos can be exceptionally sound investments. Before financial managers use repos, they must understand the nature of their investment and financing uses so that funds are not lost.

Repurchase agreements became particularly popular in the 1970s when interest rates reached new heights. Interest rates were so high that banks were barred from paying interest on short-term deposits by regulations limiting interest rates. By investing in an overnight repo, however, financial managers could effectively create demand deposits that paid interest. Financial managers were able to use repos to earn high yields but retain liquidity.

Repos can be somewhat expensive in terms of paperwork and complexity, especially overnight repos. Other instruments, such as overnight commercial paper, can provide better returns with less administration. When funds arrive late in the day, however, there is often no other investment vehicle available for the funds. Delivery transactions generally must be made before noon Eastern time. However, a repo that is executed with a local bank often can be executed later.

(b) Definitions

The term repurchase agreement refers to the basic feature of the instrument. A repo involves the temporary sale of a security that is repurchased at a later time. To a securities dealer, the repo represents a borrowing at a fixed interest rate for a specific period of time. (Interest is payable upon maturity and rates are generally lower than those on federal funds loans or deposits because the transaction is backed by collateral.) By nature, therefore, a repo involves two simultaneous agreements, one under which the security is sold at a specified price and another under which the security is repurchased at a higher specified price on a date that can be anywhere from one to 360 days later. The interest, of course, is the difference between the sale and repurchase prices. What happens, in essence, is that investors give funds to the dealer and receive collateral (the security) in return. When the funds are returned, investors receive interest.

When entering into a repo transaction, financial managers should seek to receive securities with a slightly higher market value than the funds they are lending, especially if the agreements last for more than a few days. This is to protect the investor (lender) if the seller defaults. It also protects the investor in the event that the market value of the securities declines before the conclusion of the agreement. A repo agreement may also include a provision requiring the investor to return a portion of the securities to the borrower if they increase in market value. Some financial managers seek to limit risk further by limiting repo activities to banks that have high credit ratings and to primary dealers monitored by the New York Federal Reserve Bank.

(i) Reverse Repurchase Agreements. A reverse repo is one viewed from the side of the counterparty, or dealer. A borrower puts up Treasury, government agency, or other securities as collateral and borrows funds against them for a specified period of time. A reverse repo, therefore, is not an investment but a loan with securities used as collateral. To a financial manager, reverse repo is a means of borrowing funds, while a repo is a means of lending them. In fact, every repurchase agreement because it involves two agreements consists of a repo on one side and a reverse repo on the other. When a transaction is viewed from the dealer's point of view, it is a reverse repurchase agreement when the customer delivers the securities to the dealer. An investor that needs funds for a short period of time should consider a reverse repo instead of an outright sale of a security.

An institution's financial manager can derive two benefits from reverse repos. First, they provide a relatively low-cost source of short-term debt. Second, the funds obtained through a reverse repo often can be used to make investments that will pay a higher return than the rate at which they were borrowed. (The difference between the cost of borrowing the funds and the yields received from reinvesting them is a form of interest arbitrage.)

In considering a reverse repo, a financial manager must determine the credit quality of the dealer with which the securities are placed. If it is insufficient, the dealer may not be able to return the securities upon conclusion of the agreement, even when the securities appreciate during the agreement. The amount of the loan is generally 85 percent of the value of the securities used as collateral in a reverse repo; the lender is thus protected against a decline in their value.

(ii) Brokered or Matched Repurchase Agreements. These repos are tied to reverse repurchase agreements. Rather than placing collateral directly with the lender, the borrower places the collateral with a third party, a dealer or a bank. The collateral is placed with an investor by the third party. In exchange for this service, it receives a "spread," the difference between the cost the third party charges the borrower and the return it pays the lender.

(e) Risks of Repo Transactions

Repurchase agreements contain three sources of risk. The first involves control over the securities that are being used as collateral. The investor should seek to obtain control by using one of the custodial arrangements discussed at the end of the next section or by taking physical possession of the securities. In that way, there will be no misunderstanding of whether there are liens on the securities. Even when an investor has control over the securities, however, questions over the ability of the investor to see these securities in the event of a default by the borrower may still arise.

The second source of risk in repo agreements involves changes in market conditions. If the value of the securities used as collateral in the agreement falls, the collateral may not be of sufficient value to compensate the investor in the event of a default. The seriousness of market risk, of course, depends on the length of the agreement; an overnight repo contains very little market risk. In recognition of this risk, many repo agreements contain margin requirements. An investor lending $10 million, for instance, generally will require that the securities dealer put up securities having a market value of $10,100,000 to $10,500,000, depending on their volatility. Such agreements can also include provisions that the borrower put up additional cash if market conditions threaten the value of the securities during the agreement.

The third source of risk is the possibility that the securities dealer or bank may fail during the term of the repo. This risk was reported extensively during the early 1980s, when several securities dealers and banks failed for reasons unrelated to repos. Unless steps are taken to safeguard capital, such failures can subject an investor to losses. Examining the capital position of the securities dealer is one step an investor can take. However, it is often difficult to make that examination because many dealers are not regulated, which means they are not subject to examination by an independent agency.

The possibility that a dealer may fail should not be taken lightly. A string of failures and near failures ended with losses suffered by clients of E.S.M. Government Securities, Inc. Other failures in recent years include the 1982 failure of Lombard-Wall, the 1983 bankruptcies of RTD Securities and Lion Capital Corporation, and the collapse of Drysdale Government Securities in 1984. Drysdale, for instance, got into trouble because it used a quirk in the repo market to assemble a massive securities portfolio without having much cash. When bonds are bought or sold, the amount of accrued interest is added to their price. Drysdale ignored that accrued interest in its repo transactions. When it sold the securities, the firm profited from both the sale price and the accrued interest. The practice caught up with the company when the interest payments came due and it did not have the cash to pay them. As a result, investors no longer ignore accrued interest in repo transactions.

When Lombard-Wall filed for bankruptcy in 1982, its repo customers were left without recourse. The investors had made repo agreements with Lombard-Wall because they believed they were not really loaning money to an unstable firm but rather were purchasing government securities. The bankruptcy court ruled, however, that a repo was not a separate purchase-and-sale transaction. It ruled instead that a repo was a collateralized loan, and Lombard-Wall's collateral was millions of dollars less than it needed to cover outstanding repo loans. Even after the 1984 Drysdale failure, investors still did not examine the creditworthiness of their counterparty dealers closely enough. Congress has since amended the Bankruptcy Code so that repurchase agreements are exempt from a provision freezing a bankrupt corporation's assets, so that lenders can now liquidate the securities immediately.

The question of collateral takes on extreme importance in light of past failures. A financial manager should realize that the institution's collateral is likely to be used by the dealer or bank as collateral on a repo with another client. The dealer will lend an organization money against its collateral at one rate and then use the same collateral to borrow in another repo transaction. The dealer thus makes interest on the spread, the difference in rates between the two transactions. Dealers are required to provide investors with written notice of the possibility that their collateral may be used in other transactions. These agreements are called substitution agreements, as the dealer is effectively substituting one group of securities for another.

(d) Reducing Repo Risk

Because of the repurchase agreement market's history of dealer failure, it is of utmost importance that an investor not rely solely on collateral when examining the quality of a repo dealer. The dealer's creditworthiness should be the foremost consideration. Investors should also take the following seven steps to guard against the risk of exposure in a repo transaction:

1. Verify that the dealer, even if it is a bank, is a creditworthy institution; it should have a high credit rating from a major investment-rating service

2. Confirm that the repo's collateral is delivered to a safekeeping agent if the repo term is seven days or longer (see the following subsection)

3. Monitor the collateral's market value to ensure that it is always greater than the amount invested in the repo

4. Make certain when entering into the transaction that the collateral meets the organization's investment guidelines for credit quality

5. Sign a written repurchase agreement before executing the transaction

6. Ensure that the repo rate is in accord with the quality of the securities used as collateral

7. Ascertain the dealer's substitution policy, and obtain a higher rate if the dealer retains the right to substitute collateral

(i) *Custodial Arrangements.* Custodial and contractual arrangements can lessen the risks of repos. The custodian is a third-party institution that takes delivery and control over the securities used as collateral in a repo transaction. Financial managers can choose among three types of custodial arrangements: (1) delivery repo, (2) three-party repo, and (3) letter repo.

(ii) *Delivery Repo.* The delivery repo is generally considered to be the most secure arrangement. The securities used as collateral in the transaction are physically delivered to the investor. In the case of "book entry" instruments, the dealer wires the collateral securities into the custodian bank's Federal Reserve account. If the securities are in "physical form," they are physically delivered to the investor or its custodian against payment. Despite the security of delivery repos, however, they are expensive; delivery costs can erode the investor's return on the repo unless the transaction is large or lasts more than a week.

(iii) Three-Party Repo. The original custodian of the securities retains physical possession, but it acknowledges that it is holding the securities of a three-party repo in the investor's own safekeeping account, rather than that of the securities dealer. The entity that retains custody of the securities is the dealer's clearing bank, not the investor's. The contract among the investor, dealer, and bank stipulates that the bank must transfer securities into the investor's safekeeping account against payment to the dealer. The bank then polices the repo by monitoring the value of the securities. It will also calculate the margin to ensure that the securities meet the collateral conditions of the transaction. The advantage of a three-party repo is its lower costs, because no external transfer of securities is involved (both the investor and dealer use the same custodian). In addition, the custodian makes sure that no securities are transferred until funds are transferred as well.

(iv) Letter Repo. Under a letter repo, the securities dealer sends a letter of confirmation to the investor that it is holding the securities in the investor's account. These are risky deals, and letter repos have been nicknamed "trust-me repos." Many Repo transactions with transfer of securities by dealer's clearing bank from dealer's account to customer's account investors use letter repos, however, because no transfers are involved, which means costs are minimized. The key determination a financial manager must make before entering into a letter repo is that the dealer's integrity is impeccable. Legal counsel should also approve such transactions.

(e) Alternatives to Repos

Repurchase agreements are not the only alternative to flexible short-term investing; there are other instruments that provide a similar degree of credit quality and flexibility for investments of between one and 30 days. In fact, it is wise for financial managers to diversify investment exposure by investing funds in other instruments. The instruments, discussed in previous sections, that are alternatives to repos include government agency discount notes, commercial paper, master notes, Eurodollar time deposits, and money market funds.

13.14 SUMMARY

One of the jobs performed by investment bankers and securities underwriters is devising new and different investment instruments that will strike investors' fancies and cause them to part with their funds. In many cases, the creativity of investment bankers has worked to the benefit of institutional investors. At the same time, however, many innovative instruments have caused more problems than they have solved. CMOs, for example, were designed to solve the problems inherent in the repayment of principal and interest in mortgage-backed securities. However, CMOs have disadvantages distinctively their own.

Accordingly, financial managers must weigh all of the possible problems of new and unusual securities. Such securities often have yield advantages over other types, but frequently the yield advantages are destroyed due to the following three reasons:

1. The accounting effort to maintain the securities in an investment portfolio is costly.

2. Interest income is lost because principal is not paid on time.

3. Most new instrument types have limited initial market activity. Therefore, a weak market can destroy the liquidity and further adversely weak market can destroy the liquidity and further adversely affect the market price of the instruments, thus lessening the additional income they pay should they have to be sold.

Financial managers should examine all the consequences of investing in new and exotic instruments, estimate any yield problems, and evaluate the problems against the benefits before buying the instruments.

A derivative is an investment or other financial instrument whose value is dependent on, or derived from, another asset. For example, a stock option is the right to purchase (or sell) a specific company's stock, and the value (price) of the option is linked to the price of the company's stock. Major types of derivatives are options, forwards, futures, and swaps. Although few nonprofits have used derivatives as part of their financial management processes, a number of endowments and foundations have lost money in investment derivatives such as collateralized mortgage obligations (CMOs). In this appendix a checklist of evaluation factors is provided to guide your organization, should it decide to use derivatives.

WHY DERIVATIVES?

The use of derivatives can actually reduce the riskiness of an organization's cash flows, although the main cases that get into the newspaper are those in which a speculative position was taken (mostly bets on the direction of interest rates) and the value of the underlying asset resulted in a large loss to the derivative user. When an organization uses derivatives to reduce risk, it is said to be *hedging*. Organizations such as Orange County (CA) were not using derivatives to reduce risk, but to take on additional risks. Formally, hedging is defined as protecting an existing business position by counterbalancing the position with an exactly offsetting position. The existing business position may be a foreign exchange exposure, meaning the organization's cash flows will be less if a specific currency depreciates or appreciates vis-à-vis the dollar. Or, it may be interest rate risk, meaning the organization's cash flows will be less if interest rates increase or decrease. Illustrating, one Colorado-based charity had to lay off 20 percent of its headquarters staff because short-term interest rates declined, reducing the cash flow from its investment reserves that it had been depending on for covering this overhead expense. Two possible hedging positions your organization may wish to consider are the use of interest rate futures or forward contracts and exchange rate futures or forward contracts. A forward contract is "an agreement reached at one point in time calling for the delivery of some commodity at a specified later date at a price established at the time of contracting," whereas a futures contract is "a forward contract traded on an organized exchange with contract terms clearly specified by the rules of the exchange."[1] The futures of most value to your organization are financial futures, which are based upon underlying financial instruments. *Foreign currency futures* allow for delivery of a specified amount of foreign currency, at an agreed-upon future date, in return for a specified payment of U.S. dollars. The underlying financial instrument for an *interest rate future* is a debt instrument such as a Treasury bill or Treasury bond. Correspondingly, the contract is fulfilled by delivering the specified amount of T-bills or T-bonds. With *stock index futures*, there is no delivery of underlying assets at the contract's expiration, but rather a cash payment linked to the change in the underlying stock index (such as the Standard & Poor's 500 index).

FORWARDS VERSUS FUTURES

Although very similar, forwards differ from futures in three main ways:

1. *Advantage:* They may be customized as to dollar amount and maturity.
2. *Disadvantage:* They are not traded on exchanges, and finding a trading partner wishing to take the exact opposite position to that we wish to hedge may be very difficult.
3. *Disadvantage:* They are difficult to reverse, meaning that if our organization wishes to end its hedge before the agreed-upon date, it may be costly or impossible to reach agreement with the trading partner.

Based on these considerations, your organization may be more or less inclined to use forward versus future contracts.

GUIDELINES FOR DERIVATIVES USE: A CHECKLIST

The following are some of the considerations to be addressed to guide the use of derivatives:[2]

[1]Robert W. Kolb, *Financial Derivatives,* 2nd edition (Cambridge, MA: Blackwell Publishers, Inc., 1996), 2. We strongly recommend study of Kolb's book for those needing more information on derivatives.
[2]The first seven guidelines are quoted from The Group of Thirty (G30) Global Derivatives Study Group, *Derivatives: Practices and Principles* (1993). The eighth is from Greenwich Treasury Advisors, and found in Jeffrey Wallace, "Controlling Derivatives Activities," *TMA Journal,* September/October 1994. The final listing is from James Kurt Dew and Neil Murphy, "Managing the Use of Derivatives," *TMA Journal,* March/April 1997, 57.

- Determine at the highest level of policy and decision making the scope of its involvement in derivatives activities and policies to be applied.
- Value derivatives at market, at least for risk management purposes.
- Quantify its market risk under adverse market conditions against limits, perform stress simulations, and forecast cash investing and funding needs.
- Assess the credit risk arising from derivatives activities based on frequent measures of current and potential exposure against credit limits.
- Reduce credit risk by broadening the use of multi-product master agreements with close-out netting provisions, and by working with other participants to ensure legal enforceability of derivatives transactions within and across jurisdictions.
- Establish market and credit risk management functions with clear authority, independent of the dealing function.
- Voluntarily adopt accounting and disclosure practices for international harmonization and greater transparency, pending the arrival of international standards.
- Have clearly defined policies dealing with interest rate risk and foreign exchange risk, including:
  - Clear policy objectives
  - Board approval of the policy
  - Specified reporting requirements, such as nature and frequency of reports to the board
  - Defined exposure definitions
  - Limits to exposure
  - Specified authority for who may make trades, including annual letters to the banks identifying these individuals
  - Segregation of duties, so that traders do not handle the accounting or funds transfers
  - Credit limits on counterparties (those with whom the derivatives contracts are made)
- Before entering into derivatives usage, the organization should have an organization risk management plan meeting three criteria:

- Does it demonstrate to top management that the use of derivatives can produce a reduction in the variability (volatility) of the organization's financial results (as evidenced through the Statement of Activity, Statement of Cash Flows, and/or Statement of Net Assets)?

- Does it include quantitative measures of both the forecast profitability (financial advantage of using the derivative) and risk associated (what is the possible loss to the organization of using the derivative, if any) with derivatives-enhanced activities

- Are the actual results of derivatives activities identifiable and verifiable by accounting (and internal auditors, if the organization has them) independently of input from the trader? Systems or guidelines should be in place to prevent the trader from making his position look better than it really is.

A few final comments will provide some added guidance. Not only should the direct user ("trader") of the derivatives be knowledgeable and competent, but your board and senior management should have some background in derivatives. Including in-house accounting, audit, and legal personnel in your organization's derivatives training is essential. Additionally, make sure that the most suitable instrument is used. Many times there are multiple instruments for a particular situation: forward and futures contracts, options, and another derivative known as swaps may be eligible. The swap (exchange of cash flows linked to the movement of interest rates, for example) has counterparty risk (risk of nonperformance, perhaps due to financial difficulties, of the opposite party) that is nonexistent with futures or options. These types of considerations are important in determining suitability. Finally, get more than one opinion. If one bank tells you their approach is foolproof, check with another bank. Shopping around for a better deal is sometimes also prudent, all other things equal. Bear in mind that few people understand how many of the new derivatives operate, and many of the models upon which the expected performance of these derivatives were based failed to anticipate real-world market performance. Caution is advisable in the use of any derivative, and your organization will likely limit its use to hedging known risks.

CHAPTER FOURTEEN

Safeguarding the Organization's Assets, People, and Property: Risk Management and Audit

14.1 What Is Risk Management? 538
    (a) Who Is Responsible for Managing Risk in the Nonprofit Organization? 539
        (i) Leadership Sets the Tone 540
        (ii) Communicate Policy 540
14.2 Identifying Risk 540
14.3 Safeguarding People 540
    (a) Physical Safety 542
    (b) Emotional Safety 542
    (c) Protecting the Organization from Lawsuits and Grievances 542
    (d) Dealing with Difficult or Problem Employees 543
    (e) Grounds for Immediate Termination 544
    (f) Compensation 544
    (g) Personal Use of Organizational Resources 545
    (h) Conflict of Interest 546
    (i) Getting the Most "Bang for Your Buck" 546
    (j) Staff and Volunteers—What Motivates Them? 547
    (k) What Qualities Does Leadership Possess? 549
        (i) Concern 549
        (ii) Connectivity 549
14.4 Directors' and Officers' Liability 549
    (a) Methods by Which Boards Can Protect Themselves 550
    (b) Bonding 550

14.5 Safeguarding Your Property 551
    (a) Insurance 551
14.6 Safeguarding People and Property 551
    (a) Internal Controls 551
    (b) External Review or "Audit" 552
        (i) Audit 553
        (ii) Review 554
        (iii) Compilation 554
    (c) How to Begin the Assessment Process 554
        (i) Due Diligence—Compliance with Policies,
            Procedures, and Guidelines 555
        (ii) Solutions: To Reduce Risk and Stay Out
            of Court 555
        (iii) Disaster Preparedness 556

14.1 WHAT IS RISK MANAGEMENT?

Effective risk management is the process of evaluating and guarding against potential losses to the organization. The Chief Financial Officer of a nonprofit organization should be very concerned about risk management issues because they directly affect the use of financial and other resources. Effective risk management can save significant resources, which ultimately translates into money.

Risk management has two major components:

- Loss prevention
- Loss control (reduction of loss)

In general, most leaders and managers fail to understand that risk management involves matters of risk associated with their assets. An asset is "the entire property of all sorts of a person, association, corporation, or estate applicable or subject to the payment of its debts."[1] In financial terms, assets are things owned by the organization and reported on the organization's balance sheet. In more general terms, assets are resources or anything that gives great value to the organization, whether tangible or intangible. The major types of assets include:

- People (employees, members, volunteers, independent contractors)
- Property and equipment (monies, property, equipment, trade secrets, service workers, goodwill)

Exhibit 14.1 presents a checklist for setting up a risk management program.

[1]*Webster's Ninth New Collegiate Dictionary* (Springfield, MA: Meriamm Webster Inc. Publishers, 1984).

Exhibit 14.1.   Checklist for Setting Up a Risk Management Program

- Leadership sets the tone and demonstrates their compliance.
- Leaders stay informed and demonstrate their interest and concern for this area.
- Education and training convey policies and procedures as well as organizational attitudes toward the safeguarding of assets.
- Risks are known.
- Risks are prioritized.
- A Safety Officer is appointed.
- Counselors, consultants, and practitioners (private, public, or pastoral) are consulted and used when necessary.

In order to be effective, risk management must be proactive. Proactive steps include:

- Acknowledge critical importance of risk management at the highest level
- Define risk management roles and responsibilities
- Delegate or assign risk management responsibilities and accountabilities
- Incorporate a regular inspection where losses could occur
- Review the organization's risk management program in detail regularly .
- Communicate that risk management issues must be considered when evaluating the cost of doing business, including the review of existing and new programs

(a) Who Is Responsible for Managing Risk in the Nonprofit Organization?

The Board of Trustees is responsible for setting policy and assigning responsibility for risk management functions in the nonprofit organization. In the event of a loss and subsequent legal exposure resulting from this loss, it is likely that the Board could be held accountable for losses if appropriate policies and procedures do not exist. Risk management issues are broad and pertain to paid staff and volunteers, as well as the general public who may be involved with the organization. Risk management is part of the cost of doing business and should not be ignored by the Board of Trustees.

As responsible leaders, Board members:

- Know the rules in the organization, including by-laws, policies, and procedures
- Understand the process

- Stay informed in this complicated world about issues such as law, litigation, compliance, ethics, and disclosure

(i) Leadership Sets the Tone. Control cues are the written and unwritten messages sent to an organization by its leadership, management, and staff on what is expected of the entire work force to safeguard its resources. These messages continually communicate by word and action that the work force is responsible and accountable for protecting and preserving the organization's assets so that they are available to carry out its mission.

(ii) Communicate Policy. In order to be meaningful and effective, policies must be communicated to all who have a business need to know or a role to play in adherence to the policy. Development and distribution of a policies and procedures manual are traditionally used to accomplish this task. Keeping the manual updated is required to maintain its relevance and effectiveness. However, a policy and procedures manual, per se, is not the only way to effectively communicate policies, roles and responsibilities, and expectations. Any method of communicating that works effectively for the organization is acceptable.

14.2 IDENTIFYING RISK

Your organization's people and property invite and cause risks in several distinct areas. Exhibit 14.2 summarizes some major areas of risk with specific examples.

14.3 SAFEGUARDING PEOPLE

A nonprofit organization's most valuable asset is the people who contribute resources (service and monies) in support of its mission. The staff and volunteers in your organization perform these needed activities and tasks and both groups use and develop resources.

First and foremost, you must provide a safe working environment for your staff and volunteers, regardless of whether work is performed on-site, at your organization's offices, in the field, in a donor's home, or in the staff or volunteer's residence or place of business. While you cannot completely safeguard your staff and volunteers outside your organization's place of business, you may be at risk if you are aware of a potential hazard and do not take action to protect the individual from harm.

Exhibit 14.2. Major Areas of Risk

Major Area of Risk	Examples
Legal records	Articles of incorporation Bylaws Meeting minutes List of members
Officer's and director's liability	Theft (assets, ideas, credibility) Compliance
Members of the nonprofit organization	Loss
Employees	Theft Lawsuits Safety Productivity losses
Volunteers	Exposure Space
Personnel and payroll	Employee benefits Sexual harassment
Financial management	Budget Cash handling Bonding Confidentiality of records Loan management Net assets
Investment management	Risk Image with constituents
Child care	Injury
Counseling	Liability insurance
Insurance	Rates Ranking
Fire protection	Insurance Fire alarms Disaster preparedness Emergency procedures
Injury prevention	Unenforced policy
Vehicles	Accident Theft Inappropriate or personal use
Copyrights and publications	Theft Inadequate protection
Programs and activities	Productivity losses Reputation
Miscellaneous	Disasters (any kind)

(a) Physical Safety

- Your facilities (electrical, plumbing, fire sprinklers, etc.) should comply with standard codes for your region.
- Doorways and fire exits should be kept clear and accessible.
- If crime (such as assault or theft) is prevalent in your locale, doors should be locked after hours, and individuals should be escorted to parking structures or accompanied to their transportation sites.
- Emergency service numbers, such as 911 stickers, should be placed on telephones.
- Basic safety procedures, such as what to do in an emergency, should be included in your staff and volunteer assimilation materials.
- If staff or volunteers use vehicles to conduct work (other than traveling to and from their work site), you need to ensure that they have a good driving record, have up-to-date insurance coverage, and understand their responsibilities with respect to chauffeuring others in their own or company vehicles.
- If staff or volunteers need to move heavy items, such as furniture, inventory, or stock, these individuals need to be provided with safe-lifting instructions, lift belts, and proper tools such as ladders and hand trucks.

(b) Emotional Safety

- Employee workplace guidelines specific to sexual harassment should be distributed to all individuals and supervisors, and managers should receive training on how to recognize a potential harassment situation and what steps or actions to take if it does occur.
- Staff and volunteers should be instructed on how to report a potentially harmful situation if their supervisor or manager creates unnecessary stress for their subordinates.
- When considering expansion, growth, or organizational changes of any kind, the risk, stress, or burden on the staff and volunteers should be appropriately evaluated as one of the costs of the change.

(c) Protecting the Organization from Lawsuits and Grievances

The most obvious way to prevent lawsuits and employee grievances is to comply with all laws, regulations, and policies that affect your region and organization. In addition to protecting the organization from lawsuits and grievances, you need to ensure that your staff and volunteers are protected.

(d) Dealing with Difficult or Problem Employees

Regardless of how careful the organization may be in the selection process for hiring new employees, eventually it may be faced with terminating a problem employee who does not perform up to standard. To avoid financial risk to the organization the following actions should be taken:

- Each employee has an up-to-date and accurate job description detailing his or her work assignments and responsibilities.
- Periodic evaluations should be performed, using only the tasks and assignments on the job description as criteria for evaluating employee performance.
- Once a problem employee is identified, the supervisor must document all conversations, meetings, job complaints, assignments, errors, omissions, or violations of policy; discuss them with the employee; and maintain copies of these documents in the employee's personnel file.
- The first step to termination is a counseling session to notify the employee that his or her performance is not satisfactory. Reasonable steps to provide additional assistance or training, areas to improve, and other specific information should be discussed with the employee, and a written document detailing the discussion should be given to the employee, with a copy maintained in the personnel file. If termination appears to be imminent, a time period (or deadline) within which the employee's performance must be up to standard should be determined and discussed with the employee. Interim sessions to monitor progress, or lack of progress, should be conducted and documented.
- The decision on whether to terminate or ask the employee to resign should be evaluated carefully. Very often, problem employees are willing to resign if offered an attractive severance package. The costs of the severance package should be evaluated and compared against the potential risk of lawsuit or grievance, as well as the increase in unemployment insurance if the employee is terminated. Often, tensions become high when an employee needs to be separated from the organization. The decision to fire someone may seem warranted but may not be the most appropriate action for the organization. In many cases, there will be less of a financial burden and risk to the organization if the employee is willing to resign as opposed to being terminated.
- Employees can only be terminated (*fired*) for cause. Separating an employee for lack of work, lack of funds, or change in mission or responsibilities is not considered "termination for cause."

This is generally referred to as a "layoff" and will have a financial impact in the form of workers' compensation increases. When a lay-off is performed, the only criteria that may be used are seniority, job title or description, employee skills, and how critical the person's job or responsibilities are to the organization. Performance or specific salary level cannot be used as the reason for selecting one employee over another for layoff. If an employee is laid off out of order of seniority, it is critical that you document legitimate and legal reasons for performing a lay-off in this manner.

(e) Grounds for Immediate Termination

There are instances where it is necessary to remove an employee immediately. Labor relations laws vary from state to state, and a lawyer specializing in human resources issues should be consulted if there is a question about the legality of the termination. Generally, there are grounds for immediate termination when the employee places the organization, its staff, or its volunteers at substantial risk:

- Theft or fraud
- Threatening or lewd behavior in the workplace
- Lying about use of sick leave
- Using illegal drugs or other illegal substances in the workplace
- Bringing weapons and other dangerous or hazardous items into the workplace

Even with the severity of the examples listed above and the assumption that "everyone should know they cannot do this stuff at work," it is important to document in your personnel policies those behaviors or actions that will warrant immediate termination.

Many companies place employees on "investigatory leave" (leave without pay) if allegations of any of the above activities are suspected. This benefits the organization by removing the employee from the workplace immediately, and providing time to investigate and confirm the allegations prior to the completion of the actual separation. If it is determined later that the employee was falsely accused, back wages can be paid and the employee can be restored to his or her position. Again, policies and procedures for placing employees on investigatory leave should be documented in the organization's personnel policies, with copies provided to all employees when hired.

(f) Compensation

The intangible rewards of working in a nonprofit environment enable organizations to hire qualified individuals who are dedicated to the mission of the organization at wages below industry or local average for the region. Taking advantage of this situation can greatly aid the organization in keeping its employee compensation rates down; however, there may be hidden costs in using this practice recklessly or assuming that employees will work indefinitely for low wages.

- Eventually, even the most dedicated employee will succumb to offers for better wages. High employee turnover reduces productivity and creates an unstable image in the eyes of donors and a general sense of unease and instability with other staff and volunteers.

- Ineffective or unqualified staff or volunteers use resources. Oftentimes, one highly qualified individual can perform the task of several underqualified staff and lower the overall cost to the organization. In addition, productive staff and volunteers may lose morale if unproductive staff and volunteers are allowed to remain with the organization.

- A low-paid development staff or director may be less effective at raising money than a higher-paid individual. The net effect to the organization will be a decrease in overall resources—"penny wise and pound foolish."

- Specifically in the financial arena, a highly qualified individual may be able to forecast and manipulate resources in a way which greatly benefits the organization and protects it from loss, while a lesser-qualified individual may be careless and less savvy in managing resources.

(g) Personal Use of Organizational Resources

Unless there are specific policies and active monitoring of resource use in your organization, a substantial loss can result in the personal use of resources by volunteers or staff:

- Phone
- Fax
- Photocopying equipment
- Typewriters
- Computers
- Offices supplies (paper, pens, etc.)

While all of us at one time or another have accidentally placed a pen or pencil belonging to another in our purse or pocket, this practice is theft if done consciously. If your organization has a policy prohibiting its resources from being used for personal use, then staff and volunteers need to be reprimanded when minor infractions, such as those listed above, occur. Many organizations adopt a policy that allows staff and volunteers to use organizational resources as long as it does not become excessive (e.g., using the phone to call home, the copier to copy an occasional legal document, the fax machine to send an important document). The difficulty of this type of policy is the definition of *excessive* may vary for each individual. One employee who lives close to his or her work site and calls home during breaks may not incur a significant cost to the organization; however, another employee who lives much further away and does the same may result, over time, in a significant cost to the organization. It is important for limits to be established that do not discriminate from one employee to the next. If a policy places a $5 maximum on personal telephone calls per month as opposed to a time limit for personal use, it may be interpreted as unfairly penalizing one employee. It is important to remember that the organization is not required to allow any of its resources to be used for personal use.

(h) Conflict of Interest

A conflict of interest may exist when a decision is made that may personally benefit an employee or volunteer. For example, a staff member may have a spouse who works for a travel agency. Using that particular travel agency may be viewed by potential donors or auditors as unfair. However, if the travel agent agreed to reduce travel expenses by 5 percent, the decision to use this particular vendor might be the most financially advantageous to the organization.

A potential conflict of interest does not mean that the organization cannot do business with friends or family of its staff or volunteers. It is critical in these circumstances to have full disclosure of the connection to this particular individual and to have someone other than the individual who may benefit make the final determination.

Development of and compliance with a carefully drafted conflict of interest policy will lessen the financial risk to the organization as well as reduce the appearance of impropriety with respect to donors.

(i) Getting the Most "Bang for Your Buck"

If the organization is not utilizing a resource to its fullest potential or purpose, the organization is actually wasting it. If staff or volunteers have special skills and abilities that are not being utilized, if they are not mentored properly to work to their fullest potential, or if they are not trained or given sufficient flexibility to perform their tasks or responsibilities, your organization is wasting resources. In addition, if staff or volunteers are performing unsatisfactorily, they are consuming resources.

(j) Staff and Volunteers—What Motivates Them?

Three qualities of all productive staff and volunteers are listed in Exhibit 14.3.

- Commitment
  - To their work
  - To their constituents
  - To their customers
  - To their community
  - To themselves

Exhibit 14.3. Motivation Factors

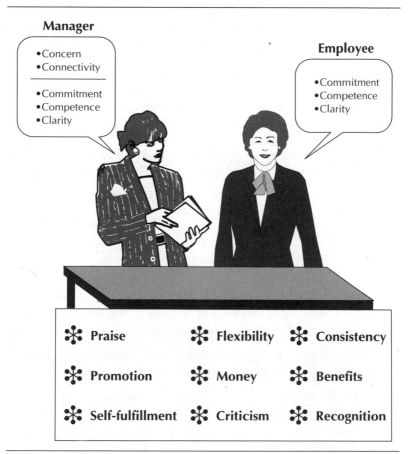

- Competence
  - In their work
  - In their relationships with other staff and volunteers
  - In dealing with donors
- Clarity
  - About their roles and responsibilities
  - About the purpose of the organization and its mission

As discussed earlier, salaries paid to employees in nonprofit organizations are often below the for-profit market level. This means that individuals accept positions with nonprofits because there are motivating factors beyond income. This commitment to the organization should be recognized and, wherever possible, acknowledged and rewarded in nonfinancial ways.

On the negative side, it is also reasonable to assume that some individuals will gravitate towards positions with nonprofits that pay lower wages because they believe the work load and expectations will be lower, commensurate with the pay scales. Thus, an individual's commitment to the organization should be evaluated on a case-by-case basis. It should never be assumed that a willingness to work for lower pay constitutes a high degree of commitment to the organization.

Paying someone below market wages does not necessarily mean that you will have substandard employees. If wages were the only motivating factor in a person's decision to accept or remain in a position, individuals would change jobs much more frequently, as offers for higher pay were offered. In each position, a staff or volunteer also evaluates the intangible rewards:

- Sense of community: relationships with co-workers and friends
- The mission and goals of the organization
- Logistical factors (e.g., proximity from home to workplace)
- Educational or learning opportunities
- Working hours
- Access to other individuals and community (e.g., a museum attracting aspiring artists or a library attracting aspiring writers)
- Feeling of pride and receipt of praise and attention for their efforts

Beyond the intangible rewards, individuals also evaluate the tangible rewards that nonprofits can offer:

- Benefits (vacation, sick leave, health insurance)
- Discounts or "freebies" (e.g., educational discounts; mentoring opportunities; ability to attend performances, screenings, or presentations at little or no cost)

It is important to remember that each individual has his or her own set of motivators for doing good work:

- Praise
- Benefits
- Money
- Recognition
- Flexibility
- Criticism
- Consistency

(k) What Qualities Does Leadership Possess?

Supervisors, managers, directors, and Board members must have the qualities, motivators, and skills of all staff and volunteers, as well as the following:

(i) Concern.

- For the staff and volunteers
- For donors and community
- For the integrity of the workplace
- For the success and failure of the organization

(ii) Connectivity.   To the infrastructure of the community (global and local), both nontechnological and technological.
It is the responsibility of leadership to:

- Set vision
- Establish goals and priorities
- Motivate and mentor staff, volunteers, donors, and community
- Establish a personality for the workplace
- Foster integrity
- Demonstrate support for rules, laws, fiduciary responsibility, and compliance

14.4   DIRECTORS' AND OFFICERS' LIABILITY

A major concern of nonprofit Boards is the unprecedented liability exposure faced by their Directors and officers. A significant rise in the number of liability suits and in insurance costs has made it increasingly difficult for officers and Directors to protect themselves.

This situation affects the quality of governance and leadership that nonprofit organizations can attract.

(a) Methods by Which Boards Can Protect Themselves

It is critical for the nonprofit organization to review its liability coverage for Directors and officers and make the required adjustments, if the organization is underprotected. Along with obtaining and acting on the liability insurance information, a Board can take other actions to protect itself and limit its liability and risk. They include:

- Ensure Board minutes are complete and accurate
- Engage paid legal counsel
- Expand management information
- Review organizational policies
- Formulate conflict-of-interest policy
- Add and/or recruit new Board members to include specific expertise
- Form new Board committees
- Bring in outside experts
- Strengthen the Finance Committee
- Strengthen legal expertise
- Strengthen insurance expertise
- Strengthen audit and accounting expertise[2]

(b) Bonding

Bonding is a precaution that a nonprofit organization should consider in its corporate stewardship. Bonding buys insurance on those handling money for the organization and ensures its constituency that the finances are being handled properly.

Some nonprofit organizations are reluctant to bond money handlers, in the belief that it questions the integrity of the people involved. Unfortunately, irregularities in the handling of money in nonprofits occur often enough that this potential cannot be ignored. If the money handlers are not bonded, the organization should safeguard its money and money handlers by engaging an annual audit. There is a wide variety of bonding patterns. In some instances the individual is bonded; in others the position is bonded, so that a change in personnel does not affect coverage. Group bonds cover everyone who handles the money.

[2]KMPG Peat Marwick, *Directors' and Officers' Liability: A Crisis in the Making* (Peat, Marwick, Mitchell & Co., 1987).

Costs of bonding vary widely, depending on the number of individuals involved and the amount of money handled. The insurance carrier for the organization is the best source to begin the process of determining how to meet its bonding needs.

14.5 SAFEGUARDING YOUR PROPERTY

(a) Insurance

Insurance does not mitigate all risk-management issues in your organization. Some of the reasons are:

- Insurance does not cover every risk
- Coverage may be limited
- Claims today may raise premiums tomorrow
- Claims may be rejected if negligence is discovered by the insurance company

Risks to an organization can be reduced, but they cannot be eliminated. Fires, floods, thefts, property damage, earthquakes, will occur despite the best efforts of your organization in the area of risk management.

Know what the insurance choices are and why the organization has made them. Exhibit 14.4 presents a checklist of factors to consider when choosing insurance.

In general, you should know the limitations and exclusions of policies and perform periodic reviews of coverage to verify that they are up-to-date for claims and losses in your region.

14.6 SAFEGUARDING PEOPLE AND PROPERTY

(a) Internal Controls

In the broadest sense, internal controls include a large number of systems and business practices combined together which, when observed, protect the assets of the organization and thereby reduce the risks associated with loss of resources.

Six important elements of an internal control system are:

1. Set the tone through leadership (control cues)
2. Communicate the policy
3. Segregate the duties
4. Keep records
5. Prepare and monitor budgets
6. Report to all stakeholders

Exhibit 14.4. Checklist of Factors to Consider When Choosing Insurance

What does the policy cover?
- ☐ Property or liability risks
- ☐ Risks from all causes
- ☐ Named perils such as earthquake, flood, lightning

What are you covered for?
- ☐ Theft by employees and/or others
- ☐ Legal negligence
- ☐ Personal injury
- ☐ Sexual misconduct
- ☐ Negligence of member, employee, or any other person associated with the organization
- ☐ Medical bills
- ☐ Volunteer activities
- ☐ Vehicular-related activities
- ☐ Auto insurance
- ☐ Workers' compensation insurance
- ☐ Inventory

What do you know about your policy?
- ☐ Are there exclusions?
- ☐ How much coverage do you carry and based on what? Are these amounts up-to-date?
- ☐ Is actual cost or replacement cost covered?
- ☐ Is replacement cost at 100 percent vs. other percentages?
- ☐ How is depreciation handled?
- ☐ Are the contents or inventory of buildings accurate and up-to-date?
- ☐ Are rare or other especially valuable items covered such as art, or other precious objects?
- ☐ Is your policy contingent upon construction codes in your area? If so, do you comply and have proof of compliance?
- ☐ Do you have a physical inventory, pictures, and other documentation that could be used as proof of loss?

Taken together, these policies outline the acceptable boundaries for fiscal decisions, govern the way resources are allocated, provide information for evaluation, and define the processes to be used in carrying out the organization's mission.

(b) External Review or "Audit"

An external review of an organization's financial and business records provides significant benefit to the organization and its constituents. Such an examination supports the integrity of the organization and those inside the organization who have responsibility for these functions and tasks.

Depending on the size and resources of the organization, the independent accountant may have expertise that is not available elsewhere within the organization. An independent accountant can advise the organization on a number of financial, business, and management issues and can serve as an excellent referral resource to other professionals whose services may be needed by the organization at some time. Professional accountants can also keep the organization informed about changing tax laws, trends, and other legal requirements.

Accounting firms can assist in the development of new or revised accounting systems, financial structures, and other vehicles required to manage the organization and achieve its mission.

The term *audit* is often used to refer to any examination of the organization's financial and/or business records. An audit is one of three types of reports that an independent accountant performing audit functions may issue to an organization as a result of its review of the organization's records.

There are three types of examinations:

(i) Audit. An audit is the most comprehensive and expensive process. An audit requires specific testing of records and a stated opinion by the auditor or auditing firm. Specific testing means that particular items are tested and verified and transactions are followed from beginning to end. If the financial statement of the organization shows there is $10,000 in the bank, the auditor contacts the bank to verify in writing that the $10,000 is, in fact, in the bank.

The second characteristic of an audit is the opinion of the auditor or auditing firm. The opinion states that the financial statements are presented in accord with generally accepted accounting principles. By making this statement, the auditor risks his or her professional reputation on the accuracy of the financial statement. If the audit is used as a basis for other financial arrangements (i.e., bank loan) and the financial statement is found to be erroneous, the auditor or audit firm may be held liable.

If a full external audit cannot be performed annually for your organization, the following situations in the organization should require an external audit to be performed:

- When a Treasurer is being replaced and records are being turned over to a successor, providing protection for both parties involved.
- If, for any reason, the integrity of the individual responsible for handling funds is questioned, the audit documents the person's integrity.
- If, for any reason, the integrity of the organization's financial status is questioned.
- If the cash-handling system, or any of its subsystems, for the organization is questioned.
- If a financial institution requires an audit before making a loan.

(ii) Review. A review is a process through which the overall financial records are examined to determine if they appear reasonable. A detailed examination of the records is not done in a review nor does the auditor or audit firm offer an opinion on the accuracy of the financial records. Only an audit offers an opinion subject to the detailed examination of the records and subrecords.

The cost of a review is substantially less than the cost of an audit.

(iii) Compilation. A compilation includes a testing of the accuracy of the records. It assesses the financial statements from a bookkeeping point of view. The cost of a compilation is less than that of a review, and substantially less than that of an audit.

(c) How to Begin the Assessment Process

An organization with no history of having an external review of its financial records may want to begin with a compilation and move to a review and audit in the future. If the organization is unable to afford the costs associated with an external review of the entire financial program, it has the option to engage the external examination on important specific parts of the financial statement or program. Examples of specific external examinations to be considered, if a full examination is not possible, are:

- Review policies and procedures manual for completeness, accuracy, and availability
- Perform a proof of cash on one, some, or all of the bank accounts of the organization
- Scan canceled checks accompanying the bank statement for any unusual payees or endorsements
- Confirm contributions made by donors
- Confirm loan balances with lenders
- Confirm all payments made during a specific period with some or all vendors
- Compare annual operating budget to operating expenses, and analyze variances
- Inquire as to how transactions are processed (for example, deposits made, bills approved and paid) to ensure proper system of internal controls and detect errors
- Perform a financial or management review of a specific program
- Perform an examination to determine the accuracy of inventory
- Check for control of petty-cash funds

- Check savings accounts for amounts, interest, and conditions
- Check to determine if designated (restricted) funds are used only for the purpose contributed
- Investigate checks outstanding for more than 30 days
- Review all bank account reconciliations for timeliness and accuracy
- Examine payroll records to ensure compliance with government regulations related to payroll, payroll taxes, income taxes, etc.
- Account for all checks used

(i) Due Diligence—Compliance with Policies, Procedures, and Guidelines. Documenting your policies and procedures is the first step in managing your risks and establishing a willingness to follow proper business practices. The next step is to verify that, at all times, policies and procedures are being followed.

During an audit, the benchmark used (beyond that of acceptable business practices) is the organization's own policies. Failure to comply with existing organizational rules can cause the most harm.

In the event of a lawsuit or a dispute, the organization's proof of compliance and an opinion by the courts are arbitrators of whether or not the company showed due diligence with respect to laws, guidelines, regulations, policies, and procedures. To verify that adherence to these documents, a periodic internal review of procedures should be conducted, and the resulting reports or documentation should be presented for review to the Board of Trustees.

(ii) Solutions: To Reduce Risk and Stay Out of Court.

- Education
  - New resources
- Training
- Adequate insurance coverage
- Loss-prevention programming
  - Films
  - Books
  - Consultants
- Conflict resolution
- Training
- Arbitration

(iii) Disaster Preparedness. Is the organization prepared in the event of a disaster? Regardless of whether the organization has liability coverage for such disasters, important documents, records, and other properties need to be protected. While an insurance company may pay for the cost of computers and other office equipment lost in a fire, it cannot restore the data or other vital informational assets lost during the disaster. Liability insurance will not provide the protection from loss of trade secrets, data, contacts, or other business information used by the organization on a day-to-day basis.

To be disaster prepared, your organization needs to determine which items or information are needed to continue to be a viable operation after the disaster. These items should be replicated, copied, vaulted, or whatever action is necessary to assure that they will be available after a disaster. The manner in which these items

Exhibit 14.5.   Basic Disaster Preparedness

Data	In addition to routine periodic backups of computer data to prevent loss from normal occurrences, such as computer shutdowns or power surges, additional copies should be made for off-site backups and/or fire-resistant vault storage.
Records, files	Duplicate copies of all important records should be kept in fire-resistant vaults either on the premises and/or in another location.
Staff and volunteers	During fire, flood, earthquake, or other disasters that places your workplace at risk, your staff and volunteers should be protected through emergency exit plans and earthquake kits (water, food, etc.).
	During an actual emergency, the ability to account for all persons on your premises will be vital to assisting emergency workers with locating and rescuing individuals. Team captains or safety officers should be appointed and given responsibility for communicating with emergency workers and assisting them in locating these individuals at the work site.
Physical inventory	A physical inventory (pictures, lists, bills of lading) that would be used to prove loss in an insurance claim should be duplicated and stored off-site as well as in fire- and flood-protection vaults on the premises.
Contact information	During and after a disaster, the ability to contact staff and volunteers should be maintained by assigning specific individuals this responsibility and by maintaining copies of employee and volunteer contact information in their homes and vehicles, so all staff and volunteers can be contacted and/or accounted for after a disaster.

and information are protected depends greatly on the type of disaster. The region may have specific types of natural disasters that are not common in other areas. For example, earthquakes are prevalent in the western United States. The aftereffects of earthquakes may include fire as well as access difficulties to the original premises. Off-site backups of items and information are necessary in earthquake regions. In the midwestern United States, floods, fire, and tornadoes are more threatening disasters. Storm shelters and fire- and flood-resistant vault storage are necessary to protect items in these regions (see Exhibit 14.5).

Your insurance company can be a valuable ally in disaster preparedness. Most insurance companies can provide general guidelines for dealing with and preparing for emergencies in your region.

CHAPTER FIFTEEN

Financial Policy—
Internal and External

15.1 Introduction   558
    (a) What Is Policy?   558
    (b) Why Are Policies Required?   559
    (c) Complying with and Establishing Policy
       and Procedure   560
    (d) Who Sets Policy?   560
    (e) Where to Start?   562
15.2 Establishing Procedures   566
15.3 Additional Resources   567

> A policy is a temporary creed liable to be changed, but while it holds good it has got to be pursued with apostolic zeal.[1]

15.1   INTRODUCTION

Establishing and complying with policy is the fundamental charge of the CFO, director, or fund manager. Internal policies are your organization's set of policies. External policies are provided by outside organizations and are agreed to as part of the acceptance of their funds.

(a) What Is Policy?

There are two general definitions for policy and procedure, authoritative and practical:

[1]Mohandas K. Gandhi, Letter, 8 March 1922, to the general secretary of the Congress Party, India.

	Authoritative	Practical
Policy:	A definite course of action adopted as expedient or from other consideration	A set of guidelines or principles defining an organization's philosophy toward how business shall be conducted
Procedure:	The act or manner of proceeding in any action or process; conduct	Steps and/or actions to be taken to comply with a specific policy

There has been a stigma associating policy with red-tape or bureaucracy. Phrases such as, "I'm sorry, that's not our policy," as a method of telling someone "no" contributed greatly to the perception that policy interferes with productivity, efficiency, and good customer relations. Certainly, in many instances, the negative association with policies is legitimate; many governmental bodies and regulatory agencies are mired in policy that is ineffective and out of date. Also, many policies have become a method of preventing lawsuits, rather than what they are intended to be: a set of guidelines (laws, rules) or principles for how day-to-day business should be performed.

(b) Why Are Policies Required?

Policy is the rule of law for an organization. Policies establish a common understanding of the overriding principles behind all that we do. Good policies merge all of the laws, rules, and regulations from all sources (both internal and external) into a cohesive instrument. Rather than providing a new staff member with copies of all the various laws, codes, and policies from all of the agencies and organizations that they may work with, policies condense all that information into one set of guidelines, eliminating inconsistencies and redundancies.

Even if policies are not written down, all organizations have policies. Sometimes, to avoid the negative association with the term, organizations may refer to them as guidelines, work rules, or job *instructions*. Regardless of what they are called or the form they take, they do exist.

If we did not have policies, a method or plan would have to be established each time someone needed to do something. If someone needed to buy something, they would have to find out what rules applied and what steps or actions needed to be taken every single time. In addition, policies enable us to share information by requiring that certain actions be performed and information be gathered in a consistent manner.

(c) Complying with and Establishing Policy and Procedure

One of the jobs of the CFO, as well as all the leadership in an organization, is to promote and establish a positive attitude toward the compliance with policy, either external or internal. If there is no support at the top, there will be no compliance at the bottom. Before staff and managers will comply with policy, they need to receive a clear message from executive management that the organization supports and actually insists on compliance with policy.

Depending on the nature of your organization and the specific policy, internal or external noncompliance can range from fraud to poor business management, from felony to raised eyebrows.

(d) Who Sets Policy?

- *Internal:* internal policies are those that are in effect within your organization. These policies must indicate compliance with external policies. See Exhibit 15.4 for methods to develop these policies. The Board establishes policy, and each department within the organization develops a set of policies that detail compliance with the policy established by the Board.

- *External:* external policies are those that affect day-to-day operations but are in the charge of an entity outside of the organization, such as the government or other regulatory agency.

Policies are very similar to laws: they have a hierarchical structure. The law hierarchy of the U.S. government is shown in Exhibit 15.1.

All laws must be consistent with the Senate or House Regulations, the Senate and House Regulations must be in compliance

Exhibit 15.1. Simplified Hierarchy of Laws

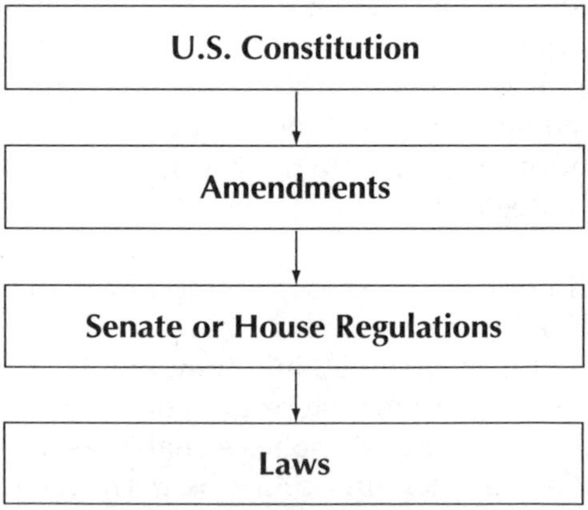

```
┌─────────────────────────────┐
│      U.S. Constitution      │
└─────────────────────────────┘
               │
               ▼
┌─────────────────────────────┐
│        Amendments           │
└─────────────────────────────┘
               │
               ▼
┌─────────────────────────────┐
│ Senate or House Regulations │
└─────────────────────────────┘
               │
               ▼
┌─────────────────────────────┐
│           Laws              │
└─────────────────────────────┘
```

with the U.S. Constitution and Amendments. Your organization also has some form of hierarchy. The Board of Directors sets the mission and goals of the institution; The Board communicates this mission to the executives who, in turn, communicate it to the units under their jurisdiction; and so on. At each step in the process, policy is being established.

Organizations that are part of the U.S. government, or do business with it, are required to comply with all U.S. government policies. Within the U.S. government, there is a hierarchy of policies. A simplified diagram of this hierarchy is shown in Exhibit 15.2.

Exhibit 15.2 illustrates how the CancerNet must comply with the policies in the Office of Management and Budget (OMB), as well as the National Institutes of Health (NIH) and the National Cancer Institute (NCI). The CancerNet also has its own set of policies with which it must comply. Any organization doing business with the CancerNet must comply with this same set of policies. If each time the staff in an organization dealing with the CancerNet had to decipher all of the policies in the hierarchy, they would not be able to do anything productively; however, if they had a set of policies that included the requirements of the CancerNet as well as any other agency with which they did business, work could be conducted both efficiently and effectively.

When the NIH developed its policies, it interpreted the policies provided by the OMB. In turn, the NCI developed its policies from the interpretation of the OMB policy produced from the NIH. Each time the OMB makes a policy change, it causes a ripple effect

Exhibit 15.2. Simplified Diagram of the Hierarchy of Policy within the U.S. Government

Office of Management and Budget (see Exhibit 15.3)

National Institutes of Health (NIH)	Department of Defense
Advanced Laboratory Workstation Project	Agencies under the Secretary of Defense
Division of Computer Research and Technology (DCRT)	Advanced Information Technology Services
BioInformatics Molecular Analysis Section (BIMAS)	Advanced Research Projects Agency (ARPA)
BioMagResBank Database Gateway	Armed Forces Radiobiology Research Institute
GenoBase Database Gateway	Central Imagery Office Ballistic Missile Defense Organization (BMDO)
Division of Research Grants (DRG)	Defense Commissary Agency
National Cancer Institute (NCI)	Defense Contract Audit Agency
CancerNet	Defense Finance and Accounting Service
Etc.	Etc.

Exhibit 15.3. OMB's Role

Office of Management and Budget

OMB's predominant mission is to assist the President in overseeing the preparation of the federal budget and to supervise its administration in Executive Branch agencies. In helping to formulate the President's spending plans, OMB evaluates the effectiveness of agency programs, policies, and procedures; assesses competing funding demands among agencies; and sets funding priorities. OMB ensures that agency reports, rules, testimony, and proposed legislation are consistent with the President's budget and with Administration policies.

In addition, OMB oversees and coordinates the Administration's procurement, financial management, information, and regulatory policies. In each of these areas, OMB's role is to help improve administrative management, to develop better performance measures and coordinating mechanisms, and to reduce any unnecessary burdens on the public.

---

throughout the entire U.S. government, as well as all the organizations that do business with the government. Unfortunately, many organizations within and outside of the U.S. government did not devote the time and resources to maintaining their policies, eliminating old policies or incorporating new policies. This illustrates how policies within the U.S. government can proliferate and become meaningless.

(e) Where to Start?

Since policies are very often an interpretation of another policy, the core meaning of the policy is often lost after multiple iterations—almost mirroring the telephone game played at parties.

With the proliferation of policies without proper maintenance, it is important to start at the top in developing new policies (or updating of existing policies). It is only in the original document, not the interpretation, that the policies in effect can be found. If your organization has dealings with the U.S. government, obtaining copies of the OMB publications is the best place to start (Exhibit 15.5). Even if you do not have business dealings with the U.S. government, the policies from the OMB may be a good model for the policies you develop. A list of documents available from the OMB is shown in Exhibit 15.4. After collecting required copies of external policies, the process of developing internal policies can begin as detailed in Exhibit 15.5.

In 1992, Vice President Al Gore began an initiative to review U.S. government policy with the goal of streamlining and simplifying the way the government does business. Many of the existing policies were rewritten during this campaign. Following suit, many not-for-profit institutions began an audit of their policies.

Exhibit 15.4.   OMB Circulars

OMB Circular A-1, dated 8/07/52	System of circulars and bulletins to executive departments and establishments
OMB Circular A-11 in PDF, Transmittal Memorandum #67, dated 6/13/96	Preparation and submission of budget estimates
OMB Circular A-16, dated 10/19/90	Coordination of surveying, mapping, and related spatial data activities
OMB Circular A-19, dated 9/20/79	Legislative coordination and clearance
OMB Circular A-21, Transmittal Memorandum #6, dated 4/26/96	Cost principles for educational institutions
OMB Circular A-25, Transmittal Memorandum #1, dated 7/08/93	User charges
OMB Circular A-34, Transmittal Memorandum #13 in HTML, dated 12/26/95	Instructions on budget execution
OMB Circular A-45, dated 10/20/93	Rental and construction of government quarters
OMB Circular A-50, dated 9/29/82	Audit follow-up
OMB Circular A-76 in HTML or PDF, dated 8/04/83	OMB Circular A-76 Supplemental Handbook in HTML or PDF, dated 4/01/96
OMB Circular A-76 Transmittal Memorandum #16, dated 5/23/96	

Performance of Commercial Activities

OMB Circular A-87, dated 5/04/95	Cost principles for state, local, and Indian tribal governments
OMB Circular A-89, dated 8/17/84	Catalog of federal domestic assistance
OMB Circular A-94, dated 10/29/92	Discount rates to be used in evaluating time-distributed costs and benefits
OMB Circular A-97, dated 8/29/69	Circular A-97 Transmittal Memorandum #1, dated 3/27/81

Specialized or Technical Services for State and Local Governments

OMB Circular A-102, dated 10/07/94	Grants and cooperative agreements with state and local governments
OMB Circular A-109, dated 4/05/76 (Available in hard copy only)	Major systems acquisitions
OMB Circular A-110, dated 11/19/93	Uniform administrative requirements for grants and other agreements with institutions of higher education, hospitals, and other nonprofit organizations
OMB Circular A-119, dated 10/20/93	Federal participation in the development and use of voluntary standards
OMB Circular A-122, dated 7/08/80 (Available in hard copy only)	Cost principles for nonprofit organizations

Exhibit 15.4.   OMB Circulars (*continued*)

OMB Circular A-123, dated 6/21/95	Management accountability and control
OMB Circular A-125, dated 12/12/89 (Available in hard copy only)	Prompt payment
OMB Circular A-126, dated 5/22/92	Improving the management and use of government aircraft —Attachment A —Attachment B
OMB Circular A-127, dated 7/23/93	Financial management systems
OMB Circular A-128, dated 4/12/85	Audits of state and local governments
OMB Circular A-129, dated 1/11/93	Managing federal credit programs
OMB Circular A-130, Transmittal Memorandum #3, dated 2/08/96	Management of federal information resources
OMB Circular A-131, dated 5/21/93	Value engineering
OMB Circular A-133, dated 4/22/96	Audits of institutions of higher education and other nonprofit institutions
OMB Circular A-134, dated 5/20/93	Financial accounting principles and standards
OMB Circular A-135, dated 10/05/94	Management of federal advisory committees

At one university, a policy review committee was established to produce a new streamlined set of policies as well as to reconcile the inconsistencies and redundancies in their existing policies. The charge of the review committee was to develop policies that were true to the original spirit of the policies established at the OMB as well as to comply with all of the various agencies within the

Exhibit 15.5.   Steps to Develop and Introduce New Policies

1. Establish a small committee with individuals who have a thorough understanding of existing internal policies within your organization and have the insight and knowledge necessary to understand the essential elements of these policies.
2. Charge this committee with the responsibility of simplifying existing policies.
3. Provide the committee with all of the existing rules, laws, policies, and other external documents that affect your business operations.
4. Present these new policies to your organization for review and approval and make changes as necessary.
5. Submit a draft of the policies to your regulatory bodies, if applicable, to seek their acceptance of your new policies and incorporate changes if necessary.
6. Distribute the new policies to your organization.
7. Establish training to assure compliance and understanding of the new policies.
8. Monitor compliance of the new policies.

government and nongovernmental organizations. After several months, the committee found that financial management policies could be divided into four main categories as shown in Exhibit 15.6. These simplified policies are a good model for developing a set of policies within your organization.

Exhibit 15.6.   Sample of Core Financial Management Policies

Accountability Delegations	The <Chancellor/Board/President> delegates the accountability for the financial management of resources to functional units within <Organization>. Consequently, each unit is responsible for properly managing the financial resources of the <Organization> for which they have been provided jurisdiction (e.g., earnings from sales and services, appropriations into accounting units assigned to their departments, etc.) to include identifying a designee (normally the Chief Administrative/ Financial Officer) responsible for formulating an accountability structure for each area. This structure depicts the delegation to initiate, process, and review business transactions by only qualified individuals.
Financial Management	Each operating unit requires financial resources in order to conduct their respective role in the <Organization>'s overall mission. Each organizational head or their designee is responsible for ensuring that the units under their direction manage <Organization> funds in an efficient and cost-effective manner by adopting proven financial management practices.
Data Integrity	Financial management decisions affect each organizational unit, the <Organization>, and interested outside parties. In order to make these decisions appropriately, timely, accurate, and complete data is imperative. Additionally, systems must be in place that contain and generate reliable financial information to help facilitate this decision-making process. Each unit must adopt proven data-integrity practices which provide reasonable assurance that transactions which occur are in accordance with management's general and specific authorization, and that all financial activities which occur are recorded in the financial records of the <Organization>. Each organizational head or their designee is responsible for establishing a system that ensures data integrity.
Regulatory Compliance	All individuals conducting business transactions affecting <Organization> funds must comply with all laws and regulations as well as any restrictions on the use of those funds. Each organizational head or their designee is responsible for ensuring that these units under their direction commit funds only in accordance with legal and regulatory requirements.

15.2 ESTABLISHING PROCEDURES

The purpose of policies is to combine all rules (external and internal) into one set of rules that do not conflict with one another. After policies have been established, the procedures for complying with policy can be developed.

It is important to distinguish the difference between policies and procedures as well as the difference between work instructions and procedures. *Procedures* are the steps that must be taken to appropriately comply with policy. *Work instructions* are the suggested steps that should be taken to comply with procedures.

Very often, individuals feel constricted by procedures because they confuse the literal procedure with the work instructions they have been taught. They are unable to respond dynamically to changes within the organization or special needs of constituents because they are attempting to comply with outdated job instructions.

At one nonprofit institution, a class was presented in contract and grant accounting. One of the attendees had been performing her duties in the same manner for more than 20 years. She had always saved a copy of each invoice and packing slip she received and filed it with the original purchase-order documents. During the delivery of the course, where the use of a new technology was introduced that would allow her to maintain a checklist of this same information, and the invoices and packing slips could be thrown away. She confronted the instructor, in near hysteria, claiming it was not appropriate and violated policy. What had happened was this:

1. The institution had a procedure which specified that all invoices, prior to payment, must be reconciled to the original purchase order. In addition, the merchandise must be received in good condition and as ordered (reconciling the packing slip to the order).
2. Her department had complied with this procedure by saving a copy of the invoice and packing slip. The stapling of the documents indicated that they had been reconciled.

The woman had confused the procedure with the *steps* she had been taught to comply, therefore, she refused to believe that a log would suffice as a method of complying with the procedure. This example illustrates how staff may interpret work rules as procedure and also how careful an institution must be about mandating how work should be performed.

Procedures should contain only those steps that are required by policy. If work rules or job aids are produced, staff need to un-

Exhibit 15.7. Steps to Producing and Maintaining Procedures

1. Establish a committee who will be responsible for developing procedures. The group should include individuals who perform the work as well as individuals who must audit the work.
2. Review each policy and determine if a procedure needs to be established. Some policies may not require an associated procedure.
3. Detail the requirements for compliance as indicated by the policy.
4. Verify that the steps outlined in step 3 can be performed. If not, review the steps or consult with the policy makers to better understand their intent.
5. Submit the procedure draft to your organization for review and acceptance. Make changes or modifications, as necessary.
6. Submit a copy of the procedures to your regulatory agencies, if applicable.
7. Incorporate changes and modifications.
8. Distribute procedures.
9. Develop training and/or work instructions (e.g., job aids).
10. Audit compliance.

derstand that they themselves are not policy or procedure, but only a method of compliance. Refer to Exhibit 15.7 for the steps to develop procedures.

15.3 ADDITIONAL RESOURCES

The development of effective policies and procedures is not a simple task. If you do not have the resources to devote to this effort, networking with other similar organizations may yield a solid set of policies which can be modified. In addition, government institutions must provide copies of their policies. Many policies of government and private organization may be found in your local library and on the Internet.

CHAPTER SIXTEEN

Evaluating Your Progress

16.1 Introduction 568
16.2 Evaluation 569
16.3 Evaluating Your Decisions 570
16.4 Evaluating Your Communications 574
16.5 Evaluating Your Mentoring and Supervisory Skills 575
16.6 Testing Your Supervisory and Managerial Skills 581
16.7 Evaluating the Financial Health of Your Organization 581
    (a) Criteria for Measuring Your Financial Health 585
16.8 Conclusion 589

16.1 INTRODUCTION

We have presented a variety of information in this book to assist the nonprofit financial manager in being more effective in his or her position. Much of the information presented has been tangible: steps, actions, knowledge, facts that a financial manager can apply to produce positive results in his or her organization.

Some might say that the annual balance sheet is the final exam for the effectiveness of the financial manager. While this may be a true and good measurement instrument in a for-profit organization, it is not the end-all in a nonprofit organization.

The measure of success for a nonprofit organization is how well it was able to deliver on its mission. The reviews come not singularly from the balance sheet but from a combination of elements, most importantly, from the nonprofit's customers and constituents.

In the most simple terms, if your organization was able to deliver on its goals and objectives for the year and end the year *flush*, a basic level of success has been achieved. The next step is to evaluate how the actions taken this year will affect your organization's ability to perform in subsequent years.

Throughout this book we have presented and examined:

- How to manage your day-to-day operations
- How to achieve short- and long-term financial objectives
- How to establish policies and procedures to streamline the organization
- The unique requirements of the nonprofit's funding sources
- How technology can be best applied in the organization
- How to manage and affect positive external relationships
- Ways to limit liabilities and protect and increase resources

To evaluate the effectiveness of the financial manager in a nonprofit organization, we need to evaluate two vastly different categories:

1. Tangible results
   - Fund balances
   - Interest income
   - Resources inventory
   - Assets, etc.
2. Intangible results
   - Risk taking
   - Working environment
   - Fluidity

To evaluate the tangible results, an audit of the financial well-being of the organization can be performed by reviewing the financial reports.

As the manager of the financial resources, you have taken every care in monitoring the day-to-day activities of your organization. The previous chapters of this book have provided information to assist you in doing your job effectively and measuring that success. How do you know if you have done a good job? How do you know if your organization is doing well? This chapter presents a method for evaluating the less tangible skills that a financial manager brings to a nonprofit organization.

16.2 EVALUATION

Effective, quality financial management requires that you are in a constant state of review, remaining fluid in your procedures and priorities and making changes and corrections where needed.

- Were your decisions appropriate?
- Have you communicated effectively with others in the organization?

- Are the staff and volunteers performing optimally?
- You may have met payroll and paid expenses, but what is the financial health of your organization in relation to accomplishing its mission and goals?

These questions may be used to begin evaluating your own performance as well as the performance of the organization.

16.3   EVALUATING YOUR DECISIONS

Hindsight is 20/20 is a term we are all familiar with in evaluating anything that we have done in the past. Certainly there will be new information available that would have had a bearing on a decision you have made. Those considerations are not necessary in evaluating the effectiveness of your decisions. You do not have a crystal ball, you cannot foresee dramatic changes, but you can factor in recurring changes in market activity, and seasonal changes, and prepare for potential disasters.

Determining whether you made the *right* decision requires an understanding of what *right* is. Often, we confuse the term as being either *"yes,* it was correct" or *"no,* it was wrong," but there is a range of correctness and appropriateness in almost every decision (see Exhibit 16.1).

Within the range of correctness, you can evaluate your decisions using the following criteria:

- Did the decision stand the test of time?
- Would you make the same decision today?
- If any, what factors would you have weighted more heavily now than you did then?
- Would you have sought the advice of the same individuals?
- Were reference materials, literature, or any other information available that you did not review but would review now?
- Were there signals, clues, reports, or advice that you ignored or would have considered more heavily?

Exhibit 16.1.   Decision Scale

| Wrong | Right | Wrong |

Exhibit 16.2. Decision-Making Evaluation

The charts and questions that follow allow you to evaluate your decision-making abilities. Before beginning the evaluation, reflect over your decisions of the last several months.

Determine which five decisions you plan to evaluate:

1. _____

2. _____

3. _____

4. _____

5. _____

For each of the questions below, consider each of the decisions above and determine which score most accurately applied in that specific case.

In all the questions below, do not consider new information that was not available at the time you made the decision, unless it was information which you either neglected to consider or chose to ignore.

A. Would you come to the same conclusion today and make the same decision?

Decision	Yes, without reservation Score = 5	Yes, but with minor modification Score = 4	Yes, but with reservation Score = 3	Probably not Score = 2	Definitely, no Score = 1	Score
1						
2						
3						
4						
5						
Total:						

B. With each decision made, there are generally facts and information that conflict. You evaluated those inconsistencies and ruled out specific information. Would you rule out the same information today?

Decision	Yes, without reservation Score = 5	Yes, but with minor modification Score = 4	Yes, but with reservation Score = 3	Probably not Score = 2	Definitely, no Score = 1	Score
1						
2						
3						
4						
5						
Total:						

(Continues)

Exhibit 16.2. Decision-Making Evaluation (*continued*)

C. You sought the advice of others and considered their advice or opinion when making your decision. This information may have been gathered over time and not specifically at the time you made the decision. You either rejected this individual's advice or used their opinion as a major justification for the decision. Would you come to the same conclusions today?

Decision	Yes, without reservation Score = 5	Yes, but with minor modification Score = 4	Yes, but with reservation Score = 3	Probably not Score = 2	Definitely, no Score = 1	Score
1						
2						
3						
4						
5						
Total:						

D. You may have reviewed reports, evaluated literature, or done other types of research when you made your decision. Would you use that same information today as a justification for your decision or weight it as heavily?

Decision	Yes, without reservation Score = 5	Yes, but with minor modification Score = 4	Yes, but with reservation Score = 3	Probably not Score = 2	Definitely, no Score = 1	Score
1						
2						
3						
4						
5						
Total:						

E. Decisions often have long-term consequences for your organization. A decision that was appropriate in the short term may become detrimental in the long term. When making decisions, you need to consider both the short- and long-term impacts. Considering how this decision has impacted your organization in both the short and long term, would you make the same decision today?

(*Continues*)

Exhibit 16.2.   Decision-Making Evaluation (*continued*)

Decision	Yes, without reservation Score = 5	Yes, but with minor modification Score = 4	Yes, but with reservation Score = 3	Probably not Score = 2	Definitely, no Score = 1	Score
1						
2						
3						
4						
5						
Total:						

Totaling your score:

   Copy the scores from each of the above questions into the table below, then total your score for each question and for each decision:

Decision	Question A	Question B	Question C	Question D	Question E	Total Score	Average (total/5)
1							
2							
3							
4							
5							
Total:							

Reviewing your scores:

   For each question and for each decision, there is a maximum total score of 25 and a lowest possible score of 5.

- A score of 25 indicates that you have exceptional decision-making abilities.
- A score of 20–25 indicates that your decision-making skills are very good.
- A score of 15–20 indicates that your decision-making skills are fair but could use some improvement.
- A score of 10–15 indicates that your decision-making skills are in need of improvement.
- A score of 5–10 indicates that your decision-making skills were poor in this particular set of instances.

(Continues)

Exhibit 16.2.　Decision-Making Evaluation (*continued*)

General indicators:

- If there is a significant difference between the totals in the score column for each decision, it may indicate that you are inconsistent in the effectiveness of your decision making. It may also indicate that you are sometimes forced to make decisions without having the time to appropriately consider or weigh the information to make an effective decision.
- For each of the questions, if there is a low or high score in a particular area, consider what was unique in that instance that caused you to make an inappropriate decision; conversely, in areas where you made a good decision, consider what was unique about that particular situation.

For the future:

When making decisions in the future, you can refer to the following checklist before making your final decision:

- ☐　I have weighed conflicting information, based on my experience and the integrity of the information in the past, and have chosen to ignore specific information for legitimate and appropriate reasons, or I have chosen to weight heavily specific pieces of information.
- ☐　I have considered the opinions of others and, based on my experience of the soundness of their advice, I am either ignoring their advice or factoring it highly in making this decision.
- ☐　I have reviewed all materials that may impact this decision. I have either chosen to follow the advice gleaned from these materials or, based on my experiences in the past, chosen to disregard this advice.
- ☐　I have considered both the short-term and long-term impacts of this decision after carefully weighing the risks and benefits.
- ☐　I have taken the time to carefully consider all the information available to me and am not making this decision in haste without properly evaluating the appropriateness or legitimacy of this decision.

16.4　EVALUATING YOUR COMMUNICATIONS

Communicating the problems, goals, status, and issues in your area is one of your main responsibilities. As discussed earlier, we make decisions based on the information available to us. The leader in your organization base their decisions on the financial information you are providing to them. As the individual responsible for financial management, you have special skills and abilities that allow you to understand the intricate details and nuances of the finances in your organization; others do not. One of your major responsibilities is communicating to others, in a manner that matches their ability to understand the financial implications of their decisions (Exhibit 16.3).

If others in your organization are continually making decisions that have a detrimental financial impact to the organization, the following questions should be considered:

- Does your communication strategy or style need to improve?
- When speaking to individuals or groups, is their body language open and interested?
- Are you respectful and thoughtful in considering differing points of view?
- Are your recommendations being ignored? If so, why?
  - Is there a thorough understanding of the information you are providing?
  - Are your reports, memos, and correspondence easy to understand?
  - When presenting your information at meetings or answering questions are you using lay terms or financial jargon?
  - When you are presenting your opinion, are you thoroughly explaining your reasons or the facts that you considered when making that decision?

16.5 EVALUATING YOUR MENTORING AND SUPERVISORY SKILLS

As a leader in your organization, part of your responsibilities is to supervise staff, volunteers, functions, areas, or tasks. One of the ways you can evaluate your own performance is to evaluate the successes of those reporting to you and the areas for which you have responsibility.

When evaluating the performance of other individuals, there are two main factors to consider and evaluate:

1. *Your skills:* your skills in effectively managing, supervising, and mentoring this individual
2. *Their skills:* the individuals' capabilities, skills, willingness to perform and learn, dedication to his or her jobs and personal growth, and integrity

Managing staff and coordinating volunteers require a set of skills unique to these particular disciplines. Some may have

Exhibit 16.3. Evaluating Your Communication Skills

Before beginning the evaluation, reflect on your communications over the last several months. These will include meetings, correspondence or memos, and impromptu and telephone conversations.

Choose five instances to evaluate that provide a general sampling of your communications over the last several months:

1. _____

2. _____

3. _____

4. _____

5. _____

An effective communication interchange requires that the individuals involved have a willingness to communicate effectively, openly, and honestly. There may be individuals who do not meet these criteria. At any particular time, there also may be other factors that make a meaningful exchange difficult (such as if the person you are speaking to is ill or under considerable personal or work stress at that time). Unless you were insensitive to an individual's specific problems or situation, do not factor these situations in your answers.

A. Were you respectful and thoughtful in your communication?

Interchange	Yes, without reservation Score = 5	Yes, but with minor modification Score = 4	Yes, but with reservation Score = 3	Probably not Score = 2	Definitely, no Score = 1	Score
1						
2						
3						
4						
5						
Total:						

B. How an individual ranks in your organization may determine the amount of detail or summary you provide. Often, upper management does not require communications with elaborate details, while staff performing clerical-type duties may require specific details. One of the major skills in communication is providing *enough* information, without miring an individual with unnecessary details. In each interaction, finding the balance between detail and summary is your main challenge. Did you provide the appropriate level of detail or summary in this exchange?

(Continues)

Exhibit 16.3. Evaluating Your Communication Skills (*continued*)

Interchange	Yes, without reservation Score = 5	Yes, but with minor modification Score = 4	Yes, but with reservation Score = 3	Probably not Score = 2	Definitely, no Score = 1	Score
1						
2						
3						
4						
5						
Total:						

C. In order for others to accept and consider your opinions, you need to provide them with your reasoning or logic for coming to a specific conclusion. This requires that you provide information that illustrates how you came to a particular conclusion or assumption. In this exchange, did you provide information that allowed the individual to understand your opinion and point of view?

Interchange	Yes, without reservation Score = 5	Yes, but with minor modification Score = 4	Yes, but with reservation Score = 3	Probably not Score = 2	Definitely, no Score = 1	Score
1						
2						
3						
4						
5						
Total:						

D. Your special skills and abilities in the financial arena allow you to understand terminology specific to the discipline. Others may not have this same level of understanding. In order to have an effective communication, you need to use the appropriate level of technical and lay terms to present your information. The use of technical terms and jargon with an individual who does not understand them

(Continues)

Exhibit 16.3. Evaluating Your Communication Skills (*continued*)

would lead to an ineffective exchange. In this engagement, did you use the appropriate level of terminology?

Interchange	Yes, without reservation Score = 5	Yes, but with minor modification Score = 4	Yes, but with reservation Score = 3	Probably not Score = 2	Definitely, no Score = 1	Score
1						
2						
3						
4						
5						
Total:						

E. Often, individuals are giving us clues as to whether or not he or she understands the information presented. There may be obvious clues, such as the individuals stating that he or she doesn't understand. There may be less obvious clues, such as the same or similar question being asked repeatedly or closed body language. In this engagement, were you factoring in these clues as a measure of the effectiveness of your exchange and making adjustments in your presentation based on these clues?

Interchange	Yes, without reservation Score = 5	Yes, but with minor modification Score = 4	Yes, but with reservation Score = 3	Probably not Score = 2	Definitely, no Score = 1	Score
1						
2						
3						
4						
5						
Total:						

(*Continues*)

Exhibit 16.3.   Evaluating Your Communication Skills (*continued*)

Totaling your score:
Copy the scores from each of the above questions into the table below, then total your score for each question and for each interchange:

Interchange	Question A	Question B	Question C	Question D	Question E	Total Score	Average (total/5)
1							
2							
3							
4							
5							
Total:							

Reviewing your scores:
For each question and for each interchange, there is a maximum total score of 25 and a lowest possible score of 5.

- A score of 25 indicates that you have exceptional communication skills.
- A score of 20–25 indicates that your communication skills are very good.
- A score of 15–20 indicates that your communication skills are fair but could use some improvement.
- A score of 10–15 indicates that your communication skills or style is in need of improvement.
- A score of 5–10 indicates that your communication skills are poor or your style of communication is ineffective.

General indicators:
- If there is a significant difference between the totals in the score column for each interchange, it may indicate that you are inconsistent in your communications or your style is not always appropriate or effective. There may be other factors that caused this particular exchange to be effective or ineffective, such as information that was not available at the time of the interchange or political issues within your organization that prevent a meaningful exchange.
- For each of the questions, if there is a low or high score in a particular area, consider what was unique in that instance that made that particular exchange effective or ineffective.

For the future:
When interacting and communicating in the future, you can refer to the following checklist:

(Continues)

Exhibit 16.3. Evaluating Your Communication Skills (*continued*)

☐ I am sensitive to the unique needs of each individual, including their diversity.

☐ I consider the skill level of the individuals in this exchange and am speaking or writing in a manner that matches their ability to comprehend.

☐ I consider the ranking or position of each individual and provide the appropriate level of summary or detail.

☐ I present an image and a style that allow others to comfortably question my opinions.

☐ I demonstrate a willingness to be wrong, am open to suggestions and differing points of view, and am certain that my motives are appropriate and in the best interest of the organization and my constituents.

exceptional skills in financial management and analysis but may lack the skills necessary to effectively supervise and motivate individuals who report to them. Individuals also may be performing well, despite being ineffectively managed. Some individuals may also have exceptional expertise in a particular subject matter but are ineffective in sharing that information and training other staff and volunteers.

Exhibit 16.4 highlights the skills needed to be an effective leader, supervisor, or manager.

Exhibit 16.4. Effective Leadership

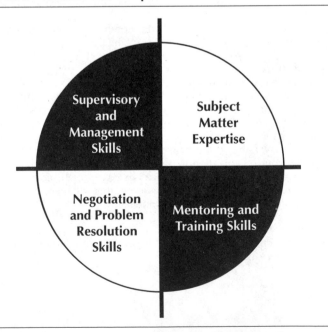

- *Supervisory and management:* These are traditional skills that we often think are the only skills in managing and supervising others. These skills include the ability to monitor the activity of others, keep proper records of attendance and performance, write and conduct performance appraisals, counsel staff, and so forth. Clear instructions motivate.

- *Subject matter expertise:* A supervisor needs to have a level of competency regarding the tasks or functions that his or her staff perform in order to accurately evaluate their performance. It is not necessary for a supervisor to possess the same or superior skills as all his or her staff, but he or she must have a general understanding, sufficient to comprehend and communicate effectively with them.

- *Negotiation and problem resolution:* Regardless of how efficiently an organization may function, there will be situations where competent staff and volunteers will have conflicting opinions, goals, or plans. A supervisor will be responsible for resolving these conflicts in a manner that leaves all parties feeling validated and needed.

- *Mentoring and training:* Above and beyond supervising an individual, a manager accepts responsibility for the personal growth of the individuals in his or her area. Whether or not the organization has formalized programs for career-succession planning or training, it is the manager's responsibility to foster excellence in his or her staff and assist them with advancement, either within the same managerial area or within the organization.

16.6   TESTING YOUR SUPERVISORY AND MANAGERIAL SKILLS

If you do not have supervisory responsibility for staff or volunteers, skip this portion (Exhibit 16.5) of the evaluation. If you supervise less than five individuals, limit your evaluation to that number. You may also choose to list a staff member or volunteer who is no longer with the organization.

16.7   EVALUATING THE FINANCIAL HEALTH OF YOUR ORGANIZATION

The previous evaluations have measured the quality of your specific skills. In this section, you will assess the financial health of your organization to evaluate how effectively you are performing.

Exhibit 16.5. Testing Supervisory/Managerial Skills

Select five staff members or volunteers you supervise.

1. _____

2. _____

3. _____

4. _____

5. _____

    There may be situations, hopefully rare, when you will be responsible for supervising an individual who may be suffering from severe psychological problems or have an alcohol- or substance-abuse problem, which has a significant impact on his or her ability to function. These individuals may pose a physical threat to the staff and volunteers in your organization. The unique set of skills required to handle this, are not typically thought of as a management requirement. Outside experts may need to be called upon (psychologist or psychiatrist, police officer, crisis specialist) to either handle the situation directly or give you guidance in handling the situation. If you are experiencing a situation with this severity, the following questions will not apply.

    A. Have you maintained proper records of your staff or volunteers' attendance, performance, and job descriptions?

Staff or Volunteer	Yes, without reservation Score = 5	Yes, but with minor modification Score = 4	Yes, but with reservation Score = 3	Probably not Score = 2	Definitely, no Score = 1	Score
1						
2						
3						
4						
5						
Total:						

    B. Do you possess sufficient knowledge or familiarity with the responsibilities of a staff member or volunteer to accurately determine if he or she is performing the job optimally?

Staff or Volunteer	Yes, without reservation Score = 5	Yes, but with minor modification Score = 4	Yes, but with reservation Score = 3	Probably not Score = 2	Definitely, no Score = 1	Score
1						
2						
3						
4						
5						
Total:						

(Continues)

Exhibit 16.5. Testing Supervisory/Managerial Skills (*continued*)

C. When in meetings or conversations with more than one individual, are all individuals given equal participation in the exchange and are each individual's opinions, problems, and issues given equal consideration?

Staff or Volunteer	Yes, without reservation Score = 5	Yes, but with minor modification Score = 4	Yes, but with reservation Score = 3	Probably not Score = 2	Definitely, no Score = 1	Score
1						
2						
3						
4						
5						
Total:						

D. Assuming that an individual possesses the skills necessary to assimilate new or more challenging responsibilities, has your training (either formal or informal) been effective?

Staff or Volunteer	Yes, without reservation Score = 5	Yes, but with minor modification Score = 4	Yes, but with reservation Score = 3	Probably not Score = 2	Definitely, no Score = 1	Score
1						
2						
3						
4						
5						
Total:						

E. At some point you may become ill, go on vacation, or leave your organization. Is there an individual or group of individuals who have sufficient understanding of your job to assume responsibility for it, if you were to be unable to perform your duties?

Staff or Volunteer	Yes, without reservation Score = 5	Yes, but with minor modification Score = 4	Yes, but with reservation Score = 3	Probably not Score = 2	Definitely, no Score = 1	Score
1						
2						
3						
4						
5						
Total:						

(Continues)

Exhibit 16.5. Testing Supervisory/Managerial Skills (*continued*)

Totaling your score:
 Copy the scores from each of the above questions into the table below, then total your score for each question and for each interchange:

Staff or Volunteer	Question A	Question B	Question C	Question D	Question E	Total Score	Average (total/5)*
1							
2							
3							
4							
5							
Total:							
Average†							

*If you are evaluating less than five staff members or volunteers, divide your total by the total number of staff members or volunteers listed.

†Calculate this row only if you used less than five staff members or volunteers for your evaluation.

Reviewing your scores:
 In this section, it is possible that your totals will not correspond to the totals below. Please use the average totals in the last column instead of the overall totals to determine your results.
 For each question and for each interchange, there is a maximum total score of 25 and a lowest possible score of 5.

- A score of 25 (average 5) indicates that you have exceptional supervisory and managerial skills.
- A score of 20–25 (average 4) indicates that your supervisory and managerial skills are very good.
- A score of 15–20 (average 3) indicates that your supervisory and managerial skills are fair but could use some improvement.
- A score of 10–15 (average 2) indicates that your supervisory and managerial skills are in need of improvement.
- A score of 5–10 (average 1) indicates that your supervisory and managerial skills are poor.

General indicators:
- If there is a significant difference between the totals in the score column for each staff member or volunteer, it may indicate that you are inconsistent in your supervisory and managerial delivery. There may be other factors, such as inconsistencies in staff responsibilities, personal attitudes, political issues, or other unique situations that may cause this fluctuation.
- For each of the questions, if there is a low or high score in a particular area, consider what in that instance made that particular supervisory and managerial situation unique.

(Continues)

Exhibit 16.5.   Testing Supervisory/Managerial Skills (*continued*)

For the future:
    When managing and supervising your staff and volunteers, you can refer to the following checklist:

☐   All the job cards or descriptions of my staff and volunteers are accurate and up to date.

☐   All my staff and volunteers have received a copy of their job descriptions and have received a performance appraisal, where applicable.

☐   When faced with a conflicting situation or plan, I have considered the opinions of all staff and volunteers when determining which situation or plan to approve.

☐   I have trained or am in the process of training an individual or group of individuals to perform my job in the event I am unable to perform it temporarily or if I decide to leave the organization.

☐   I have carefully documented issues, meetings and conflicts, and have taken a proactive approach to assuring that the staff and volunteers under my responsibility are performing optimally, and I have taken the necessary actions to remove staff or volunteers who are not performing effectively.

Defining *financial health* can be somewhat difficult. You may have sufficient resources to cover your payroll and pay your outstanding invoices, but:

• Have you used your resources wisely?

• Have you made purchasing or other financial decisions that may have negative short-term impacts but wise long-term implications?

• Has your conservatism in financial matters limited your organization's ability to accomplish its mission and goals?

• Did you take unnecessary risks that may have put your organization at risk?

• Did you fail to take limited risks that might have positioned your organization better for the future or made it better able to accomplish its mission and goals?

(a) Criteria for Measuring Your Financial Health

• Your bank may determine that financial health means that you have money in the bank and have managed your cash flow between your checking and other longer-term interest-bearing accounts.

• Your creditors may determine that you are financially healthy if you pay your invoices on time.

- Your contributors may determine you are financially healthy:
  - If you have the lowest possible overhead
  - If you accomplished or achieved your mission and goals
  - If your expenditures were appropriate and legitimate
- Your Board of Directors may determine that you are financially healthy if you have positioned the organization well, balancing the needs of all your constituents, and assisted the organization in successfully meeting its mission and goals.

To determine whether your organization is financially healthy, you must consider all the factors mentioned above. The evaluation detailed in Exhibit 16.6 will assist you in evaluating your organization's financial health.

Exhibit 16.6. Financial Health Evaluation

A. Did you make any financial or purchasing decisions that had short-term benefits but long-term negative impacts to your organization?

Yes	Probably, yes	Maybe	Probably not	Definitely, no
Score = 1	Score = 2	Score = 3	Score = 4	Score = 5

B. At any time in the evaluating period did you incur expenses (such as bank penalties or fines, short-term loan charges) that could have been avoided if expenditures and investments would have been more appropriately delayed or handled differently?

Yes, often	Yes, occasionally	Seldom	Almost never	Never
Score = 1	Score = 2	Score = 3	Score = 4	Score = 5

C. Did you take unnecessary risks?

Yes, often	Yes, occasionally	Seldom	Almost never	Never
Score = 1	Score = 2	Score = 3	Score = 4	Score = 5

(Continues)

Exhibit 16.6. Financial Health Evaluation (*continued*)

D. Did you take appropriate and well-calculated risks?

Never	Almost never	Seldom	Yes, occasionally	Yes, often
Score = 1	Score = 2	Score = 3	Score = 4	Score = 5

E. Is your overhead or percentage of expenditure on overhead versus programmatic expenses consistent with other similar organizations?

Below average	Slightly below average	Near or matching	Above average	Exceeding average
Score = 1	Score = 2	Score = 3	Score = 4	Score = 5

F. At any point during the evaluation period did you restrict the use of resources that could have been used more appropriately to accomplish the organization's mission and goals?

Yes	Probably, yes	Maybe	Probably not	Definitely, no
Score = 1	Score = 2	Score = 3	Score = 4	Score = 5

G. At any point during the evaluation period did your actions put the organization at unnecessary risk or where you unable to meet expenses?

Yes	Probably, yes	Maybe	Probably not	Definitely, no
Score = 1	Score = 2	Score = 3	Score = 4	Score = 5

H. At any point during the evaluation period did you allow an inappropriate or illegitimate expenditure or transaction without taking necessary action to stop or rectify it?

Yes	Probably, yes	Maybe	Probably not	Definitely, no
Score = 1	Score = 2	Score = 3	Score = 4	Score = 5

I. During your evaluation period, did you ever fail to pay your invoices on time or take advantage of net discounts and rebates?

(Continues)

Exhibit 16.6. Financial Health Evaluation (*continued*)

Yes	Probably, yes	Maybe	Probably not	Definitely, no
Score = 1	Score = 2	Score = 3	Score = 4	Score = 5

K. At any time, did you suffer an increase in loan rates or other negative impacts due to a bad credit rating?

Yes	Probably, yes	Maybe	Probably not	Definitely, no
Score = 1	Score = 2	Score = 3	Score = 4	Score = 5

Transfer your scores and total below:

A. _____

B. _____

C. _____

D. _____

E. _____

F. _____

G. _____

H. _____

I. _____

J. _____

K. _____

Total: _____

Reviewing your scores:

- A score of 45–50 indicates that your organization tests well and your organization could be considered financially healthy.
- A score of 35–45 indicates that your organization tests well and while improvement may be needed in specific areas, is relatively healthy.
- A score of 25–35 indicates that your organization did not fair well in this test and there may be cause for concern or changes in managing your organization's financial resources.
- A score of 15–25 indicates that your organization's health may be at significant risk and major changes are indicated.
- A score of 5–15 indicates that your organization is not healthy, and serious changes and a re-examination of priorities need to occur immediately.

16.8   CONCLUSION

None of these evaluations should be taken out of context or used as a justification or reason for making significant changes in your organization. It is important to use these evaluations as one of many tools for measuring your performance, as well as that of your organization. There may be unique factors in these evaluations that cause your scores to be inaccurately high or low. Performing this evaluation quarterly and averaging your results after a year may also provide a better picture of your performance. Performing this evaluation over time ensures that you are as effective as you can be for the organization you serve.

Index

A

Academic affairs committee,
1.3(b)(iv)
Accountability
defining structure for,
3.4(a)(g)
establishing policy regarding, 3.4(c)
ethics and, 3.4(d–f)
for financial reports, 6.3(c)
general policy statements,
3.4(c)(i)
monitoring, 3.4(g)(i)
policy interpretation,
3.4(c)(ii)
purpose of, 3.4(b)
scheduling reviews of,
3.4(g)(ii)
special focus for nonprofits,
6.2(c)
Account analysis statement,
9.2(c)
Accounting activity evaluation, 3.3(b)(iii)
Acquisitions
financial manager's role in,
4.7(c)
financial problems and,
6.6(f)(v)
financial projections for,
4.7(f)(iii)
financial synergy and,
4.7(d)(ii)

motives for, 4.7(d)
programmatic synergy and,
4.79(d)(i)
Activity-based management,
3.3(b)(i–ii)
Activity statements, 6.6(c)(i)
Advised lines of credit, 10.8(c)
Aggregation level, in budgeting, 5.4(c)
Alternative equities, defined,
12.11(i)
AMBAC Indemnity Corpora-
tion, 13.9(e)(xii)
American depository receipts,
appendixes 11F–G
American Institute of Philanthropy, 2.2(c)
Annual compound return,
12.10(b)
Annual financial statements,
6.6(c)
activity, financial position,
and cash flows, 6.6(c)(i)
financial ratio analysis,
6.6(c)(ii)
Annual necessary investment,
4.7(b)
Annual reports, 6.6(a)
Annuity trust, 8.14(d)
Application evaluation, in
borrowing, 10.4(b)(iv)
Archival data gathering, in
budgeting, 5.4(d)

Area-specific strategies, 4.2(a)
Articles of Incorporation,
1.1(b)
Asset allocation, 11.2(c)
    alternative investments,
        11.2(c)(iv)
    defined, 12.11(i)
    equity instruments,
        11.2(c)(iii)
    fixed-income instruments,
        11.2(c)(ii)
    investment instruments,
        11.2(c)(i)
    socially conscious investing,
        11.2(c)(v)
Asset-backed securities,
    appendixes 11E and G
    government, 13.9(e)(x)
Asset-based lending, 10.8(c)
Asset classes
    non-traditional, 12.12(c)
    traditional, 12.12(c)
Asset ratio, 6.6(c)(ii)
Asset redeployment, 6.6(f)(iv)
Asset sales, 6.6(f)(iv)
Audit committee, 1.3(b)(iv)
    financial responsibilities of,
        3.1(b)(iii)
Audits, 3.3(d), 14.6(b). See
    also External reviews
Automated clearing house, 9.3
Automation, 3.3
Awards, potential, 8.3(a)

B
Balance sheet, 2.5
Bank Administration Institute,
    9.2(b)
Banker's acceptances, appen-
    dix 11E, 13.12(a)
Banking relations, rating,
    2.5(a)
Banking services
    account reconcilement,
        9.3(g)

cash management and,
    9.2(a)
investments, 9.3(i–j)
managing charges, 9.2(c)
monitoring balances and
    transactions, 9.3(d)
purchasing, 9.2(b)
security safekeeping, 12.6(c)
short-term borrowing,
    9.3(h)
sweep accounts, 9.3(j)
Bank obligations, appendix
    11E
Base case budget worksheet,
    5.6(b)
Bequests, 8.4, 8.14(i)
Better Business Bureau, 6.2(c)
Bills of exchange, 10.8(c)
Board committees, 1.3(b)(iv)
Board of Trustees
    committee support of,
        3.1(b)
    endowment management
        and, 12.6(e)(i)
    financial responsibilities of,
        3.1(a)
    responsibilities, appendix
        1A
Bond anticipation notes,
    13.9(e)(xxiii)
Bond funds, corporate,
    13.12(d)
Bonding financial personnel,
    3.3(d)
Bond Investor Guarantee,
    13.9(e)(xii)
Bond Power form, 12.6(b)
Bonds, 12.10(c)
    annual compound return
        of, 12.10(b)
    document preparation,
        10.11
    municipal bonds, 10.9, 10.11
    taxable, 10.11(b)
    underwriting firms, 10.10

Borrowing. *See also* Loan approval process
alternative sources of, 10.4(c)
from banks, 6.6(f)(v), 10.8(a)
domestic short-term bank loans, 10.8(b)
financial proposal preparation, 10.6
international short-term bank loans, 10.8(c)
leasing compared, 10.12(a)
loan approval process, 10.4(b)
presentations for, 10.7
requirements of, 10.3(b)
short-term, 9.3(h), 10.2
lending trends, 10.8(d)
steps in, 10–4
strategic objectives and, 10.3(a), 10.5
understanding debt, 10–4(a)
Bottom-down budget approach, 5.4(c)
Budget Director, function of, 5.4(a)(i)
Budgeting. *See also* Forecasting
annual necessary investment and, 4.7(b)
approval of, 5.5(e)
cash budgeting. *See* Cash budgeting
cautions in, 5.5(f)
collecting data or projections for, 5.4(e)
consistency with targets, 5.5(f)(iii)
developing and improving, 5.4
establishing policy for, 5.4(b)
example of, 5.5(d)
expenses and, 5.5(c)
financial control and, 2.2(a)

flexible, 4.6(b)
gathering archival data, 5.4(d)
hindrances in, 5.5(f)(ii)
interim reports and, 5.4(c)(ii)
managing from, 6.6(f)
nonfinancial targets and, 5.6(a)
ploys in, 5.5(f)(i)
preparation for, 5.4(a)
preparation philosophy and, 5.4(c)
principles of, 5.4(c)
program establishment, 5.6(c)
purposes of, 5.4(b)(i)
rating, 2.5(a)
revenues and, 5.5(b)
revisions, 5.4(c)(i)
setting amounts, 5.5
targets, 5.4(c)
uses of, 5.4(b)(ii)
zero-based, 5.6(d)
Budget variance analysis, 6.6(b)
capital budget, 6.6(b)(ii)
cash budget, 6.6(b)(iii)
deferred giving, 6.6(b)(iv)
operating budget, 6.6(b)(i)
Building and grounds committee, 1.3(b)(iv)
By-laws, appendix 1B, 1.1(b)

C
Calenderization, in budgeting, 5.6(d)
Campus Crusade for Christ, Intl., 2.1
Capital budget, 6.6(b)(ii)
managing, 4.6(c–d)
Capital erosion, 5.4(c)
Capital expenditure, 4.6
analysis of, 4.6(a–b)
Capital project restrictions, leasing and, 10.12(a)

Capital ratio, improving,
12.3(f)
Capital rationing, 4.6(c–e)
Cash. *See also* Cash budgeting;
Cash flow
analysis of, 6.6(e)
banking environment and,
9.2(a)
bank service charges, 9.2(c)
conversion cycle, 2.5(b)(i)
creative sourcing of, 3.3
determining disbursements,
5.7(c)(ii)
determining receipts,
5.7(c)(i)
emphasis on, 6.6(f)(iv)
forecasting, 5.7(c), 9.3(e)
functions of, 9.2
fund raising and, 8.8(b)
as gift, 8.4
management of, 2.5
position, 6.6(f)(ii)
ratios, 6.6(c)(ii)
Cash budgeting, 5.7. See also
Budgeting
collecting historical information, 5.7(b)
forecasting in, 5.7(c)
purpose of, 2.5(b)(ii)
steps in, 5.7(b)
uses of, 5.7(a), 6.6(b)(iii)
Cash flow, 2.3
estimating, 9.3(f)
forecasting liquidity funds,
12.2
mergers and acquisitions
and, 4.7(d)(iii)
statements, 6.6(c)(i)
system, 2.2(b)
time lines for, 2.2(c)
Cash managers, upgrading,
9.3(l)
Cash reserve ratio, 6.6(c)(ii)
Causal method of forecasting,
5.5(a)(i)

501(c)(3) corporations, 1.1(a)
Certificates of deposit. *See also*
Time deposits
definition of, appendix 11E
Eurodollar, 13.12(b)(iii)
government, 13.9(e)(xvii)
negotiable, 13.12(b)
variable-rate, 13.12(b)(i)
Yankee, 13.12(b)(iv)
Certificates of participation,
13.9(e)(xviii)
Chairman of Board
financial responsibilities of,
3.1(c)
responsibility listing, appendix 1A
role of, 1.3(b)(i)
Charitable gift annuity,
8.14(e)
Charitable giving, 8.10
deferred gifts, 8.14
donor motivation, 8.12
outright gifts, 8.13
planned giving programs,
8.11
valuation and, 8.14(m)
Charitable lead trusts, 8.4,
8.14(f)
Charitable remainder trusts,
8.4, 8.14(c)
Check collections, 9.3
Check payment reconciliation,
9.3(g)
Checks and balances, 3.3(d)
Chief Executive Officer
financial responsibilities of,
3.1(c)
responsibility listing, appendix 1A
Chief Financial Officer,
1.3(b)(ii)
accountability focus, 6.2(c)
financial responsibilities of,
3.1(d)
objective targeting by, 6.2(b)

responsibility listing, appendix 1A
Church of God Missionary Board, 6.3(d)(ii)
Church of the Brethren, 6.3(d)(i)
Collateralized mortgage obligations, appendix 11G
government, 13.9(e)(ix)
Collection periods, and borrowing, 10.3(b)
Collection systems, 9.3
Commercial paper, 13.11(a)
defined, appendix 11E
issuing formats, 13.11(a)(i)
types of, 13.11(a)(ii)
Committed facility, 10.8(c)
Common stock, appendixes 11F and G
Communication, 3.3
skills evaluation, 16.4
Compatible asset mixes, calculating, 12.10(b)
Compensation issues, employee, 14.3(f)
Computer platforms, 7.2(a)
Computer usage, and performance improvement, 2.5(a)(i)
Conduits, 2.2(b)
Confidential information, 7.5
Conflict of interest, 14.3(h)
Consolidated budget, 5.4(c)
Constituents, financial role of, 3.1(e)(i)
Contractors, independent, 1.3(b)(viii)
Contracts, 8.3
financial reports and, 8.3(c)
locating potential awards, 8.3(a)
managing, 8.3(b)
Contribution ratio, 6.6(c)(ii)
Controlled disbursement, 9.3(c)

Controller
financial responsibilities of, 3.1(d)
functions of, 3.3(a)
Controls
effective, 3.3(d)
maintaining, 3.3(c)
Convertible debt instruments, appendix 11G
Convertible preferred equity issues, appendix 11G
Convertible securities, appendix 11F and G
Core products, 4.7(a)
Corporate bonds, appendix 11E, 13.11(d)
Corporate debt instruments, 13.11
commercial paper, 13.11(a)
corporate bonds, 13.11(d)
corporate notes, 13.11(c)
high-yield bonds, 13.11(e)
loan participations, 13.11(b)
master notes, 13.11(f)
Corporate notes, appendix 11E, 13.11(c)
Cost analysis
evaluating, 3.3(b)(ii)
per year, 4.6(b)
Cost coverage, 6.2(b)
Council of Better Business Bureaus, 2.2(c), 6.3(c)
Credit card payments, 9.3
Credit lines, 9.3(h)
Credit quality, government securities, 13.9(a)
Credit rate, 9.2(c)
Credit-rating firms, 12.3(c)(i)
Credit risks, 9.3(m)(i), 12.3(c)(i)
Currency
denomination, 11.2(e)(ii)
as gift, 8.4
Current ratio, 6.6(c)(ii)
Custodian services, 12.6(a)

Customer base, knowledge of, 2.3

D

Daily reports, 6.6(ii)
Data collection, budgetary, 5.4(a)(ii)
Debt, understanding, 10.4(a)
Debt ratio, 6.6(c)(ii)
Decision evaluation, 16.3
Deferred gifts, 8.14
  administration of, 8.14(n)
  annuity trust, 8.14(d)
  bequests, 8.14(i)
  charitable gift annuity, 8.14(e)
  charitable lead trusts, 8.14(f)
  charitable remainder trusts, 8.14(c)
  complementary services and, 8.15(o)
  endowments, 8.14(j)
  life income gifts, 8.14(a)
  pooled income fund, 8.14(b)
  retirement plans, 8.14(k)
  special considerations, 8.14(l)
  testamentary gifts, 8.14(h)
  trusts, 8.14(g)
  valuation of, 8.14(m)
Deferred giving report, 6.6(b)(iv)
Deficit, budget, 5.4(c)
Delivery *versus* payment system, 12.6(a)
Deposit reconcilement, 9.3(g)
Derivatives checklist, appendix 13A
Developmental Officer
  Chief Financial Officer's support of, 8.8
  role of, 8.7
Development committee, 1.3(b)(iv)
Difficult employees, 14.3(d)
Directors, choosing, 1.3(a)

Direct payment guide, appendix 9A
Disaster preparedness, 14.6(c)(iii)
Disbursement management, 9.3(b)
Disclosure of information, 7.5
Discounted cash flow analysis, 4.6(b)
Discretionary revenue, 5.4(c)
Diversification, 12.10(e)
  by asset class, 12.10(e)(i)
  defined, 12.11(i)
  by geography, 12.10(e)(v)
  by global investing, 12.10(e)(vi)
  by industry sector, 12.10(e)(iv)
  by investment type, 12.10(e)(i)
  by manager, 12.10(e)(ii)
  by type of issuer, 12.10(e)(iii)
Donation costs, calculating, 8.9(a)(ii)
Donation-dependent nonprofits, 2.3
Donors. *See also* Charitable giving
  bill of rights, appendix 8A
  cultivation of, 8.7(a)
  fatigue, 3.3
  mailings, 6.7(a)(ii)
  motivation for, 8.12
Downsizing, 6.6(f)(iv)
Due diligence, 14.6(c)(i)

E

Early warning signals, financial, 4.5(b)
Earnings credit rate, 9.2(c)
Economic projections, 5.4(e)
Economic trends, borrowing and, 10.3(b)
Economies of scale, 4.7(d)(ii)
Economies of scope, 4.7(d)(iii)

Education, organizational, 8.6
  guidebooks, 8.6(a)
  simplifying policies, 8.6(a)
Efficient markets, defined,
  12.11(i)
Electronic book entry, 12.6(b)
Electronic check presentment,
  9.3
Emotional safety, 14.3(b)
Endowment
  characteristics of, 12.8
  defined, 11.1
Endowment management,
  12.7
  asset allocation, 12.8(b),
    12.10(a)
  assets, 12.8(c)
  bonds, 12.10(c)
  characteristics of, 12.7(a)
  creation of endowment,
    12.7(c)
  definitions used in, 12.11(i)
  directing of, 12.7(d)
  diversification in, 12.10(e)
  equities, 12.10(d)
  growth, 12.9(c)
  implementation issues,
    12.11(g)
  importance of, 12.7(b)
  inflation and, 12.11(f)
  investment policy, 12.9(a),
    12.11(b)
  investment return, 12.9(d)
  managing risk, 12.10(g)
  modern portfolio theory,
    12.7(h)
  monitoring performance,
    12.10(h)
  responsibility for, 12.7(e)
  spending policy, 12.11
  spending rates and,
    12.10(b), 12.11(e)
  strategies, 12.7(f)
  time horizon, 12.10(f)
  total return spending,
    12.11(d)

Uniform Management of
    Institutional Funds Act,
    12.7(g)
  withdrawals from, 12.8(a)
Endowment pool, defined,
  12.11(i)
Endowments, 8.14(j)
Equipment obsolescence, leasing and, 10.12(a)
Equity instruments, appendix
  11F, 11.2(c)(iii)
Equivalent annual cost analysis, 4.6(b)
Estate distributions, charitable, 8.12(b)
Ethics, 3.4(d)
  ethics check, 3.4(e)
  making ethical decisions,
    3.4(f)
  range of, 3.4(d)
Eurodollar certificates of deposit, 13.12(b)(iii)
Eurodollar time deposits,
  13.12(b)(ii)
Evaluation, 16.2
  of communications, 16.4
  of decisions, 16.3
  of financial health,
    3.3(b)(iii), 16.7
  criteria for, 16.7(a)
  of mentoring, 16.5
  of program alternatives, 4.7
  of projects arising from ex-
    isting programs, 4.6
  of supervisory skills, 16.5,
    16.6
Executive committee, 1.3(b)(iv)
Executive Director, 1.3(b)(v)
  financial responsibilities of,
    3.1(c)
Expansion strategy, 6.6(f)(iv)
Expenses, budgeting, 5.5(c)
External reports, 6.7
  activity statements, 6.7(a)
  cash flow, 6.7(a)
  financial position, 6.7(a)

External reports, (*Continued*)
  usage of, 6.2(c)
External reviews, 6(b). See
  also Audits, 14
  due diligence, 14.6(c)(i)
  partial, 14.6(c)

F

Fannie Mae. *See* Federal National Mortgage Association
Farm credit system securities,
  13.9(e)(i)
Feasibility evaluation, 2.5(a)(i)
Federal Farm Credit Banks,
  13.9(a)
Federal Home Loan Bank securities, 13.9(e)(ii)
Federal Home Loan Mortgage
  Corporation securities,
  13.9(e)(ii)
Federal National Mortgage
  Association securities,
  13.9(e)(iv)
Finance committee, 1.3(b)(iv)
  financial responsibilities of,
  3.1(b)(i)
  responsibility listing, appendix 1A
*Financial and Strategic Manage-
  ment in Nonprofit Organization*, 3.1(e)(i)
Financial difficulties, 2.2(c),
  6.6(f)(iii)
Financial electronic data interchange, 9.3(l)
Financial Guarantee Insurance Company,
  13.9(e)(xii)
Financial management, 2.2
  cash flow system, 2.2(b)
  structure of, 2.2(a)
  treasury management im-
  portance, 2.2(c)
Financial objectives, 2.4(c)(ii)
  achievement of, 2.4(c)(iii)

hindrances to, 2.4(c)(v)
  operational efficiency and,
  2.4(c)(iv)
  overlap of, 2.4(c)(ii)
Financial planning
  basics of, 4.5(b)
  borrowing and, 10.3
  early warning signals, 4.5(b)
  long-range, 4.5(a)
Financial policy
  beginning, 15.1(e)
  compliance to, 15.1(c)
  definition of, 15.1(a)
  establishing procedures for,
  15.2
  reasons for, 15.1(b)
  resources required, 15.3
  responsibility for, 15.1(d)
  sample of, 15.1(e)
  simplifying, 8.6(a)
Financial position statements,
  6.6(c)(i)
Financial proposal preparation, 10.6
  contents of, 10.6(c)
  plan overview, 10.6(b)
  term sheet, 10.6(a)
Financial reports. *See also* Reporting system
  accountability and, 6.3(c)
  accountability focus, 6.2(c)
  differences from for-profit
  businesses, 6.2
  external reports, 6.7. See
  also External reports
  external usage, 6.2(c)
  major reports, 6.5
  mission attainment and,
  6.3(b)
  objectives of, 6.3
  primary focus of, 6.2(a)
  reporting system design, 6.4
  restricted *versus* unrestricted assets, 6.2(d)
  timely reflection of situation
  and, 6.3(a)

turnaround management
and, 6.3(d)
Financial risk. *See also* Risk
management
types of, 9.3(m)(i)
Financial structure
development of, 3.1(e)(iv)
importance of, 3.1(e)(iii)
soundness of, 3.1(e)(v)
Financial synergy, in mergers
and acquisitions, 4.7(d)(ii)
Fixed costs, 5.5(c)
Fixed-income instruments, appendix 11E, 11.2(c)(ii)
Fixed income securities. *See
also* Yield analysis
choosing, 13.7
corporate debt instruments,
13.11
fixed-time de-posits, appendix 11E
interest rate decline and,
13.4(b)
interest rate rise and, 13.4(a)
interest rates and longer
maturities, 13.5
money market instruments,
13.12
municipal floating-rate instruments, 13.10
price movement on, 13.4
repurchase agreements,
13.13
U.S. government agency securities, 13.9
U.S. treasury securities, 13.8
yield calculation, 13.4(c)
Flash reports, 6.6 (ii)
Flexible budgeting, 5.5(c),
5.6(b)
Floating-rate notes,
13.9(e)(xxiv), 13.10
Forecasting, 5.5(a)
techniques for, 5.5(a)(i)
Foreign investments,
11.2(e)(ii)

Form 990, 6.7(a)(i)
Form 990-T, 6.7(a)(i)
Foundation listing, 8.3(a)
Foundations On-Line, 8.3(a)
Fraud, 9.3(m)(ii)
Freddie Mac. *See* Federal
Home Loan Mortgage
Corporation
Functional budgets, 5.4(c)
Fund accounting, 6.2(d)
Fund balance ratio,
6.6(c)(ii)
Funding ratios, 6.6(c)(ii)
Funding risks, 9.3(m)(i)
Fund raising management. *See
also* Gifts
basic, 8.2
campaign expenditures,
6.6(d)(ii)
contracts, 8.3
efficiency ratio analysis,
6.6(d)(iv)
evaluation, 8.8(a)
financial problems and,
6.6(f)(v)
general, 8.5
general mailings, 8.9(c)
grants, 8.3
mid-campaign evaluation
and redirection,
6.6(d)(iii)
philosophy and major ob-
jectives, 6.6(d)(i)
pledge drives, 8.9(b)
post-campaign effective-
ness, 6.6(d)(iv)
promotions, 8.9(a)
rating, 2.5(a)
restricted *vs.* unrestricted,
8.5
source protection, 3.3
special events, 8.9(a)
telemarketing campaigns,
8.9(c)
Funds management system,
structuring, 9.3(c)

G

General obligation bonds, 13.9(e)(xiv)

General obligation securities, 13.9(e)(xi)

Gifts. *See also* Fund Raising
annuity, 8.4
deferred. *See* Deferred gifts
outright. *See* Outright gifts
treasury management and, 2.2(c)
types of, 8.4

Ginnie Mae. *See* Government National Mortgage Association

Government National Mortgage Association securities, 13.9(e)(vi)
adverse features, 13.9(e)(vii)
pass-through securities, 13.9(e)(viii)

Granting agency reports, 6.7(a)(iv)

Grants
financial reports and, 8.3(c)
locating potential awards, 8.3(a)
managing, 2.2(c), 8.3(b)

Grievances, staff, 14.3(c)

Guidebooks, financial, 8.6(a)

H

Hard money, 5.4(c)

Hedging, defined, 12.11(i)

High-yield bonds, 13.11(e)

I

Income tax deductions, donations and, 8.12

Index funds, appendices 11F and G

Inflation rate
defined, 12.11(i)
effects of, 12.11(f)

Information management, 3.3

Information technology, 3.3

In-kind gifts, 8.4

Insurance
liability, 4(a), 14
property, 14.5(a)

Interest rates
investment prices and, 13.4(a)(b)
market prices and, 12.3(c)(ii)

Interim reports, 5.4(c)(ii)

Intermediate term, defined, 11.1

Internal controls, 3.1(e)(v)

Internal reports, 6.6
annual financial statements and ratios, 6.6(c)
annual reports, 6.6(a)
budget variance analysis, 6.6(b)
cash and liquidity, 6.6(e)
fund-raising management and evaluation, 6.6(d)
managing from, 6.6(f)

Internet, financial information on, 2.2(c)

Inventories, 2.5
management of, 2.5(a)

Investment. *See also* Investment operations; Portfolio management
asset allocaton. *See* Asset allocation
benchmarks for comparing, 12.10(h)
case study, 12.3(g)
checklist for, 11.3
criteria for, 12.3
grade, appendix 11G
guideline review, 11.2(f)
guidelines, appendix 11A, 11.2
instruments, 11.2(c)(i)
level of risk, 11.2(e)
liquidity and, 12.3(b)
long-term, 1.1(b)

management fees, defined, 12.11(i)
managers review criteria, 12.12(e)
measurement of, 11.2(d)(i)
money market instruments, 12.3(f)
operating authority for, 11.2(b)
operating procedures, 12.5
outside advisers. *See* Outside investment advisers
policy, defined, 12.11(i)
pooling of funds, 12.3(h)
principal safety and, 12.3(a)
reinvestment requirements, 12.3(e)
reporting, 11.2(d)(ii)
responsibility for, 11.2(a)
risk and, 12.3(c)
short-term, 1.1(a), 9.3(i)
speculation and, 12.4
timing of funds usage, 12.3(d)
written policy, 11.1
Investment center, 3.3(b)
Investment committee, 1.3(b)(iv)
asset allocation and, 11.2(c)
endowment management and, 12.6(e)(ii)
financial responsibilities of, 3.1(b)(ii)
role of, 11.2(a)
Investment consulting firms, 12.12(c)
Investment operations, 12.6
bearer *versus* registered form, 12.6(b)
custodian selection, 12.6(a)
executing transactions, 12.6(d)(i)
maturity ticklers, 12.6(d)(iii)
reporting transactions, 12.6(d)(vii)

securities safekeeping, 12.6(c)
technology tools, 12.6(d)(v)
transaction memos, 12.6(d)(ii)
using outside investment manager, 12.6(e)
verifying transactions, 12.6(d)(vi)

J
Job descriptions, 1.3(c)
samples, appendix 1A
Joint ventures, 4.7(e)
financial projections of, 4.7(f)(iii)
Junk bonds, 13.11(e)

K
Key financial success indicators, 6.3(a)

L
Large-cap stocks, defined, 12.11(i)
Lawsuits, protecting against, 14.3(c)
Leadership
evaluation of, 16.5
skills, 14.3(k)
Leasing, 10.12
Legal risks, 9.3(m)(i)
Lenders
concerns of, 10.4(b)(iii)
repayment, 10.4(b)(v)
Letters of credit, 10.8(b–c), 13.9(e)(xii), 13.11(a)(ii)
Leverage, 10.4(a)(ii)
Liability, 14.4
bonding and, 14.4
insurance, 14.4(a)
protective steps, 14.4(a)
trustees, 3.1(a)
Life income gifts, 8.14(a)
Life insurance, donation of, 8.13(d)

Lilly study, 2.4(a), 5.4(c)
Line item budget, 5.4(c)
Liquidity, 12.3(b). See also
    Liquidity funds
  analysis of, 6.6(e)
  defined, 11.1, 12.11(i)
  as financial objective, 6.2(b)
  fund raising and, 8.8(b)
  investment, 11.1, 11.1(e)(i)
  leasing and, 10.12(a)
  ratios, 6.6(c)(ii)
  risks and, 9.3(m)(i)
  targeting, 6.6(c)(i)
  treasury securities and,
    13.8(b)
Liquidity funds. *See also*
    Short-term investment
  cash flow forecasting,
    11.2(a)
  managing, 12.2
  strategy, 11.2(b)
Loan approval process, 10.4(b).
    See also Borrowing
  application evaluation,
    10.4(b)(iv)
  basic preparation for,
    10.4(b)(i)
  concerns of lenders,
    10.4(b)(iii)
  lender repayment,
    10.4(b)(v)
  reasons for borrowing,
    10.4(b)(ii)
  refinancing, 10.4(b)(vi)
Loan participations, appendix
  11E, 13.11(b)
Lockbox processing, 9.3(a)
Long-range planning, 3.1(e)(i)
Long-term, defined, 11.1
Long-term investment, 1.1(b)
  policy sample, appendix
    11D

M

Mailings, general, 8.9(c)
  description of, 8.9(c)(i)

financial considerations,
    8.9(c)(ii)
Management by objectives,
    5.6(a)
Management objectives,
    2.4(c)(i)
Management services, for giv-
    ing programs, 8.14(n–o)
Management skill evaluation,
    16.5, 16.6
Marketing, 1.2(b)(iv), 3.1(e)(i)
Market risk, 9.3(m)(i),
    12.3(c)(ii)
Master notes, 13.11(f)
Maturity, investment,
    11.2(e)(i)
Maturity ticklers, 12.6(d)(iii)
Mentoring evaluation, 16.5
Mergers
  financial manager's role in,
    4.7(c)
  financial projec-tions of,
    4.7(f)(iii)
  financial reports and,
    6.6(f)(v)
  financial synergy and,
    4.7(d)(ii)
  management team for,
    4.7(d)(iii)
  motives for, 4.7(c)
  programmatic synergy and,
    4.7(d)(i)
Misappropriations, 5.4(b)(ii)
Mission
  attainment, 6.3(b)
  defining strategic decisions,
    4.2(b)
  development, 4.2
  importance of, 2.4(b)
  organizational, 1.2(a)
  strategy and bottom line,
    4.2(a)
Modern portfolio theory,
    12.6(h)
Money market instruments,
    13.12

banker's acceptances, 13.12(a)
bond funds, 13.12(d)
mutual funds, 13.12(c)
negotiable certificates of deposit, 13.12(b)
overview, 12.3(f)
time deposits, 13.12(b)
Money market mutual funds, appendix 11E, 13.12(c)
Monthly reports, 6.6(i)
Motivation, 14.3(j)
Moving average, 5.5(a)(i)
Multiple regression model, 5.5(a)(i)
Municipal bond insurance, 13.9(e)(xii)
Municipal Bond Investors Insurance Company, 13.9(e)(xii)
Municipal bonds, 10.9
issuance of, 11.11(a)
market changes in, 10.9(a)
Municipal debt instruments, government, 13.9(e)(xi)
Municipal notes, 13.9(e)(xx)
Municipal securities, appendix 11E

N
National Charities Information Bureau, 6.3(c)
Natural disasters, 9.3(m)(ii)
NCIB Standards in Philanthropy, 6.2(c)
Negotiable Order for Withdrawal, 9.3(j)
Net cash flow, 6.6(b)(iii)
Net operation ratio, 6.6(c)(ii)
Net present value, 4.6(a)
analysis of, 4.6(b)
Net surplus, 6.6(c)(ii)
Networking, with other organizations, 3.3(d)
New Era Philanthropy scandal, 2.1

Nominating committee, 1.3(b)(iv)
responsibilities, appendix 1A
Nonfinancial targets, in budgeting, 5.6(a)
Nonprofit organizations
characteristics of, 1.2
definition of, 1.1
language of, 1.4
spectrum of, 2.3

O
Office of Management and Budget, 8.3(b), 15.1(d)
Officers, 1.3(b)
Chairman of Board, 1.3(b)(i)
Chief Financial Officer, 1.3(b)(ii)
President, 1.3(b)(i)
Secretary, 1.3(b)(iii)
Treasurer, 1.3(b)(ii)
Off-site storage, financial data, 9.3(m)(ii)
Operating budget, 6.6(b)(i)
Operating ratios, 6.6(c)(ii)
Operational risks, 9.3(m)(i)
Organizational changes, technology and, 6.2(g)
Organizational resources, personal use of, 14.3(g)
Outright gifts. See also Charitable giving
life insurance, 8.13(d)
real estate, 8.13(b)
securities, 8.13(a)
tangible property, 8.13(c)
Outside investment advisers, 12.12
compensation of, 12.12(e)
reasons for using, 12.12(b)
selection of, 12.12(d)
types of, 12.12(c)
working with, 12.12(f)

Overdrafts, 9.3(g)
  services for, 10.8(c)
Overspending, 5.4(b)(ii)

P
Partnerships, 4.7(e)
Pass-through securities,
  13.9(e)(viii)
Payables, 10.1
  management, 2.5(a)
Pension plans, overfunded,
  10.4(c)
Performance improvement
  measures, 2.5(a)(i)
Performance reviews,
  3.4(g)(ii)
Permitted yield, 10.11
Personal property, as gift, 8.4
Personnel committee,
  1.3(b)(iv)
Philanthropy standards, 6.2(c)
Physical safety, 14.3(a)
Planned giving programs. *See
  also* Charitable giving:
  Deferred gifts; Outright
  gifts
  administration of, 8.14(n)
  donor motivation, 8.12(a)
  marketing charitable
    planned giving, 8.12(c)
  organizational fit, 8.11(c)
  role of governing board in,
    8.11(a)
  role of nonprofit financial
    manager in, 8.11(b)
  taxes and, 8.12(d)
  wills and, 8.12(b)
Planning committee, 1.3(b)(iv)
Pledge drives, 8.9(b)
  description of, 8.9(b)(i)
  financial considerations,
    8.9(b)(ii)
Policy, written, 3.1(e)(v)
Pooled income fund, 8.4,
  8.14(b)
Pooling, funds, 12.3(h)

Portfolio review, 12.5(a)
  trading activity, 12.5(a)(ii)
  unrealized gains and losses,
    12.5(a)(i)
Positive pay, 9.3(g)
Preferred equity redemption
  cumulative stock, appendix 11G
Preferred stocks, appendices
  11F and G
Pre-refunded bonds,
  13.9(e)(xvii)
Presentations to investors,
  10.7
  answering objections,
    10.7(b)
  personalizing, 10.7(c)
  question importance,
    10.7(a)
President, 1.3(b)(i)
  financial responsibilities,
    3.1(c)
Price variances, in budgeting,
  5.6(b)
Principal
  preservation
    in long-term investments,
      11.1(b)
    in short-term invest-
      ments, 11.1
  safety of, 12.3(a)
Problem employees, 14.3(d)
Problem resolution evaluation, 16.5
Procedures
  establishing, 15.2
  financial, 3.1(e)(v)
Profit center function, 3.3(b)
Program budgeting, 5.4(c),
  5.6(c)
Program committees,
  1.3(b)(iv)
Program expense ratio,
  6.6(c)(ii)
Program managers, financial
  responsibilities, 3.1(e)(i)

Programmatic synergy, in mergers and acquisitions, 4.7(d)(i)
Programming, 4.7
Promotions, 8.9(a)
    description of, 8.9(a)(i)
    financial considerations and, 8.9(a)(ii)
Property safeguards, 14.5
Prospecting for funding, 8.7(a)
Publicly available reports, 6.7(a)(ii)
Public relations, 1.3(b)(iv)

Q
Quarterly reports, 6.6(i)
Quasi-endowment, defined, 12.11(i)

R
Ratio analysis, 6.6(c)(ii)
Real estate donations, 8.13(b)
Real Estate Mortgage Investment conduits, appendix 11G
Receivables management, 2.5(a)
Re-engineering, of financial management, 2.2(c)
Refinancing, 10.4(b)(vi)
Refunding bonds, 13.9(e)(xvi)
Regulatory changes, 10.3(b)
Reinvestment requirements, 12.3(e)
Reporting formats, 2.5(a)(i)
Reporting system
    design of, 6.4
    improvement of, 3.3
Reports. See Financial reports
Repurchase agreements, appendix 11E, 13.13
    alternatives to, 13.13(e)
    brokered, 13.13(b)(ii)
    custodial arrangements, 13.13(b)(d)(i)
    definitions of, 13.13(b)

delivery repo, 13.13(d)(ii)
    introduction to, 13.13(a)
    letter repo, 13.13(d)(iv)
    reverse repurchase agreements, 13.13(b)(i)
    risk reduction, 13.13(d)
    risks of, 13.13(c)
    three-party, 13.13(d)(iii)
Request for information, 9.2(b)
Request for proposal, 9.2(b)
Resource-attraction products, 4.7(a)
Resources, treasury management, 2.2(c)
Responsibility checklist, 3.2
Restricted assets, 6.2(d)
Retained life estate, 8.4
Retirement plan donations, 8.14(k)
Return on invested capital, 4.6(a)
Return ratio, 6.6(c)(ii)
Revenue anticipation notes, 13.9(e)(xxii)
Revenue bonds, 13.9(e)(xv)
Revenues
    budgeting, 5.5(b)
    seasonality of, 10.3(b)
Reverse repurchase agreements, 13.13(b)(i)
Revolving credit agreement, 10.8(b)
Reward, in debt pricing, 10.4(a)(i)
Rights (corporate action), appendix 11F
Risk, 12.3(c). See also Risk management
    case study, 12.3(g)
    credit risk, 12.3(c)(i)
    in debt pricing, 10.4(a)(1)
    investment, 1(b), 11, 11.1(e), 11.2(e)
        currency denomination, 11.2(e)(ii)

Risk, (*Continued*)
  maturity limitations,
    11.2(e)(i)
  managing, 12.10(g)
  market risk, 12.3(c)(ii)
  mergers and acquisitions,
    4.7(d)(iii)
Risk management. *See also* External reviews: Staff issues
  checklist for, 14.1
  disaster preparedness,
    14.6(c)(iii)
  external audits, 14.6(b)
  identifying risk, 14.2
  internal controls, 14.6(a)
  issues, 9.3(m)
  liability, 14.4
  major areas of risk, 14.2
  overview of, 14.1
  rating, 2.5(a)
  reducing risk, 14.6(c)(ii)
  responsibility for, 1(a), 14
  safeguarding people, 14.3,
    14.5, 14.6
Rule 144 stock, appendix 11F
  and G

S
Safeguards, staff and volunteers, 14.3
Salle Mae. *See* Student Loan
  Marketing Association
Seasonality, of revenues,
  10.3(b)
Second Harvest, web page,
  6.2(c)
Secretary, 1.3(b)(iii)
  responsibilities, appendix
    1A
Secured loans, 10.8(b)
Securities
  clearance, 12.6(a)
  dealers, 10.10
  donation of, 8.4, 8.13(a)
  safekeeping, 12.6(c)

Securities and Exchange Com-
  mission Rule 415, 13.11(c)
Security. *See also* Risk manage-
  ment
  of information, 7.5
  issues regarding, 9.3(m)
Semivariable costs, 5.5(c)
Service center function, 3.3(b)
Service portfolios, 4.7(a)
Service pricing, 2.3
Services, as gifts, 8.4
Sexual harassment, 14.3(b)
Short-run fluctuations, 5.4(c)
Short-term, defined, 11.1
Short-term borrowing, rating,
  2.5(a)
Short-Term Financial
  Management Score,
  2.4(c)(iii)
Short-term investment, 1.1(a)
  examples, appendix 11B
    and C
  guidelines, appendix 11A
  optimizing return, 12.2
  rating, 2.5(a)
Simple regression model,
  5.5(a)(i)
Small-cap stocks, defined,
  12.11(i)
Socially conscious investing,
  11.2(c)(v)
Soft money, 5.4(c)
Software
  designing or purchasing,
    7.4
  financial programs, 6.2(d)
Special events
  description of, 8.9(a)(i)
  financial considerations,
    8.9(a)(ii)
Specialty managers approach,
  12.11(i)
Spending policy. *See also* Cash
  defined, 12.11(i)
  endowment, 12.11

Spending rates
   calculating, 12.10(b)
   defined, 12.11(i)
Staff issues, 14.3
   compensation, 14.3(f)
   conflict of interest, 14.3(h)
   determining strengths and
      weaknesses, 3.4(g)
   emotional safety, 14.3(b)
   hiring, 1.3(b)(vi)
   immediate termination,
      14.32(e)
   lawsuits and grievances,
      14.3(c)
   leadership, 14.3(k)
   motivation, 14.3(j)
   physical safety, 14.3(a)
   problem employees, 14.3(d)
   support for financial man-
      agement, 3.1(e)
   use of organizational re-
      sources, 14.3(g)
   using full potential, 14.3(i)
State financial requirements,
   6.7(a)(iii)
Statement of cash flows, 5.7(c)
Stewardship, in treasury management, 2.2(c)
Stock market crash, 12.3(c)(iii)
Stocks. *See* specific fund type
Strategic alliances, 4.7(f),
   6.6(f)(v)
   financial aspects of, 4.7(f)(ii)
   motives for, 4.7(f)(i)
Strategic decision making
   decision-making process, 4.4
   defining, 4.2(b)
   financial resources and, 10.5
   management process and,
      4.3
   strength and weakness de-
      termination, 4.4(a)
Strategic planning. *See also* Financial planning; Mission
   development

   area-specific strategies,
      4.2(a)
   for change, 4.5
   compared to management
      control, 4.1
   definition of, 4.1
   implementing, 4.7(g)
Streamlining business
   processes, 3.3(b)(i)
Strengths, organizational, 4.4(a)
Student affairs committee,
   1.3(b)(iv)
Student Loan Marketing Association securities,
   13.9(e)(v)
Subject expertise evaluation,
   16.5
Supervisory skills evaluation,
   16.5
Supplementary products,
   4.7(a)
Support service expense ratio,
   6.6(c)(ii)
Support structure, 3.1(e)(ii)
Surplus, budget, 5.4(c)
Swap exchanges, 10.8(b)
Sweep accounts, bank, 9.3(j)

T
Tangible property donation,
   8.13(c)
Target liquidity level, 6.6(c)(ii)
Taxable bonds
   organizational use of,
      10.11(b)(i)
   qualifications to issue,
      10.11(b)(iii)
   short-term financing
      through, 10.11(b)(ii)
Tax anticipation notes,
   13.9(e)(xxi)
Taxes
   charitable deductions and,
      8.12(d)
   leasing and, 10.12(a)

Technical terms glossary, appendix 7A
Technology security issues, 9.4
Technology tools. *See also* Software
  benefits of, 7.2(d)
  checklist, 7.2(a)
  choosing, 7.2(a)
  cost of, 7.2(f)
  growth analysis and, 7.3(a)
  implementation strategy, appendix 7B
  limitations of, 7.2(e)
  need for, 7.2(c)
  needs assessment, 7.6
  organizational changes and, 7.2(g)
  planning and, 7.3
  refusing to use, 7.6(e)
  requirements and, 7.2(b)
  staff use, 7.6(e)
Telemarketing campaigns
  description of, 8.9(c)(i)
  financial considerations, 8.9(c)(ii)
Termination, employee, 14.3(d)(e)
Term loans, 10.8(b)
Testamentary gifts, 8.14(h)
Tiger teams, 3.3
Time deposits, 13.12(b). *See also* Certificates of deposit
  Eurodollar, 13.12(b)(ii)
Time horizon investment, 12.10(f)
Time series models, 5.5(a)(i)
Timing, of fund usage, 12.3(d)
Tools, financial, 3.1(e)(ii)
Top-down budget approach, 5.4(c)
Total quality management, 9.3(k)
Total return, defined, 12.11(i)

Transactions
  executing, 12.6(d)(i)
  logs, 12.6(d)(iv)
  memos, 12.6(d)(ii)
  reporting, 12.6(d)(vi)
  technology tools, 12.6(d)(v)
  verifying, 12.6(d)(vi)
Transformers, 2.2(b)
Treadway Commission, 3.3(d)
Treasurer, 1.3(b((ii)
  financial responsibilities of, 3.1(d)
  function of, 3.3(a)
  responsibilities, appendix 1A
Treasury bills, 13.8(b)(i)
Treasury bonds, 13.8(b)(iii)
Treasury functions
  benchmarking, 9.3(k)
  upgrading, 9.3(l)
Treasury management
  diagnosis framework, 2.5(b)
  importance of, 2.2(c)
  improvement of, 2.5
  objectives, 2.3
Treasury Management Association, 9.2(b), 9.3(l)
Treasury notes, 13.8(b)(ii)
Treasury strategies, 6.6(f)(iv)
True endowment, defined, 12.11(i)
Trustee committee, 1.3(b)(iv)
Trustees, choosing, 1.3(a)
Trusts, 8.14(g). See also Deferred gifts
Turnaround management, 6.3(d)

U
Underspending, 5.4(b)(ii)
Underwriting firms, 10.10
Uniform Management of Institutional Funds Act, appendix 12A, 12.6(g)
Unrestricted assets, 6.2(d)

U.S. Department of Health and Human Services, 8.3(b)
U.S. Government Agency obligations, appendix 11E
U.S. government agency securities, 13.9
advantages of, 13.9(b)
asset-based securities, 13.9(e)(x)
bond anticipation notes, 13.9(e)(xxiii)
certificates of participation, 13.9(e)(xviii)
collateralized mortgage obligations, 13.9(e)(ix)
credit quality, 13.8(b)
farm credit system securities, 13.9(e)(i)
federal home loan bank securities, 13.9(e)(ii)
federal home loan mortgage corporation, 13.9(e)(iii)
federal national mortgage association, 13.9(e)(iv)
floating-rate notes, 13.9(e)(xxiv), 13.10
general obligation bonds, 13.9(e)(xiv)
government national mortgage association, 13.9(e)(vi)(vii)
municipal bond insurance, 13.9(e)(xii)
municipal debt instruments, 13.9(e)(xi)
municipal notes, 13.9(e)(xx)
pass through securities, 13.9(e)(viii)
pre-refunded bonds, 13.9(e)(xvii)
refunding bonds, 13.9(e)(xvi)
revenue anticipation notes, 13.9(e)(xxii)
revenue bonds, 13.9(e)(xv)
sale methods, 13.9(c)
student load marketing association, 13.9(e)(v)
tax anticipation notes, 13.9(e)(xxi)
types of, 13.9(e)
"when issued" trading, 13.9(d)
zero coupon municipal bonds, 13.9(e)(xviii)
U.S. government awards, 8.3(b)
U.S. Treasury Securities, appendix 11E, 13.8
background, 13.8(a)
liquidity and market, 13.8(b)
treasury bills, 13.8(b)(i)
treasury bonds, 13.8(b)(iii)
treasury notes, 13.8(b)(ii)

V
Valuation, charitable giving and, 8.14(m)
Variable costs, 5.5(c)
Variance analysis, budget, 6.6(f)(i)
Variance report checklist, 6.6(b)(i)
Volume variances, in budgeting, 5.6(b)
Volunteers
financial control, 2.2(a)
recruiting, 1.3(b)(vii)
responsibilities, appendix 1A

W
Warrants, appendix 11F
Watchdog agencies, 2.2(c)
Weaknesses, organizational, 4.4(a)
West's Annotated California Codes, appendix 12B

When issued trading, 13.9(d)
Wills, charitable giving in,
    8.12(b)
Workforce, understanding, 1.3
Working capital, 2.5
Work instructions, 15.2
Workload reduction, 3.3(b)(i)

Y
Yankee certificates of deposit,
    13.12(b)(iv)
Yield
    defined, 12.11(i)
    in long-term investments,
        11.1(b)
    pooling of funds and, 12.3(h)
    in short-term investments,
        11.1
Yield calculation, 13.4(c)
    to call, 13.4(c)(iv)

current yield, 13.4(c)(i)
to discounted cash flow,
    13.4(c)(iii)
to maturity, 13.4(c)(ii)
total realized compound
    yield, 13.4(c)(v)
Yield curve analysis, 13.2
    factors influencing, 13.2(a)
    riding the yield curve,
        13.2(c)
    using yield curve, 13.2(b)
Yield spread analysis, 13.3

Z
Zero balance account, 9.3(c)
Zero-based budgeting, 5.6(d)
Zero coupon bonds,
    12.3(c)(ii)
Zero coupon municipal
    bonds, 13.9(e)(xix)